# Pioneer Mikes

## Cover Captions

### Front Cover:

(Top Row, from left) KMED-AM studio production, c. 1931 [Courtesy of the Southern Oregon Historical Society, photo 9544]; Cheetah participates in a 1981 KSOR-FM interview [Western States Museum of Broadcasting (WSMB) collection]; KGW-TV cooking program with Konnie Worth and chef Gino Airaldi, 1956 [Courtesy of the *Oregonian*].

(Middle Row, from left) KGW-AM live 1938 remote interview [Courtesy of the *Oregonian*]; KGW-AM Hoot Owls decal, c. 1927 [Courtesy of www.pdxhistory.com]; KWJJ-AM mainstay morning announcer, Sammy Taylor, c. 1950 [WSMB Collection]; Bill Clark at KOTI-TV, c. 1957 [Smullin Collection, WSMB].

(Bottom Row, from left) Bill Smullin hosting KBES-TV's *The Answer Man*, c. 1955 [WSMB Collection]; Barret Hansen, who went on from Reed College's KRRC-FM to become *Dr. Demento*, 1976 [Courtesy of Barret Hansen]; KATU-TV weatherman Jim Bosley, c. 1968 [Courtesy of KATU/Fisher Broadcasting Company]; KGMG-FM's IGM automation system, 1959 [Courtesy of the *Oregonian*].

### Back Cover:

(Top Row, from left) Susanne Waldron, Tarantula Ghoul on KPTV-TV's *House of Horror*, c. 1957 [Courtesy of the *Oregonian*]; Frank Kincaid as KOIN-TV's Mr. Duffy, 1966 [WSMB Collection]; KMED-TV news director Hank Henry, c. 1965 [Ray Johnson Collection, WSMB].

(Middle Row) The KISN-AM "Good Guys" donned wigs anticipating the Beatles' U.S. arrival, January, 1964 [Courtesy of Gino Rossi].

(Bottom Row) A Hood River county farm family gathered to listen to their radio in 1925. [Courtesy of the Bettman/Corbis Archive].

# Pioneer Mikes

## A History of
## Radio and Television
## in Oregon

### POPULAR EDITION

## Ronald Kramer

**Western States Museum of Broadcasting
and JPR Foundation, Inc.**

Ashland, Oregon

In cooperation with
**The Oregon Association of Broadcasters**

*Dedicated to the memory of the*
*KGW Hoot Owls whose heart,*
*hope and humor epitomized the*
*highest ideals of broadcasting and*
*what the public should expect of*
*the radio and television industry.*

Design by David Ruppe, Impact Publications.
Typesetting by Christy Collins

Printed in the United States.

Library of Congress Control Number: 2009929422

ISBN: 978-0-615-30030-6

# Contents

## The 1950s
# Inventing TV Land and Radio's Rebirth

## The 1960s
# In Full Color

## The 1970s & '80s
# TV Roars, FM Soars

# Preface

Although I didn't realize it at the time, *Pioneer Mikes* began in 1993, when I was asked by the Southern Oregon Historical Society to write a history of broadcasting in southern Oregon. Having seen that work, the Oregon Association of Broadcasters approached me in 2001 about undertaking an effort to chronicle the entire state's broadcasting history. While I thought I was reasonably well-acquainted with Oregon's broadcasting history, my research rapidly revealed that my knowledge was, at best, superficial. The story of the unfolding of the radio and television industry in Oregon is the story of 20th century Oregon itself—its urbanization, expansion, unfolding political life and natural disasters—its challenges and its triumphs. It's a story filled with vision, heroism, leadership and humor—and a story that has in many respects been lost to time.

It is impossible to cite the full range of individuals who deserve to be acknowledged for their role in building radio and television in the Beaver State, although some individuals loom larger than life in that story. I've attempted to credit as many as can practically be acknowledged—but inevitably have missed some who should have been noted.

While others have assembled histories of radio and television in other states, Oregon has an unusual number of nationally notable stories to tell—and it seems particularly fitting to salute the founders and practitioners of broadcasting in Oregon, and their accomplishments, as Oregon is celebrating its own 150th anniversary.

A few comments about the scope of *Pioneer Mikes'* scope should be offered.

First, *Pioneer Mikes* has been prepared in two editions. This popular edition is taken from an academic reference edition, which was prepared for placement in selected research libraries around the state. The academic reference edition contains 25 percent more information, and greater detail, than this popular edition and you may wish to consult it if you're looking for either greater depth than this volume contains or more specific source information (since footnotes on sourcing have been pruned by about 50 percent in this popular edition). The academic edition also contains fully-developed chapters for stations of the 1970s and 1980s that have, to save on space, been reduced to a largely tabularized summary in this edition.

While this is, in many respects, the story of the people who built radio and television in Oregon and their accomplishments, the Federal Communications Commission (FCC) dictates that broadcasting is structured around licensing *stations*. Thus, *Pioneer Mikes* is centrally organized around *stations*. To the best of my ability, *Pioneer Mikes* chronicles every radio and television station ever licensed in Oregon (through 1982) including, to a limited degree, some interesting, but failed efforts. Because most individuals worked for a number of broadcasting stations during their careers, the stories of particular individuals are generally contained within the profiles of the stations with which they were associated (with the index then providing detailed references to their appearances within multiple stations' profiles).

Regarding stations, I have used a call sign convention of using *no* service type (i.e., AM, FM or TV) prior to World War II since all stations were AM during that period. Following World War II, when FM and TV stations came into existence, I have rendered call signs as KGW-AM or KJIB-FM even if the station's legal call sign would have been KJIB(FM)—for a station such as KJIB which had no AM counterpart. This approach seemed likely to me to be the least confusing for readers.

Additionally, the publisher of this volume, the JPR Foundation, is currently engaged in developing the Western States Museum of Broadcasting (WSMB), a new cultural facility in Ashland, in connection with a large collection of equipment, photographs, files and memorabilia that has been donated by various parties. Accordingly, many photographs and footnote references throughout this book are cited from the "WSMB Collection," deriving from materials owned by the WSMB.

In general, *Pioneer Mikes* covers the period 1922–1982. While a few ownership or other changes have been included past that ending date, my attempt to be both comprehensive and inclusive ends with Oregon broadcasting's 60th anniversary in 1982, with some stations founded afterward being included in the table which appears in chapter 27.

Because the names of some towns and institutions (and some people) have changed over time, I have used the name in use at the time a city, college or institution first appears with a parenthetical note regarding the current name, e.g., Marshfield, Oregon (now Coos Bay, Oregon). From that point forward, all references are made using the current name, e.g., Coos Bay.

Because some stations span many decades, the unfolding of their histories has been handled in two ways. For the 1920s and 30s, where an individual station's emergence or alteration materially affects the story of Oregon radio as a whole, stations either have commanded their own unique chapter(s) or have been incorporated within chapters which describe larger evolving events. Beginning in the 1940s, however, Oregon possessed so many stations that a different approach has been taken. For new stations that signed-on following World War II, a station's full history (through 1982) is contained at the point at which that station began. For stations which signed-on prior to World War II, a 1940s decade "update" chapter called "Across the Dial—Around the State" contains their further histories through 1982.

So many have contributed to this work in essential ways that it is impossible for me to acknowledge all who have helped. For those not identified, please know that your contributions have been of inestimable value and are profoundly appreciated. Some parties, however, played such central roles that, without them, this book absolutely couldn't have been written. For their invaluable assistance, I am especially indebted to the staff at the National Archives and Records Administration at College Park, Maryland, in particular to Tab Lewis and David Pfeiffer; and to the Oregon Historical Society, and its research librarian, Mikki Tint. My editors, Alan Reder and Paul Westhelle, John Baxter and George Kramer, were instrumental in strengthening *Pioneer Mikes*.

Two Oregon institutions have also played key roles. The Oregon Association of Broadcasters (OAB) provided both the stimulus for this book as well as assisted in financing its costs. Perhaps of even greater importance, the OAB, through its members and president, Bill Johnstone, opened numerous doors which helped me secure stories and illustrations that would otherwise have been unavailable. The reader will also readily see that the *Oregonian* is a central character in *Pioneer Mikes*. Early on, the *Oregonian* brought its already longstanding traditions for courageous journalism and public service to radio and younger readers will, perhaps, be surprised at how fundamentally the *Oregonian* shaped modern broadcasting in Oregon through its ownership of KGW. As I set about writing *Pioneer Mikes*, the *Oregonian* again played a new role in facilitating my research. I am deeply grateful to the *Oregonian*, its editor Sandy Rowe and—in particular—the paper's librarian, Carole McMinniman and its assistant photo editor, Drew Vattiat, for generously providing me both access to the newspaper's library as well as the use of numerous photographs from its collection.

Lastly, I wish to acknowledge a deep debt of gratitude to Craig Adams of Portland. Craig, himself a longtime radio announcer/DJ, has a consuming passion for the history of broadcasting and, long before *Pioneer Mikes* was ever contemplated, had methodically assembled a great deal of information about many stations in Portland and across the state. That foundation, which Craig graciously shared, afforded me the luxury of far deeper and more detailed research at the National Archives and elsewhere, than I could have attempted without the "building blocks" which Craig provided. For his constant help in tracking down elusive data, his thoughtful notes on my drafts and for fact-checking this entire manuscript, Craig has been an essential and valued collaborator. I am profoundly grateful for his help.

That said, errors of fact or omission contained in *Pioneer Mikes* are purely and solely my own responsibility.

As one who has worked in broadcasting for over 40 years, it has proven both a privilege and a challenge to pursue this story. Broadcasters across the region have been generous in sharing their memories and files and it has been tremendously gratifying to be able to relate the stories of colleagues and friends. At times, it has also been a bit challenging to try to impartially recount some events in which I was a participant.

*Pioneer Mikes* turned out to be a far more extensive and complex undertaking than I ever anticipated. At the same time, it has proven vastly more rewarding than I had ever hoped. I have tried to tell a history, a tale as it were, of an industry which has fundamentally touched the lives of all Oregonians in powerful, exciting and, at times, tragic ways.

It is a story which I am truly honored to have the opportunity to share with you.

Ronald Kramer
March 2009

# The 1920s
# Inventing Radioland

# 1

# Signing-On

In 1921, the crackle of distant voices and music began reshaping Oregon's landscape as people, wearing primitive headphones, listened to simple "crystal set" radios.

At the time, Oregon was a very different place than it is today, economically, politically and socially. The state's 784,000 citizens were equally divided between urban and rural settings. Only one in eight Oregonians owned a car, and more than 18 percent of Oregon homes lacked electricity.[1] Portlanders were inflamed over the proposal by the Portland Railway, Light and Power Company—which was teetering on insolvency—to raise street car fares from six to eight cents, while students at Corvallis' Oregon Agricultural College (now Oregon State University) were voting to ban formal attire at all campus social events due to "the general feeling that dress suits and democracy do not go together."[2, 3]

The previous year, Oregon had battled a severe flu epidemic, and Albany and Klamath Falls were particularly hard hit. In February 1920, state officials were concerned over "petty interference with local agencies engaged in combating the influenza epidemic," and threatened to quarantine Klamath Falls from the rest of the state. While the armistice that ended World War I had taken effect in November 1918, some peace-time military-to-civilian conversions were still in progress as the 1920s dawned. It took the federal government until March 1 of that year to return control of its railroad lines to the Southern Pacific Company.

Social patterns were also in flux. While the National Prohibition Act (known popularly as the Volstead Act) had officially made the U.S. a nation of tee-totalers, whisky was still readily available. Smuggled in from Canada, it was worth as much as $300 a case in Portland.

The social aftershocks of World War I had been profound. The Allies' victory over the Axis had stirred many patriotic passions—and the Ku Klux Klan (KKK) was holding successful rallies in Ashland, Medford and Astoria—discovering that Oregon was fertile ground for

KGW's studio in the *Oregonian* building tower, c. 1923

its hate-filled rhetoric. The KKK's marches somewhat paralleled the Nazi movement, which Germany was finding increasingly compelling following its defeat in the war. Having been well-received in Oregon's rural areas, the Klan quickly moved into Portland, which soon became the group's *de facto* headquarters for all states west of the Rocky Mountains. Responding to several Klan-organized "neck-tie parties" (near-lynchings) in the spring of 1921, Oregon Governor Ben Olcott pleaded for enforcement of existing law and, ultimately, requested federal assistance.[4] Three years later, the Klan was largely responsible for electing both Walter Pierce as Oregon's governor as well as much of the Oregon Legislature.

The Klan's "Roaring Twenties" Oregon activities are nearly unthinkable in the 21st century but, in 1920, found acceptance in much of the Beaver State. Oregon was a place where men and women were struggling with thorny political issues surrounding individual rights and the very meaning of citizenship. On January 12, 1920, Oregon became the 25th state to ratify the nineteenth amendment to the U.S. Constitution (the Equal Suffrage Amendment), which gave women the right to vote.

Yet, on January 24, 1920, U.S. Secretary of Labor William B. Wilson branded the Communist Party "revolutionary," and sought to deport Communist aliens. Perhaps in response, the Executive Committee of the National Board of Fire Underwriters published an ad in the *Oregonian* on February 9, 1920, headlined **"Let Us Americanize America!"** It described "the present emergency as great as that presented by the War."[5]

While some were feeling threatened by foreign and other "outside" elements, Oregon's traditional agrarian and labor interests were feeling shut out. On January 30, 1920, the then-powerful Oregon Grange announced the formation of a new political party, the Land-Labor Party of Oregon. Farmers and workers were invited to "join in one great movement for the regeneration and purification of the Oregon system."[6]

Politics are fueled by access to information. Yet, before radio provided instantaneous news, most Oregonians lived in relative isolation from the nation's nerve centers. They relied on the state's daily and weekly newspapers for event coverage, and the more distant they were from urban centers, the more isolated they were from Oregon and the nation's cultural and political heartbeats.

For leisure, Oregonians (like most Americans of the time) tended to entertain themselves to a great degree. Cultured homes had pianos around which people gathered to sing. Town bands of amateur and semi-professional musicians were common. Lectures and debates attracted crowds as new ideas were ventilated.

For inexpensive professional entertainment, Oregonians turned to "photoplays" (silent moving pictures)—an industry that had already established a firm hold. You could see Harold Lloyd or Pola Negri at well-attended theatres like the Rivoli, Blue Mouse, Liberty, Majestic, or the Columbia in Portland. In Eugene, there was the McDonald and, in Medford, the Page or Rialto Theatres—all places where one could catch Charlie Chaplin in *The Idle Class* or Lon Chaney in *Bits of Life*. In Portland, one could attend D.W. Griffith's hit silent film, *Way Down East*, which was playing at the People's Theatre "at popular prices"—replete with music by the People's Orchestra.

For more elaborate professional entertainment, Portlanders could attend performances at the Pantages (at the corner of Broadway and Alder) or the Hippodrome (Broadway and Yamhill), where vaudeville circuits offered entertainment like Will Rogers or Reginald deKoven's comic opera *Robin Hood*. In most Oregon towns of any size, theatres and "opera houses" offered similar fare. Musical reviews played at Portland's Heilig (at the corner of Broadway and Taylor), and in the early 1920s Portlanders could enjoy "big city" entertainment, such as Metropolitan Opera contralto Sophie Breslau appearing with the Portland Symphony.

But Oregon's entertainment options were soon to be profoundly changed by the new "wireless telephone," or "raidio," which quickly became "radio." People couldn't initially decide just what to call it or even how to spell it. Yet, it was a powerful new force that soon would shatter the isolation of Oregon and its various regions.

It was a time of hope, stress and change—all playing out in an Oregon that would be forever altered by the new marvel called radio.

## How radio arrived

Like most major military conflicts, World War I had stimulated major technological developments, including the field use of new Morse code radio transmitters and receivers. While voice transmission had been experimentally undertaken as early as 1906, sound transmission remained generally impractical throughout the Great World War. But some military men, trained in the fundamentals of wireless (radio) transmission, returned from the war with a fascination for radio's potential. Its ability to electronically "connect" people seduced them. Tinkering with this primitive toy, they explored ways to harness it for entertainment and exchange of information.

As the 1920s dawned, radio was so primitive that transmitters were still being licensed by the Department of Commerce's (DOC) Bureau of Navigation, which had received shipboard transmitter licensing responsibility following the Titanic's 1912 sinking. As non-maritime

"My Radio Gal," a popular song about radio, 1922

WSMB Collection

transmitters came into use, the Bureau of Navigation licensed such transmitters as "Special Land Stations" (what we would come to think of as radio stations) to distinguish them from the anticipated norm of radio transmitters' nautical uses.

As radio experimentation grew following World War I, the number of requests for such Special Land Station licenses started to grow. DOC staff, under the guidance of Secretary of Commerce Herbert Hoover (who spent his teenage years living with an uncle in Newberg, Oregon, following the death of his parents) saw radio licensing much like automobile licensing—a registration process through which essentially anyone who asked for a license was granted one. Like an automobile's license plate number, each radio station was issued a call sign and federal regulations required each station to broadcast its call sign to identify itself when it began and ceased transmission (a regulation which still exists). In the 21st century, with many stations operating 24/7, the public often doesn't hear stations perform this obligation, but in radio's early years stations often broadcast only for short periods and gave their call signs when they turned on their transmitters. Hence the term "signing-on" became common both inside radio and in the public mind.

Slowly, in Oregon and around the nation, experimentation with this wondrous new device was growing.

Radio seemed an almost mystical force, perhaps compounded by the fact that its ultimate significance and potential uses remained uncertain. In the summer of 1922, the *Ashland Weekly Tidings* reported that "Marconi, the Italian radio wizard hopes to receive messages which he suspects the inhabitants of Mars are trying to send to earth." A photo showed the inventor with his complex receiving equipment. Six months later, the *Oregonian* ran the front-page story "Radio Love Tests Declared Success—Diagnosis by Wireless Said to be Based on Electronic Reactions' of Passion," which reported that San Francisco doctor Albert Abrams claimed that "Love can be diagnosed by a distance by radio in connection with the 'electronic reactions.'"[7]

Radio was mysterious and alluring.

As 1922 dawned, the national interest in radio began to explode. Suddenly, popular songs even started to be written about this mysterious, marvelous new portal to the world.

## Identifying Oregon's First Radio Station

Identifying most "firsts" depends on how one defines the achievement. For radio, some scholars count the "amateur" Special Land Stations, which later went on to become "professional." On that basis, KGN has a strong claim dating back to 1921. However, Ashland electronic tinkerers William J. Virgin, Floyd Rush and Elmer Morrison, without the benefit of a federal license, assembled a five-watt transmitter in Morrison's Ashland barn in the fall of 1921. Virgin later reassembled that apparatus at his father's flour mill in Central Point, from which he reportedly broadcast sporadic programming. Virgin later applied for a professional station license as KFAY, which the DOC authorized on July 6, 1922. KFAY inaugurated broadcasting on

September 23, 1922, from studios located at the Jackson County Fairgrounds (see also chapter 2), but the station's activities date back to the preceding fall.

While KFAY's license was renewed in October 1924, it ceased broadcasting a month earlier. However, Virgin started Medford's KMED in 1926. That station claims to be Oregon's oldest radio station based on Virgin's original unlicensed work in the fall of (see chapter 4).

What really was Oregon's "first" radio station? Let's consider the efforts that led to the development of licensed professional stations.

## Special Land Stations

In 1921, eight parties, stretched between Portland, Corvallis and Enterprise, secured licenses for Special Land Stations from the DOC. Schools like Oregon State University and Washington and Benson Polytechnic High Schools were among them, along with a few individuals. Oregon seemed thirsty for radio.[8]

Three of these Special Land Stations, 7XF, 7XG and 7XI, would prove to be unusually important.

## 7XF/KGN Portland

7XF was started by Charles L. Austin, hailed by some as the father of radio in Oregon, whose Northwestern Radio Manufacturing Company played a key role in radio's development in the state. Austin's interest in radio dated from an early age. At the age of 15, while living with his family in Portland's Mt. Tabor district, he was an active member of the Portland Progressive Club, whose goal was "to promote interest in wireless telegraphy."[9, 10] A largely self-taught electronic experimenter, after graduating from high school Austin worked as a radio operator

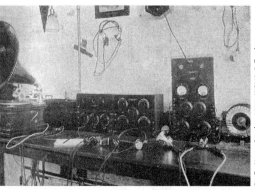

Charles Austin's 7XF in 1921 showing the Remick Song Shop phonograph, at left, used to broadcast recordings.

on the ocean liner S.S. Rose City. Following his World War I military service as chief electrician and radio inspector of the Portland Naval District, he secured a license for a Special Land Station early in 1921 under the auspices of his newly formed Northwestern Radio Manufacturing Company.[11] It was given the call sign 7XF. While 7XF operated sporadically, its broadcasts clearly seemed intended for the public (which at that time would largely have consisted of similarly interested radio hobbyists). In October 1921, *Radio News* reported that Clyde Freeman, the manager of Portland's Remick Song Shop, heard the broadcasts and offered the use of a new phonograph and recordings of the very latest in jazz dance music, songs and classical recordings for broadcasting in exchange for on-air acknowledgements. Preceding the playing of each record, Austin would announce the name of the record, its label identification number, the make of phonograph on which it was being played—and Remick's shop location.[12]

In addition to broadcasting music, Austin also offered public health bulletins on Tuesday and Friday evenings at 8:45 and industrial news on Monday evenings. Beyond radio's inherent allure, Northwestern Radio Manufacturing clearly saw radio as a growth industry, and in February 1922 the company applied to the DOC for a license for a new "professional" station. That application, approved on March 28, 1922, authorized KGN's operation.

Hawley's Irvington home (c. 1930) located at 1914 NE 22nd Street, Portland, from which 7XG/KYG operated. Hawley installed two large wooden poles on the property to support KYG's antenna wires.

*Courtesy of the Oregon Historical Society, photo CN021628*

## 7XG/KYG Portland

In February 1922, while planning KGN, Charles Austin built and installed the equipment for another experimental station, 7XG, for prominent Portland businessman Willard P. Hawley Jr. Hawley's father, Willard P. Hawley Sr., had made his fortune in paper-related businesses, including a large Oregon City plant later purchased by Crown-Zellerbach—which his son managed.

Hawley Jr.'s elegant Irvington mansion in east Portland featured impressive front columns and a large crescent-shaped driveway. There, he installed 7XG's studio in a large basement ball-room. In operation, it offered programming similar to 7XF's.[13, 14]

Hawley invited teachers from Benson Polytechnic High School and others to talk, sing and play over the air, after which Hawley would feed them ice cream and cake. With a pioneering nod toward commercialization or, at the least, a flair for promotion, Hawley periodically mentioned what was apparently an unusual delicacy at the then-popular high school hang out, the Sugar Bowl located on Broadway between 15th and 16th Streets, saying: "Hello, Sugar Bowl! Hello, Sugar Bowl! I wish we had some of that nice French Salad [sic] ice cream here right now."[15] Promptly, a messenger from the Sugar Bowl would arrive with a couple of gallons for Hawley to serve to his in-studio guests.

In part, Hawley used the station to amuse his guests, but he also enjoyed announcing, having been trained to speak on the radio by Sgt. Richard C. Travers at San Francisco's Presidio-based Signal Corps. Travers reportedly possessed the "best carrying and clearest sounding [radio] voice of any man in California" and was known as the "Man with the Million Dollar Voice."[16]

In March 1922, when 7XG was only a few weeks old, Hawley applied to elevate his station to professional status. Having already spent $6,000 on 7XG's construction, he ordered additional equipment costing another $4,000 for improvements. With 7XG's power increased to 100 watts (from 5 watts), the station was re-licensed as KYG on March 28, 1922, and inaugurated broadcasting with great fanfare. KYG was even nationally hailed as in the May 20, 1922, *Radio Digest Illustrated* article "WYW, KYG and WDZ All Famous." Hawley often receiving up to 40 letters a week from widely scattered listeners.[17, 18]

# 7XI/KGG Portland

Another significant broadcasting develop-
ment was the 1921 founding of Hallock and
Watson's Radio Service, whose "Fifteen Years in
Radio" motto apparently took account of the
combined experience of its co-founders, Joseph
H. Hallock and Clifton H. Watson.[19, 20]

Joe Hallock and Clif Watson had been boyhood friends in Oregon and were later class-
mates at Oregon State University. They shared a
keen interest in radio throughout their formative
years.[21] Following college graduation, Watson
worked as a radio operator on Alaskan coastal
steamers for a time and then, in 1915, the two
young men worked together installing transmitters for the Montana Power Company. In 1916,
they did similar work for the Northwestern Electric Company and then went their separate ways
for a time.[22] Watson took a position as radio
inspector for the DOC in Seattle, and Hallock
worked as an operator at the United Wireless
Company's Astoria wireless telegraph station,
whose call sign was PC.[23] When the U.S. entered

Ted Hallock Collection, WSMB

Joe Hallock cavorting atop a 600-foot tall radio
tower in San Diego, where he was installing a
"high power" station when he and Clif Watson
were making contract radio installations, 1916.

World War I, Hallock joined the Navy and was put in charge of a huge Navy "arc" station in
Bordeaux, France.[24] After the war, Hallock and Watson again worked together installing transmitters in 1920 for the Republic of China.

Returning to Portland in 1921, they established their radio manufacturing business, Hallock and Watson, with the former as president and the latter as treasurer.[25] The company first
applied for an "experimental" license as 7XI, but only a few days later applied for a station with
professional status, KGG.

Licensed on March 15, 1922, KGG broadcast its inaugural atmospheric romp that same
evening. Indeed, KGG had probably jumped the gun, since newspaper accounts of the broadcast report that it was the "second news broadcast sent out" by the station.[26] The radio log
published in the March 16, 1922 *Oregon Journal,* reported that the Northwestern Radio Manufacturing station would provide news daily from 7:30 p.m. to 8 p.m., that Willard P. Hawley's
station would offer music on Tuesday and Wednesday evenings from 8 p.m. to 8:45 p.m. and
that Hallock and Watson's station would offer news from 7:15 p.m. to 7:30 p.m. The *Oregon
Journal* was in the forefront of radio development and very early established the *Oregon Journal
Radio Service,* which provided the reading of news from the newspaper and its wire service
over the Portland radio stations not associated with its rival newspaper, the *Oregonian.* The
*Journal* described its purposes thus: "The *Journal* bulletin news service is broadcasted [sic] in
cooperation with President Charles L. Austin of the Northwestern Radio Manufacturing Com.,
Willard P. Hawley, Jr. and the Hallock and Watson Radio Service. The wave length is always 360
meters" (the equivalent of 833 KHz).[27] The Hawley transmissions were still occurring under the
owner's amateur license as 7XF and 7XG but Hawley was, nevertheless, regularly offering music
and news programming under those call signs. For those without radios, Meier & Frank, Portland's largest department store, obligingly set up a large radio receiver with an oversized "horn"

Many broadcasters got into radio through manufacturing or servicing radio receivers, which were primitive. Northwestern Radio Manufacturing Company (NORCO), operator of KGN, made this two-unit set in 1921 (right). One step above crystal set radios which a radio enthusiast could personally build, this radio consisted of the SR-2 tuner, on the right, and the SR-1 amplifier, on the left, electronically joined by four metal bands. The tuner alone, which required an external detector like a crystal, allowed listening on headphones. Purchasing the SR-1 detector/amplifier additionally permitted powering a speaker. The holes on the amplifier enabled viewing the flow of the filaments to ensure that the expensive tubes weren't fed too much voltage, which could cause them to burn out. Hallock and Watson, operator of KGG, manufactured this model TRF-5 in 1925, by which time a radio's tuner and amplifier sections were combined into one unit (left). Both the NORCO and Hallock and Watson sets used three large dials to "tune" a station, with the smaller knobs for controlling other settings, and both used large external batteries.

Photos courtesy of Sonny Clutter, www.radiolaguy.com

speaker on the company's fifth floor, or sometimes on the street below. Reportedly, KGG was initially located in the window of Hallock and Watson's Park Street store, and Hallock would give station breaks, saying: "KGG—King George George."[28] Not long after, the *Journal* established a radio studio in its building, from which KGG also frequently broadcast by late 1922.

Thus, by mid-March 1922, three Portland parties had applied for Special Land Stations that had evolved into professionally licensed stations: Northwestern Radio Manufacturing Company's 7XF/KGN; Willard P. Hawley, Jr.'s 7XG/KYG and Hallock and Watson Radio Service's 7XI/KGG.

## KQY Portland

The last entry in the 1922 race to operate radio in Portland came from the Stubbs Electric Company. Stubbs Electric, with Osmon Stubbs as its president and R. W. Stubbs its corporate secretary, was a mainstay Portland electrical supply house that had been founded in 1897. Gradually, the company branched into wireless and radio parts and equipment—and Stubbs' key radio man in that effort was Wilbur Jeffrey Jerman.

Jerman was born in Silverton on June 11, 1901, and developed an interest in radio at an early age when Alfred Adams, the owner of the Silverton Opera House, introduced young Jerman to radio.[29] Soon, the youth set up a place in the basement of the family home to tinker with radio.[30] The Jermans moved to Portland when young Wilbur was 10 or 11. He continued to putter around with radio and chose Benson Polytechnic for his high school in order to further that exploration. Badly bitten by the radio bug, Jerman

Wilbur J. Jerman collection, WSMB

Osmon Stubbs pictured in 1947 in Stubbs Electric's 50th Anniversary brochure.

decided to seek his fortune rather than complete his education and, shortly after leaving Benson, went to work for Stubbs Electric, where he was employed by 1917. Never formally schooled in radio electronics, Jerman's remarked that he just kind of "picked it up."[31] He was, by his own account and that of many others, a born tinkerer.

In early 1922, Stubbs Electric landed a contract to install a radio station for the *Calgary Daily Herald* and Jerman was sent to Calgary to build CHCQ—a considerable responsibility for the 21-year-old.[32, 33] He managed a crew that erected two towers (which held the antenna wire stretched between them) on the Herald's roof, as well as the instal-

(Left) CHCQ's antenna, strung with colored lights for the station's first night on the air to signal that it was broadcasting, May 1, 1922. (Right) Wilbur J. Jerman atop the *Calgary Herald*'s roof.

lation of the studio and transmitting equipment on the newspaper building's top floor. When CHCQ was completed, Jerman demonstrated a flair for promotion by having the rooftop tower installation decked out with electric lights, which made a bold statement against the night sky. With entertainers drawn from the bill of the nearby Palace Theatre, the station's inaugural program was a huge hit, and Jerman basked in his accomplishment. His photo, taken on the Herald's roof next to one of the towers, reflects a satisfied, slightly jaunty air.

Having observed radio's growth, Osmon Stubbs decided it was time to set up his own station and submitted a license application in January 1922. Shortly before leaving for Calgary, Jerman built the station that was inspected by the Seattle-based DOC radio inspector on February 11 (the same day as KGG's inspection), although Stubbs' station license as KQY wasn't issued until March 30. The station signed-on March 31 with 10 watts.

KQY must have struggled. To boost its visibility, the station persuaded Ernest Jorgensen, a *Portland News* editor, to broadcast news two or three times daily. It was a prominent KQY offering. While the station received polite press coverage, it was on nowhere near the scale enjoyed by KGW, KGG, KGN or KYG (the latter three no doubt benefiting from their "association" with the *Oregon Journal*). By September 24, 1922, KQY had raised its power to 100 watts, with its old transmitter going to KFBM, Astoria (see chapter 2), and was operating from the second floor of the Stubbs Electric building. But KQY had no allocated nighttime broadcasting hours according to the Portland area radio schedule published in October 1922.

| New Night Broadcast Schedule[34] | | | | | | | |
|---|---|---|---|---|---|---|---|
| Time | Sunday | Monday | Tuesday | Wednesday | Thursday | Friday | Saturday |
| 7:00–7:30 | OR | Quiet Hour | | | | | |
| 7:30–8:00 | | HW | HW | HW | HW | HW | HW |
| 8:00–9:00 | Quiet Hour | OR | Quiet Hour | OR | Quiet Hour | OR | HW |
| 9:00–10:00 | HW | NW | RSB | NW | MF | Quiet | RSB |

OR = KGW, *Oregonian* station    HW = KGG, Hallock and Watson station    NW = KGN, Northwestern Radio Mfg. Co. station
RSB = KYG, Radio Service Bureau station (successor to Willard Hawley)    MF = KFEC, Meier & Frank station

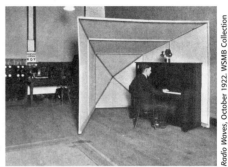

(Left) KQY broadcasting a quartet, Jerman holding telephone-style mike. (Right) KQY broadcasting "horn" as constructed by Jerman.

Jerman was Stubbs' chief operator and must have also functioned in a general oversight role for KQY because he took it upon himself to do what was necessary. Because Stubbs had allocated space for KQY in an unsuitably large room in the company's building, Jerman constructed a large wooden horn to focus the sound. Sizeable enough to hold a piano and performing cast, the horn made the allotted studio space acoustically functional. Radio was still a rag-tag idea with few resources. Once, Jerman appropriated a bookcase out of Stubbs' office when his boss was away on a business trip. "He was angry with me about that," Jerman recalled.

KQY made an occasional programming splash, sometimes engaging in live entertainment such as an October 1922 broadcast by the thirty-piece Apostolic Faith Church Concert Band. But at the time of that broadcast, the published Portland-area radio schedule (above) didn't even list KQY. The station struggled against its more prominent competitors until its final broadcast—"Vocal and Instrumental Selections" from 6 p.m. to 7 p.m. on May 1, 1923.[35] KQY gave up the next day and must have immediately notified the DOC by wire or phone, as the station's license was deleted on May 3, 1923.[36]

Stubbs wasn't the only broadcaster who had begun to question the wisdom of entering the radio field. Willard Hawley also decided that KYG was something he could do without. Beginning in late September 1922, he briefly allowed a potential purchaser of the station, a company called Radio Service Bureau, to operate KYG from his home. Stories differ as to whether Hawley actually sold KYG to that company, although Hawley acted as though he had completed the sale. While Radio Service Bureau seemingly took possession, it lacked the funds to complete the purchase and had apparently only been soliciting potential local investors for that purpose.

Notwithstanding such behind-the-scenes activities, Radio Service Bureau announced plans to relocate KYG to the Gasco Building at 11th Avenue and Washington Street, where it intended to install a "high-class station," which was supposed to sign-on October 23, 1922. It never did. The DOC radio inspector, suspicious over apparent misstatements made in the company's license application, canceled KYG's license on November 7, 1922, upon determining that the station had never been built at the new location.[37] Another version of KYG's demise holds that Radio Service Bureau initially sought to operate from the *Portland Telegram* building but couldn't secure city approval to erect the necessary towers on its roof.[38] In any event, KYG was no more.

## Listeners' Experience: Installing a Radio

At radio's onset, receivers were both primitive and scarce. Oregon newspapers were known to report the installation of a residential radio receiver as front page news. Such installations often made press, such as when the *Oregon Journal* noted that Hood River resident H. G. Ball had installed the first powerful regenerative-circuit set in that city.

In 1922, a listener's experience was vastly different than today. Sets could be simple: a crystal set receiver could be easily constructed using a coil of wires, often wound on a round Quaker Oats tube, with a few additional commercial parts available at electronic supply stores. For those willing to spend more money, commercially made crystal sets were also sold. At first, all listening occurred on headphones. In a very simple setup, two listeners might share a two-receiver headset (one side designed for each ear) by putting their heads together. As opposed to such sharing, or passing the headphone sequentially among family members, combining "jacks" could be purchased and allowed the connecting of several sets of headphones to the radio set so that multiple family members could listen simultaneously. As the radio craze grew, Oregon telephone company officials complained that "radio fever" was prompting the theft of countless receivers (headphones) that had been appropriated from public telephones for home radio listening.

As radio receivers became more sophisticated, headphones gave way to horn speakers, which essentially consisted of a headphone playing into a horn that spread the sound. This allowed communal listening and eliminated the need for headphones. Soon, horn speakers were replaced by cone-type loud speakers that could fill a room with better- quality sound. As radios required more signal to power these speakers, crystal set receivers gave way to vacuum tube sets.

While the tube-style sets also received signals at greater distances and were better able to selectively tune among competing station signals, vacuum tubes that could be powered from a home's AC wall-socket were five years away. Thus, the first tube radios ran on batteries that required an expensive, awkward array. Initially, these radios used two types of batteries that were designated A and B to distinguish their differing size and function. The 6-volt A batteries wet cells were similar in size to present-day car batteries and contained the same highly corrosive acid. The 45-volt (later 90-volt) B batteries at first were glass-tube wet cells but eventually graduated to dry cells like those used in modern flashlights. Later, the C battery, a 4.5-volt dry cell, came into use because its addition improved receiver performance. In radio's early years a receiver required at least two, if not all three, of these types of batteries.

Thus, a radio receiver in 1922 or 1923 was a fussy, complex and frequently smelly affair. Large A batteries sometimes leaked acid with serious consequences for carpeting or household furnishings. Radios were expensive to purchase and to operate. The A batteries required frequent recharging, and many households used battery recharging services that picked up a spent battery, provided a loaner set of charged batteries and returned the customer's recharged A batteries the following day. At a time when the new Ford Model T cost $300, operating a radio receiver could easily cost $6 a month for batteries, plus occasional tube replacements at $10 each. Tubes were so expensive that, even after numerous decades had passed, many early radio enthusiasts remembered inadvertently breaking a tube with sharp bitterness.

Radios came to use smaller, less power-hungry tubes over the next few years, tubes that allowed sets to operate on less expensive, and more convenient, dry cell batteries. But it was not until 1927 that radios utilizing AC (or DC) power from wall sockets came to the market.

These radio sets were far less sensitive than modern receivers and, throughout the 1920s and much of the 1930s, they required large external antenna wires—often stretched between the home and a handy tree (or garage). Radio set owners also had to install a good ground (a connection to some metal that was driven into the ground) for the radio to work decently. A cold-water pipe would often suffice but, if faced with poor reception, it was a good idea to drive a copper stake into the ground and connect it by copper wire to the radio receiver chassis. In order to give adequate service, early receivers all required the extra signal that a good ground provided.

Thus, in radio's earliest years a receiver was so far removed from our era of transistors and microchips that even the most flamboyant 1920s science fiction writers couldn't have envisioned a Walkman.

## Listeners' Experience: Using a Radio

Just as the *Oregon Journal* story mentioned earlier noted that "the wave length is always 360 meters," all radio stations in the nation initially broadcast on the same frequency. As a holdover from radio's military usage, this was expressed in meters (equal to the length between the crests of the radio wave that a transmitter emitted). Radio stations and the public did not begin referring to a station's wave length by the now more popular designation of frequency (the number of waves transmitted per second) until the end of the decade. There was an inverse relationship between the two measurement systems. Higher frequency stations emitted more densely packed waves which, consequently had shorter wave lengths. A 360-meter station, at 833 KHz, had a longer wave length than a 200-meter station operating at 1500 KHz. It was all somewhat confusing and technical for the average person. In the same way that early personal computers later became the province of the young and technologically inclined (at least initially), parents were often content to let their children tune in a radio for the family's enjoyment.

Because they all shared the same frequency, stations would sign-on for an hour or two, or even for just a few minutes, and then sign-off to give another station a chance. When misunderstandings occurred, or gentlemen's agreements about frequency sharing failed, two stations might operate simultaneously, resulting in serious interference for listeners. Radio programming was primitive. On June 22, 1923, the *Oregonian*, for example, reported that KGN would offer music from 7 p.m. to 7:30 p.m. and KGG would offer "news, market and police reports" from 7:30 p.m. to 8 p.m. Both stations, of course, operated on the same frequency.

Radio consisted almost entirely of live amateur and semi-professional entertainers and phonograph recordings, all relentlessly trying to be heard over these primitive systems. Notwithstanding the varying technical and artistic quality of the entertainment, radio's intrigue stimulated people like Portland residents Mr. and Mrs. A. C. Stevens, who announced an "innovation in diversions" in the form of a radio party, when they invited ten guests to listen to KYG with them in April 1922.

Listening to something occurring far away was thrilling and seemed like magic. Distant reception (known as DX) was an important part of the radio hobby, and communities voluntarily observed a "silent night" when no local stations broadcast. With each city's silent night differing among communities, local radio enthusiasts were given the chance to tune in distant stations without the interference of local signals. This practice, also a voluntary gentlemen's agreement among stations, continued for several years throughout the nation.

## Oregon's First Radio Station – KGW

It's difficult to define "firsts" in radio and depends heavily upon the criteria used. For example, several radio stations compete for the title of America's "first" radio station. From the standpoint of public awareness that there was even a radio station to listen to, that honor is often accorded to KDKA of Pittsburgh, Pennsylvania, whose November 1920 broadcast of election returns is sometimes cited as the first real radio broadcast. During 1921, a total of 29 stations signed-on the air with voice transmission in the U.S.[39] Some saw themselves as full radio stations and applied for real "call signs" such as KDKA, but most were more what we would now refer to as amateur (ham) stations.

Defining the "first" Oregon radio station solely around the use of a professional (rather than an amateur) call sign can also be misleading. KGG was licensed on March 15; KGW on March 21; KGN on March 28; and KQY on March 30 – all in 1922.[40] Yet, KGG apparently was on the air by the time of KGW's March 28 sign-on and continued broadcasting until fall 1924, when the station abandoned its license.

## KGW

All corporate bravado by partisan contestants aside, a strong case can be made that Oregon's first and lasting professional radio station was the *Morning Oregonian*'s KGW.

Newspapers across America watched the launch of radio with a mixture of interest and antagonism. Radio had captured the public's imagination and could hardly, therefore, be ignored. At the same time, newspapers worried that radio might prove a serious rival for the delivery of news, and they weren't too interested in promoting a potential competitor. Various papers handled the dilemma differently. Some daily newspapers deeply embraced radio to the point of starting their own stations. For example, Detroit's *Daily News* started WWJ in 1920 (which also allows WWJ to claim the disputed title of the nation's first professional radio station).[41] Other newspapers reported on the "radio craze" with columns of technical advice about the best circuit to use for building your own receiver but avoided printed references to any local radio station.

Portland's *Morning Oregonian* must have been watching the unfolding interest in radio, both locally and nationally, for some time. Its major Portland competitor, the *Oregon Journal,* had closely allied itself with all three broadcasting enterprises in operation in Portland by mid-March, 1922, by offering "news bulletins" from the *Journal*'s newsroom for broadcast over all three stations. On March 23, 1922, the *Journal* proudly proclaimed it was "the first Portland newspaper to establish a regular news broadcasting service." Eventually, the *Journal* formalized its relationship with Hallock and Watson's KGG. On October 15, 1922, the *Journal* proudly trumpeted that KGG had set a distance record for its recently installed 50-watt higher power transmitter with a reception report from Topeka, Kansas. By March 1923, the *Journal* was referring

*Courtesy of the Oregonian*

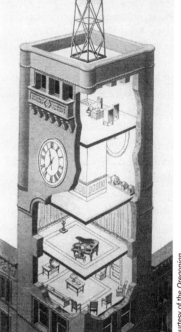

*Courtesy of the Oregonian*

The *Oregonian* building was located on the corner of Portland's SW Sixth Avenue and Alder Street. The first steel-frame building in the western U.S., its four-story corner "tower" was the structure's most distinguishing feature and was prominently referenced in the Hoot Owls artwork and promotional literature (see chapter 3). (Top) *Oregonian* tower with KGW antenna stretching across Alder Street. (Bottom) *Oregonian* tower cut-away view with KGW radio layout.

(Left) Edgar B. Piper, editor (1910–28), *Oregonian* newspaper. (Right) KGW Inaugural Program performers (left to right), Giorgio Polacco, Edith Mason, Edgar Piper, March 25, 1922.

to KGG as the "official broadcasting station for the *Journal*." The newspaper's radio log for that time reflects that KGG signed-on with "The *Journal* Chimes" (no doubt picked up from the paper's well-known clock tower, a local architectural landmark).

Watchful but close-mouthed, the *Oregonian*'s interest in starting its own station must have been a closely held secret. Where other newspapers, such as the *Calgary Daily Herald*, heavily trumpeted advance plans for a radio station, the *Oregonian* was silent about seeking one. Indeed, the station had already been completely constructed by the time the *Morning Oregonian* first announced its intentions. On March 19, 1922, the newspaper reported that construction of a new radio station had been completed the previous day with an 18-foot by 18-foot radio studio installed on the *Oregonian* building's 11th floor and the transmitter located on the 13th floor. The antenna was stretched between a tower located on the *Oregonian*'s roof and another located on the adjacent Northwestern Bank building.[42]

The paper reported that, following testing, KGW would commence regular broadcasting in about a week. Drawing on radio's maritime heritage, the *Oregonian* hired the Shipbuilders Radio Service, a maritime supplier, to install the station.[43] On the licensing documents, Shipbuilders was actually first shown as the 50-watt station's licensee, and one of the company's employees, Jesse Weed, was the station's architect and chief operator. Portending its intention that KGW would aspire to higher standards, the *Oregonian* noted that "Unlike radiophone broadcasting so far done in Oregon, the *Oregonian* will not confine its musical service to phonograph records. There will be a piano and other musical instruments in the broadcasting station and instrument and vocal selections by visiting artists will be sent together with the work of local musicians."[44]

Radio, still in its infancy, was quite primitive. At the time of KGW's birth, transmitters, for example, often failed to operate for an entire evening or even a complete program. Studio equipment was scarcely better. The *Oregonian* later recalled that KGW's "original carbon 'mike' was a temperamental thing. When not in use it was stored in a wooden box heated with electric lights to dry out the carbon particles. In use, as soon as the carbon became dampened by the breath of a speaker or singer, it started to hiss."[45]

Yet, KGW was clearly seeking to set a different radio standard. Following daily news coverage of its transmitter testing, the new station signed-on with great fanfare and an inaugural program that did indeed raise the bar for radio in Portland.

KGW's inaugural broadcast on March 25, 1922 was a star-studded event—at least by Portland standards. Stepping through "a clutter of wires and gadgets," *Oregonian* editor Edgar B. Piper signed-on KGW by saying: "The *Oregonian* offers the enjoyment of a great invention to the people of the Northwest. We plan to give you the best in music, addresses by good speakers and news bulletins."[46]

With the Portland opera season just opening, KGW borrowed members from the Portland Opera cast for its noon inaugural. Ms. Edith Mason, a famous soprano with the Chicago Grand Opera, was accompanied by the Chicago Grand Opera principal conductor, Giorgio Polacco, at KGW's piano. Estimating the radio audience at 50,000 (which must surely have included those listening to receivers set up in such public places as Meier & Frank), listeners heard Mason inaugurate KGW with selections from "Madame Butterfly" and other arias.

Engineer Vern Haybarker adjusts the KGW transmitter, January 1, 1924.

It seems clear that Piper was the driving force for the *Oregonian*'s entry into radio. He took a personal and professional interest in it as is evident both from correspondence and his comments at KGW's inauguration. Moreover, while most stations had an excellent relationship with the Seattle-based DOC radio inspector, O. R. Redfern, KGW's became troubled. In Piper's view, KGW held great promise of glory and public service, which warranted the paper's sizeable investment. Piper believed that the federal government's appointed representative had, however, failed to share either that same vision or to fully appreciate the depth of the *Oregonian*'s commitment and capabilities in radio.

Believing Redfern was insufficiently supportive of KGW's efforts, an irritated Piper wrote Secretary of Commerce Herbert Hoover (with whom he was friendly) on August 31, 1922, complaining about Redfern's "antagonistic attitude" and "irritating and detrimental friction" over KGW's aspirations. Piper went so far as to accuse Redfern of outright prejudice in favor of other stations to KGW's disadvantage.[47]

A wounded Redfern took exception and defended himself to his supervisor, D. B. Carson, Commissioner of Navigation/DOC, saying:

> In all my dealings with this station (I) merely endeavored to enforce the United States radio laws as I am supposed to do. The only friction which I recall was at the time when the *Oregonian* entered the radio field with a 50-watt station and refused to adopt a schedule of hours as agreed upon by the other broadcasting stations in Portland. At a conference held at that time between the broadcasting station owners, Mr. H. E. Thomas, city editor of the *Oregonian* made the statement that inasmuch as Mr. Piper was a personal friend of the Secretary of Commerce, the *Oregonian* intended to broadcast whenever they felt like doing so.[48]

Unwilling to let the matter drop there, Piper again complained of new harassment by Redfern in a letter to Carson dated September 11, 1923. When KGW sought to increase power to

Courtesy of the Oregonian

THE OREGONIAN · RADIO · K·G·W·

Radios were scarce in 1923, and KGW used its "Loud-speaker Automobile" to play KGW's programming on the streets of Portland to expand the station's audience.

500 watts and install a new transmitter in November, Redfern traveled to Portland to inspect the facilities and wrote a very favorable report that helped mollify the *Oregonian*.

Reception reports poured in, including Ashland resident Lloyd P. Crowson's: "You came in very loud." "This is the finest thing that has ever come into the life of farmers," said Mrs. R. A. Webster of Mill Plains, Washington. Little was known about radio's reach and the next day's *Oregonian* carried the story "How Far Radio Music Can Be Heard is Not Known."

By April 1, 1922, Portland had five radio stations in operation: the *Oregonian*'s KGW; the *Oregon Journal*'s Hallock and Watson station, KGG; Charles Austin's Northwestern Radio Manufacturing Company's KGN; Willard Hawley's KYG and Stubbs Electric's KQY. Air time on the five stations was divided as follows:

| Time | Sunday | Monday | Tuesday | Wednesday | Thursday | Friday | Saturday |
|------|--------|--------|---------|-----------|----------|--------|----------|
| 12:00–12:30 | NW | NW | NW | NW | NW | NW | NW |
| 12:30–1:00 | | | | | | | |
| 1:00–1:30 | Vacant | Vacant | Vacant | Vacant | Vacant | Vacant | Vacant |
| 1:30–2:00 | | | | | | | |
| 2:00–2:30 | Vacant | OR | OR | OR | – | – | – |
| 2:30–3:00 | NW | NW | NW | NW | NW | NW | NW |
| 3:00–3:30 | | | | | | | |
| 3:30–4:00 | OR | OR | OR | OR | OR | OR | OR |
| 4:00–4:30 | | | | | | | |
| 4:30–5:00 | HW | HW | HW | HW | HW | HW | HW |
| 5:00–5:30 | | | | | | | |
| 5:30–6:00 | | | | | | | |
| 6:00–6:30 | Stubbs | Stubbs | Stubbs | Stubbs | Stubbs | Stubbs | Stubbs |
| 6:30–7:00 | | | | | | | |
| 7:00–7:30 | OR | HW # | NW | NW | NW | NW | NW |
| 7:30–8:00 | | OR | HW # | HW # | HW # | HW # | HW # |
| 8:00–8:30 | Listening Hour | NW | NW | OR | Listening Hour | OR | Hawley |
| 8:30–9:00 | | Listening Hour | | | | | |
| 9:00–9:30 | NW | NW | Hawley | OR | Hawley | NW | HW |
| 9:30–10:00 | | | | | | | |

**OR** = KGW, *Oregonian* station    **HW** = KGG, Hallock and Watson station    **NW** = KGN, Northwestern Radio Mfg. Co. station
**Hawley** = KYG    **Stubbs** = KQY    **#** = *Journal* Radio News Bulletin Service

Portlanders line the Park Blocks to listen to KGW's broadcast of President Calvin Coolidge's speech on October 23, 1924.

The stations cooperated in more ways than just sharing airtime. On April 1, 1922, the *Oregonian* reported that "the new motor generator in The *Oregonian* radio tower displayed a wild and unaccountable streak of artistic temperament last night," which required KGW to transport baritone Dr. Stuart McGuire and accompanist Miss Ida May Cook to KYG's studios. KYG obliged KGW by transmitting the thus-delayed program. Since both stations were on the same frequency it was an easy, thought perhaps embarrassing, substitution. Apparently, such difficulties occurred often enough that the stations worked reciprocally in that way. On July 13, 1922, KYG's facilities failed and the *Oregonian* reported:

> An excellent musical programme scheduled to be broadcast from the Willard P. Hawley, Jr. station last night at 9 o'clock had to be canceled on account of the transmitting apparatus breaking down. That radio fans who were "standing by" for the programme might not be disappointed, another local station broadcast a number of phonographic records to fill up the time.

As the first radio stations signed-on, people were uncertain about what to call the new radio phenomenon. The *Oregonian*'s headline writer was prone to use the term "aerophone," as in the front-page "Herbert Gould sings to Aerophone Circle," on April 11, 1922, and "National Guard Unit Will Hold Unique Radio Dance and Entertainment Friday—Music from The Oregonian Aerophone Tower" on April 23, 1922.

While Portland had spawned five stations by the end of 1922, Hawley's KYG had been abandoned. The license for Stubbs' KQY was deleted on May 2, 1923, and Austin's KGN broadcast its last program a few weeks later on May 31, 1923.[49] Hallock and Watson's KGG endured until May 1924 but was largely inactive in its last months. Each station—depending upon how one might credit time spent broadcasting under an amateur call sign, the date of first broadcast under a professional call sign or the issuing date of the station's license—might variously claim being first.

Yet, it was KGW that had entered radio as a serious, enduring business and set the standard for professionalism. Indeed, KGW rapidly became one of the nation's leading radio stations.

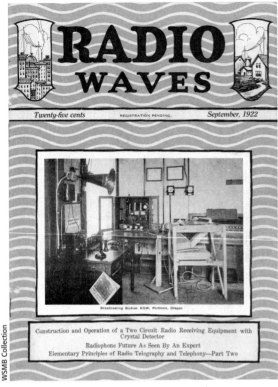

WSMB Collection

KGW pictured in *Radio Waves,* September, 1922.

In terms of the public's understanding of what a radio station should be, KGW seems to have a persuasive claim as Oregon's first.

As Oregon's first radio stations finished signing-on, radio was new and not well understood. Nearly everything on radio was a potential "first": the broadcast of a band concert, a sermon, a wedding, a graduation address, a women's club meeting, an organ recital, a dance concert (listeners obligingly scheduled dance parties in their homes to utilize the service) or an army band concert or chorus. Each of these "firsts" was claimed and reported as news.

Yet, out of these early attempts at grandstanding, these fledgling radio stations were beginning to assemble a new kind of community. By the late 1920s, radio personalities started to refer to their listeners as inhabitants of Radioland." WDSU, in New Orleans, published *Selected Poems and Philosophies* for its Radioland audience. In Toronto, DeForest-Crosley published the 1931 booklet *Personalities in Radioland,* and Fawcett Publications began publishing *Radioland* magazine in 1933. It was a hypothetical term for a new phenomenon. It acknowledged the rise of something new and unique: a large number of physically distant people who felt connected to one another and—more important—to the voices of distant speakers, whose unseen images they could only imagine. But listeners' imaginations were unbelievably powerful as they conjured up images of those distant radio personalities. It caused a deeply etched sense of personal attachment and loyalty—a sense of community—among listeners.

Radio had captured the imaginations of Watson, Hallock, Hawley and Austin. More important, it had captured the imagination of the public. Yet fundamental questions remained. With more stations failing than succeeding, how would radio be sustained?

Doubtlessly hoping to fuel public enthusiasm (and likely in part as an outlet for their own zeal), Watson, Hallock and Austin joined with Walter Haynes, a radio instructor at Portland's YMCA, and in March 1922 began publishing a slick monthly magazine, *Radio Waves,* which endured for more than a year.[50] Published primarily for the Portland area, it featured pictures of local (and San Francisco) stations, technical tips and radio news, and advertising for the growing number of stores that sold parts necessary for building radios. In its first issue, *Radio Waves* wondered about radio's future:

> Now that the public has been initiated into the wonders of entertainment via the air, who will foot the bill? It is not the course of events that such luxuries continue to come "free gratis." The time is not far hence when artists will charge for their services. Thus will the

problem present itself. Whether radio will be maintained by subscription, a subtle form of advertising or furnished by the government remains to be seen. However, now is the time to get in while the getting is good.[51]

Radio had arrived in Oregon, and the announcers had it right. Listeners and performers alike were suddenly all citizens of an evolving Radioland—a place these Oregon radio pioneers had created in the Beaver State.

# Endnotes

1. The economic and social conditions described in the opening paragraphs are largely taken from *The Oregon Story 1850–2000*, Staff of the *Oregonian* (Portland, OR: Graphic Arts Publishing, 2000).
2. This institution became Oregon State Agricultural College in 1927 and Oregon State College on April 17, 1956, before becoming Oregon State University.
3. "Dress Suit Banned by O.A.C. Students," *Oregonian*, February 12, 1920, 1.
4. Rev. Lawrence J. Saalfield, *Forces of Prejudice in Oregon 1920-1925*, (Portland, OR: Archdiocesan Historical Commission, 1984), 2–5.
5. Advertisement, *Morning Oregonian*, February 9, 1920, 9.
6. "Third Party in Oregon is Urged," *Morning Oregonian*, January 30, 1920, 1.
7. *Sunday Oregonian*, January 14, 1923, 1.
8. One earlier station, 7YB, had been authorized in March 1920 and licensed to the University of Oregon in Eugene.
9. Art Redman, "Northwestern Radio Manufacturing Company, *Antique Radio Classified*, September, 2005.
10. *Oregonian*, May 24, 1908, 4.
11. While the company started in 1921, it was actually incorporated on April 19, 1922, with capital stock of $50,000, by Frank Phillippi and Joe H. Page—in addition to Austin as its principal founder. (*Oregonian*, 3/20/22, 15)
12. "Advertising by Radio," *Radio News*, October 1921, 281, 348.
13. Originally at 400 E. 22nd St. N, the address under the current Portland street addressing system is 1914 NE 22nd Avenue. The home is now a bed and breakfast.
14. The "7" prefix in these "amateur" radio call signs indicated that the stations were licensed in the nation's seventh "radio district" which consisted of the Pacific Northwest. These "amateur" call signs distinguished their radio stations as not intended, either by their owners or the federal government, to be professional broadcasting stations such as KDKA, Pittsburgh or WWJ, Detroit.
15. "Behind the Mike," *Oregonian*, March 18, 1942. French Salad ice cream must have been a unique ice cream specialty of the Sugar Bowl. This unusually named ice cream is otherwise unknown.
16. "Behind the Mike," *Oregonian*, March 18, 1942.
17. *Radio Digest Illustrated*, May 6, 1922, 6.
18. "Behind the Mike," *Oregonian*, March 18, 1942.
19. Joseph Homer Hallock, born April 23, 1891, was a former naval radio engineer who was assistant engineer in the construction of the U.S. Navy's then largest-in-the-world station at Bordeaux, France. (*Portland Oregon Journal*, April 2, 1922, 16). He later worked for the Federal Telegraph Company. (*Oregonian*, May 28, 1922 Sec 3, 5)
20. Watson also had a U.S. Navy background having been in charge of the U.S. Naval Radio Laboratory at Mare Island, CA. (*Oregonian*, May 29, 1922, Sec 3, 5) Watson was born in Oregon around 1893. (US Census 1920)
21. Watson's first name has frequently been spelled "Cliff." His name being Clifton, rather than Clifford, the correct spelling is with a single 'f.'
22. Information regarding their 1915–1916 activities comes from "Hallock and Watson," by Art Redman, *Antique Radio Classified*, June, 2006.
23. United Wireless Station at Astoria "PC," article in SOWP Wireless Pioneer. (Hallock Files, WSMB Collection)
24. Arc stations transmitted telegraphy, rather than telephony (voice) using a primitive method of a spark-generated carrier wave. The Bordeaux arc station was reportedly the largest, most powerful in the world.
25. "Popular Communications," 1957, and Joseph Hallock's photo album. Ted Hallock, Joseph Hallock's son, reports that Roy Young was also a partner. (Ted Hallock. Interview with author. Tape recording. Portland, OR. October 13, 2004).
26. *Oregon Journal*, March 15, 1922, 1.

27. *Oregon Journal*, March 16, 1922, 1.
28. "Behind the Mike," *Oregonian*, March 18, 1942.
29. Jerman, Wilbur J. Interview by author. Tape recording. Portland, OR. October 2, 2002. Jerman died on March 17, 2004. (Social Security Death Index)
30. KQY article from Jerman papers (WSMB Collection).
31. Jerman interview.
32. CHCQ signed-on as CQCA on May 2, 1922. The station's call changed to CHCQ on May 9, 1922, and to CFAC on August 26, 1922. It was owned by the *Calgary Daily Herald*. (http://www.broadcasting-history.ca/listings_and_histories/radio/histories.php?id=155&historyID=59)
33. "Station KQY," *Radio Waves*, October 1922, 197.
34. *Oregon Journal*, October 15, 1922, Sec. 2, 6.
35. *Oregon Journal*, May 1, 1923.
36. Department of Commerce handwritten notation on final KQY license (KQY file, NARA, College Park MD).
37. This account of KYG's demise is based upon the KYG Broadcast *Pro-File* record and accounts in the *Oregon Journal* as reported by Craig Adams.
38. "Behind the Mike," *Oregonian*, March 20, 1942.
39. Radio Service Bulletins 51 and 57, US Department of Commerce, Washington, DC.
40. Application filed January 20, 1922; station inspected by O. R. Redfern on February 11, 1922. The station was originally licensed for limited hours (4 p.m. to 10 p.m. for general broadcasting, later modified to 10 p.m. to 12 Midnight). By November 1922 the station's licensing reflected "unlimited hours" authority.
41. In the book "WWJ – the Detroit News," published in 1922, the *Detroit News* reports that it was broadcasting regular music and news programming beginning in August, 1920.
42. Information based upon Port of Portland website: http://www.radiotowersite.com/rt_kgw_history.asp)
43. The Department of Commerce Bureau of Navigation/Radio Service license application contained blanks for the applicant to identify its "per word" and "minimum per radiogram" charge for ship-to-shore message traffic, and what came to be called "Limited Commercial" professional stations filled in the technical portions of the application leaving the message charge sections blank.
44. *Oregonian*, March 19, 1922, 8.
45. "Twenty Years Behind the Mike," *Oregonian/Northwest Magazine*, March 22, 1942, 4.
46. "Silver Anniversary: KGW's Quarter Century on the Air," *Oregonian*, March 23, 1947.
47. August 31, 1922. Letter from Edgar Piper to Herbert Hoover. (KGW file, NARA, College Park, MD).
48. September 7, 1922. Letter from O. R. Redfern to D. B. Carson, Commissioner of Navigation, Bureau of Navigation, Department of Commerce. (KGW file, NARA, College Park, MD).
49. Craig Adams, www.pdxradio.com.
50. "Behind the Mike," *Oregonian*, March 19, 1942.
51. Originally *Radio Waves*, March 1922, as quoted in "Behind the Mike," *Oregonian*, March 19, 1942.

2

# Radio Reverberates Across Oregon

America's preeminent broadcast historian, the late Erik Barnouw, once described 1922 as the nation's "era of euphoria" over radio. While Portland had been home to the state's first stations, other communities across Oregon were soon caught up in that bubbling enthusiasm.

## KQP Hood River

Interest ran high in Hood River, for example. The *Hood River News* reported on April 21, 1922, that E. A. Franz had purchased the community's first "radio telephone." Having gone to Portland to purchase routine items at a hardware store, Franz had his first encounter with radio. After "'listening in' on a radio concert, he fell just as hard as every other man and woman who has ever 'listened in' to a radio concert," the paper reported. Franz bought the necessary items and made plans to install the set in his Hood River hardware store for his customers' amusement.

Radio seemed to offer a variety of potential benefits. On April 21, 1922, the *Hood River News* also observed that "Many a rancher has raised his boys and girls to the age at which they have become useful only to lose them because there is nothing but work and no amusement in ranch life. But radio has come and will furnish a never-ending variety of entertainment."

Portland's KGG was popular in Hood River, but the idea of launching a local station was also afoot. In late March 1922, Lloyd H. Stimson, a naval veteran who had worked in wireless during World War I, filed a license application in the name of his Blue Diamond Electric Company. His station, KQP, signed-on April 29, 1922, offering Edison Diamond Disc phonograph records "and was probably heard over a radius of about 1000 miles."[1] By late May, KQP (which was located on a hill above State Street) was in full operation and carrying news reports from the *Oregon Journal* just like the Portland-based stations. Radio had taken hold in Hood River. On June 2, 1922, the *Hood River News* observed: "A few days ago we heard a man say 'radio is just a fad that will be here today and gone tomorrow.' But this man will find that he is as mistaken as were those who declared that the phonograph and the movies were merely passing fads." On June 30, 1922, the paper reported the names of various residents, identifying their sets and the distant stations they had been able to hear.

Clearly, the *Hood River News* had also been smitten by radio. The paper's July 28, 1922, issue reported that the *News* would install its own station to be "operated from the home of the *News*' editor on 13th Street. The *News* will be the first newspaper outside of Portland in the state to install a radio transmitter and, as far as is known, the first weekly newspaper in the United States to be equipped with this new and wonderful utility."

The *News* made no mention of KQP, but Stimson clearly didn't wish to compete. When editor/publisher H. G. Ball filed the *News*' radio application a few days later, it must have been accompanied by a letter from Stimson authorizing the transfer of the KQP call sign to the newspaper. By July 26, KQP was the property of the *Hood River News* and being operated by Stimson for the newspaper. On September 29, 1922, the *News* proudly reported that the "Promise of Radio Is Now Fulfilled" and noted that local residents had listened to radio "concerts" from Calgary, Great Falls, Wallace, Idaho, Seattle, Tacoma, Yakima, Denver, Portland, Salt Lake City, Los Angeles, El Monte, San Francisco and Stockton during the past week.

By then, Harry Read's Hood River Radio Shop had moved into the Blue Diamond Electric Company's building. But by late January, notwithstanding the *News*' crowing about KQP's "remarkable record last month" of being received in Milford, Connecticut, the reality of operating a radio station in a small community had finally caught up with the paper, and the *News* was exploring ways of relieving itself of the burdens that KQP imposed. If the *News* was not up to the task, it seemed unlikely that another commercial enterprise would have an interest in taking over the station—so a noncommercial alternative was explored. Local resident Carroll Mansfield led the effort by local radio enthusiasts to establish the Apple City Radio Club, which assumed responsibility for programming and operating KQP. That change also provided an opportunity for Harry Read to play a larger role in the station. Turning the station over to the club must have been discussed for months before its consummation, because the federal licensing papers appear to have been filed late in February, immediately following the club's actual formation on February 22.[2] Charter club members included Ball, who signed the license transfer application as club secretary, and Read, who was designated the station's "operator."[3]

The club's regular 25-cent monthly dues for charter members helped pay the costs of operating the station, which were anticipated to be quite low, and radio enthusiasts under the age of 18 were encouraged to apply as associate members at no cost. Among the club's first decisions was that the executive committee, consisting of the officers, would rule on the suitability of all programs to be broadcast.

## KDYQ Portland

Another new arrival in radio found a home in Portland's YMCA Building, at Sixth and Taylor Street, which was the home to the Oregon Institute of Technology (an organization entirely unrelated to the university of the same name later established in Klamath Falls). The Y offered

KDYQ, Portland.

a variety of vocational classes, including accounting, automotive and electrical engineering, stenography and business, as well as Elementary School for Men and a college prep curriculum. This Oregon Institute of Technology leaped into radio as a vocational opportunity and brought in L. S. Simpson, formerly of Hood River, as principal of the radio program. The radio students even formed a fraternity, "'I Tappa Kee' to foster a spirit of comradeship and promote progress in radio operation."[4] The group's goal was to "constitute a legion of honor with its aim the preservation and observance, through appropriate ritual, ceremony and example, of the noble traditions which in the past have inspired courage to make the supreme sacrifice in the hearts of those valiant knights of the key—those radio men who have gone down with their ships in fulfillment of their duty and trust."[5] While clearly focused upon telegraphy, the school applied for a radio station license as KDYQ. Granted on May 4, 1922, the station was located on the building's fourth floor and signed-on May 9, 1922.[6]

Oregon's first presidential radio broadcast was a big event in 1923. KDYQ's Lloyd Stimson coordinated the arrangements for hearing KGW's broadcast of president Warren G. Harding's Independence Day speech in Portland on July 4, 1923. At Hood River, 1.5 miles of wire were run (by Harry Read) from the *Hood River News'* publisher's home to the KQP studios, from which the signal was re-broadcast to radio receivers placed in public locations throughout the town. "Radio Triumphant Here on the Fourth," proclaimed the *Hood River Glacier*. "The address of the president was heard plainly; even the sibilant S's were heard."[7] Even the smallest aspects of radio were still considered newsworthy. Installation of a radio set by the Fire Department, and L. O. Meacham's installation of an aerial in Hood River's tallest tree (150 feet), both made ink in the October 4, 1923 *Hood River Glacier*.

# KDYU Klamath Falls

As newspapers across the nation entered radio, virtually all the Portland-area newspapers allied themselves either with stations they owned or with which they were closely associated. As the *Oregonian* built KGW and the *Oregon Journal* associated itself variously with KGN, KGG, KQY and KYG, other Oregon newspapers took notice. In southern Oregon, the Klamath Falls *Evening Herald* didn't want to miss out, and in April 1922 publisher F. R. Soule applied for a radio station license in the Herald Publishing Company's name. Southern Oregon's first federally authorized station, KDYU, was licensed on May 4, 1922, to be operated from the back of the newspaper's printing plant on Eighth Street. Like the *Oregonian*, the *Herald* said nothing about its radio application in print although it ran a "Radiograms" column in May and June of 1922 that offered tidbits about radio's growth across the nation. Perhaps this was an attempt to try gauge the community's interest in radio. When the series of articles abruptly ended in late June, the paper ceased mentioning radio and it is doubtful that KDYU was ever constructed. The *Herald* abandoned KDYU's license in November 1922.[8]

# KDZJ Eugene

Eugene's first radio station was the creation of Garrett Lewis, a University of Oregon student, whose license for KDZJ was granted on May 26, 1922. The station operated from his home at 1271 Emerald Street.[9] Using the business name Excelsior Radio Company, Lewis announced plans to broadcast "assembly speakers at the University of Oregon and musical concerts held by the 'associated students' of the University."[10] Lewis, who had been a naval operator with training in the Harvard Radio School, reportedly hadn't discussed his programming plans with the University but anticipated that "there will be no difficulty in obtaining permission [to broadcast]." By August, KDZJ was regularly broadcasting on Mondays, Wednesday and Fridays. Presumably awaiting the opening of fall University of Oregon classes (and potential programming material), Lewis was looking for partners.[11]

Lewis' enterprise in establishing KDZJ reflected considerable initiative but apparently produced little business results. Indeed, the Eugene *Daily Guard* observed that summer that it thought the radio craze had passed. Lewis was clearly in no position to sustain the effort that KDZJ required, and he let the station's license expire in November 1922.

# KFAT Eugene

Eugene dentist S. T. Donahue applied for a license in June 1922 and was granted KFAT on July 6 of that year. Operating from his dental office in the Zumwalt Building at 681 Willamette Street across from the Heilig Theater, KFAT was on the air before September 20, 1922, when the *Eugene Daily Guard* favorably reported on the previous day's broadcast. According to historians Will McKenzie and Gene Lane, "KFAT was more 'amateur' than professional, kept sporadic hours and was apparently operated from the dentist's office more for his pleasure than that of whatever small audience may have been listening."[12] Since KFAT apparently began broadcasting around the time KDZJ expired, some have theorized that Lewis sold his KDZJ equipment to Donahue. This seems possible, since both stations' technical descriptions in their DOC license applications are similar. That interpretation is further supported by the report that Lewis became KFAT's chief engineer and, along with another fellow radio enthusiast Paul Hoppe, rebuilt the KFAT equipment to achieve an increase in power to 100 watts, which was later approved.

Eugene broadcast historian Raleigh Wildman reported that "During New Year's Eve of 1922, KFAT was on the air with a special broadcast and it was rumored that some of the stories told got pretty 'raucous,' and that there were many telephone calls and letters of complaint from listeners. This very well could have been a factor in the station's decision not to seek renewal of KFAT's license in the spring of 1923 when its license expired."[13]

## KFAB Portland

Meanwhile, back in Portland, another radio entrant appeared—albeit briefly. On June 1, 1922, Charles C. Coleman and Carson P. Niles, previously dealers for radio sets and equipment, filed incorporation papers for the Pacific Radiofone Company. Located at 675 Brazee Street, the company's KFAB was licensed on June 14, 1922, and held the first call sign issued west of the Mississippi in the newly opened "KF" four-letter call letter series. The need for four-letter call signs arose because radio's growth had exhausted the KA through KE three-letter series. As a result, the DOC began using four-letter call signs, beginning with KF. KFAB lasted less than a month, having begun broadcasting around July 25, 1922, and signing-off late in August. To raise cash, the station's 10-watt transmitting equipment was sold to Frank S. Barton of the Salem Electric Company, a supplier of electric supplies who had recently begun selling radios. The KFAB unit was used to found Salem's KFCD.

## KFCD Salem

While KFAB's license was not formally cancelled until mid-November 1922, Barton applied for his radio station license as KFCD in late August, and it was approved on September 9, 1922. The station didn't sign-on until October 27, 1922, having been "held up pending the engagement of a qualified operator."[14] The "qualified operator" turned out to be C. Meredith Landaker, a Salem High School junior, who had recently passed his federal radio license exam. Landaker agreed to serve as KFCD's operator in exchange for use of the station for his amateur ham radio operations during off hours.

KFCD had high hopes of presenting "a number of fine attractions, mostly from local musicians; it is not planned to use much if any phonograph music; it will be the real stuff."[15] Much of the station's offerings relied upon the Salem Apollo Club, which debuted on KFCD on November 13, 1922. The club, a branch of the main Apollo Club in Portland, was dedicated to semi-professional vocal and instrumental music performances and offered "60 voices of Salem, Oregon." The Apollo Club broadcasts were expected to be "the finest boost that Salem ever had in musical or direct advertising way. The singers will make it a genuine concert that ought to give all [listeners] this side of Chicago a whole evening's pleasure. It is believed that no other such pretentious number has yet been offered anywhere in the west."[16]

KFCD made a good deal of press in its first few weeks—but not much thereafter. One practice that appeared to be common in radio's early days was for small stations lacking local entertainment sources to "pick up" the signal of another distant station and re-broadcast it live. It was a practice considerably at odds with later performance rights and copyright. On November 24, 1922, *Oregon Statesman* reported that KFCD had, the previous night, presented "The Hotel Statler Orchestra, at St. Louis, Mo., [which] played one of its peppiest dance programs for the benefit of Salem radio fans. The strains came into the Salem Electric radio station as clear as if the players were in the next room." A July 2, 1922, *Oregonian* article had also reported that the Salem Electric station would rebroadcast KGW's signal some evenings.

Salem Electric was located in the Masonic Lodge building on the northwest corner of State and High Streets, and KFCD operated from a first-floor display window so the public could observe. KFCD broadcast approximately four hours daily, Monday through Saturday, from noon to 1 p.m. and 5 to 8 p.m. each evening. Studio audiences for live music performances were seated in the electric store. The station offered local programming, including Dr. Sites' Salem Symphony, the performance of a Boy Scout troop from the Salem Heights Community Hall, the Whitney Boys Chorus and the Presbyterian Church Quartet Singers. On Fridays, Barton offered gavel-to-gavel coverage of the Salem Women's Club.[17]

While KFCD seems to have done a fine job of reflecting the Salem community in its programming, the station failed—apparently largely for technical reasons. KFCD's studio and transmitter were surrounded by four motion picture theatres whose carbon arc projectors, along with an adjacent 6,000-volt power transmission line near KFCD's antenna, created so much interference that the station's signal was unreliable. However, Salem historian Douglas Stingley also credits antagonism by the afternoon *Capitol Journal* newspaper with starving the station of support necessary to its survival. Reportedly, the paper ran a "scare campaign centered on the many dangers to the public created by radio waves."[18]

KFCD signed-off January 26, 1924, and Salem was without a local radio station for another decade.[19] Early in 1925, Barton wrote in an *Oregon Statesman* radio column: "Many friends of KFCD have expressed regrets that the 50-foot towers are a thing of the past and Salem will no longer be represented on the broadcasting maps."[20]

## KFAY Medford

Further south, radio beckoned William J. Virgin Jr, whose father, William J. Virgin Sr., had moved to Oregon to open a profitable Central Point flour mill near the turn of the century. Virgin, Jr., who had been born in Ashland, was about 20 when his father's death required him to assume management of the family's mill.

Late in 1921, Virgin and some friends gathered in Elmer Morrison's garage at 1049 Ashland Street to tinker with radio. In addition to Morrison and Virgin, those present included Sam Jordan, owner of an automotive and electronics shop, and Floyd Rush, a veteran military radio operator. The men assembled a small, five-watt radio transmitter and stretched an antenna wire from the garage to a large tree. Without benefit of a license, they transmitted southern Oregon's first radio broadcast.[21] In December, Rush reportedly constructed the first permanent radio receiving set in Jackson county for Virgin.

As interest in radio grew, local newspapers began running stories about "wireless concerts" that newly developing radio stations were offering in other parts of the country. On March 15, 1922, the *Ashland Daily Tidings* reported that a Medford man had used "a radiophone" in his rooms at the Medford Hotel to listen to broadcasts from as far away as Chicago and San Francisco.

Inevitably, Virgin and his friends soon devised ways to combine fun with commerce. On May 25, 1922, the *Medford Mail Tribune* reported on discussions among electronics dealers about building a local radio station. Central Point had been suggested as an ideal site because of its central location between Josephine and Jackson County listeners. The town offered $200 toward such a construction if Medford, Ashland and Grants Pass would contribute the balance.

Virgin sprang into action. On July 21, 1922, *Medford Mail Tribune* reported that he was building a station, presumably at the flour mill in Central Point, and that the newspaper would participate in the project by providing news and market reports for broadcast.

Virgin's license application was filed early in August and approved, as KFAY, on August 16, 1922. While KFAY was licensed solely in Virgin's name, the men who had initiated the effort in Elmer Morrison's garage the previous fall remained nominally associated with it. The *Medford Mail Tribune*, in its coverage of KFAY's inauguration, even credited KFAY as co-owned by Virgin and Sam Jordan, and it seems likely that Jordan retained some type of unofficial ownership. Later station employees recall successor radio station KMED broadcasting commercials for Jordan's electric company without charge years after Bill Virgin's death (see chapter 4).

KFAY signed-on September 23, 1922, with a broadcast of Launsbach's Dance Orchestra from the Jackson County Fairground's pavilion.[22] Interested parties were invited to view "the first broadcast station in Southern Oregon."[23] Hallock and Watson built KFAY's transmitter, which Clif Watson installed, and L. Darrell Minkler operated the station that night.[24] Reportedly, the broadcast began inside the pavilion but, due to concern that the room was acoustically unsuitable, the orchestra moved outside for the remainder of the broadcast.[25] The *Mail Tribune* hailed KFAY as a great success: "Radio station K.F.A.Y. located at Medford Oregon is getting excellent results. Last Saturday night, when broadcasting dance music by Launsbach's orchestra on low power with the aerial incomplete, they were picked up by Santa Cruz Calif, Sedro Woolley, Wash., Salt Lake City, Utah and other equally distant points. Last night, with the completed aerial and high power they probably reached over a radius of 1,500 miles."

Bill Virgin's first transmitter in 1922. Likely located in Central Point, it probably operated briefly from there before he submitted his formal application for a radio station license.

The newspaper also encouraged community participation by reporting that "the owners of the station wish the public to consider the installation of a [radio station] as a community affair and wish the support of all local talent to make it a success. They wish all musicians to register with them who are willing to sing or play over the radio-phone."[26]

Following its sign-on, KFAY continued operating several days a week, mostly with local talent but also using phonograph recordings. While initially licensed to downtown Medford, Virgin eventually secured permission to operate KFAY from the Jackson County Fairgrounds, and the station was re-licensed to that location in spring 1923.

KFAY received national press coverage when Virgin showed up after a week's absence on April 19, 1923, and discovered that the entire station had been stolen. Since the transmitter was a "breadboard affair" (parts placed on a board) and the microphone was also a simple matter, the theft wouldn't have been difficult. While local stories persisted for years that the theft was actually a prank pulled by Virgin's friends, it was indeed a crime. Emery (Buster) Tull and Paul Wright, the latter a bellboy at Medford's Hotel Holland, were arrested a day later, and the stolen equipment was found sitting on the porch of H. L. Bowman's Central Point home. The equipment, which had apparently been scheduled to be shipped to Seattle the next day to be sold or re-used, had sustained significant damage. Bowman was booked on complicity in the

Early radio stations needed radio receivers in order to ensure that no one else was broadcasting (since all stations used the same frequency) when they wanted to sign-on. This was KFAY's reception equipment in 1922.

crime but was later released when it became clear the boys had tried to implicate him to lighten their own burden. The two thieves were sent to the State (Juvenile) Training School in Salem.

KFAY had clearly become popular and Virgin decided radio—rather than the family flour mill—was the business for him. In an October 2, 1922, letter to the Department of Commerce radio inspector in Seattle, he reported that he had sold his flour mill and started Virgin's Radio Service. He asked to have KFAY's license and call letters transferred to the new company's name.[27]

By then, Virgin was devoting himself full-time to the sale of radio sets and parts through the Virgin's Radio Service store and the operation of KFAY. The theft must have prompted Virgin to consider relocating KFAY away from the County Fairgrounds and, after first exploring installing the station at the Medford Natorium, he joined forces with a radio sales competitor, Paul's Electric Store.[28] In October 1923, they jointly rented space in the newly remodeled Medford Building at 33 North Central Avenue for their shops and for KFAY.[29]

For a time, the station operated from the back of Paul's Electric store. Later, it was moved to Virgin's radio shop with the transmitter's dynamotor generator located in the Medford Center Building's basement.[30, 31]

There was an irony to radio's meteoric rise. Newspapers like the *Oregonian*, hobbyists like Willard Hawley and institutions like the YMCA, had all built radio stations for altruistic purposes. Operating non-commercially, their public success soon proved to be a major economic headache for these entrepreneurs. Once radio's initial thrill had passed, radio performers began expecting payment for their services. Businesses that had been operating stations purely for the good of the community were soon subject to demands for more elaborate programming, which could no longer be secured for free. No one had yet figured out how to generate the revenue needed to meet the operating costs fueled by the public's radio craze.

Bill Virgin sought various ways to offer quality entertainment inexpensively. In the days before concerns about copyright were prominent, long-time Medford postmaster Frank De Sousa recalled that Virgin set up an antenna "three or four miles out of town" to pick up KNX from Los Angeles and used "a telephone connection to the station" to rebroadcast programming.[32]

Before long, Bill Virgin began selling advertising on KFAY, something that was not widely done at that time. For example, KGW did not "go commercial" until 1925 and KFJR until 1927. According to KMED historian Art Chipman, Virgin, who was his own advertising salesman, "would make the rounds of people he thought might wish to advertise that day and then go over to the station in the evening and broadcast until such time as the advertising had been used up."[33]

But by 1924, KFAY was forced to compete with programming offered by corporate-supported "big city" stations heard distantly in Medford. Competition from these larger stations in Portland, Seattle and California, as well as more distant stations beginning their first network-affiliated "chain" broadcasts from the eastern United States, meant that KFAY needed more power, more paid staffers and more quality programming to effectively compete—all of which would require additional capital. It proved too steep a challenge, and KFAY signed-off for the last time in September 1924.[34] Although KFAY had "gone silent," Virgin continued to operate his radio equipment supply business from various retail outlets located along Main Street. But Virgin wasn't quite finished with radio (see chapter 4).[35]

## KFBM Astoria

Astoria's two newspapers, the *Morning Astorian* and the *Astoria Evening Budget*, were both watching other Oregon newspapers' foray into radio with interest. On August 22, 1922, a license application signed by Lloyd Foster was filed jointly by Cook and Foster's Radio Service and the Astoria Hardware Store for station KFBM, which they established in cooperation with the *Morning Astorian*. With a transmitter that duplicated the one Wilbur Jerman had built CHCQ Calgary, and which reportedly he had originally constructed for KQY Portland, the station initially operated from the Astoria Hotel.[36]

Assuming that Truman Cook and Lloyd Foster would have likely purchased KQY's original 10-watt transmitter for KFBM, it is likely that the KFBM installation in Astoria occurred shortly after KQY's power increase to 100 watts in September 1922.

KFBM signed-on Monday evening, October 16, 1922, with a piano and an Edison talking machine (furnished by Cline Music Company) from a studio located in the newspaper's Fellman Building offices. Ralph D. Wylie, a recent graduate of Oregon Institute of Technology, was the station's operator. On successive evenings, the station featured performances by the Columbia Orchestra (actually a 6-piece ensemble) and the Dreamland Orchestra, which performed works such as "I Wish I Knew," "Say it While Dancing" and "Time After Time." After a brief relocation to the Astoria Hotel, KFBM moved to the back of Kelley's Bakery on Duane Street between 14th and 15th Streets, where it had "a small studio with a piano."[37]

On November 8, 1922, the *Morning Astorian* reported "KFBM Plays Big Part Sending Election News" the previous evening. The paper obviously foresaw potential tie-ins between radio and publishing and, in a large display ad on November 15, 1922, offered a free crystal receiving set in exchange for soliciting specified numbers of new subscriptions to the paper.

## KFGG Astoria

The *Astoria Evening Budget* decided it needed to compete with the *Morning Astorian*'s radio venture and set about securing its own station. Unfortunately, the paper unwisely chose a partner. In early November, the *Evening Budget* announced an arrangement under which a new Astoria business, the Radio Sales and Service Company, would build and operate the newspaper's radio station, which was licensed as KFGG. In mid-November, the *Evening Budget* proudly announced that broadcasts from KFGG were imminent. It is clear that the station was actually constructed, with studios reportedly located at 183 12th Street and transmitting towers variously reported to have been located on the Page Building and/or the Weinhard Hotel.[38, 39] Then on November 23, 1922, with no comment in the *Astoria Evening Budget*, the *Morning Astorian*—under the headline "Budget Radio Station Closed Up is Report,"—gleefully reported:

> The radio broadcasting station operated by the *Astoria Evening Budget* and the Radio Sales and Service Company has closed its doors and no attempt will be made to send out programs. It is understood that the proprietors of the R.S.S. have left the city.[40]

With no stated reason for the Radio Sales and Service Company's exit, either technical deficiency, larceny or both may have figured in the hasty departure.

With KFGG abandoned, KFBM continued to have Astoria's local airwaves entirely to itself with the *Morning Astorian* offering programs such as entertainers from the Blue Mouse Theater or Ralph Wylie playing his steel guitar. Following each evening's broadcast, the newspaper printed a report on the previous day's KFBM programming.

Then—on December 7, 1922—Astoria was suddenly engulfed in flames. In one of the most serious disasters to ever hit the community, much of the city's downtown was destroyed. Early reports held that the fire had been deliberately set in two locations by "radical incendiaries."[41] On December 8, 1922, "thousands of persons living in the northwest received their first news of the Astoria disaster through the *Oregonian* high-power broadcasting station. The early reports were sent out from KGW at noon and created a sensation. At 2 o'clock in the afternoon a complete story of the disaster was broadcast."[42]

Among the businesses that burned up were Cook and Foster Hardware, Astoria Hardware and the *Morning Astorian* itself. As the front end of Kelley's Bakery was burning, the KFBM transmitter was jerked loose from its connecting wires and removed, and the station's piano was kicked downstairs to the basement where it was consumed by flames.

Astoria suddenly had greater issues to face than the loss of a small radio station—and neither KFBM nor KFGG was ever rebuilt. KFBM's license was allowed to expire in January 1923 and was deleted in March 1923. While the transmitter had been salvaged, Cook later wrote: "We did not foresee the future value of the radio franchise and sold the station to Ernie Marsh [projectionist at the Liberty Theatre] (see chapter 4). A couple of weeks later he tried to sell it back but we could not spare the money [needed in] getting our business set up."[43]

# KFFE Pendleton

Eastern Oregonians were regularly listening to the Portland stations when William E. Snodgrass decided it was time for Pendleton to have a station of its own. A photographer by trade, Snodgrass had a studio above the Pendleton Drug Store in 1921 but also had an interest in radio.[44] In October 1922, he applied for a station license in the name of the Eastern Oregon Radio Company, Inc. Inspected by O. R. Redfern on October 19, the station was licensed as KFFE on October 24, 1922, located in the Penland Building above the Tallman Drug Store.[45]

The *Daily East Oregonian* was likely not enthusiastic about the advent of a local radio station, for the paper was totally silent about KFFE. The paper's only stories dealing with radio were a few reports of upcoming programs from stations located in Oregon's western areas, and its only references to KFFE occurred in the Eastern Oregon Radio Company's paid advertising as in a November 25, 1922 ad, when the company was identified as located in Room 2 of the Penland Building. In a December 16, 1922 display ad devoted to selling the Magnavox horn speaker, "The Reproducer Supreme," the company noted in small type, "Operating Radio KFFE, Room 2 Above Tallman Drug Company, First and Only Broadcasting Station in Umatilla County."[46]

Transmitters such as KFFE's were small and the studio was simple which made relocating the 10-watt station easy. By early 1923, KFFE apparently relocated to what was then City Hall where, local legend holds, Snodgrass was allowed to set up his transmitter and antenna in the cupola.[47] A. O. "Monk" Cardon, a long-time Pendleton resident who later entered broadcasting, was a teenager when KFFE signed-on (see chapter 13). Cardon later recalled acquiring a headphone from the remodeled phone system at the Temple Hotel, purchasing a crystal detector from Harold Brock at Taylor Hardware, and "requisitioning" a discarded teepee pole from the

Round-Up grounds to carry 100 feet of wire between the pole and his bedroom—all in order to listen to fledgling KFFE.[48]

Little is known about KFFE's programming, although the station endured until 1924. While broadcasting had ceased, its license was deleted in November of that year. In Pendleton's 1925 city directory, Snodgrass was shown working as a salesman.

## KFEC Portland

Oregon's largest department store, Meier & Frank, was poised to become a major radio entrant. A Portland institution founded in 1857, the company probably entered broadcasting because it was already selling radio sets. A major purchaser of newspaper display advertising, the store perhaps thought operating a high-quality station of the type it intended would boost radio set sales. This was, after all, a time when no talent was paid to perform, and a radio station's expenses were essentially limited to technical operating costs. Meier & Frank's KFEC was licensed on October 3, 1922, and signed-on October 19, 1922, with a broadcast featuring Earl Fuller's Famous New

GOOD NEWS FOR RADIO FANS

Meier & Frank's Own Radio Broadcasting Station—

KFEC

(Wave Length 360 Meters)

Will Officially Open Tonight With a Splendid Program—From 9 to 10 o'Clock—Presenting Among Other Features

EARL FULLER'S FAMOUS NEW YORK JAZZ BAND

This—the first of a series of super programs to be broadcasted by Meier & Frank's every Thursday between 9 and 10 P. M.—will give Radio Fans an opportunity to hear the man who introduced jazz to "The Great White Way"—Earl Fuller—for six years featured in the world-renowned Rector's Cafe, New York. On tonight's program Mr. Fuller will present

Julia Dawn, the Girl From Rector's

in two song numbers: "I Wish I Knew" and "Mighty Lak a Rose." The balance of the program for the radio hour will be diversified and entertaining, embracing vocal and instrumental numbers by talented artists, including Tommy Tobin singing Larry Franklin's Fox Trot Ballad "Love Thief," a local composition with Larry Franklin at the piano; also Winifred Campbell, soprano soloist.

We Invite Radio Fans

to "tune in" on this concert tonight and to tell us what they think of it; what they enjoyed most; what they would have us broadcast at the next Thursday night concert and afterwards.

You can call Atwater 4600 during the radio hour and ask for the radio operator. You can let us know by letter or otherwise how the different renditions came in and make any suggestions you please.

*Meier & Frank Co.*

Meier & Frank promoted KFEC's sign-on in this October 19, 1922 *Oregonian* advertisement.

York Jazz Band and Julia Dawn, the "Girl from Rector's." KFEC and its programming were mentioned in all of the store's display advertising. With KFEC's antenna located on the roof of Meier & Frank's 16-story building, the station's studios were installed on the fifth floor, where the studio and transmitter shared a room with heavy curtains draped between them for acoustic separation. During periods when KFEC wasn't broadcasting, its studio was used as a library and reading room for store employees.

Meier & Frank's prominence, along with its abundant print advertising schedule, gave KFEC a real advantage. KFEC also broadcast performances by Herman Kenin and his Oregon Grille Orchestra, a group that was more or less the KGW "house orchestra."[49] No doubt Meier & Frank's advertising clout with the *Oregonian* allowed KFEC rights to intrude upon KGW's "performer territory" in a manner that might have been off limits to other radio stations. But in 1929, KFEC would come to an interesting end (see chapter 7).

## KFBH Coos Bay

With Marshfield (renamed Coos Bay in 1944) residents listening to radio from northern Oregon, the local Thomas Music Company, run by Lou L. Thomas, thought it would be useful to operate a local station. Perhaps, like Meier & Frank, it sought to stimulate its sale of radio sets.

Thomas, a prominent citizen and future Coos Bay mayor, applied for a radio station license while his store was located at East 73 Central Avenue. Licensed as KFBH on August 4, 1922, the station was inspected by O. R. Redfern on November 25, 1922.[50] Technical expertise for KFBH was supplied by Mason Mears, Thomas Music Company's radio specialist, who had gained radio experience through World War I military service and who also established a radio school in Coos Bay in conjunction with the station.

By October 5, 1922, KFBH was broadcasting every Tuesday, Thursday and Saturday evening, but the results were likely disappointing to Thomas. Good local entertainment was hard to come by and phonograph "concerts" could readily be heard on distant stations. Moreover, Thomas Music Company was busy planning for its move into the spacious new quarters in the Elks Temple Lodge #1160, which was under construction in late 1922. The company's decision to move to the Elks Building may also have been influenced by the large July 1922 fire that destroyed four commercial blocks in downtown Coos Bay immediately adjacent to Thomas Music Company's Central Avenue location.

The Thomas Music Company relocated to this Elks Building in early 1923 but decided not to bring KFBH to its new location. When KFOF signed-on under different ownership, it also operated from this building (see chapter 4).

Courtesy of Jack Slattery Collection, Coos Historical and Maritime Museum, photo 992-8-1038

When the Thomas Music Company celebrated its grand opening in the Elks Building on February 16, 1923, it did so without KFBH. On January 3, 1923, Thomas notified the Department of Commerce that he was abandoning KFBH, although Thomas Music Company did continue to sell and service radios from their new location.[51]

## KFDA Baker City

Lou Thomas wasn't alone in seeking to connect his music store with radio broadcasting. In Baker City, Sanford Adler, who owned Adler's Music Store, also wanted to start a radio station. With a license application submitted in September 1922, KFDA was licensed on October 2 of that year. Equipment was supplied by Hallock and Watson Manufacturing in mid-December.[52] Like some other newspapers, the Baker City *Morning Democrat* saw a potential relationship with radio and indicated that it would print daily program listings for the station.

By January 1, 1923, KFDA was receiving reception reports from as far away as Rhode Island and Long Island, NY, with engineer E. R. Marshall as the station's operator. Picking up on "radio fever," local theatre manager K. L. Burk scheduled *The Radio King*, "a stirring ten-chapter movie serial starring Roy Stewart" at both the Empire and Orpheum theatres beginning on January 18, 1923. The *Morning Democrat* gave a door prize, a Brownie radio receiver, "as a means of increasing interest in radio." But the challenge of maintaining KFDA was too great, and the station only operated until May 1924, when its license was cancelled at Adler's request.

# KFDJ Corvallis

Oregon's last 1922 entry into the growing world of radio occurred when the Department of Physics at Oregon State University (OSU) applied for a radio license in late November.[53] Interests associated with OSU had been involved with radio as far back as 1919 when, on October 4, a U.S. Army colonel, W. F. Sharp, had wired the Department of Commerce requesting application forms to establish a radio station for the Field Artillery Reserve Officers Training Corps at the university.[54] Subsequently, the university secured a license for a Special Land Station, 7YJ, to be used for "technical and training."

Like any new technology, much effort was devoted to technical experimentation primarily aimed at improving a signal's reach, clarity and reliability. As a result, technical aficionados were among early radio's primary figures. Just as the Oregon Institute of Technology's KDYQ was created to explore the science of radio and its technical career opportunities, OSU's Department of Physics had been experimenting with radio for some time through work conducted by Professor Jacob Jordan. Following Colonel Sharp's lead, the school first obtained a license for experimentation over 7YJ in May 1921 and used that station to learn and teach about the physics of radio.

But at the same time, radio's public communication opportunities were becoming clearer to Jordan. In fall 1922, OSU relinquished 7YJ's license in favor of a new radio station license, approved as KFDJ, on December 7, 1922. KFDJ apparently didn't officially sign-on until shortly after New Year's Day, having completed transmitter tests on that date. Some test broadcasts may have commenced as early as October 7, 1922 under 7YJ's license or another experimental license, 7XH, held by the school. In any event, a Corvallis vs. Toledo OSU football game was broadcast prior to the school's formally submitting KFDJ's license application.[55] It was common by that time for Special Land Stations like 7YJ, or Northwestern Radio Manufacturing's experimental station 7XF, to offer programming for the general public, even though such stations were technically not licensed for such general broadcasting.

KFDJ broadcasts continued using the 7XH call sign until "official" service as KFDJ commenced after New Year's Day, 1923. OSU claims the station officially signed-on January 25, 1923, with a broadcast by the OSU Band "under the direction of Captain Harry L. Beard including opera, fantasy, popular music, and jazz."[56] The 60-piece band was crowded into room 212 in Apperson Hall along with KFDJ's transmitter. By 1925, the station's studios had been moved to the third floor of the OSU administration building (later renamed Benton Hall), although the transmitter remained in Apperson Hall about 400 feet away.[57] Regardless of location, KFDJ's studio was quite primitive. No acoustic treatment was applied to the walls and the microphone (being held on the right of photo below) was the type designed for telephone use.

Professor Jordan had not only personally constructed the transmitting apparatus but also served as the station's operator. Early KFDJ programming consisted of music and lectures, and the initial KFDJ staff consisted of Wallace Kadderly, station director; Professor Jacob Jordan, who also served as the station's chief engineer; Grant Feikert, station operator and student Webley Edwards, announcer. Edwards was KFDJ's first student manager.

Following his college graduation, Edwards went on to a significant broadcasting career. Having relocating to Hawaii in 1928 to work as an automobile salesman, in 1935 he launched *Hawaii Calls*, a weekly radio program broadcast throughout the U.S. from Waikiki's Moana Hotel. The program endured until 1972, when ill-health forced Edwards to end the series. During World War II years, Edwards also worked as a CBS Radio reporter and is believed to be

Inaugural KFDJ broadcast, OSU band, January 25, 1923.

the first person to have announced the Japanese attack on Pearl Harbor on December 7, 1941 (see chapter 13).

Kadderly later went to work for KGW (see chapter 15). Feikert became KFDJ/KOAC's chief engineer in 1932 and went on to become one of Oregon's principal radio engineering consultants, practicing into the 1970s.

These early stations were all noncommercial, and at radio's inception no one really envisioned advertising as its economic support model. As that idea began to emerge, it was considered unseemly by many—including then-Secretary of Commerce Herbert Hoover. It was Hoover who first sought to convene the annual industry-wide conversations (which eventually led to the founding of the National Association of Broadcasters), and at the first such gathering in spring 1922, he admonished: "It is inconceivable that we should allow so great a possibility for service, for news, for entertainment, for education, and for vital commercial purposes, to be drowned in advertising chatter."[58]

Across Oregon, from Hood River to Medford, Astoria to Baker City, Pendleton to Coos Bay—just as in Portland—electronics enthusiasts were intrigued by radio's promise and launched small stations with little thought to their long-term viability. And, just as in Portland, while most failed to muster sufficient resources or resolve to endure, a few did. In 1922, interest in radio continued to burgeon across the state as Oregonians huddled around their radios to listen to their local station—if they had one—or distant signals from Portland, Seattle or San Francisco.

There was magic was in the air—magic called radio.

# Endnotes

1. *Hood River News,* May 5, 1922, 1.
2. *Hood River News,* March 2, 1923, 1.
3. *Hood River Glacier,* March 1, 1923.
4. "Radio Group Organized," *Morning Oregonian,* November 20, 1922, 11.
5. Ibid.
6. Craig Adams' notes.
7. *Hood River Glacier,* July 12, 1923.
8. The license was reported deleted in the 12/1/1922 Radio Service Bulletin.
9. *Oregonian,* August 6, 1922, Sec. 5, 6.
10. Ibid.
11. *Eugene Daily Guard,* August 8, 1922, 6.
12. Eugene radio history website, http://www.angelfire.com/or/erg/page2.html.
13. Ibid., 4.
14. *Oregon Statesman,* October 26, 1922, 6.
15. Ibid.
16. *Weekly Oregon Statesman* (Salem, OR), November 14, 1922, 4.
17. KFCD description from "The KFCD Story: A Short Radio Life," by Salem historian Douglas H. Stingley, an unpublished paper.
18. "Salem's First," Douglas Stingley, *Popular Communications,* October 1993.
19. Bruce W. Bjorkman, History of Salem's First "Salem Electric Co.," (unpublished article) Salem, OR: WSMB Collection).
20. Ibid.
21. Art Chipman, *KMED The First Half Century* (Medford, OR: Pine Cone Publishers, 1972), 4.
22. Launsbach worked at Medford's Weeks and Orr furniture store and ran the music department where he so successfully oversaw the sale of Brunswick phonographs and Sherman and Clay pianos that he had to abandon his orchestra work in October 1923. (*Medford Sun,* October 14, 1923).
23. *Medford Mail Tribune,* September 28, 1922, 8.
24. Minkler was an amateur radio operator who, in 1912, received the first radio operator's license issued in southern Oregon. Sometime after his work with KFAY, Minkler left Medford, worked for Brunswick Records and eventually co-founded Radio Recorders in Hollywood, California, a major transcription recording company for the radio industry. ("Radio in Southern Oregon," a March 28, 1973 reminiscence written by Minkler and Donald Runyard in connection with KMED's 50th anniversary celebration. Ray Johnson Collection, WSMB).
25. Power, Everett E. 1982. Letter to Pinecone Publishers dated August 18. (Ray Johnson Collection, WSMB). Power was an Oakland, California, attorney who grew up in Medford and attended the KFAY sign-on. His recollections are contained in a letter written in response to Art Chipman's history of KMED, *KMED: The First Half Century.* Minkler, who Power reports operating during KFAY's sign-on, went on to operate Minkler's, a radio and TV sales and service store in Medford.
26. *Medford Mail Tribune,* September 28, 1922, 8.
27. Located in the back of a shop on the east side of Central near the intersection of Main and Central in Medford.
28. *Medford Mail Tribune,* April 23, 1923, 6.
29. Later known as the Medford Center Building and the M&M Department Store Building.
30. The station's studios were likely located on the first or second floor but the motor generator plant seems to have been located in a wire-enclosed cage in the basement based upon the author's inspection of the premises in 1995.
31. It would appear that, in preparing to move into the Medford Center, Virgin first set up his shop and KFAY in a small space off the alley directly across Central Avenue from the Medford Center Building, which was then under construction. (*Medford City Directory,* 1923)
32. De Sousa statement in KFAY file (WSMB Collection). This reference refers to either KFAY or KMED operation.
33. Chipman, *KMED: The First Half Century,* 7.
34. A December 8, 1924, letter from Redfern to Commissioner of Navigation, DOC, Washington DC, reports that Virgin's Radio Service had "dismantled their station and request that their license be cancelled and their call letters deleted." (KFAY file, NARA, College Park, MD)
35. Reportedly, the station last broadcast in September 1924. Subsequently, Virgin's Radio Service formally requested cancellation of its license. O. R. Refern, District Supervisor of Radio, reported that request, and

confirmation that the station's equipment had been dismantled, in a December 3, 1924 letter to the Commissioner of Navigation, Department of Commerce. [KFAY file, NARA, College Park MD] KFAY's license was cancelled that same day.

36. Undated letter from Truman Blair Cook to Chester R. Lamont, Clatsop County Historical Society.
37. Ibid.
38. 545 Commercial Street.
39. Located on the northeast corner of 12th Street. The locations of studio and transmitter are based upon DOC records and the Portland Radio History website listings of Craig Adams.
40. *Morning Astorian*, November 23, 1922, 4.
41. *Oregonian*, December 8, 1922, 1.
42. *Oregonian*, December 9, 1922, 2.
43. Truman Blair Cook letter in Clatsop County Historical Society files.
44. Located at 751 Main Street according to 1921 City Directory.
45. Located at 114 W. Alta according to Craig Adams' files.
46. Tallman & Company Druggists was located at 653 Main Street according to the 1921 City Directory.
47. The building, now known as the Old City Hall, still stands at the renamed location of 34 SE Dorian Street. The station is shown as located there in its January 1923 license renewal.
48. Ted Smith, "History of Radio in Umatilla County," *Pioneer Trails* (Pendleton: Umatilla County Historical Society, Spring 2003), 11.
49. Kenin was an important figure in broadcasting both in Oregon and nationally. The Portland native began playing violin in George Olsen's band—which frequently appeared on Portland radio in the 1920s—while in college. After forming his own "big band," Kenin performed on many Portland stations, and the short-lived ABC Network (see chapter 9) in San Francisco and Seattle, before enrolling in the Northwestern School of Law in Portland where he opened a legal practice in 1931. Dividing his time between law and music, Kenin was elected president of the American Federation of Musicians (AFM) Portland local in 1936 and remained in that office for 20 years. On the 1958 retirement of the AFM's international president, the controversial James C. Petrillo, Kenin was elected international president, a post he held until his 1970 death. He was instrumental in the founding of the National Endowment for the Arts (NEA) and the National Endowment for the Humanities (NEH). ("Musician Union Leader, Herman Kenin Found Dead," *Nevada State Journal*, July 22, 1970, 3.)
50. This is how the address was rendered by Thomas in KFBH's DOC license application.
51. Handwritten DOC notation on KFBH's final license.
52. Adler's was located at 2013 Main Street.
53. The application was signed by G. (Grant) A. Covell, Dean of the School of Engineering.
54. Telegram from W. F. Sharp to Radio License Department, DOC, Washington, DC (KFDJ file, NARA, College Park, MD)
55. *Sunday Oregonian*, January 28, 1923, Sec, 5, 9.
56. Ibid.
57. Station description contained in November 3, 1925, letter from Kenneth Clark to Commissioner of Navigation, DOC, Washington, DC, in which Clark reports upon Redfern's November 1 inspection of the station (KFDJ file, NARA, College Park, MD).
58. Herbert Hoover. *The Memoirs of Herbert Hoover: the Cabinet and the Presidency, 1920–1933*. (New York: Macmillan and Company, 1952), 140.

# 3

# Late-Night Clubs:
# The Hoot Owls Roost in
# KGW's *Oregonian* Tower

"The 'Hoot Owls' do not sound like regular radio stuff. They sound as though there was a dandy party going on in the next room and somebody had left the door open," wrote *Wireless Age* magazine in May 1924. Ten months after signing-on, KGW launched the "KGW Hoot Owls" and created a national sensation.

## The Hoot Owls, KGW Portland

Officially known as the "**K**eep **G**rowing **W**iser Order of Hoot Owls," (with a clever play on the letters K, G and W), the Hoot Owls are the stuff of which legends are made. A group of prominent Portland businessmen joined some professional entertainers, and created a weekly 90-minute entertainment revue that quickly took the nation by storm—and set the standard for public service.

Stories about the program and its originators abound. One holds that the program's concept originated with *Oregonian* associate editor Ronald G. Callvert, who was an inveterate radio buff. Supposedly, Callvert happened to listen to the *Nighthawks Frolic* program from WDAF Kansas City, when that station was only seven months old.[1] An alternative story is that *Oregonian* editor Edgar Piper was traveling in late December 1922 and either heard the *Nighthawks* while passing through, or staying in, Kansas City.[2]

A third version was later told by Richard Haller, an *Oregonian* staffer who was assigned to KGW when the station

WSMB Collection

Hoot Owls logo, drawn by Tige Reynolds, as used on the cover of *Hoot Owl Classics, Vol 1,* 1928

signed-on. Haller, who had graduated from the University of Michigan and the Sorbonne, first worked at the *New York Journal* before coming to the *Oregonian* as its book editor. Soon conscripted to KGW assignment, he went on to manage the station for six years. By the time Haller left KGW in 1929, to become director of production for the ill-fated American Broadcasting Company network in San Francisco, he was acknowledged as "the dean of broadcasting in the northwest" by the *Oakland Tribune* (see chapter 6).[3] Even after leaving KGW, Haller maintained an association with the Hoot Owls, and as late as December 9, 1932, he sang on the program by recording.[4]

Haller recounted the Hoot Owls' founding as stemming from his tiring of announcing station breaks—"This is KGW"—every few minutes. Believing that listeners were probably as tired as he of that litany, he thought that a more personal relationship needed to be developed between KGW and its listeners, and the idea of a radio "fraternity" came to him.[5]

The real circumstances of the Hoot Owl's founding may, like many other events, have unfolded nearly simultaneously from several like minds as an undertaking whose time had come.[6]

Clearly, the Hoot Owls were at least partially inspired by the Nighthawk broadcasts, which began on December 4, 1922. Kansas City's WDAF had been granted use of the Class B 400-meter frequency in November, and the higher-quality frequency assignment precluded the station's broadcasting phonograph recordings (see chapter 4). Trying to fill a late-night time period, the station settled on broadcasting the Coon-Sanders Novelty Singing Orchestra, which was appearing at the Plantation Grill of Kansas City's Hotel Muehlebach. A popular local band, the group was headed by Joe Sanders and Carlton Coon, who was reportedly unhappy that they were to be broadcast without receiving any additional payment. Their first broadcast occurred on Monday, December 4, 1922, at 11:45 p.m. Coon was apparently unaware his microphone was on when he remarked that "No one would stay up to listen to this but a bunch of nighthawks." The aside quickly drew 60,000 pieces of mail from listeners in 31 states who proclaimed that they were, indeed, nighthawks.[7] The strong listener response prompted WDAF to quickly rename the program the *Nighthawk Frolics* and the band, sensing a good thing, quickly changed its name to the Coon-Sanders Nighthawks.

The Nighthawks' program was an early radio dance band remote broadcast, which was distinguished by inviting listeners to send telegrams with requests for songs, which were performed on the spot. Listeners could also request membership in a Nighthawk chapter. Announcer Leo J. Fitzpatrick, a *Kansas City Star* police reporter with no previous radio experience who was assigned to the Nighthawks' debut program, acknowledged each new membership by ringing a gong and saluting the listener as a "Brother Night Hawk." It was a fairly simple program—an announcer, the band, listener feedback and the sense of belonging to the new and exciting world of radio. The program drew extensive national attention, and Callvert and Piper were among those captivated.

KGW's only internal written history credits Callvert with the idea for a late-night program but, regardless whether it was Piper or Callvert who first heard the Nighthawks, it was Callvert who reportedly made the suggestion to KGW's program director, Dick Haller—who may have been harboring some thoughts of his own about a fraternity-type program.

Once the idea of launching a new program had been advanced, Haller sought out Charles F. Berg, an amateur theatrical performer better known as the owner of a Portland women's apparel store located at 615 SW Broadway Avenue. Frank Sardam, an insurance agent with a background in amateur theatre, joined Berg in that conversation. The invitation to Berg and Sardam likely stemmed from theatrical "frolic" performances that Berg, Alan "Punch" Green and others had previously presented for the Portland Advertising Federation (unofficially known as the "Ad Club"), which had just presented its most recent Follies production in which Portland's most prominent businessmen had participated.[8] While the Ad Club's membership records no longer exist, it seems likely that senior members of *Oregonian* staff, such as Piper would have been Ad Club members. Inviting the Ad Club troupe to serve as the core cast for the late-night program would have been an easy connection to make.

In early January 1923, Callvert, Berg (and likely Haller) met in Piper's office to brainstorm the program's concept, and then ensnared a cadre of others to join them in writing and performing it. Capitalizing on the sense of belonging that the Nighthawks had developed, they decided to stylize KGW's offering as a club or lodge. From a radio station's standpoint, Haller's fraternity idea had value. It was decided early on that one membership requirement was a commitment to "attend" the group's weekly meetings—albeit by radio. Having decided upon a late-night time slot, the Hoot Owls' name was an obvious alternative

Richard Haller at the KGW microphone

*Radio Digest Illustrated, December 6, 1924 (WSMB Collection)*

Charles F. Berg in 1929

Harry S. Grannatt Collection, WSMB

to the Nighthawks, but KGW took ownership of the name by using its call letters to denote the owls' supposed penchant for wisdom. Thus, the *Keep Growing Wiser Order of Hoot Owls* became the program's official name.

Walter Taylor Sumner playing the Owlorgan

The Hoot Owls' first broadcast occurred on Monday, January 29, 1923, and consisted of the best Ad Club Follies with Portland mayor George Baker, Piper and others participating.[9] Listeners were invited to send in requests, comments, suggestions and membership applications.

Contrary to most of what has been written about the Hoot Owls, like the Nighthawks, the program was initially broadcast on Mondays, with some occasional Friday broadcasts interspersed. The program was also of irregular length. Soon, however, the Hoot Owls settled into a regular 90-minute program commencing on Friday night at 10:30 p.m.

At its inception, the program's central characters and theme were somewhat different from their later iterations. On the eve of the first broadcast, the *Oregonian* wrote:

> The first meeting will be devoted to launching the club, considering the election of officers, and swearing in the charter members. Charlie Berg, the 'Bubo,' or 'Eagle Owl' will preside and the Ignavi, or 'Grand Duo Owls,' will support him. Juhasz and Natanson have contributed the Manilla String Sextet to furnish music and Larry Franklin, the local composer of popular music, will hold forth at the piano.[10]

The next day, the *Oregonian* reported:

> At 11 o'clock tonight Charles F. Berg, Grand Bubo of the KGW Order of Hoot Owls, will assemble his Ignavi on the limb of the Hoot Owl trees and they will start something.[11]

Supposedly, the first program included a burlesque travelogue, "A Trip to Cuba."[12] By the broadcast on February 12, 1923, however, Berg's title had evolved from Bubo to Grand Screech, the title which he retained for the rest of his life.

While the program's style evolved over time, the Hoot Owls always used a somewhat formal program structure arising from its founding concept as a club. The program opened with a roll call of Hoot Owl officers—known as the Degree Team—followed by a "business meeting," during which typical club business was handled including the reading of correspondence, answering questions, acknowledging gifts and considering membership applications. The Hoot Owls' "rites" at each meeting included singing of the official Hoot Owl song (printed later in this chapter) to Owlorgan (a circus calliope) accompaniment and the riding of the group's imaginary mascot, a goat named Sweet William, by newly initiated members. *Sunset Magazine*, which dubbed the Hoot Owls the "Laughter Lodge of the Air," described the Owlorgan as "a music-making contraption that makes a racket like nothing

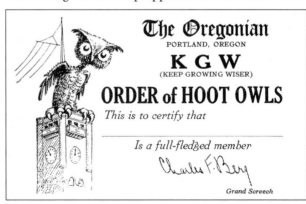

The Oregonian
PORTLAND, OREGON
K G W
(KEEP GROWING WISER)
ORDER of HOOT OWLS
*This is to certify that*

_____
*Is a full-fledged member*

*Charles F. Berg*

*Grand Screech*

Later version of the Hoot Owls membership card

ever heard on land or sea."[13] Following these rites, the program unfolded with both semi-scripted and extemporaneous patter from members of the Degree Team.

The Hoot Owls might best be described as an early *Saturday Night Live* on the radio. They also had a slight Marx Brothers (who were members of the Hoot Owls and occasionally appeared on the program) quality, although one listener described them as "more cerebral than slap-the-knee funny."[14] *Sunset Magazine* described the show as making "no attempt to uplift or elevate the brows of the audience; there is not even stereotyped announcing. It is a period of frivolity and fun, a radio 'get together' of which the fan *feels he is a part*" [emphasis in original].[15]

Stylized as a mythical lodge, the program featured poetry, skits, music and spontaneous tomfoolery all in the guise of a meeting of the Order—a "secret society of the air." Listeners submitted membership applications and those who were accepted were inducted in a formal on-air ceremony. The Hoot Owls' distinctive logo was created by *Oregonian* cartoonist C. L.

Initial Hoot Owls Degree Team in promotional picture (clockwise from top: Charles F. Berg, Frank J. Sardam, Alex Riley, Henry Metzger, Dick Haller, Barney Goldstein, Tige Reynolds, Steve Juhasz.

*Radio Digest Illustrated*, December 6, 1924 (WSMB Collection)

Smith, and lucky inductees received highly prized membership cards featuring that symbol.[16] Smith's role as the Hoot Owls' cartoonist was later assumed by another *Oregonian* cartoonist and future member of the Degree Team, "Tige" Reynolds. Successful membership applications supposedly required demonstration of some type of significant talent or accomplishment, but the term was generously interpreted.

Officers of the Hoot Owl Order, the Degree Team, varied over the program's life but initially consisted of:

| Charles F. Berg | Grand Screech |
| --- | --- |
| Frank J. Sardam | Grand Scream[17] |
| Dick Haller | Holder of the Grand Goat |
| Alex Riley | Grand Skipano (from 1923–26)[18] |
| Jim Albert | Grand Shout[19] |
| Bill Strandborg | Grand Talon |
| Bill Hoffman | Grand Scratch |

One author, Lori Shea Kuckler, has speculated that the satiric hyperbole of the Hoot Owls' Degree Team titles was really an attempt to poke fun at the Ku Klux Klan which had, by the time of the Hoot Owls' inception, made uncomfortably strong inroads in Oregon politics.[20] If true, one can easily imagine the city fathers who founded the Hoot Owls not wishing to openly link their humorous Hoot Owl titles to their antipathy for the Klan (see chapter 1).

The background of the principal individuals and the offices they held reveals a great deal about the program.

| Name | Profession | Hoot Owl Office | Years |
|---|---|---|---|
| Alan "Punch" Green, Sr. | Stockbroker/Entertainer | Grand Songsmith | 1926–1927 |
| Alex Riley | Musician, Sherman and Clay Company | Grand Skipano (previously Grand Piano) | 1923–1926 |
| Ashley C. Dixon, Sr. | Owner, KFJR radio | Grand Scratch | 1926–1928[21] |
| Barnett "Barney" Goldstein | Attorney, Fmr. Us. District Attorney, Exalted Ruler of the Elks | Grand Schmoos | 1923–1929 |
| Bill Hoffman | Multnomah Hotel mgr. | Grand Silence | 1923–1925 |
| Bill Strandborg | Pepco | Grand Talon | 1923–1925 |
| Charles F. Berg | Owner, Charles F. Berg's | Grand Screech | 1923–1932 |
| Charles O. Chatterton | KGW manager | Grand Scotchman | 1929–1933 |
| Charles "Chuck" Whitehead | Musician, orchestra leader | Grand Piano | 1926–1927? |
| Cliff Engle | KGW staff[22] | Grand Scribe | 1928–1931 |
| Dean Collins | Portland Telegram, feature writer | Grand Sonnet | 1926–1933 |
| Dick Haller | KGW program director | Holder of the Grand Goat | 1923–1929 |
| Edward S. "Tige" Reynolds | *Oregonian* cartoonist | Grand Sketch | 1926–1931 |
| Forrest Berg | Son of Charles Berg | Grand Squeak | 1929–1933 |
| Frank J. Sardam | Northwestern Life Insurance Company, local manager | Grand Scream[23] | 1923–1933 |
| Fred Spoeri | Pacific Telephone & Telegraph, manager | Grand Central | 1923–1925 |
| George Hotchkiss Street | Vocalist and singing teacher | Grand Uproar | 1924–1925 |
| Harry S. Grannatt | Insurance agent | Grand String Bean[24] | 1926[25]–1933 |
| George Smith | Meier & Frank Display Dept. | Grand Songster | ?–1930 |
| Henry Metzger | Fleishner, Mayer and Company, salesman | Grand Szan | 1923–1925 |
| James M. (Jim) Albert | Guaranty Trust Company, Sales Mgr. | Grand Shout[26] | 1923–1927 |
| Josephine "Jo" Grannatt | Daughter of Harry S. Grannatt | Brussel (sic) Sprout | ? –1933[27] |
| Mel Blanc | KGW announcer | Grand Snicker | 1927–1931 |
| R. G. Callvert | Oregonian assoc. editor | Grand Skidoo[28] | 1926–1933 |
| Sid Goodwin[29] | KGW staff | Holder of the Grand Goat | 1929–1931 |
| Walter Taylor Sumner[30] | Episcopal Bishop of Oregon | Grand Sermon | 1926–1933 |
| William Robinson Boone | Music teacher | Grand Skipano | 1926–1933[31] |

Others also joined in the fun. William Boone, who was teamed with local writer Dean Collins in the popular "Dill Pickle Duets," would often play Beethoven's "Moonlight Sonata" on the Owlorgan. In an era when the press was somewhat more collegial, the *Oregonian*'s sponsorship of the program was no bar to participation by staff from rival newspapers.[32] There were more additions in 1926, such as Ashley C. Dixon, who owned rival KFJR and wrote extensively for the program. Among Dixon's contributions was the "Hoot Owls Midnight Ode," which closed the program and for 40 years thereafter remained KGW's official sign-off. The "Midnight Ode" poignantly captured the Hoot Owls' sense of humanity intertwined with the romance of their weekly kilocycle club.

### Midnight Ode

*Friends, the midnight hour is at hand and tomorrow will soon become today.*

*What has gone is done.*
*Each song, or laugh, or jest far flung, is on its way to join the ages of the past.*
*Here we stand, the center of a mighty web of golden rays; radiant beams*
*which travel as thought to countless thousands, to happy homes*
*and cheerful firesides;*
*But as well, to some less fortunately blessed by kindly fate.*

*And should any ask us, "Why the Hoot Owls?"*
*This our answer—"To spread a little sunshine."*
*And this our earnest prayer.*

*That to those who laugh we may send our mirth to mingle.*
*But to those to whom the past has been most unfair,*
*To those deprived of sunshine and the joy of living, with each song our laugh*
*or jest we sent our blessing.*
*We send our hope that to some pale lips we may have brought a smile, and*
*to others a moment's rest from pain.*

*As this day is ending and another being born,*
*By the symbol of the chimes we voice our hope that tomorrow*
*may be happier than today for friends whose portion has been*
*most hard to bear.*

[the chimes of hope ring]

*Today is Yesterday and Tomorrow is Today.*[33]

Notwithstanding the program's general level of frivolity, dealing as it did with spreading a message of hope for a better future, the "Midnight Ode" was taken very seriously and could only be delivered by a member of the Degree Team or a very distinguished guest. According to Hoot Owls cast member Edris Morrison: "It was considered a great honor to be asked to do it. One time someone asked to give the [Ode] and he [Charlie Berg] didn't feel that the man was worthy of it. Charlie was pretty violently upset about it."[34]

Dixon wrote numerous Shakespearean burlesques for the Hoot Owls, including "Richard the Thirteenth," "The Curing of Hamlet," "The Merchant of Venice, California," and "Twelfth Night—that became the Thirteenth." Dean Collins composed many of the Hoot Owl song lyrics, including the Dill Pickle songs and a verse segment called "Bedtime Stories." One key addition to the Hoot Owl cast was Melvin Jerome Blank, who became Mel Blanc when he went on to thrill millions as the voice of Bugs Bunny, Daffy Duck, Elmer Fudd, Porky Pig and a host of other animated characters. The young Blanc contributed fables in dialect and other comic voices on the Hoot Owls.

Blanc, a recent Lincoln High School graduate, was playing violin in Herman Kenin's Orchestra when Degree Team member Harry Grannatt (pronounced GRAN-ite) heard him sing and play his ukulele during one of the Multnomah Hotel's *Breakfast Club* programs. When Blanc was asked to perform the popular standard "Juanita" (to which he knew the lyrics) on the Hoot Owls, he readily agreed only to discover on arriving at the KGW studio that special lyrics had been prepared. Blanc began his professional broadcasting career singing the following into the KGW microphone:

**Wanita**
*(to the tune of "Juanita")*

*I'd be a wreck when I got the check*
*I prayed that she'd get indigestion*
*But such luck, it was out of the question.*
*They say nanny goats can eat soda cans and such,*
*My girl eats things nanny goats won't touch.*
*I call her my sweet Wa nita:*
*"Wanna eat, wanna eat," Wanita.*[35]

Blanc also regularly created sound effects, for which he also later became famous (such as his voicing the sputtering automotive personality of Jack Benny's Maxwell car). Another Hoot Owls performer, particularly in the program's later years, was Clarence H. "Toley" Tolman, a singer and musician who remained a prominent member of the KGW musical staff well into the 1940s.[36]

The Hoot Owls seemed to "have a thing" about goats, although they didn't actually use an animal in the broadcast. Hoot Owls who were newly initiated in person (as opposed to by mail), were required to recite the Hoot Owl oath from memory. If they made a mistake they went through a hilarious ceremony including much ribbing and a ride on a mythical goat, Sweet William, a totally uninhibited animal given to butting. A wooden paddle, handled by Frank Sardam, provided the sound effects for the goat's butting encounters. During the first Hoot Owls broadcast, Portland mayor George L. Baker "took the ride and spent the rest of the hour getting even."[37]

The Hoot Owls were also devoted to Shakespeare in their own way. In addition to the many burlesques performed, the Bard's ode to the Hoot Owls went like this on an early broadcast:

**The Hoot Owl Poets' Corner**
*(non-member's Soliloquy)*
*By William Shakespeare*

*To screech or not to screech? That's the question.*
*Whether 'tis nobler to listen in, safe in our obscurity,*
*And laugh when they kid the other fellow,*
*Or boldly come forth, ride the goat and perch securely on the roost forever after,*
*To perch, to hoot, perchance to be hooted at—ay, there's the rub,*
*That makes us rather bear the ills already ours*
*Than fly to others that we know not of.*[38]

No recordings of the Hoot Owls exist.[39] Our best understanding of the program comes from scripted skits written for the program, which were published in two books, and from some surviving scripts.[40] From these sources, we know that the program opened with a short song sung by the cast. This was the program's initial Hoot Owl Song:

**Hoot Owl Song**
(c. 1923)

*The Hoot Owls, The Hoot Owls*
*Keep Growing Wiser Hoot Owls*
*We are a razzy, jazzy crowd*
*We Hoot each Friday night out loud*
*To be good Hoot Owls we are proud*
*Keep Growing Wiser Hoot Owls.*[41]

Not long afterward, it was replaced by another simple opener:

*The Hoot Owls are hooting tonight*
*All together again*
*The Hoot Owls are hooting tonight*
*Starting at half-past ten.*[42]

By 1924, the program had adopted a more elaborate opening, beginning with the orchestra playing an overture followed by a different Hoot Owl song:

**Hoot Owl Song**
(c.1924)

*When we gather for the meeting*
*And they put us on the air*
*We will send a friendly greeting*
*To the people everywhere.*
*So accept our invitation*
*Hear each merry jest we bring*
*Turn your dials and get the station*
*And listen while we sing:*

*Hello, Everybody,*
*Here we are again;*
*Growing wiser, Hoot Owls,*
*Friday, half-past ten.*
*Everybody's happy*
*No use feeling blue*
*So Hoot, Hoot, Hoot Owls, Hoot!*
*From KGW.*[43]

In 1927, Dean Collins wrote a new opening song, which was sung to the tune "Funicula, Funicula" and opened the program throughout 1928. In the fall of 1929, about the time Harry Grannatt started writing the majority of the program, the program began using the final chorus from the 1924 show opener as its theme, which became known as the "Hello Everybody" song.[44]

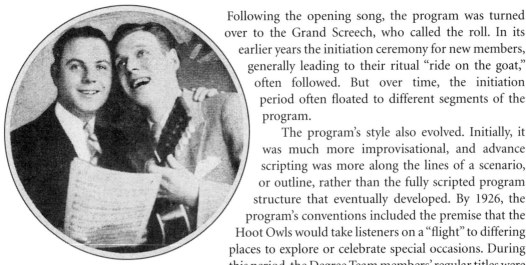

Forrest Berg (left) with George Smith, the "Village Blacksmith," in a Hoot Owls promotional photo.

*Radio Digest,* June, 1930 (WSMB Collection)

Following the opening song, the program was turned over to the Grand Screech, who called the roll. In its earlier years the initiation ceremony for new members, generally leading to their ritual "ride on the goat," often followed. But over time, the initiation period often floated to different segments of the program.

The program's style also evolved. Initially, it was much more improvisational, and advance scripting was more along the lines of a scenario, or outline, rather than the fully scripted program structure that eventually developed. By 1926, the program's conventions included the premise that the Hoot Owls would take listeners on a "flight" to differing places to explore or celebrate special occasions. During this period, the Degree Team members' regular titles were expanded to include appropriate military or aviation terms such as Commander or Squadron Leader.

The program's evolution took a considerable step when Harry S. Grannatt was invited to join the Degree Team in 1926. Grannatt, an insurance man who got his start in radio in San Francisco as an avocation, was an incredibly prolific writer of both words and music, as well as fine a performer with a keen wit. Gradually, Grannatt began providing increasing amounts of fully scripted material for the program in addition to performing. By 1929, when Grannatt had become the program's principal scriptwriter, the Hoot Owls moved to a fully scripted format (although script for individual bits were still contributed by other members of the Degree Team for which Grannatt simply left holes in his full program script).

An important addition was made to the Degree Team on September 20, 1929, when Grand Screech Charles F. Berg's 29-year-old son, Forrest, was inducted as Grand Squeak to the accompaniment of the Hoot Owl Band playing "Sonny Boy." Following the death of Berg's wife when Forrest was just 18 months old, the boy had been raised by his mother's family in San Francisco, where he successfully entered the retail clothing business as a young man. While father and son apparently had only moderate contact for many years, Forrest was invited to come to Portland in 1922 as the second-in-command of his father's store. There, he took over "modernizing" the business. Later in the decade, when his father's appearances on the Hoot Owls became somewhat erratic due to both travel and health issues, Forrest increasingly substituted for his father as the presiding Hoot Owls officer. By late 1931 and early 1932, Forrest emceed the Hoot Owls as frequently as his father.

The Hoot Owls used numerous running gags. For example, one cast member reportedly once tried to tell a story involving a blonde woman sitting across from a man in a Pullman car and was interrupted by other cast members. Ten minutes later, he tried to continue and was again shouted down. Some minutes later, he again tried to finish his story unsuccessfully. As he attempted to finish the story over the next three programs, he was continuously interrupted either by the Degree Team or the orchestra. Intrigued listeners began inquiring about the conclusion. Once, an old woman even came to the studio—presumably to see what the program looked like—and, on departing, demurely asked a secretary if she could be told the end of the story. But the end of that story has never been told.

A program could typically include a song like "The Cuspidor My Father Left to Me," or "In Hay Fever Time I'll Meet You In McMinnville:"

> *In hay fever time I'll meet you in McMinnville,*
> *All the handkerchiefs are gone but I still sneeze.*
> *I've used pillowslips and skirts,*
> *Napkins, tablecloths and shirts,*
> *And now I'm using father's B.V.D.'s.*[45]

Another audience favorite was the "Cheese Opera" (set in Tillamook) whose lyrics included: "And that's why the Swiss Cheeses have all the holes—when it's Limburger needs ventilation." The plot involved a lead soprano named Listerine and her lover, Freddy (an imprisoned bootlegger), who sings to Listerine from his jail cell: "My heart is the garbage can of love—Left standing on the fire escape above."[46]

To say the program was spontaneous would be an understatement. In May 1931, Oregon governor Julius Meier appointed Harry Grannatt and Ted Baum to the State Fair Committee with the assignment of assisting in the fair's publicity planning. During their broadcast on May 8, Portland chief of police Jenkins interrupted the Hoot Owls' live show to arrest Grannatt and Baum on air "for stealing police badges in the state capitol." The pair had apparently purloined them as a prank, while attending a meeting of the State Fair Committee, in a pre-arranged stunt to promote the fair. Dean Collins was also arrested on air "for making a nuisance of himself" when he interfered with Jenkins' efforts to arrest the other two.

Following the arrests, the remaining cast members were left to finish the program on their own. The badges "weren't worth 39¢" according to Governor Meier, who nevertheless stated that he believed the badges were an emblem deserving respect. Meier appointed a special prosecutor, Multnomah County judge William A. Ekwall (himself an occasional performer on programs like the Hoot Owls), while the arrested trio retained defense counsel. On the premise that they were arrested in the hearing of thousands of radio listeners, it was decided that the preliminary hearing should also be broadcast live during the following week's Hoot Owls program. In succeeding weeks, various on-air "trials" carried on the prank, although no records exist on the outcome of this good-natured stunt.

The original Hoot Owl programs were so boisterous that listeners began to inquire whether any intoxicants were being used to stimulate the entertainment. Perhaps that had been the case because Ronald Callvert was then formally given the assignment of assuring that suitable alcoholic restraint was observed—which explains the derivation of his Degree Team title, Grand Skidoo. Actress and amateur historian Helen Platt, who served as KGW's public affairs director in the 1950s, wrote in an unpublished history of KGW:

> The Hoot Owl hilarity was the natural result of a congenial group of exceptionally clever and talented men, born entertainers, who loved to clown, putting on a show for the fun of it and

## HOOT OWLS' SHRIEKS MAKE NIGHT HIDEOUS

PORTLAND, ORE.—The Hoot Owls are making the night hideous with their hoots in the vicinity of Portland several nights each week, since KYG, the Portland Oregonian broadcasting station, has organized this order of Radio maniacs. Members are initiated both in person and via the ether. So far hundreds of night owls all over the nation have been initiated.

*Radio Digest,* March 1923 (the magazine incorrectly identified the broadcast on KYG instead of KGW.)

having a wonderful time. That was the secret of the program's amazing popularity. It wasn't the show itself, good as it was, it was the gusto of the performers, the exuberant, carefree spontaneity that the audience loved.[47]

The Hoot Owls were simply unlike anything else on the radio. The program lays claim as being the first radio variety show, the first radio variety show broadcast from a script, the first radio quiz show and the first live audience program broadcast from a remote location.[48]

## Membership in the Hoot Owls

The Hoot Owls were an immediate sensation. Within hours of their first broadcast, membership applications poured in by telephone and wire—but all were rejected because the Hoot Owls insisted that applications be submitted by written letter. Hoot Owl members also had to be male (there's more to be said about that later in the chapter) and had to agree to abide by the Hoot Owls' simple pledge to "scatter sunshine, help Brother Hoot Owls in distress and to attend the meetings."[49] Bishop Frederick W. Keater of Tacoma was inducted "and he had no more brushed the goat hair off the seat of his trousers and plucked the owl feathers out of his hair when some of his Tacoma friends were on the long distance telephone congratulating him for entering such a lively organization."[50]

Within two days of the first broadcast "the mail for [the Hoot Owl] department broke all records," the *Oregonian* reported. On the third program, it was announced that membership applications had been received from King Tutankhamen (who noted that he enjoyed the program while excavators were fussing around outside his bedroom) and the entire Elks Club of Redding, California (who were listening on a Magnavox amplifier and horn speaker), among others.

Five months later, a typical Hoot Owls broadcast might include membership inductees from most western states as well as Wisconsin, Oklahoma, Texas, Montana, Ohio and Pennsylvania, plus several Canadian provinces. The Hoot Owls were also traveling to make distant personal appearances such as at a meeting of the Marysville, California, Hoot Owls chapter on June 11, 1923.[51]

Nearly a year after their debut, the Hoot Owls had members in 44 states, five Canadian provinces, Alaska, Hawaii and Mexico. In Mexico City, the largest movie theatre had the Hoot Owl program as a regular feature each week with an on-stage radio that played KGW live from Portland.[52] Hoot Owl chapters were formed from Sacramento to the Arctic Circle, as well as among the crews of ships at sea where the program could be heard across the Pacific Ocean thousands of miles from North America.

Interest in the program was broad, and by October 1924 the Hoot Owls were simultaneously broadcast over KFRC San Francisco and CFAC Calgary, Alberta (with those stations presumably picking up the program off-air). In 1925, KLX San Francisco joined in. At various times the program also seems to have been simulcast over KFOA Seattle, KHQ Spokane and, in 1929, over KFJI Astoria (likely using the Northwest Triangle network circuits since KGW and KFJI were two of the four stations comprising that network). On special occasions, such as New Year's Eve or the Hoot Owls' own anniversary programs, they were also broadcast over the NBC Red radio network.

Newspapers across the country, including the *Galveston News,* the *Iowa City Press-Citizen,* the *Lancaster Daily Eagle* (Pennsylvania), the *Salamanca Press-Republican* (New York) and the *Zanesville Times-Recorder* (Ohio), included the Hoot Owls in their published listings of radio programs. Frequently, the Hoot Owls were identified as one of the editor's "Best Bet" picks,

Radio Digest Illustrated, January 9, 1925 (WSMB Collection)

At right is Hoot Owl degree team—left to right, Frank J. Sardam, Grand Scream; Henry W. Metzger, Grand Slam; Dean Collins, Grand Bonnet; Bishop W. T. Sumner, Grand Sermon; Alan (Punch) Green, Grand Songsmith; Barnett H. Goldstein, Grand Schmoos; Wm. Robinson Boone (seated at piano), Grand Skipano; R. G. Calvert, Grand SHdeo; Chas. F. Berg, Grand Screech; A. C. Dixon, Grand Scratch, and "Tige" Reynolds, Grand Sketch.

KGW Hoot Owls (left to right) Frank Sardam, Henry Metzger, Dean Collins, Reverend Sumner, Punch Green, Barnett Goldstein, William Boone (at piano), Ron Callvert, Charles Berg, Ashley Dixon, Tige Reynolds (on piano).

such as in the *Bismarck Tribune* (North Dakota), the *Clearfield Progress* (Pennsylvania), the *Dunkirk Evening Observer* (New York), the *Frederick Post* (Maryland), the *Mexia Daily News* (Texas) and the *Sheboygan Press Telegram* (Wisconsin). Eventually, KGW hired a staff of three secretaries whose full-time assignment was to answer Hoot Owl mail.

More than 90,000 Hoot Owl membership cards were ultimately issued. Members included county jail inmates; presidents Harding and Coolidge; admiral Byrd; the mayors of San Francisco and New York; sportscaster Graham McNamee; prize fighters Gene Tunney, Gentleman Jim Corbett and Jack Dempsey; Babe Ruth; Don Gilman (later vice president of NBC); preacher Billy Sunday; showman Alexander Pantages; and three Oregon governors. Since there was no age requirement, it was not unusual for a proud new father to seek membership for a newborn son.

Association with the Hoot Owls was apparently considered an impressive credential, and an astonishing number of well-known figures later identified themselves as having been associated with the program early in their careers. Likely, this meant they made some occasional appearances since the core of the program consisted of regulars from either the community or KGW's own staff, and no reference to these many names appear in the *Oregonian* or other published sources.

A crisis of sorts erupted during the Hoot Owls' debut program when an eastern Oregon listener wired in a $5 donation. Since the Hoot Owls charged no membership fee, this presented a challenge. Debate over how to use this bounty continued for weeks until, near the end of one broadcast, the $5 disappeared. "This may stop the progress of attending to business matters until it is found because there would be very little to fight over if there was no treasury," the *Oregonian* reported on February 8, 1923. The $5 was alternately lost and found during weeks of ensuing broadcasts, and disposition of the contribution apparently was never settled.

Membership was distinctly male. Only men and boys were eligible to join, and membership was granted only upon a unanimous vote of the Degree Team.[53]

In the then-recent wake of the successful Women's Suffrage movement, the program's male-only membership policy naturally provoked controversy. Following the very first Hoot Owls program, women petitioned for membership. On February 1, 1923, the *Oregonian* reported that "the debate on whether women will be allowed to join the Hoot Owls reached new heights

Hoot Owls promotional decal, c. 1927
Courtesy of www.pdxhistory.com

yesterday. Women are demanding to be admitted and say they will bring the matter to open debate by radio. Several write that they have to fight with their husbands for the headphones to hear the Hoot Owls meet and they'll fight just as hard to be members. It is expected that some action will be taken on the matter when the next meeting takes place." One woman thought she deserved membership because listening to the Hoot Owls was at least keeping her husband home one night a week. She sent regular reports, and when the program was on more than once a week, she reported that he had now advanced to staying home at night twice a week. Some men, however, submitted membership applications with the condition that exclusion of female membership be continued.

The debate over admitting women went on and by February 12, 1923, the issue had been reframed from "Will we take them in?" to "How can we keep them out?" The broadcast on February 23, 1923 was thrown into a furor when Grand Talon Bill Strandborg suggested that female applicants form an auxiliary, the "Ground Owls," who could sit beneath the Hoot Owl tree. It was a suggestion not kindly received by aspiring female applicants.

All membership cards issued during the program's life went to men—save one.[54] Nellie Revell, a female circus press agent, was stricken ill while visiting Portland and was subsequently confined to bed for four years. To support herself, she wrote a book that the Hoot Owls promoted via their continuing debate over whether they should induct women. They ultimately did induct her—but by proxy. The debate and her initiation helped her sell her book and successfully cope with the financial challenges caused by her illness.

One of the Hoot Owls' most ardent fans sent regular letters signed "Ima Kidder." Reportedly a nurse at a local hospital, she asked that no attempt be made to learn her real identity and the cast respected her wish.[55] She regularly sent greetings, as well as cake and cookies for each Hoot Owl cast member's birthday—which they consumed with gratitude expressed on air to her pseudonym. A veteran fan, Kidder even visited Charles F. Berg's store but, when the unknowing Berg personally waited on her, she didn't reveal her identity.[56]

Each Monday (and later on Wednesdays), the Degree Team was hosted by the *Oregonian* in a weekly lunch at the Portland Hotel (later moving to the Benson) during which they planned the following Friday's program. *Oregonian* editor Edgar Piper generally presided while the men reviewed the past week's local and national, seeking fodder for their satires, and brainstormed improbable songs and skits. Finally,

Courtesy of Sonny Clutter, www.radiolaguy.com

The Hoot Owls broadcast using this mantle clock style Western Electric 7A microphone beginning around 1928.

having decided upon what was "fit to be aired," they turned things over to Grannatt, Collins or Dixon to write the appropriate songs, skits and spoofs.

Planning and writing the program was a huge assignment for these active business leaders. For the actual broadcasts, however, they could also draw upon KGW's own internal entertainment resources, which included announcers and musicians. In a time still considered the heyday of vaudeville, the Hoot Owls also often included visiting vaudeville entertainers from the Fox, Broadway or Pantages Theatres. Performers like Ernestine Schumann-Heink, Eva Tanguay, the Marx Brothers or the Duncan Sisters frequently appeared on the program. One appearance by comedy duo Olson and Johnson led to an association between them and Harry Grannatt, which resulted in the Broadway team's negotiating the use of some of Dean Collins' Dill Pickle Songs and other Grannatt material in their performances.

Courtesy of Oregon Historical Society

Hoot Owls' Hungari program cover, 1926

Leaving the KGW studios for a more public location, the Hoot Owls created an annual benefit dinner, the Hungari, to celebrate the anniversary of their founding.[57] The inaugural Hungari, held on December 26, 1924, was broadcast from the ballroom at the Hotel Portland by "wire telephony" and featured Walker's Old Time Fiddlers from Forest Grove along with the regular cast. It was arguably the first use of a studio audience in radio and a sold-out show; 300 people attended the program. As many as 500 guests joined the annual Hungari in subsequent years.

The fourth annual Hungari in 1927 was broadcast live over KMO Tacoma, KFOA Seattle and KHQ Spokane—in addition to KGW. The program included a contribution from the Sage of Yamhill, who continued his lecture on "Synthetic Sausages."

During its ten-year run, the program was always "sustaining"—meaning that KGW accepted no commercial announcements during the broadcast. "[It was] a gift to the people of Portland from KGW and the *Oregonian*," former KGW announcer Bob Thomlinson recalled.[58] While it appears that musicians and some other entertainers were paid, the Degree Team, which wrote and centrally performed the program, did so entirely as volunteers.

In 1924, the Hoot Owls (after due deliberation in "business meetings" held on the air) authorized jeweler Frank Haener's creation of "Hoot Owl pins" which sold quickly. Offered in silver for 75¢ or gold for $1.50, proceeds went to charities selected by the Degree Team. Following the initial joint effort with the Police Department, which resulted in the creation of the Hoot Owls Sunshine Division in 1923, the Hoot Owl pin sales of 1924 seem to have crystallized the program's succeeding, long history of using the broadcasts for broad charitable purposes.

Heavily influenced by Episcopal Bishop Walter Taylor Sumner's energy and interests, the Hoot Owls eventually focused their charitable initiatives in two areas which they referred to as their "divisions." The Rainbow Division and the Sunshine Division eventually became so well-known that they ceased to be referred to with any Hoot Owls' reference. They simply became

Patients at Doernbecher Children's Hospital, Portland, gather around a radio donated by the KGW Hoot Owls Rainbow Division.

known as the Rainbow Division and the Sunshine Division, each commonly understood to be elements of the "Keep Growing Wiser Order of Hoot Owls."

The Rainbow Division, which was formed to provide radio sets to "shut-ins who otherwise would be without this or any other form of entertainment," began very early in the program's history. Under its auspices, 1,300 radios were installed by KGW technicians in such locations as the Oregon State Tuberculosis Hospital and the Multnomah County Farm. The Rainbow Division also established a trust fund to provide medical care for orphans.

Illustrations by Tige Reynolds from *Hoot Owl Classics, Vol. 1*

Two volumes of material written for the Hoot Owls were published in *Hoot Owl Classics Vols. 1 & 2,* in 1928 and 1929. The first, subtitled "Bed-Time Stories," contained material penned by Dean Collins; the second, by Harry Grannatt, included poems, jingles and short stories. The volumes also contained unattributed cartoon art by Tige Reynolds. Both volumes were published under the imprimatur of the Rainbow Division, Portland, Oregon, with paper and printing all donated. All proceeds supported the Rainbow Division's work.

The Sunshine Division began as a Christmas distribution of holiday food baskets and trees. Previously, the Portland police had been collecting and distributing these items themselves, augmented by police reserves and a group of volunteer citizens known as the Portland Vigilance Police. With Christmas 1923 approaching, the police asked the Hoot Owls for help in securing donations. The program, already operating the charitable Rainbow Division, established the Sunshine Division for that purpose. While initially a Christmas effort, it later grew to a year-round enterprise. Reports of need regularly came in and were broadcast on the program throughout the year, and listeners always responded quickly and generously.

Once, when the Hoot Owls were seeking fuel for needy families, the Grand Scream was called to the phone during the broadcast. A Hoot Owl listener reported: "There will be a flat car loaded with 18 cords of forest wood delivered to you in the Portland freight yard tomorrow morning for the Hoot Owls, charges prepaid." A call for a wheelchair brought in eight of them. The program's appeals proved so successful that the Sunshine Division had to use a donated warehouse to handle the volume of contributed goods.

As the Great Depression reached its depths, the Hoot Owl Cannery was established for a week when the owner of McMinnville's Mione Packing Plant offered to can, without charge, fruits and vegetables that had been donated by farmers in response to Hoot Owl appeals. Distant Hoot Owl chapters in other cities set up efforts similar to those in Portland and, thus, the effect of the Hoot Owls' charitable enterprise extended broadly outside the "home roost."

Portland Police Patrolmen W. B. Stram (left) and H. Rekdahl in Sunshine Division promotional photo.

*Oregonian photo courtesy of Sunshine Division/ Oregon Historical Society, photo 021604*

Through the Hoot Owls' efforts, the Sunshine Division became a permanent part of the Portland police. As long as they remained on the air, the surviving Hoot Owls periodically rendered fundraising assistance to the Sunshine Division long after the regular Hoot Owls broadcasts had ended.[59]

The Sunshine Division's structure, established through the Hoot Owls' efforts, endured until 1987 when the City of Portland withdrew the cash appropriation that had funded some Police Department staffing. Beginning in 1988, the Sunshine Division agreed to reimburse the Police Department for the salary expense of the department's officer who supervised the division and established itself as a separate non-profit corporation. As of this writing 85 years after the Hoot Owls' founding efforts, the Sunshine Division continues to coordinate with the Portland Police Department and run its emergency food relief program by soliciting and distributing donations of cash, food and services.

In early 1933, the Hoot Owls ended their ten-year KGW run. Creating and presenting the program on a largely volunteer basis was tiring but the passage of time had also taken its toll. Some cast members, like Haller and Blanc, had moved on. Then, in late April 1931, death claimed Tige Reynolds, the *Oregonian* cartoonist whose on-air presence and visual representations of the Hoot Owls had helped cast the program's spell. The Hoot Owls cancelled their intended May 1 program and gathered for a spontaneous Reynolds memorial before the KGW microphones.

Unfortunately, that event proved a sad rehearsal for the program's greatest loss: on September 1, 1932, a heart attack killed Grand Screech Charles F. Berg. He had a history of ill-health, and it was his first heart attack in 1922 that brought his son, Forrest, to Portland to assist in his father's business.[60] Berg, one of Portland's "most energetic civic leaders and keenest business minds," was editorially mourned by the *Oregonian* as: "[a] rare cavalier, far-visioned, competent, boyish of heart, with a mature wisdom and purpose. [H]e believed, as essential to living, that laughter is the tonic of the race. In twenty years there has been little of constructive moment to the city of Portland that did not summon Charlie to an unselfish task. Charlie Berg was one of the few."[61]

The death of this beloved Portland figure occurred on a Thursday evening late in the Hoot Owls' summer-long vacation from radio. Although it was their summer hiatus, on the following day, the Hoot Owls gathered before the KGW microphones for a brief, unscheduled broadcast eulogy:

> These are the Hoot Owls assembled in regular meeting in the home roost of KGW. We are gathered tonight to pay brief and simple homage to Charles F. Berg, grand screech and founder of the Hoot Owls, whose sudden passing gives us pause to scatter that sunshine which he radiated throughout his life to his family and countless friends.
>
> Ten years of happy service by Mr. Berg made his name synonymous with the name Hoot Owls and we aim to carry on, as he would have us do, his simple creed – "service to fellow men."[62]

KGW music director Abe Bercovitz played "Ehli, Ehli," a Jewish song of mourning, on the violin (both Berg and Bercovitz were Jewish), and the Degree Team and the Hoot Owls' audience all broke down on air.

Following Berg's death, the Degree Team reported their firm intention to continue, but it wasn't meant to be. Following the Berg eulogy and the conclusion of their summer hiatus, the Hoot Owls returned to their regular broadcasting schedule on September 30, 1932. They promoted a significant Hoot Owls skit, "Africa Squeaks," for their program on October 21 (replete with a silly promotional press photo), but their spirit seemed to be waning. Likely heavily preoccupied with personal and professional matters, Forrest Berg never returned to the regular program following his father's death.[63]

By 1933, Grannatt, Blanc and some other Degree Team members were involved in other programs on KGW and KEX that featured satirical and zany humor similar to the Hoot Owls'. The prolific Grannatt was writing the *Circus Court of the Air*, heard on KEX, and seems also to have been involved in *Powers Pied Piper*, a vehicle created for Blanc, so his determination to preserve the Hoot Owls in the face of Charles F. Berg's passing may have been waning. As one cast member put it: "With Charlie and the Bishop gone, the heart went out of it."[64] Rallying for the traditional Sunshine Division Christmas broadcasts of 1932, the Hoot Owls limped into the New Year with their program on January 6, 1933 but without Berg the void in their roost must have seemed increasingly overwhelming.

It seems unlikely that, as the Hoot Owls entered the KGW studio for their 518th program on January 6, 1933, they intended it to be their final broadcast. Given the program's history and prominence, it seems that a grand finale would have been prepared if the program's conclusion had been anticipated. A skit had been prepared for the program and the customary advance publicity appeared—all without hint that it would be the Hoot Owls' final weekly episode.

But it was. Perhaps during the broadcast the Hoot Owls realized just how difficult it was to go on. Perhaps they had some sense that the program wasn't up to their customary standard following the deaths of Charles F. Berg and Tige Reynolds and the departures of Blanc, Sumner, Forrest Berg and others. Whatever the circumstances that caused the program's conclusion, no public explanation was given for their sudden exit. The following morning, on January 7, 1933 the *Oregonian's* "Behind the Mike" column contained their simple one-sentence epitaph: "The Hoot Owls last night broadcast their final program and retired to their woods for good."[65]

On December 8, 1933, some surviving cast members briefly re-assembled the first of three successive Friday night broadcasts to raise funds for the Sunshine Division. Returning for the broadcast of what the *Oregonian* described as "KGW's ace presentation in the old days" were Harry Grannatt, Bill Boone and Dean Collins. They initiated Portland mayor Carson and Portland police chief Lawson and "auctioned off songs and acts for a price, as in former years," with proceeds benefiting the Sunshine Division.[66]

The last of this three-program series on December 22 featured a celebration of Custard Pie night.[67] According to Helen Platt, Carey Jennings—then manager of KGW and KEX—was the last person initiated into the Hoot Owls in 1933. Jennings must have been initiated on either the January 6 or December 22 broadcast.

In ensuing years, surviving members of the Degree Team occasionally gathered to broadcast. In 1935, they made an appearance on Ashley Dixon's KFJR for that station's tenth anniversary. Focusing on charitable purposes, the Hoot Owls fluttered back into the KGW studios for a combined KGW/KEX broadcast on April 30, 1940. And on January 23, 1947, surviving Degree Team members made a March of Dimes appearance on KALE.

As time passed, their appearances became increasingly rare. Radio remained a continuing interest for some central cast members and, while not using the Hoot Owls name, they occasionally appeared on other radio programs, including KEX's *Circus Court of the Air* (which was fed to NBC). In 1941, the *Oregonian* reported that insurance man Harry Grannatt, who had a fine background in classical music and occasionally gave lectures for the Portland Symphony, was the announcer/host for KXL's weeknight *Concert Hour* program. Surviving members of the Degree Team also reportedly gathered under the Hoot Owls name for some early KGW-TV telecasts more than 20 years after the program's demise. However, the Keep Growing Wiser Order of Hoot Owls essentially disbanded on January 6, 1933, when they departed their home roost.[68]

The Hoot Owls had made history—and compelling radio filled with humor and humanity.

## Other Late-Night Clubs

Skating on the success of programs like the Hoot Owls and the WDAF Nighthawks, other stations created their own zany "membership" programs. WBBM Chicago called theirs the *Nutty Club* with Guy Lombardo and His Royal Canadians serving as the official Nutty Club Orchestra. San Francisco's KFRC had its *Cuckoo Club*. In Oregon, several stations launched their own efforts which, unlike post-World War II late night radio programs, all centered on live music and skits. But, compared to the Hoot Owls, these other late-night Oregon radio programs had modest impact and are now little known.

*Howling Order of Portland Tomcats,* **KXL Portland:** This program issued membership cards like the Hoot Owls and wisely avoided direct competition with the Hoot Owls by meeting on Thursday evenings. From the membership card's reference (below) to the Multnomah Hotel, it appears they may have invited members into the studio (unlike the Hoot Owls who generally gave only special permission entrance tickets). The KXL Tomcats apparently were in operation for only one or two years in the later 1920s.

*Insomniacs Club,* **KEX, Portland:** When KEX Portland was being constructed in 1926, it engaged in some late-night technical tests and apparently spontaneously programmed while conducting them. According to an *Oregonian* news story, the broadcasts caught sufficient favor that it

KXL Howling Tomcats membership card, signed by Harry Read, c. 1927

Crew of the good ship Pretzel, which sailed every Wednesday evening with the Wind Jammers Club over KFWV

encouraged the station to schedule what it called the *Insomniacs Club* on a regular basis. The program doesn't appear to have been of particularly long duration, however.

**The Wind Jammers Club, KFWV Portland:** KFWV's entry into the locally-produced late-night variety program effort was known as the *Wind Jammers Club*, usually heard at 10 p.m. on Wednesdays. The Wind Jammers supposedly occupied a ship, initially called the Pretzel (which was later renamed the Black Maria) and sailed to various locales such as Sweden and Norway. The ship was captained by Charles Becsey, "one of Portland's most prominent entertainers," joined by Frank L. McGuire, Judge W. A. Ekwall, Portland commissioner Stanhope Pier, City of Portland purchasing agent Frank Coffinberry and local attorney Frank Lonergan.[69] The Portland Police Quartet and the Associated Oil Trio were among those who provided music counterpoint to the travelogue skits.

The Wind Jammers generally broadcast from KFWV's basement studio in the Sovereign Hotel and were a major source of pride to the station.[70] Even as he passed his 100th birthday, KFWV owner Wilbur Jerman continued to fondly identify the Wind Jammers as one of the station's most memorable accomplishments.[71]

*Cuckoo Club,* **KOIN Portland:** [see chapter 9]

*Crater Lake Frolics,* **KMED Medford:** Another station that boasted a membership program was KMED Medford, which signed-on in 1926 and at least briefly offered a "frolics" *a la* the Hoot Owls. The program centered on the Medford area's proximity to Crater Lake, which was the program's supposed setting. The *Crater Lake Frolics* does not appear to have been long-lived.

*Pelican Club,* **KFJI Klamath Falls:** When Klamath Falls got its first radio station, KFJI, in 1932, the station launched a late-night frolics program called the *Pelican Club* (see chapter 10).

Beyond the availability of talent, which differed between communities, the stations that seem to have had the most success with late-night club programs were those whose licenses afforded them higher power and premium nighttime coverage. Radio listening typically diminished late at night, and stations relied upon a larger potential audience to achieve listener levels that justified such programming. Stations with broader nighttime coverage often found it easier to create and sustain late-night programming including clubs of the types discussed in this chapter. Smaller stations without significant nighttime rights, like KMED and KFJI, faced significant hurdles in establishing successful late-night club programs.

# Endnotes

1. Callvert remained with the *Oregonian* for many years. Upon Edgar Piper's 1928 retirement, Callvert succeeded him as editor and, in 1939, Callvert won a Pulitzer Prize for editorial reporting. [Wikipedia.org] The paper always publicly identified him as R. G. Callvert.
2. "Multi-Voiced Mel Blanc Recalls Days of Ad-Lib Portland Radio High Jinks," *Oregonian,* May 9, 1945, 40.
3. "Pacific Coast Studio's Dean Goes to S.F.," *Oakland Tribune,* February 17, 1929, 4.
4. He sang "Lady Do Not Trust A Stranger" on that day's Sunshine Division fundraising program. *Morning Oregonian,* December 9, 1932, 9.
5. Marguerite Davis, "Are You a Hoot Owl?," *Sunset Magazine,* December 1924, 49.
6. The *Oregonian* also credits Portland mayor George L. Baker as an originator of the program although no other information about his role has come to light. "Twenty Years Behind the Mike," *Oregonian/Northwest Magazine,* March 22, 1942, 4.
7. Edmiston, Fred W., *The Coon-Sanders Nighthawks: The Band That Made Radio Famous"* (McFarland and Company: Jefferson, North Carolina, 2003), 85.
8. For example, on April 8, 1920, Degree Team members Charles Berg and Alan "Punch" Green had presented "Lombardi Ltd" at the Marquam Grand. (Oregon Historical Society, photo 017280)
9. Writing in advance of the premiere broadcast, the *Oregonian* of January 26, 1923, pg. 11, refers also to W. J. Hoffman as a Hoot Owl officer charged, with Berg, with organizing the first program "interest in [which is] growing hourly."
10. *Oregonian,* January 28, 1923, Sec. 1, 18.
11. *Oregonian,* January 29, 1923, 7.
12. Helen Platt, *KGW—Portland's Pioneer Radio Station* (unpublished manuscript) (Portland, OR: Helen Platt Collection, Oregon Historical Society Research Library, MSS1134), 8.
13. Davis, "Are You a Hoot Owl?," *Sunset Magazine,* December 1924, 49.
14. "Back Fence—Don't You Just Love Reminiscing About Those…," *Oregonian,* March 8, 1924, D2.
15. Davis, "Are You a Hoot Owl?," *Sunset Magazine,* December 1924, 49.
16. While Smith created the original Hoot Owls logo, it was adopted and refined by Tige Reynolds who, from 1926 until his death in 1931, was the graphic designer for all Hoot Owls materials.
17. Sardam performed many characters on the Hoot Owls, including the Sage of Yamhill, Dr. Sedative P. Seidlitz, A. Gardner Diggs, the Ridgepole and Santa Claus. He was also the author of the Hoot Owl oath, Hi Mocha Si.
18. Skipano is a comic reference to the piano and denotes the musical director for the program. He was also known as Prof. All Spradeloutski. Juhasz was also the first musical director of the program.
19. He conducted the Hoot Owls quiz program segment, "Hittie McGinn's Questions and Answers Department."
20. As suggested by Lori Shea Kuechler, author of *The Portland Police Sunshine Division: An Early History* (Portland, OR: Sunshine Division, 2003).
21. Dixon's departure from the Hoot Owls may have something to do with personal tragedy, which befell him in 1928 (see chapter 17).
22. In 1930 Engle is identified as hosting the "KGW Spotlight," an "afternoon matinee program given with full orchestra and a wide variety of other talent." ["KGW and the Pacific Northwest: What They Offer the Radio Advertiser," (Portland, OR, KGW, c. 1930), 4.

23. Sardam was born November 21, 1880 in Colorado and died May 17, 1954 in Los Angeles. (California Death Index)

24. Harry Selleck Grannatt, born June 17, 1898, in Colorado, was extremely tall and thin. While Mel Blanc, in his autobiography "That's Not All Folks!," reports that Grannatt was nearly seven feet tall (p. 16), Grannatt's medical records indicate that he was 6 feet 4 inches tall. Being extremely thin, he appeared even taller than his considerable stature (Grannatt family records, Harry S. Grannatt Collection, WSMB).

25. Grannatt's induction date into the Hoot Owls is based upon his handwritten correction to a 1948 newspaper story which incorrectly reported him as an original cast member (WSMB collection).

26. He conducted the Hoot Owls quiz program segment, "Hittie McGinn's Questions and Answers Department."

27. Jo Grannatt Davis regularly appeared on the program. Her status as a Degree Team member is based upon her father's handwritten additions of her name—along with Forrest Berg's—to the listing of Degree Team members printed at the back of his copies of the Hoot Owls' Volume 2 pamphlets of published material.

28. Callvert was also King of Hungari.

29. As a youth, Sidney L. Goodwin was a vaudeville performer. Hired by the *Oregonian* to cover police, drama and radio news, he transitioned into KGW from the paper and also wrote "Sid's Column," for *Radio Waves* (see chapter 1) just as the Hoot Owls were getting their start. ("Behind the Mike," *Oregonian*, March 19, 1942.) Around 1930, Goodwin left KGW to go to NBC's San Francisco studios where he remained for some years (*Radio Digest*, December 1931, 69). He later moved on to NBC Hollywood, where he was a network announcer and, later, a network executive. (Rollie Truitt interview, KGW 50th Anniversary celebration recording, 1972. Portland, OR: Oregon Historical Society collection.) He left NBC in 1938 to freelance ("Behind the Mike," *Oregonian*, March 20, 1938, 9). In the late 1940s, he was an ABC Radio staff director (www.radiogoldindex.com).

30. Sumner died September 4, 1935, at Good Samaritan Hospital in Portland.

31. Replacing Riley as Grand Skipano and music director.

32. The sense of commercial competition apparent in the contemporary broadcasting industry doesn't seem to have much existed then. Not only did KFJR's Dixon participate in the Hoot Owls, but Harry Grannatt was also active at KOIN, having been a vocalist in that station's programming virtually from the station's sign-on (Craig Singletary, *Radio Station KOIN: A Case Study of Music Programming*, M.A. Thesis, University of Oregon, August 1963, 16).

33. The text of this version of the Midnight Ode differs slightly from that officially published by the Hoot Owls. This text is taken from a letter from Dixon sent to Mrs. Margaret Porter, July 21, 1927, in response to a request for the text of the Ode. It is also the version published in *Hoot Owl Classics – Vol. 1*. It is presumably, therefore, closer to its author's original intent.

34. Edris Morrison interview, "KGW Reminiscence on the occasion of KGW's 50th Anniversary," Oregon Historical Society collection.

35. Mel Blanc and Philip Bashe, *That's Not All Folks!*, (New York: Warner Books, 1988), 17.

36. Toley died on June 9, 1995. "Toley Tolman of Radio's Hoot Owls Dies," June 17, 1995, *Oregonian*, D2.

37. "Broadcasting from KGW," *Oregonian*, January 31, 1923, 11.

38. *Oregonian*, March 17, 1923, 13.

39. While KGW was the first Portland radio station to acquire program recording equipment, it didn't arrive until about four years after the Hoot Owls' last broadcast. A recording of Harry Grannatt reading the Midnight Ode, and the sound of the KGW Chimes that followed, is contained on a recording of KGW's 1972 50th Anniversary program. However, it is unclear whether that recording was recreated for the 1972 anniversary or comes from an earlier original rendition. An "original" KGW recording of that station's 50th Anniversary Program is located in the KBPS Archive of the National Public Broadcasting Archive, University of Maryland, College Park, MD. A copy of that recording is in the WSMB Collection. The only known contemporary recordings by a Degree Team member are two songs sung by Alan "Punch" Green, "All I Want Is You" and "I'm Back In Love Again," which appeared on Columbia 948–A/B and were recorded around 1927.

40. *Hoot Owl Classics – Volume 1*, Dean Collins, Portland, OR, 1928 and *Hoot Owl Classics – Volume 2*, Harry Grannatt, Portland, OR, 1929. Profits from the sale of both books were used to help support the Hoot Owls' charities. It is some measure of the program's continuing popularity that Volume 2 went into a second edition in 1930.

41. Hoot Owls Program 390 script, January 3, 1930. (WSMB Collection)

42. Ibid.

43. "Peeps Into Broadcast Stations: Hot Hoot Owl Stuff," *Wireless Age*, May 1924, 40.

44. Hoot Owls Program 373 script, September 6, 1929. (WSMB Collection)

45. Harry Grannatt, *Hoot Owl Classics – Volume 2*, (Portland, OR, Sunshine Division, 1929), 22

46. "Hoot Owls Provided Light Touch in the 20s," *Oregon Journal*, December 16, 1971, Sec. 2, 1.

47. Much of the preceding Hoot Owls material comes from Platt's history, graciously made available by the Oregon Historical Society, Helen Platt Papers, Oregon Historical Society, MSS 1134.

48. List of "firsts" taken from Helen Platt, "The Fabulous Hoot Owls," *History of KGW* (unpublished manuscript) Oregon Historical Society.

49. Davis, "Are You a Hoot Owl?," *Sunset Magazine*, December 1924, 76.

50. Ibid.

51. "Broadcasting from KGW," *Morning Oregonian,* May 16, 1923, 9.

52. Davis, "Are You a Hoot Owl?," *Sunset Magazine*, December 1924, 77.

53. *Wireless Age,* April 1924, 40.

54. While Harry Grannatt's daughter, Josephine, appeared on the program, she was apparently was not considered a member since Helen Platt's official history of KGW reports that Revell was the only woman to ever receive membership.

55. Letter from Ima Kidder to Hoot Owls (Harry S. Grannatt Collection, WSMB).

56. Ibid.

57. The word Hungari was taken from one of the mystic references in the Hoot Owl oath.

58. "Multi-Voiced Mel Blanc Recalls Days of Ad-Lib Portland Radio High Jinks," *Oregonian,* May 9, 1945, 40.

59. Information about the Sunshine Division is heavily drawn from research initiated by ret. Sgt. Ralph O'Hara, founder of the Portland Police Historical Society, and Dr. Charles Tracy, Chair of the Administration of Justice Department at Portland State University, as published on the Internet at: www.sunshinedivision.org/history.htm.

60. Forrest Talbot Berg Oral History, November 6, 1982, Oregon Historical Society.

61. *Oregonian,* September 3, 1932, 4.

62. *Oregonian,* September 3, 1932, 3.

63. Forrest Berg may have participated in the December 1933 gathering for three Christmas charity fundraising programs. A December 18, 1933, *Oregonian* ad for the program indicates that the old Degree Team, including the Grand Screech, was reassembled. Since no cast member took over Charles F. Berg's Grand Screech title on the weekly program following his death, and assuming that ad's text was correct, the most likely member to have assumed that title in December 1933 would have been Forrest Berg.

64. Platt, "The Fabulous Hoot Owls," 21.

65. *Oregonian,* January 7, 1933, 5.

66. Quoted material from *Oregonian,* December 8, 1933, 9.

67. *Oregonian,* December 22, 1933, 7.

68. The most extensive history of KGW radio was written by Helen Platt who was given the assignment by Dorothy Bullitt shortly after Bullitt purchased the station in 1953. Platt came from a distinguished Portland family and became personally close with Dorothy Bullitt, who generally stayed at Platt's home when visiting Portland. The Platt manuscript and associated papers, previously cited, are in the possession of the Oregon Historical Society. Platt's manuscript, essentially an "authorized biography," is written from an insider's perspective and by someone who clearly had unusual access to station personnel and records. Platt's manuscript, however, rarely cites sources. Nevertheless, information from Platt's KGW history has been invaluable in preparing *Pioneer Mikes*. One apparent error in Platt's manuscript was her citation that the Hoot Owls programs ran until 1934. Presumably based upon that source, 1934 has often been cited, without further substantiation, in other published accounts. However, the *Oregonian*, which still owned KGW at that time and published detailed program listings for the station, carries no listings for the Hoot Owls past the January 6, 1933 program, other than the 3-program December 1933 series. It is on this basis that the program's ending date has been established in *Pioneer Mikes*.

69. "Wind Jammers Promise Fun," unidentified newspaper clipping dated January 6, 1926 (Wilbur J. Jerman Collection, WSMB).

70. Undated news clippings from Wilbur J. Jerman papers (Wilbur J. Jerman Collection, WSMB)

71. Jerman, Wilbur J. interview by author. Tape recording. Portland, OR, October 2, 2002.

# Now a Word from Our Sponsor: Becoming Commercial

## 1923

As 1923 came to a close, Oregon appliance stores were promoting a "Radio Christmas." Families dreamt that a new Radiola or Atwater Kent might find a place under their Christmas tree. Many did—but the radio stations to which they would be listening were changing rapidly.

At the outset, no one really envisioned radio as a *broadcast* medium. With stations all initially operating on a common frequency of 360 meters (833 KHz), the licensing structure hadn't contemplated an individual station broadcasting more than occasionally.[1] Yet, it quickly became evident that stations who possessed greater access to talent, capital or both were in a position to provide programming that was superior. For those stations and the public, sharing the single 833 KHz frequency minimized opportunities to fully exploit radio's potential.

The shared frequency scheme also produced squabbling between stations over operating hours. In response, Secretary of Commerce Herbert Hoover allocated a second frequency in mid-1922—400 meters (750 KHz)—for use by "better quality" stations. The original frequency, 833 KHz, was to be used by "Class A" stations, and the new frequency was reserved for the higher-quality "Class B" stations.

Since any real attempt by a federal agency to define distinctions in program content bordered upon censorship, which was constitutionally prohibited, Class B stations were defined on purely technical grounds—as stations that operated at higher power than Class A stations and that broadcast no phonograph records. Larger, better-financed stations quickly jumped to Class B operation and, in communities where more than one station jumped to the new dial position, they again had to voluntarily devise sharing for the new 400-meter frequency.

Thus, with these changes, a single station could be licensed for any combination of 360-, 400- or 485-meter (used for weather reports) operation depending upon their equipment and programming. Many stations possessed authority to operate on more than one, or all, of these bands.

By 1923, it was apparent that the public's burgeoning radio appetite had made the 360–400–485 frequency allocation system obsolete. In April, the Department of Commerce (DOC) responded by announcing a whole new scheme more similar to the radio band familiar to modern radio listeners. All the original 360-meter stations, newly reclassified as Class C, were assigned the lowest priority but could continue to share 833 KHz. Over time, however, stations that chose to meet specified standards and raise their power could aspire to either Class A or Class B status (Class A broadcasting at higher power than Class B) on unique frequencies that were separated in 10-KHz increments. This scheme roughly translates to stations using the frequencies between 550 and 1350 KHz on the contemporary AM radio dial. Under Congressional pressure, the DOC attempted to allocate the new, better frequencies on a geographically equitable basis across the nation.

For stations that qualified for these superior wave lengths, changes in frequency assignments were rolled out over a period of months in 1923. Along with the new Class C assignments, the government also began referring to stations' operating frequencies in kilocycles rather than meters. Throughout the 1920s, however, the public continued to refer to stations' wavelengths (measured in meters, rather than in kilocycles).[2] Whether expressed in meters or kilocycles, most small stations chose to remain in their original 360-meter dial spots, although some did make the move to the better, unique dial spots.

KGW led the way in switching to a better frequency and, on May 12, 1923, moved to 492 meters, equal to 609.3 KHz. On February 22, 1925, KGW became the first Oregon station to move to a kilocycle-assigned frequency when it moved a tad up the dial to 610 KHz (equal to 491.5 meters).

As stations matured to Class A or Class B operation and were able to broadcast more hours each day (since they didn't have to share frequencies), the public's radio appetite grew even more. Amidst these changes, 1923 saw the failure of a pioneer Oregon radio station. KGN suspended operations on May 31, 1923. From that point on, radio pioneer Charles Austin confined himself to equipment manufacturing.[3] But, with the radio craze in full swing, other new stations continued to emerge.

## KFFO Hillsboro

KFFO, a tiny 5-watt Class A station, signed-on in Hillsboro, on March 23, 1923. Owned by Dr. E. H. Smith, an M.D.D.O. physician and surgeon, the station was located in his offices at 2nd and Main Streets. The doctor licensed the station to broadcast "entertainment and like matter."[4] Apparently operated essentially as a hobby, the station does not appear to have attracted much attention and its license was deleted upon its expiration on March 12, 1924.

## KFGL Arlington

KFGL filed its license application in March 1923 and set up shop in the Arlington Garage in the tiny town of Arlington, population 700, located 135 miles east of Portland. Initially licensed

Twelve-year-old Carl Severinsen when he won a cornet concert, 1939

in the garage's name, KFGL was built and owned by Earl Wilcox Snell, the future Oregon secretary of state and governor who lost his life in a tragic 1947 plane crash near Lakeview. Snell operated the garage in partnership with Earl Lemon, who does not appear to have been involved with KFGL.

While licensed in 1923, it appears that KFGL didn't spread its radio wings until 1924. A broadcast on January 4, 1924 drew front-page attention in the *Arlington Bulletin*, which described "the initial performance by the local station" as "highly successful."[5] A Thursday, January 10, broadcast by the Arlington High School Trio also was reported to have been greatly enjoyed.

Snell must have soon realized that operating KFGL represented a greater challenge than he had anticipated. The Arlington General Hardware Store sold radio equipment, and there was town gossip that its owner, J. K. Irby, seemed to be "developing a radio bug. About the next thing you will hear is that Irby will have a broadcasting station."[6] Needing help with KFGL, Snell brought Irby in as a partner. Irby likely believed the move would help him sell more radio sets. Thus, KFGL's next license renewal, filed in March 1924, was jointly in the name of Snell and Irby. Both men must have found station operation too taxing, because when that license expired in June 1924, the owners didn't renew it. KFGL left the air permanently that spring.[7]

Other than Earl Snell, Arlington's most famous broadcasting product was trumpeter Carl "Doc" Severinsen, an Arlington native who gained fame as Johnny Carson's musical sidekick on the NBC-TV "Tonight Show" in the 1970s. Before leaving Oregon, Severinsen was a performer on The Dalles' KODL in the late 1940s (see chapter 13).

## KFHB, Hood River

Perry Beardwell of Hood River's Rialto Theatre was among the folks in Hood River who were watching radio's development. A radio enthusiast, Beardwell apparently persuaded theatre owner A. S. Kolstad to allow him to build and locate a radio station in the theatre. A license application was filed in March 1923, and the station was on the air by April 12, 1923, although Beardwell got into trouble while building the station. On March 23, 1923, the *Hood River News* reported that Beardwell had to be rescued by the volunteer fire brigade from the top of a tree while installing the lead-in to a "cage aerial" after he "over-reached himself and dislocated his shoulder. He was absolutely helpless."[8]

Rialto Theatre at the time of KFHB's operation with antenna towers visible on adjacent roof

Initially licensed jointly to Beardwell and Kolstad/The Rialto Theatre, KFHB's subsequent license renewals were all issued solely in the name of Kolstad and the theatre.

Between KFHB and KQP, the latter was clearly the larger of Hood River's two stations. With KQP offering a regular schedule of music (the Hood River Radio Saxophone Quartet was prominently featured) and talks, KFHB's more meager listings consisted of an occasional program by the Rialto's organist but sometimes nothing more involved than the baseball scores.[9] Hoping to improve KFHB's coverage, Beardwell installed a new 114-foot-mast transmitting antenna on May 18, 1923. KFHB was clearly struggling, however, and presumably seeking alliances. In late 1923, Beardwell arranged for Harry Read to assume the position of KFHB's operator, in addition to his corollary assignment at KQP.

Hood River was, however, having enough difficulty sustaining one radio station, much less two. KFHB, which apparently operated well into 1924, allowed its license to expire in June 1924. While a renewal application was submitted in early January 1925, no renewal application was submitted as the station's April 14, 1925 license expiration date neared. KFHB had, in fact, ceased operation nearly a year before. The station's license and call sign were deleted in June 1925 "on account of expiration."[10]

## KFIF/KBPS Portland

Students at Portland's Benson Polytechnic High School had a longstanding interest in radio. Initially, Benson had operated experimental Morse code station 7YK for physics and electronics students. However, as regular radio stations developed in 1922 and early 1923, the operation of this "spark gap" station became impractical because of the interference it caused with regular radio reception.

Since Willard Hawley had abandoned KYG in October 1922 and his successor, the Radio Service Bureau, had quit a month later, an opportunity arose (see chapter 1). By February 1923, the KYG transmitting equipment, which had been built by Charles Austin's Northwestern Radio Manufacturing Company, was sitting in Stubbs Electric's display window and was advertised for sale at $1,500. Popular legend holds that some passing Benson students saw the transmitter and went back to the school to persuade officials to purchase it, in the student body's name, to replace 7YK. In reality, the purchase was far less casual. Having acquired the transmitter, Stubbs apparently offered it to Benson's principal, C. E. Cleveland, who appointed a faculty/student committee to consider the matter.[11] According to W. D. Allingham in a 1955 interview, the primary motive for Cleveland and his faculty members in purchasing the transmitter was the hope that a radio station would help boost school enrollments and build better community relations for the still relatively new school.

On March 16, 1923, the *Oregonian* reported that "the former KYG broadcasting equipment has been purchased by the Benson Polytechnic school and will soon be in the air again with a series of educational features according to C. E. Cleveland, principal of the school."[12] John Herz, a student and commercial radio operator, was to be in charge of the station, and chemistry instructor Fred A. Brainerd was in charge of programming. Since KYG's license had been abandoned, the school needed to file a new Department of Commerce application in which it requested reinstatement of the KYG call sign. Learning that wasn't possible, the station signed-on as KFIF on May 4 in conjunction with the Fifth Annual Benson Tech Show.

Radio as an industry was still evolving from a point-to-point emergency and government communication medium into the popular entertainment vehicle it was rapidly becoming. Thus, at first, KFIF operated for an hour each evening, broadcasting for 13 minutes at a time and then going silent for two minutes "to listen to distress calls."[13]

Originally licensed in the name of the Benson student body, the licensee was changed to the high school itself on August 27, 1924. For decades, one of the school's ongoing challenges was securing periodic federal authority to sign-off KFIF during Benson's vacation periods (each instance having to be individually federally approved). KFIF changed its call sign to KBPS in 1930.

The school's foresight in acquiring KFIF in 1923 propelled Benson Polytechnic into the role of operating one of the nation's first, and most durable, educational radio stations.

## KFJI Astoria

Liberty Theatre's Ernie Marsh was interested in radio. Seven months after the devastating Astoria fire, which had consumed both KFBM and KFGG, Marsh purchased KFBM's transmitter and applied for a license for a new station—KFJI—which Marsh signed-on July 19, 1923, from the Liberty Theatre.

Radio was a much more casual affair than contemporary readers might appreciate, and the Department of Commerce was more concerned with regulating wave

*Oregonian* ad, January 21, 1924

WSMB Collection

lengths and other technical parameters than it was in carefully attributing station ownership. Examples of such licensing confusion include the Arlington Garage/Earl Snell and Hood River's Rialto Theatre/Perry Beardwell. Such was also the case in Astoria. Marsh, the theatre's manager and projectionist, apparently built and owned the station personally, although it was housed at, and licensed in the name of, the Liberty Theatre.

The station and the theatre clearly were intertwined. Movie display advertising in the Astoria newspapers frequently also promoted KFJI, which was important to the community and appears to have been reasonably well-supported.

# 1924

## KFOH Portland

One of Portland's shortest-lived radio stations signed-on March 23, 1924, using the transmitter of Charles Austin's by-then-defunct KGN. KFOH was owned and operated by Eric H. Chambers, who also operated a radio sales/repair business known as The Radio Doctor (located at 41st and Taggart Streets), which was also the location of KFOH's 15-watt transmitter. KFOH used the on-air slogan "The Radio Bungalow" and offered regular programming in March and April—including performances by pianist Miss Vera Beatrice Frank and violinist Miss Harriet Avery. When the station's license routinely expired on May 27, 1924, Chambers did not seek its renewal. The last published program listing for KFOH appeared in the *Oregonian* on May 30, 1924.

# KFOF Coos Bay

Following the demise of Coos Bay's KFBH, the community was without a local radio station until Rohrer Electric Company, owned by Landis Rohrer, filed a Department of Commerce radio station application in February 1924. Licensed as KFOF on February 28, the 10-watt station was operated from Rohrer Electric's store at 245 Central Avenue.

Interestingly, KFOF appears to have been a cooperative venture by Rohrer and L. L. Thomas of Thomas Music Company, the licensee of the defunct KFBH. According to the *Southwestern Oregon Daily News* of February 6, 1924, KFOF started broadcasting on February 5 from Thomas Music Company's store, and E. T. Treen, the music store's radio engineer, was in charge of the station. Perhaps KFOF's location at the music store stemmed from changes going on at Rohrer—which moved to a temporary location at 449 Central Avenue on March 25, 1924, while awaiting completion of its permanent new headquarters in the elegant Hall Building, located at 245 Central Avenue (commonly known as the Elks Building).

Rohrer and Thomas were unclear about the station's utility. Reflecting indecision about KFOF's value, the station's license was allowed to expire on May 27. In August, a request for reinstatement was submitted, and was approved on August 25. Yet, KFOF's license was again allowed to expire on November 24, 1924. By that time, Rohrer Electric had relocated to the Elks Building—and no reinstatement was sought.

# KFQN Portland

Oregon's first religious station got its start on June 19, 1924, when the Third Baptist Church, located at the corner of Vancouver and Knott Streets in Portland, signed-on KFQN using the transmitter that had formerly been KGG's. Perhaps Joe Hallock was a member of the congregation, or perhaps he just saw the opportunity to sell the KGG equipment to the church. Either way, it was Hallock who signed the May 1924 license application on behalf of the church and apparently maintained the equipment. The church's Reverend W. Arnold Bennett presumably appeared on the station's regular broadcasts on Wednesdays and Fridays from 8:00 p.m. to 9:00 p.m., and on Sundays from 9:45 a.m. to 10:30 a.m. and 9:00 p.m. to 10:00 p.m. When KFQN filed for a license renewal in 1925, it was denied due to the station's irregular and infrequent schedule. By 1925, the DOC's Radio Division was attempting to ensure that stations given the increasingly scarce frequencies would make the fullest possible use of them.[14]

# KFRQ Portland

One of the Portland radio community's more colorful early stations, KFRQ, signed-on in November 1924. Owned by Harry M. Schultz under the name of Radio Market Service Company, the station was authorized to operate on 1410 KHz on November 11. Reportedly, the station was used to promote stock sales for the Allen Brokerage Company owned by H. M. Allen, who had a reputation for employing "shoddy business practices [and] duping prospective clients".[15] Reportedly, the brokerage would broadcast coded stock quotes over KFRQ— a practice that government officials considered illegal. KFRQ ceased broadcasting in June 1925.

# KFJR Portland

The last addition to the Portland air waves in 1924 was Ashley Dixon Sr.'s KFJR. Ashley Clayton Dixon Sr. and his wife, Jessica, had both been born in Illinois—where they married.

Craig Adams Collection, WSMB

KFJR in 1925

Their son, Ashley C. Dixon Jr. was born in 1909, while the couple was living in Chicago. In 1916, the Dixons moved to western Montana's Bitterroot Valley and, with a background in banking, the reasonably well-to-do Dixon purchased land just north of the Three Mile Trading Post near Stevensville, Montana. There, he developed a McIntosh apple orchard and helped organize Stevensville's First National Bank.[16] Both father and son shared a deep interest in radio, which they expressed as early as 1919 through their operation of an amateur radio station.[17] In March 1923, they secured a broadcasting license and established KFJR, which was, at least initially, "more amateur than broadcast" according to a federal radio inspector.[18]

KFJR, which reportedly signed-on August 23, 1923, used the slogan "The Bitterroot Broadcasting Station" and operated modestly from the Dixon's home with power drawn from the farm's lighting plant.[19] Dixon frequently broadcast his own talks, but "occasionally a group of men from Stevensville would form an orchestra and travel to Dixon's home for a short broadcast."[20] For reasons that remain unclear, the Dixons relocated to Portland in 1924.

At the time of his move, it seems unlikely that Dixon envisioned radio as an occupation. Certainly, it wasn't economically feasible for the noncommercial station to support the family and, on arriving in Portland, Dixon drew upon his banking background and took a sales position at the Ralph Schneelock Company, one of the city's largest dealers in municipal and government bonds. An application to move KFJR, operating at 1140 KHz, from Montana to Portland was authorized by the Department of Commerce on November 12, 1924, although the station did not sign-on until May 18, 1925. The Schneelock Company's offices were in the Lumberman's Building, and it is likely that Dixon's familiarity with these premises helped lead to KFJR's relocation to the Lumberman's Building in 1927 (see chapter 9).

Signing-on from the Dixons' Eastmoreland home—with studios above the garage—the elder Dixon was the station director (equivalent to general manager) and Dixon Jr., who was 16 when the station signed-on in Portland, was the station operator.[21] KFJR devoted serious effort to local programming which included the *Kiwanis Club Frolic* (perhaps an attempt to mount a program similar to the KGW Hoot Owls) offered on alternate Tuesday evenings beginning in

The Dixon Home, at SE 56th and Glenwood, in 1926. KFJR was located on the second floor of the garage (to the right of the home).

October 1925 (before Dixon himself joined the Hoot Owls in 1926).[22]

Originally operating with 50 watts, KFJR inaugurated a five-year partnership on April 6, 1926 with the *Oregon Journal*, which sponsored many programs, including the long-running children show *The Journal Junior*. Later, the *Journal* also sponsored KFJR's popular *Music of the Masters* series as well as *News & Markets* (also known as *Oregon Journal News*). In June 1926, KFJR increased power to 100 watts and adopted the slogan "The Eastmoreland Broadcasting Station."

With radio burgeoning, Secretary of Commerce Herbert Hoover struggled to lead the government regulatory apparatus that was increasingly necessary to provide the public with a better service and the industry with clear regulations. When he convened the annual National Radio Conference in 1924, his comments revealed a dismal view of the role of commercialism in radio. He observed: "If a speech by the president is to be used as the meat in a sandwich of two patent medicine advertisements, there will be no radio left." A year later, at the 1925 conference, he spoke out against "the use of radio broadcasting for direct sales effort."[23]

Content issues aside, however, Hoover's real struggle was with the fact that the minimal federal authority over radio which existed was clearly inadequate to deal with the industry's explosive growth.

# 1925

## KGW Portland

Three years after Oregon's first stations signed-on, radio was beginning to look more like a business than a hobby—and KGW was a bellwether indicator. Since its inception, KGW had been entirely noncommercial—fully sustained by the *Oregonian*—but by 1925 radio was changing. Following a trial experiment earlier in the year, the *Oregonian* switched KGW to commercial status on September 1, 1925 and the station began accepting regularly sponsored programming.[24] Reportedly, its first commercial program was the *Check Seal Program* featuring the Rose City Trio (of which violinist Julius Walter, later of KOIN, was a member). It was heard daily at noon (see chapters 6 and 9 for continuation of KGW's history).

With the move to commercial operation, KGW claims to have created and broadcast the first singing commercial in the nation (although the exact date is unknown). Sears Roebuck was the advertiser, and the jingle was sung by station announcer Stephen Gaylord early in KGW's commercial life.[25]

Courtesy of the Oregonian

KGW's broadcast of President Coolidge's October 23, 1924, speech at Portland's Civic Auditorium was a complex technical achievement indicative of the station's growing scope of operation and aspiration.

**RADIO STATION**
**K-G-W**
Morning Oregonian
Portland, Oregon

Operating under Class B license, 500-watt power transmission, 492 meter-wave length.

WSMB Collection

KGW promotional brochure, c. 1924

## KFWV Portland

By 1925, Wilbur Jerman had been involved in the construction and operation of quite a number of radio stations. When Stubbs Electric was contracted by Willard Hawley to build KYG, it was Jerman who constructed that station. He also worked for Meier & Frank's KFEC and, when Stubbs decided to create his own station, KQY, Jerman built and essentially managed that station as well. Yet, while working as a salesman and technician at Stubbs, Jerman clearly had higher aspirations. In 1925, he applied for a license for a station of his own—KFWV.

The five-watt KFWV was located in Jerman's home on East 58th Street South.[26, 27] In short order, however, Jerman decided to build his own 50-watt transmitter, which was federally inspected on July 25, 1925, and licensed on August 5.[28] It was that transmitter with which KFWV officially signed-on October 6, 1925, "giving so much volume that it had to be cut down."[29] The station's studio was set up in Jerman's living room, "with the walls draped from ceiling to floor with heavy monk's cloth to absorb the echoes."[30] The transmitter was located in the home's second-floor bedroom.

Charles Austin of Northwestern Radio Manufacturing was a good friend of Jerman's and lived across the street. The two young men collaborated often. Radio was a young person's fancy at the time, and the Portland radio community must have been small and tightly knit. When Austin purchased a "superhet" radio, the newest circuit on the market, the two eagerly set it up for a trial run in Wilbur's bedroom, where it performed admirably.[31]

Launching KFWV must have been quite a gamble for Jerman, who had quit Stubbs Electric to establish the station. When an anticipated investor named Allen backed out and money was scarce, Jerman feared that a collection agent would seize the station's equipment, which he surreptitiously moved to his father-in-law's farm on Portland's outskirts. There, he stretched the transmission antenna wire between a conveniently located windmill and the house.[32] Radio was still a pretty casual, and it was feasible to move a station in the dark of night and return to the air the following day.

While Jerman was clearly KFWV's technical wizard, he also displayed an acumen for marketing and dubbed KFWV the "Voice of Mt. Tabor," (a rather large hill on Portland's east side) to distinguish it from the downtown stations. Even while operating from Jerman's home, the station maintained an active set of phone circuits used to broadcast from a variety of remote locations, including the Broadway, Liberty, and People's Theatres and the W.O.W. Hall.[33]

Eventually John C. Egan, a display advertising salesman for the *Oregon Journal*, approached Jerman about forming a partnership. Egan was twenty years' Jerman's senior, and Jerman, who was still a rather young man, saw himself as providing KFWV with technical, rather than administrative, strength. Egan's seniority and broader background must have appealed to Jerman. The two established a partnership and made plans to relocate KFWV to downtown Portland (see KFWV/KWJJ later in this chapter).

## KTBR Portland

Oregon's next application for a radio station license came from Brown's Radio Shop in Portland, which was owned by Milburn E. Brown, who always identified himself as M. E. Brown.[34] With the call letters KTBR requested, Brown's station was licensed on September 21, 1925, and signed-on September 24 from its three-room studios located on the radio shop's second floor.[35] The inaugural broadcast featured an address by Portland mayor George Baker. KTBR clearly had ambitious goals when it adopted the slogan "Tell the World By Radio." KTBR's path onto the radio dial was paved with a voluntary "share time" agreement Brown struck with Ashley Dixon's KFJR. Under the terms of that agreement, the stations equally divided use of KFJR's 1140 KHz frequency. Air time was becoming increasingly scarce, and perhaps KFJR was finding it difficult to make full use of its frequency so this arrangement apparently helped both stations. In 1926, Brown turned over management of his radio shop to Charles W. Hunter and his son (and it eventually became Hunter's Radio Shop) in order to devote himself full-time to KTBR (see chapter 9 for continuation of KTBR's history).

## KFDJ/KOAC Corvallis

Oregon's last addition to radio in 1925 wasn't really an addition. Rather, it was a change. On December 21, 1925, KFDJ at Oregon State University in Corvallis officially changed its call sign to KOAC, and it remains so to the present (see chapter 16 for a continuation of KOAC's history).

# 1926

The year 1926 opened against a backdrop of high radio drama in Washington, DC. With near-universal agreement that regulation of broadcasting by the Department of Commerce had failed, various political interest groups were maneuvering to establish a new federal agency to oversee radio. Much of the public's complaint was about interference, such as Pacific Grove resident George A. Killian's letter to KNX Los Angeles: "Is there no way to correct the encroachment [sic] of shyster radio broadcasting stations from taking advantage of the present lack of radio restrictions? Every time I try to tune in your wonderful station I get the wail of some semi-human on a pirated wave length."[36]

Additionally, educators and like-minded forces were seeking a licensing system that would impose formal public service responsibilities on the radio industry. In contrast, radio station owners favored a more *laissez faire* approach. Following a battle that raged throughout 1926, Congress passed the Radio Act of 1927, which President Coolidge signed into law on February 23, 1927. The Radio Act, which created the Federal Radio Commission (FRC), largely favored the broadcasters' interests—as opposed to the educators'—although it did establish the standard of the "public interest, convenience and necessity" as the basis for the FRC's regulation of radio. It also divided the nation into five geographic zones, each with its own appointed radio commissioner charged with special oversight responsibilities for that area. As a body, the five commissioners and their staffs were charged with regulating the nation's burgeoning radio industry (see Federal Radio Commission later in this chapter).

In its battle to establish the FRC, however, Congress failed to either complete the appointment of a full complement of five commissioners or to allocate funds for offices and staffing. Accordingly, the FRC started with "one desk, two chairs, a table and a packing box" according to radio historian Eric Barnouw.[37] Commerce Secretary Hoover graciously allowed the new commission to use a Commerce Department office as the commission began the tasks of figuring out just which stations were operating on the increasingly crowded airwaves and what to do about the signal interference that such congestion produced.

December 1926 was a busy month for radio in Oregon with new stations signing on in Portland, Eugene and Medford.

## KGEH/KOOS Eugene

In Eugene, Harold H. Hanseth was making plans for his own radio station to be located on the second floor of the Eugene Hotel at 229 Ninth Street (now East Broadway).[38] While Dick Bollam initially co-owned the station with Hanseth, Bollam's name does not reappear following the station's opening. Reportedly, KEGH's call letters were selected to help promote the hotel's identity.[39]

KGEH was eager to sign-on and complained on December 28, 1926, in a wire to the Department of Commerce that, although construction had been completed ten days earlier, the necessary authority to commence broadcasting hadn't arrived.[40] With federal approval wired on December 29, the station's first broadcast (operating with 50 watts at 1370 KHz) was at noon on December 30. It was sponsored by Laraway Music Company.

KGEH's official dedication occurred a day later as a New Year's Eve celebration and featured the head of the Eugene Music Studios—Hugh Winder—as master of ceremonies. Musicians from Winder's organization provided entertainment while civic and religious leaders appeared at the KGEH microphone to both ring in the New Year and welcome the station to the community. KGEH's published schedule included a "local feature group on Friday nights" who took to the air upon completion of the KGW Hoot Owls' weekly romp.

Hanseth must not have seen himself as a programmer because it was announced on January 4 that Winder would become the station's announcer and assume responsibility for KGEH's local radio programs. Among the programs that Winder quickly scheduled were live broadcasts of Eugene's Rotary Club and entertainment from the Kiwanis, the Chamber of Commerce and the Lions Club, as well as the Eugene Gleemen—but Winder's burst of activity must have been too much. In February 1927, KGEH suspended operations but was back on the air in April, with Hanseth again in charge and with added studio locations in the McDonald Theatre and on the University of Oregon campus. In May 1927, Hanseth leased KGEH to Curtis G. "Shrimp" Phillips and his close friend, Frank L. Hill.[41] The two were recent graduates of the University of Oregon who shared a great interest in radio.

Reportedly, KGEH paid no rent to the Eugene Hotel, whose only compensation was the promotion afforded by the station's presence. Eventually, the hotel must have deemed that an inadequate return. While it has been reported that the station moved to the adjacent *Eugene Register Guard*, building that location isn't recorded in federal records. Rather, in spring 1927

KGEH moved its studios and transmitter to room 432 of the Miner Building at 140 East Broadway (with the antenna remaining atop the hotel).[42]

In 1927, KGEH announced grand plans for maintaining remote broadcasting circuits to two churches, the University of Oregon's Schools of Music and Theatre, and the Eugene Hotel, in addition to programming from the station's own studios. As 1928 dawned, KGEH was actively programming. On January 22, the station broadcast an address by University of Oregon president Arnold Bennett Hall entitled "America and World Politics," and on February 8, the American Legion Drum Corps made its radio debut over the station.

But these would turn out to be KGEH's expiring gasps. Amid a confused financial situation, Phillips defaulted on lease payments due to Hanseth while he simultaneously sought to renew KGEH's license in his own name. Hanseth, seeking to retain control, filed an application to move KGEH to Coos Bay—all of which led the FRC's radio inspector, O. R. Redfern, (who by now had transferred to the still-new FRC from assignment in the Department of Commerce) to "suggest investigation to definitely determine who owns this station."[43]

Perhaps sensing disaster, Phillips apparently solicited the submission of endorsements to the Department of Commerce Radio Division. One was submitted by J. E. Shelton, president of the Eugene Chamber of Commerce, who opined that "taking inventory of the things of which the City of Eugene could feel proud, I found myself placing Eugene's radio Broadcasting Station, KGEH, near the top of the list."[44]

In unusually frank language for a federal employee, Redfern also wrote to his supervisors "During my inspection trip through Oregon last summer I was informed that a Mr. [name concealed] of Portland, Oregon, had actually furnished the money for this station [apparently to Phillips] although in my investigation I was unable to definitely prove this. Mr. [name concealed] is a very notorious character in Portland. Information furnished by reliable parties in Portland indicate that Mr. [name concealed] is in reality a moral leper and has been in difficulties with parents of young girls."[45]

Eugene, Oregon, had handed the Federal Radio Commission a hot potato.

## Federal Radio Commission

Under the Department of Commerce's stewardship, the radio industry had burgeoned in ways that no one, certainly not the framers of that agency's authority, could have anticipated. Secretary of Commerce Hoover had earlier attempted to temper federal regulation with an approach that anticipated a somewhat self-regulated industry—an approach that stimulated his convening the annual conferences for the radio industry. But Hoover's approach increasingly foundered as radio grew exponentially. Seeking to regulate the interference resulting from too many stations competitively occupying too few frequencies, he attempted to impose order and was rebuffed in a 1926 court decision that struck down his efforts to *assign* stations to particular frequencies and operating powers. As the public purchased more and more radios only to suffer from a growing interference, the need to pass a new law and create an agency that could effectively regulate what was quickly becoming a wild-and-wooly radio environment was becoming increasingly clear. Pressure mounted throughout 1926, leading to the passage of the Radio Act of 1927, which established the Federal Radio Commission. President Coolidge signed the Radio Act into law on February 23, 1927.

It took months, however, for the successor to the Department of Commerce to set up shop for the regulation of radio via five very newly appointed Federal Radio Commissioners. It wasn't until November 1927 that Congress even got around to appointing the fifth and final FRC commissioner. Under the system established in the Radio Act of 1927, the FRC commissioners would make policy (including licensing) decisions while the DOC and its staff would continue to be the on-the-ground forces responsible for implementing those policies—including the administrative (but not the policy) functions associated with licensing. The DOC also investigated any alleged violations of the new legislation.[46]

Harold A. Lafount, a businessman from Salt Lake City, Utah with a background in radio manufacturing, was appointed commissioner and given responsibility for the FRC's northwestern zone (which included Oregon). But the newly installed FRC commissioner Lafount received radio inspector Redfern's recommendation to investigate KGEH just as Hanseth was peppering Lafount with inquiries about his application to move the station to Coos Bay. On January 24, 1928, Lafount wrote Hanseth: "Mr. Phillips asks that this station be re-licensed to operate in Eugene and you ask that it be allowed to move to Coos Bay. The Commission would like to know definitely the actual ownership of the station."[47]

Hanseth replied "[the] Eugene station was leased to Phillips who being unable to pay rent signed full release on station January twenty first." In a telegram dated January 16, 1928, Hanseth asked that the station's call sign be changed to KOOS.

The FRC authorized moving KGEH (now KOOS) to Coos Bay on February 7, 1928.[48]

Eugene was again without a local radio station.

## KEX Portland

Portland's most powerful radio station, KEX (operating at 670 KHz), signed-on Christmas Day 1926. As the Federal Radio Commission sought to reduce the interference produced by the 733 licensed radio stations for which the FRC had inherited regulatory responsibility, KEX was literally the last station licensed under the old regime. Authorized at 20 kilowatts, it was also among the west's most powerful stations, the second largest on the West Coast. Owned by Seattle-based Western Broadcasting Company, which also owned KJR Seattle, KEX operated from studios in the Terminal Sales Building at 446 SW Morrison Street. Built at a cost of $35,000, KEX called itself "Oregon's Most Powerful Station." KEX signed-on with the radio writer of the *Oregon Journal*, Arnold M. Grosse, "throwing the switch" for the station's broadcast with Herman Kenin's orchestra, which was followed by the Telephone Quartet and the Amaizo five-piece orchestra.[49]

KEX had a fascinating evolution. The station generated technical complaints over interference to other stations and in 1931 went through a complex share-time negotiation with the New Mexico College of Agriculture's (now New Mexico State University) radio station, KOB. KEX also pursued a regional strategy seeking to connect the Seattle-Portland axis for broadcasting purposes, a strategy successfully employed by KGW with its Triangle Network. However, as Portland's only station owned by out-of-town interests, KEX had difficulty attracting advertisers, who apparently resented the "foreign" control. Seeking to capitalize on its regional vision, KEX was also involved in the formation of the short-lived American Broadcasting Company, a Seattle-based radio network that began in 1928 and folded ten months later (see chapter 6). KEX went into receivership shortly after the collapse of this ABC network (see chapter 9 for continuation of KEX).

Harold A. Lafount, Federal Radio Commissioner for stations in the Pacific Northwest, 1929

WSMB Collection

Herman Kenin's Orchestra seated on the steps leading into the ballroom of the Multnomah Hotel, December 16, 1928.

## KMED Medford

Meanwhile, Bill Virgin was back at it in southern Oregon. While his KFAY had gone silent in September 1924, his interest in radio continued. On April 12, 1926, he inquired with the Department of Commerce about securing a license for a new 50-watt station. His application for such a station—with backing from the *Medford Mail Tribune*—arrived in Washington, DC on December 13, 1926.[50] Reportedly, the newspaper's publisher Robert Ruhl established a 50-50 partnership with Virgin in the new station for a $1,500 investment. Likely the arrangement was, like Virgin's earlier relationship with Sam Jordan in KFAY, an informal handshake since Virgin submitted the required DOC application solely in his own name (see chapter 2). In any event, the *Medford Mail Tribune* trumpeted the station's pending arrival.

Initial planning included consideration of establishing a small, two-station network by connecting KMED with Wilbur Jerman's KFWV in Portland. According to Virgin's account in the *Mail Tribune*, "programs put on in Medford would be re-broadcast at Portland putting Medford's station before additional thousands of radio fans."[51] However, it doesn't appear that any such arrangement actually developed.[52]

With studio and transmitter initially located in a single room on the second floor of the Sparta Building, located at the corner of Riverside and Main Streets, KMED signed-on December 28, 1926, at 6:00 p.m.[53] It was the successor station to KFAY. The opening broadcast featured *Mail Tribune* news reports, an address by Professor Irving Vining of Southern Oregon Normal School (now Southern Oregon University) in Ashland, vocal offerings by members of the Maddox family, assorted musical performances, old-time dance music by Nick Kime, and a special

"Frolic" presented by Medford's Crater Club that included a tongue-in-cheek proposal to enlarge Crater Lake as a harbor for the City of Medford. Unlike KFAY, KMED sported a new commercially manufactured Western Electric transmitter. The station's transmission plant featured two 85-foot-tall towers purchased from the local grange. Their presence on the Sparta Building's roof created an imposing sight in downtown Medford.

Perhaps allured by KMED's newspaper association, sponsors appeared in profusion. *Music by Wolf,* featuring Nick Kime, was offered by the Armory Service station. McPherson's men's clothing store, Jackson County Creamery and Young's Garage offered programs. People's Electric sponsored the performances of Mr. and Mrs. Carleton Janes. The Associated Buick Dealerships of Southern Oregon offered the Buck Master Six Orchestra, and Russell's Department Store offered a live performance of Gilbert and Sullivan's *Pirates of Penzance.* On May 13, 1927, KMED ordered a phone circuit to broadcast live the second anniversary of Walker's Old Time Ball from the upstairs ballroom in the Medford Center Building, where Virgin had earlier established both his radio shop and KFAY.

But KMED's driving force, Bill Virgin, was afflicted with Bright's Disease, and the 41-year-old died unexpectedly on January 28, 1928. It appears that Virgin personally handled significant announcing duties, and KMED didn't operate for several days following his death. The station quickly hired Earle Davis, formerly of KFWB Hollywood, and KMED returned to operation. On Virgin's death, the *Medford Mail Tribune*—doubtless trying to be helpful—publicly reaffirmed its support for the station and inaugurated a plan that gave newspaper advertisers associated commercial time on KMED. Bill Virgin's sudden death left his widow, Blanch, in sole charge of the station.[54] While she was not the first woman in America to own a radio station as has sometimes been reported, she was nevertheless among the first—and a notable exception to the almost universally male management of the nation's radio stations.[55] Blanch Virgin relied heavily on business counsel from William "Pop" Gates, owner of Medford's Groceteria and a close friend of her deceased husband, as she assumed sole responsibility for KMED.[56] Over time, Blanch Virgin successfully developed the station into a major community resource of considerable commercial value (see chapter 10).[57]

A Civic Enterprise!

MEDFORD'S NEW

# RADIO BROADCASTING STATION

*Means Much to Southern Oregon*

WSMB Collection

*Medford Mail Tribune* headline, October 27, 1926

"LISTEN IN" for

# KMED

*Medford's New Radio Broadcasting Station Is*

## Now on the Air!

The Mail Tribune-Virgin Station Will Present Carefully Prepared Radio Programs Every Afternoon and Evening

Music of All Kinds--Church Services
News Items and Market Reports

K. M. E. D. will broadcast on a 250 wave length. Turn your dial to this station and enjoy the programs—Don't miss them!

The Whole West Coast Will "Tune In" on Programs from Medford

*These Firms Will Be Among the First "On the Air" With Entertainment for You*

| | | |
|---|---|---|
| Chamber of Commerce | Jackson County Creamery | California Oregon Power Co. |
| People's Electric | King Radio | Terminal Hotel |
| American Laundry | Riverside Barber Shop | Young's Garage |
| Virgin Radio Service | Wolff Furniture Store | Fischer-Schaffel Electric |
| Russell's Department Store | Armory Service Station | Merrick's Oriental Gardens, |
| McPherson's Men's Store | Jarmin & Woods Drug Store | Featuring the "Nite Hawks." |
| J. N. Cole | Pantorium Cleaners | Methodist Church |
| Liberty Meat Market | Piggly Wiggly Grocery | Christian Church |
| Armstrong Motor Co. | Medford Realty Board | |

WSMB Collection

Ad, *Medford Mail Tribune,* December 26, 1926

## KROW Portland

The last radio station to arrive on the scene in 1926 was also the one with the shortest life. On December 26, the Oregon Broadcast Company, owned by John C. Egan, received a license for a 50-watt station to operate on 1300 KHz. Egan, an advertising salesman for the *Oregon Journal* (who also partnered with Wilbur Jerman in KFWV/KWJJ), received the call letters KROW for his new station on December 29. Later, he claimed to have signed-on the station that same day from studios located in the Sovereign Hotel (with the transmitter located on the roof of the adjacent Broadway Theatre).[58, 59]

Egan had acknowledged his earlier association with Wilbur J. Jerman and originally told the DOC that he had purchased a 50-watt transmitter from Jerman for KROW's use. However, in January 1927, Egan told the DOC that he hadn't purchased Jerman's transmitter and, instead, decided to build a different 250-watt unit. The DOC concluded that KROW had falsified its sign-on date, and when KROW's license expired in March, it was not renewed. A radio inspector visited the Broadway Theatre in April and concluded that KROW had "never broadcast any programs" and that Egan and his associates had "fraudulently obtained [a] license [as] owners of a station which they did not own" (with reference to the KFWV transmitter).[60]

# 1927

1927 saw two new radio stations join the Oregon air waves.

## KWBS Portland

On February 11, 1927, Portland's new 10-watt KWBS began broadcasting on 1490 KHz. Owned by Schaeffer Radio Company, the station's call sign stood for the initials of William B. Schaeffer, the company's owner and a local radio set manufacturer. The studios and transmitter were located at 226 SE 14th Street. The station adopted the slogan "Know, Watch, Boost, Serve" and mostly played phonograph recordings.

In April 1928, while little more than a year old, KWBS raised its power to 50 watts and announced that it was moving to a new studio plant on the mezzanine of the Francis Motor Car company at 405 SE Hawthorne (at the corner of Grand Avenue and Hawthorne Boulevard). The station's relocation was tied to the power increase, which had been approved by the FRC, and KWBS formally opened its new Eastside Studio plant at 7 p.m. on May 7 with a program including S. W. Lawrence, president of the East Side Commercial Club; Frank Shull, president of the Portland Chamber of Commerce; Clarence Francis, of the Francis Motor Car Company; and D. Al. Griffis, president of the Specialty Merchants Association (see chapter 7 for additional information on KWBS).

## KLIT Portland

Barely a week after KWBS's arrival, Portland's last entrant to the airwaves in 1927 joined the radio community. KLIT—whose call sign honored the station's founder, Lewis I. Thompson—signed-on February 18, 1927, at 1450 KHz with 7.5 watts. Thompson had filed his application in January, noting that he would "greatly appreciate station call letters KLIT" being assigned, and was promptly licensed to operate from 475 21st Street. KLIT seems to have been a casual affair that enjoyed a peripatetic existence. In 1928, the station drew a letter from the

Department of Commerce radio inspector, who complained that "It is noted that you state that you are operating this station on 860 kilocycles at the present time. According to records of this office you are licensed to operate KLIT on a frequency [of] 1450 kilocycles. A statement from you regarding this matter will be appreciated."[61]

Apart from technical issues, KLIT's problems involved its core purposes. Less than a year after it signed-on, Supervisor Redfern reported that Thompson appeared to have departed from the statement of use given in its original license application. Thompson had originally indicated that KLIT was to be a service for Portland's Broadcast Listeners Association, and would broadcast only after midnight. In January 1928, Redfern wrote to the DOC, saying, "the Broadcast Listeners Association is in no way connected with this station."[62]

On January 21, 1928 Redfern reported that "this station has put on one or two programs [phonograph]. This station absolutely does not and has not served any useful purpose.[63] It is merely a plaything [sic] of the owner."[64] Perhaps sensing a non-renewal of KLIT's license in the winds, Thompson put KLIT on the market on January 23 and it was promptly sold to Messrs. Curtis G. Phillips and Frank Hill, of Eugene. Thompson quickly filed an application to authorize moving KLIT to Eugene and transferring station ownership to the two former operators of KGEH.

In a telegram, Commissioner Lafount had already indicated he viewed such a change favorably. Nearly simultaneously, Lafount had notified Thompson by letter that KLIT's Portland operation did not meet "the interest of public convenience, interest and necessity" and would not be renewed.[65] In the same letter, Lafount indicated his understanding that Thompson contemplated moving to Hollywood (demonstrating a somewhat remarkable degree of awareness about this local station by a federal official). There were, in short, many reasons to support Thompson's sale of KLIT to Phillips and Hill and for the station to be moved to Eugene.

On March 12, 1928, KLIT was formally sold to the Eugene Broadcast Station (owned by Phillips and Hill), and relocated. The community of Eugene once again had a local station of its own (see chapter 7).[66]

# KFJR Portland

A significant sign of the times was Portland's KFJR's switch to commercial operation on November 7, 1927, a full two years after KGW's pioneering step into commercial operation.

Prior to 1927, KFJR operated "on a noncommercial basis." The station moved into a new studio plant—occupying a suite of three rooms on the top floor of the Lumberman's Building at the corner of SW Fifth Avenue and Stark Street—still during its noncommercial period but likely contemplating the added revenue commercial operation would create. Clearly aiming for "state of the art," the new plant featured an air-handling system that could completely recycle the studio's air in three minutes, a glass announcing booth, and a signaling system to allow cueing between different areas of the station. A reception room was "furnished for the convenience and comfort of visitors."[67] The *Journal Juniors* program, which was scheduled

KFJR begins commercial operation
Oregon *Journal*, November 6, 1927.

WSMB Collection

KFJR covers a special event in 1926, in its studios. From left to right: R. T. Thompson; Portland Mayor Baker; Ashley C. Dixon; Oregon Governor Pierce; announcer Joseph H. Hallock.

Photo apparently used in a later KALE/KPOJ promotional publication (given its caption). While labeled as taken in 1926, it is more likely from 1927, after KFJR moved from Dixon's garage to the Lumberman's Building studios. Note presence of Joseph Hallock (far right) as KFJR announcer.

two nights a week, arose from KFJR's formal association with the *Oregon Journal*, and featured "many talented boys and girls who have won wide fame by their singing and playing."[68]

## KFWV/KWJJ Portland

The last 1927 change in Oregon radio occurred on June 24, when Wilbur J. Jerman's KFWV became KWJJ, a call sign honoring its owner's initials. In early 1926, while still operating from Jerman's east side home/studio, the station had opened business offices (but apparently not studios) in the Sovereign Hotel. The station's aspirations were clearly growing. Having started as Jerman's personal property, it had apparently been incorporated in 1926.

Originally a simple partnership, the company was restructured in October 1926 as KFWV Broadcast Studios, Inc., with Jerman as president and Egan (who had abandoned his KROW venture some months earlier) as secretary/treasurer. A power increase from 50 to 500 watts was approved in November. By the time the station applied for a license renewal in April 1927, KFWV was maintaining studios in both the Sovereign and Benson Hotels, as well as the Broadway and Liberty Theatres. In a September 1926 DOC application, Jerman proposed changing the station's call sign to KWJJ and indicated that he was adding a new, and presumably principal, station location, which he referred to as the "K.W.J.J. Visible Studio," to be located at 328 SW Salmon Street. Jerman also indicated that new remote studios were being established at the People's Theatre at 127 West Park Street and the W.O.W. Hall at East 7th Avenue and Alder Street. Jerman noted that KFWV/KWJJ was now "the official station of the east side Business men's Club and also of the W.O.W. Multnomah Camp No. 77."[69] Although Jerman was president of the corporation, KWJJ was typically managed by Egan with Jerman functioning as chief engineer (see chapters 9 and 13 for continuation of KWJJ's history).

John Egan was clearly responsible for a considerable portion of the station's growing success. His advertising sales background at the *Oregon Journal* must have been helpful to Jerman, whose own background was heavily in engineering and operations. In the 1926 Pacific Radio Show Exposition's brochure, Egan is identified as KFWV's director.

KFWV officially became KWJJ on June 24, 1927. In 1929, Egan and Jerman established a more formal partnership when Jerman brought Egan into the KWJJ Broadcast Company, Inc., by officially transferring all of his personal interest in the station to the corporation and installing Egan as the secretary/treasurer.[70] The step was apparently at least partially taken in response to friendly advice offered to Jerman by commissioner Lafount, who had suggested ways in which Jerman could most effectively acknowledge Egan's contributions to KWJJ's growing success. With his own skills more technically focused, Jerman relied on Egan's familiarity with commerce and had indicated to Lafount that the station's "growth and popularity is due to the co-operation of us both."[71]

Radio was still a reasonably casual affair and KFWV/KWJJ maintained numerous phone lines to permit remote broadcasts from throughout the city, often because someone had purchased time on the station to have a program originate from their location. Jerman recalled a series of broadcasts from a dance hall on 15th Avenue, where the station had installed the lines but hadn't deployed an engineer to staff the broadcast at the remote end. "We didn't really break the law, but he'd open up a board on the stage, and turn the amplifier on, and that'd feed the station" directly without a local announcer/operator on duty.[72]

The *Oregonian*, April 3, 1927

WSMB Collection

Reportedly, Egan periodically departed KWJJ but always seemed to return, and Egan and Jerman continued to operate the station in partnership— under their common corporate umbrella—until the station's 1952 sale.

The entry of KWBS, KLIT and KROW, as well as the problems at KGEH, all give evidence of the overcrowded radio dial that the FRC had been created to solve. Change was in the air, and it was clear that the FRC would eventually shut down some stations to relieve the congestion. Radio had undergone explosive growth but by 1927 was in an uncertain time. Stations naturally worried about their future, even those as prominent as KGW, which prompted the *Oregonian* to publish an ad (above) only four days after the FRC assumed jurisdiction:[73]

## Endnotes

1. A second frequency, 485 meters, was also available and was specifically reserved for broadcasting weather and market reports. Typically, a station would sign-off of 360 meters, change the transmitter to 485 meters, broadcast the weather/market report for five or ten minutes, and sign-off to return to 360 meters for entertainment programming.
2. The Kilocycle unit was changed to Kilohertz in 1960 by an international tribunal to honor early electromagnetic wave scientist Heinrich Hertz.

3. Craig Adams www.pdxradio.com. Austin installed a radio system for the Portland Police Department in 1932 and continued to work in radio for some time thereafter. Eventually, he left radio entirely. He died in Blue River, OR, on June 11, 1980, at age 90. (Oregon Death Index and Social Security Administration records).

4. Department of Commerce, Bureau of Navigation, Radio service, "Applicants Description of Apparatus" station application, (KFFO, File No. 1062, NARA, College Park, MD).

5. "Arlington Radio Station Broadcast Is Big Success," *Arlington Bulletin*, January 11, 1924, 1.

6. "Arlington Merchant Has Up-To-Date Radio Plant," *Arlington Bulletin*, January 25, 1924, 1.

7. Department of Commerce, Bureau of Navigation, Radio Service (KFGL file, NARA, College Park, MD).

8. *Hood River News*, March 23, 1923, 1.

9. E. A. Kincaid, Charles Zolla, J.C. Meyer and Ed. Poirer, *Hood River News*, April 20, 1923, 10.

10. Handwritten note on KFHB final license (KFHB file, NARA, College Park, MD).

11. Committee members included W. D. Allingham, a faculty member in the Drawing Department and an enthusiastic amateur "ham" operator, and Roy T. Stephens, a physics instructor who was later instrumental in the station's operations. Allingham served as the station's first technical advisor, later program manager until he resigned to enter commercial radio in 1941. Stephens was the station's representative to the Federal Radio Commission (later the Federal Communications Commission) from the station's inception. "Interesting Historical Facts About KBPS," probably written by Patricia Green Swenson, KBPS general manager, circa 1955 (KBPS history files, WSMB Collection). Also, Patricia L. Green Swenson, "Radio in the Public Schools of Portland, Oregon" (Ph. D. dissertation, School of Education, New York University, 1958), 5.

12. *Oregonian*, March 16, 1923, 11.

13. Swenson, "Radio in the Public Schools of Portland, Oregon," 10.

14. Most of the information about KFQN comes from Craig Adams' www.pdxradio.com site.

15. Craig Adams www.pdxradio.com.

16. Ron P. Richards, "A History of Radio Broadcasting in Montana," (MA thesis, Montana State University, 1963), 11.

17. It has been reported by Richards in "A History of Radio Broadcasting in Montana" that their ham station was licensed as 7IT which seems incorrect since that call sign then belonged to an amateur in Ketchikan, AK. This author has found no evidence that a regular amateur call sign was issued to the Dixons in Montana. Based upon Richards' account, *Voice in the Big Sky: History of Montana Broadcasting,* by C. Howard McDonald, referred to the Dixons' pre-1923 Montana operations as "clandestine" or "pirate" (i.e., unlicensed) which seems possible.

18. The Federal Radio Inspector commented, in his notes, that the station operated "more amateur than broadcast." Craig Adams Broadcast *Pro-File* report.

19. "Behind the Mike," by William Moyes, *Oregonian*, March 20, 1942.

20. Richards, "A History of Radio Broadcasting in Montana," 11.

21. 1350 E. 36th Ave., Craig Adams www.pdxradio.com.

22. "Kiwanis Club Frolic," *Oregon Journal*, October 13, 1925, 13.

23. Erik Barnouw, *A Tower in Babel* (New York: Oxford University Press, 1966), 177–178.

24. Arden X. Pangborn interview conducted by Cathy Walsh, March 5, 1978, (Portland, OR: Oregon Historical Society).

25. Platt, *KGW—Portland's Pioneer Radio Station,"* Chapter, KGW Firsts. Also, KGW 50th Anniversary Program, a 1972 recording from collection of WSMB, Courtesy of National Public Broadcasting Archive–KBPS Collection, University of Maryland, College Park, MD. On Richard Haller's exit from KGW, Gaylord took over for a short tenure as station manager. He later left radio to enter the fruit and produce business. (Platt, 6).

26. According to Federal Radio Inspector Redfern's notes, Jerman was using the transmitter previously at KFRQ although Jerman, in 2002, disclaimed any recollection of such an arrangement. The license date is from Craig Adams www.pdxradio.com.

27. The actual address was 385 58th Street S. under the "old" Portland street numbering system.

28. DOC Inspector Redfern's note on the license application indicates that KFWV had been constructed with the equipment from H. M. Schultz's abandoned KFRQ, a point that Wilbur Jerman disputed in a 2002 interview with the author. It seems probable, however, since KFWV was subsequently reconstructed with new transmission equipment of Jerman's own construction in October 1925. Since KFWV did not formally begin broadcasting until October, it seems likely that Redfern may have inspected an installation, using the KFRQ transmitter for the authorized KFWV plant, that Jerman never actually used.

29. "Portland's Newest Station Has Volume," *Sunday Oregonian*, October 11, 1925, Sec. 3, 5.

30. "Newest Broadcast Station Opens with Big Set," *Oregonian*, October 11, 1925, Sec. 3, 5.

31. Jerman interview.

32. Jerman interview.

33. Respectively located at 202 Broadway, 103 Broadway, 127 West Park Street, and East 7th and Alder Streets. At this time, while the transmitter apparently remained at Jerman's home, the station's main studios were at the KWJJ "Visible Studio," at 328 Salmon Street. The station also added studios at the Benson Hotel and the Sovereign Hotel shortly thereafter. (Application for Radio Station Construction Permit, September 26, 1927, KWJJ file, NARA, College Park, MD).

34. The shop was located at 172 Tenth Street, Portland, according to the *Sunday Oregonian*, September 20, 1925, Sec. 4, 8. Brown never used his first name, signing documents as M. E. Brown.

35. A proud KTBR asset was the station's Chickering Ampico reproducing piano ("Test Program from New Portland Radio Station," *Oregon Sunday Journal*, September 20, 1925, Sec. 2, 4).

36. Letter from George A. Killian to Radio Station KNX, July 22, 1926. (KQW file, San Jose, CA, file, Department of Commerce, NARA, College Park, MD).

37. Erik Barnouw, *A Tower in Babel* (New York: Oxford University Press, 1966), 214.

38. Hanseth was clearly interested in getting into radio but apparently not as certain that Eugene should be the focus for his efforts. On July 16, 1926, he had written Secretary of Commerce Herbert Hoover requesting an application form to establish a new 500-watt radio station in Santa Rosa, CA (KGEH file, NARA, College Park MD).

39. Roger Houglum, "Early Day Broadcasting in Lane County," *Lane County Historian* (Eugene, OR: Lane County Historical Society), Vol. XIX, No. 1, Spring, 1974, 4.

40. Hanseth, Harold H. 1926. Wire to Commissioner of Navigation, DOC, Washington, DC dated December 28 (KGEH file, NARA, College Park MD).

41. Craig Adams www.pdxradio.com.

42. Application for Federal Radio Commission License dated August 4, 1927 (KGEH file, NARA, College Park, MD).

43. Radio supervisor's report contained in KGEH "Application for Renewal of Radio Broadcasting Station License," filed January 11, 1928, by Curtis Phillips (KGEH file, NARA, College Park, MD).

44. Shelton, J. E., 1927. Letter to Curtis G. (Shrimp) Phillips dated December 30 (KGEH file, NARA, College Park, MD).

45. Redfern, O. R., 1928. Letter to Department of Commerce dated January 12 (KGEH file, NARA, College Park, MD).

46. While it was originally intended that the DOC would serve this supporting role for only one year, at the end of that period the resolution of pending interference/frequency allocations was nowhere in sight and the DOC's term of service to the FRC was repeatedly annually extended. It was not until July 20, 1932, that the DOC field staff was formally absorbed by the FRC (Marvin Bensman, *Beginning of Broadcast Regulation in the Twentieth Century*, [Jefferson, N.C./London: McFarland and Company, 2000] and email from Bensman to author].

47. Lafount, Harold A., 1928. Letter to H. H. Hanseth dated January 24 (KGEH file, NARA, College Park, MD).

48. Lafount, Harold A., 1928. Telegram to H. H. Hanseth dated February 8 (KGEH file, NARA, College Park, MD).

49. "KEX On the Air," *Oregon Sunday Journal*, December 26, 1926, 8. The Telephone Quartet probably meant that the group consisted of accomplished amateurs drawn from the ranks of the local phone company staff.

50. Virgin, W. J. 1926. Letter to O. R. Redfern dated April 12 (KMED file, NARA, College Park, MD).

51. "Mail Tribune to Rebroadcast Its Radio Offerings," *Medford Mail Tribune*, November 26, 1926.

52. When interviewed in 2002, at age 101, Jerman did not recall ever meeting Virgin, which would suggest that the discussions about a KFWV–KMED association may have transpired by phone or mail.

53. KMED's original installation occupying only a single room comes from an account in the *Medford News*, December 24, 1948, 1.

54. Blanch Virgin's name has often been spelled "Blanche." Her handwritten correspondence and obituary both reflect that she did not include an "e" in her name.

55. Broadcast historian Donna Halpern credits Eunice Randall as the first woman radio station owner at Boston's WGI.

56. Gates was apparently formally recognized as a KMED representative by the Federal Radio Commission as evidenced by his sending a November 15, 1928, telegram on behalf of the station in which KMED requested special nighttime broadcasting privileges to report upon weather for the Rogue Valley's fruit growers.

57. Gates was identified as KMED's manager in a 1930 affidavit filed by Alfred Robinson, a federal radio inspector, in connection with an FRC Rules violation occasioned by the station operating for a brief period without a licensed operator on duty. Chief engineer Floyd Rush claimed he was delayed in returning to Medford after visiting his brother in Grants Pass. The station was found by the inspector to be in the care of a young, and apparently somewhat frightened, Lee Bishop, who promptly signed-off KMED when confronted by the inspector. Bishop later became a major figure in Oregon radio (KMED file, NARA, College Park, MD).

58. Located at 1207 SW Broadway.
59. Located at 1008 SW Broadway.
60. Report of April, 1927 inspection by FRC representative as quoted (likely from Broadcast *ProFile*) by Craig Adams, www.pdxradio.org.
61. Redfern, O. R. 1928. Letter to Lewis I. Thompson dated January 23 (KLIT file, NARA, College Park, MD).
62. Redfern, O. R., 1928. Letter to Department of Commerce, Radio Division, Washington, D.C. dated January 23 (KLIT file, NARA, College Park, MD).
63. Meaning that, because of the station's licensing, it was obligated to broadcast more frequently and not solely broadcast phonograph recordings.
64. "Application for Renewal of KLIT's license," dated January 21, 1928, supervisor's notes dated January 21, 1928 (KLIT file, NARA, College Park, MD).
65. Lafount, Harold A. 1928. Letter to Lewis I. Thompson, dated February 11 (KLIT file, NARA, College Park, MD).
66. Reportedly for approximately $5,000. Craig Adams www.pdxradio.com.
67. "New KFJR Studio To Open Monday Night," *Oregon Sunday Journal*, November 6, 1927, Sec. 2, 6.
68. "Journal Juniors To Be Heard on Air Two Nights," *Oregon Sunday Journal*, November 6, 1927, Sec. 2, 6.
69. KFWV/KWJJ DOC Construction Permit Application, receipt date stamped September 26, 1926 (KFWV file, NARA College Park, MD).
70. FRC Application for Voluntary Assignment of Radio Station License dated October 29, 1929 (KFWV file, NARA, College Park, MD).
71. Egan, John C., 1929. Letter to Harold A. Lafount, dated November 5 (KFWV file, NARA, College Park, MD).
72. Jerman interview.
73. *Oregonian*, April 3, 1927, Sec. 5, 9.

# 5

# Harry Read: KQP, KOIN, and KXL

One of Oregon's most influential and colorful pioneer broadcasters was Harry B. Read.[1] Born in Seattle, Washington on August 29, 1892, Read grew up in Bremerton, Washington. The son of Louis B. and Elizabeth Read, he was one of four children, including sisters Phoebe and Faith and an elder brother, Walter.[2] Like Joe Hallock, Clif Watson and Charles Austin, Harry Read became infatuated with wireless at an early age, perhaps through exposure from his brother, Walter, who later reported that he "had been [bitten] by the radio bug when in knee pants."[3] Read's interest in radio grew during a stint in the Merchant Marines, after which he wound up in Portland working for Hallock and Watson. Around 1921, Read moved to Hood River, where he set up the Hood River Radio Shop and played a prominent role in launching and sustaining KQP, which signed-on in 1922 (see chapter 2).[4] Oregon's Johnny Appleseed of early radio, Harry Read would eventually either launch or own seven early stations across the state.[5]

By 1924, with the failure of KFHB, KQP was Hood River's only local radio station (see chapter 4). Yet, despite backing from the *Hood River News* and participation by some of the community's prominent citizens, KQP was also struggling. While Read was the chief operator of both KQP and KFHB (until its demise), the task of operating KQP under the Apple City Radio Club's ownership increasingly proved to be a challenge.[6] KQP's struggle was complicated by the fact that the

Harry Read (1892–1948). c. 1947

interests of the Apple City Radio Club members were both in the welfare of radio generally (such as minimizing the interference that then-common "regenerative circuit" sets could cause), in addition to the responsibilities of operating KQP. As radio set ownership grew between 1922 and 1924, the club must have assumed that the majority of Hood River set owners would join the club, pay dues and help support KQP's costs. Club membership did increase, but by the beginning of the fall 1923 "radio season," insufficient funds were available to operate KQP. Moreover, the club was still appointing volunteers to determine KQP's programming—a strategy not designed to compete well with the better-funded urban stations which KQP increasingly faced.

At that time, radio had "seasons" that were dictated by atmospherics. Reception was best in the crisp, winter weather and worst during the summer, when lightning caused severe static. With reception always stronger at night than during the day, many stations devoted little effort to daytime summer programming and only scant attention to nighttime summer operation. By the time the 1924 radio season ended, the Apple City Radio Club's enthusiasm for KQP had ebbed, and responsibility for the station increasingly had fallen on Read's shoulders—as evidenced by the station's fall 1923 license applications submitted in the name of "Apple City Radio Club (H. B. Read)" instead of solely in the club's name as had previously been the case.

KQP doesn't appear to have returned to the air following the 1924 summer doldrums. Its license was allowed to expire in December 1924, and in a letter dated November 25, 1924, O. R. Redfern reported to his supervisor that the Apple City Radio Club of Hood River had requested that KQP be placed on the "inactive" list and that their call letters be reserved for a period of one year.[7] What seems clear in light of later events is that Harry Read had taken over KQP. Moreover, Read understood operating KQP in Hood River was financially impractical and began developing plans to relocate.

In July 1925, Read requested reinstatement of KQP's license. Granted on July 10, 1925, the approval contained the unusual notation that "call letters of this station were reserved in Nov. 1924"—a process for which there appears to have been little precedent (remember KFIF's unsuccessful effort to retain Willard Hawley's KYG call sign when Benson Polytechnic bought the Hawley transmitter). The Hood River KQP license was issued for a term expiring on October 9, 1925.

It seems doubtful that KQP ever again broadcast from Hood River. Instead, Read left Hood River for Portland in October 1925 and took up residence in the Portland Hotel on Sixth Avenue. From that location, he asked the DOC to delete KQP's Hood River license on October 10, 1925, and simultaneously filed an application for a new station.[8] The new higher power 500-watt station—licensed in his own name to serve Portland—requested KQP's former frequency and "reserved" call letters. The *new* Portland KQP license application was received and granted simultaneously with the request to delete the *old* KQP—a series of transactions that seem to reflect the unusual flexibility of federal officials at that time. Read was always an engaging figure, with a contagious enthusiasm for radio, and they must have liked him.

Portland's KQP signed-on November 9, 1925, from studios in Room 544 of the Portland Hotel.[9] With its transmitter located in Portland's Sylvan Hills, KQP was the first station north of San Francisco to operate with a remotely controlled transmitter—a fact that doubtless reflected Read's fascination with technology. At the same time, KQP's antenna also demonstrated Read's flair for the exotic and consisted of "a 120-foot wooden mast [with] 16-wires forming a loop, with 4 to each guy, held in a vertical umbrella shape by 4 guy wires."[10] It must have been quite a sight.

KQP was now the sole property of Harry B. Read. While Read's move of KQP to Portland had virtually sailed through federal officials, the station's relocation to Portland proved to be anything but smooth operationally. Yet, Read had big plans.

In December 1925, not satisfied with sharing time with Jerman's KFWV, Read explored methods of gaining more air time and more transmitting power. Based upon the unfolding events, it seems that Read either had only modest interest in actually operating KQP himself or had seriously overextended himself financially—or both. Effective February 7, 1926, he leased all of KQP's air time to the *Portland News,* which had become interested in radio at its 1922 onset. The station began identifying itself on the air as "KQP and the *Portland News.*" Charles W. Myers, the *Portland News*' business manager, also assumed KQP's management. But less than a month later, on March 1, 1926, KQP was sold to the Northwestern Trust Company for $2,400 plus payment of all outstanding bills Read had incurred in constructing the station.[11]

Northwestern Trust Company promptly appointed Dolph Thomas as KQP's station manager and established an order with Hallock and Watson to "place this station in as high class condition as is possible regardless of the cost."[12]

It all unraveled quickly, however. On March 11, 1926, Read publicly proclaimed that he had been "swindled by [Northwestern's] Mr. Stockman" and that the new owners of KQP "were an unsavory group."[13] At the same time, the *Portland News* discontinued its association with KQP. More pertinent is a telegram from Redfern to the DOC on March 13, 1926, in which he reversed his previous recommendation that KQP's sale to Northwestern Trust be approved.[14] Redfern reported that "Read, the former owner of Station KQP, claims that the Northwest [sic] Trust Company swindled him out of his station. The Better Business Bureau, of Portland, makes a very unfavorable report on the officials of this company and the Manager of the *Portland News* informed me over long distance telephone that Mr. H. E. Ervin, the President of the Northwest [sic] Trust Company, is at the present time under Federal Indictment at Los Angeles for fraudulent use of the Mails."[15]

Read had considerable leverage in the dispute because, at that time, despite protests from broadcasters, American Telephone and Telegraph had adopted the position that all commercial radio transmitters required a license from AT&T, which claimed control of relevant patent rights. While some stations courted litigation by failing to take out such a license, KQP had complied and its license was still in Read's name. Read simply refused to transfer it, thereby rendering KQP legally inoperable. Moreover, on March 15, 1926, the DOC informed Redfern that a special temporary authority to operate KQP that had previously been granted to Northwestern Trust Company, "has expired and the Northwestern Trust Company has no authority to continue operation of this station."[16] Redfern personally delivered that message to C. W. Myers, who relayed it to Northwestern Trust, prompting Northwestern's H. E. Ervin to explode that "he would never rest until he had caused [Redfern] to lose [his] job and that he [Ervin] would 'get' anyone in Portland who dared to oppose H. E. Ervin."[17] When Ervin's response was reported to Redfern, he laconically observed, "This illustrates the class of officials which compose the Northwestern Trust Company."[18]

To resolve the impasse, Redfern suggested that KQP go silent while matters were sorted out. According to a telegram in the Federal Radio Commission files, Read secured financial assistance from the *Portland News* and took possession of the station—in the name of KQP, Inc.—on March 15.[19] He took KQP silent on March 25 and the next day sold stock in the station to Joe Hallock and Clif Watson. They promptly took over and requested a new call sign, telling the Department of Commerce Radio Division that "KQP suffered from a bad reputation while in the hands of its former operators." On April 6, 1926, KQP officially became KOIN.[20]

The renamed and reborn KOIN officially returned to the air at 3 p.m. on April 12, 1926, once again associated with the *Portland News*. Spelling out the station's acronym, the station's slogan was "**K**now **O**regon's **I**ndependent **N**ewspaper." Dolph Thomas was again the studio director, station manager and voice of KOIN, which began referring to itself as the "*Portland News*-Halowatt Broadcasting Station" (referring to both newspaper and Hallock and Watson's line of radio receivers).

The station was progressing quickly. Soon, its name became part of the station's programming when the KOIN orchestra was founded. On June 21, the station moved to the basement of the Heathman Hotel (at what is now 731 SW Salmon Street).[21] In August, the licensee name was officially changed to KOIN, Inc., and on November 8, 1926, KOIN, Inc. was officially purchased by the *Portland News*.[22] Clif Watson remained at KOIN as the station's chief engineer, a position he held until June 1930.[23]

During KOIN's founding, an elegant New Heathman Hotel was rising across the street from the old Heathman, and on December 17, 1927, KOIN moved its studios to the grand mezzanine of the new hotel.[24] There, it enjoyed a large lounge that allowed guests to look into the station through double plate-glass windows, and a large 40-foot-by-20-foot main studio.[25] Reporting on that move, the *Oregon Sunday Journal* observed: "the suite on the mezzanine floor of the New Heathman promises to lead the coast for arrangement and beauty. Furnishings are to be of 'art moderium' type with special brightly colored drapes. Special finish will be applied to the pianos to blend with the studio art work."[26]

Finally having achieved stable ownership, KOIN began assembling a large, talented and ultimately legendary staff, which served the station and community well for decades. On November 4, 1928, Art Kirkham joined KOIN as an announcer, and Owen "Red" Dunning joined the KOIN orchestra as assistant director in 1929.

But while KOIN grew and prospered, the ambitious Harry Read wasn't content.

Contemporaneous with selling KQP/KOIN in spring 1926, Read jumped into his next venture—KXL, a call sign he specifically requested. The tumult at KQP/KOIN makes one wonder about the adventuresome, innovative Harry Read, who reportedly sold his shares in KOIN, Inc., at the station's November 1926 sale. He must have been working on his next radio station all during mid-1926 because, by the time of KXL's November 1926 license application, Read was KXL Broadcasters, Inc.'s, secretary-treasurer. When KXL was licensed for 50 watts on 750 KHz on November 27, 1926, the station's studios and transmitter were identified as located on the top floor of the Mallory Hotel at 171 Lownsdale Street.[27]

KXL signed-on at 6:30 p.m. on December 13, 1926 (the day the Atwater Kent radio manufacturers sold their millionth radio)—with performances by the Mallory Hotel Quartet and the Lyle Lewis Dance Orchestra.[28] Thus began one of the most colorful periods in Oregon broadcasting history.

Read's penchant for tinkering was newly tickled. Going from the 500-watt KQP to the 50-watt KXL must have gnawed at him. Radio's chaotic conditions also worked against KXL's growing in the manner Read might have anticipated. On February 17, 1927, KXL changed frequency to 770 KHz. By mid-1927, KXL was being described as a "haywire operation" in a federal radio inspector's report. In June, the station moved to 1360 KHz, and on September 19, 1927, the studios relocated to the seventh floor of the Bedell Building at 530 Sixth Street. At that location, KXL's roof-top antenna was located directly across the street from KGW's antenna (on the roof of the adjacent *Oregonian* building). That proximity resulted in massive interference and produced numerous complaints to the Federal Radio Commission. On investigation, the FRC generally found KXL to be at fault.

In April 1928, KXL raised its power to 250 watts and, on November 6, 1928, both KXL's studios and transmitter were relocated to the Multnomah Hotel, where two new 70-foot towers were erected on the hotel's roof—a step that resolved the interference that had existed at the Bedell building. But on November 11, 1928, a major national frequency reallocation forced KXL to move to 1250 KHz. That month, the station increased its power to 500 watts but added a new nighttime sharing arrangement with Boise High School's KFAU in Idaho.[29, 30] Then, on November 11, 1929, the FRC ordered KXL to move to 1420 KHz and to downgrade to 100 watts, an arrangement in which it shared time with Benson Polytechnic's KFIF (later to become KBPS).

As that sequence of events suggests, it was a frenzied time—reflecting both radio's growth as well as the maddening changes created by the FRC's attempt to establish order out of the chaotic airwave conditions it had inherited. The radio inspector's characterization of KXL as "haywire" suggests that KXL was more frenzied than most others.

Read must have intended that KXL would become a major Portland radio force. Unlike some stations like KTBR or KFJR, which operated from small storefronts, KXL made its home on the mezzanine of one of the city's finest establishments, the Multnomah Hotel. Read also envisioned the station as having a newspaper alliance and held discussions with the *Portland News* while planning KXL, although he ultimately recruited the *Portland Telegram*. A newspaper alliance was important to effectively compete with KGW (owned by the *Oregonian*) and KOIN (associated with the *Portland News*). KXL's relationship with the *Portland Telegram,* which the newspaper claimed to be "one of the most important transactions involving radio broadcasting in the Pacific Northwest," formally commenced on June 4, 1928 and was inaugurated with a 161-hour continuous programming marathon during which the *Telegram* gave away "thousands of dollars in prizes," including an "Auburn sport model sedan."[31]

Read was also likely thinking about the financial investment that would be necessary when opportunities to raise KXL's power presented themselves, and he was perhaps hoping that a newspaper association would help attract the necessary capital. Clearly, he was thinking big.

But radio's tumultuous state was at odds with Read's vision for KXL's prominence. The FRC's efforts to reduce interference required the commission to take various steps, including eliminating some stations and rigidly mandating power reductions and time-sharing between others. Captive of these restrictions, KXL's chances for further increasing its power—something Read considered of preeminent importance—were significantly worsened. The share-time allocations with high-school-owned stations in Portland and Boise must have especially chafed him. Meanwhile, his repeated pleas to FRC Commissioner Harold Lafount for a power increase were falling on deaf ears. As Read became increasingly frustrated, his propensity to tinker went into high gear.

In 1929, interference complaints suddenly started to roll in at the Federal Radio Commission's offices, such as one from Portland's G. G. Gerber, "the Radiator Man," who wrote: "Is there any possible way in which local station K.X.L. could be held on its wave length?" Another Portlander, Gilmore Verdery, wrote that: "KXL is using more power than [it] could be [while] still radiating a sharp wave." Other complaints came in from throughout the West. On July 26, 1929, FRC Inspector Edwin Lovejoy visited KXL and found:

> "the transmitter being operated by a young man giving his name as Shirrel, [sic] who possessed no operators license of any kind (and) entirely new transmitting apparatus installed, for which a Construction Permit or Station License had never been obtained. It would appear that power output far in excess of the 500 watts [for KXL] was being used by the station."[32]

On August 26, 1929, the Federal Radio Commission's general counsel sent KXL a copy of that report asking for an explanation. In an affidavit dated September 12, 1929, Read responded by offering a series of transmitter diagrams and a slew of technical language, which avoided directly answering the FRC's inquiry.

In a second affidavit issued that same day, Read stated that "with the approval of O. R. Redfern, the late supervisor of radio in the seventh district, record programs were formerly sometimes run by the station announcer, for the purpose of relieving the operator, but that there was at all times a licensed operator in charge of KXL and on the premises." Read observed that Sherill [sic] was a station announcer, that he (Read) was a licensed operator and on the premises and that, on receiving the letter dated July 26, 1929, he had added another licensed operator to the staff.

On September 27, 1929, acting in response to a request by the commission's assistant general counsel to interpret Read's affidavit, the radio commission's acting chief engineer filed a memorandum reporting that Read's affidavit essentially contended that, while the transmitter was capable of considerable power, it could not achieve it with the level of DC power being supplied to the transmitter. He further noted that, while the radio commission's forms didn't ask for specifications on power source equipment, "there can seem no reason why this high power transmitter should have been installed unless a greater power than that which the station is licensed for was intended to be used."[33]

On October 15, 1929, the Federal Radio Commission notified KXL that it was "not satisfied that public interest, convenience or necessity would be served" by granting KXL's latest license renewal application and that the FRC had designated KXL's renewal application for hearing on January 9, 1930. In radio terms, this was the equivalent of being indicted by a grand jury.

On October 18, KXL's chief operator, Jack Nichols, wired commissioner Harold Lafount "Realizing the predicament here I know of no time that more than 800 watts input has been used here. There must be some error as this is a nice station and everything has been on the square."[34] An unidentified FRC staff member wryly made a marginal note on the telegram "only allowed 100 [watts]."

A handwritten note in the FRC's files dated October 23 indicates that, while KXL's renewal had been set for hearing in a standard fashion, perhaps suggesting that step had been premature. The implication was that the FRC's true interest was in getting to the bottom of what really was going on. Perhaps the commission received some further inquiry, either from newspaper or congressional interests or other parties favorable to KXL, because—while no instruction to this effect seems to now exist in the FRC's KXL files—Lovejoy was apparently directed in a November 1, 1929, telegram (which no longer exists in federal archives) to further investigate and seek a suitable solution.

Few stations engaged in a license revocation hearing would venture forth without legal counsel, and so it seems odd that FRC files contain no evidence that KXL was being represented by counsel during this proceeding. Less than a year later, the station was being represented by Judge John C. Kendall, who continued as Read's lawyer for many years both in connection with KXL and Read's later stations. Kendall was well-connected at the FRC and, indeed, his good friend Ben S. Fisher had just arrived at the commission as assistant general counsel (see chapter 7). Perhaps Kendall was informally involved in pleading KXL's case for leniency before the federal officials, and such contacts helped produce the now-missing November 1 instruction to Lovejoy. On the record, however, Harry Read was handling his 1929 FRC problem entirely on his own.

What resulted was essentially a "no-contest" plea by Read. On November 5, Lovejoy reported that he had inspected KXL that same day and "the so-called auxiliary transmitter has been entirely disconnected and partially disassembled and according to the statements of Harry B. Read 'no further attempt will be made to use any part of it.'"[35] Lovejoy further reported that he had clearly observed that the KXL transmitter was now properly adjusted to broadcast only at its authorized 100-watt power.

An affidavit dated November 5, 1929, contemporaneously submitted both by KXL Broadcasters, Inc., as well as Read personally, was attached to Lovejoy's report. In them, KXL affirmed that its "auxiliary transmitter, heretofore used in connection with KXL Broadcasting station at Portland Oregon, has been disconnected and partially dismantled; and that said apparatus will be removed from the premises, and that said apparatus will not be used in the future in connection with KXL Broadcasting station."[36]

The scheduled license renewal hearing was quietly cancelled. Harry Read had narrowly averted the disastrous result of his penchant for tinkering—and had saved KXL. But while his tinkering had been halted in terms of KXL's transmission power, it flourished in other areas of station operation.

Read had always been distrustful of big business and, in particular, utility monopolies. He hated the power and telephone companies with a vengeance, and perhaps the most widely known "Harry Read story" springs from that antipathy. Having moved to Portland from Hood River, Read was loathe to order telephone lines from the phone company for live remote broadcasts. In Hood River, it had been easy enough to run wires around town for broadcasts such as KQP's relay of KGW's broadcast of a Portland address by President Warren G. Harding on July 4, 1923 (see chapter 2). Read brought to Portland both his desire to originate programs from around the city along with his Hood River sense that he should be free to do so without leasing circuits from the phone company. So, he sought alternatives.

From KXL's Multnomah Hotel studios, Read discovered his workaround. He could flush a tennis ball—to which a wire was attached–down a men's room toilet.[37] He would then flush a similar tennis ball down a toilet at the intended broadcast location and, after carefully studying the Portland sewer system and identifying the manhole cover under which both wires would arrive, he would retrieve the two wires with a fishing pole, connect them and complete his desired remote broadcasting circuit. Read became a true scholar of Portland's underground sanitary and storm drains and grew adept at "wiring" the station's studios to different remote broadcast locations using his "sewer system" of interconnection. Although KXL was young, it is generally understood that Read's unique method of "floating" remote circuits sprang more from his dislike of the phone company and his sense of challenge, rather than from a lack of funds to lease circuits.[38] Reportedly, Read used this system for years until the phone company tipped off the city public works officials, who reportedly put a stop to Read's self-installed remote broadcast circuits.

A variant of this story has Read scheduling a remote hookup for a station advertiser and then flushing a tennis ball down his own office toilet, a second through the toilet in the client's office, and then finding the two balls in the sewer to connect the wires they respectively carried. Supposedly, this arrangement worked for two years "with no one the wiser."[39]

Increasingly, remote broadcasts began to originate outside a station's home community, and Harry Read was up to the challenge. Reportedly, when he wished to broadcast a legislative meeting from Salem, 40 miles south of Portland, he flushed lines from the station's studios through the sewers to a location near the old Portland railroad tracks along the Willamette River. There, he attached one wire to each rail and then "picked up the circuit" by connecting wires to the tracks in Salem and flushing wires from the tracks to the capitol to complete the circuit.[40] One can only theorize how bad a broadcast connection the arrangement must have produced.

David Rees, later of KMED and KSYD (which later became KMJC) in Mt. Shasta, California, went to work at KXL "as one of Harry Read's boys" in 1929. Rees was hired as a licensed station operator but was also the announcer (and salesperson) for the station's *Red Top Taxi of the Air* evening program. On more than one occasion, Rees observed Read hooking up the remote lines for a broadcast using the sewer system line routing. Such conduct doubtless contributed to KXL's reputation for being haywire.

Read's sewer system of remote broadcast circuits became legendary in Portland radio circles and has variously been attributed incorrectly to several other early broadcasters. From this writer's research, however, it seems clear that the story is uniquely attributable to Harry Read and was reasonably well-known at the time. For example, on November 8, 1935, an *Oregonian* "Behind the Mike" column by William Moyes reports that "Hairy Reed [sic] of KXL has not discovered any new sewers lately, although he goes on a sewer hunting expedition occasionally? [sic]"[41] Notwithstanding pressure from Portland city officials, Read appears to have never entirely given up his unique "remote" system. A 1938 *Oregonian* column glowingly praised Read's later Salem station, KSLM's, "remote system," which allowed connection to "40 or 50 remote pickup points"—a scale of operating expense that could hardly have been expected of KSLM using leased phone company circuits.

Another Harry Read story dates from the time KXL was quite young and while located in the Multnomah Hotel. Reluctant to order from the power company the direct current power needed to provide plate voltage for the station's transmitter, Read apparently tapped into the hotel elevator motor circuit.[42] The system appeared to work tolerably well during mid-day. But mornings and late afternoons, when the elevator was unusually busy with hotel guests checking in and out, power variations made the KXL transmitter unstable. KXL engineers/operators were instructed to go to a bank of tapered resistors that Read had installed (of the type commonly used in electric space heaters at the time) and insert/remove these resistors from the circuit. Those actions compensated for the fluctuating DC power levels occasioned by the hotel's guest load.[43]

A licensed pilot, Read is said to have built functional microphones from cigar boxes, repaired tubes and transmitters in "down home" ways rather than replacing them with new ones, and was known to cool his transmitter with tap water that exited through a bathtub.[44]

Read was both smart and innovative, particularly in technical areas. William B. Smullin, later owner of a variety of radio and TV stations and one of Oregon's pioneer television broadcasters, would visit Read to ask questions when he was first learning broadcasting (see chapters 10 and 17).

According to Smullin, "[He] was a 'wire guy,' he played with the wire and was always in hot water with the engineers and the FCC for not being on frequency. Judge John C. Kendall got him to buy a brand new Western Electric transmitter, except Harry at night would take it apart."[45]

According to Smullin, Read often reassembled it differently than the manufacturer or designer had intended.

Blaine Hanks began working at KSLM in 1946 after Read had sold the station. However, Read liked to hang around and Hanks tells of Read having earlier rigged up the KSLM transmitter to secure DC power from a dynamotor connected to an old Ford engine. The car engine turned the dynamotor to create the electricity to run KSLM. According to Hanks it was a smelly, smoky and somewhat "Rube Goldberg" affair. A contemporary newspaper account reports that Read had set the engine to run at 27 mph—a speed he had calculated it could maintain for years without breaking down. Consuming $50 worth of gasoline each month, the engine produced huge quantities of heat—enough to raise the temperature of the studios to an uncomfortably warm degree. The basement, where the engine was located, was stiflingly hot. Read, ever disdainful of waste, thought about selling the excess energy to neighbors for their use in heating water and for other household purposes.

Harry Read "running remote broadcast circuit." Illustration from *Of Mice and Men*, by Jane Woodfin.

Read also had a things for ceilings. It's said he sometimes liked to think while standing high on a ladder. At KSLM, he had a clock mounted on the ceiling above a couch in his office so that he could nap and still keep track of the timing for broadcasts as he would occasionally open his eyes. In his Salem home, he mounted a clock at ceiling height because he had always disliked the difficulty of reading a clock located on a dark mantel. At the station, he also had a high-quality radio mounted on the ceiling. His official rationale for its unusual location was that it would prevent tinkering and damage to the speaker grille cloth.

Read's waged his quintessential assault against utility monopolies while a Salem resident. Having started station KSLM Salem in 1934, Read's business used considerable amounts of electricity. He had grown up in the Seattle area, where power had been relatively inexpensive, and he chafed at paying KSLM's monthly power bill. Rebuffed following an approach to the Salem power provider about more favorable pricing, and resenting what he perceived as the company's arrogant attitude, Read threatened to "build his own" generating capacity.

Doubtless perceiving him as an idle threat, the power company hadn't bargained for Read's tenacity and sense of invention. The Bonneville Power Administration (BPA) was just being created to provide a source of inexpensive power for municipal and non-profit cooperative power systems. Read monitored that development, and when BPA began operating in 1938, he incorporated Salem Electric Company with three other Salem residents. The company promptly hired him as its manager. After a three year struggle to secure access to BPA power, Salem Electric began operating in 1941.

As he fought the well-established, well-funded and politically sophisticated incumbent power provider, both Salem Electric's lower prices and Harry Read's personal magnetism helped sell the system. Battling the City of Salem for a franchise, which the city may have been reluctant to grant due to the incumbent commercial power provider's influence, Read was arrested on at least three separate occasions for installing power lines over city streets "without adequate authority." Given Read's earlier sewer adventures, one can imagine that securing city authority wasn't much on his mind. The outspoken Read litigated each arrest, and ultimately the Oregon Supreme Court overturned his convictions.[46] In 1943, Read sold KSLM and concentrated entirely on his work at Salem Electric (see chapter 10).

Courtesy of William Read

Walter Read, c. 1940

In his last months, Read's health failed, and he died in a Salem hospital on October 9, 1948. His elder brother, Walter, was a beneficiary under his will, and his adopted son, Bill, worked for Salem Electric as a journeyman lineman, retiring in 1993 after a 35-year career.

Walter Read had earlier been involved with his brother Harry in both KXL, KOOS and KORE, as well as with Sheldon Sackett in KVAN. Shortly following Harry's death, Walter and his wife, Genevieve, moved from their Los Angeles home to the Coquille area, where Walter had shortly before established KWRO. Around 1953, Walter and Genevieve moved to Salem, but Walter does not appear to have again been involved directly in radio station operation. From 1953 to 1957, he worked for Salem's Lou Johnson Company, and then for Willamette Radio Supply, until leaving Salem around 1964. Returning to Salem around 1975, he lived out his last days in the Elderest Nursing Home until his death in July 1985.

The Read brothers made an enormous contribution to the founding and flowering of radio in Oregon. The scope of their collective influence is striking. Ever the visionary, Harry is the more remembered of the two brothers. Salem Electric continues to serve Salem-area residents with power, and the legend of its founder remains solidly embedded in the company—just as Harry Read's KSLM continues to broadcast to Salem listeners.[47]

Across Oregon, the legend of Harry Read endures—his vision, his singular style and his total commitment to achieving goals that served the public interest as he interpreted it.

## Endnotes

1. While Read's name is variously spelled Read and Reed in Federal licensing documents, newspaper accounts and other records, based upon family records Read is correct.
2. Obituary, *Oregon Statesman*, October 12, 1948, 9.
3. *Vancouver Sun,* November 17, 1939.
4. A more detailed account of Read and his Hood River Radio Shop is discussed in chapter 2.
5. Read started KFHB, KQP, KOIN, KXL, KSLM, KORE and KOOS.
6. It was also variously known as the "Radio Shop of Hood River."
7. Redfern, O. R. Letter dated November 25, 1924 to Commissioner of Navigation (KQP/KOIN file, NARA, College Park, MD).
8. KQP's "number" in the DOC radio licensing system was 637. It was therefore significant that the "new" KQP, licensed to Portland, was given a different number (1875) and was therefore treated as a distinct, new station although given the use of the "old" KQP call sign, which Read had "reserved."
9. Clark, Kenneth, Acting Supervisor of Radio, Seventh District. Letter dated November 23, 1925, to O. R. Redfern (KQP/KOIN file, NARA, College Park, MD). The letter goes on to describe the studio as having "walls of brick construction, plastic covered, with burlap hangings, and then draped with Monks Cloth. Over the doors and windows are two thicknesses of heavy velour drapes, with heavy padding between. The floor is covered with four layers of deadening felt, covered with heavy Wilton carpet. [The studio] was especially built for a music studio by the Hotel Management. All programs will be supervised by Mr. and Mrs. H. B. Read."
10. *Portland Tribune*, November 21 or 22, 1925, as reported by Craig Adams.
11. J.B. Eakin, President; Jay Stockman, Secretary-Treasurer

12. Redfern, O. R. Letter dated November 25, 1924 to Commissioner of Navigation (KQP/KOIN file, NARA, College Park, MD].

13. Broadcast *Pro-File* notes from Craig Adams in email dated November 23, 2005. In a March 13, 1926, letter from Redfern to DOC, Washington DC, Redfern relates Read's claim that Northwestern Trust Company, while negotiating purchase of KQP with him, incorporated the station as KQP Incorporated, listing the names of H. E. Ervin, John B. Eakin and J. Stockman as principals, omitting Read, later telling Read that his omission was a "typographical error." Northwestern Trust had "entered into a partnership with the *Portland News*, which had an excellent reputation, as part of its purchase of KQP and Redfern had recommended approval of the sale on the strength of the *Portland News*' involvement. When C. W. Myers, Business Manager of the *Portland News* dissolved that partnership as a result of his investigation of Northwestern Trust with the Better Business Bureau, Redfern reversed his recommended approval of the sale.

14. Telegram is referenced in Redfern's March 15, 1926, letter to DOC, Washington DC (KQP file, NARA, College Park, MD).

15. Redfern, O. R. 1926. Letter dated March 11 to DOC, Washington, DC (KQP file, NARA, College Park, MD).

16. Tyrell, A. J., Acting Commissioner of Navigation, DOC. 1926. Letter dated March 18 to O. R. Redfern (KQP file, NARA, College Park, MD).

17. Redfern, O. R. 1926. Letter dated March 15 to DOC, Washington, DC (KQP file, NARA, College Park, MD).

18. Ibid.

19. Redfern, O. R. 1926. Telegram dated March 27 to Bureau of Navigation/DOC, Washington, DC (KQP file, NARA, College Park, MD).

20. Information concerning the evolution of KQP into KOIN comes from various sources but principally from Craig Adams who has, in turn, relied upon contemporary accounts in the *Portland News* as well as the Broadcast *Pro-File* listing for KOIN.

21. Led by conductor Misha Pelz.

22. The *Portland News* was actually a Scripps-Howard paper at the time, and the group's president, Harry W. Ely, was therefore officially president of the station's corporate owner.

23. *In Tune with the West*, KOIN promotional brochure, 1931.

24. The newer hotel was built directly across the street from the original Heathman and its official name was New Heathman to distinguish it from the original. The "new" wasn't dropped until the original Heathman ceased operation.

25. Ibid.

26. "Ultra Modern Studio Being Built for KOIN," *Oregon Sunday Journal*, November 6, 1927, Sec. 2, 7.

27. KXL Broadcasters included Harry Read and Love Electric Company of Tacoma, WA. The latter had presumably advanced capital to construct the station and was the owner of the transmitting apparatus in the station's first license application. O.E. Yates was president of KXL Broadcasters and Harry B. Read was secretary-treasurer (Broadcast *Pro-File* prepared for Ray G. Watson).

28. The station's offices were initially located in the Pantages Building, Room 501, but shortly after the station's inauguration were relocated to KXL's Multnomah Hotel studio.

29. Data in this paragraph from Broadcast *Pro-File* of KXL.

30. KFAU went commercial and changed its call sign to KIDO in 1928.

31. *Portland Telegram*, May 26, 1928.

32. Lovejoy, Edwin W. 1929. Report to DOC, Washington, DC dated July 26 (KXL file, NARA, College Park, MD).

33. Sutton, George O., Acting Chief Engineer, Federal Radio Commission, 1929. Memorandum to the Legal Division, Federal Radio Commission, dated September 27 (KXL file, NARA, College Park, MD).

34. Nichols began announcing KXL's nighttime program *Sleepwreakers*, heard from 1 a.m. to 7 a.m. on March 9, 1929 (Source: Craig Adams).

35. Lovejoy, Edwin W., 1929. Letter to Department of Commerce Radio Division, Washington DC dated November 5 (KXL file, NARA, College Park, MD).

36. Read, H. B., 1929. Affidavit of KXL Broadcasters executed by H. B. Read, president dated November 5 and Affidavit of H. B. Read, an individual, dated November 5 (KXL file, NARA, College Park, MD).

37. Some people attribute the locale of this story to KXL, and its location in the Multnomah Hotel, which Read later owned.

38. This story is corroborated by former KXL employee Stan Bennett in an interview conducted by Hugh Rundell c. 1976 which appears in Washington Association of Broadcasters, "They Took To the Air" (unpublished manuscript, 1989), 11 (WSMB Collection).

39. John R. Ross, *Against the Odds!* (Portland, OR: Salem Electric and Carolina Pacific Publishing Company, 1991), 7.

40. Corroboration for this incident appears in Evelyn Sibley Lampman's *Of Mikes and Men*, 78.

41. The misspelling of Read's name is intentional since the column consisted of a collection of humorous anecdotes and news updates about various Portland radio personalities as purportedly submitted by a perhaps mythical Winnie Winchell of Portland.

42. The story of DC power tapped from an elevator has also been attributed to Wilbur J. Jerman in connection with the installation of O. B. Stubbs' Portland station, KQY, in Rodney Johnson's autobiography, Rodney Forney Johnson and Robert Artman, *A Tiger By the Tail* (Portland, OR, privately published, 1985), 107.

43. This version of the story is corroborated by the previously cited Stan Bennett/Hugh Rundell "They Took To the Air" interview.

44. Ross, *Against the Odds!*, 7.

45. Ibid.

46. Much of the information about Read's founding of Salem Electric comes from the company's self-published history, Ross, "*Against the Odds!*"

47. On February 12, 2007, KSLM abandoned its historic call letters in favor of KKSM. The KSLM call sign endures in the Salem area, however, and is now held by a Low-Power TV station, operating on channel 14.

# 6

# On Many of these Same Stations: Network Radio Comes to Oregon

At its beginning, radio was entirely local. The first radio stations in America simply broadcast phonograph recordings and put amateur performers in front of their microphones. The quality of the entertainment was secondary—the immediacy of hearing others at a distance was enough.

But as listeners' expectations gradually grew, stations needed to offer more professional programming which was expensive to create locally. Larger communities developed such programs more easily and stations in smaller communities struggled as their local listeners were attracted to distant stations offering more elaborate attractions. In its early years, Medford's KMED, for example, signed-off in the evenings because it couldn't effectively compete with programming from the Portland and San Francisco stations.[1]

Creating high-quality programming in urban centers and distributing it to client stations seemed like a cost-effective solution. But how could that be done?

## WEAF/AT&T and WJZ/RCA Networks

Boston department store owner John Shepard started WNAC Boston and then set up an experiment with AT&T and its New York station WEAF to bring that station's programming to WNAC over phone lines. When the January 4, 1923, simulcast by the two stations—AT&T's first "chain station" effort—succeeded, WNAC continued to regularly broadcast

WEAF's programs.[2] A station in Round Hills, Massachusetts, then asked AT&T for the same arrangement.

Soon, AT&T began connecting a network (although it was then called a chain) of stations for special broadcasts such as presidential speeches, sports events and early musical/variety programs including the *Atwater Kent Hour* (sponsored by radio manufacturer Atwater Kent), the *Cliquot Club Eskimos* (sponsored by soft drink manufacturer Cliquot Club soda) and the *Eveready Hour* (sponsored by Eveready Batteries). While lacking AT&T's extensive phone network, the Radio Corporation of America (RCA), which owned WJZ Newark, New Jersey, used Western Union Telegraph Company circuits to establish a second primitive network.

As radio grew, AT&T—a major force in early radio—increasingly drew complaints that it was establishing a radio monopoly partially because it refused to lease its circuits to RCA for network operation and partially because of its attempts to enforce certain patent, radio-related rights it believed it owned (see chapter 5). Tiring of bad press, AT&T decided to abandon radio station and network ownership and sold its stations and radio network to RCA in fall 1926. RCA quickly formed a subdivision, the National Broadcasting Company (NBC), which then became the owner/operator of two radio networks—the AT&T/WEAF chain and the RCA/WJZ network—in addition to a number of stations. To distinguish the two networks, NBC dubbed the old AT&T/WEAF chain "NBC Red" and the old RCA/WJZ chain "NBC Blue." Legends abound regarding the origin of the colors, including an account suggesting that an engineer drew the networks' circuit routing on a map in colored pencil with colors that "stuck."

## NBC Red and Blue Networks

NBC made its broadcast debut on the evening of November 15, 1926, with a mixed network of approximately 24 stations drawn from the ranks of both Red and Blue.[3] That inaugural broadcast was a star-studded gala featuring the New York Symphony, soprano Mary Garden

WSMB Collection

NBC's November 15, 1926, inaugural broadcast originated from the ballroom of New York's Waldorf-Astoria Hotel (now the site of the Empire State Building). Numerous celebrities gathered to observe. Charles A. Lindberg is seated at the far left and Amelia Earhart is next to him.

singing from Chicago, Will Rogers (mimicking President Coolidge on a circuit from Kansas City) and dance bands from various locations. Broadcaster Ben Gross overheard one society dowager in attendance in the New York studio exclaim: "My dear, I had no idea! We simply must get one of these radios."[4]

NBC's opening was a huge success—but it wasn't heard in western America. Because AT&T's telephone circuits hadn't originally been designed to relay radio broadcasts, new lines (which were still unavailable) were required to reliably distribute network radio programming across the country. So despite its name, NBC wasn't really a *national* network at its inception. When NBC began, network radio circuits weren't available west of Chicago—so Oregonians were left to read about the NBC's debut in the *Oregonian* and await its real arrival in the west.

## NBC Orange Network

That wait lasted four and one-half months. On April 5, 1927, KGW was part of the seven-station inaugural broadcast over NBC's new "Orange" network of Pacific coast stations (the other stations consisted of KFI Los Angeles, KPO San Francisco, KGO Oakland, KFOA and KOMO Seattle and KHQ Spokane).[5] Listeners to these seven stations heard a three-hour inaugural program featuring the San Francisco Symphony, Chicago Light Opera artists, a popular singing group known as the Duncan Sisters and San Francisco organist Wallace A. Sabin (who performed remotely on the Bohemian Grove's instrument). It was a grand, star-studded event that the *Oregonian* predicted "the radio fraternity would long remember."[6] NBC had rushed to open its west coast studios, located in San Francisco on the 22nd floor of the Hunter-Dolin Building at 111 Sutter Street, but they weren't finished in time for the Orange Network's debut. Instead, the inaugural broadcast originated from the St. Francis Hotel.

Following this inaugural event, NBC Orange went silent for a week while its Sutter Street studios were being completed. Then, NBC Orange launched its only program, *Eight Neapolitan Nights*, which was broadcast under the sponsorship of Shell Oil from 8 p.m. to 9 p.m., Monday and Saturday, and 9 p.m. to 10 p.m., Tuesday through Friday.[7]

NBC Orange was a regional network, however, since NBC wasn't really connected "coast-to-coast." Until September 1928, the connection between Denver and Salt Lake City (which was required to connect the San Francisco/Orange Network stations to the eastern Red Network) was still a temporary one, accomplished by the network placing a long distance telephone call to complete the circuit.

Programming on the NBC Orange Network was actually a wisp of NBC Red's offerings.[8] Lacking an effective method of linking NBC's eastern branches to the western Orange, NBC assembled a full cast of directors, announcers, singers and musicians in San Francisco. Following eastern NBC broadcasts, the network sent the scripts and musical scores by Railway Express to San Francisco so that the same programs could be re-created, a week delayed, for Orange Network listeners.[9]

Because recreating eastern programs for NBC Orange was cumbersome and costly, NBC increasingly began creating original programs in San Francisco—and elsewhere in the west—uniquely for the Orange Network stations. One such program, which grew to become one of western America's most respected, popular and long-lived offerings, was the *Richfield Reporter,* which began in 1931 and was sponsored by the Richfield Oil Company. In later years, the program billed itself as "America's Oldest Newscast."[10] The Richfield Oil Company (which became Atlantic Richfield Company/ARCO in a 1966 merger) operated a prominent chain of western automotive service stations, which the *Reporter* sponsorship promoted. The program's signature opening was a grand fanfare, and during its long life, the *Reporter*—generally 15 minutes long—was heard over different networks (moving from NBC Red/NBC to ABC in September 1947). The program remained extremely popular with western listeners for more than 25 years. Its signature close "That's 30 for tonight, friends" (referring to newspaper jargon for identifying a story's conclusion when submitting copy to an editor) became well-known.

## Founding of Columbia Broadcasting System (CBS) Network

Interest in network radio programming was clearly growing. In 1927, a major competitor to NBC developed when the Columbia Broadcasting System (CBS)—under the leadership of the scion to a wealthy family with tobacco interests, William Paley—acquired a floundering network that had been launched the previous year by interests associated with the Columbia Phonograph company. CBS inaugurated programming on September 18, 1927, but was also not a truly national network at its inception since it also had no phone circuits to connect to western stations.

Because western stations didn't initially have wire connections to eastern radio programming, they tended to invest more deeply in developing higher-quality locally produced programming. When national network programming subsequently became available to these western stations, they naturally were reluctant to abandon the local programming they had developed and sought ways to cost-effectively capitalize on their already-successful efforts. That led to the development of regional networks through which stations could share their best programming, as well as supply their programs to NBC or CBS for national distribution. Reflecting the west's sense of individualism, such arrangements also caused some to wonder about creating a western-based national radio network to compete with NBC and CBS (see ABC later in this chapter).

## Syndicated Networks

An early alternative to the wire-distributed network programming of NBC and CBS was the effort by station WMAQ, home of the wildly successful *Amos 'n Andy,* to achieve national coverage for that program by mailing disc recordings to stations. Commencing in March 1928 and lasting until the program moved to NBC on August 19, 1929, this experiment with disc syndication wasn't deemed successful in 1928, even though it led to others in the 1930s through the 1950s. In Oregon, KFEC carried *Amos 'n Andy* during its disc syndication period.

Another approach for sharing programs involved the somewhat limited instances in which stations in the west simultaneously broadcast the same programs either by capturing one another's signal off-air or through the use of telephone or other lesser-quality wire circuits. For example, KGW's *Hoot Owls* programs were simultaneously broadcast by stations in Seattle, Tacoma, Spokane, Calgary and San Francisco either through off-air pickup or wire connection.

## Northwest Triangle Network

KGW was an early participant in what was called the Northwest Triangle Network, which also included KOMO Seattle and KHQ Spokane (and KAST Astoria for a brief period). The Northwest Triangle Network utilized Postal Telegraph Company lines that were normally used for telephone (as opposed to telegraph) communications during the day. As a result, the circuits were more suitable for radio programming than Western Union's circuits had been for the 1924 RCA/WJZ Network and, because their long distance rates were lower than AT&T's, the Postal Telegraph circuits proved attractive for regional radio use in the Pacific northwest.

According to Homer Pope, a longtime Seattle engineer who worked at KOMO when the Northwest Triangle Network was in operation, these circuits could be rented cheaply at night because, while they were busy during the daytime, they were silent in the evening. The Northwest Triangle Network, therefore, concentrated on evening programming when programs were shared among the network's three stations. It is likely that the early *Hoot Owl* broadcasts, which KGW shared with KOMO, were distributed in this fashion even before the Northwest Triangle Network was officially formed.[11]

Regional networks like the Northwest Triangle, however, were an order of magnitude smaller than NBC and CBS' full-scale national undertakings. Would anyone in the west try to compete on that scale?

## American Broadcasting Company (ABC) Network

Beating CBS to actual West Coast programming capability was a young upstart—the American Broadcasting Company (ABC)—which was created by the Western Broadcasting Company. Western Broadcasting, which owned KJR Seattle, KEX Portland and KGA Spokane, was headed by Adolph H. Linden, a prominent Seattle entrepreneur who had built Seattle's stylish Camlin Hotel and other major establishments. Linden, who was also president of Seattle's Puget Sound Savings Bank, had purchased KJR from its founder, early Seattle radio figure Vincent Kraft. Linden used KJR to anchor the ABC network, which made its Oregon debut over KEX on October 3, 1928.

On October 8, 1928, ABC connected with CBS, which lacked western distribution, to relay CBS programs over ABC's three stations. According to Craig Adams, different nights of the week were dedicated to either ABC's programming or to CBS's. ABC initiated a reasonably significant schedule of its own programs, and its national aspirations were reflected in its rapid addition of stations in other areas. By December 24, ABC had expanded into California and added KYA San Francisco, KMTR (now KLAC) Hollywood and KHJ Los Angeles to its chain. These California stations also provided ABC with programming including the Mark Hopkins Hotel dance orchestra and music from the Los Angeles Biltmore Hotel's orchestra.

KYA also provided ABC with the San Francisco origination of Herman Kenin's Orchestra—which had originally been a prominent feature of early 1920s radio fare in Portland over KGW and KEX.[12] In January 1929, KDYL (now KCPX) Salt City and KLZ Denver joined ABC, which was then renamed the ABC Western Chain. This new name distinguished it from other regions, since ABC had also added midwest and east coast stations to its line-up. On June 1, 1929, ABC began midwest service over WIBO Chicago. WIL St. Louis; WHRM Minneapolis (now WLB); WOQ Kansas City, Missouri; KFA Lincoln, Nebraska; and KTNT Muscatine, Iowa, soon joined.[13] On July 13, 1929, ABC Western added KFBK Sacramento and, at the end of the month, announced plans to become a fully national independent network by October—with the addition of other stations along the eastern seaboard, including WOL Washington, DC.

ABC offered a significant program line-up although, during its early months, the network didn't successively program all hours of the day. By the summer of 1929, however, the ABC schedule was continuous and growing in quality. In addition to its many music programs, which often involved band remotes, ABC also offered situation comedy/dramas such as the *Olympic Rangers, Histories of Paul Bunyan, Harper's Corners, The Chronicles of Katz* and *The Great American Appleburys*. Adolph Linden was known for spending lavishly, and enough money was being spent on programs like *The Great American Appleburys* that leather-style gold-embossed script holders were provided to its cast members. ABC was also relaying CBS programs such as the *Sonatron Tube Program, The Majestic Theatre of the Air*, the *Old Gold*

*Cecil and Sally* (whose real names were Johnny Patrick and Helen Troy) was an early program about a couple named Cecil and Sally Epps, originally heard over the short-lived ABC network. Following ABC's failure, they moved to the NBC Orange Network in 1929 and were heard over KGW into the early 1930s. The program was produced by the San Francisco media firm MacGregor & Sollie, Inc., and was mailed on large electrical transcription discs (ETs) to many radio stations such as KXL, KMED and KFJI, who plugged *Cecil and Sally* into their local schedules at convenient times. Patrick, who was born John Patrick Googan, deliberately flunked his West Point and University of California entrance examinations to pursue a radio career. Originally a switchboard operator at KYA San Francisco, he got his start as a writer/actor on *Cecil and Sally* at that ABC station and jumped to KPO San Francisco when ABC failed. Between 1929 and 1933, he wrote over one thousand scripts for the *Cecil and Sally* program and then went on to a distinguished writing career including the Pulitzer Prize-winning play "The Teahouse of the August Moon." (left) KMED promotional card, 1930. (right) Promotional photo issued during ABC Network run.[16, 17]

*Program with Paul Whiteman and his Orchestra* and the *Doctor West's Toothpaste Program*—all originating from CBS's New York studios.

On its face, ABC provided a plausibly competitive challenge to NBC and CBS—which perhaps explains why the relationship between ABC and CBS increasingly became uneasy. In order to become an entirely independent network, ABC announced plans on July 31, 1929 to sever its connection with CBS within three months. [14, 15]

CBS had been relying upon its relationship with ABC for western coverage. Following that announcement, CBS faced a real challenge since its president, Bill Paley, believed AT&T couldn't provide CBS with new western circuits before January 1930. Yet, on the strength of CBS's reputation, KOIN Portland announced on August 12, 1929, that it would affiliate with CBS.[18]

Trouble was brewing for ABC. Only days after KOIN's August announcement about its affiliation, reports started circulating that ABC was experiencing financial difficulty. Unable to secure additional financing to maintain the network's program circuits, Linden soon relinquished control of ABC's leased circuits to CBS so the latter could continue to feed its programs to western stations (including KOIN)—a step that effectively ended the ABC network. FRC files include a memorandum to the commissioners, dated August 26, 1929, transmitting a telegram "relative to the closing of Stations KJR, KGA and KEX, along with other stations comprising the American Broadcasting Chain."[19] The American Broadcasting Company, embodying Linden's dream of creating a major western-based radio network, was dead.

# Don Lee Broadcasting System

Automobile dealer Don Lee was an early force in California radio. He purchased station KFRC San Francisco in November 1926, and a year later, in December 1928, he acquired KHJ Los Angeles and leased a phone circuit to share programs between KFRC, KHJ and several other California stations.[20] In 1929, CBS sought to add the Don Lee-connected stations to its network—essentially to at least partially replace CBS's connection with ABC, which was unraveling (see ABC elsewhere in this chapter). With financing provided in part by CBS, Lee established a new network, the Don Lee Broadcasting System (DLBS), which connected stations in California and the Northwest. Ultimately, DLBS also added stations in the Rocky Mountain states. The CBS-DLBS association allowed CBS to feed its western stations and, when CBS was silent, DLBS offered its programs on these circuits under its own name. On November 10, 1929, KOIN (which was CBS-DLBS's only Oregon affiliate) broadcast its first program from this collaboration. The CBS-Don Lee partnership officially commenced operation as the Columbia-Don Lee Network on January 1, 1930. [21, 22]

# Northwest Broadcasting System (NBS) Network

Because CBS was now able to program western stations through the DLBS circuits, it no longer needed the ABC lines it had assumed when ABC collapsed and those circuits reverted to the KJR, KEX, KGA group—which had been taken over by Ralph A. Horr under the new name of the Northwestern Broadcasting Company. Using the ABC circuits it had inherited, this group formed a new network, the Northwest Broadcasting System (NBS), and shared programming among its three stations. Perhaps sensing competition and wanting to avoid another challenge such as ABC had mounted, NBC announced on October 16, 1931, that it had purchased the Northwestern Broadcasting System, its stations (including KEX) and the NBS regional network.

# United Broadcasting Company (UBC) Network

On November 5, 1930, another network was launched when the United Broadcasting Company (UBC) made its debut over a nine-station hookup. Originating from KFWB Los Angeles, UBC's Oregon outlets were KXL Portland, KORE Eugene and KMED Medford. It was each station's first network affiliation. On February 26, 1931, UBC and NBS merged—although both networks continued to operate independently—and on February 29 KEX became a UBC affiliate.

UBC began at an inauspicious time. The Depression was moving toward its darkest moments and, perhaps as a result, the network suspended operations on April 1, 1931. Despite an announcement a week later that programming would resume the following week, UBC appears to have never returned to operation. Thus, when NBC purchased NBS in October 1931, there was little left of UBC for NBC to also acquire.

# Mutual Broadcasting System (MBS)/
# Don Lee Broadcasting System

The Mutual Broadcasting System grew out of an eastern regional network, the Quality Network, which had been founded in 1929. It consisted of WOR New York, WLS Chicago and WLW Cincinnati.[23] Led by WOR, the network was renamed the Mutual Broadcasting System (MBS)

AIMEE

LYLE BARDO

MEL VENTER

# THE BREAKFAST GANG
## DON LEE BROADCASTING SYSTEM

SWEENEY

PRETTY POLLY

Rockin Jones, Sandy Sanford, Dick Lotter, Billy Shuart, Carlton Ackley, Tex Langston
Norvell Price, Willard Spencer, Al Cicerone, Paul Rosen, Zolly Zollman

OLD POKEY

RUDY

WSMB Collection

Don Lee's answer to the NBC Blue (later ABC) Breakfast Club, c. 1944

on October 15, 1934. At that point, WGN Chicago replaced WLS and WXYZ Detroit was added to make that station's programs—in particular *The Lone Ranger*—nationally available.

In 1936, Mutual took a major step beyond its original purpose of sharing programming between the network's four key stations. In September, it began an aggressive national expansion by adding affiliates in five major markets plus the 13 stations of the New England states' Colonial Network.

Relations between CBS and Don Lee, which had been releasing CBS programs in the west, became strained in 1935. On December 29, 1936, CBS and Don Lee ended their association. In 1937, the ten stations of the Don Lee Broadcasting Service joined Mutual, which then replaced CBS as the national programming source for DLBS stations. In the west, the network was known as the Mutual Don Lee Network and, on September 26, 1937, it made its northwest debut at 4:30 p.m. with a 90-minute special program, *Welcoming, From The East.*

Mutual Don Lee Network's Northwest Unit consisted of KOL Seattle, KALE Portland (which later became KPOJ), KMO Tacoma, KORE Eugene, KSLM Salem, KRNR Roseburg, KIT Yakima, KVOS Bellingham, KGY Olympia, KPQ Wenatchee, KXRO Aberdeen, and KIEM Eureka.

The network's programs were offered to these stations. During periods when Mutual fed no programs, Don Lee often fed its own programs to the stations as well as other Don Lee Broadcasting Service affiliates. In 1940, Don Lee took a minority stock interest in Mutual, whose stock had previously been held solely by the network's four key stations. By 1946, Mutual Don

Lee had, at 400 stations, more affiliates than any other network and was an important component of Oregon radio.[24]

Because national telephone circuits had lagged in the west, regional networks developed greater influence there than in the eastern and midwestern states. Consequently, networks like DLBS and the Intermountain network, in the Mountain time zone, continued to offer regional programming well into the 1950s. Where more powerful major market stations were easily received in many smaller communities in the eastern U.S., the more sparsely populated west contained many small-town stations of relatively little interest to the big networks—NBC and CBS. Don Lee and Mutual provided many of these stations with their first network affiliations. The resulting relationships, and the regional programming that Don Lee created, helped give radio in Oregon and throughout the west a uniquely regionalized flavor, which nicely complemented the efforts of NBC and CBS.

# Endnotes

1. Bishop, Lee. Interview by author. Tape recording of telephone conversation. October 29, 1993.
2. The WEAF log book, as reported in Gleason Archer's *History of Radio to 1926*, 287, shows the entry "7:55–8:00 P.M. Saxophone solo by Nathan Glanz, Lovelight in Your Eyes. Program to be broadcast jointly by WEAF and WNAC." The extensive AT&T history with WEAF, in the company's semi-authorized history *Commercial Broadcasting Pioneer: The WEAF Experiment: 1922–1926*, by William Peck Banning, reports (on pages 159 and 164) that the simulcast ran for three hours' based upon a contemporary account in *Radio Digest Illustrated*.
3. The number of stations on the initial NBC broadcast has never been clearly established and has been variously reported as between 19 and 26. On the occasion of its 60th anniversary, NBC used the number 25, although the author's own investigation suggests that 24 is the correct number.
4. Barnouw, *A Tower in Babel*, 191.
5. The first program carried by the Orange Network was a special broadcast of President Coolidge's Washington, DC, address on the 200th anniversary of George Washington's birth (Platt, *KGW – Portland's Pioneer Radio Station*, 9).
6. *Morning Oregonian*, April 4, 1927, 1, and April 6, 1927, 1.
7. "The NBC Pacific Coast Network," by John F. Schneider, online at http://members.aa.net/~jfs/nbc.htm, copyright 1997 by John F. Schneider.
8. The "color" references to the networks supposedly originated with the AT&T Long Lines Division's use of different colors to code the lines for the various radio networks that were emerging. The AT&T Network lines were red and, when NBC acquired the AT&T radio properties, the lines that NBC leased for what had been the Western Union line-connected stations became the NBC Blue. In addition to the Orange, for some years NBC operated the NBC White Network, connecting its shortwave international stations, as well as an NBC Gold Network from 1931-March 1933. NBC Gold made its debut on October 18, 1931, heard in Oregon over KEX, and carried many of the NBC Blue programs heard in the East. CBS, while it never used the name, was the Purple in AT&T coding.
9. Orange Network listeners heard *The RCA Hour, The Wrigley Program, The Standard Symphony Hour, The Eveready Light Opera Program* and *The Firestone Hour*, among others, under this method once Orange Network's San Francisco operations hit their stride. These programs were identified by the announcer saying: "This program came to you from the San Francisco studios of the Pacific Coast Network of the National Broadcasting Company" (Schneider, NBC Pacific Coast Network).
10. Promotional postcard featuring *Richfield Reporter* anchor John Wald advertising the program's switch from NBC to ABC Radio on September 26, 1947.
11. The Northwest Triangle Network's use of Postal Telegraph lines is more fully described in an interview with Loren Stone conducted by Hugh Rundell, "They Took To the Air," Washington Association of Broadcasters, 488 (WSMB Collection).
12. ABC Network Program Schedule, Week of March 24, 1929 (KEX file, NARA, College Park, MD).
13. ABC Network Program Schedule, Week of Sunday June 9, 1929 (KEX file, NARA, College Park, MD).
14. Craig Adams from *Oregon Journal*, July 31, 1929.
15. http://www.oldradio.com/archives/stations/sf/fotoarch.htm accessed on August 12, 2008.

16. The program was scheduled at 7:15 a.m. and p.m. on KXL in 1931 and, after some absence, returned to the KXL schedule in 1935 (Craig Adams email to author).

17. "Clever Entertainers—Cecil and Sally," *Radio Digest*, August 1930.

18. Elizabeth McLeod reports (http://members.aol.com/jeff560/cbs.html) that the date of KOIN's CBS affiliation is December 15, 1928, the date that CBS apparently also celebrates. In view of the more detailed newspaper announcements from KOIN about the CBS affiliation in 1929, it seems as though CBS has informally adopted a somewhat generalized date, prior to KOIN's formal affiliation, based upon the ABC–CBS split of the ABC lines feeding KOIN.

19. Terrell, W. D. (Chief, Radio Division, FRC), 1929. Memorandum to the Members of the Commission dated August 26 (KEX file, NARA, College Park, MD).

20. Elizabeth McLeod reports that the stations thus interconnected were the McClatchy Newspaper stations plus KOIN Portland, KVI Tacoma (since relocated to Seattle) and KFPY Spokane. KOL Seattle, joined the CBS roster in 1930.

21. The *Sunday Oregonian* identifies it only as a "chain program" in its KOIN program listing on that date, [Sec. 4, 10).

22. "History of KFRC San Francisco and the Don Lee Network," John Schneider, *www.adams.net/~jfs.*

23. The Quality Network stations consisted of WOR New York, WLS Chicago, WLW Cincinnati and WXYZ Detroit (optional outlet) (Broadcast Archive, www.oldradio.com, Barry Mishkind).

24. Broadcast Archive, www.oldradio.com, Barry Mishkind.

# The End of the Roaring Twenties

Radio was still new and exciting but, while some "portable" sets were being manufactured, they were extremely bulky and few Americans traveled with radios in the late 1920s. Capitalizing on radio's appeal, tourist camps began promoting themselves as "radio tourist parks." This meant, simply, that they possessed a radio and a large speaker, which was placed outside at night for lodgers to communally enjoy. Radio Park, in Sunny Valley, Oregon (about 20 miles north of Grants Pass) was one such locale. While the tourist camp and radios are long gone, the park's heritage still lives on at that site, which retains the name.

The late 1920s was also a period when what came to be called programmatic architecture developed. Buildings such as Holly-wood's Brown Derby restaurant, shaped like a hat, and other buildings in the likeness of coffee cups and donuts, were constructed across the nation. Oregon had at least one programmatic building, a "novel radio store" constructed in 1927 at 2186 East Stark Street in Portland. Because its owner, H. A. Hall, was the Orpheum radio distributor in eastern Multnomah County, the building was designed to resemble an Orpheum radio set.[1]

It was a time when the radio community was adapting to its increased prominence and exploring the social responsibilities and economic opportunities that such growth implied. For example, stations often had staff hostesses, whose job was to make each visitor feel welcomed. Many stations published formal visiting hours as did nine out of Portland's ten stations in 1928. At KFEC, one could view the station's sixth-floor studios through a heavy glass window, while KOIN was deliberately situated so that one could enter a lounge and observe programming. KGW welcomed visitors, particularly

Radio Park in Sunny Valley, Oregon (originally called Grave Creek)

in the afternoons, and KWBS, KFJR and KTBR openly welcomed the public at all hours of the day. KWJJ's studios welcomed visitors from noon to 1 p.m. daily, while KEX was open to the public as early as 6:45 a.m.

Against this backdrop, stations continued to develop across Oregon.

## KGEH Eugene/Coos Bay

The year 1928 opened with a full-scale radio melee in Eugene, inaugurated by H. H. Hanseth, who had successfully regained control over his station KGEH and was filing to relocate it to Coos Bay. When the FRC approved KGEH's move to Coos Bay, Eugene was left without a local radio station. Various interested parties, including Messrs. Hill and Phillips (who had lost KGEH to Hanseth) stepped in. Virtually simultaneously, as Hanseth was setting up his Coos Bay station KOOS, Hill and Phillips applied for a new Eugene frequency (see KLIT/KORE section in this chapter and chapter 10).[2]

## KOOS Coos Bay

Coos Bay was clearly interested in radio, having been without a local station since KFOF signed-off in 1924. On February 10, 1928, the *Coos Bay Times* reported that the town would "be the seat of a high powered broadcasting station within 30 days." This was according to Thelma E. Cullen and H. H. Hanseth (both of Eugene), who told the paper that they would move *their* station to Coos Bay once the FRC approved.[3] Since there had been no mention of Cullen during KGEH's tenure in Eugene, the use of "their" was notable. Miss Cullen proposed opening a retail radio sales store to help finance the station.[4] KOOS Radio Sales and Service was incorporated on February 23 for these purposes with Cullen, Hanseth and Irene G. Pratt as incorporators.

With its relocation approved by the DOC on February 24, KOOS made plans to sign-on March 12 from studios located at the corner of Broadway and Market. Augmented by plans for remote lines to local churches, an advisory council of noted citizens from different areas of the community and "considerable talent [which] has been secured for the opening," KOOS proposed an elaborate schedule that included broadcasting a *Housewives Hour* daily from 10 a.m. to 11 a.m., a *Luncheon Hour* from noon to 1 p.m., a *Matinee Hour* from 3 p.m. to 4 p.m. and a *Dinner Concert Hour* from 6 p.m. to 8 p.m.[5]

*Oregon Journal* photo

Novel radio Building, 2186 East Stark St., Portland, 1927

KOOS actually signed-on March 15, 1928, with remarks from Miss Cullen preceding a program anchored by station announcer Jesse Weed (who had been KGW's pioneer operator/announcer).

KOOS quickly organized a Broadcaster Club with dues of $1.00 a year to help support the station, and the *Coos Bay Times* urged the public on. "Let's Put' Er Over Big, JOIN! JOIN!" trumpeted a March 17 ad.

In succeeding weeks, KOOS broadcast church services, local musicales, children's programs and speeches by local officials—but starting a radio station in Coos Bay proved daunting.

Little is known about Hanseth and even less about KOOS' other two incorporators. The son of Norwegian-born parents, Hanseth was born in 1901 and reportedly grew up in Selma, Oregon. By age 19, he was living in Portland and working as a truck driver.[6] Thelma Cullen appears to have been only 20 at the time of KOOS' founding and, therefore, a somewhat odd choice for a business partner by the 27-year-old Hanseth. Perhaps the young man had developed a romantic interest in Cullen or Pratt. If so, the romances failed.

When KOOS was just two months old, Cullen and Pratt jointly wired commissioner Lafount on May 27:

> Station KOOS has been off the air one month. It was discovered Coos County does not need radio station [sic]. KOOS to remain off the air permanently by decision of KOOS Radio Sales and Service, Inc. *Please cancel our license permanently* by order of our Board of Directors.[7]

The statement was not underlined in the telegram but, rather, by the FRC staff as an action item. With the FRC seeking to eliminate stations to reduce interference, KOOS was the first in the nation to voluntarily surrender its license. In a letter dated July 28, the FRC's acting secretary thanked KOOS for its cooperation "in relinquishing your license."[8]

Hanseth was unaware of these events—and had then lost his radio station twice in a one year. He quickly contacted the FRC seeking to regain control of KOOS's license. Because he had personally retained ownership of the equipment, all he needed to operate the station was a license. But since KOOS's license had already been deleted, the station technically no longer existed. Hanseth learned in June that he would have to apply for an entirely new station—no easy matter as the FRC was thinning the nation's stock of stations. The November 3, 1928, *Coos Bay Times* reported Hanseth's filing such a license application, which was strongly endorsed by the Coos Bay Chamber of Commerce. At a November 8 hearing in Washington, DC, favorable testimony was also given by Oregon senator Charles McNary, and it was intimated that a new KOOS license would be issued shortly.

A re-born KOOS returned to the air in December with a transmitter located in the Blanc & Nicould Building at Second and Anderson Streets. It was clearly a Spartan operation with the station's studio located in a spare bedroom in Hanseth's home located at 1056 Central Avenue.[9, 10, 11] Programming was simple: phonograph records, announcements "and an occasional studio feature with local talent." When Hanseth filed a financial statement with the FRC in 1933, he reported that the company had $9.90 cash on hand and 10¢ in savings. At that point, KOOS, the "Furtherest [sic] West Station in the U.S.A.,"[12] had operating losses of $1,005.56 and a negative asset value of $895.84 on its balance sheet.[13] KOOS remained in Hanseth's bedroom until about 1930, when it relocated to the fifth floor of the Hall Building and placed its antenna on the building's roof.

## KLIT/KORE Portland/Eugene

Eugene saw a slightly less colorful close to its radio circumstances in 1928. Following H. H. Hanseth's relocation of KGEH/KOOS to Coos Bay, Eugene lacked a station of its own. Phillips and Hill, were trying hard to either stay in, or get back into, the radio business, depending upon how one interpreted the state of their control over KGEH. While Hanseth was fighting to regain control of KGEH and move it to Coos Bay, Phillips and Hill were fighting to retain the station, behaving as though it was still both a viable concern and *their* property.

Newspaper accounts indicate that they explored renaming the station KROW (the call sign of the short-lived, ill-fated Portland station owned by John Egan in 1926–27). As it became clear that they would lose control over KGEH to Hanseth, Phillips and Hill found a new opportunity. On February 11, 1928, radio inspector O. R. Redfern wrote Lewis I. Thompson, regarding his application to renew the license of KLIT Portland:

> After making a careful examination, [we] find that this station is very seldom on the air and is not being operated in the interest of public convenience, interest and necessity and, therefore, a license will not be issued for its continuance.[14]

On February 15, Phillips and Hill filed an application in the name of Eugene Broadcast Station to move KLIT to Eugene, proposing its location on Broadway between Oak and Pearl Streets. Since the application didn't contain any certification from Thompson that he was selling the 10-watt KLIT, Lafount insisted upon their submitting verification of the station's sale—which was provided in a March 8 telegram. Following the FRC's March 28 approval, KLIT relocated to Eugene and filed an application on April 5 requesting a new license and the new call sign KORE. Thus, KLIT became Eugene's KORE, whose call letters developed a distinguished history.[15] Early in KORE's life, the station left its location in the Miner Building, which had been home to KGEH, and moved to Hills Drug Store (owned by Frank Hills' father).

Much of what has been written about KORE's early years entirely ignores Hanseth's role as KGEH's founder. Some reports suggest that Hill and Phillips simply moved to change the call sign from KGEH to KORE as though it were a single continuing station—but that clearly wasn't the case. Other aspects of KORE's founding are also murky. It has been reported that Hill and Phillips established KORE by purchasing a 50-watt transmitter from KFEC Portland, when that station was sold in March 1929, but that seems unlikely. A more plausible account holds that Tommy Thompson, who later founded KPIR (which became KPNW), and Paul Hoppe traveled to Portland to pick up the KLIT transmitter for KORE.

After only a brief interval of local radio silence, the city of Eugene once again had its own radio station. As the *Eugene Daily Guard* pointed out, "it is a really great advertiser of Eugene and vicinity."

## KWBS/KVEP and the Oregon Wildcat

In Portland, William Schaeffer's KWBS was charting a difficult course. National-scale talent, heard on such programs as the *Atwater Kent Hour, Roxy and His Gang* (live from the Capitol Theatre) and the *Wrigley Gum Program with Guy Lombardo and Wendell Hall*, was regularly being presented over local stations with network hookups. Long-established local independent stations, like KEX and KWJJ, provided entrenched competition. Facing such odds, Schaeffer Radio Manufacturing's KWBS was struggling—but Schaeffer tried valiantly. On May 7, 1928, the 50-watt station boosted its power to 100 watts and relocated to the mezzanine of the handsome Francis Motor Car Building on the corner of SE Hawthorne Boulevard and Grand Avenue. Perhaps seeking a more sharply etched presence, on August 28,

Robert G. Duncan, as pictured in his Statement of Independent Candidate for Third Congressional District, 1922 General Election Voters Pamphlet.

1929, the station changed its licensee name to Schaeffer Broadcasting Company and its call sign to KVEP, which stood for the "**V**oice of **E**ast **P**ortland." Wilbur Jerman had recently moved KFWV/KWJJ to downtown Portland, so Schaeffer may have seen an opportunity to fill a perceived void in eastside Portland radio.

But he couldn't catch a break. A little more than two months after moving the station, the stock market crashed on Black Tuesday and almost immediately KVEP was in decline. Given these conditions, Schaeffer was only too pleased to sell two hours of nightly air time to one Robert Gordon Duncan. While it was later rumored that Duncan at least partially owned KVEP, that wasn't true. He was just an advertiser—albeit a *very* important one.

Duncan was a flamboyant character, self-styled as the "Oregon Wildcat," who, according to some accounts, had modeled his fiery broadcasts after radio agitator W.H. Henderson of Shreveport, Louisiana. Duncan was a man of vigorous conviction—most of which he directed to railing against big business and big government. As far back as World War I, he had been politically active and ran two recall campaigns against public officials. During his unsuccessful 1922 Congressional race, his slogan was "Kick the corporations out of politics."[16]

As the 1920s advanced, he grew increasingly outspoken. And as the Depression deepened, he reserved special venom for chain stores and banks/brokerages, particularly singling out Sears-Roebuck, although he also railed against "Merrill-Lynch and the rest of the banking gang."[17] Previously, he had started a small publication to spout his views and at that time considered himself to be a publisher. But with air time suddenly available on KVEP, the "Wildcat" quickly switched media gears and principally focused on radio—using KVEP to vehemently articulate his political and social views each night.[18]

The FRC was still seeking to better organize the spectrum, hoping to eliminate rampant interference, and ordered KVEP to share its 1500 KHz frequency with KUJ Longview.[19] KVEP objected to the FRC's order, refused to honor the time-share and operated as it wished "on top of" KUJ. This promptly produced interference and listener complaints flowed into the FRC.

**RADIO**

# K V E P

*Commercial Broadcasting Station*

**"The Voice of East Portland"**

OFFICE STATION AND STUDIOS
495 HAWTHORNE AVE. -:- PHONE EAst 7117

PORTLAND OREGON

KVEP Stationery letterhead, c 1929

When KVEP refused to amicably resolve the matter, the radio commission took the only step open to it. When KVEP's license expired on May 29, 1930, the commission refused to renew it. KVEP signed-off May 30 with a furious Schaeffer seeking judicial review of the commission's action.

In July, the station's equipment was attached by creditors and, when the station's license was formally canceled by the FRC on September 15, 1930, and Schaeffer's pleas for judicial relief had all been rejected, KVEP was just a memory.

But that is only a small part of the KVEP/Robert Gordon Duncan story.

KVEP had totally inflamed the Portland establishment with Duncan's vitriolic attacks. Indeed, while Duncan was only an advertiser, he was commonly thought to control the station, and the *Oregonian* referred to him as KVEP's "mascot."[20] As far back as December 1928, shortly after Duncan's broadcasts began, rumors reached the FRC that Schaeffer had lied about his citizenship when he first applied for KVEP's license.[21] On December 29, 1928, FRC secretary Carl H. Butman wrote Schaeffer inquiring about the matter. Schaeffer replied in a December 29, 1928, telegram that the station had "no aliens either officers or directors." He followed up with a sworn written affidavit to the same effect on January 12, 1929—but the matter didn't end there.

The Portland establishment's outrage over Duncan's acidic speeches was surging. Between March and May 1930, a host of entities began pummeling the Federal Radio Commission with complaints—centered on Duncan—over the then-pending KVEP license renewal.

The following is a sampling of the numerous public comments received by the FRC.[22]

Bond house Freedman, Smith and Camp Company, stated "Duncan, a former patent medicine faker, is conducting a campaign of vilification and abuse of respectable citizens and intimidation against businesses, large and small, for the purpose of securing 'contributions' to his campaign."

The Portland Better Business Bureau complained that Duncan "uses radio to black mail independent retailers into financing [the] campaign of vilification he is waging against chain stores and businesses owned outside of Portland."

The Advertising Club of Portland "hereby records its disapproval of the character of utterances which for several weeks have taken place over Radio Station KVEP, Portland, Oregon, upon the ground that said utterances are indecent, obsene [sic] and profane."

The *Oregon Journal*'s Managing Editor Donald J. Sterling wired the FRC his "protest against KVEP now operating by sufferance of your body because of nightly broadcasts of one Robert G. Duncan. For weeks this person has been broadcasting slanderous attacks upon individuals and institutions using obscene and indecent language. That radio should be thus prostituted is an insult to decent people."

R. J. Benjamin, editor of the *Portland News*, wrote Oregon senator Charles McNary: "There seems to be no other way to rid Portland of this lunatic radio station than by Federal action such as cancellation of its license. For this reason we are certain that the best interests of the people of Portland will be served by putting station KVEP off the air permanently. Shall a mad dog be permitted to roam at large simply because it bears a federal license?"

An impressive list of civic, business, religious and military forces further lined up against Duncan and KVEP. To organize this opposition, they hired Judge John C. Kendall to formally contest KVEP's license renewal.

Both Schaeffer and Duncan were clearly aware that major forces were lining up against them and things rapidly turned ugly. Against the backdrop of technical complaints regarding KVEP's violation of frequency time-sharing, the FRC began monitoring the station's frequency on an almost daily basis for technical compliance. The FRC compiled a record of frequency variations of minor, and sometimes major, proportions. That produced a torrent of FRC notices to the station about operating off-frequency. KVEP responded with descriptions of various transmitter failures and explanations of pending plans for procuring more precise equipment.

Responding to the impending crusade mounting against him, Schaeffer filed a formal complaint with the U.S. Attorney, alleging that a former KVEP employee had falsely represented himself as an FRC employee (presumably at the behest of the FRC) in order to "secure information [from current employees] concerning the manner in which K.V.E.P. was operated to the detriment of the property rights of W. B. Schaeffer."[23] No prosecution resulted.

Schaeffer then alleged that FRC representatives had conspired to trick a KVEP operator into briefly leaving the station in order that the authorities could then find the station "without a licensed operator on duty"—an allegation the federal officials hotly denied. The FRC eventually cited KVEP for that offense.

And then there was Congress. FRC files contain numerous letters and telegrams from congressional members either asking the commission what all the fuss was about or specifically complaining about Duncan and asking that the FRC take appropriate action to stop KVEP's broadcasts.

In May 1930, the FRC sprang into action. Taking a cue from a complaint by the Portland Advertising Federation, which doubtless had been orchestrated by Judge Kendall, the commission sent Schaeffer a notice that it had scheduled a hearing over the station's application for license renewal based upon technical violations as well as charges that the station had broadcast "profane, obscene or indecent" programming in violation of the Radio Act of 1927.[24] It was alleged that in a various broadcasts that spring, KVEP had committed various violations of that statutory provision. It was the first time anyone in the nation had been charged with such a violation, and it attracted enormous attention.

Duncan had incited a truly impressive coalition of enemies. Beginning in February 1930, MacMarr Stores, Inc. had secretly arranged to have a court stenographer record verbatim transcripts of many of Duncan's nightly two-hour broadcasts. These were regularly and secretly forwarded to the FRC, who thoroughly reviewed them when setting KVEP's renewal hearing. Indeed, federal agents continued to literally "shadow" Duncan for months, filing reports both on his public utterances as well as how he appeared to be received by his audiences.

But KVEP's problems ran still deeper. In the renewal hearing, the FRC also charged that Schaeffer, who was foreign-born and had become a naturalized U.S. citizen, had misrepresented his citizenship status to the FRC when KWBS was first licensed. Schaeffer Radio Manufacturing Company had originally been a partnership between Schaeffer and one Fred Spear. Since FRC licensing provisions at the time limited a non-U.S. citizen to one-sixth ownership of a radio station, that partnership had been structured with Spear holding five-sixth of the interest in the station. Schaeffer later became a naturalized citizen and terminated his partnership with Spear—but that termination occurred some months prior his naturalization's completion. Therefore, it was alleged that between April and December 1927 (when he was naturalized), he was the sole owner of the station and had concealed that fact. The FRC was also unhappy about

KVEP's failure to stay on its assigned frequency and to honor its time-sharing arrangements. Those charges were added to the list of transgressions to be considered.

KVEP was clearly not profitable without Duncan's advertising income. Schaeffer was likely also worried about possible investigation into the citizenship issue, and both considerations caused him to explore selling the station. As early as January 1928, he engaged in discussions with individuals (who incorporated as the Pioneer Radiocasting Service) with the intention of their assuming significant responsibility for KVEP. In response, the FRC's Harold A. Lafount turned to the Portland Better Business Bureau for a background report on Pioneer Radiocasting Service. The Better Business Bureau responded that the new company's principals were significantly involved with "a new political organization called the Minute Men" and had previously been associated with the Oregon Ku Klux Klan. "While definite information concerning the Minute Men is not available," the Portland Better Business Bureau reported, "it seems to be a sort of revival of the Klan movement and there may be some political aspects of the plans of these gentlemen to get into the radio field."[25] One can only speculate about Schaeffer's own political views in noting that the parties with whom he engaged in sales discussions clearly tended toward an anti-establishment, anarchistic or vigilante bent.

Schaeffer also discussed selling KVEP to Duncan, although nothing came of it. Finally, in early September 1929 he did "sell" the station to one George A. Dunn. One can almost feel sorry for Schaeffer, who was either a very poor judge of character or remarkably unlucky. In a frantic telegram to the FRC on September 24, 1929, Schaeffer reported that:

A certain Geo A Dunn with whom I had preliminary arrangements for partnership and who persuaded me to make a temporary transfer of license to [him] absconded with the company funds and payroll. Warrants for his arrest are out on many bad checks, fraud and government [sic] and larceny. Geo A Dunn has turned plain crook taking with him a new automobile and several radio sets belonging to Portland merchants as well. He abandoned a car at Seattle and is evidently now in Canada. I urgently ask that you cancel [my] sent application of license transfer.[26]

The commission obliged and disregarded the application to transfer KVEP's license to Dunn.

Thus, by the time the FRC designated KVEP's license renewal application for a hearing in May 1930, KVEP had already acquired an unusually bizarre record. The hearing opened on May 27, 1930, in Washington DC, with portions of Duncan's broadcasts read into the record, along with the numerous public complaints they had drawn. The testimony regarding the text of Duncan's speeches must have curled the commissioners' toes. "This is the strongest stuff I have heard as having gone over the air since I became a member of this commission," said FRC chairman Ira E. Robinson.[27]

Schaeffer tried to dodge responsibility by explaining that Duncan had purchased the time and, under the terms of his advertising agreement, the station had no control over the content of his speeches. That argument failed to impress anyone other than Duncan. The hearing—the first U.S. prosecution of profanity, obscenity or indecency in radio—was attracting international attention.

Oregon had fielded major players for the event. John C. Kendall had been hired by the coalition of business owners, civic interests and concerned members of the public to oppose KVEP's license renewal. Educated at the University of Minnesota Law School, Kendall had moved to Coos Bay, where he must have been an impressive figure. Appointed circuit court judge in 1921, he was elected to the same office in 1924 but resigned in 1927 to relocate to Portland and resume a private practice. Kendall was already quite interested in radio, and it quickly became a major focus of his practice. Eventually, he wound up representing a huge number of Oregon stations in addition to having some broadcast ownership interests of his own. A respected Portland figure, the *Oregonian* consistently referred to him as Judge Kendall, despite the fact he no longer held that office.

The Federal Radio Commission was represented at the hearing by its assistant general counsel, Ben S. Fisher, an attorney who went into private practice in Coos Bay immediately following World War I. Fisher remained in Coos Bay for about a decade, married a local girl in 1920 and had a son, Ben C. Fisher, in 1923. By 1929, financial conditions in Coos Bay were terrible and Fisher was considering his professional options. While he knew nothing about radio—"[he] had no experience with radio except how to turn on a set," according to his son—he was a good Republican with strong political connections, including friendships with powerful Oregon senators McNary and Steiwer. Not long before the KVEP case, he was offered the position of the Federal Radio Commission's assistant general counsel and promptly relocated to Washington, DC.

Not surprisingly, Kendall and Fisher were close friends from their common time in Coos Bay. Given Kendall's extensive background in radio law, it is conceivable that he played some role in Fisher's move to the FRC staff. [28] Memoranda between Kendall and Fisher before, during and immediately after the KVEP hearing clearly indicate the two men were close and coordinated their work during the hearing.

At the hearing, Schaeffer pleaded that KVEP's financial viability rested on its advertising revenue from Duncan.[29] Yet as the two-day hearing unfolded, what appeared to be an increasingly apprehensive Schaeffer finally offered to take Duncan off the air if it would preserve his license—but it was too late for that.

Besides Schaeffer's claim that his advertising contract prohibited him from censoring Duncan's speeches, Duncan separately claimed that, as a candidate for congressional office (during a portion of the time his broadcasts were in dispute during the hearing), neither Schaeffer nor the FRC had legal authority to censor him.[30]

Judge John C. Kendall, 1923

Ben S. Fisher, c. 1945

On May 30, 1930, the FRC issued its decision and declined to renew KVEP's license, saying that it had "indisputable proof that the station has broadcast obscene language."[31] The FRC's private notes indicate that, in addition to consideration of the charges on the record, the commissioners had also become convinced that Duncan was engaged in an extortion scheme under which he would demand payment from various individuals or businesses to avoid their being made the subject of his on-air attacks.

Courtesy of the Oregonian

Tige Reynolds' cartoon, May 30, 1930, the day the Federal Radio Commission denied KVEP's license renewal.

But even that wasn't the end of Schaeffer's problems.

Concurrent with the FRC's denial of KVEP's license renewal, Duncan was arrested on June 2, 1930, by a U.S. marshal on charges that he had violated the 1927 Federal Radio Act's prohibition against broadcasting "obscene, indecent or profane" programming (a criminal offense). He was released on a $2,500 bond.

On June 10, 1930, Duncan was found guilty in Judge Mears' Portland district court of "electioneering on election day." The jury deliberated all of ten minutes. He was sentenced to ten days in jail and a fine of $75, a sentence that Duncan appealed although it appears that he ultimately served.

Claiming he couldn't secure a fair trial on the federal indecency charge in Portland, Duncan asked for a change of venue, and the case was moved to Medford, which had no federal court at that time. All of the witnesses and attorneys traveled to Medford, where federal Judge Bean heard the case on October 8, 1930. The government's argument was heavily based upon testimony by Robert M. Mount, manager of the Portland Better Business Bureau, to the effect that Duncan had made "various vicious statements in radio broadcasts over KVEP," some of which Duncan defended by asserting that he had been speaking on behalf of the Anti-Chain Store League.[32] Newspapers covering the trial, likely in deference to contemporary tastes, did not describe the offending remarks in much detail.

One complaint, that *was* detailed in the press, was Duncan's on-air assertion that the blindness of a beloved Portland figure, B. F. Irvine, was caused by his contraction of a "loathsome disease."[33] From 1919 to 1937, the widely respected Irvine was editor of Portland's *Oregon Journal.* He was occasionally mentioned as a potential Oregon gubernatorial candidate. But as a young man, Irvine's eyesight had been compromised from a work-related injury that was subsequently compounded by a blow to the head sustained during a boxing match. The combined injuries had caused sudden and total failure of his optic nerve years before the KVEP fracas.

Duncan's baseless charges particularly infuriated both Irvine's press colleagues and the community. Denouncing the right of a broadcaster to engage in such unfounded attacks, U.S. Attorney George Neuner argued that "the protection [from scurrilous attack] of 125,000,000 radio listeners [throughout the nation] was at stake." Assistant U.S. attorney John W. McCulloch argued that "this is the first time in the history of the United States that a jury has been called upon to decide a criminal matter of this kind under the Federal Radio Act. This is not an ordinary case. It doesn't involve only a few dollars and only one man, but all of the people of these United States and their children."[34]

If found guilty on all five alleged indecency counts, Duncan would have faced five years in prison but the Medford jury acquitted him on four. Reportedly, the jury would have found him guilty on all five counts but for one staunch juror who nearly hung the jury. Duncan was sentenced to six months in county jail and fined $500, the first individual ever found guilty of broadcasting indecent material on the radio. Both sides claimed victory—but neither was happy with the verdict.

That was hardly the end of Wildcat Bob Duncan. After his release from jail, he turned up on KWJJ in 1932 with a program similar to the one that occasioned his KVEP difficulties. Sufficiently controversial to prompt FRC personnel to again monitor his activities, these broadcasts drew a letter from Lovejoy to the Washington, DC, FRC office on May 11, 1932. A subsequent follow-up letter from W. D. Terrell to Lovejoy reported that Duncan was still ranting about his typical subjects such as chain stores and tariff reform, but "in a rather suppressed manner."[35]

The details of Duncan's activities over the next several years are unclear, but in 1936 he decided to run for the Oregon senate and purchased air time on KEX. His 30-minute program ran Tuesday through Friday, at 8:30 p.m., for 26 weeks. While still commonly referred to as the Oregon Wildcat, he seems to have also restyled himself as the Blue Eagle while he continued his tirades over KEX. The *Oregonian*, describing him as "radio's most picturesque talker," reported that he also had scheduled three broadcasts in Salem and two in Eugene.[36]

What had Duncan broadcast over KVEP that so inflamed Portlanders in 1930? Unquestionably, he engaged in vicious name-calling. He labeled individuals as crooks, prostitutes and moral reprobates with abandon.[37] He threatened to shoot any number of individuals with whom he disagreed—and kept a gun next to his microphone during broadcasts.

He was particularly explicit in his tirades about U.S. congressman Franklin Korrell, who he essentially accused of engaging in gay sex. "Mr. Korrell is admittedly an ex-room mate and bedfellow of Clarence Brazell who forfeited a heavy bond to prevent trial for crimes of moral perversion with Portland youths."[38] Calling upon all "natural men" among his listeners, he urged them to turn Korrell out of office so that Oregon would not be represented by "a sissified Sodomite." Radio was only eight or nine years old at the time, and nothing of this nature had ever been encountered on American airwaves. While libel prosecutions for printed transgressions were occasional, the broadcast equivalent, slander, hadn't really been perfected as a legal basis for pursuing claims of defamation. Clearly, Duncan was guilty of slander but the mechanism for prosecuting for that type of defamatory speech really didn't exist in 1930.[39]

Besides defamation, Duncan's utterances occasionally included references to the "damn" chain stores or other parties whom he damned. However, it would be hard to conclude that Duncan's vitriolic utterances were either obscene or profane by 21st-century standards. His "crime" seems to have had more to do with trodding on the prevailing public sense of indecency which, although vague, was prohibited discourse under the Federal Radio Act.

KVEP, a relatively small station whose contribution to the Oregon radio community was reasonably brief and undistinguished, made the record books over its combustible finale.

## KFEC Portland

1929 saw the end of some of Oregon's founding radio influences. Charles Austin's Northwestern Radio Manufacturing Company, which had been a pioneer in radio broadcasting and manufactured 100,000 receivers over eight years, closed following a difficult patent litigation.

Meier & Frank's KFEC—Portland's second oldest radio station—was also facing an uncertain future. Born with high hopes under the stewardship of one of Portland's most notable institutions, the station had grown from its original 10-watt transmitter—albeit only to a 50-watt operation.[40] By 1929, it was still housed in the department store's massive downtown headquarters on Morrison Street between Fifth and Sixth Avenues.

Originally, the station's programming had been prominently featured in the store's many newspaper ads. "Meier & Frank's Own Radio Broadcasting Station will Give a Splendid concert Tonight." "Meier & Frank's Own Radio Broadcasting Station will Give Children's Program." "Play-by-play sports coverage of the St. Mary's-Multnomah Club football game"[41] and "Election Returns Service—Editions Throughout the Evening in concert the Oregon Journal" were typical headlines of KFEC programming included in the department store's newspaper ads. Clearly, it was Meier & Frank's goal to set the same standard for public service in radio for which it was well-known in retail.

In its pursuit of success, KFEC had tried various national associations, including scheduling the first run of radio's famous *Amos 'n Andy* series, which made its KFEC debut on November 23, 1928 (see chapter 6). In late December 1928, KFEC also hired Joseph Sampietro as the station's musical director. A violinist, Sampietro was a member of the Portland Symphony and a frequent participant in radio broadcasts. Some months later, he would become KOIN's music director. His hiring by KFEC in 1929 suggests that the station intended to reinvigorate its presentation of live music.

These hardly seem the actions of a station headed toward extinction—but Aaron M. "Bud" Frank (father of Gerry Frank), 36-year-old son of Meier & Frank co-founder Sigmund Frank and manager of the store, was frustrated with KFEC. Radio had changed. Portland's more prominent stations had grown larger, secured higher transmitter powers and acquired prestigious network affiliations that were not available to a small 50-watter like KFEC. In general, despite Frank's best efforts other stations were offering radio in a grander manner than KFEC. The station had simply been passed by, notwithstanding attempts at significantly re-invigorating itself by scheduling *Amos 'n Andy* and hiring Sampietro. By 1929, KFEC was largely offering phonograph recordings drawn from the Meier & Frank music department stock.

The terrible interference dilemma also hung over stations' heads. Congress had stipulated that all new licenses issued by the FRC include a waiver under which the applicant disclaimed any property rights in the frequency it used. The requirement was designed to give the commission the authority to weed out lesser stations by whatever evaluation system it might devise and clear the airwaves of interference, which had become a serious public concern. Even larger stations such as KGW were concerned over the uncertainty of the situation (see *Oregonian*/KGW ad in chapter 4).

When it came time to renew KFEC's license in 1928, Aaron Frank was not amused by the requirement that he execute such a waiver. In a January 12 letter to Redfern accompanying KFEC's license renewal, Frank wrote: "We wish to protest the requirement of a waiver as a prerequisite to being granted a renewal of our license. We do not know by what authority, if any, we are bound to make this waiver."[42]

In the course of the FRC's efforts to reduce interference, it had changed stations' frequencies and required some to share frequencies. In 1927, KFEC was ordered to share time with Benson Polytechnic High School's KFIF. In 1928, KFEC was made to share time with Astoria's KFJI. It must have seemed to Frank that KFEC was increasingly seen as a second class station by the FRC—which was totally at odds with his vision for the station. If anything, Frank wanted to see KFEC as an industry leader. Just the previous year, Meier & Frank had litigated five lawsuits filed by a variety of music publishers, who alleged that KFEC was infringing upon their rights by broadcasting recordings of their music. Meier & Frank successfully defended against these suits and, in doing so, won a major victory for the entire radio industry on May 12, 1928. But now KFEC was sharing time with tiny KAST in Astoria.

In addition to protesting the frequency waiver in his January 12 letter to Redfern, Frank also sketched out his plans for expanding Meier & Frank's commitment to the station. He reported to the FRC on having installed new towers on the store's roof "approximately forty feet above our large Meier & Frank Company electric sign," and expressed his commitment to creating more expensive and engaging KFEC programming—with Sampietro's engagement being just a hint—if only the FRC would give the station a better, more powerful frequency. However, that was not to be.

Other changes were looming. In 1928, Frank was considering expanding the store. Meier & Frank ultimately solicited bids for a major expansion of the building (which had previously covered three-quarters of a full city block). The $2 million construction project eventually expanded the store to a full block, and KFEC just didn't fit as clearly into those plans as might have been the case when the station was launched in 1922.

Accordingly, in April 1928, Meier & Frank sought FRC approval to relocate KFEC to the store's large warehouse in one of Portland's industrial areas.[43] In a last gasp, KFEC purchased KTBR's transmitter and increased its program schedule to 14 hours daily, consisting primarily of phonograph recordings—but with some studio programs, as well. Apparently, the results weren't enough to satisfy Aaron Frank's sense of what Meier & Frank's radio ventures should reflect.

## The End of KFEC

Notwithstanding its December 1928 initiatives, in early January 1929 Meier & Frank firmly decided to sell KFEC and quit the radio business. Perhaps the idea was initiated by a prospective buyer. A. E. Kern Company of Portland, headed by Alfred E. Kern, was eager to purchase the station, and Meier & Frank filed an FRC application seeking authority to sell the station to him in late January. The sale was publicly announced.[44]

In retrospect, the purchaser would seem an odd choice. For decades, the A. E. Kern Company had been a Portland-based job publisher and produced a wide variety of materials, including the Rose Festival program booklets. But the company was also closely associated with what in later years would come to be called the German-American Bund. It produced a German-language Portland newspaper, *Nachricten*, and was reportedly connected to a variety of what would later be identified as pro-Nazi sources. Eleven years later the *Oregonian* editorially branded "*Nachrichten* a disgracefully traitorous publication, presumably subsidized in some manner by the Nazis."[45] For Meier & Frank, a company started by two German-Jewish immigrants, the choice of Kern as a buyer seems incongruous. Perhaps, Aaron Frank came to that same conclusion.

The FRC was also unhappy about KFEC's proposed sale, having apparently concluded that moving the station to another city would better resolve some of the chronic interference conditions that plagued Portland's radio reception. It seems unlikely that the FRC would have declined approval of the sale, but it is entirely possible that commission staff made it clear that a sale keeping KFEC in Portland was not viewed favorably. For whatever reason, the Kern sale was abandoned.

But Meier & Frank was now firmly committed to selling KFEC and did so several weeks later—to Carl Haymond, who already owned KMO Tacoma. KFEC was to be moved to Yakima under Haymond's ownership. In March, the FRC approved the sale, and KFEC promptly signed-off and was dismantled and shipped to Yakima. It signed-on there as KIT on April 9.[46] Bob Hartzog, KFEC's operator and announcer of many years, was essentially "sold" along with the station and moved to Yakima to assume similar responsibilities at KIT.[47]

As the decade came to a close, Meier & Frank, a founding influence in Oregon radio, was out of the broadcasting business, and KFEC was just a memory.

## Endnotes

1. "Novel Radio Store," *Oregon Journal*, November 6, 1927, Sec 2. 7.
2. Hanseth, Harold H., 1928. Telegram to Federal Radio Commission (requesting the KOOS call sign despite the fact that approval of his move to Coos Bay was still pending) dated January 16 (KOOS file, NARA, College Park, MD).
3. Newspaper coverage of the KOOS move implied that Cullen had been part-owner of the station in Eugene although no references to her have been found in connection with KGEH.
4. "Coos Bay Gets Radio Station," *Coos Bay Times*, February 10, 1928, 1.
5. "Station KOOS To Be On Air Here Monday," *Southwestern Oregon Daily News*, March 6, 1928, 1.
6. Following his sale of KOOS c. 1935, Hanseth lived in California for a period in connection with his founding KIEM Eureka. He died in April 1980 in Grants Pass (Social Security Death Index).
7. Cullen, Thelma E. and Pratt, Irene G., 1928. Telegram to Commissioner Harold A. Lafount dated May 27 (KOOS file, NARA, College Park, MD).
8. Clearman, W. J., (Acting Secretary), 1928. Letter to KOOS Radio Sales and Service, Coos Bay, OR, dated July 28 (KOOS file, NARA, College Park, MD).
9. The FRC's Radio Service Bulletin dated December 31, 1928, reports that the station was authorized during December. The *Oregon Journal* reported on December 11, 1928, page 17, Edwin Lovejoy, of the Seattle FRC office had "just announced" the issuance of the construction permit. It is likely KOOS signed-on very shortly thereafter.
10. Blanc & Nicoud operated a radio set sales store at that location.
11. The address is taken from Hanseth's FRC Application of June 28, 1928, and identification of the address as Hanseth's residence from Peterson, Emil R., and Powers, Alfred, *A Century of Coos and Curry* (Coquille, OR: Coos-Curry Pioneer & Historical Association, 1952), 497.
12. Slogan on the letterhead on which the financial statement was submitted.
13. Attachments to FRC application received May 23, 1933 (NARA, College Park, MD)
14. Redfern, O. R., 1928. Letter to Lewis Irvine Thompson, Portland, OR, dated February 11 (KLIT file, NARA, College Park, MD).
15. Material in this paragraph is taken from KORE files at the National Archives in College Park MD.
16. Oregon Secretary of State, State of Oregon Statements and Arguments of Political Parties and Independent Candidates, Multnomah County General Election, November 7, 1922. Statement of Robert G. Duncan, Independent Candidate For Representative in Congress, Third Congressional District, 35.
17. Craig Adams, www.pdxradio.com.
18. Parties who were attacked by Duncan included C. C. Chapman, Editor of the *Oregon Voter*; U.S. congressman Franklin F. Korell (who had defeated Duncan in the May 16, 1930, Republican primary); George Sandy, American Legion official; Robert M. Mount, manager of the Portland Better Business Bureau; A. M. Work, Portland businessman; the KGW Hoot Owls; the Portland Breakfast Club; the *Oregonian* and the *Oregon Journal* according to the October 11, 1930, *Oregonian*.
19. The station later moved to Walla Walla, Washington.
20. *Oregonian*, May 29, 1930, 1.
21. At that time FRC regulations required that a radio station be 5/6th owned/controlled by individuals holding American citizenship.
22. The quotations which follow are part of the KWBS/KVEP files, NARA, College Park, MD.
23. Schaeffer's complaint, filed May 15, 1930, with, and investigated by, the Federal Bureau of Investigation, Portland, OR, office, alleged that Robert E. Schmidtz had impersonated an FRC employee to assist the FRC. Schmidtz denied the charge (KVEP file, NARA, College Park, MD).

24. Lovette, Frank H., FRC Acting Secretary. 1930. Letter to Radio Station KVEP, Schaeffer Radio Company dated May 3, 1930 (KVEP file, NARA, College Park, MD).

25. Mount, Robert M. (Manager of the Portland Better Business Bureau, Inc.) Letter to Harold A. Lafount, Federal Radio Commission, dated January 26 (KVEP file, NARA, College Park, MD).

26. Federal Radio Commission (KWBS/KVEP Correspondence File, NARA, College Park, MD)

27. *Oregonian,* May 29, 1930, 1.

28. Fisher's appointment to the FRC position had been a political one. With the sweep of Democratic Federal 1934 elections, he left the Radio Commission's employment just as the FRC was being succeeded by the Federal Communications Commission and set up a Washington, DC law practice that same year. The firm, which later became known as Fisher, Wayland, became one of the first, and most prominent, law firms representing broadcasting clients. Kendall had a son, John W. Kendall, who also became an attorney. Fisher hired the younger Kendall fresh out of Georgetown University law school in 1936, and in 1941, the younger Kendall returned to Portland to join his father's firm (which became Davis, Wright, Tremaine). He remained in practice in Portland until 1980. Fisher's son, Ben C. Fisher, also entered the practice of law and joined his father's Washington, DC, firm—a position he continued to hold (although now largely retired), in 2008. The original Fisher firm has been successively merged into various others and has been known as Shaw Pittman since 2000.

29. Schaeffer asserted that he had between $12,000 and $15,000 invested in KVEP and that he had fixed monthly expenses of $500 for the station. KVEP's contract with Duncan called for him to pay KVEP $650 per month for the daily, two-hour air time.

30. A provision in the Radio Act of 1927, that survives in the Communications Act of 1934 (which replaced it and remains in force), forbids broadcasters from censoring or otherwise influencing political broadcasts by federal electoral candidates.

31. *Oregonian,* May 30, 1930, 6.

32. "Jury at Medford Will Take Duncan Case After Final Arguments Today," *Oregonian,* October 8, 1930, 1.

33. Ibid.

34. Ibid.

35. Lovejoy, Edwin W., 1932. Letter to Supervisor of Radio, Department of Commerce, Washington, DC, dated May 11 (KVEP file, NARA, College Park, MD).

36. *Oregonian,* April 1, 1936, and April 7, 1936.

37. On May 9, 1936, speaking of the Portland Labor Council: "The infernal crooks that manipulate that labor ticket down there are an infernal bunch of cheap-skate bribe-takers."

38. Duncan, Robert Gordon, 1930. Letter to the Federal Radio Commission dated May 22. Duncan cites his "bona fides" in the letter as: The Oregon Wildcat, The Apostle of Democracy, Editor of Duncan's Trade Register (KVEP file, NARA, College Park, MD).

39. One of the earliest cases in the U.S. involving defamation by radio was Sorensen v. Wood, 123 Neb. 348, 243 N.W. 82 (1932), which held that radio defamation was actually a libel rather than a slanderous act. Other cases later in the decade tended to treat radio defamation as slander but case law on such actions didn't start to codify until late in the 1930s and into the 1940s. Law involving defamation resulting from political broadcast utterances of a candidate for public office was not resolved by the U.S. Supreme Court until 1959 in Farmers Educational & Cooperative Union of America v. WDAY, Inc. 360 U.S. 525, 79 S.Ct. 1302 (1959) (Harold L Nelson and Dwight L. Teeter, Jr., *Law of Mass Communication: Freedom and Control of Print and Broadcast Media* (Mineola, New York: The Foundation Press, Inc., 1969), 66–71).

40. The store billed itself as "The Quality Store of Portland."

41. November 1, 1924, 12.

42. Frank, Aaron M., 1928. Letter to O. R. Redfern dated January 12 (KFEC file, NARA, College Park, MD).

43. Using the street names then current, the warehouse was bounded by Everett, Flanders, 14th and 15th Streets.

44. Unfortunately, the application to sell KFEC to A. E. Kern Company cannot now be located in the National Archives.

45. Editorial, *Oregonian,* September 26, 1941.

46. KIT sign-on date from Broadcast *Pro-File.*

47. Other than where otherwise indicated, details in this paragraph come from "Meier & Frank Radio Plant Going to Yakima," *Sunday Oregonian,* March 24, 1929, Sec. 4, 6.

"Covered Wagon Days" Compliments of
Gevurtz Furniture Company
Corner Second and Morrison, Portland.

"A Little Down On A Big Bill!"

KEX

Earl Fagen
Master of Ceremonies
W. Painter's Mishts
Organization

# The 1930s
# The Depression

# Entering the Depression

# 8

Radio emerged during the flapper era of prosperity and allowed Oregon to more fully enter the nation's mainstream through the heightened connection it brought to a largely rural state. Then suddenly, the Roaring Twenties screeched to a halt. In October 1929, the stock market crash signaled a new era—one filled with challenge, austerity and uncertainty. Many Oregonians initially thought the economic turn would prove only a short-term dislocation. Few anticipated the length and depth of the upheaval at hand. Yet, the fall 1929 economic barometric readings were sobering.

By January 1930, Portland's retail index was down 50% compared to the previous year.[1] Portland banks lost $3 million in deposits in 1930, and some, such as Portland's Bank of Hibernia, closed immediately after the crash. Initially, Portland's urban retail-centered economy was hit far harder than the rest of the state, with the area's unemployment standing between 10,000 and 20,000 in 1930. Outside Portland, where agricultural and timber economies predominated, communities were initially less affected. But as Oregon's major industry, timber, fell victim to the crash, economic devastation gradually spread throughout the state.

At the Depression's dawn, both government officials and business leaders tended to view the downturn as nothing more than a temporary challenge to be weathered. Writing on New Year's Day, 1930, the *Oregonian* editorialized: "That Oregon prosperity will continue throughout the new Decade and far into the indefinite future seems is as assured as things can be."

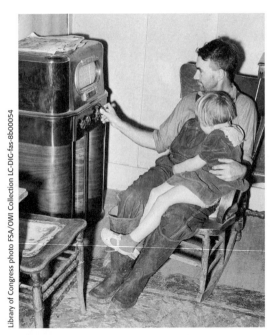

Father and daughter listening to radio, 1940.

But things looked different by April 1930, when customary seasonal job fluctuations should have produced increased employment and no upturn materialized. By the fall, the construction industry had also failed to rebound—and concern escalated dramatically. In response, KGW's Hoot Owls augmented their customary Christmas efforts to feed and clothe the numerous needy by sponsoring the erection of they called the World's Largest Christmas Tree to encourage charitable giving. That Christmas, the Hoot Owls distributed 1,200 food baskets—an effort mitigated only a small portion of the Depression's deepening hardships.

Still hopeful, the City of Portland raised its 1931 budget after first reducing its tax levy. But when anticipated revenues failed to materialize, Portland struggled with an unbalanced budget. That same year, Multnomah County property tax delinquencies soared to 29 percent. Statewide the figure stood at 39 percent. By 1933, half of Multnomah County's property owners were in tax arrears. Aaron Frank, the Meier & Frank store scion who was also an official of the newly formed Civic Emergency Committee, later said: "There was virtually a tax strike in Multnomah County." Deposits at the United States National Bank, Portland's largest, plummeted by $10 million between December 1931 and June 1932, and Meier & Frank hurriedly deposited millions of dollars in Portland's fourth largest bank, the American National, to keep it solvent.

Efforts like those of the Civic Emergency Committee, the Hoot Owls' Sunshine Division and the Portland Community Chest all valiantly sought to meet the growing demands for assistance—but the challenge was too great for private resources alone. Oregon was sinking deeper into the Depression.

On January 1, 1931, the Portland Police imposed a 6 p.m. curfew in the city's skid row area. Anyone on the street afterward was arrested. When a soup kitchen line got too long, the police arrested a jobless man when he took a second slice of bread. When a tenant tried to run out on his rent payment of 80¢, his landlord murdered him. Tensions mounted, and as the crisis deepened, government ratcheted up efforts seeking to address the deteriorating conditions. Ultimately, the federal government was providing 89¢ of every dollar directed to economic relief efforts in Oregon.

Where 1920 had seen social unrest reflected in Ku Klux Klan marches in Portland and Medford, by 1930 public demonstrations were focused on economic issues as hungry, frightened Oregonians pressed for reform. Nationally, those forces produced fiery, influential political radio commentators such as Father Charles E. Coughlin. In Portland, they stoked popular interest in the radio broadcasts of Robert G. Duncan, the Oregon Wildcat (see chapter 7).

In southern Oregon, which had been one of the KKK's bastions, some of the same people who earlier had donned white night-riding robes turned their attention to the perceived failings of local government. In Jackson County, two local newspapers editors funneled these frustrations into a movement that lasted several years and culminated in the founding of the Good Government Congress (GGC). The GGC and its allied forces were quietly, but staunchly, opposed by Robert Ruhl, editor of the *Medford Mail Tribune*. Violence became frighteningly common and caused Ruhl to have good reason for concern over his family's personal safety. Another newspaper editor, who also opposed the GGC, was dragged into the street and publicly horsewhipped. Newspapers posted 24-hour guards over their printing plants. In a fight for control of county government, GGC forces stole the ballot boxes that held the fall 1932 election results and destroyed most of the ballots. Eventually, one of the GGC's principal leaders shot and killed a Medford policeman, who had been dispatched to arrest him in connection with the ballot theft. Ultimately, governor Julius Meyer was forced to send in the state police to help restore order. In 1934, Ruhl's *Medford Mail Tribune* won a Pulitzer Prize for meritorious public service in its courageous coverage of the Jackson County Rebellion. The story is widely believed to have been the basis for Sinclair Lewis' 1935 novel *It Can't Happen Here*.

Amid these events, radio played an unanticipated role. While KMED was formally owned by Blanch Virgin, the station's association with the *Medford Mail Tribune* was prominent (see chapter 4). Reportedly, GGC supporters sought to purchase air time on KMED to promote their views and were rebuffed by the station. According to Lee Bishop, who worked at KMED at the time, Mrs. Henrietta B. Martin, former president of the GGC, filed suit in federal court against KMED over the issue—and lost.[2] Such a case was one of the earliest in the nation to establish the principle that radio stations weren't common carriers and couldn't be compelled to sell air time to anyone who sought a public soapbox.

While Herbert Hoover had used radio to broadcast a few of his speeches, it was the newly-elected Franklin D. Roosevelt who intuitively understood radio's capacity to rally the nation's spirit. Roosevelt masterfully used radio for his legendary Fireside Chats. A shaken and worried nation hung on his words, hoping the federal government would solve the nation's illnesses. Families commonly placed a photograph of Roosevelt on the radio, all the better to appreciate his virtual visits.

Eventually, radio produced an almost familial bond between the public and their president. People routinely wrote to him following his broadcasts, as if he were a beloved uncle. C. Lee Curtis of Portland wrote: "More power to you for your speech of last night. My only complaint is that it didn't come sooner."[3] Portlander Mrs. Frank Taylor wrote: "God bless you always dear Mr. President, and may He comfort, guide and protect you in your hours of need. I send you also my deepest gratitude for the work you have given my husband on the W.P.A."[4]

It was, in many respects, a very dark time. Yet radio rose to serve a different role during the Depression, one largely consisting of entertainment, which helped the public escape during fearsome times. Radio provided a free replacement for the vaudeville entertainment that had been so popular in the previous decade—although, along with the Depression, it killed live vaudeville in the process. But, it also created a new home for many famous vaudeville performers.

Like movies of the era, radio often spun an air of elegant pretension. Announcers and orchestra members wore tuxedos, regardless of whether they had a live in-studio audience to see them. Most radio stations sought to reflect the same visual elegance in their studios that was found in the movie palaces being built by Paramount, MGM and Loews around Oregon and the nation. NBC's newly constructed network production centers in New York, Chicago, Los Angeles, Denver and San Francisco were designed in *art deco/art moderne* style. Apart from soap operas, radio programs either ignored life's problems or offered glimpses of a brighter future. Even the soap opera *Our Gal Sunday* revolved around the fictional tale of a poor Colorado orphan who marries England's most eligible bachelor and then confronts life's challenges from within the security of an enviable marriage. It was a time when both radio and movies offered their patrons momentary escape, generally to a world in which the inhabitants of a largely care-free society found happiness in the end.

Journalist William R. Lindley, who graduated from Benson Polytechnic High School, and eventually worked at the *Eugene Register-Guard* and the Associated Press, grew up in Portland's Eastmoreland district during the Great Depression. He later wrote that "on the radio, comedy shows were the favorites with the entertainers taking people's minds off those scarcely hopeful days. Comedians who successfully brought their vaudeville stage acts to radio included Jack Benny, Eddie Cantor and Fred Allen."[5]

Radio in the 1920s had offered a magical diversion. In the decade of Depression, it offered hope and escape.

## Endnotes

1. Information regarding economic and social conditions taken from William H. Mullins, *The Depression and the Urban West Coast 1929-1933: Los Angeles, San Francisco* (Bloomington, IN: Indiana University Press, 1991).
2. Undated letter from Lee Bishop to Ray Johnson, likely written in 1972 in connection with KMED's 50th Anniversary (Ray Johnson Collection, WSMB).
3. From a letter dated March 16, 1937 (Lawrence W. Levine and Cornelia R. Levine, *The People and the President* (Boston, MA: Beacon Press, 2002), 193.
4. Ibid., From a letter dated September 12, 1941, 382.
5. Walter R. Lindley, *Hard Times, Good Times in Oregon*, (Manhattan, KS: Sunflower University Press, 1995), 26.

# 9

# Portland Area Radio in the 1930s

By the late 1920s, KOIN was flourishing. The station's December 1927 move from the old Heathman Hotel's basement to the New Heathman Hotel's mezzanine gave it one of the west's most lavish radio studios. While the honor of serving as the first major Portland network affiliate went to KGW, KOIN chose CBS just as that network was achieving national reach. The CBS affiliation, which began in 1929, launched a relationship that endured in radio for over 40 years—and which remains in place in television almost 80 years later. While larger stations tended to focus on live music in the 1930s, KOIN pursued that philosophy with unusual vigor. Its musical staff was so vast that KOIN soon became an anchor point for regional and national network programs to a far greater degree than was KGW's circumstance with NBC.

In November 1931, KOIN launched its first network program, *Isle of Golden Dreams* hosted by Johnnie Walker, which was sent to the northwest leg of the Don Lee Broadcasting Service. *Radio Digest* repeatedly extolled the "haunting and exquisite" program and praised its melodious "unique combination of pipe organ, vibraharp and steel guitar" as the "weekly ideal for lovers of soft, soothing and restful melodies."[1, 2] Walker's haunting *Golden Dreams* sign-off especially drew listener comments. Perhaps it had originally been prepared for use as KOIN's station sign-off, if the station thought about taking a cue from KGW's *Midnight Ode* (see chapter 3), but was instead used as *Golden Dreams'* closing "invocation." *Radio Digest* thought it was particularly "apropos to the atmosphere on the *Isle of Golden Dreams*."[3]

Panoramic view of the KOIN reception lobby on the New Heathman Hotel's mezzanine. The station's studios are visible in the background. *In Tune With the West*, KOIN publication, 1931.

Soon, KOIN created other programs to send to the DLBS network:

❦ *Magic Mirror* on Wednesdays, from 9 to 9:30 p.m.

❦ *Modernistic High Jinks* on November 30, 1932 (fed to the network's northwest leg)[4]

❦ *Slumber Boat* (which had premiered locally in 1931) in December 1932 on Tuesday evenings at 10:30

❦ *Romantic Moods*, featuring the KOIN salon orchestra

❦ *Rainbow Moods*, in 1936 featuring a ten-piece orchestra, each evening from 11:30 p.m. to midnight.

Felt KOIN pennant used on mike stand, c. 1935

By 1934–35, KOIN was regularly originating music programs for both DLBS and CBS, and at one point it was feeding a total of four and one-quarter hours of programming weekly to the Columbia Pacific Network. It was not until the late 1950s, when the high cost of originating so much live music became impractical, that KOIN broadcast its first commercial phonograph recording in its history.

KOIN was admirably equipped for its role in creating such a huge quantity of live radio music. The studios were large, flexible and elegant—and the huge "KOIN" neon sign on the New Heathman Hotel's roof for decades served as a beacon boldly proclaiming a hub of major radio enterprise.

KOIN entered the 1930s with a core staff that established a foundation on which the station successfully operated for decades. At KOIN's height, as many as 120 staff worked in the studios. C. Roy Hunt, who had taken over management of the station in 1929 after honing his skills at KXL, was aided by station accompanist, and his executive secretary, Ruth Bjork. It was Hunt's early programming philosophy that established KOIN as a home for live music, and it was the talented crew he assembled that made it enduring. While KOIN's programming was centered on music, the station's major news offering was the 10 p.m. *Five Star Final*, which debuted in May 1937 anchored by James Wyatt. For 20 years, Wyatt anchored

*Slumber Boat Program*. From *In Tune With the West* (1931), KOIN promotional brochure. (left to right) Frank Trevor, Gene Baker, Cecil Teague, Anson Bush, Dorothy Robinson, Owen "Red" Dunning.

the high-profile nightly program until his death on October 10, 1956—and one of his signature phrases, "Wottaworld," [sic] became regionally famous.

But music was at KOIN's core. It was said that the station maintained the largest full-time staff of musicians in Oregon radio. By 1930, the KOIN staff included pianist Geraldine France, who had been with the station since its 1926 sign-on and had the reputation of *always* being on time for rehearsals and broadcasts; Johnnie Walker, a Portland radio veteran who began hosting KOIN's popular nightly *Merry Go Round of the Air* program (from midnight to 1 a.m.), and the musically versatile Owen "Red" Dunning. All would remain with KOIN for decades.

In 1930, songs by KOIN's handsome, young Irish tenor, Howard Davis, were causing female KOIN listeners to swoon. His appearances on the station's *Cuckoo Club* (KOIN's contribution to the *Hoot Owls* radio genre) just added to his allure. Even station engineer Earle Denham doubled as a staff tenor. Frank

KOIN's C. Roy Hunt, c. 1940

Trevor was both a pianist and director of the Rose City Beavers, a talented and highly versatile group that formed the nucleus of the station's musical forces.[5, 6] Red Dunning said the group could play anything "from Bach to boogie," although they often appeared on the air under other names associated with a given sponsor such as the *Stetson Syncopators*, *Jack Cody's Bohemians* or the *Blue Blowers*.[7] KOIN frequently re-labeled its musical forces to serve the interests of sponsors, including the fairly sizeable *Hop Gold Orchestra*, which was named after a Portland brewery.

The Rose City Beavers appeared across the KOIN program schedule. By 1930, they were also being fed to the CBS Network and became so popular that the station frequently had them perform independent of broadcasts in venues such as the Multnomah Hotel.

The station's powerhouse musical ensemble, however, was KOIN's orchestra, which boasted:

KOIN Cuckoo Club membership card, c. 1930

- Frank Keller, flute
- Rudy Schultz, percussion
- Carl Clogston, bass
- Ferdinand Sorenson, cello
- Charles Clow, trumpet
- Lloyd Welfare, trombone
- George Phillips, trombone (one trombone apparently wasn't enough!)
- Anson Bush, violin
- Frances Pozzi, harp (she had been at the station nearly from its inception and remained for decades)
- Gene Baker, vocal music director and announcer
- Owen "Red" Dunning, cornet, violin, bass and a number of other instruments

WSMB Collection

KOIN's Hop Gold Orchestra in a public performance, c. early 1930s

Courtesy of www.pdxhistory.com

KOIN Klockers in 1940. (left to right) Ivan Jones, Frank Trevor and Walter Stewart

Dunning had come to KOIN after originally performing in Herman Kenin's Multnomah Hotel Orchestra. Musically ubiquitous, he was almost an orchestra unto himself and also wrote the majority of the orchestrations performed by KOIN's various ensembles. Presiding over the entirety of KOIN's musical forces was conductor Joseph Sampietro, who came to KOIN following his brief employment at KFEC (see chapter 7). Sampietro remained at his KOIN post until his death in 1942.[8]

While the station also maintained sizeable dramatic forces—Clay Osborne, for example, was director of skits, and several other members of the staff were hired as actors and writers—KOIN's major emphasis was clearly on music.[9]

From this constellation of musicians KOIN broadcast an entire day of music each and every day. Its mainstay programs, including *KOIN Klock*—the station's "rise 'n shine" effort—and the noon-time *Come and Get It*—which opened with the sound of a triangle and the call "Come and Get It"—remained on the KOIN program schedule for more than 40 years (see chapter 22).

KOIN was clearly Portland's music station.

## KGW Programs and Staff

KGW was also thriving in 1930. Graduating from its 1922 birth in the *Oregonian*'s tower, the station had proved sufficiently valuable that the newspaper created new KGW studios on the building's seventh and eighth floors. Regular NBC programming had arrived at KGW in 1927, while vestiges of KGW's pre-NBC days, its Northwest Triangle Network regional hookup, allowed the station to exchange quality regional programming with its Triangle partners in addition to having its choice of the NBC Red and Blue offerings. According to listener surveys, a majority of Portlanders preferred KGW to all other stations combined.[10]

Indeed, KGW had always been a leader, the Hoot Owls being but one example. In 1924, *Oregonian* editor Edgar Piper had taken on the Associated Press (AP) when it objected to KGW's broadcasting AP news material from the *Oregonian* on election night. For that infraction, the newspaper received a meaningless $100 fine.[11] But at the AP's annual meeting in 1925, Piper successfully sponsored an amendment to the AP Bylaws—amid strong opposition from the *New York Times*—that established the right of newspapers like the *Oregonian* to broadcast "news deemed of transcendent importance" over their radio stations.[12] Yet, it was an uneasy peace between press and radio. In 1936, the *Oregonian*, which by then owned both KGW and KEX, became an early subscriber to the Trans Radio News Service to assure the availability of suitable news material for its radio stations.

When KGW joined NBC in 1927, all NBC programs were originating from San Francisco, but soon KGW began feeding some of its own programs to the network—including *The Arabian Nights, John Doe's Music* and the *Saturday Nite Dance Jamboree.* Indeed, even before feeding programs to NBC, KGW's *Montag Fireside Hour* had been a feature on the old Northwest Triangle Network.

*Silk banner used by KGW for remote broadcasts, c. 1940*

WSMB Collection

Following an assignment as radio editor of the *Oregonian*, Paul R. Heitmeyer became KGW's general manager in April 1929, succeeding Dick Haller.[13] Heitmeyer was the youngest key executive at any major station on the west coast and quickly expanded KGW's broadcast day to 17 hours. KGW achieved significant commercial success under his management, but Heitmeyer left in early 1931 to manage Longview, Washington's, KUJ, which he had purchased.

KGW was heavily involved in broadcasting sports, education and public events. Dick Haller, originally a KGW announcer and manager, broadcast football games "from a cramped and very inadequate booth on the north roof of the Multnomah Stadium."[14] When Haller left KGW in 1929, Jimmy Richardson handled the play-by-play coverage until 1934.

But in sports announcing, no one made a bigger splash than Arthur Roland "Rollie" Truitt. He entered radio as a KXL announcer and graduated to sports coverage. Truitt came to KEX in 1933, when the station acquired broadcast coverage rights to Portland Beavers' baseball, and he quickly became the station's key sports announcer. Another early KGW staffer, Janet Baumhover, dubbed him "Mister Baseball"—a nickname by which he eventually became widely known.[15] Truitt remained at KEX for decades, although he "followed the team." When KEX ceased airing the Beavers, the station permitted Truitt to announce the games for other Portland stations like KWJJ.

Initially, many play-by-play game broadcasts were presented as re-creations. Teletype descriptions of plays on the field were sent by a Western Union telegraph operator from the baseball stadium to another Western Union operator seated next to the broadcast announcer, who typed out the dots-and-dashes description to hand to the announcer, who extemporaneously re-created the game on the spot. For many years, these re-creations consisted solely of the announcers' voices with no sound effects permitted.

WSMB Collection

Singer Louise Gillhouse was KGW's entry in the 1930 Madison Square Garden New York competition for the year's most beautiful radio artist, pictured here in *Radio Digest,* April 1931.

Rollie Truitt, 1945

Originally, the Portland Beavers would only allow re-creation broadcasts of away games and no home games were broadcast. Truitt reportedly wasn't enthusiastic about adding sound effects (i.e., a ball being hit or a crowd cheering) because he thought it was the announcers' voices and enthusiasm that carried the day. In 1933, when the Beavers and Truitt moved to KEX, the team began allowing the broadcast of the last three innings of home games. In 1936, the full broadcast of all home and away games commenced—still without sound effects. Finally in 1937, Truitt relented and some sound effects were introduced. When the *Oregonian* sold KEX in 1944, Beaver baseball migrated back to KXL—with Truitt again following the team. He remained the Portland Beavers' radio voice over various stations until 1963 and continued as the team's public address stadium announcer for some years thereafter. When he died in 1971, the universally liked Truitt was saluted, locally and nationally, for his major contributions to sports broadcasting and the remarkable span of his career.

## KEX and ABC

While KGW enjoyed steady growth and the stability of *Oregonian* ownership, KEX faced challenges.

In the early 1930s, KEX's manager was Bill Norman. Jack Barnett had preceded him as manager but, by the early 1930s, was KEX's key announcer. Local talent was still scarce and "Everybody was invited to go on the air in those days," according to Clyde Bruhn who worked at KEX at the time.[16] "A bootlegger and a policeman took off from their respective duties to come up and sing. Anything went," Bruhn described.[17] During the period of time that NBC owned the station, writer Evelyn Sibley Lampman was working at KEX. She described one of her early efforts, *Elmer and Gweny,* as "a small, 15-minute homey character study program sponsored by Lubliner Florists." As described in the memoir of her radio career, *Of Mikes and Men,* the program was a local attempt to replicate the national phenomenon created by NBC's *Amos 'n Andy.* Lampman noted that the cast included Howard "Brick" Hooten and Claribel Signer. Because Hooten was Lubliner's delivery boy, Lampman noted, "they did not have to pay him extra for performing. Claribel got $5 a program."[18] Lampman also described the station's 11 p.m. broadcast of a walkathon for cash prizes in a former dance hall, and the incredibly boring radio resulting from the announcer's attempt at describing people perambulating.[19]

Notwithstanding with some colorful local programming, KEX faced challenges. When the Seattle-based American Broadcasting Company (ABC) collapsed on August 25, 1929, it took the Western Broadcasting Company (which owned both the network and three of the network's key stations, including KEX) down with it (see chapter 6). KEX barely remained on the air. ABC had been relaying some CBS programming that KEX carried, but just days after ABC's collapse KEX permanently lost CBS to KOIN on September 1 (see chapter 6).

Following ABC's collapse, a bankruptcy court appointed Seattle's Ralph Horr receiver of the Western Broadcasting Company's assets, and he promptly renamed what remained of ABC as the Northwest Broadcasting System (NBS). KEX was struggling, and on December 22, 1929, began carrying programming from the new regional network, which was based at KJR Seattle.[20]

That network's programming wasn't really competitive with other networks, and with much of KEX's broadcast day being programmed from it, the effort proved little more than a stopgap attempt that ultimately failed.

On February 29, 1931, KEX also joined the United Broadcasting Company's (UBC) regional network chain which billed itself as "The Silver Network." But UBC folded just over a month later on April 1, 1931 (see chapter 6).[21]

In short, KEX was having a tough time.

## KEX Sold to NBC and then the *Oregonian*

With the Depression in full stride, both KEX and its parent network, NBS, were struggling. NBC, in contrast, was thriving. With the NBC Red Network clearly dominant, NBC Blue's western coverage was complicated by the frequent, often abortive network start-ups of ABC, NBS and UBC—which forced NBC to vie for Blue Network affiliations. Sensing that the best solution was to "clear the field," NBC purchased NBS on October 31, 1931 by acquiring all of NBS' stock. Although technically NBS operated KEX under this arrangement, in practice KEX functioned like an NBC-owned property. Since NBS held 100 percent of the stock of KEX's licensee, the Western Broadcasting Company, NBC effectively acquired ownership of KEX, KJR and KGA, and all three stations then became solid NBC Blue outlets. On October 18, KEX broadcast the inaugural program of the newly created NBC Gold Pacific Network (essentially a western subset of the NBC's Blue Network).[22] Yet, KEX was continuing to lose considerable amounts of money (the three-month period of May 1 through July 31, 1933, showed $19,690 in losses).[23]

NBC's acquisition of these stations raised concerns among NBC's Red affiliates in Seattle and Portland who feared that NBC might treat its owned stations more favorably than its affiliated ones in the same market. Stations owned and operated by networks are, in the broadcast industry, referred to as O&O's. KEX's ownership by NBC from 1931–33 had given Portland (and Oregon) its only network O&O prior to the media conglomeration ownership realignments of the late 1990s. These tensions with the western affiliates NBC's Red Network led to what has been incorrectly stylized as the *Oregonian*'s purchase of KEX from NBC, which was submitted to the FRC for approval around August 9, 1933.

KEX's Earl Fagan on remote broadcast, early 1930s

While even that letter to the FRC on August 9th refers to the transaction as a sale, it was actually something akin to a lease under which NBC transferred to the *Oregonian* KEX's license, use of the KEX assets and all KEX operational responsibility, including the right to program and maintain the station, for a period ending June 14, 1938. NBC executed this agreement, however, with the clear expectation that it would eventually re-acquire the property.

Upon conclusion of the agreement's term, the *Oregonian* was obligated to transfer the license and all other KEX property back to NBC and restore NBC's ownership as it existed prior to the 1933 "sale." Moreover, once the agreement reached its second year, the *Oregonian* had the right to prematurely terminate the agreement (and its KEX ownership) on 90-days' notice. Alternatively, the *Oregonian* could extend the agreement for an additional five years by giving notice prior to November 1, 1937.[24]

The *Oregonian* did renew this lease in 1937. What neither party had contemplated was that changes in FCC rules would undo KEX's eventual reversion to NBC. The FCC's 1943 adoption of its Duopoly Rule (which prohibited any party from owning more than one radio station in the same community) essentially eliminated any possibility that NBC could take KEX back. Moreover, it also put the *Oregonian* in the position of owning two radio stations, KGW and KEX, in the same community—something which the Duopoly Rule also prohibited. Accordingly, the *Oregonian* sold KEX to Westinghouse on November 28, 1944 to comply (see chapter 13).

## KGW-KEX

The *Oregonian*'s acquisition of KEX proved the dawn of a new, successful era for the station. Having received full control over KEX, in 1933 the *Oregonian* quickly moved to consolidate its position

KGW-KEX stationery letterhead, early 1940s

as owner of Portland's NBC Red and Blue stations. At the time of the *Oregonian* purchase, Larry Allen was managing KEX (as an NBC employee). Unbeknownst to him, the *Oregonian* had made the KEX acquisition conditional on securing his services to manage the combined KGW-KEX.

While KEX had relatively lavish radio studios at the time it was sold, KGW was then engaged in remodeling its *Oregonian* studios. The newspaper's plans were quickly modified to allow the incorporation of KEX, which dedicated its new seventh-floor *Oregonian* studios on August 30, 1934. The newspaper proudly labeled the new KGW-KEX studios "the "Most Modern In the West."

Larry Allen proved a fortunate addition to KGW, where his vision and drive sparked new strength for the two stations' combined operation. Interestingly, Allen was reportedly the prototype for the inspiration for the character Barry Alden, a station manager in Evelyn Sibley Lampman's fictionalized history of early Portland radio, *Of Mikes and Men* (see chapters 5 and 7).

Where KOIN tended to specialize in lavish musical offerings, KGW-KEX—while hardly ignoring music—focused on drama, variety programming and news. In 1933, KEX launched the weekly program *Covered Wagon Days*, a huge studio production heard on Tuesday evenings under Gevurtz Furniture Store's sponsorship. Fledgling KGW-KEX announcer and newsman Chet Huntley, later of NBC-TV fame, played Randolph Jordan, the program's romantic male lead.[25] Originally written by Robert L. Reed,[26] *Covered Wagon Days* featured a large orchestra conducted by Abe Bercovitz and a huge cast. A typical episode might involve a cast of

KGW-KEX New Studio A, 1934

KGW's *Covered Wagon Days* postcard, c. 1937

more than 20 people, which makes the fact that the program toured the Pacific Northwest all the more remarkable.

*Covered Wagon Days*, one example of a program KGW-KEX sent to the Northwest Triangle Network, ultimately led to a labor dispute. Janet Baumhover, a KGW staffer who later became deeply involved in the organized labor movement, was an actress on *Covered Wagon Days*. According to Baumhover, "Ordinarily we'd get paid two and a half, I was paid two and a half for the show no matter how many hours we rehearsed. I guess it [*Covered Wagon Days*] was a half hour show. When we did the [Northwest Triangle] network with Seattle and Portland and Spokane we got $3.50."[27] Dispute over these wages ultimately led to the American Federation of Radio Artists (AFRA) securing representation rights for Portland radio artists.

Among *Covered Wagon Days'* cast members was Joe Hallock (formerly of Hallock and Watson), who came to work at KGW around 1932 when his company fell on hard times during the Depression.[28]

Hallock and Watson's radio receiver manufacturing business began suffering in 1926 when the patent holder on the then-new superhetrodyne circuit began suing companies like Hallock and Watson, who were making "superhet" sets without a patent license.

Chet Huntley took over the romantic role of Randolph Jordan in KEX's *Covered Wagon Days* from Lawrence Keating. He is shown here rehearsing with Cora May Christopher, who played baby Tomathin Mackay, September 20, 1936.

Consequently, Hallock and Watson abandoned manufacturing and went into consulting and industrial installations. While Hallock and Watson limped along, Joe Hallock took an announcing job at KGW, at least part-time, until the Depression finally extinguished his company.[29] "We made a lot of money in the 11 years we were in business," he later said, "but the Depression wiped us out."[30]

Hallock had come to radio performing circuitously. As an Oregon State University student, he had acted in student productions and later toured with the Dufferin Players and the company of Hollywood actor Leo Carrillo (likely in Carrillo's own production, *Lombardi, Ltd.*).[31] The Carrillo production had played in Portland, and that is perhaps where Hallock met the popular western actor. Following his radio manufacturing career, Hallock was thus well-equipped for radio acting. He played various parts on *Covered Wagon Days*, including Sergeant Frost, with "a phony Irish accent," and Mountain Man Joe Dowger.[32, 33] Phil Irwin, who joined the KGW announcing staff in the mid-1930s, was the *Covered Wagon Days* announcer.

Another major KEX program of the period was *Homicide Squad*, a precursor of the famous *Dragnet* television program that debuted in 1949. A Monday night offering, *Homicide Squad* was a major studio production with a full orchestra and a sizeable cast. One of the program's distinguishing features was its opening signature scream. Actor Ron Myron recalled it thus:[34]

| | |
|---|---|
| Announcer: | The Homicide Squad is on the air. |
| Woman: | No, no. Don't shoot. Don't shoot. |
| Woman: | (Blood curdling scream) |
| Announcer: | The murder has been committed. |

The scream was done by either Barbara Bird, Edris Morrison, Peggy Williams or Isobel Errington, who was particularly known for the blood-curdling quality of her scream.[35] Errington later married *Oregonian* associate editor and Hoot Owls co-founder Ronald Callvert.

Newly joining KGW-KEX in 1938 as the stations' promotion manager was H. Quentin "Q" Cox, who would later become prominent as the station's general manager (see chapter 13).

A major event for both KGW-KEX occurred in February 1938, when the stations installed RCA transcription recording equipment. No practical system for recording radio programs had existed until 1934, when a system was developed using 16-inch recording blanks. Cut on a recording lathe, each side of a record held about 15 minutes of programming, and these "instantaneous recordings" could be immediately replayed. Since networks did not allow the broadcast of prerecorded material, this system (which NBC referred to as its "Instantaneous Reference Recording" system) was used to provide copies for sponsors and performers as well as to be retained for legal purposes.

Perhaps because of the period when NBC owned KEX, and the personnel swap of Allen to KGW at the time of KEX's sale, NBC and KGW-KEX maintained an unusually close relationship. Not only did KGW-KEX originate considerable programming for the NBC Red and Blue Networks, but KGW became well-known as a stepping stone to NBC employment. Perhaps that contributed to KGW-KEX's assembly of a stellar personnel roster during the 1930s.

The station's announcers, such as Archie Presby, Ralph Rogers, Frank Hemingway and Phil Irwin, were consummate professionals. Hemingway, who had started at KBND Bend and then moved to KAST in Astoria, was a KGW-KEX mainstay before moving to a network career in Los Angeles. One of his signature programs on KGW-KEX, and later on an NBC Blue regional hookup, was a news program sponsored by Tillamook Cheese. The voice of Folgers Coffee in later years, he was still being heard on the ABC Radio Network in the mid-1970s. Phil Irwin came to KGW from the training program at the Portland Civic Theatre Academy, where he had been coached by Ron Myron, and was a widely loved and respected KGW staffer until his death from leukemia in 1950 (see chapter 11).

Another KGW-KEX star, Mel Blanc, "graduated" from the Hoot Owls and tried out the big city of Los Angeles—but he returned to Portland, where he began a quirky, eccentric and spontaneous program on KEX called *Cobwebs and Nuts*. With significant help from his wife, Estelle, the program proved enormously successful and eventually moved from KEX to the more-prominent KGW. Ultimately, Hollywood again beckoned, and Blanc left KGW-KEX for good in 1935.

It was truly a golden age for KGW-KEX.

## KTBR and KFJR Become KALE

KTBR stationery letterhead, early 1927

KTBR began in the M. E. Brown Radio Shop, with its six bronze antenna cables impressively strung between two masts on the shop's roof. By 1927, the station was operating from studios in the Commodore Hotel at 16th and Morrison Streets but broadcasting an intermittent schedule due to its time-sharing obligation with KFJR. While KTBR offered church services, it specialized in sports coverage and boasted the exclusive contract for carrying the Pacific Coast League baseball games and hockey games from the Portland Coliseum. It was also the "appointed official station of the Oregon State Motor Association (the AAA of Oregon) giving out reports of road conditions each evening."[36]

In its January 1928 FRC license renewal, the station proudly included the Northwest Radio Listeners' "Results of Straw Vote on Portland Stations," which reported that KGW, KTBR, KOIN and KFJR were respectively the first, second, third and fourth most popular Portland stations.[37] Some months later, on March 3, 1928, the FRC granted Brown's application to raise KTBR's power to 500 watts, although the station was still sharing 50 percent of its air time with KFJR.

Following these somewhat promising developments, the Depression hit KTBR hard. By the spring of 1932, the station was seriously in arrears and was operating under an attachment by its creditors. By then, Brown was characterizing KTBR as having "never been a financial success."[38] At the same time, KXL had observed KTBR failing and had prospectively filed an FRC application seeking KTBR's frequency. Not surprisingly, Brown was actively exploring emulating Meier & Frank's sale of KFEC and the possibility that someone might purchase the station and relocate it outside of Portland. Before anything along those lines matured, however, a conversation arose between Brown and C. W. Myers of KOIN and the *Oregon Journal*.

KTBR was in sad shape, and the equipment, which had cost over $17,000, was only worth $5,361 by 1932. The station owed $9,000, and its monthly expenses outstripped revenue by 27 percent.[39] Brown was happy to sell KTBR lock, stock and barrel to KOIN's owners for $9,000—all of which went go to his creditors, save for the $1 that went to Brown. The new owners (officially incorporated as KALE, Inc.) requested the new call sign KALE—Yiddish slang for "money," which provided a humorous counterpart to KOIN.

In December 1932, KALE relocated its studios, which had been in the Weatherly Building, to the KOIN's Heathman Hotel studios. On November 3, 1933, KALE began broadcasting programs from both the Columbia and Don Lee Networks that had previously been carried on KOIN. This freed KOIN air time for the locally originated music programming in which the station specialized. In 1934, Theodore Kooreman became KALE's general manager.

While Ashley C. Dixon Sr.'s KFJR had been prominent in its earlier years, it ultimately failed to maintain a leading role in Portland radio, its fate seriously compounded by a Dixon family tragedy.

Dixon Sr. and his young son, Ashley C. Dixon Jr., had been jointly involved in KFJR since the station's inception in Montana (see chapter 4). The younger Dixon carried major responsibilities at KFJR, and his father doubtless anticipated that he would eventually take over the station. But those plans were shattered on July 22, 1928, when Ashley C. Dixon Jr. was killed in the family home when a revolver he was cleaning accidentally discharged. Dixon came home to find his 21-year-old son dying on a bloody living room floor. Ashley C. Dixon Jr. died in an ambulance en route to the hospital. The tragedy likely contributed to the Dixons' divorce early in the 1930s.

Also likely due to his son's death, Dixon left the Hoot Owl Degree Team in 1928. Dixon carried on at KFJR well into the 1930s, capturing off-network programs such as *Little Orphan Annie* when it left NBC in 1934 and developing local efforts, such as the *Oregon Journal Juniors* program. Yet, it seems likely that the changes in his personal life must have contributed to his decision to sell KFJR in 1936.

Prior to 1936, KALE had been sharing time with KFJR, but that arrangement ended on November 18, 1936, when Kooreman engineered the purchase of KFJR and combined the stations. The most important result was joining their time-sharing allocations, which made KALE full-time on the 1300 KHz frequency. The station adopted the slogan "Portland's biggest little station."[40]

Although KFJR's license was deleted effective with the sale, Dixon remained in radio. KALE's purchase agreement either formally or informally included a provision that Dixon would work for KALE, where he remained an announcer for many years. Occasionally also working as a sales executive, his *Luncheon Concert* program celebrated its 15th year on the KFJR/KALE schedule in 1942.

In 1937, Roy Hunt became KALE's manager and remained in charge until his death on May 22, 1942. On September 26, 1937, the Mutual Broadcasting System made its northwest debut on KALE—along with 11 other affiliated stations—over the Don Lee Broadcasting System's lines. KALE's becoming a full Don Lee affiliate allowed KOIN to once again become a full CBS affiliate. In early 1938, KALE raised its power to 1 kilowatt, and by December 1939, the station was using the slogan "KALE-The Journal" while KOIN was using "KOIN-The Journal."

A successful KALE had been formed from the foundations of some of Portland's pioneering stations.

## Harry Read Sells KXL

KXL had signed-on in 1926 and survived its troubles from 1929 to 1930 when the FRC believed the station had used unauthorized power. Still, KXL had to share its nighttime broadcasting rights with other stations, and Harry Read doggedly, but largely unsuccessfully, pursued both higher power as well as exclusive nighttime rights. KXL filed seemingly endless such requests to no avail. Ensconced in its longtime Multnomah Hotel home, with its flat-top antenna gracing the hotel's roofline, the station remained active in the community and continued to offer frequent remote broadcasts—doubtless aided by Read's subterranean audio routing system (see chapter 5).

KXL's Tom Symons at the mike, c. 1940

KXL's success also brought success to Read, who was being depicted as a tycoon in the local press by 1936. Yet, Read's adventuresome nature still summoned him to climb new mountains. His attention turned toward Salem, and he began planning a new station, KSLM, for Oregon's capital (see chapter 10). The Depression years were tough on the nation and Oregon, and Read likely was also thinking it might be time to cash out of KXL. Shopping for a buyer, he settled on Ed Craney and Thomas W. Symons Jr., who had been partners in the broadcasting business all the way back to their 1922 start in Spokane, Washington. Craney, a resident of Butte, Montana, had been long-time owner of KGIR in that city. Symons, a resident of Spokane, was the principal stockholder of Symons Broadcasting Company, long-time licensee of KFPY, Spokane. Read was in a position to dictate who KXL's new owner would be, since he owned 88 percent of the company's stock, and the new owners took over in 1937. [41]

## Prosperity Clubs

Harry Read negotiated selling his KXL stock to the two men for $20,000 but, in the midst of the negotiations, Read again got himself into a scrape. In the tough economy, Portlanders had begun participating in "prosperity clubs," which were described in news accounts as chain-letter brokerages that allowed parties to invest varying amounts of money and charged a brokerage fee for each investment. As many as a half-dozen such operations sprang up in the city as hopeful Portlanders invested in anticipation of huge returns. Payoffs were supposed to occur within days or weeks, but press accounts soon began to report on gulled individuals who were wondering where their money had gone.

On May 12, 1935, when a new chain calling for a $100 investment sprouted up with a half-dozen new clubs, the Portland Police arrested the operators and charged them with running a lottery. [42] The problem was that KXL had been airing advertising for nine different prosperity clubs, and neither the FCC nor local officials were amused. KXL's license renewal application was designated for an FCC hearing.

Read explained that he was out of town when his staff members had accepted the advertising accounts on a Saturday and that on his return on Monday he promptly consulted with his business attorney who assured him the announcements were legal. The next day, Read said he consulted his FCC counsel, John C. Kendall, who advised him to immediately take the announcements off the air, which he did.

The investigation of the prosperity club issue involved many of the same FRC/FCC staff members who had labored through Read's earlier imbroglio over unauthorized transmitter power. It must have had a déjà vu quality for them. Since Read's application to sell his KXL stock to Craney and Symons was before the commission—concurrent with KXL's pending license renewal—it was obvious that the sale couldn't go forward unless the prosperity club issue was resolved and KXL's license was successfully renewed.

The commission held a hearing on these issues at which KXL was defended by John C. Kendall, this time joined by Ben S. Fisher, who had gone into private practice. Once again, Read got off the hook and, in renewing KXL's license, the commission generally praised KXL's overall record. Read's application to sell his KXL stock to Craney and Symons was also approved and the two took over on May 11, 1937. The Symons-Craney partnership slowly augmented the station, which then applied for a change in frequency—from 1420 KHz to 750 KHz—and a significant increase in power to 10 kilowatts daytime only. Symons, however, suffered a fatal heart attack on October 12, 1941—two weeks before the power increase was implemented (for a continuation of the KXL story, see chapter 15).

## KVAN Signs-On in Vancouver, Washington

KVAN of Vancouver, Washington, originated under a partnership between Walter L. Read (Harry Read's older brother) and Sheldon F. Sackett. Read had become acquainted with Sackett, publisher of the *Coos Bay Times* (now the *Coos Bay World*), when Read owned/managed KOOS in Coos Bay. In 1938, Walter Read sold KOOS to Sackett. By that time, they must have already discussed Read's next project because shortly thereafter he filed an application—which was approved by the FCC on November 1, 1938—for a new station in Vancouver in which Sackett was a participant. Filed in the name of the Vancouver Radio Corporation, KVAN was essentially a Portland station in terms of signal coverage and population served, and it eventually located both its studios and transmitter in Portland.

KVAN stationery letterhead, c. 1943

Walter Read entered the Vancouver arena with an impressive resume. Following work with his brother, at Harry's KXL in 1926, he spent four years in Seattle radio before returning to KXL around 1931. KOOS was then managed by Wallace Brainard, who left for KIEM Eureka in 1933, at which point Walter Read went to Coos Bay and took over as KOOS' manager. In 1936, he purchased the station from its owner, Harold Hanseth, and after selling KOOS to Sackett in 1938, pursued his Vancouver project (see chapter 10).

KVAN signed-on October 30, 1939, with 250 watts on 880 KHz and the station's official dedication was held on November 19, 1939, with Read as the general manager. KVAN had already established an association with the Vancouver *Sun*, and the newspaper favorably covered its activities. As publicly announced, the station's initial staff included:

- ‹ Walter L. Read, owner-manager
- ‹ Paul Spargo, technical supervisor and assistant manager
- ‹ George Volker, sales promotion
- ‹ Stuart Stockenburg, announcer/newscaster
- ‹ Ray Baty, sales promotion
- ‹ Forest Kleinman, sales promotion
- ‹ Leon Crager, program manager/chief announcer
- ‹ S. W. "Bill" McCready, commercial manager.

While press accounts identified Walter L. Read as KVAN's "owner-manager," the actual situation seems to have been more nuanced.

# Sheldon F. Sackett

Read's partner in KVAN, Sheldon F. Sackett, was a visionary, charismatic figure. According to later KWJJ owner Rod Johnson, Sackett's personal motto was "Don't think ant, think elephant."[43] Widely respected, his tremendous energy often propelled Sackett to the professional grand gesture—but he was also a troubled man.

Sackett began his newspaper career as a reporter in McMinnville, and in 1928 purchased Salem's *Oregon Statesman.* The acquisition began a long string of newspaper purchases.[44] In reporting Sackett's 1968 death, the *Oakland Tribune* observed that he "bought newspapers the way some people collect antiques."[45]

A man of deep political conviction, Sackett was unambiguous about expressing his views. Endorsing Herbert Hoover in 1932, Sackett—

*Sheldon Sackett, 1947*

still registered as a Republican—became an "FDR Democrat" and a solid Roosevelt supporter. On May 8, 1930, he took over control of the *Coos Bay Times,* which he owned until his death. Propelled by Sackett's boundless energy, the *Times* became an extremely influential Oregon paper, as well as a highly personal one. During his 1959 divorce proceedings, for example, the paper ran huge close-up photographs of Sackett's bare legs in an attempt to secure a delay in his court appearance based on a medical condition.

Suffering from mental illness for much of his life, Sackett would likely today be diagnosed as manic depressive. One writer has said, "during one period he would be sensitive, almost shy. Then, he would turn flamboyant and arrogant."[46] In his manic phases, he was wildly expansive, developing grand plans to purchase newspapers, radio stations and even entire radio networks. In the reciprocal depressions that followed, he would be at best introspective and at worst largely disconnected or vacant. In one of his later expansive phases, he purchased radio station KROW San Francisco, after having acquired the weekly Oakland *Olympic Press* just days before.[47] Likely during a similar phase lasting several weeks in 1944, he:

- ❧ purchased the Vancouver, Washington, *Sun* newspaper
- ❧ bought a Portland weekly paper (also named the *Sun*)
- ❧ placed a $1 million down payment on a Portland printing plant
- ❧ acquired the aging *Seattle Star* for $400,000.

That expansive burst was short-lived. As *Time* magazine observed: "Three months ago, Oregon publisher Sheldon F. Sackett was expanding like a pigtailer's wad of bubble gum but, by last week Sheldon Sackett was pinched for cash. He hastily unloaded the Portland weekly and implored Smith Davis, the Cleveland newspaper broker, to take the *Seattle Star* off his hands."[48]

In 1950, Sackett made news when he again purchased—for $150,000—the building and presses of the defunct *Seattle Star* and announced plans to establish a new Seattle daily newspaper, the *Seattle World.* In 1952, he announced plans to file TV station applications for Walla Walla and Medford. But like many of his other pronouncements, action failed to follow. In

*Van Koover*

Van Koover
cartoon used as
a logo by KVAN,
mid-1950s

1953, Sackett made national news when he stepped forward to rescue the foundering *Los Angeles Daily News.* A week later, the deal was in shambles and was ultimately aborted. Sackett's peripatetic career was strewn with such purchases, announcements, successes and failures.

It is now hard to say just whose vision conceived KVAN. Vancouver Radio's original FCC application listed Sackett as president and 50-percent stockholder in the corporation. While the FCC granted that application, which reported that the corporation's financing derived from stock equally subscribed by D. Elwood Caples and Sheldon F. Sackett (who had each supposedly purchased 25 shares for $5,000 and subscribed equally to another 150 shares to be issued subsequently), in fact each man had only purchased 11 shares. Caples then sold 60 shares to Read for $6,000 on December 17, 1938, shortly after the FCC approved KVAN's construction.

Because the stock that had been subscribed hadn't been fully purchased, the company lacked funds, and Read personally loaned the station the money it needed for construction in 1939. When Sackett was called upon to pay his subscription, he instead entered into an agreement to sell Read his total shares in Vancouver Radio Corporation for $2,500 plus assumption of the $7,000 subscription for shares that Sackett had never fulfilled. It was those transfers of stock to Read that triggered Vancouver Radio Corporation's required filing of an FCC application to transfer control of the corporation from Sackett to Read.

These complex transactions caused the FCC to question whether Read had been the real party in interest in the original 1938 application it had granted or whether Sackett had essentially used Read as his agent and concealed that relationship from the commission. It proved easier to avoid the discussion, and on advice of Vancouver Radio Corporation's attorney, Ben S. Fisher, the application for transfer of control was withdrawn on September 19, 1940. Thus, while press accounts of KVAN's inauguration all refer to Read as owner-manager, his ownership of the station at the time must have been fractional at most. The title seems to have referred more to the appearance of ownership than actual fact.

At the same time, KVAN's real ownership was further confused by the station's announcement on October 9, 1940, in the Vancouver *Columbian,* that Sackett was purchasing the station from Read and that Read was leaving KVAN "to enter another field of radio."[49] Although the announcement may have only been an attempt to report Sackett's purchase of Read's stock, it was also the signal for Read's departure from the station.

Concurrently, Sackett assigned his KOOS manager, Ben E. Stone, to assume KVAN's general management responsibilities and exercise his authority from Coos Bay. Under this arrangement, S. W. "Bill" McCready continued as KVAN's commercial manager under Stone's supervision.[50] This absentee management continued until 1942, when McCready became KVAN's on-site general manager.

When KVAN signed-on, it operated from studios in the Evergreen Hotel, and the station's 880 KHz frequency prompted its use of the slogan "At the Center of the Dial." In 1945, the station changed frequency to 910 KHz and moved to the Clark County Bank Building with Fred F. Chitty succeeding McCready as general manager. One of the announcers during this period was Don Rickles, who later moved to KGW and eventually to NBC in Hollywood.

During the 1950s, Sackett attempted to enter the Portland television market and applied for channel 21, as KVAN-TV, in 1952. Given the struggles of UHF television, he later unsuccessfully attempted to transfer his construction permit to channel 3 but, as his broadcasting affairs were winding down in the late 1950s, he abandoned that effort.

Sackett owned KVAN until 1959, but by then, his best days were behind him. The always-colorful Sackett called a press conference at Portland's Benson Hotel to announce KVAN's sale. Walking in coatless and shoeless with a "fistful of telegram carbons, he stared fiercely at [the press]. 'Wayne Morse,' he called out. 'Didn't come,' he mumbled, throwing the wire on the floor. He did the same for twenty other celebrities, none of them present. Then he sat down and announced that the station had been sold for a half-million dollars to Don Burden (see chapter 23)."[51] Portland newspaper columnist Doug Baker described the 1959 party held to announce KVAN's sale saying: 'Everybody who ever had been anybody was there…a complete collection of has-beens…. Even then, Sheldon Sackett was living in the past…The only ones he could attract were has-beens."[52]

## Willie Nelson

One of the last notable moments of Sackett's KVAN ownership was the station's hiring of future country-and-western star Willie Nelson.

Really a musician, it was music that first brought Nelson into radio. He was still in high school when Bud Fletcher, who regularly booked him for performances, arranged for Hillsboro, Texas, station KHBR to hire him. Nelson thought it was the ideal situation—he was getting paid to play and sing on the radio and had a following. After high school graduation and an Air Force tour, Nelson got married, became a father and started working at KCNC Fort Worth, Texas, to pay the bills. Money was tight, and unable to afford his own home, he brought his family to Portland to live with his mother-in-law. He also took a job at KVAN "making a living [in radio], more or less and playing music on weekends."[53] KVAN promoted his arrival by saying that Nelson had come to Oregon "lock, stock and barrel" and that he "liked the rain" in Portland-Vancouver. Hosting

KVAN ad for Willie Nelson's *Western Express* program, 1959

the station's afternoon *Western Express* "Texas Willie Nelson"—as he was known on KVAN—was heard from 2:30 to 3:30 p.m. Monday through – Saturday with "the best country music."

While working for KVAN, Nelson reportedly made his first recording—*No Place for Me*—in a Portland garage. He also reportedly wrote the Christmas song *Pretty Paper* while at KVAN.

It was a chance meeting during Nelson's time at KVAN that sparked his meteoric career. Mae Axton, mother of singer Hoyt Axton, was assisting Colonel Tom Parker—who had just taken over as Elvis Presley's manager—in artist promotion. One day, she stopped by KVAN to be interviewed by Nelson, who followed her into the station lobby after her on-air appearance. She later reported that when he played some of his music, her jaw hit the floor. "If I could write half as well as you, I'd be the happiest woman on earth," she told him. She advised him to immediately get out of radio, go back to Texas and concentrate on his music career.[54] After six months at KVAN, neither the money nor the conflict between his weekend gigs and radio were working out—so Nelson following Axton's advice and returned to Texas to make his way.

(Because there have been three different radio stations that all used the call sign KVAN at different periods, sometimes on more than one occasion in their life, the KVAN call sign can be confusing. In the interest of simplicity, we'll henceforth refer to the station described in this chapter as KVAN #1. The KVAN#1 story continues in chapter 23.)

# Endnotes

1. Singletary, *Radio Station KOIN: A Case Study of Music Programming*, 32.
2. "Pacific Coast Echoes," *Radio Digest*, December 1932, 43–45.
3. "KOIN-Portland Fans Helpful," *Radio Digest*, April 1932, 58.
4. Information regarding KOIN programs fed to DLBS and CBS from Singletary, *Radio Station KOIN: A Case Study of Music Programming*, 38–39, 57.
5. C. Roy Hunt had caused the Rose City Beavers to be founded New Year's Day, 1928, on his own arrival at KOIN.
6. Craig Adams reports that the Rose City Beavers also had their own program on KXL, at 7:30 p.m., in January 1929 although it is unclear how long the Beavers remained on the KXL schedule.
7. Singletary, *Radio Station KOIN: A Case Study of Music Programming*, 22.
8. Information regarding the musical, and other, KOIN staff early in the 1930s is taken from a 50-day series of staff profiles published by the *Portland News*, in 1930, as contained in an unidentified listener-assembled scrapbook held in the WSMB Collection.
9. Another notable program was a two-hour daily talk show hosted by Janet Baumhover on which the Rose City Beavers would also appear. (Baumhover, Janet. Interview by Nellie Fox. Tape recording. Portland, OR, June 6, 1989. (Portland, OR: Oregon Historical Society collection.)
10. *KGW and the Pacific Northwest: What They Offer the Radio Advertiser* (Portland, OR: KGW Radio, 1930), 3 (WSMB Collection).
11. Elliott Parker (Central Michigan University), "The News Box: Re-evaluating Radio News in the 1920s," (paper presented at the Association for Education in Journalism and Mass Communications Conference, 1996)
12. *Oregonian*, November 21, 1941. In an editorial published on that date, the paper observed: "It is rather pleasant to reflect that The *Oregonian*'s policy adopted sixteen years ago, of news co-operation with radio, has been so widely vindicated in practice and is now accepted by the strongest objector of that day."
13. He followed Haller, Gaylord, Harry Anderson (each of whom served somewhat briefly) and the *Oregonian*'s business manager, W.E. Hartmus, who was responsible for the station for a short period prior to Heitmeyer's appointment. (Platt, *KGW—Portland's Pioneer Radio Station*).
14. Truitt, Rollie. Interview conducted for KGW Radio 50th Anniversary Celebration. Tape recording, Portland, OR, 1972 (Portland, OR: Oregon Historical Society collection).
15. Baumhover, Janet. Oral History Interview by Nellie Fox, June 6, 1989 (Portland, OR: Oregon Historical Society collection).
16. Charlie Hanna, "Behind the Mike," *Oregonian*, December 27, 1986, 7.
17. Ibid.
18. Lampman, Evelyn Sibley. Scrapbook, undated. Special Collections Department, University of Oregon Library.
19. Based upon the Earl Fagan/KEX photo it would appear that the venue was Lotus Island and the promoter was Al Painter.
20. NBS consisted of KJR Seattle, and KGA San Francisco, in addition to KEX.
21. Craig Adams, UBC and NBS: Networks Connect the West, part IV, www.pdxradio.com.
22. Source for most of the paragraph is Craig Adams, www.pdxradio.com.
23. Western Broadcasting Company, Inc., Purchase Agreement for sale of KEX from Western Broadcasting Company to *Oregonian*, Exhibit C—Financial Statement dated August 7, 1933 (KEX file, NARA, College Park, MD).
24. Ibid. Terms contained in the Purchase Agreement, Exhibit D (KEX file, NARA, College Park, MD)
25. Huntley was at KGW in 1936–37 following a career that began at KPCB, Seattle, in 1934. He next went to KHQ Spokane, in 1935 before arriving in Portland. From KGW he went on to Los Angeles, a move that eventually led to his career first with the CBS network, then the ABC network and ultimately with NBC News (David Blair Richardson, *Puget Sounds: A Nostalgic Review of Radio and TV in the Great Northwest*. (Seattle, WA: Superior Publishers, 1981), 72, and Lyle Johnston, *Good Night, Chet* (Jefferson, NC: McFarland and Co, 2003), 20–30.
26. Succeeded by Dave Drummond and Fred White. (White, Fred. 1972. Interview in connection with KGW 50th Anniversary. Tape recording. Portland, OR: Oregon Historical Society).

27. Baumhover interview.
28. By 1926, Hallock and Watson had taken in Roy C. Yonge as a corporate officer involved with their two apparently separate organizations, Halowatt Radio Corporation and Hallock and Watson Radio Service. For a time, the companies operated in two different locations but, in 1929, Hallock and Watson became Hallock-Watson and Yonge and the two companies consolidated locations. Halowatt Corporation was defunct by 1932. While Joseph Hallock remained secretary of Hallock and Watson, by 1933, he was already employed full-time at KGW. By 1936, when Clifton H. Watson had become president of General Lithograph Company, Hallock had left KGW to work for the FCC and their business relationship had ended. (Polk Directories)
29. By 1926 or 1927 Hallock was working, at least part-time, as an announcer at KFJR (see chapter 8).
30. Redman, "Hallock and Watson," *Antique Radio Classified*, June 2006.
31. Details on *Lombardi, Ltd*. from Carrillo, Leo. *The California That I Love*, (Englewood Cliffs, NJ, Prentice Hall, 1961), 194.
32. Hallock left KGW, reportedly in 1935, to work for the FCC and was assigned to the Tampa, FL, Field office. He later was transferred to the FCC's Portland office where he became Engineer-in-Charge in February 1953. (Redman, "Hallock and Watson," *Antique Radio Classified*, June 2006.) He retired from the FCC in 1960 (Hallock, Joseph. 1960. Memo to Chief, Field Operating Division dated July 11 contained in Joseph Hallock scrapbook, WSMB Collection) and died in Lake Oswego, OR, in 1976 ( "Behind the Mike," *Oregon Journal*, February 18, 1953).]
33. Hallock, Theodore "Ted." Interview by author. Tape recording. Portland, OR, October 13, 2004.
34. Myron's legal name was William Myron Cox although he was always professionally known as Ron Myron. (Decision, FCC 54-926, p 12. NARA, College Park, MD).
35. Williams later married Mel Bailey, a future KEX program director (Ted Hallock interview with the author).
36. "Application for Radio Station Construction Permit," Federal Radio Commission application dated September 27, 1927 (KTBR file, NARA, College Park, MD).
37. Ibid.
38. The quoted material, along with the other information provided in this paragraph, comes from an August 31, 1932, letter from C. W. Myers, President of KOIN, Inc. to the Federal Radio Commission (KTBR file, NARA, College Park, MD).
39. Ibid.
40. Craig Adams, www.pdxradio.com.
41. The remaining 12 percent was owned by Erick Houser, John C. Kendall, J. N. Hart and Walter Read. *In the Matter of KXL Broadcasters Consent to Transfer of Control of Corporation*, FCC Docket 4088, May 11, 1937, 2 (KXL file, NARA, College Park, MD).
42. "Chain Letter Broker Faces Lottery Charge," *Oregon Journal*, May 13, 1935.
43. Johnson and Artman, *A Tiger By The Tail*, 108.
44. Sackett made several attempts at establishing partnerships in the Salem paper but they didn't go smoothly. He generally proved unhappy without exercising total control and in 1939 he acquired sole ownership of the paper.
45. "Sheldon Sackett, Publisher, Dies," *Oakland Tribune*, September 2, 1968, ES 55.
46. Joseph Russell Sand, Sheldon *F. Sackett: Flamboyant Oregon Journalist* (MA thesis, University of Oregon, 1971), 3.
47. The KROW purchase price was $250,000. Sackett continued to operate KROW until May 1959, when he sold the station to Gordon McLendon and his father, Barton, for $800,000. McLendon renamed the station KABL.
48. *Time*, Vol. 50, No. 3, July 21, 1947, 68.
49. Vancouver *Sun*, October 11, 1940.
50. McCready had been chief engineer of KXL Portland, in 1935 but was part of the sign-on team at KVAN in 1939.
51. "As Kisn Folds," Francis Murphy, *Oregonian*, September 4, 1976.
52. Sand, *Sheldon F. Sackett: Flamboyant Oregon Journalist*, 92.
53. Willie Nelson with Bud Shrake, *Willie, An Autobiography* (New York: Cooper Square Press, 2000), 83.
54. Ibid., 123.

# 10

# Radio Across Oregon in the 1930s

## KFJI/KAGO Astoria and Klamath Falls

Throughout the 1920s, radio in Astoria had been moderately successful. Following the 1922 fire that destroyed the community's local stations, KFJI had been enthusiastically welcomed in 1923. The small KFJI (originally only 10 watts) survived under the tender care of Liberty Theatre manager/projectionist Ernest E. Marsh. When the station began, Department of Commerce licensing was casual and it wasn't totally clear whether the theatre or Marsh owned the station. Eventually, that was clarified. Marsh owned the station personally, and he did a good job of building its community significance and success.

However, in 1928, KFJI was at a crossroads when Marsh's employer transferred him to Portland. Quickly, he worked out a $500 sale of the station to George Kincaid, who owned Astoria's Kincaid News Service.

A Portland native, Kincaid got his first job in the circulation department of the *Oregon Journal* and later worked for the *Vancouver World* in Vancouver, British Columbia. After leaving the newspaper field for a time, he moved to Astoria, where he opened an agency office for the *Oregonian* in addition to operating an auto freight business, and married Marguerite Schamberger Frost, a member of a prominent local family. Where Marsh appears to have operated KFJI more or less as a side project, Kincaid approached the station with grander, strongly commercial, ambitions.

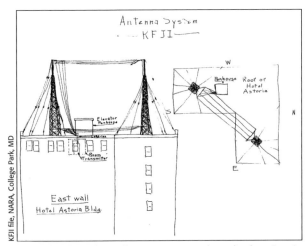

Drawing of KFJI's roof-top towers, and studio location in Hotel Astoria as shown in October 1929 FRC license renewal application.

With Marsh no longer at the Liberty, Kincaid moved the station to studios in the Stokes Building at 12th and Commercial Streets. Later, he moved it to the more prime location of the Hotel Astoria—the community's tallest, most imposing building—where he installed a grand single studio on the mezzanine. On August 19, 1929, Kincaid applied to transfer the station from his personal ownership to a new corporate entity, KFJI, Inc., with Kincaid as vice president and treasurer and his father, J. A. Kincaid, as president.

In 1931, a Federal Radio Commission submission described the KFJI studio as "well-draped and neatly furnished. Microphones, with the exception of one composite condenser microphone, are the carbon type."[1] The station maintained "a number of remote control connections to broadcast church services, theatre entertainments, Chamber of Commerce meetings, dance programs and maneuvers of the Oregon National Guard at Camp Clatsop. The value of the studio furnishings and equipment is in excess of $2,000."[2]

After purchasing KFJI, Kincaid had clearly made a significant investment in expanding its influence. Even today, the station stirs strong memories among some of Astoria's more senior citizens. For example, at 10 a.m. on Saturday mornings, KFJI invited Astoria's children into the studio for the *KFJI Pirates Club*. Children would come either to the Liberty Theatre studios or the Hotel Astoria's elegant mezzanine studios and sing live on the radio. Sometimes, children were required to bring a designated item, such as canned food that was donated to charity, for which they received a ticket to the movie theatre following their radio performance.[3] In 2005, Evelyn Haenkel still vividly recalled the KFJI *Pirates Club* theme song, which she sang on the air with fellow club members each Saturday:

> **KFJI, Astoria Oregon**
> **Pirates Club Theme Song,** *c. 1930*
> (*As recalled by Evelyn Haenkel*)
>
> We are pirates bold,
> As in days of old.
> We're searching everywhere,
> For treasures that are rare.
> If you join us, you'll have to find,
> The keys to kindness and warm sunshine.
> Our chest of treasures like these,
> But you must use the keys.

KFJI seems to have been commercially successful. By 1931, it had six full-time employees, a monthly payroll of $750 to $800 and was producing a monthly profit of between $100 and $150.[4] Notwithstanding this success, Kincaid decided to move the station to Klamath Falls.

Judge John C. Kendall was retained to handle the FRC relocation application, which proposed operating in Klamath Falls on a new 1210 KHz frequency with a power of 100 watts.[5] In that application, Kincaid described his motive for the move:

> During the past year KFJI has endeavored to interest Astoria business men in the use of talent, radio programs and electrical transcriptions in order to eliminate the use of phonograph records as much as possible. We have found it almost impossible to interest them in any sort of program where expense would be one bit greater than where phonograph records would be used. Klamath Falls offers us a much larger field for the production of studio programs and also the opportunity to interest sponsors in presenting high class electrical transcription programs to the radio audience there.[6]

A hearing on the proposal was held on September 28, 1931. Surprisingly, Astorians seem to have been unaware of the proposal, and no objections were raised.

On December 4, 1931, the FRC—acknowledging that KFJI had "rendered a generally meritorious service" in Astoria—approved the move and noted that because of Klamath Falls' larger population, more people would benefit from KFJI in its new location. Kincaid wasted no time and requested permission to cease operating in Astoria on December 14. On December 24, he requested authority to begin broadcasting from Klamath Falls on January 1, 1932.

Given the speed with which the move was accomplished, KFJI must have begun preparing its Klamath Falls studios in the Willard Hotel at Second and Main Streets shortly after the hearing examiner issued his favorable recommendation on October 22. Kincaid scheduled a complimentary New Year's Eve reception and dance at the Willard so that local residents could inspect the station, which signed-on at noon the next day.

And so as 1932 dawned, Klamath Falls' first local radio station had arrived—and KFJI was just a memory in Astoria.

Klamath Falls was excited. On January 9, a local store known as Momyers, signed up as KFJI's first advertiser when it agreed to sponsor *Momyer's Melody Makers* the following Sunday.[7] The station seems to have also brought its *Pirates Club* to Klamath Falls, because a KFJI schedule published in 1934 notes that such a program aired at 4:30 p.m. on Saturday afternoons.

Kincaid's intuition about Klamath Falls proved accurate, and the station was immediately successful. In March 1932, the KFJI schedule featured local programs sponsored by Better Baking, Troy Laundry, Klamath Cleaning, Johnson Grocery, Star Drugstore, Baldwin Hardware, Dunham Auto and Moe's Women's Store among others. The 1934 schedule shows added local entertainment programs sponsored by a long list of local businesses, including LaPointe's women's clothing store, the Klamath Falls Creamery, Balsiger Motor Company and Copco power company. KFJI also carried syndicated programs such as *Cecil and Sally* and *Chandu, the Magician*.[8, 9] Each morning the station signed-on with the *Alarm Clock Program* and frequently broadcast live music from the Palm Café.

It seems likely that not all of the KFJI staff relocated from Astoria. The dapper Dave Morris was KFJI's announcer by mid-1932. In October 1932, KGW's Bill Norvell came from Portland to become KFJI's station manager and worked under Kincaid.

In an enormously ambitious undertaking, KFJI sought to create its own version of the KGW Hoot Owls in the *KFJI Pelican Club*. Following KGW's model, KFJI sought out venerable local citizens to stage the program.[10] Initially broadcast on Wednesday evenings at 9 p.m., the program seems to have moved to the same time on Tuesdays by 1933. Like the Hoot Owls, it focused upon charitable purposes.[11] The program raised about $15,000 for local needy families before its charitable responsibilities were transferred to another local organization in 1935.

KFJI Announcer Dave Morris, 1932

While successful in business, George Kincaid encountered difficulty in his personal life in Klamath Falls. Around 1934, he was divorced from Marguerite and in February 1935 married Helen Criger of Portland. The couple became prominent and well-respected. When his father died on May 20, 1943, Kincaid acquired the balance of the company's shares and became the sole stockholder of KFJI, Inc. Despite this boon, his personal life was unraveling. Within a year, Kincaid began the process of selling the station to Willard D. Miller, a Klamath Falls hotel owner. Several months after Kincaid filed the required FCC license assignment application, Helen filed for divorce in September 1944. While the FCC had not yet approved the sale, Kincaid's ownership of the station he had laboriously moved from Astoria to Klamath Falls was nearly at an end—and so was his marriage.

At 5 p.m. on October 21, 1944, KFJI commercial manager Jack Keating, found an unconscious Kincaid at his Lakeshore Drive home. The 47-year-old Kincaid had ended his life by firing a Luger pistol into his head. He left a note detailing his despondency over personal matters and the coroner ruled his death a suicide.

On January 2, 1945, Kincaid's estate completed the sale of KFJI to W. D. Miller's KFJI Broadcasters, for which Keating continued to serve as commercial manager. Miller had also purchased KWIN radio in Ashland and had a variety of other business interests, including the Maywood Hotel in Corning, California; the Big Meadows Ranch in Marion, Montana, and the W. D. Miller Construction Company in Klamath Falls, in addition to the W. D. Miller Lumber Company in Etna, California. Richard Maguire was secretary of KFJI Broadcasters, as well as KFJI's general manager. Robert McVay was the station's program director (and became commercial manager when Keating left), and Ed Boyd was KFJI's chief engineer.

Miller quickly moved to upgrade KFJI. On February 25, 1946, he filed an application to increase the station's power to 1 kilowatt unlimited time and to change frequencies to 1150 KHz. On March 12, 1946, a large crowd, including local dignitaries, gathered for an open house. They viewed KFJI's newly remodeled and enlarged Willard Hotel studios and danced to the Baldy Evans Orchestra in the hotel's banquet room, where a buffet supper was served following the event.

After another ownership change, the station's call sign was changed to KAGO October 21, 1959. [12]

## KAST Astoria

Astoria was quick to feel KFJI's absence, and senior Astorians still recall the community's sense of loss over the station's departure for Klamath Falls.

The ever-enterprising Wilbur J. Jerman, of Portland's KWJJ, initially sought to fill the gap by forging a relationship with a short-lived Astoria newspaper, the *Daily Messenger.* Together they created *The Voice of the Lower Columbia Newspaper of the Air,* which was added to KWJJ's schedule. The paper reported that beginning April 9, 1933, "every evening, from 6:30 to 7:00 o'clock [sic], there will be a SPECIAL RADIO BROADCAST for Astoria and all of the Lower Columbia Region, via STATION KWJJ [emphasis in original]."[13] The program offered a "Free Service for [newspaper] Subscribers" who could include personal news items, greetings to friends, dedication of songs and special music numbers [and] the use of time on the air by any Lower Columbia Region civic, patriotic or fraternal organization."

While the *Messenger* obligingly printed the full KWJJ program schedule each day, the effort (which continued for much of 1933) was not sufficiently rewarding for either KWJJ or the *Daily Messenger* and was abandoned, as was the newspaper itself, in 1934.

Astoria businessman Abraham Shapiro decided to remedy KFJI's departure. In 1934, the Federal Communications Commission (FCC) superseded the Federal Radio Commission. Shortly after the FCC's formation, Shapiro filed an application to construct a new station using the frequency previously used by KFJI in Astoria.[14] Shapiro, who was 66 at the time of the application, had lived in Astoria since 1922. In 1933, having sold his other business interests (which included a general merchandise store), he possessed the financial capacity, time and interest to construct a new radio station that he estimated would cost $9,000. Shapiro planned to return the station to the Hotel Astoria, albeit with its studios fronting the Commercial Street side, rather than in KFJI's old mezzanine location.

Over 1,200 Astoria community members signed petitions urging the FCC to grant Shapiro's application. It was also endorsed by numerous city councils, civic organizations and local officials. Shapiro's application, however, was opposed by KSLM Salem—which was represented by Judge Kendall—because Shapiro proposed using the same 1370 KHz frequency as KSLM's. While the Salem station had originally been authorized for daytime-only operation, when KFJI departed for Klamath Falls, KSLM had secured nighttime rights by using the coverage previously allocated to KFJI in Astoria. To settle the dispute, Shapiro amended his application, requesting daytime-only. The revised application was readily approved.

Shapiro requested call letters KAST and, with a large photo of the Astoria Column (no doubt to suggest the station's commitment to prominent local involvement), published a small brochure announcing the station's impending arrival. "A New Station Now Opens Up A New Field—Only Station Giving Complete Coverage in the Lower Columbia River Area!," it proclaimed.

KAST signed-on from its Hotel Astoria studios on Monday, July 1, 1935, at 10:30 a.m. with recorded music leading to a three-hour-long dedicatory program that started at 6 p.m. It featured dignitaries who spoke from a Hotel Astoria meeting room and talent who performed in the main studio in the hotel. Astoria once-again had a radio station to call its own.

KAST was highly successful under Shapiro. Having accomplished his major goal of again providing Astoria with a local station, he sold KAST for $8,500 to the newly formed Astoria Broadcasting Corporation on October 1, 1936. Astoria Broadcasting consisted of stockholders Hattie S. Brown (who owned 51 percent of the stock), M. R. Chessman and Ted W. Cooke, who had worked at KORE Eugene since 1931. Cooke and William H. Sandiford were KAST's general manager and assistant manager, respectively. It has sometimes been reported that in 1937, the Astorian-Budget Publishing Company purchased Cooke's stock with a loan from the U.S. National Bank. More likely, it was not the publishing company itself that took control but rather its president, M. R. Chessman, who purchased a large block of the Astoria Broadcasting Company's stock. In October 1937, Cooke and Sandiford resigned, and James C. Wallace, who had previously worked on the *Astorian-Budget*'s advertising staff, became KAST's manager (see chapter 15 for a continuation of KAST's history).

# KSLM – Harry Read Moves to Salem

Harry Read believed Oregon's capital city was ready for a radio station of its own—something it had not enjoyed since KFCD's abrupt demise in 1922. For such a venture, he either needed or desired partners. Forming a new corporation, Oregon Radio, Inc., Read purchased one-third of its stock, his brother Walter (who was then managing KOOS in Coos Bay) another third and John C. Kendall the remaining third. Each party invested $2,500. They applied for 1370 KHz with a power of 100 watts.

At the time, the nation was still operating under a provision of the old Radio Act of 1927 which, in an attempt to equalize access to radio signals, had divided the nation into five zones and allotted spectrum rights to each. The resulting zone frequency capacity quotas were complex, and each new station or change in an existing station's power level had to be accounted for in a way that didn't unfairly benefit one region of the country to the detriment of another.

In order for the 1370 KHz frequency to be used in Salem at 100 watts, it was necessary to convert KOOS Coos Bay from an unlimited 24-hour a day station to daytime-only, and assign KOOS' nighttime rights to the new station. H. H. Hanseth, Inc., licensee of KOOS, approved a resolution to that effect on April 4, 1934, and the FRC then approved Oregon Radio's application on May 22, 1934. KSLM signed-on October 3, 1934.

There is no indication that Hanseth received any consideration for abandoning his station's nighttime rights, although it may be assumed that part of Walter L. Read's contribution to Oregon Radio, Inc., was persuading Hanseth to reduce KOOS's facilities. Conceivably, money changed hands but there is nothing in the Federal Radio Commission files to substantiate that scenario. Alternatively, Hanseth's concurrent development of a new station in Eureka, California, with William B. Smullin, may have been a factor (see KOOS elsewhere in this chapter). Officially, however, Coos Bay's loss was simply Salem's gain.

Harry Read was thinking bigger and subsequently launched the telephone-line-connected Oregon Network consisting of stations KSLM, KOOS and KORE.[15]

Read moved to Salem in 1935 to manage KSLM. Several years earlier, had had married Mary Zorovitsch, and by 1939, Mary Read was listed as vice president Oregon Radio, Inc.[16] Harry and Mary Read divorced around 1942, and at about that time, Read decided to exit radio. In 1943, he sold his shares in KSLM's licensee, Oregon Radio, Inc., to Glenn E. McCormick and Paul V. McElwain for $69,000. McElwain, who had a significant interest in KBKR Baker City at

Courtesy of Salem Electric

KSLM's first studio, 1934

the time, was a partner in Coos Bay's Buick and Chevrolet dealership, Bay City Motors. McCormick, who had been manager of KBKR for two years, assumed the presidency of Oregon Radio, Inc., and McElwain became secretary-treasurer. The formal ownership transfer occurred on March 1, 1944.

KSLM had previously been an affiliate of the Keystone Broadcasting Service, a syndicator who distributed programming on discs. One of the new owners' first actions was affiliating KSLM on March 20, 1944, with the Pacific Broadcasting Company, a regional network owned by Carl Haymond through his station KIT in Yakima, Washington (see chapter 7).[17] Pacific Broadcasting essentially represented Mutual/Don Lee to smaller stations and distributed their programming, as well as Haymond's own, over the Mutual/Don Lee circuits.

With the sale of KSLM, Read formally left radio, although he continued to "hang around" the station according to Blaine Hanks (who joined the KSLM staff in 1946) and Read's adopted son, Bill. By the time Read sold KSLM, he was increasingly devoting himself to establishing Salem Electric, the power cooperative of which he was president at the time of his death in 1948 (see chapter 5).

## KORE Eugene

The story of KORE's birth is inextricably bound up with the confusing transition of interests involving Harold Hanseth, Curtis G. "Shrimp" Phillips, Frank L. Hill, KGEH and KOOS (see chapter 4). By the time the dust settled in 1928, Phillips and Hill had their new station on the air. KORE (standing for **K-ORE**gon) operated on 1500 KHz with 50 watts, initially from the Eugene Hotel.

KORE operated from a variety of locations before the station finally settled into its new studios above Hills Department Store (also known as Hills Economy Store) at 731 Willamette Street. That location, which was owned by Frank L. Hill's father, provided far grander accommodations than the station had previously enjoyed. According to Roger Houglum (a Eugene broadcaster, educator and historian), the new location provided space for a new control room, a "formal" studio suitable for live performances and a transmitter room, as well as office and storage areas.

One feature of these new studios was a carbon-button microphone, commonly used in radio at the time, which required a DC current to function. At KORE, this voltage was supplied by a battery that would periodically run down, forcing the station to sign-off for a half hour until it could be recharged. KORE's transmitter could also be fussy. Don Hunter, then a high school student who took over a KORE high school news program in 1933, recalls the station's chief engineer Harold Gander recommending to him that kicking the transmitter at a precise point was a solution that worked well.[18]

Programming was simple and consisted largely of phonograph records borrowed from McMorran and Washburne's Department Store in exchange for on-air promotional credit. One early station employee believed that, for its first ten years, KORE didn't own a single record—all were borrowed.[19]

Another historian of Eugene radio, quoting Roger Houglum's *Early Day Broadcasting in Lane County*, writes:

> Some of the early [KORE] programming included live talent show remote from the McDonald Theater, a Man-on-the-street interview with George Herbert, wrestling matches broadcast from the Eugene Armory and remote broadcast of U of O football games from Hayward Field with sportscaster Day Foster.

Frank Hill's wife, Violet, took an early role in station programming and operations [including] monitoring station broadcasts for poor musical selection, mispronounced words or other problems.[20]

KORE evolved from a business that was not very profitable and functioned more like a hobby into an increasingly successful enterprise.[21] Along with other emerging small-market stations, KORE affiliated with the new United Broadcasting Company (UBC) on November 5, 1930. When UBC collapsed on April 1, 1931, KORE was left without a network affiliation and remained an independent until it joined the Don Lee/Mutual Broadcasting System on September 26, 1937. During the course of the decade, KORE changed frequencies several times—operating on 1490 KHz, 1500 KHz and then 1420 KHz. In March 1941, KORE switched to 1450 KHz and raised its power to 250 watts.

KORE Observers Lounge, Willamette Avenue Studios, 1937

On April 27, 1937, KORE dedicated its new studios at 2600 Willamette Avenue in a building that had previously housed the Eugene Country Club. The next year, University of Oregon student Dolph Janes came to the station as a part-time announcer and remained at KORE on a part-time basis for the magnificent sum of $10 per week. When Janes graduated and needed full-time work, he took a job at KBND Bend and his replacement at KORE was Duke Young (who later started KFMY-FM in Eugene). Janes returned to KORE as a full-time employee in 1940 and remained at the station until joining the military during World War II. In 1948, following a stint in the hospital recuperating from wartime injuries, Janes returned to KORE as news director. He remained there for many years before taking a senior position at the Oregon Museum of Science and Industry.

Other KORE staff in the early 1940s included station manager Lionel Trommilitz; staff announcer Bruce Nidever; chief engineer Floyd Viken, who replaced Gander; and Laura Plank, who hosted a women's program.

## Herbert W. Armstrong/Radio Church of God

One of KORE's early programs grew to unanticipated proportions. In the early 1930s, the station offered a weekday morning devotional program from 7:45 a.m. to 8:00 a.m. It was programmed by representatives of the local houses of worship, who assumed a weeklong obligation to broadcast. Lining up clerics was apparently proving difficult when Herbert W. Armstrong, who had come to religion at the age of 36 and been ordained only two years earlier, presented himself at KORE in late September 1933 and was quickly given a week's use of the time slot. As Armstrong later observed, "October 9th was surely a great big day in my life—the day of my very first experience before a microphone, ON THE AIR! I took this opportunity very seriously. It was an opportunity to speak to several HUNDRED people at once! I had never spoken to that many before [emphasis in original]."[22]

When introduced by the announcer, Armstrong uttered what became his trademark opening—"Greetings, Friends"—and promptly froze. Struggling through his first five minutes, he gradually gained composure. Following his second broadcast, KORE manager Frank Hill summoned Armstrong to his office and reported that the station had received very positive audience response to his first appearance—something that had never happened with other clerics. Hill suggested that Armstrong take on a regular KORE Sunday morning broadcast and offered to sell him the air time for $2.50 per week, a sum that seemed immense to Armstrong. Soliciting funds on air from those sympathetic to his ministry, Armstrong began his weekly Sunday morning broadcasts in early 1934.

Herbert Armstrong's program steadily expanded to include KXL Portland and KSLM Salem—both stations at that time owned and/or managed by Harry Read— on his Oregon Network.

What began as Armstrong's three-station Oregon hookup further expanded to become the Radio Church of God—later renamed the World Church of God. In 1939, his program was renamed *The World Tomorrow*, following the theme of the 1939 World's Fair. It achieved national network coverage.

Beginning in 1934, Armstrong's magazine, *The Plain Truth*, was launched as an adjunct to his radio broadcasts. In 1946, he relocated his headquarters to Pasadena, California. As television arrived, he added the ABC-TV network to his weekly broadcast schedule. Armstrong's radio broadcasts also expanded to international coverage.

In the early 1960s, son Garner Ted Armstrong, born in Portland in 1930 but largely raised in Eugene, took over much of the broadcast work. His announcing style, modeled after Paul Harvey's, was unique and compelling, but his flamboyant

Herbert W. Armstrong, with his wife, Loma, seated beside him during a radio broadcast, c. 1950.

lifestyle created problems for the World Church of God. His father eventually denounced him for having fallen into "the arms of Satan," and in 1978 both removed him from the broadcasts and excommunicated him. Following Herbert Armstrong's death in 1986, *The World Tomorrow* continued with a replacement pastor until leaving America's airwaves in 1994. And it all started in 1934 at Eugene's KORE.

## KOOS Coos Bay

Harold Hanseth apparently managed KOOS by himself until Wallace E. Brainard, who had a technical background but no previous radio experience, was engaged as manager in July 1931. With Brainard in charge of KOOS, Hanseth was free to pursue other interests, which soon focused on founding a new station, KIEM in Eureka, California, in partnership with Bill Smullin.

KOOS stationery letterhead, early 1943.

As KIEM's construction began, Hanseth apparently "transferred" Brainard to Eureka in 1933, which created a vacancy at KOOS.

Hanseth may have been contemplating selling KOOS, as opposed to again personally assuming its management, when he brought in Walter Read from Portland, who had an extensive radio background (see chapter 5). Read became the KOOS manager around 1934.

Following KORE's release of its nighttime power rights in favor of Harry Read's KSLM, Walter Read purchased KOOS on March 3, 1936, under the name Pacific Radio, Inc.[23] Apparently, Walter's brother Harry was also a minority KORE stockholder during this period.[24] Arriving at KOOS in 1935 was a recent OSU graduate, Stanton D. Bennett, who became the station's chief engineer—a post he retained until 1938.

That same year, Walter Read sold KOOS, by then a 250-watter located on the fifth floor of the Hall Building in downtown Coos Bay, to Sheldon Sackett, who also owned the city's daily newspaper, the *Coos Bay Times* (now the *Coos Bay World*). Walter Read left Coos Bay to pursue developing KVAN in Vancouver, Washington. Following his time in Vancouver, he wound up in Los Angeles as a sales representative for Gates Radio—a major manufacturer of broadcasting equipment. Under Sackett's ownership, J. B. Toles took over as KOOS manager and Ben Stone as program director. An independent station in its earlier years, KOOS joined the Mutual Broadcasting System on June 1, 1938 (see further discussion of Sackett in chapter 9).

## KBKR Baker City

Baker City had not had a local radio station since Sanford Adler abandoned KFDA in 1924. In 1939, 100 watt KBKR was founded by Louis P. Thornton, a Gresham, Oregon resident with no prior connection broadcasting. The station, which was solely owned by Thornton, signed-on KBKR at 1500 KHz, with studios located in the Weil Building at

KBKR stationery letterhead, 1940

2019 Main Street (with the transmitter on H Street near the city limits). Having secured an increase in power to 250 watts and a change in frequency to 1490 KHz on March 29, 1941, he sold the station for $12,000 in June 1941 to the newly-formed Baker Broadcasting Company, which consisted of Paul V. McElwain of Coos Bay and Glenn E. McCormick (who came to KBKR from Eugene's KORE.) The new owners relocated the studio to 1900 First Street. Subsequently, the station was sold to Inland Radio, Inc., which also owned KLBM, La Grande. Lee Jacobs, president of Inland Radio, presided over both stations and, by 1952, the station's studios had moved to 2030 Auburn Avenue.

## KBND Bend

Bend got its first radio station in 1938 when KBND, owned by the *Bend Bulletin*, signed-on December 19 at 1310 KHz with 250 watts. Located in the basement of the Pilot Butte Inn, the station was built by its chief engineer, Stan Bennett, who came to Bend from KOOS and went on to work at numerous stations in the Pacific Northwest. He was assisted by young August "Augie" Hiebert, who came to KBND in fall 1938 from KPO Wenatchee, Washington, for what he later described as "a meager $60 a month which no self-respecting engineer would work for."[25]

In June 1939 when Bennett left to build KFAR Fairbanks, Alaska, Hiebert—who built his first ham radio at age 15—became KBND's chief engineer at a salary of $125 per month. When Bennett asked Hiebert to join him in Fairbanks, Hiebert resigned from KBND, to be replaced by Gene Lovejoy. In mid-August 1939, Hiebert followed Bennett to Alaska, where he pursued a distinguished broadcasting career that caused him to later be dubbed the "father of broadcasting" in that state.

On December 19, 1938, KGW marked KBND's birth with a special on-air salute that included performances by KGW-KEX Ensemble, which performed "Oregon, My Oregon." Palmer Hoyt, editor of the *Oregonian*, and John C. Kendall, the attorney for both KGW-KEX and KBND, also participated in the 7 p.m. dedication program. Signing-on KBND, *Bend Bulletin* editor Robert W. Sawyer spoke for the station:

> We may be pardoned, we trust, for the pleasure we take in the reception given KBND. From all sides the kind messages have been pouring in. From now on KBND will speak for itself but here today we want to express our thanks for all the evidences of friendship that have come to us in this new undertaking. It is our hope that KBND will be made an instrument to service to Central Oregon and it may always merit the good will with which it has been received.[26]

The station, which billed itself as the "Voice of Central Oregon," featured news programming prepared by the *Bend Bulletin* and music offerings such as *Morning Swing, Moods in Rhythm, Hollywood Boulevard, Home Folks Frolic* and *Light Symphony*.

The initial KBND announcing staff included Chet Wheeler and Frank Hemingway, who came to the station with a theatrical background but no radio experience. Hemingway's brother was a Bend physician who knew that KBND needed an announcer, and he encouraged Frank to leave Montreal and apply. Hemingway was hired as a newsman, announcer and sales-

KBND Staff Sign-on Day Publicity Photo, December 1938 (left to right: Frank Loggan, Chet Wheeler, Frank Hemingway, unknown woman, unknown man, Stan Bennett, Augie Hiebert)

From "Airwaves Over Alaska"

person and is remembered for his extreme professionalism, all the more notable since KBND was his maiden radio experience.[27] Hemmingway went on to Portland's KGW before moving to a major career as a network radio announcer (see chapter 15).

KBND joined the Don Lee/Mutual Broadcasting System on March 1, 1944, and was sold to the Central Oregon Broadcasting Company in 1946. The buyer's president, Frank H. Loggan, who had been at KBND since sign-on, owned and managed the station with great distinction for decades. The station moved to 1270 KHz with 1 kilowatt in 1950 and to 1110 KHz on October 2, 1951. By then, the station had ten full-time employees, including program director Kessler Cannon and chief engineer Robert Dickinson. In its 1951 license renewal, the station noted that it "takes particular care in the presentation of broadcasts of public issues to find individuals to represent each side who are thoroughly experienced and qualified in the problem under discussion."

In 1952, KBND moved into its new studios in the Coble Building and in 1958 raised its power from 1 kilowatt to 5 kilowatts (along with another studio move to 5000 Studio Road). While continuing its Mutual affiliation, the station added an ABC Network affiliation on April 26, 1959, but dropped MBS in 1960 and ABC in 1967. Another power increase, this time to 10 kilowatts daytime, went into effect by 1972. The station secured an increase in nighttime power to 5 kilowatts around 1985, but the station was required to operate with a directional nighttime pattern (meaning that a station used multiple towers to achieve a signal pattern that wasn't omnidirectional, and thus provided required interference protection to other existing stations). The station took on a CBS affiliation around 1981.

By 1990, KBND-AM was co-owned with a new FM station KLRR Bend, which had signed-on in 1985 on 101.7 MHz with 8.2 kilowatts. Both stations went bankrupt and were purchased on April 27, 1990, by Combined Communications of Eugene. KBND then switched to a talk-radio format.

## KUIN/KAGI Grants Pass

Grants Pass had flirted with radio since the crystal set days, when the *Grants Pass Daily Courier* expressed a clear interest in the fledgling medium by installing a "radiophone" receiving set in its

A KUIN studio production possibly created in conjunction with the Josephine County Fair. Far right is Ed Malone, long-time KUIN staff member. Others are unidentified.

offices in 1922 in order to listen to news reports. The paper also used what it called a "loudspeaking system" to present local musical talent shows and sporting events to crowds gathered outside the paper's Sixth Street offices.

Amos Voorhies, the newspaper's publisher, was called by some the dean of Oregon newspapermen. He gradually expanded his loudspeaking system to a bunch of "tubes, transformers, condensers, resisters, coils and dials crammed on a three by five foot table" which was used to broadcast events and recruit volunteers for firefighting and other public purposes.[28]

Voorhies seemed fascinated by the loudspeaking system, which was as close as Grants Pass had come to having its own radio station. Thus, when a young William B. Smullin approached him in 1938 about a radio partnership, Voorhies was favorably predisposed.[29] Smullin was aware that Walter L. Read had sold his interest in KOOS Coos Bay to Sheldon Sackett and, that Read had filed an application to construct a new 500-watt station on 1320 KHz in Grants Pass. Smullin, a visionary Stanford graduate, sensed an opportunity.[30]

Smullin got his start in the newspaper business working as managing editor of the *Southwestern Oregon News* in Coos Bay. There, he got his first taste of radio and proposed a partnership to Hanseth, "if they could find something to get into with 'four bits'" (Smullin at that time having only his energy to invest). Initially, nothing came of this approach, but when Smullin was later working in Portland, radio was "still eating at him" and he decided that Eureka, California, should be the site for his first radio venture.

Smullin reconnected with Hanseth, and the two men established a partnership under which they successfully submitted an FRC application to construct what became KIEM Eureka. Hanseth was president of their Redwood Broadcasting Corporation, as well as KIEM's general manager. But KIEM steadily lost money in its early years, which caused Smullin to take over as general manager in April 1937. A year later, he bought out Hanseth and the only other stockholder and then persuaded Don O'Kane and Jack Crothers, publishers of *Eureka Standard* and the *Eureka Times* respectively, to purchase minority interest positions in Redwood Broadcasting.[31]

Smullin must have had expansion in mind when he took in O'Kane and Crothers, because he soon persuaded them to develop media holdings at the "northern entrance" to the Redwood Empire. With an introduction arranged by his partners in Eureka, Smullin approached Amos Voorhies one afternoon, knowing that any venture in which Voorhies was associated would immediately command credibility. Smullin proposed a 50-50 handshake partnership with Voorhies to build a radio station in Grants Pass. It was a relationship that endured for decades.

Securing a Grants Pass frequency required, however, overcoming two competing applications—both of which had been submitted by Walter Read under different ownership structures. Read's ploy in submitting two Grants Pass applications apparently irritated the FCC, which dismissed one of them on technical grounds and the other as redundant of the first.

Still, the Voorhies/Smullin partnership, under the name Southern Oregon Broadcasting Company, had to appear at an FCC hearing to determine whether Grants Pass needed, and could support, a radio station. Voorhies and Smullin both had close Congressional connections, which they used to further their cause along with endorsements from a legion of local supporters they had recruited.

They were successful in convincing the FCC and securing a license. KUIN signed-on December 16, 1939, with 100 watts at 1310 KHz.[32] The station's call letters were taken from the maiden name (Quinn) of the fiancé of John Bauriedel, a Coos Bay native whom Smullin had recruited to radio during the latter's studies at Stanford. Bauriedel, whose assignment was to sign up enough advance advertising to ensure the station's financial success, went on to manage KUIN.

KUIN began with a 17-hour daily broadcast schedule offering programs ranging from "orchestrations and vocal numbers to several drama series, three news broadcasts and a morning devotional."[33] The station also used syndicated transcriptions from the World Broadcasting System, Lang Worth and C. P. MacGregor of Hollywood, California, which included *Stars Over Hollywood*, *Lang Worth's Hillbillies* and the *House of MacGregor* drama program.

J. Edwin Arnold, who joined KUIN on January 1, 1959, went on to manage the station for decades—including its call sign change to KAGI in 1959. The station was donated to Southern Oregon University's Jefferson Public Radio in the summer of 1990.

## KLBM La Grande

There were clear expressions of early interest in radio in La Grande. For example, the *Eastern Oregon Weekly Republican* carried an article on September 30, 1922,

KLBM stationery letterhead, c. 1940

"Union to Have Radio System," which reported upon a radio receiver that was being installed at La Grande's Union Hotel. But Union County had no radio station of its own until 1938, when Harold M. Finlay applied for an FCC construction permit for what would become KLBM (which stood for **K**-**L**and-of-the **B**lue-**M**ountains).

Finlay, a former publisher of the *La Grande Eastern Observer*, brought in chief engineer Charles S. Breeding from Los Angeles to handle technical matters; James "Swede" Carlson came from Weister, Idaho, to assist him, and Barry Turner, from Walla Walla, was KLBM's first program director.

KLBM, the Voice of Eastern Oregon, signed-on at 1420 KHz with 250 watts at 7 a.m. on September 30, 1938, and maintained a close association with the newspaper, through which it had access to the United Press wire service.

The station's studios were located on the second floor of the Sacajawea Hotel at 1402 Adams Avenue, with the transmitter located one mile east of La Grande on U.S. Highway 30. Subsequently, the studios were moved to the Bouvy Building at 1120 ½ Adams Avenue, just up the street. On March 29, 1941, KLBM changed frequencies to 1450 KHz, and a few months later, on November 4, 1941, KLBM was sold for $15,000 to Ben E. Stone (program director at KOOS Coos Bay since 1938). One of Stone's changes was relocating the studios to the transmitter site. Stone, however, only held the station for three years and then sold it to Inland Radio, Inc., in September 1943. Inland, whose motto was "Serving Eastern Oregon," consisted of Marshall E. Cornett, president, and Lee W. Jacobs, general manager. It also operated KBKR Baker City, Oregon.

Kenneth L. Lillard became a major force at KLBM. Having started at KVAN Vancouver, Washington, in 1944, he moved to KLBM in December of that same year. Likely originally an announcer, he was the station's commercial manager by 1949 and by December 1952, general manager as well. He eventually took on both the general manager and program director functions by December 1962. On January 1, 1973, Lillard purchased the station through the company he founded, KLBM, Inc. He launched KLBM-FM in 1977 and later sold both the AM and FM stations on January 14, 1985. Having been at the station for almost 40 years, to many he *was* KLBM.

## KRNR-AM/KSKR-AM Roseburg

KRNR signed-on at 3:30 p.m. on December 11, 1935, with a quotation from the biblical Book of Books: "Canst thou send lightnings [sic], that they may go and say unto thee, Here we are?' Job 38:35."[34]

KVAN stationery letterhead, c. 1943

KRNR was owned by Southern Oregon Publishing, which also owned the local newspaper, the *Roseburg News-Review*, and was additionally connected to the *Klamath Falls Herald and News* and the *Medford Mail Tribune*.[35] KRNR was managed by the paper's J. B. Toles (who came to Roseburg from KOOS Coos Bay). The 100-watt daytime station inaugurated programming with performances by "Speed" Rober's orchestra and Joe Shirey's dance band, presumably broadcasting from the station's Umpqua Hotel basement studios, which were lined with Nu-Wood, a new Oregon-manufactured acoustic wall covering.[36] The studios also featured a grand piano that hinted at the station's commitment to locally created entertainment programming.

The *News-Review* held great hopes for KRNR, which it promised would "sparkle with brilliant entertainment features in addition to a liberal amount of time devoted to ever-popular news broadcasts."[37] *News-Review* editor Harris Ellsworth, who eventually became KRNR's station manager, scheduled himself to host a daily discussion of the news of the day at 4 p.m. called *The Editor Views the News*. The 1500 KHz station, at the very top of what was then the authorized AM band, billed itself as "at the opposite end of the dial from KOAC (whose 550 KHz frequency was at the low end of the AM dial)."[38] KRNR joined the Mutual Broadcasting System on September 26, 1937.

Along with many other stations affected by a national radio frequency realignment, KRNR switched to 1490 KHz on March 29, 1941, and was given permission to raise its nighttime power to 250 watts on September 24, 1941.

At the time of the Pearl Harbor attack in December 1941, Marshall N. Pengra had been promoted to general manager, accompanying the commercial manager assignment he had held since 1938. Gilbert Walters was program director, and Henry J. Chandler Jr. was chief engineer.

After World War II, KRNR moved its studios to room four of the Kohlhagen Building at 134 North Jackson Street, and by December 1949 had also joined the Keystone Broadcasting System transcription network. By then, Leroy Hiatt was KRNR's general manager, and Ralph Smith was chief engineer. Lyle Fenner arrived as program director in 1950 and also handled agricultural reporting under the title of farm director. Bob Grant was both news and sports director, while Max Dick, who later became chief engineer at KXL, held that title at KRNR in 1950.

KRNR partially affiliated with CBS on October 10, 1952, but on losing its Mutual affiliation to KRXL Roseburg, it became a full-time CBS affiliate on August 1, 1953.

KRNR went through a series of staff changes, with H. J. Chandler becoming general manager by December 1955. He was succeeded by Aaron Boe in 1957 and by James E. Doyle in 1959.

On March 1, 1961, KRNR was sold to Douglas County Tricasters, Inc. Robert F. Johnson was president of the buyer, as well as KRNR's general manager. Other officers were Joe Maierhauser, vice president and James H. Johnson, secretary-treasurer and commercial manager.

By 1963, James H. Johnson had replaced Robert F. Johnson, and David A. Coplin was KRNR's chief engineer. The station raised its daytime power from 250 watts to 1 kilowatt by December 1965 and by the mid-1970s had adopted a country-and-western format.

By December 1981, James M. Macke was KRNR's chief engineer. By December 1985, the station had increased its nighttime power to 1 kilowatt and V. Faye Johnson was president, David Weisman was general manager and Ernest T. Evans was program director.

On December 21, 2004, KRNR was sold to Brook Communications, Inc. On June 7, 2008, it became KSKR.

WSMB Collection

Lyle Fenner pictured in a 1956 edition of *TV-Radio Prevue*.

## KMED Grows

While founder Bill Virgin's death in 1928 was a great blow to KMED, his widow, Blanch, quickly took over the station while relying heavily upon William Gates for advice. Gates, who lived next to the Virgins on Medford's Crater Lake Avenue, had been a close friend to both Bill and Blanch and was one of Medford's leading businessmen as owner of the Groceteria Market. Gates helped teach Blanch how to manage a business and remained her close counselor for many years. He also had a tangential relationship to radio through his nephew, Parker Gates, who had founded Gates Radio Company in Quincy, Illinois. With a $1,500 loan from Bill Gates' to his brother, the company eventually became a major supplier of broadcasting equipment.[39] As Blanch Virgin learned the radio business, she also conducted women's programs, served as the station's program director in earlier years, wrote broadcast copy and occasionally announced.[40]

One of Blanch Virgin's closest associates was Gladys LaMar, who was originally a vaudeville and radio performer in San Francisco. LaMar may have had her introduction to KMED when she headlined a January 17, 1927, musical broadcast on the station sponsored by the Medford Realty Board. While a San Francisco radio entertainer at the time, she must have liked Medford and gotten on well with the Virgins, because she began working at KMED later that same year, presumably as a performer. While she returned to San Francisco on January 1, 1928, and had her own programs on KFRC, KPO, KGO, KJES and other Bay Area stations, she returned to Medford in 1934 to serve as KMED's program director at a weekly salary of $60. A close friend of Blanch Virgin's (who referred to her as "Buster"), LaMar remained at KMED until its 1950 sale, after which she retired to Portland and got married.[41, 42] An accomplished pianist, LaMar frequently accompanied musicians on KMED's grand piano.

Lee Bishop had been intrigued by radio ever since he performed as a youth with a band which broadcast in Iowa.[43] At 21, he took a job with the Pacific Fruit and Produce Company in Seattle and was dispatched to the company's Medford office to serve as office manager. But radio still called to him. While in Medford, Bishop wrote to Blanch Virgin asking for a job, even though he had no radio experience.

KMED, "The Voice of a Great Country," was located on the second floor of the impressive, white-tiled Sparta Building at the corner of Riverside Drive and Main Street. But KMED was a

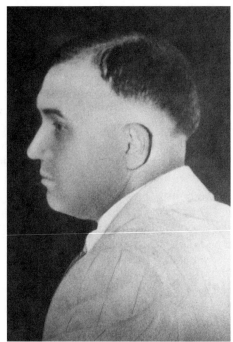

(Left) Blanch Virgin Randle, c. 1930. (Right) In a silent tribute to the station's founder, this photo of Bill Virgin hung on the wall above the KMED transmitter during the station's years in the Sparta Building, c. 1927.

small station that had only one studio and no recording equipment. It therefore had no way of auditioning talent other than by putting someone on the air and listening to the broadcast. A few weeks before the stock market's Black Tuesday crash on October 29, 1929, Bishop was put on the mike while Mrs. Virgin and her advisor, Bill Gates, went to John Dennison's radio shop across the street to evaluate him. Bishop was hired on the spot.[44]

In addition to Virgin and Bishop, the early 1930s KMED staff consisted of chief engineer Floyd Rush, who also had a regular announcing shift; assistant engineer Dave Rees, who had come down from KXL Portland and who also announced; salesman Art Adler; and announcer/public relations director Jerry Jerome. While hired as an announcer, Bishop also soon became KMED's commercial manager.[45]

Describing the early KMED programs, Bishop recalled:

A very interesting morning program [was done] by Glenn Faybrick Sr., owner of the Domestic Laundry, who would come to the studio and do a very good book review, every Monday morning. In the early days, pre-network, we had what amounted almost to a network, and that was the big sixteen-inch transcriptions—and *Ma Perkins*, which was very, very popular, practically stopped work in the Medford area every morning at ten o'clock.[46]

One of KMED's most ambitious local programming efforts was the *COPCO Players*, named after its sponsor, the California Oregon Power Company. The dramas, written by a local female member of the Ames family, used local actors and musicians.

KMED was too small a station to be of interest to the major radio networks such as NBC or CBS. As a result, KMED participated in several sporadic attempts to launch new networks. One such attempt was the United Broadcasting Company Network in 1930 which was anchored from KFWB in Hollywood and included KXL Portland and KXA Seattle. None of these new networks ultimately proved successful, and it was not until 1937 that NBC allowed KMED into its fold. Once an NBC affiliate, the station secured the status and revenue a major network affiliation carried. A curiosity of the NBC affiliation was that KMED needed to bring local listeners up to speed, given the NBC soap operas' character and plot complexities. For several weeks before inaugurating its NBC service, KMED broadcast synopses of the main characters and plot lines.

When Lee Bishop arrived, KMED didn't broadcast on Sundays—"although that soon changed"—and the station began operating from roughly 7 a.m. until 7 p.m. the other six days unless special event coverage dictated later operation.

Floyd Rush, also associated with KMED's predecessor station, KFAY, had been KMED's chief engineer since the station's 1926 sign-on. As the 1930s dawned, KMED was growing and Blanch Virgin was again eager to raise its power—a step that was complicated by the station's home in the Sparta Building. While the location had been eminently suitable for KMED when the station signed-on in 1926, the two 85-foot-tall windmill towers placed on the building's roof, with KMED's transmitting wires stretched between them, used a ground system that had serious limitations. In 1931, KMED replaced its 50-watt Westinghouse transmitter with a 100-watt model designed and installed by Rush—but the growing station had stretched the limits of the Sparta Building location to capacity.

The 100-watt transmitter had to be crammed into KMED's Sparta Building studio—rather than in the control room—and the heat it produced was often a problem. Windows had to be opened during warm weather, and when the city's fire station siren—which was mounted on a power pole next to the building—sounded, announcing was all but impossible. The transmitter could also be fussy, and guests were warned not to touch the front panel, which could impart a hefty shock.

Besides raising its power, KMED was growing in other respects and, had expanded to fill much of the Sparta Building's second floor by 1931.[47] Virgin wanted the expanded studios to make a

KMED's Sparta Building control room, mid-1930s.

KMED in the Sparta Building, c. 1932. The station's studio area eventually consisted of five windows on the left, beginning with the fourth from the left-most window.

KMED's Sparta Building studios featured elegant Chinese decor. The technical plant was similarly grand. Note the traveling boom-mounted condenser microphone, which could easily be adjusted to pick up performance groups of different size. A condenser microphone was state-of-the-art and not frequently found in smaller-market stations in 1931, the approximate date of this photo.

(Left) A KMED studio production, c. 1931
(Right) KMED's initial transmitter installation on Ross Lane, 1933

statement about KMED's growing influence, and she remodeled the studios in a stylish Chinese motif—which everyone thought elegantly reflected the station's growing success.

In 1933, Blanch Virgin again wanted to raise KMED's power, and with the Sparta Building's capacity exhausted, the station began exploring new locations for the transmitter plant. Floyd Rush left KMED in 1932, resigning in a fit of pique with the unfulfilled expectation that Blanch Virgin would quickly plead for his return.[48] His ploy failed, and Virgin immediately appointed Dave Rees to succeed him. Rees located land on Ross Lane that, according to Gerry Latham (later the *Medford Mail Tribune*'s publisher) had the highest water table in the entire valley—a highly desirable feature that would boost a station's coverage. Virgin purchased the property, and in 1933, KMED installed a new 250-watt transmitter—designed and built entirely by Rees—at the new Ross Lane site. While the Sparta Building's towers were removed, KMED's studios remained there until 1941.[49]

## One Man's Family

Another result of KMED's NBC affiliation was its ability to broadcast *One Man's Family*, arguably the most influential radio soap opera ever developed. Originating from NBC's San Francisco Sutter Street studios, the program began in disc syndication in April 1932, jumped to NBC's West Coast Network a month later and graduated to the full NBC Network in May 1933. It was the first program originated on the west coast to be heard nationally. Unlike most soap operas, *One Man's Family* was broadcast in the evening, and like television's *Dynasty*, became a mega-hit. The program was influential, enormously

Cralton E. Morse with some of his *One Man's Family* scripts in a promotional photo.

profitable and extremely long-lived—remaining on the NBC radio schedule until 1959.

The Peabody Award-winning *One Man's Family* was the brainchild of writer/director Carlton E. Morse, whose father owned land in Jackson County and for whose family Ashland's Morse Avenue is named. Carlton, who considered the program to be a family drama (as opposed to a soap opera), spent his teenage years in Ashland and Talent and wrote many *One Man's Family* episodes in southern Oregon while visiting family.

## KMED—New Quarters in 1941

KMED again wanted to raise its power in 1941, and the station broke ground for a new combined studio and transmitter plant on Medford's Rossanley Drive near the transmitter building the station had used since 1933. According to Rees, the new building, which was constructed by a Mr. Whiteside, was designed in *art moderne* style by Blanch Virgin. "That's what she wanted. That's the way she pictured it in her own mind," Rees said.[50] Rees installed KMED's new 1 kilowatt transmitter in the station's new quarters, and KMED signed-on from its new location in March 1941.

KMED studio-transmitter building in the mid-1940s

Courtesy of the Southern Oregon Historical Society, photo 15242

## Endnotes

1. Quoted material from "Statement of Facts, Grounds for Decision and Order of the Commission," Application of KFJI Broadcasters, Inc., for construction permit (to move to Klamath Falls), Docket 1264, December 4, 1931 (KFJI file, NARA, College Park, MD).

2. Ibid.

3. Haenkel, Evelyn, and other Astoria residents. Interview with author. Tape recording. Astoria, Oregon. July 13, 2004.

4. Application of KFJI Broadcasters for construction permit (to move to Klamath Falls), December 4, 1931, 2.

5. The station originally proposed operating on 1370 KHz in Klamath Falls, but during the relocation hearing process, amended its request to 1210 KHz (the frequency that was finally approved).

6. Application for Radio Broadcasting Station Construction Permit, Exhibit A, KFJI, Inc., July 13, 1931 (KFJI file, NARA, College Park, MD).

7. *Klamath Falls Evening-Herald*, January 9, 1932, 3. The program featured local talent including Bob Constans (guitar), Roy Larson (viola), Ed Murphy (violin) and George McCoy (ukulele).

8. *Cecil and Sally* was shown as scheduled daily in the station's October 1933 published schedule contained in the KFJI 1934 FRC Application for License Renewal (KFJI file, NARA, College Park, MD).

9. Shown as being carried at 8:00 p.m. daily on the March 1932 program schedule published in the *Klamath Komic Kapers*, March 25, 1932, 6.

10. Prominent in the program were Dr. E. D. Lamb, the Rev. J. Henry Thomas, a former archdeacon of the Episcopal Church. (Sisemore, *History of Klamath County Oregon: Its Resources and Its People*, 429).

11. The Tuesday, October 3, 1933, program was called the *Pelican Charity Program*.

12. Information on J. A. Kincaid's death, the sale to Willard Miller and the KAGO call sign change from Barry Mishkind's www.oldradio.com/research.

13. Advertisement, (Astoria) *Daily Messenger*, April 7, 1933, 6.

14. 1370 KHz both daytime and nighttime.

15. *Broadcasting Magazine*, June 15, 1934, 30.

16. She is first identified as his wife in the Polk's Portland Directory, 1932.

17. The station was originally Meier & Frank's KFEC, Portland, which Haymond purchased and moved to Yakima as KIT.

18. Hunter, Don. Interview with author. Tape recording. Eugene, OR. April 20, 2005.

19. Roger Houglum, *Early Day Broadcasting in Lane County*, 8.
20. Quoted material from www.angelfire.com/or/erg/rewind.html.
21. It is important to note that Phillips and Hill had lost the station to Hanseth in 1928 because they couldn't meet their lease obligations to him on the station.
22. Herbert W. Armstrong, *Autobiography of Herbert W. Armstrong, Vol. 1*, (Pasadena, CA: Worldwide Church of God, 1987), online version at http://www.thetrumpet.com/index.php?page=book&id=1423&section=1558, Chapter 30.
23. Email from Barry Mishkind dated October 15, 2008, reporting transcription of FCC records as the source for this date.
24. Federal Communications Commission Examiner's Report No I-319 Application of KXL Broadcasters for Renewal of License and Consent to Transfer of Control of Corporation, Docket Nos. 3340 and 4088, November 28, 1936, 2. (KXL file, NARA, College Park, MD).
25. In 2005 Hiebert was the first inductee into the Gold Circle of the National Academy of Television Arts and Sciences-Northwest Chapter.
26. "Thank You," *Bend Bulletin*, December 20, 1938, 4.
27. Stan Bennett. Interview. *They Took To the Air*, Washington State Broadcasters Association, Oral Histories, 11.
28. J. Edwin Arnold, *WmB* (unpublished manuscript) (Grants Pass, OR: Smullin Collection, WSMB), 46–47.
29. Early in his career, Smullin used the nickname "Bill" and often signed correspondence in that fashion. To distinguish himself from his father, William B. Smullin Jr. and other another Bill Smullin in his extended family, Smullin adopted "William B," abbreviated as "WmB," as a nickname. He was generally referred to as "William B" by associates, signed memos "WmB" and memos were addressed to him in that manner. However, from this point forward, the author will continue to refer to him as Bill Smullin, the name by which he was generally known in the first portion of his career.
30. J. Edwin Arnold, *WmB.*, 44.
31. Phil Johnson, manager of the Buster Brown Shoe Store in Coos Bay, whom Hanseth had recruited at the outset of planning for KIEM. (J. Edwin Arnold, *WmB.*), 23.
32. The station's call letters were changed to KAGI in 1959.
33. "KUIN Goes on Air 17 Hours Daily," *Grants Pass Daily Courier*, December 16, 1939, 1.
34. "Radio Station KRNR Of Roseburg Flashes Its Initial Program," *Roseburg News-Review*, December 12, 1935, 1.
35. Information taken from an "Opinion of the Legal Department," Broadcast Division, Federal Communications Commission, filed in connection with a 1941 KRNR application to increase power to 250 watts day and night. (KRNR file, NARA, College Park MD)
36. The original licensee of the station, Southern Oregon Publishing Company, was majority-controlled by the News-Review Company. In March 1937, the station was authorized for 250 watts daytime and 100 watt nighttime power.
37. "Fine Entertainment and Daily News Will Feature Broadcasts from KRNR," *Roseburg News-Review*, December 2, 1935, 1.
38. *Roseburg News-Review*, November 30, 1935, 6.
39. Chipman, *KMED: The First Half Century*, 10.
40. Information on Blanch Virgin's radio-related work taken from KMED FCC Application for Modification of License, Exhibit No. 6—Plans for Staffing Station, dated February 4, 1947, filed to secure a daytime power increase from 1 to 5 kilowatts (KMED file, NARA, College Park, MD).
41. Blanch Virgin Randle's nickname for LaMar is noted in an October 15, 1972, letter from the Randles to KMED written in connection with the station's 50th anniversary celebration. LaMar's last name has been spelled in many different ways in press accounts. It is rendered here as LaMar based upon various records including Blanch Virgin Randle's reference to her in this 1972 letter. (Ray Johnson Collection, WSMB).
42 Details of LaMar's career taken from KMED FCC Application for Modification of License, Exhibit No. 6—Plans for Staffing Station, dated February 4, 1947, filed to secure a daytime power increase from 1 to 5 kilowatts. (KMED file, NARA, College Park, MD).
43. Over station WHO, Des Moines, Iowa.
44. Bishop, Lee. Interview with author. Tape recording. October 29, 1993.
45. Adler came to KMED in 1933 (Exhibit No. 6—Plans for Staffing Station, dated February 4, 1947 (KMED file, NARA, College Park, MD).
46. Bishop interview.
47. KMED's studio expansion is recounted in a story in the *Medford News,* December 24, 1948, 1.
48. Rees, David. Interview with author. Tape recording. November 2, 1993.
49. "The Sparta Building, Medford, Nomination Form for listing on the National Register of Historic Places," March 1, 1992, Section 8 (WSMB Collection).
50. Rees interview

# Naked in the Studio: Learning to be an Announcer

# 11

In the 1930s, when most local radio programming consisted largely of live music or drama, radio stations played a remarkably central role in a community's cultural life. Stations maintained strong connections with local musical organizations and theatrical groups, whose members often found either paid or volunteer work at radio stations, who needed such talent on a daily basis.

Yet, local radio programming also required skills for which there was no "minor league" or training program available in most communities. Radio *announcing* was a new type of job, and there were few places where one could train.

In the 21st century, it is hard to appreciate the glamour and esteem that were attached to the new profession of radio announcing. When radio began, announcers were frequently individuals with a modest musical or general business background who were thrown into the studio to give some on-the-air order to the collection of sequential volunteers who passed before the microphones. To prevent these voices from growing too popular and then demanding exorbitant salaries, the early radio industry borrowed a practice from the early motion picture industry—making announcers anonymous just as the stars of early "talking pictures" were not given screen billing. Accordingly, early radio stations often required announcers to identify themselves on-air using only their initials. Yet despite these steps, announcers rapidly grew in prominence. Network announcers, such as Milton Cross, Ted Husing and Graham

The KOIN announcing team, 1931. Announcing was considered a very formal responsibility, and it was accordingly expected that announcers would dress formally while on duty. Top row (left to right): Ron Myron, Johnnie Walker, Billy Sandiford, Gene Baker. Bottom row (left to right): Milton Swartwood, Art Kirkham (chief announcer), Stephen Gaylord (from "In Tune With the West," a KOIN publication.

McNamee became as big stars as the performers they were introducing. Across America, young men wondered how they might join that select fraternity.[1] In short, radio announcing became a distinct, highly regarded profession.

In 1930, the magazine *What's On the Air* described the changing requirements for being an announcer:

> Whereas, a few years ago almost anyone who had the 'gift of gab' was considered eligible for the position of radio announcer, to-day [with the networks and largest stations] the requirements are more severe. A working knowledge of German, French, Italian and Spanish, as well as a fairly complete knowledge of music, must accompany the pleasing voice and pose and presence expected of a master of ceremonies.[2]

Magazines such as *Meet Your Favorite Announcer* were published in the same vein as movie fan magazines. Announcers' fan clubs formed and magazines published ballots so readers could vote for their favorite announcers. It was a high-status, glamorous profession, and the public held announcers in the kind of high regard later accorded airline pilots and astronauts. At all but the smallest stations, it became commonplace for announcers to dress formally, wearing tuxedos for evening broadcasting and often morning coats for daytime work. In probably the best development for the English language that ever occurred in the United States, proper diction and precise enunciation became announcers' obsessions. Given the broad intellectual, vocal and charismatic qualities required, radio announcing—especially at large stations and the networks—became a relatively highly-paid profession.

As radio grew throughout the 1920s and stations no longer broadcast for limited hours unless they had a frequency sharing arrangement, the demand for announcers steadily rose. Where

Group photo of KGW's announcing staff, July 17, 1932: (left to right) Cliff Engle, Bob Thomlinson, Henry Blank, Archie Presby.

earlier a station might have employed a single announcer, broadcasting from early morning to late at night required an entire crew of announcers. In order to establish and maintain proper announcing standards among the three to five announcers that might typically be on staff, most stations appointed a chief announcer, who was expected to be the professional's professional—the final arbiter of standards for diction and decorum. Generally, the chief announcer had the power to make announcing assignments based upon either skill level, "fit" or personal preference. Many radio stations retained staff positions with the title of chief announcer well into the 1970s. But the position's role clearly started to fade as local radio became disc-jockey-oriented and staff announcers were no longer the on-air presiding officers as had traditionally been the case for studio announcers.

But as the 1930s dawned, the need for trained announcers was growing fast. Where could stations find these supermen of the air waves?

In smaller communities, they had to be home-grown. KMED's Lee Bishop was the office manager of a produce distributor—and had no prior radio experience—when he was given a live on-air audition at KMED. He was hired on the spot and trained on the job (see chapter 10).

In Portland, the Portland Civic Theatre stepped into the breach and founded the Portland Civic Theatre Academy. The Civic Theatre, which had itself only been formed through the merger of two smaller amateur theatrical companies in November 1929, established its academy in 1932.[3] Primarily designed to teach dramatic skills to aspiring amateur actors, the academy also developed a series of "radio announcer" courses and offered specific instruction for students interested in this field. The first tuition charge was $3 per semester for any or all classes.

The Portland Civic Theatre Academy helped fill two personnel needs for local stations: actors and staff announcers. Actors such as Janet Baumhover, Edris Morrison, Helen Platt and Ron Myron (who also was an instructor at the academy), all worked steadily at the Portland stations while honing their skills at the Portland Civic Theatre and its academy.[4] In 1972, Ron Myron described how Phil Irwin "was a student of ours in the first Civic Theater School and KGW called up one day, as other stations would do when they needed an announcer and said, 'Do you have any promising material?' We had Phil as a student and he was very promising,

NEW HOME OF THE NATIONAL BROADCASTING CO., INC.
Circled in the center foreground is the NBC studio section in Radio City.

*Radio Announcers* magazine, 1934

so we sent him and he got the job. He had a beautiful voice and he was very serious about it."[5]

Irwin was a Portland radio success story. He quickly rose in stature at KGW, eventually becoming the station's chief announcer. In 1945, Irwin was the recipient of NBC's highly coveted H. P. Davis National Memorial Announcers Award, named for a founding figure in radio. The award proclaimed Irwin as "America's outstanding radio announcer of the year" and the *Oregonian* editorially praised him "the best radio announcer in America."[6] His premature death from leukemia in 1950 was widely mourned and led to an annual charitable effort by KGW and the Portland community to raise funds for leukemia research.

Another notable announcer of the period was Art Kirkham, who got his start in radio at Oregon State University's KFDJ (later KOAC) as assistant announcer. On November 4, 1928, Kirkham joined KOIN, rising to the position of chief announcer by the following September. While earning his degree at OSU and working at KFDJ, Kirkham was deeply involved as a singer in the university's musical activities, including the Glee Club. On arriving at KOIN, Kirkham immediately joined the Portland Light Opera Company, where he was a soloist for several years.

Despite his singing background, Kirkham's duties were solely those of an announcer at KOIN. Occasionally, he also did sports announcing at what would become KOIN's sister-station KALE. Kirkham's most visible project at KOIN was the *Newspaper of the Air,* for which he would select two or three lead stories from the daily paper, in addition to some lesser feature stories, to summarize and read on the air. The program remained on the KOIN schedule for decades.[7] Kirkham became quite popular, and the station published a collection of his essays entitled *This and That* in 1939.

Arthur Rolland "Rollie" Truitt, born in Boulder, Colorado, in 1901, moved with his family to Douglas County when he was quite young. His first encounter with radio occurred when, listening on a crystal set, he heard KGW's Sid Goodwin announcing a Portland Beavers' baseball game. When the Beavers hit a home run, Goodwin's signature phrase was "Oh lady! Oh lady!" and young Rollie Truitt was fascinated. He knew then that he wanted to do what Goodwin was doing. Starting out at KXL in 1926, Truitt began sports announcing when the Beavers' broadcasts moved to KXL in 1928. He was given the play-by-play assignment—the role that had originally captivated him as performed by Goodwin—a year later. When the Beavers moved to

KGW-KEX in 1933, Truitt came along and became a major Portland radio fixture. "What a job for a guy who had never played baseball," he wrote in 1953.[8] At his death in 1972, he was nationally acknowledged as having inspired the career aspirations of numerous well-established broadcasters, including Galveston's Woody Carlson.

Amid such formality, gravity and responsibility, it's not surprising that radio employees sought relief in humor. Like the captain of a ship, announcers were expected to remain totally professional and in complete command under all circumstances. So naturally, their co-workers wanted to challenge their ability to remain focused under fire.

One of the more common in-studio pranks was setting fire to an announcer's script while he was reading it on the air, defying the butt of the joke to both maintain composure as well as read at a clip that allowed finishing the announcement before fire consumed it.

For stations large enough to possess electrical transcription (ET) disc cutters, these 16-inch discs were used both to record programming for delayed broadcast as well as to pre-record commercials. Particularly during World War II, when aluminum (aluminum formed the base of the blank discs to which the recording medium's coating was applied) wasn't available, glass was substituted. These glass discs were fragile and had to be carefully handled. Sometimes after a particularly difficult recording session, or perhaps when a record was being transcribed very close its broadcast time, a control booth prankster would hold up a disc that was broken in half and let the poor announcer sweat over the careless handling that had destroyed the recording. Usually, it was a dummy disc instead of the real McCoy.

More adventuresome types might start to undress a helpless announcer while he was on the air. They might start with his belt, sequentially moving to his shirt, shoes and socks, while the announcer had to control his voice and bodily movements to avoid giving the hint that anything unusual was transpiring. Time permitting, the prankster might continue on to remove the announcer's trousers and….

Also in the embarrassing category, it was not entirely unheard of for a prankster to import a woman into the studio in an abundantly flowing cloak—who was stark naked underneath. The sudden loss of her wrap was intended to break the announcer's concentration and composure—at least fleetingly.

One can imagine the other types of pranks that might have been pulled—and they probably were.

# Endnotes

1. There were virtually no female announcers in radio at the time. It was believed that women's higher-pitched voices were inherently less pleasant for listeners.
2. "Want to be a Radio Announcer?" *What's On the Air*, October 1930, 31.
3. Schilling, Jr., Lester Lorenzo. *The History of the Theatre in Portland, Oregon 1846–1959* (MA thesis, University of Wisconsin, 1961), 429.
4. Platt went on to work for KGW in public relations and was assigned by Dorothy Bullitt, in the mid-1950s, to write KGW's history. Her unpublished manuscript has been extremely valuable to the author.
5. Myron, Ronald. Interview recorded in connection with KGW Radio's 50th Anniversary celebration. Tape recording, Portland, OR. 1972 (Oregon Historical Society).
6. *Oregonian*, October 26, 1945.
7. Material about Kirkham in this paragraph taken from Oral History Interview with Art Kirkham conducted by Glen Meek, January 22, 1980. Oregon Historical Society Collection.
8. Truitt biographical material from Paul Andresen and Kip Carlson, *The Portland Beavers* (San Francisco: Arcadia Publishing, 2004), 44.

# Invasion!
# The War of the Worlds

As one of the nation's larger cities, Portland had a total of seven radio stations in 1938—with each national network having an affiliated station. Smaller communities with fewer stations, such as Eugene and Medford, didn't have an affiliated station for each network, but because there were fewer stations on the air at that time, and AM radio signals travel greater distances at night, listeners in smaller areas received network programming not carried by local stations by tuning into distant ones. To help listeners find those programs, newspapers routinely listed the frequencies of non-local stations such as in the "On the Radio Chains" box, shown on page 176, which originally appeared in the *Medford Mail Tribune* on October 30, 1938.

In order to effectively use the table, listeners had to know that KGW, KOMO, KFI, KPO and KOA were NBC Red stations; KEX, KJR, KGA and KGO were NBC Blue stations; and KOIN, KNX and KSL were CBS stations. The *Mail Tribune* apparently didn't think the Mutual network's stations were worthy of inclusion.

With relatively few radio stations on the dial, and no other sources of instant news, listeners deeply trusted radio's news coverage. In a world without Internet, television or satellite communication, they also had fewer news sources against which to evaluate something heard on the radio.

**ASHLAND** DAILY **TIDINGS**

Vol. LXII.      ASHLAND, OREGON, MONDAY, OCTOBER 31, 1938.      No. 51.

# FANTASTIC WAR BROADCAST; NATION IN PANIC

*Ashland Daily Tidings* headline, October 31, 1938
WSMB Collection

## H.G. Wells' *War of the Worlds,* CBS, 1938

Three thousand miles from Oregon, the Columbia Broadcasting System had recently given over one of its premiere status symbols, the sustaining (meaning a program without a sponsor) *Columbia Workshop* program, to the rapidly rising *enfant terrible* of radio, Orson Welles. Only 24 years of age in 1938, Welles had first made his mark in live theatre before bursting onto the radio scene with great drive and a stentorian voice that was much in demand for both announcing and acting assignments. As the voice of Mutual's *The Shadow* and an actor on numerous other programs, he was often heard live on one program only minutes before his live appearance on another network. His radio performance calendar was so heavily booked that, when he had a tight schedule to meet in New York, he customarily hired ambulances to ferry him between NBC's Radio City and the other networks' studios.

CBS's *Columbia Workshop* had been founded by the brilliant and innovative radio producer Irving Reis. For a sustaining program, it had a significant budget and its charter was to explore radio's artistic boundaries. Capitalizing on Welles' celebrity, upon his arrival CBS had even saluted the repertory company—with whom he had regularly worked in various off-Broadway theatrical assignments and which he imported to the *Workshop*—by renaming the *Columbia Workshop* the *Mercury Theatre of the Air.*

With Halloween 1938 fast approaching, Welles needed a suitable *Mercury Theatre* subject. Apparently without much thought, he decided to adapt the H. G. Wells book, *War of the Worlds,* for radio. A 19th-century tale about Earth's invasion by hostile Martians, Welles worried that the story was too hokey to be effective but assigned CBS staff writer Howard Koch to adapt it. When it was completed, he feared it didn't meet the need for a suitably scary Halloween offering and made various changes including restructuring the script as a purported live big band remote broadcast, which was periodically interrupted by "news flashes." He also updated the geographic references to have the Martians land in the obscure town of Grover's Mill, New Jersey. Supposedly, Koch warned Welles' that the changes made the script *too* believable—although Welles later denied that.

## The Martians Land

On Sunday, October 30, 1938, at 8:00 p.m. Eastern Standard Time, CBS's *Mercury Theatre* took to the air with an opening announcement clearly stating that what followed was a dramatization. The experimental

**On the Radio Chains**

STATIONS.
Where to Find Them on the Dial:
KEX, Portland, 1180; KFI, 640, Los Angeles; KGA, 1470, Spokane; KGO, 790. San Francisco: KGW, 620. Portland: KJR, 970, Seattle; KNZ, 1050. Los Angeles: KOA, 830, Denver: KOIN, 940, Portland; KOMO, 926, Seattle; KPO, 680, San Francisco; KSL, 1180, Salt Lake.

"Grandpa" Bill Dock of Grover's Mill, NJ, took his rabbit gun in hand the day after the Mercury Theatre's *War of the Worlds'* broadcast and re-staged for photographers how he had intended to fight off the invading Martians.

*Mercury Theatre*, however, was somewhat like public radio of a later age—it was a minority taste. Most listeners were tuned to one of radio's most popular programs, NBC Red's *Chase and Sanborn Program with Edgar Bergen and Charlie McCarthy*. However, that program had opened with a vocalist whose performance apparently didn't hold great appeal, and a signifi-cant number of listeners switched to the *Mercury Theatre* program on CBS—too late to hear the announcement that the program was a dramatization. They tuned in just in time to hear a short burst of music, ostensibly a dance remote broadcast, interrupted by a "news flash" about a meteor falling in a field near Grover's Mill, New Jersey.

Before the hour was over, the meteor turned out to be a spacecraft inhabited by Martian invaders, who subdued New Jersey and then turned their attention to New York City, which they totally vanquished—including destroying the CBS headquarters. A forlorn residue of human civilization remained until the Martians were mercifully defeated by common Earth bacteria—against which they had no biological defense.

The program completed the Earth's destruction in sixty minutes! It sounds entirely implau-sible—and it was. Even so, approximately six million Americans took the broadcast seriously, and a national panic erupted. While CBS later asserted total surprise that the broadcast was being taken as fact by millions, CBS clearly knew something was amiss halfway through the program when Davidson Taylor, esteemed administrative supervisor of the broadcast, entered the program's control room ashen-faced. But he didn't stop the program.[1]

When the broadcast ended, all hell broke loose as police and reporters invaded the studio. The network promptly confiscated all copies of the script and wouldn't let the cast leave the building without handing them over. Clearly concerned about liability, CBS issued a statement:

It was neither Columbia's nor the *Mercury Theatre*'s intention to mislead anyone, and when it became evident that a part of the audience had been disturbed by the performance; five announcements were read over the network later in the evening to reassure those listeners.[2]

Across the country, police departments, churches and newspapers were inundated with anxious inquiries—and numerous hysterical listeners required medical attention. The next morning, newspapers across the nation were filled with reports of the national panic.

## Reaction in Oregon

Because all network radio programs were aired live, the *Mercury Theatre* was heard at 5 p.m. in Oregon. Like audiences across the country, Oregonians listening to Portland's KOIN, Los Angeles' KNX, Seattle's KIRO or Salt Lake City's KSL, also panicked.

The *Baker Democrat Herald* reported that "Residents of Baker Also Frightened by War Scare On Radio."[3] In Pendleton, it was reported that the program had caused panic among many, including National Guard captain M. A. Boyer, who called the police to report that the entire United States was in danger and to express his concern that America's weapons were powerless against the Martians.[4]

The *Grants Pass Daily Courier* recounted "a Grants Pass minister reported that after Sunday night's fantastic invasion of the United States by men from Mars, several persons called his home seeking the benefits of religion."[5] In Klamath Falls, the *Evening Herald* wrote that the local police had received numerous inquiries asking if the invasion story was true.[6] In Eugene, the *Register-Guard* reported that Mutual affiliate KORE was swamped with calls from concerned listeners of the rival network's program and that the newspaper itself had received a similar load of phone calls.[7]

In Ashland, the Police Department received numerous calls from worried residents, including three from city attorney Frank van Dyke. The residents of the Ashland Convalescent Home were "almost made nervous wrecks" according to staff member William Barber.

In Portland, CBS affiliate KOIN reported that it answered 800 calls and took complaints from three women who fainted during the broadcast—one of whom required a doctor's care. Several persons rushed into the *Oregonian*'s business offices demanding information, and the newspaper's switchboard was swamped.[8] An *Oregon Journal* staff member stopped for gas only to be told by the station attendant "There's no use buying any gasoline. The world's coming to an end."[9]

Some saw through the drama. The *Astoria Evening Budget*, for example, proudly reported that "Astoria Fails to Fall for Radio War." That city apparently had no incidents to report.[10]

In the days that followed, many Oregon newspapers offered editorial comments on the panic. The *Eugene Register-Guard* huffed: "Amusing and pathetic is the story of the nationwide hysteria induced by a radio dramatization of H. G. Wells' War of the Worlds."[11] The *Grants Pass Daily Courier* smugly observed: "For the real news, the daily newspaper is still a pretty safe source to turn to."[12] The *Klamath Falls Evening Herald* cautioned, "Whether it be when listening to a radio or to a conversation, or reading a newspaper or magazine, it is well to look for the whole meaning, and above all, to be wary of wrong conclusions."[13] In an editorial titled "The Tragedy of Radio," the *La Grande Evening Observer* worried over the consequences of "the power of radio if that same realism is put into insidious propaganda—and in war time it will be."[14] The Salem *Oregon Statesman* wrote: "All that is necessary is that the incident sober ambitious broadcasters who take too lightly their opportunity to affright the public."[15]

The *Oregonian* editorialized:

That an almost completely literate nation, with public schools, and abundant universities, and other educational and cultural advantages, should go into a screaming tail-spin over a dramatized broadcast of H. G. Wells' "The War of the Worlds" would have challenged belief no longer ago than yesterday—but today the singular seizure is a demonstrated fact. When the Columbia Broadcasting System released the super-horror tale of an invasion by Martians it achieved the artistic ultimate. The radio production was much too realistic. An unprecedented and admittedly embarrassing triumph of radio realism was the result.[16]

Congress and the Federal Communications Commission were indignant, which resulted in a new FCC regulation—still in effect—that requires stations to plainly identify as a dramatization any fictional material that might logically be construed as real news coverage.

Within days, the Martians and the hysteria had evaporated. Oregon and the nation were once again safe from extra-terrestrial challenge.

# Endnotes

1. Photo from http://www.historylink.org/essays/output.cfm?file_id=4002.
2. Ibid.
3. "Residents of Baker Also Frightened By War Scare on Radio," *Baker Democrat Herald*, October 31, 1938, 1.
4. "Reaction Here," *East Oregonian*, October 31, 1938, 1.
5. "Local People Frightened by Newscast," *Grants Pass Daily Courier*, October 31, 1938, 1.
6. "Local Scare," *Klamath Falls Evening Herald*, October 31, 1938, 1.
7. "Eugene Radio Fans React To Thriller Too," *Eugene Register-Guard*, October 31, 1938, 1.
8. "'War of Worlds' Shakes Portland", *Oregonian*, October 31, 1938, 2.
9. "Many Portlanders' Hair On End During Broadcast," *Oregon Journal*, October 31, 1938, 1.
10. "Astoria Fails To Fall For Radio War," *Astoria Evening Budget*, October 31, 1938, 1.
11. "Minds Set For Hysteria," *Eugene Register-Guard*, November 1, 1938, 4.
12. "Technique Makes Old Thriller Live," *Grants Pass Daily Courier*, October 31, 1938, 4.
13. "Radio Incident," *Klamath Falls Evening Herald*, November 1, 1938, 4.
14. "The Tragedy of Radio," *La Grande Evening Observer*, November 1, 1938, 2.
15. "Radio Caution Needed," *Oregon Statesman*, November 1, 1938.
16. "The Things From Mars," *Oregonian*, November 1, 1938, 10.

UNITED PRESS
MILITARY STRATEGIST'S
MAPS *of all Fronts*

90 FLAG
INDICATORS
to keep
pace with the
daily military
movements

NORTH AFRICA · SOLOMON IS.
MEDITERRANEAN · EUROPE
GUADALCANAL · NEW GUINEA
WORLD · PACIFIC · ALASKA

*Featuring* NAVAL & AIR BASES · SUPPLY ROUTES · MILITARY
HIGHWAYS · RAILROADS · BOMBER FLYING RANGE · PLANE & SHIP DISTANCES
BETWEEN MILITARY OBJECTIVES · VITAL MILITARY RESOURCES
*Distributed by* UNITED FEATURE SYNDICATE

K X L

10,000 WATTS                    750 K. C.

Best wishes always
Sincerely
Jane Powell

# The 1940s

# World War II and Post-War Years

# The War Years

Three new Oregon radio stations, KWIL, KODL and KWRC, signed-on prior to the Japanese attack on Pearl Harbor.

## KWIL Albany

On January 14, 1941, the *Albany Democrat-Herald* launched its radio station. The newspaper's subdivision, the Central Willamette Broadcasting Company, signed-on KWIL (**K-WIL**lamette) with a power of 250 watts on 1210 KHz. The station, which was known as the "Voice of the Heart of the Willamette Valley," was managed by Chet Wheeler (who came from KBND) and operated from a studio/transmitter site at Queen Avenue and Elm Street. Lacking furniture at the time, program director Herb Davidson (who later went to KPOJ and KOIN) read the 6 p.m. sign-on seated on a nail keg. The following day, the station joined the Mutual Network. On March 29, 1941, the station moved to 1240 KHz.

## KODL The Dalles

Virgil Barney Kenworthy was born August 5, 1900, in Wayne, Indiana. As a youth, Kenworthy's hobby was wireless, and as radio grew, it matured into a deep interest for him. Working as a farmer in Portland during his teen years, Kenworthy was managing a theatre in Syracuse, Oregon (Linn County), by 1930. Following more than a year's planning, he

Paul Walden at work in his KODL office, c. 1950.

formed the Western Radio Corporation, which filed an FCC application for a new station in The Dalles. According to later KUMA owner Ted Smith, Kenworthy's silent partner in the venture was the Loren Hicks family of Salem.[1]

Paul Walden was the engineer who helped install station KODL (**K-O**regon **Da**L**l**es). It signed-on October 21, 1940, on 1200 KHz with 250-watts daytime and 100-watts nighttime power. The station's studio and transmitter were housed in a 36-by-46-foot building, located on Sunset Hill at 2112 Scenic Drive. Based on a commercial house floor plan, the building was constructed so that it could be converted into a residence in case the station proved a failure.[2] On March 29, 1941, the station moved to 1230 KHz and on September 1, 1953, became an ABC Radio Network affiliate. Eventually, Walden was appointed KODL's manager.

In 1967, Kenworthy sold KODL to Seattle resident Frederic A. Danz for $125,000. Danz, who had extensive holdings in regional movie theatre and real estate, took over KODL on October 1, 1967. One of his first changes was putting the station on a format of "contemporary easy listening—pleasant music, appealing to the adult audience," in addition to adding classical and semi-classical music on Sunday evenings. The station also began a regular program editorializing on local issues.

KODL's sale also provided the impetus for Paul Walden, the station's manager for 20 years, to move on. In 1967, Walden purchased KIHR Hood River.

In 1972, KODL changed its call letters to KGLX and on April 14, 1975, joined CBS Radio. In 1982, KODL was sold to Larson-Wynn, Inc., who changed the call sign back to KODL.

## KWRC/KKID/KTIX Pendleton

Having completed construction of KODL, Kenworthy—who lived in The Dalles—set about building a station in Pendleton which principally received radio service from Walla Walla's KUJ. The station was nearly ready to sign-on when Pearl Harbor was attacked on December 7, 1941.

KWRC (K-Western-Radio-Corporation) signed-on December 10, 1941, at 1240 KHz with 250 watts from studios at 1000 SW Sixth Street. The station also used the letters in its call sign as an acronym for Pendleton's own slogan, "World's Roundup City."[3]

Henry Hogue was KWRC's initial general manager and was supported by staff members Paul Walden, who succeeded him as manager, Richard Pooley and Mary Jane Hodgen.

Ted Smith was a Pendleton High School student who hung out at KWRC during its construction, and then worked part-time as an announcer while still a student. Following his high school graduation, Smith worked full-time for KWRC before entering the Navy Air Corps in 1943. Returning after the war, Smith contacted KWRC manager Paul Walden. "He [Walden] was always one of my favorite people [and] I just wanted to say hello to him and he said 'Oh, I'm glad you're home. Can you come and help me out?'"[4] Walden immediately re-hired Smith, and he quickly rose through the ranks to become KWRC's manager in 1947.

KWRC became KKID on December 23, 1958, when it was purchased by WSC Broadcasting Company of Oregon, Inc. Fred W. Stevens was the president and general manager of KTIX, and Paul Ward was the station manager.

Roderick Sound, Inc., purchased the station on July 16, 1961. Robert W. Roderick was president and general manager, and his wife, Donna, was program director. On August 1, 1967, the Rodericks sold the station for $135,000 to Eastern Oregon Broadcasters, Inc., a wholly owned subsidiary of Juniper Broadcasting, Inc., which also owned KGRL Bend and held a majority interest in KACI The Dalles. In 1981, Capps Broadcasting, Inc., which had taken over Juniper's interest in KTIX, sold the station to Agpal Broadcasting, Inc. for $400,000.

KWRC's birth was inextricably tied to America's shock over Pearl Harbor. Just as the station was preparing to sign-on, the world changed completely—and dramatically—as war entered the American scene.

## First Network Announcements

Sunday, December 7, 1941, began quietly. Published radio schedules anticipated a wide variety of programs. The New York Philharmonic was slated for its weekly Columbia network broadcast at noon, for example. A half-hour news round-up, *The World Today*, was scheduled to precede it. Mutual's *Swing Time String* was on KALE's schedule. NBC Blue had booked an hour-long edition of its regular Sunday *Great Plays* series, that week featuring "The Inspector General." KEX listeners were expecting that program to be followed by a panel of academics, journalists, politicians and business leaders who would be debating economic and political issues. KGW had nearly a full hour of news and commentary from H. V. Kaltenborn on its noon schedule with the erudite *University of Chicago Round-Table* discussion program preceding it. KWJJ had scheduled *Novelty Entertainers* at noon and planned on broadcasting a pipe organ concert from Oaks Park amusement park at 12:30 p.m.

Suddenly, Oregonians heard distant network announcers interrupting programs with news bulletins. At 11:29:50 a.m. Pacific Standard Time, just moments before the *University of Chicago Round-Table* discussion was to begin, Portland listeners to KGW heard NBC announcer Robert Eisenbach interrupt NBC Red with a bulletin about the Japanese attack on Pearl Harbor. Few listeners had ever heard of Pearl Harbor, and even fewer knew its location. NBC Blue's *Great Plays* was on KEX at that same moment.

Since CBS already had a news program scheduled, announcer John Charles Daly didn't have to interrupt a scheduled program to report the news. He opened *The World Today* at 11:30 a.m. with the shocking announcement and continued to anchor the unfolding coverage. CBS got through to London for a report from Robert Trout, who was followed by American commentator Elmer Davis' extemporaneous thoughts. But Daly interrupted Davis at 11:49 a.m.—and then switched to CBS's Ford Wilkins in Manila who reported that the Philippines were under attack. Suddenly, Wilkins's report was cut off. War-time censorship had entered the world of radio.

In 1941, radio networks were unaccustomed to interrupting scheduled programming—and CBS's New York Philharmonic concert went on the air on time as did most other programming on all the networks. But radio began to gear up for the unprecedented challenge the war presented, and soon the phrase "We interrupt this program" became familiar to Americans as the concept of breaking news developed.

# Oregonians Hear the News

University of Oregon student Ancil Payne was a native of Mitchell, Oregon, who later became general manager of KGW and president of King Broadcasting. But that Sunday morning in 1941, Payne was setting a dining room table at the Tri-Delta House in Eugene. "The announcer broke into the [Glenn Miller song] 'Chattanooga Choo-Choo' to say that Pearl Harbor had been bombed. We didn't even know where Pearl Harbor was, but we found out shortly thereafter."[5]

Pendleton was three days away from getting a new radio station, KWRC, which wasn't yet ready to sign-on that Sunday. Pendleton High School senior Ted Smith was in the studio that morning. "The station's staff stood around watching the teletype bark out the horrible news and they couldn't do a thing about it," he recalled.[6]

KFLW's (later KFLS) Floyd Wynne was on his regular Sunday shift at the station that morning. "We had a church program on and in the middle of the program this fellow came on saying, 'The Japs are bombing Pearl Harbor!' And from that point on, we were on the air 24-hours-a-day. Up to then, we normally signed-off at midnight."[7]

KWIL's young promotion manager, Herbert Davidson (he shortly thereafter became the station's chief engineer and, in 1956, went on to a 20-year run as KPOJ's chief engineer), heard the news over KGW. Bursting into KWIL's studios, he told a reluctant engineer to interrupt the church service broadcast and put him on the air to make the announcement—which he did to station manager Chet Wheeler's consternation. "Don't ever interrupt a church service again," Wheeler admonished.[8]

Lee Bishop had been at church for his second daughter's baptism and tuned in KMED on his car radio as he and his wife, Hester, were driving home. "That's war," Lee said to her. "And from then on things were different."[9]

NBC eventually modified its famous three-chime signature of the notes G-E-C, adding a fourth chime, a repeated C—which was an alert to local stations and listeners that the network was interrupting for a war bulletin.

The nation was at war, and radio was suddenly called upon to play a vital new role. News had never been radio's forte. As far back as the *Oregonian*'s fight with the Associated Press over KGW's access to AP news, the press had tried to suppress radio's role as a news source (see chapter 9). But suddenly, the first war to be electronically brought into America's homes was at hand.

# Early Effects on Local Stations

No one knew just what to do that first Sunday of World War II. For years, KXL had been filing FCC requests seeking authority to broadcast during evening hours for various special events—and all such requests had been routinely denied. But on December 7, 1941, KXL requested—and received—permission to broadcast throughout the night on the uncertain tide of events. All three networks reported that they expected the war to have little impact on broadcasting—but they were wrong.

President Roosevelt scheduled an address for 9:30 a.m. PST on Monday, December 8, and all radio networks and their affiliated stations carried it. Concerned that Japanese aircraft might use stations' signals as directional aids for bombing runs, the government ordered all stations to sign-off that evening. The night of December 8, America's air waves were silent for the first time since radio's inception.

Stations returned to the air the next morning but were again ordered off the air on Tuesday evening, immediately following another presidential address. The next day, they operated knowing that they could be ordered off the air by the FCC at any time on just five minutes' notice.

KGW and KEX (the *Oregonian* had taken to referring to its stations as "KGW-X") set up loudspeakers outside its building at Sixth Avenue and Alder Street to relay news in case the radio stations were off the air during important news developments. KGW manager Arden X. Pangborn issued a new policy that "his stations would interrupt local broadcasts whenever hot war news is received by the wire services but will not interrupt network programs, except in case of a war flash of local importance."[10, 11]

The radio industry didn't exist during the first World War, and in 1941 the federal government was struggling with the security issues of the hundreds of private radio stations who had the potential to inadvertently provide useful information to an enemy. Stations were ordered to place permanent guards at their transmitters and used either "federal troops, private watchmen, state, county or municipal employees" for the purpose.[12] Stations also had to make secure arrangements for quickly extinguishing their FAA-required tower lights in the event that a blackout was ordered.

Ever since the late 1930s, when European political tensions began escalating, audiences had been warming up to the idea that radio could be a source for breaking news. At the time of the 1938 German invasion of Czechoslovakia, a marathon series of news broadcasts by NBC's H. V. Kaltenborn captivated listeners and stimulated similar efforts at Mutual, and CBS eventually earned great fame from Edward R. Murrow's war coverage.

Radio threw itself fully into the war effort. Where initially war news had centered on special live coverage, networks quickly added regularly scheduled newscasts. Local stations' practice of scheduling newscasts at the top of each hour originated during this period. The networks tended not to shorten their programs to create time for hourly newscasts, however. Instead, they concentrated on scheduling program-length news offerings of 15 or 30 minutes. Non-network stations such as KXL, however, did begin offering hourly newscasts facilitated by new network news services, including Trans Radio News.

Entertainment programs began to embrace wartime themes of self-sacrifice, such as the rationing of strategic goods that quickly followed Pearl Harbor.

Entercom KWJJ Collection, WSMB

This 40-page brochure, produced centrally for use by client stations across the nation, was distributed by KWJJ around the first anniversary of Pearl Harbor. In addition to fully chronicling the many war-related programs KWJJ was presenting, it also provided the insignias of other nations' aircraft for civilian defense purposes, as well as pictures of the insignia and rank emblems for all U.S. military forces.

WSMB Collection

KWJJ's John Egan looking at a promotional poster for prominent war news commentator Lowell Thomas at the station's new 1011 SW 6th Avenue studios early in World War II, c. 1942

Having gotten his start at KGW-KEX during World War II, by the time of this 1956 photo Don Kneass, surrounded by news teletype copy, had moved to KWJJ.

KXL war map, c. 1943

Soap operas adjusted their storylines to include the characters' daily confrontation of the challenges of wartime life, including the ever-present fear for the safety of loved ones in the military.

Radio stations quickly began losing some of their brightest employees to voluntary enlistment and the draft. The war thus created job opportunities for newcomers such as KOIN's Jack Lenard, KGW-KEX's Don Kneass and KUMA's Ted Smith. "All the young men are going off to war and so I'm hanging around the radio station," Smith remembered. "They offered me a part-time job, and so I worked nights and weekends until I graduated from high school, and then I worked full-time until I went into the Navy Air Corps," recalled Smith, who later owned KUMA and KJDY and was president of the Oregon Association of Broadcasters. [13]

Soon, radio was daily sending news of the war into American homes. To aid listeners in following military campaigns, stations such as KEX and KXL distributed free maps of the war fronts so that listeners could plot troop movements. In May 1942, the *Oregonian* reported that KEX had received 562 requests for the war maps it had produced as part of the newly developed *War Time News Roundup*, which aired nightly at 11:30. The program, which was billed as *History in the Making*, was simulcast on KGW and remained in production until the war was nearly over.

KGW had also scheduled a 3:45 p.m. *War Periscope* program, and announcer Don Kneass was additionally presenting a 15-minute newscast at 10:15 a.m.—a morning news presence new to radio. By 1943, Kneass, a local boy who had graduated from Grant High School before entering radio, was doing a second daytime newscast over KEX at 3:45 p.m. Arden X. Pangborn also created the program *Remember Our Men* to especially honor those in the military.

By 1942, KOIN was carrying the women's program *Victory at Home* at 8 a.m. on Wednesdays and *War Time Women* nightly at 10:30 (both from CBS), plus the full complement of CBS's extensive European coverage of the war.

The addition of so much news coverage, especially in the wake of military enlistments by announcers and other personnel, created huge new opportunities in radio. The *Oregonian* was particularly well-situated, since KGW and KEX were operated as a department of the newspaper and therefore had abundant print reportorial talent upon which to call.

## Tom McCall

Thomas Lawson McCall graduated from the University of Oregon in June 1936 with a journalism degree. After a brief career with the *Bend Bulletin*, he spent a number of years at Moscow, Idaho's, *News-Review* before campaigning for a reporter position in Portland at either the *Oregonian* or the *Oregon Journal*. The former hired him in March 1942, 15 minutes before the latter offered him a job. Thus, KGW had access to him for radio work when Ben Titus, news director of the *Oregonian*'s two radio stations, suddenly died on May 16, 1944.[14] Thus began the broadcasting career of one of Oregon's most celebrated and respected broadcasters and public figures.

McCall had been voicing some public service programming on KGW at $5 per program when the newspaper's radio columnist, Bill Moyes, heard a recording of McCall's commanding, gravely voice and exclaimed: "There is the most interesting voice in radio." Shortly thereafter, McCall, who suffered terribly from mike fright, was assigned to KGW-KEX as a news announcer. In his autobiography, McCall later recounted that station manager Arden X. Pangborn wouldn't even tell him when he was going to start because he knew McCall wouldn't sleep "between now and then."[15]

Tom McCall went on the air with only a few hours' notice, sharing a noon newscast with Mel Baldwin. The newspaper was so concerned over McCall's mike terror that it stationed an extra announcer, Mel Bailey, in the studio as a precaution. "Pang thought we ought to have another newscaster in the studio when you collapsed," Bailey explained.[16] After working in radio for a portion of the year, McCall enlisted in the military later in 1944 but returned to KEX in 1946. On his return, he increasingly devoted himself to news commentary, as opposed to newscast, announcing. His major assignment was the program *Talk of the Town* (see additional history on McCall in chapters 17 and 18).

## KOIN Portland

KOIN threw its entertainment forces into helping support the war effort. *Stop, Look and Listen* joined the station's schedule in March 1942. Broadcast at 10:45 p.m. on Wednesdays, it was designed for skywatchers (volunteers who monitored the skies for enemy aircraft) while at their outposts and featured musical requests they submitted, as well as news of special interest to that audience. *Company at Ease* joined the KOIN schedule in fall 1942. Hosted by Red Dunning, it featured servicemen, guest artists and the station's orchestra.

Early in the war, KOIN began broadcasting 24 hours a day as a service to factory and ship-

KOIN stationery logo, 1942

Courtesy of the Oregon Historical Society, photo 63745

KOIN's Red Dunning (left) in costume for a skit to sell war bonds, 1942

KOIN Radio Advertiser, August 1945

A live coast-to-coast CBS network broadcast of KOIN's *Million Dollar Club*. The series won the station the Variety Showmanagement (sic) Award as the "War Bond Station of the Nation."

yard workers on the swing and graveyard shifts. Deviating from its policy of not playing recorded music, KOIN broadcast from its World, Standard and Lang-Worth transcription libraries to fill the wee hours of the morning. The station also deployed its musicians to perform noon war bond rallies at the downtown Portland Victory Center and at local industrial plants.

KOIN suffered a crushing loss in August 1944, when long-time employee and Portland fixture Joseph Sampietro, the station's music director since 1929, passed away. Sampietro's baton, however, was smoothly passed to Red Dunning.

## KWJJ and KXL

What most Americans today might think of as U.S. Treasury savings bonds were simply called "baby bonds" when they began in 1935." Renamed "defense bonds" in March 1941, they were again renamed as "war bonds" following the Pearl Harbor attack and helped finance the war. The government realized that considerable media attention would be required to successfully fuel bond sales and requested assistance from the radio industry. Networks and stations launched bond drives, and throughout Oregon stations helped spark bond sales with special programming and events.

No station was more deeply engaged in supporting bond sales than KOIN. In 1943, the station began a weekly half-hour program called *The Million Dollar Club*, which aired at 9:30 p.m. on Tuesdays. The program recognized local individuals who had stimulated $1 million or more in bond sales. Willard Mears had joined the station in 1940 after working in radio for more than a decade in Los Angeles, where he had had largely been engaged in writing and network acting. At KOIN, Mears created such public affairs programs as *The Million Dollar Club*, which brought KOIN great praise.

On September 9, 1943, KOIN began its third war bond drive with a highly success-

KXL celebrated selling over $300,000 in war bonds, enough to build a bomber to be called "The Lucky Beaver," by unfurling this scroll containing the names of 5,000 bond purchasers. It was presented to the State Bond Administration in a 1943 Portland Beavers baseball pre-game ceremony (KXL was the "Beavers Baseball station" at the time).

ful stage program, for which there was no admission charge, at the Portland Civic Auditorium. KOIN sold $1,138,000 in bonds that day. On February 1, 1944, that effort was dwarfed when the station set a sales goal of a million dollars and at day's end had tallied $11,557,757 in bond sales. Only one other CBS station in the country sold more bonds that day (which had been established as a coordinated CBS-sponsored effort) than KOIN.[17]

During the war, KOIN was saluted by Columbia Broadcasting System's vice president, Herbert V. Akenberg, who said: "No station in the country has made a greater contribution to the radio industry than KOIN."[18]

## Jane Powell

An early Jane Powell publicity photo, c. 1945, taken shortly after her arrival in Hollywood.

One of Portland's contributions that helped boost the country's morale was a true girl next door entertainer—Jane Powell—who was born Suzanne Lorraine Burce on April 1, 1929. Her father, who worked for more than 14 years for Portland's Wonder Bread bakery, encouraged the precocious youngster, who began singing and dancing at an early age. When she was five, she began appearing on KGW's *Stars of Tomorrow*, a long-running Portland program hosted by "Uncle" Nate Cohn and sponsored by Star Furniture Company, which eventually transferred to television on Portland's

Nate Cohn presiding over a KGW *Stars of Tomorrow* radio broadcast in 1943

KLOR-TV.[19] Powell became a regular on *Stars of Tomorrow,* singing hit songs like "On the Good Ship Lollipop," which had been made famous by child star, Shirley Temple.

At age 12, Powell was named Oregon Victory Girl and began singing on KOIN. Within a year, she was appearing on two weekly KOIN programs. In June 1943, having just graduated from eighth grade at Beaumont Elementary School, Powell was preparing to enter Grant High School in the fall. But first, her family went on a summer vacation to Hollywood. Learning of the trip, KOIN's Charles Myers arranged for Powell to appear on CBS's *Stars Over Hollywood.*[20] There, her career skyrocketed and soon she appeared on many major network programs, including *The Railroad Hour, Lux Radio Theatre* and *The Chase and Sanborn Hour with Edgar Bergen and Charlie McCarthy.*

When her family returned to Portland at summer's end, it was to pack up and relocate to Hollywood, where the young Jane Powell had been signed to an MGM movie studio contract. Portland mayor Earl Riley wrote to her: "Dear Suzanne, wherever destiny takes you, Portland will be watching with interest and enthusiasm."[21] Portland had adopted the talented, petite singer as its own, and when she returned to Portland to visit, she was greeted like royalty.

## KMED and Camp White

Outside Portland, other Oregon stations threw themselves into the war effort with similar energy. Medford had been significantly affected by the Army's construction of a huge military training facility, Camp White, in Central Point (about six miles north of Medford). Several men stationed at Camp White during the war went on to play significant roles in broadcasting,

Many radio stations across the U.S. celebrated the nation's success in World War II by issuing promotional brochures chronicling radio's contribution to the war effort. *Radio in Victory* was KWJJ's offering in 1945.

including Ed Barnett, who later joined KWIN, KBES-TV and KMED-TV. KMED's James J. Dunlevy entered Camp White as a private assigned to the camp's public relations department. Soon, he became the master of ceremonies for many radio programs that KMED fed from Camp White to the Blue Network (western leg) via Portland's KGW (see chapter 15). Following the war, Dunlevy returned to KMED and then went on to manage Medford's KYJC in 1951.[22]

Radio had played an instrumental role in the lives of Oregonians throughout World War II and significantly contributed to the nation's success on the home front.

## The Oregonian Sells KEX

Notwithstanding the national war effort, in many respects some semblance of normalcy existed on the home front. However, one major change in radio resulted from the lengthy grinding of the wheels of federal bureaucracy. Prior to the war, the FCC had released its "Report on Chain Broadcasting," which examined the consequences of NBC's ownership and operation of two networks, the Red and the Blue. That structure dated back to NBC's 1926 founding and had resulted in similar dual-ownerships at the local level. For example, the *Oregonian* owned two radio stations, KGW and KEX in Portland, which were respectively affiliated with NBC's Red and Blue networks. The FCC's report concluded that dual ownership, which it named "duopoly," unfairly restrained competition between the Red and the Blue, resulting in less vigorous programming than would occur if the two networks were independently owned.

Accordingly, the FCC proposed prohibiting the ownership of two networks, or two local stations in the same market, by any single entity. NBC bitterly protested the proposal and unsuccessfully took the FCC to court. But in 1943, the FCC's duopoly rule took effect. Perhaps sensing the outcome, in 1942 NBC had begun referring to its second network as the Blue Network—as opposed to the NBC Blue Network—while still referring to its other network as the NBC Red. In 1943, Ed Noble, owner of the Wrigley Company, purchased from NBC the Blue Network and its complement of owned-and-operated stations. Noble operated the network under the name The Blue Network until 1945, when it was renamed the American Broadcasting Company (ABC).

While the duopoly rule was principally aimed at NBC, it also applied to local station ownership. Therefore, the *Oregonian*'s dual ownership of KGW and KEX was in violation. Just as NBC had chosen to sell the less profitable and prestigious of its two networks, the Blue Network, it was the Blue-Network-affiliated KEX that the *Oregonian* elected to sell.

KEX was purchased by Westinghouse Radio Stations on December 28, 1944, for $400,000. Westinghouse, which already owned a variety of other radio stations, was generally regarded as an eminently qualified buyer.

## KGW-KEX—FIRE!

On the evening of September 23, 1943, the type of calm that typically pervades a radio studio late at night was suddenly interrupted at KGW-KEX. Around 11:15 p.m., a sudden flash occurred in the booth in which Mel Bailey was announcing. Billowing clouds of smoke quickly flooded the stations' seventh-floor studios, where recording technician Andy Anderson and announcer Don Green were working. While a call was quickly placed to the fire department, the building's internal fire hose system was not in good repair and produced far too little water to suppress the fire. The radio staff evacuated to the street along with the newspaper's printing staff, who had been turning out the next morning's paper. On the street, a large crowd joined them to watch the three-alarm blaze.

When Green got to the street, he recalled that he had left his new overcoat hanging by his chair in the studio. A recently married young man on a modest salary, he decided he had to retrieve it. Somewhat foolishly, he raced back into what by then had become a raging inferno and successfully retrieved his coat. Rollie Truitt and Bob Mills had been broadcasting a banquet at a nearby location that evening. When it ended, they emerged to the street and saw a crowd gathered to watch a large fire—unaware that it was their station that was burning. Figuring out the blaze's source, a tuxedo-clad Truitt remembered that KGW musical director Abe Bercovitz had recently borrowed a $50,000 violin from Meier & Frank executive Aaron Frank—and the instrument was still in the studios. Following Green's foolhardy example, Truitt climbed up the fire truck's ladder to re-enter the studios, seven stories up, and descended with the precious violin cradled in his arms to the cheers of the assembled crowd.

The fire's source was never completely determined but was generally thought to have started in the seventh-floor battery room.[23] Regardless of its source, the fire devastated the KGW-KEX studios. KGW was able to remain on the air carrying a network feed until the studio equipment burned up—at which point the station went silent. But the outage was brief as staff raced to the transmitter site on North Denver Street (Pacific Highway) and resumed temporary operations from that location using microphones and other equipment rescued from the smoking studios.[24] Amazingly, KGW and KEX were each off the air for a total of only twelve minutes.

Ravaged by the fire, the KGW-KEX studios were a total loss. The destruction included nearly the entire record transcription library, Glenn Shelley's studio organ, the grand piano,

A KWJJ music program, c. 1945, originating from its "Big Studio," in the station's new seven-studio facilities, which were constructed just as World War II erupted. The contrast between these facilities and those newly constructed for KGW late in the 1940s is striking.

most of Homer Welch's precious sound effects devices and the studio broadcasting equipment. Almost everything not destroyed by fire was ruined by smoke and water. It also appears that most of KGW's early memorabilia collection was also a casualty of the fire.

KWJJ, which had just completed the construction of its new seven-studio home at 1011 SW Sixth Avenue, immediately offered KGW and KEX temporary space. Hard work by the radio stations' staff, along with extremely speedy attention by the phone company to re-route

Recording/transcription and transmission room, with cutting lathe turntable (far right) of the new KEX studios, 1948.

circuits to the KWJJ building, allowed KGW-KEX to sign-on the next morning.[25]

KEX didn't leave its temporary home at KWJJ until 1945, when it relocated to new temporary quarters at 815 SW Yamhill Street. On November 24, 1946, it took up permanent residence at its newly constructed Radio Center at 1230 SW Main Street.

KGW, however, continued to broadcast from its "temporary" home at KWJJ until July 1948, when a new *Oregonian* building was completed and the station moved into new state-of-the-art studios there.

The new KGW studios in a December 1950 photo

## Newhouse Buys the *Oregonian* and KGW

In 1950, Portland's oldest surviving—and in many ways most prominent—radio institution was about to be rocked to its core. The *Oregonian* had decided to abandon its home on the corner of Sixth Avenue and Alder Streets in 1946, perhaps stimulated by the 1943 fire but also likely designed to improve the efficiency of the paper's printing plant. Committed to remaining downtown, the *Oregonian* purchased a full city block just ten blocks south of its old home. Then in the hands of descendents of its founders, after World War II the Oregonian Publishing Company made a grand and ultimately fateful decision by engaging Portland's only acknowledged world-class architect of the time, Italian-born Pietro Belluschi, to conceive its new home. The *Oregonian*'s 1892 building had been designed by prominent San Francisco architects Reid and Reid, who had also designed the famous Hotel Del Coronado. Perhaps the paper's owners were eager to again make a daring architectural statement. If so, they must have been gratified by the *New York Times*' description of the *Oregonian*'s new home as a "gentle shimmering mass of glass, marble and granite."[26]

The Oregonian Publishing Company had invested heavily in the construction of its huge, new plant at 1320 SW Broadway and construction costs had reportedly soared to twice of what had been anticipated. The project's cash demands became crushing. Compounding the situation, the *Oregonian*'s new media ventures had not gone particularly well. KGW-FM was foundering economically, and the paper had unwisely abandoned its pioneering television opportunity—likely because of the cash needed to construct its new headquarters. While the *Oregonian*

New Home of *The Oregonian,*
Portland, Oregon
*Pacific Northwest's Largest Newspaper*

WSMB Collection

Postcard showing the new 1948 *Oregonian* building, whose construction forced the sale of both the newspaper and KGW.

remained profitable after moving into its new headquarters in 1948, profits were neither up to their customary yields nor sufficient to meet the demands that the new headquarters had imposed. The *Oregonian*'s newly installed president, banker E. B. MacNaughton, saw that the only way to preserve the paper was to sell it. Thus as the new decade dawned, the *Oregonian*—the oldest continuously published paper in the west and widely considered one of the finest dailies in western America—went up for sale.

Newspaper tycoon Solomon Isadore Neuhaus, who later changed his name to Samuel I. Newhouse, was already a formidable media figure. Called Sam by his family, he eventually went by S. I. Newhouse in the business world, where he tightly ran a newspaper empire under the name Advance Publications, Inc. Newhouse had his own way of doing things.

Newhouse offered $5.6 million for the *Oregonian,* a higher figure than the newspaper had anticipated, and the offer was readily accepted. Newhouse was well-known for maintaining close family control over his newspapers, and reportedly his willingness to close the *Oregonian* purchase was based on a special added factor. His eldest son, S. I. Jr., was unhappily tending one of the family's recent purchases, the *Harrisburg Patriot* in Pennsylvania. Since the *Oregonian* purchase included the option to buy KGW Radio, and KGW was also once again jockeying for a television channel after the Oregonian had abandoned its earlier KGWG-TV construction permit, the elder Newhouse temporarily assigned his son to Portland to oversee the KGW acquisition and the planning for a television station (see chapter 14 for information on the *Oregonian*'s earlier TV application).[27] He also reportedly secured his younger son Ted's agreement to fly to Portland monthly to check-up on their newest acquisition once S. I. Jr.'s Portland assignment had ended. Newhouse clearly viewed his option to purchase KGW as a key element of his *Oregonian* purchase.

The *Oregonian*'s sale was announced on December 11, 1950. It was Newhouse's first publishing venture in the west and set a record price for the purchase of an American daily newspaper. Because Newhouse's purchase initially included only the *Oregonian,* a new corporation was formed to own KGW and, with a naming salute to KGW's proud traditions, Pioneer Broadcasters, Inc., was established as the radio station's owner. Newhouse's purchase included an

18-month option to acquire all of Pioneer's stock for $350,000—which he exercised two months after the newspaper's sale. Thus, on February 21, 1951, KGW had a new owner.

Just over a month later, KGW celebrated its 30th birthday with its principal event consisting of a contest involving old radio sets. Over a period of several weeks, the public was invited to bring old radios—from crystal sets to 1920s-era battery sets to console radios—to KGW's studios, where the sets were judged for their age, condition and performance in categories such as "largest headphone set" or "oldest commercial tube set." They were displayed in the KGW Hostess House, and the winners, including Temple V. Ehmsen, won a new 1952 radio (see chapter 14).

## KGW-FM/KQFM-FM#1/KKRZ-FM Portland

KGW-FM had signed-on as the Pacific Northwest's first FM station on May 7, 1946. But by 1949, KGW-FM was struggling and the *Oregonian* (who still owned it) was looking for a way out—perhaps because its presence depressed opportunities for selling KGW-AM, which the paper was exploring. Citing the "lack of general public acceptance of the FM method of broadcasting," the *Oregonian* offered the use of the station (presumably not including its license) to the Portland School District for use as an adjunct to its AM station, KBPS. The district demurred, saying "district authorities have not had time to consider the financial obligations that would be assumed in accepting the gift," at which point the *Oregonian* decided to abandon KGW-FM and surrendered its license on February 20, 1950.[28]

Following S. I. Newhouse's purchase of the Oregonian and KGW-AM, on August 17, 1951, he announced his interest in reactivating the FM station and succeeded in returning KGW-FM to the air on February 1, 1952. Its studios were again located with KGW-AM on the new *Oregonian* Building's fourth floor.[29] The FM station, broadcasting at 100.3 MHz with its power increased to 57 kilowatts, was once again simulcasting KGW-AM and its NBC programming and operated from 3 p.m. to 10:15 p.m. daily.

The FM station must again have appeared more like a promise than a plum. H. Quentin "Q" Cox, who had been managing KGW-AM-FM since 1946, had remained with the stations through their sale to the Dorothy Bullitt/KING interests (see chapter 18). Now, Cox wanted to venture out on his own, and a friendly purchase of KGW-FM's license and equipment (but not the transmitter site itself) for $3,750 was arranged with him on October 20, 1954.

KGW had prospered under Cox's management, and his departure was widely mourned. Gordon Orput, president of Pioneer Broadcasters, Inc., said: "We are sincerely sorry to hear of Cox's decision to leave KGW. His contribution to the radio industry in Oregon and the nation has been outstanding."

Cox took ownership of the FM station in November 1954, with the *Oregonian* leasing its transmitter site to him, and he promptly requested new call letters. On December 1, 1954, KGW-FM became KQFM#1 (standing for "Q's FM") with its studios relocated to the Terminal Sales Building at 1220 SW Morrison Street (which had been KEX's original home through 1934).[30] Cox was KQFM's president and general manager, his wife, Helen, the program director, and Charles K. Dickson the station's chief engineer. KQFM broadcast music and operated from 9 a.m. to 9 p.m. Monday through Saturday. Apparently largely a family affair, the Cox's took Sunday off and so did KQFM. In January 1955, the station added Sunday to its schedule and gradually moved to a background music format.

Because King Broadcasting had donated the original KGW-FM/KQFM transmitter site to support the state's creation of KOAP-TV, KQFM had to relocate its transmitter and signed-off on October 27, 1960 to move to the KGMG tower across the street at 4636 SW Council Crest Drive (see chapter 16). KQFM returned to the air from its new location in early November.

Cox sold KQFM on March 21, 1962 to Point-O-Salescast, Inc. (headed by its president, Juan Young) for $1, plus assignment of liabilities totaling $10,000. Point-O-Salescast was founded in 1950 and used on-site tape cartridge playback equipment to insert commercial announcements to the background music systems in retail locations. Point-O-Salescast made several changes, including moving the station's studios to the 18th Avenue Building (405 NW 18th Avenue) a year later. Arlie D. Kent was general manager in 1964.

David M. Myers purchased KQFM and Point-O-Salescast, Inc. on September 1, 1969, for $59,000. Myers owned the "Music by Muzak" franchise, which had been established in 1957 by a previous owner, serving the area between Medford and Randle, Washington. Around 1970, Myers began using a KQFM subcarrier to replace leased telephone circuits to feed the Portland-area Muzak signal to subscribing businesses.

In 1970, KQFM moved its studios to shared quarters with Myers' other businesses at 2815 SW Barbur Boulevard. Jon I. Wright became KQFM's program director, and William E. Laurens was its chief engineer. By June 1970, KQFM's format was being described as "familiar instrumental music." On April 26, 1972, KQFM raised its power to 100 kilowatts, and in October Wright became the general manager. KQFM's slogan was "just good instrumental music 24 hours a day."

In August 1975, KQFM moved along with Myers' other companies to a new building in the Johns Landing area known as the Audio Group Building at 5005 SW Macadam Avenue. By 1977, KQFM's format was being described as "Soft MOR."[31] That year, KQFM was purchased by Golden West Broadcasting as a sister station to KEX (see chapter 15).

# Endnotes

1. Ted Smith, "History of Radio in Umatilla County," *Pioneer Trails,* The Umatilla County Historical Society, Vol. 27, No. 1 (Spring 2003), 10–11.
2. Rodger Nichols. Email to author. April 4, 2008.
3. Smith, "History of Radio in Umatilla County," 10–11.
4. Ted Smith. Interview with author. Tape recording. October 9, 2003.
5. Payne, Ancil. Interview with author. Tape recording. November 11, 2002.
6. Smith interview.
7. Wynne, Floyd. Interview with author. Tape recording. October 14, 2002.
8. Jim Boland. Email to author containing Davidson interview notes. March 26, 2009.
9. Bishop interview.
10. Pangborn had been born Lester Arden Pangborn. He changed his name to Arden X. Pangborn when, as a student at the University of Oregon trying to earn money as a writer, he believed that the change would favorably attract editors to his work. During the 1940s, he was managing director of KGW-KEX, later general manager of KGW, and went on to serve as vice president and general manager of WOAI Radio and TV in San Antonio, TX, before returning to Portland to join the staff of the *Oregon Journal.* He died in April 1998. ("Local Media Executive Arden X. Pangborn Dies at 91," *Oregonian,* April 15, 1998, D9).
11. "Behind the Mike," *Oregonian,* December 9, 1941.
12. Memorandum Licensed Radio Stations from the Federal Communications Commission Engineering Department, January 21, 1942 (WSMB Collection).
13. Smith interview.
14. Oregon Death Index.
15. Tom McCall and Steve Neal. *Tom MCall: Maverick* (Portland, OR: Binford and Mort, 1977), 12.
16. Ibid.

17. Singletary, *Radio Station KOIN: A Case Study of Music Programming*, 62-63.
18. Ibid., 63.
19. *Stars of Tomorrow* began on KGW around 1935, switched to KEX in 1950, then switched to KPTV in 1953, then to KLOR from 1955–57, and then returned to KPTV, where it ran until 1964. Besides Powell, Johnny Ray, Nora Martin and Kay St. Germain were among the program's "discoveries." (http://kptv.home.comcast.net/Shows/stars.htm).
20. Jane Powell, *The Girl Next Door* (New York: William Morrow and Company, 1988), 44.
21. Ibid., 48.
22. Chipman, KMED: *The First Half-Century*. At the conclusion of the war, Dunlevy, by then a sergeant, joined KMED as public service director and, in 1948, station manager under Blanch Virgin's ownership. When Virgin began preparing to sell KMED, Dunlevy became station manager of new Medford station KYJC.
23. William Moyes, "Behind the Mike," *Oregonian*, September 25, 1943, 8.
24. KEX had moved to that site in 1935 where it installed a 300-foot tower. KGW joined KEX there in 1938. Thus, it was easier for the staff to get both stations back on the air quickly when the studios were consumed by fire.
25. Much of the information about the KGW-KEX 1943 fire comes from material contained in Helen Platt's "KGW-Portland's Pioneer Station," unpublished manuscript, MSS 1134, Platt, Helen Papers, Oregon Historical Society. Other material comes from published accounts in the *Oregonian* on September 24 and September 25, 1943.
26. Pietro Belluschi obituary *New York Times*, February 16, 1994.
27. Carl Felsenthal, *Citizen Newhouse: Portrait of a Media Merchant*. (New York: Seven Stories Press, 1998), 55.
28. "KGW to Close FM Station," *Oregonian*, January 25, 1950, 1.
29. Kendall, John, 1950. Letter to T. J. Slowie, Secretary, FCC, dated February 20 (KGW-FM file, NARA, College Park, MD).
30. After the KQFM call letters were abandoned in Portland, they were later acquired by a Hermiston station, which is, therefore, referred to as KQFM-FM#2.
31. Information about Point-O-Salescast and the Myers Group purchase from Craig Adams, www.pdxradio.com.

# 14

# FM and TV Vie During Radio's Post-War Boom

## FM and TV Compete

Almost from radio's birth, scientists were busily trying to develop two different, improved broadcasting systems. Early radio stations had barely signed-on when visionaries began predicting that "radio pictures"—television—would arrive within a few years.[1] At the same time, AM radio—transmissions using Amplitude Modulation (AM)—of the 1920s and 30s was subject to interference from both local equipment (like diathermy machines) and atmospherics like summer lightning storms. Scientists worked diligently on both solving AM static and creating television.

Edwin H. Armstrong was an early colleague of Radio Corporation of America president David Sarnoff, and according to Armstrong, Sarnoff asked him to invent a system that would eliminate AM static. While it took him ten years, Armstrong subsequently developed static-immune Frequency Modulation (FM) radio. But to Sarnoff's horror, it was a system that required totally replacing AM transmitters and AM radios to be effective. "I thought Armstrong would invent some kind of a filter to remove static from our AM radio. I didn't think he'd start a revolution—start up a whole damn new industry to compete with RCA," Sarnoff reportedly said.[2]

Sarnoff and RCA were heavily committed to launching television and, as a result, made no effort to develop FM radio. A frustrated Armstrong ultimately started building his own FM stations, which operated on the original FM band

Meissner 9-1047 FM converter that allowed playing pre-World War II FM stations operating on 42–50 MHz band through an AM radio.

Courtesy of Andrew R. Mitz and www.somerset.net/arm/fm_only_photo_gallery_2.html#pre_war

WSMB Collection

Meier & Frank ad, *Oregonian*, September 21, 1939

of 42 to 50 MHz. Despite Depression economics, television's technical vagaries were finally resolved during the 1930s, and NBC officially launched its television service at the New York World's Fair on April 30, 1939. From 1939 to 1941, NBC's television service was broadcast only a few hours a week but virtually no receivers (which were quite expensive) existed to view it. Then, World War II intervened and halted all radio station construction along with NBC's television operations.

Oregonians followed these initial steps toward a national television service with great interest. On September 25, 1939, Meier & Frank set up a public demonstration in its tenth-floor auditorium of the Farnsworth Electronic Television system, an early competitor to the RCA/NBC system.[3]

With a huge investment already made in developing television, RCA did everything it initially could to stunt the widespread introduction of FM in order to boost TV. While the FCC was interested in promoting both FM and TV, it further complicated FM's growth by changing the frequencies authorized for it. While in 1940 the FCC had assigned FM stations to the 42 to 50 MHz band, the commission moved FM "upstairs" to the 88 -108 MHz band after the war. That step made all pre-war FM transmitters and radios obsolete—a considerable setback for FM radio.

The war's end thus set the stage for a historic contest. Which would catch on first? FM radio or television? Or could the nation—and the broadcasting industry—afford to pursue their simultaneous development? Broadcasters wrestled with those decisions.

## 7XAO/W7XAO-TV Portland

Oregon's first TV venture dates back to the earliest days of television experimentation. On September 20, 1925, the *Oregon Sunday Journal* announced that Wilbur J. Jerman's KFWV Radio expected to inaugurate experimental television broadcasting "inside of a week." Jerman secured an experimental television license for station 7XAO, although at that time television was so new a concept that the experimental station was licensed for "relay broadcasting" rather than specifically for visual transmission.[4] While it isn't clear what action, if any, followed Jerman's

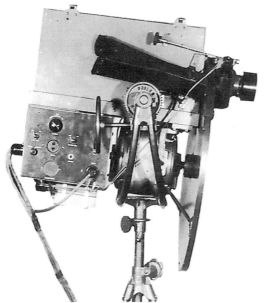

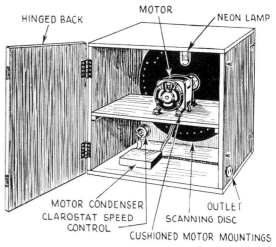

Early TV camera used by Lee DeForest for his Passaic, NJ, TV station W2XCD in 1931. The motorized "scanning disc" used in early mechanical television is clearly visible.

A TV receiver used to receive pictures produced by a scanning disc camera.
*Radio Listeners Guide and Call Book*, fall 1928. (WSMB Collection)

securing his 1925 television license, in June 1928 he announced that his station would soon "begin installation of television equipment for broadcasting of small pictures."[5]

That same month, Jerman's 7XAO license was renewed by the Federal Radio Commission specifically for the purpose of transmitting "radio pictures." It was the only TV license in the Northwest.[6] Following a change in federal licensing procedures, 7XAO became W7XAO and Jerman, enthusiastic about television, said that he expected "to broadcast moving pictures on the television license to use the projection machines in the Broadway theatre for pictures, and KWJJ broadcasting station to broadcast the sound accompaniments."[7, 8] It's important to note that the earliest experimentation in television, including Jerman's W7XAO, involved mechanical, rather than electronic, systems to generate visual images. The mechanical systems, which used a motor-driven rotating disc, could never equal the quality and convenience of electronic systems once they became practical. Jerman's experimentation was with mechanical TV and was apparently modest. His TV license was cancelled by the FRC in November 1930.[9]

## KGPP/W7XTE Portland

While Jerman was experimenting with TV, other radio exploration was underway in Oregon. On January 8, 1930, Portland police chief Leon V. Jenkins (who had often appeared on the KGW Hoot Owls) proposed to the Portland City Council the building a radio station, which he envisioned using to apprehend criminals (see chapter 3). Following some experiments, the effort resulted in the 200-watt KGPP, operating on 2442 KHz, which some claim to be the first police radio system in the nation. KGPP was constructed by Charles Austin, who then went to work for the police department as the station's operator.[10]

Austin was assisted by Temple V. Ehmsen, a policeman who also served as a KGPP operator. In 1944, Ehmsen filed an application for an experimental FM station, W7XTE, in his own name. The FCC issued a construction permit on October 30, 1944 but apparently the station was never built—perhaps because of Ehmsen's mid-1944 call to active U.S. Naval duty. The W7XTE license was cancelled in 1945.

# KGW-FM Portland

Notwithstanding its principal interest and heavy investment in television, NBC still encouraged some development of FM radio by its network affiliates. In a letter dated January 21, 1944, to KGW-AM manager Arden X. Pangborn, NBC President Niles Trammell encouraged KGW to submit an FM station application and expressed his hope for "an opportunity to discuss this matter with you in more detail." KGW must have had a long-standing interest in FM, because on October 30, 1940, it purchased the land on which KGW-FM was later constructed.

Despite the lack of experimental FM operations in Oregon, the issue of whether to invest in the development of FM or TV loomed large in 1945. The *Oregonian*, arguably the state's largest and most visible broadcast owner, didn't really know how to choose and so applied for both FM and television facilities (see KGWG-TV elsewhere in this chapter). Just more than a month after General Eisenhower ordered the D-Day landing in Europe, the *Oregonian* applied for a new FM station to operate on 46.1 MHz in the pre-war "low-band" FM allocation.[11] That application, filed on July 20, 1944, was doubtless a placeholder, that anticipated the war's successful conclusion, because construction of an FM station during the war would have been impossible. Subsequently, the newspaper amended its application to move to the newly announced "high-band" FM and requested 100.3 MHz. Then on April 27, 1945, three days before Adolph Hitler's suicide, the *Oregonian* filed a television station application.

Because its FM transmission plant hadn't been finished, KGW-FM requested and received special temporary authority from the FCC to operate with 250 watts on 95.3 MHz. Less than an hour after receiving the telegram conferring that authority, KGW-FM—Oregon's first FM radio station (and, the newspaper claimed, the first commercial FM station west of the Mississippi River)—signed-on at 5:45 p.m. on May 8, 1946, with Matt Frey, *Oregonian* general manager, and H. Quentin "Q" Cox, KGW manager, jointly throwing the transmitter switch. Announcer Bob Franklin signed-on the station saying: "This is KGW-FM—the *Oregonian*, operating on its assigned frequency of 95.3 megacycles, with a power of 250 watts as authorized by the Federal Communications Commission" and 15 minutes of news followed. [12, 13]

The *Oregonian* editorially observed that:

> The clarity of transmission of music and the human voice by The *Oregonian*'s new frequency modulation station, KGW-FM, is astonishing to those few who own an FM receiving set or have access to one in a dealer's showroom. Since there are only about a score of FM receiving sets in the Portland area KGW-FM will be an expensive service freely given to the public until there are enough sets to justify an advertising rate schedule. Station KGW-FM will be in the forefront [of FM development] and those who may obtain receiving sets are not likely to regret their early purchase.[14]

However, those dreams proved difficult to realize (see chapter 13). The station's interim authority to operate on a different frequency, and at reduced power, was routinely extended by the commission until 1949, at which time KGW-FM settled at 100.3 MHz with 54 kilowatts.

Initially, the *Oregonian* anticipated that the FM station's programming would consist of a mix of NBC Network offerings and newly contemplated local programs such as *Rollie Truitt Time* and *Your Mayor Speaks* and live music such as the *World's Greatest Hymns* with Glenn Shelley and *Rhythm Vendor* with various KGW artists. But following sign-on, such extensive local programming hardly seemed plausible for the small number of FM receivers in the community.

Originally, KGW-FM *was* programmed separately from KGW-AM but on June 27, 1948, the FM station began simulcasting KGW-AM. Nevertheless, the *Oregonian* was making investments in KGW-FM. During the period since KGW-FM had first signed-on in 1946, the station had successively grown with its power raised to 5.1 kilowatts on April 1, 1947, and to 54 kilowatts on April 1, 1948, from its newly constructed Healy Heights transmitter at 4545 SW Council Crest Drive (which was completed on March 24, 1948).

The station switched frequencies, still on an interim authority basis, to 100.3 MHz on October 10, 1947.[15] The *Oregonian* must have been carefully watching its investment in FM because on June 10, 1949, Judge Kendall, representing his client, advised the FCC that KGW-FM would reduce its operating hours to seven hours a day Monday through Saturday, with and only an extra half-hour on Sundays. Even that reduction wasn't sufficient to stanch losses, and on January 23, 1950, Kendall advised the commission that KGW-FM would cease operation at 10:30 p.m. on Tuesday, January 31, 1950.

The axe had fallen on KGW-FM, and Kendall returned the station's license to the commission on February 20, 1950.[16]

KGW-FM's demise was likely designed to distance the *Oregonian*'s from any broadcast properties that were running substantial losses as the newspaper began exploring the sale of both itself and KGW.

*Courtesy of the Oregonian*

KGW chief engineer Harold Singleton adjusts the new KGW-FM transmitter on March 31, 1948, as the station prepares to raise its power to 54 kilowatts the next day.

## KGWG-TV Portland

On May 16, 1946, just nine days after KGW-FM signed-on, the FCC approved the *Oregonian*'s application for a channel 6 TV station—KGWG. The *Oregonian* had been quick to leap into television, having filed an application for channel 4 on May 9, 1945. (During the FCC's year-long consideration of the application, the newspaper modified its request to substitute channel 6 for channel 4.) At the time, no other television applications had been filed for the Portland area, and the *Oregonian*, which had made a profit of more than $1 million in each of the two preceding years, seemed well-equipped to assume the challenge of TV. However, by the time the commission approved KGWG, few FM or TV receivers existed, and would-be station owners had to anticipate the need to operate such stations at a considerable loss until these new services gained popularity.

On further reflection, the *Oregonian* decided it was unwise to simultaneously pursue both new FM and TV stations, and in a letter dated December 22, 1947, the *Oregonian*'s counsel, John W. Kendall, reported it was abandoning its TV plans:[17]

> The Oregonian Publishing Company is now going forward with the completion of its FM station and the installation of equipment utilizing the full facilities as authorized by its FM construction permit, thereby requiring a substantial investment, for the further reason that there are a very limited number of television receivers in the Pacific Northwest, said Oregonian Publishing Company wishes to surrender its construction permit for authority to construct and operate a television station at Portland, Oregon.[18, 19]

Courtesy of John S. Kendall

John W. Kendall, attorney, son of John C. Kendall, and father of John S. Kendall. He represented numerous Oregon radio and television stations during his career. c. 1955.

The *Oregonian*'s abandonment of KGWG would prove to be momentously ill-advised and costly.

Subsequently, the newspaper explained its decision to abandon KGWG was based on two factors: 1) lack of space for television studio facilities in its new building (an assertion that seemed hard to accept at face value since the application had been filed in 1945 when designs for the new building were still in flux) and 2) that the KGW radio staff would be too heavily engaged in relocating the radio operation to its new studio location to allow construction of KGWG.[20]

In reality, KGWG's cancellation occurred because the *Oregonian* was overextended due to the construction of its new downtown headquarters. As a result, it had begun to rethink its investment in broadcasting. As far back as the 1947 abandonment of KGWG, the newspaper was likely considering the possibility that the paper itself would be sold. It is clear that by the close of the decade, the idea of such a sale was under active consideration, and new broadcasting ventures that were losing money would likely detract from its sale price. The *Oregonian* and KGW-AM were sold to S. I. Newhouse on February 21, 1951—without either FM or TV adornments.

## KTVU-TV Portland

Another television aspirant was Video Broadcasting Company, a California-registered partnership between 11 southern Californians. Its FCC application for channel 3 in Portland was apparently submitted late in 1947. Granted in February 1948, the company was authorized for a 15.5 kilowatt transmitter with offices in Portland's Heathman Hotel (which was also KOIN's home). While the KTVU call sign was assigned on April 28, 1948, construction proceeded haltingly.[21] Partially resulting from zoning problems, Video Broadcasting had to file several requests for additional construction time. In December 1948, in an obvious change of plans, Video Broadcasting reported that it had constructed a studio/transmitter building near the southeast end of South West Crest Drive but was still awaiting zoning authority to construct its tower.[22, 23]

The commission apparently concluded that Video Broadcasting was dragging its feet. This determination was influenced by the commission's confidentially learning that KTVU had entered into negotiations over a contemplating joint relationship with the *Oregonian* involving the paper's possible purchase of 51 percent of Video Broadcasting's stock, which would result in KTVU operating from the *Oregonian* studios that had originally been slated for KGWG (which, of course, contradicted the paper's earlier assertion that it returned KGWG's construction permit due to lack of space). The FCC concluded that KTVU wasn't financially viable. On November 17, 1949, it denied Video Broadcasting's request for additional time to build the station, saying: "It appears that the permittee has not been diligent in the construction of its proposed TV station."[24]

Radio was clearly a less expensive, and perhaps less uncertain, venture than television. Whereas both Oregon entities that had received TV construction permits in the 1940s had failed to construct their stations, numerous parties jumped into the new world of FM. Not all succeeded, however.

## KWIL-FM Albany

KWIL-AM made the leap into FM by applying for a 710-watt station—to operate on 101.7 MHz—which signed-on October 24, 1947.[25] KWIL-FM operated until around 1956, when it ceased broadcasting and returned its license to the FCC.

## KUGN-FM Eugene

On April 10, 1946, KUGN-AM partners Carl H. Fisher and Benjamin Phillips applied for a new FM station for Eugene—operating on 99.1 MHz with 8 kilowatts power—and signed-on, with an interim service using only 250 watts power, on October 12, 1947. They periodically sought extensions of that temporary authority while deferring construction of the more powerful transmitting plant that had originally been authorized. In 1953, after having received approximately a dozen such extensions, the station asked the FCC to allow it to abandon the eight kilowatt version of KUGN-FM and to simply consider the 250 watt version the completed station. The FCC approved the request in October 1953, and KUGN-FM began operating on a regular, as opposed to an interim, basis.

KUGN-FM never really became profitable and signed-off September 11, 1960—remaining silent for several years while KUGN, Inc., contemplated what to do with the station. It may have been dismantled, because KUGN, Inc., subsequently filed an application to "reconstruct the station at our present site."[26] In 1962, KUGN, Inc., offered to donate the station to the University of Oregon—which was operating a lower-power KWAX-FM at the time. On October 28, 1962, KUGN-FM filed an application to transfer its license to the university saying: "There is an abundance of FM stations in the Eugene-Springfield area, operating on a commercial basis, and there does not seem to be a demonstrated need for putting ours back on the air."[27] Ultimately, the university declined the gift, and on May 19, 1964, KUGN-FM requested cancellation of its license.[28] Some of KUGN-FM's equipment was donated to the University of Oregon and was eventually used to raise KWAX's power on its own frequency (see chapter 16). However, KUGN, Inc., wasn't finished with FM—and the KUGN-FM call sign resurfaced in 1978 (see chapter 21).

## KGPO-FM Grants Pass

World War II officially ended with V-J Day—victory over Japan—on August 15, 1945. On October 30, the Southern Oregon Broadcasting Company (owner of KUIN Grants Pass) filed an FCC application for a new 102.3 MHz FM station to operate as a sister of KUIN. The application was approved under the call sign KGPO—standing for K-Grants Pass Oregon—although amendments in 1946 shifted the station's frequency to 96.3 MHz. KGPO signed-on April 25, 1948, and survived until it was voluntarily shut-down in 1961. According to long-time KUIN manager, Eddy Arnold, "They shut it down in '61 for lack of listeners. There were no [FM] sets out there then."[29]

## KFLW-FM Klamath Falls

Shortly after World War II ended, KFLW-AM applied for an FM frequency and was granted 94.5 MHz at 5 kilowatts. Ultimately, the station chose not to act upon the construction permit, and KFLW-FM was not built.[30]

## KMED-FM Medford

In 1939, KMED applied to build an FM station in the then-authorized "low" FM band but those plans were shelved by World War II.[31] Following the war, other applications for FM stations were being filed in Jackson County, which must have concerned KMED. While the station renewed its FM planning after the war and secured an FCC construction permit, it ultimately decided to abandon the effort. It was more than 20 years later that KMED-FM was actually constructed (see chapter 27).

## KALE-FM/KPOJ-FM Portland

KALE Portland also wanted an FM outlet, and on July 14, 1946, station manager Charles Couche announced that the FCC had authorized construction of the 50-kilowatt KALE-FM to operate from Mt. Scott on 96.1 MHz. In making the announcement, Couche couldn't predict a sign-on date, because approval for the necessary radio equipment hadn't arrived from the post-war Civilian Production Administration. KALE-FM finally did sign-on June 6, 1948—operating at 98.7 MHz with 44 kilowatts power—on the date KALE-AM became KPOJ-AM (see chapter 15). With a quick call sign change, the FM station signed-on as KPOJ-FM.

In August 1949, KPOJ-AM-FM, owned by the *Oregon Journal*, moved from its studios at 919 SW Taylor Street to the Odd Fellows Building at 1019 SW 10th Avenue, a location it occupied well into the 1970s. In 1955, KPOJ-FM reduced its power to 4.3 kilowatts (likely to lower its operating costs).

## KEX-FM Portland

KEX owner Westinghouse signed-on the FM sister station, KEX-FM, on Thanksgiving Day, 1948. The studios were located in KEX's new Radio Center at 1230 SW Main Street in Portland, with the transmitter located on Healy Heights at 4504 SW Carl Place.[32] With a power of 56.4 kilowatts at 92.3 MHz, KEX-FM was Portland's sixth FM station.

On December 17, 1956, KEX-FM signed-off without explanation. It signed-on on August 5, 1957, as an all-classical music station, a format that then-new Westinghouse president Donald H. McGannon had decreed for the company's ailing FM properties. The move wasn't successful, and, on March 15, 1962, Westinghouse donated KEX-FM to the Oregon State Board of Higher Education as an adjunct to Portland's newly created noncommercial television station, KOAP-TV. KEX-FM left the air permanently on April 8, 1962. As a rechristened KOAP-FM, it signed-on April 30, 1962 (see chapter 16).

## KOIN-FM Portland

KOIN-AM was an early FM applicant, having received its FCC construction authority nearly simultaneously with KGW's. KOIN-FM's 50-kilowatt plant, which was originally authorized on 94.5 MHz and later reassigned to 93.1 MHz, was subsequently constructed on 101.1 MHz. The station signed-on September 12, 1948, and operated daily from 3:30 p.m. to 10:30 p.m.

KUGN-FM, KGW-FM, KOIN-FM, KEX-FM, KPOJ-FM and KGPO were typical early FM stations. Hatched as siblings of existing AM stations, they were able to share engineering facilities and personnel, which made starting a new FM station more economically feasible. Because the AM band was then largely considered be full, particularly in larger communities, FM seemed to be the only way for new would-be broadcasters to enter radio. Despite not knowing how popular FM would prove to be, many new parties across Oregon filed applications to start new FM stations with little understanding of how long it might take them to become economically viable.

## KPFM-FM/KPAM-FM/KCNR-FM/KCNR-FM/ KKLI-FM/KKSN-FM/KYCH-FM Portland

Portland's Stanley M. Goard, who had started out as a radio technician, was just such an aspiring new station owner. Following World War II, he filed an application for KPFM (standing for **K**-**P**ortland-**FM**) in the name of Broadcasters Oregon, Ltd., which he owned. The FCC issued him a construction permit in late 1945.

KPFM, Oregon's oldest surviving FM station, was constructed on Sentinel Hill in Portland's Healy Heights area, in a white building trimmed with glass, brick and aluminum. The station's front hallway sported a linoleum floor that was inlaid with the station's call letters and musical notes. Two studios had been designed for live music broadcasts, and sponsor's observation booth overlooked the largest studio. The station called it the "View Room Studio" and it was large enough to hold an orchestra if needed. The plant was relatively elegant and featured anechoic curved walls such as were found in the larger radio networks. Stanley Goard and his wife, Doris, lived in the building's first-floor basement area, which featured a commanding view of the city stretched below them.

Goard envisioned KPFM as a bastion of good music, and the station had been designed to both produce and transmit it—a sort of classical music version of KOIN's fundamental commitment to continuous live-music programming. KPFM began transmitter testing on September 3, 1946, on its 94.9 MHz frequency and was in full commercial operation by November 13 with a daily operating schedule of 2 p.m. to 10 p.m. KPFM's sold its first commercial time (Oregon's first commercial time sale on FM) to an auto and trucking company. While the station had originally been tested at 1 kilowatt, by November 13 it had jumped to 1.53 kilowatts— which made it Oregon's most powerful FM station at the time. KPFM switched to 97.1 MHz on July 31, 1947, and expanded its hours on August 1, 1947, to run from noon to 10:15 p.m. daily. In 1948, the

KPFM chief engineer Walter M. Nelson, (left) and Stanley Goard at the station's sign-on.

Flyer for FM demonstration at Benson
Polytechnic, 1948

station increased its power to 1.59 kilowatts and also
raised its antenna height, giving it greater range.[33]

By 1948, KPFM was actively promoting FM radio,
since lack of receivers was the station's greatest challenge.
In February of that year, KPFM and the Portland Council
of Radio Distributors presented a demonstration of FM
sets and reception in Benson Polytechnic High School's
auditorium.

On January 9, 1960, Stanley Goard sold KPAM and
KPFM for $200,000 to William E. Boeing Jr.'s Chem-Air,
Inc. KPFM inaugurated stereo multiplex broadcasting
(while all FM stations had previously been monophonic,
the multiplex system allowed stereo transmission by a
single FM station) on December 16, 1961, at noon, and
the station's longtime classical music format was largely
abandoned on October 19, 1964, when classical music
moved to late-night hours and popular music took over
the rest of the schedule (see chapter 21). Adverse listener
reaction was swift and flooded the station—to no avail.

On October 1, 1965, KPFM was again sold—this time to Romito Corporation. The compa-
ny's title was derived from the last names of its owners: president and general manager Walter
P. Rossman (formerly KVAN assistant manager and KXL commercial manager); Dr. Samuel L.
Miller; and Marvin R. Tonkin (owner of Marv Tonkin Ford Sales, Inc.). Rossman, Miller and
Tonkin each held a one-third interest in Romito. KPFM's $175,000 purchase price included its
sister station, KPAM-AM.

Rossman bought out his partners for $20,000 each on June 20, 1967. Then, he began simul-
casting a Top-40 format on both the AM and FM stations, including Portland's first "underground rock" program, the Saturday *Night Flight with Dan Foley*, which premiered at midnight
on March 13, 1968. The FM station used the slogan "FM 97: Taking the Town by Stereo." The
DJ roster included Craig Walker in his first Portland assignment, Bob Brooks, Peter Leyland,
and Bob Marx (real name Michael Bailey). Bob Lee was the news director and Bob King the
program director. Rossman owned the station for many years but sold it long before his death
in 1993 at the age of 79.

## KPRA-FM Portland

Wilbur J. Jerman and John C. Egan launched KPRA under a different corporate ownership
than the other station they both owned, KWJJ. The two men were already running an advertising agency, Pacific Radio Advertising Service, Inc., which purchased and re-sold air time on
their station, KWJJ. It was under that agency ownership that they filed an FCC application for a
new FM station to operate on 95.7 MHz with 250 watts. KPRA's studios were at 1017 SW Sixth
Avenue (next door to KWJJ at 1011 SW Sixth Avenue) and the station's transmitter site was
located on Healy Heights.

Portland's third FM station, KPRA signed-on September 25, 1947, with a Portland Beavers
baseball broadcast. Programmed separately from KWJJ, the station operated Monday through
Saturday from 10 a.m. to 1 p.m. and from 6:30 p.m. to 10 p.m. Its only simulcast with its sister AM station was a daily promotional feature at 12:45 p.m., *What's On FM*. A month after
sign-on, the station raised its power to 3.4 kilowatts, and on January 9, 1948, KPRA switched

frequencies to 95.5 MHz. Initially, Jerman was KPRA's manager but William E. Richardson assumed that title in 1948.

Some controversy surrounds KPRA's demise. The station signed-off on September 24, 1948, after struggling with the cost of separate programming in a market with relatively few FM receivers. Jerman later maintained that vandals had broken into the transmitter building, damaging the transmitter and smashing meters, and that the station's marginal financial standing prevented it from making repairs.[34] Industry wags suggested this was a ruse to allow the station to be gracefully retired without admitting its economic failure. It's likely that Jerman had confused the demise of KPRA, which apparently failed for purely economic reasons, with a vandalism incident that ultimately silenced his next FM station, KWJJ-FM. Seattle-based engineering consultant Ben Dawson, corroborated the KWJJ-FM version of failure at the hands of vandals by reporting that, in 1957 or 1958, he dismantled the original KWJJ-FM transmitter, which had been visibly vandalized.[35]

## KWJJ-FM Portland

Wilbur Jerman and John Egan's second FM attempt, the 3.4-kilowatt KWJJ-FM, signed-on April 30, 1949, at 95.5 MHz, the same frequency on which KPRA-FM had last operated. Presumably, KWJJ-AM acquired the license of the defunct KPRA-FM, which had been owned by Jerman and Egan under Pacific Radio Advertising, Inc. KWJJ-FM, however, enjoyed little more commercial success than KPRA-FM and ceased operation on November 14, 1950. Jerman sold the station's Healy Heights transmitter location to John D. Keating the following day (see chapter 18).

## KXL-FM Portland

Another Portland FM venture that was little more successful than KWJJ-FM was KXL's FM effort. On April 10, 1946, the FCC authorized KXL-FM on 96.5 MHz with 39.9 kilowatts. KXL, then owned by Ed Craney, explored—but did not consummate—a joint operation with KALE on its Mt. Scott transmitter site. With FM still a new technology, KXL pursued a highly unusual experimental operation in which it tested various mountain-top transmission sites using a low-power transmitter.

These mobile tests were apparently conducted somewhat intermittently, and, when the FCC urged the station to select a final transmitter location in February 1948, KXL-FM explained that roads to a possible transmitter site on Larch Mountain remained closed. Apparently, the station had broadcast in November and December 1947 and then signed-off for the winter. Intending to resume operations in the early summer of 1948, KXL-FM advised the commission that it would "probably be ready to build our station sometime this fall." But on December 1, 1948, KXL's attorneys instead asked the FCC to dismiss the station's FM authority, pointing out that "in the area the irregular terrain makes reception of FM signals somewhat doubtful. The Hooper breakdown of FM listeners shows but few points interested in FM in that area." The FCC deleted KXL-FM's call letters on December 28, 1948.

## New AM Stations Boom in Post-War Radio

World War II's end 1945 brought dramatic growth in radio. In 1941, Oregon had 22 stations; in 1950, it had 43 AM stations, plus eight FM stations—a total of 51 radio stations.[36,][37] Along with that growth, the character of radio was beginning to change. Before the war, network affiliation had been the norm: in 1945, 95 percent of all U.S. radio stations were network-affiliated.[38] But growth in the number of stations soon started to change that ratio. With network affiliations already fully committed in larger cities, new stations there tended to sign-on as independents. After 1947, as the networks' attention began to shift to television, the radio networks' role gradually began to shrink in importance, and by 1955 only 50 percent of stations in the U.S. were network-affiliated.[39] Even in smaller communities, while network affiliation still remained attractive, it was no longer as critical—all of which helped spawn the Liberty Broadcasting System (LBS).

## Liberty Broadcasting System (LBS)

Little remembered now, the Liberty Broadcasting System (LBS) was founded in 1948 by Texan Gordon McLendon, known as the "Old Scotsman." The network was organized largely around sports broadcasting and used the "re-creation" approach in which a telegrapher at the event took down the action in code and sent it over a dedicated circuit to a radio studio, where another telegrapher decoded it and was handed it to an announcer who "re-created" the event—sometimes with added sound effects. Local stations had engaged in such sports re-creation broadcasts throughout the 1930s and 40s but McLendon took this practice to the network level.

By 1952, LBS was the nation's-second largest radio network, with 458 affiliates. But when the larger baseball clubs raised the rights fees that year to an unsustainable degree, McLendon filed an unsuccessful antitrust lawsuit over the pricing which Liberty contended was collusive. Things unraveled quickly. Unable to afford the increased fees, the network abruptly shut down on May 16, 1952, and its failure affected LBS affiliates across Oregon and the nation.[40] One such station was KWIN.

## KWIN-AM/KCMX-AM Ashland

Robert Dodge developed the idea of building a radio station in Ashland and then enlisted Ed Tomlin and Roy Peck (who had an engineering background) to organize the Rogue Valley Broadcasting Company. Attorney Frank Van Dyke came in as a fourth partner. Mark Hamacher eventually bought a controlling interest and became what Tomlin described as "the power behind the wheel." Where Dodge's principal interest had been developing the station largely as a community service, Hamacher's goals focused more on business.

With 250 watts on 1400 KHz, KWIN signed-on July 30, 1946, from a studio/transmitter site at 1160 Helman Street on the edge of Ashland's northern boundary—but the site decision would eventually prove fateful. KWIN emulated Jackson County's oldest broadcaster, KMED, in a variety of ways, including the *art deco* building exterior that was intentionally modeled after KMED's.[41]

Managed by Roy Peck, the new station also had as its program director and chief engineer former KMED staffer Floyd Rush, who'd returned to the Rogue Valley from Portland.

Announcers included Glen Garvey, imported from Los Angeles as well as Vern Kuykendall of Klamath Falls, Jim Strickland of Corvallis, and Phil Schwab from Southern Oregon College (which later became Southern Oregon University). Other staff included Mrs. Margaret Richie of Ashland and Kippy St. Dell, a "Hollywood actress," both of whom were in the programming department, and Logan Niniger, KWINs commercial manager. Frank Snyder was the pianist in the musical department, and Donna Frazer was the station's receptionist.

KWIN had a difficult beginning and Peck quickly left the station to pursue a career in Los Angeles. Seeking recommendations on managerial talent, Tomlin then contacted Chet Correy, a former fraternity brother who was managing KWIL Albany. That call resulted in the station's hiring Robert Reinholdt as manager in December 1946.[42] Ten days after his arrival, the station burned to the ground. A new building was constructed on the original concrete foundation, and all of the station's interior contents were replaced.[43]

While KWIN was technically and programmatically successful when it returned to the air, its financial position remained tenuous. Reinholdt managed the station

Courtesy of the George Rambo collection

KWIN studios, 1957

until September 1948 and was then succeeded by Ed Barnett, who, following his military duty, had joined the KWIN staff shortly before Reinholdt's arrival.

On December 6, 1946, the station received FCC approval for an FM station construction permit but, given the AM station's financial position, that venture was abandoned.

Then KWIN encountered another major problem. The station had leased pasture land immediately north of its building for its tower, but the arrangement apparently didn't clearly establish rights for the buried radial field wires required for an AM tower. Eventually, a dispute arose when the landowner, Thomas Fowler, wanted to plant an area of the pasture. Rogue Valley Broadcasting wound up settling the matter by purchasing the property at a price the station it couldn't afford—an event that eventually helped push the station into bankruptcy.[44]

On March 1, 1951, KWIN ended its status as an independent station by joining the Liberty Broadcasting System (LBS). But when LBS failed in May 1952, KWIN itself became insolvent and went off the air August 1, 1952, following a claim from the Internal Revenue Service over the station's failure to pay $5,300 in back taxes. During subsequent foreclosure proceedings, Mark Hamacher, who was KWIN's major creditor, purchased the station for $20,000 in December 1952.

Radio was moving toward disc jockey (DJ) programming, a term supposedly invented by newsman/commentator Walter Winchell.[45] On April 20, 1953, KWIN resumed operations with DJ/music programming similar to its offerings prior to the LBS affiliation, and on October 15 of that same year KWIN joined the Mutual network. For the first time, Jackson County had all four major radio networks represented locally. During the late 1950s, controlling interest in KWIN was owned by Douglas D. Kahle, a resident of Pacific Grove, California.

KWIN rebounded from its earlier financial difficulties and controlling interest in the station was purchased in March 1962 by W. Henry Peck of Ashland. Peck recapitalized KWIN and moved its studios from their original location to the Mark Antony Hotel (now the Ashland Springs Hotel). The transmitter was moved to Ashland's south side, where a new two-tower directional antenna system was constructed when the station raised its power to 1 kilowatt and switched frequencies to 580 KHz—changes that went into effect on April 4, 1962, concurrent with KWIN's move. Offering 16 hours music daily, the station's fortunes seemed to have finally turned. Its country-and-western format featured Henry Peck as range boss, Wayne Loerke as trail boss, Jeanne Barlow as tally wrangler and Bill Lively (later Ashland's chief of police), Ed Tomlin, Ron Holloway and Sue Henry as trail riders. By 1966, KWIN had re-affiliated with Mutual but switched to CBS on June 5, 1967.

In June 1968, the station abandoned the hotel location and moved its studios and offices to the transmitter site. Although KWIN was purchased in October 1971 by C & W Broadcasters,

Inc., the station's country-and-western music format continued with local personalities Robin Lawson, Mel Tynan and Jim Chesky as announcers along with a call sign change to KCMX on October 12. The station also carried the *Ashland Grizzlies* and *Portland Trailblazers* games. In 1981, Pacific Northwest Broadcasting, Inc., which owned KPNW-AM-FM Eugene, purchased KCMX-AM—along with KKIC-FM—for $1 million (see chapter 27).

## KRUL-AM/KLOO-AM Corvallis

On Saturday, August 23, 1947, at 6 p.m., Pacific States Radio Company signed-on Corvallis' KRUL at 1340 KHz. It was Benton County's only commercial radio station. Supposedly, KRUL was started by a family connected to Brown and Haley, Inc., the Washington state manufacturer of Almond Roca candy, in an attempt to engage the interest of a young family member who ultimately proved uninterested in the station. Built alongside the Mary River, KRUL's tower was a short, squat unit and allegedly a Richfield Oil Company service station sign.[46] Station manager Phil Waters commanded a crew whose goal was to create a radio service that focused on music, news, "local interest broadcasts" and local sports. Emphasizing sports, one of the 250-watt station's first broadcasts was play-by-play coverage of the Oregon State University softball tournament on Sunday, August 24, anchored by KRUL's news/sports director, Clair W. ("CW") Peck, who came to Corvallis from KHIZ, Ottumwa, Iowa, and succeeded Waters as station manager in 1948. Later in the year, KRUL added OSU football and Corvallis High School home and away games to its schedule.

Reportedly, DJs had total freedom in programming and chose their own air names. Mel Palder was one of the more colorful DJs who used his real name on pop music shows, but, for *Hayloft Hoedown*, he became Sheriff Lem Redlap—a backwards spelling his name. The station owner, Pacific States Radio Company, may have run into difficulties and it appears that KRUL may have gone silent in 1957. On April 23, 1957, the station was sold to Benton Broadcasters,

Jeff E. Evans, KRUL's chief engineer/announcer, anchoring his daily 7:45 a.m. *Early Worms Club* program, 1948.

Inc., which was co-owned by Robert G. Beattie and Dale K. Allison. The station's call sign appears to have been changed to KLOO as a result of the sale. KLOO was purchased by Robert Lowell Houglum and his wife, Mimi, in 1964.

## KWRO-AM Coquille

KWRO stationery letterhead, late 1950s
WSMB Collection

Following his exit from KOOS Coos Bay, his abortive attempt to start a radio station in Grants Pass in 1938 and his 1940 sale/departure from KVAN Vancouver, Washington, Walter Read seemed to have been casting about for another radio project. Between 1941 and 1945, Read worked in radio in Juneau, Alaska, at Boeing in Seattle and in radio equipment sales in Los Angeles. Yet, he must have been planning his next radio venture during these years.[47]

Read was familiar with the community from his years at KOOS and obviously believed that a new station, serving the entire county, would be successful. William E. Walsh was a Coos Bay attorney who had represented KOOS during the time Read owned and managed that station. Walsh also served in the Oregon senate, where he had represented Coos County since 1941. Walsh and Read seem to have dreamed up the new station in December 1946. They established their partnership and, on February 5, 1947, submitted an FCC application which proposed establishing a new 250-watt radio station on 1450 KHz in Coquille.[48] After the FCC granted a construction permit in June 1947, they asked that call sign KWRO be assigned on July 28, 1947.

KWRO signed-on January 13, 1949, and Walter Read moved to Coquille around that time. One can speculate that the call sign may have been intended to stand for **K**-**W**alsh-**R**ead-**O**regon.

In the beginning, KWRO was managed by Robert Harris, who had earlier worked at KOIN, and immediately before taking on KWRO, had been the owner/manager of KTIL Tillamook. Other staffers included Curt Haynes from KOOS, engineers Phil Linn and Ralph Brown, both of KTIL and sales manager Bill Cook, who'd moved into radio sales following work at the Coos Creamery. "Coquille's Newest Asset" offered music and transcriptions from the Associated-Muzak library. The station's studio and transmitter were located in the Sanford Heights area at 1270 West 13th Street. In 1949, the partners decided to convert their business structure from a partnership to a corporation under the name KWRO Broadcasters, Inc. Walter Read sold his interest in KWRO around 1953 and moved to Salem, leaving the company in the control of his original partner, William Walsh and members of his family.

By the late 1950s, KWRO was using the slogan "Big 'K' Radio." On October 31, 1956, the station switched to 630 KHz, at 1 kilowatt daytime-only, and on June 10, 1960, it raised its power to 5 kilowatts, still daytime-only. In the mid-1950s, the station was managed by Lynn C. Thomas, who was succeeded by Leonard F. Epling in 1958. Epling's staff included operator James McCurdy, traffic manager Deloy Keeler, salespeople/announcers Lavarre Ramey and Edward Fredrickson, accountant Margaret Wylie and engineer Darrell Johnson. In 1976, KWRO Broadcasters, Inc., still owned by co-founder William Walsh, sold the station to KWRO Broadcasting Company on December 7. KWRO became KSHR on January 18, 1982. When Golden Bear Communications, Inc., purchased the station in 1984, it changed the call sign to KBEY on January 4, 1985. On March 27, 1987, both KBEY-AM and KSHR-FM were purchased by Coquille River Broadcasters, Inc. who restored the AM station's call sign to KWRO on May 1, 1987.

# KUGN-AM Eugene

Originally, Carl H. "Pop" Fisher was principally in the construction business through which he represented Lehigh Structural Steel out of Allentown, Pennsylvania. Accordingly, he erected Lehigh radio towers for stations throughout the west. Sensing a good business opportunity, in 1944 he started his own company, Tower Sales and Erecting Company, headquartered in Portland, to handle the radio construction work. While Fisher

Long-time KUGN announcer/newsman Wendy Ray on remote

was known in the construction business as "Carl," in broadcasting he went by "Pop" Fisher, the nickname given to him by his son, Carlton "Carl" O. Fisher.[49]

Observing the success of radio stations he had constructed, Fisher established Valley Broadcasting Company, in partnership with Benjamin Phillips, who was president and manager of the First National Bank of Port Angeles, Washington. They submitted an FCC application for KUGN-FM on April 10, 1946. They also established a new 250-watt station on 1400 KHz, KUGN-AM, which signed-on June 30, 1946, in Eugene.

Fisher brought in veteran broadcaster S. W. McCready to manage KUGN. McCready had started out at KXL, where he was chief engineer by 1935. In 1949, Lester S. Ready Jr. was KUGN's program director, Lytle N. Young the commercial manager, Jack L. Billings the news director, Robert R. Whitely the continuity director and William H. Green the chief engineer.

Recalling KUGN's genesis, Carl O. Fisher said: "We had a wonderful few years building radio towers because we were practically the only ones in the west doing that. After we noticed that some people were starting to do pretty well in radio we said, 'Well, we better build one of our own, so we applied for Eugene's second station and built KUGN."[50]

Fisher was an "absentee owner" and lived in Portland. Phillips, originally a 50-percent partner in Valley Broadcasting Company, wanted to sell his interest, and on November 4, 1948, he requested FCC approval to transfer his interest equally to brothers O. E. Berke and P. R. Berke for $50,000. At the same time, KUGN's ownership structure was undergoing change. KUGN, Inc., formed in April 1948, was predominantly owned by Valley Broadcasting, which held 96 percent of the company. Pop Fisher and son Carl and the Berke brothers each held an additional one percent interest.

In January 1952, Valley Broadcasting was dissolved and shares in KUGN, Inc., were acquired 50 percent by Pop and 25 percent by each of the Berkes. Pop Fisher purchased the Berkes' interests in early 1953 and in May of that year sold his 100 percent ownership of KUGN, Inc., to his son, Carl. The transaction was prompted by Eugene Television, Inc.'s successful application for KVAL-TV in April 1953 (see chapter 19). The FCC had approved the TV construction permit contingent upon Pop Fisher's divesting his KUGN, Inc., ownership. Carl Fisher sold his 50 percent interest in KIHR Hood River to his father as part of his purchase of KUGN, Inc.

KUGN initially was an ABC affiliate. A major change occurred on September 30, 1950, when KUGN switched to 590 KHz at 1 kilowatt. Two years later, on September 20, 1952, KUGN switched to NBC, remaining an NBC affiliate for many years) and November 16, 1953, it increased power increase to 5 kilowatts daytime and 1 kilowatt nighttime.

On April 1, 1973, the Fisher interests sold the station to Obie Communications (now Obie Media Corporation), a division of Obie Industries, a company headquartered in Eugene with broad media interests, including outdoor advertising. In 1977, KUGN lost its long-time NBC Network affiliation to KPNW and affiliated with CBS on December 5 when KASH lost its CBS connection (see KASH section in this chapter).

## KERG-AM Eugene

The last new newspaper-owned AM station of the 1940s was the *Eugene Register Guard*'s KERG (**K**-**E**ugene **R**egister **G**uard). Operating from the *Register-Guard*'s offices at 37 West 13th Avenue, the station signed-on November 18, 1949, with its transmitter located on Coburg Road. KERG joined the CBS Radio Network on October 5, 1951, and raised its power on September 19, 1954, to 5 kilowatts daytime and 1 kilowatt nighttime. Subsequently, the station would change call signs to KWOW, KQAK and KDUK. It was eventually donated to the Lane County School District 4J on January 10, 1997, where it became KRVM (see chapter 16).

## KASH-AM/KEED-AM/KOPT-AM/KOPB-AM Eugene

Radio Air Ways, Inc., was conceived during World War II by Portland's E. L. Kincaid, who filed an FCC application for 1520 KHz in Eugene on November 8, 1944. Original company stockholders included H. Day Foster, who had worked in radio at KORE, KUJ Walla Walla and KSLM before relocating to Portland to work at KGW-KEX in 1943 (where he served as program manager). It was originally intended that Foster would manage the new Eugene station, with the call letters KASH. The other original stockholders were G. G. Van der Vlugt, who held 76 percent of the stock, and Kincaid, who held 23 percent. Foster owned the balance of the company.

The war, among other events, caused a number of planning changes. Early in the application process, Radio Air Ways modified its application to seek 1550 KHz. Foster passed away, and his stock was surrendered to the corporation, which in turn, sold it to Clyde W. Kincaid. Following the FCC's granting of a construction permit for a 1 kilowatt station (day and night) on 1550 KHz, Radio Air Ways asked to switch frequencies to 1600 KHz with a nighttime directional pattern in October 1946. On January 23, 1947, the FCC authorized that change. Originally, the station contemplated housing its studios in the Eugene Hotel, but by the time construction began space wasn't available there and the station instead established studios at a newly constructed transmitter building on Day Island Road.

Initial planning for the station had been heavily Portland-based. Besides Foster, Rollie Truitt was set to be news editor and announcer. At the time of Radio Air Ways' 1944 FCC application for KASH, Truitt was in his third year as a freelance sports announcer—broadcasting on KGW, KEX, KWJJ and KXL as circumstances warranted—and was apparently willing to relocate to Eugene for a full-time assignment. Other anticipated staff included Paul Harden as chief engineer (who had previously worked for a number of Oregon radio stations) and Marjorie Allingham (previously an actress and then a secretary at KGW-KEX in Portland). By the time the station actually signed-on, time had wrought change. With Foster's death, E. L. Kincaid assumed the station manager role, with Clare Mattingly as assistant station manager. William Riley was the chief engineer and Laura Nidever the program director.

EUGENE, OREGON
TELEPHONE 5-3357
POST OFFICE BOX 1600

RADIO AIR WAYS, INC. • "TOP O' THE DIAL" *1600*

KASH stationery letterhead, c. 1950
WSMB Collection

The 1-kilowatt KASH signed-on September 20, 1947, operating at 1600 KHz ("At the Top of the Dial"). The station's first day on the air featured University of Oregon football coverage, the *KASH Party Line,* local music and news programming and the *Top of the Morning* program from 6 a.m. until the 8:30 a.m. *Bible Fellowship Hours.* The station also focused significantly on agricultural programming such as the 6:55 a.m. *Sears Farm Fair* and the 12:15 p.m. *Farm Digest.*

The owners were gratified by KASH's growth, and E. L. Kincaid rapidly assumed a greater role. In 1952, he purchased the corporation's remaining unsubscribed stock, which considerably boosted his leverage. However, relations between Kincaid and G. G. Van der Vlugt, a resident of John Day, were deteriorating. While Van der Vlugt had been the major investor at the outset, Kincaid now rivaled his position. Moreover, Kincaid strongly believed that the company should venture into television, a move that Van der Vlugt adamantly opposed. Accordingly, in May 1954, Kincaid bought out Van der Vlugt's interest in the company for $75,000 "to settle all controversies existing between G. G. Van der Vlugt and Erven L. Kincaid."[51] By the time Kincaid purchased his adversary's shares, the company had already, under the name Television Air Ways, sought channel 26 in Eugene (see chapter 19). Conceivably, the tensions surrounding the Kincaid/Van der Vlugt relationship contributed to Television Air Ways' subsequent lack of success in the television proceeding.

On August 1, 1976, KASH took on a short-lived affiliation with CBS Radio but relinquished it on December 5, 1977. On April 1, 1985, KASH changed call signs and took over the call sign of another Eugene station, KEED. The station again changed call signs on April 22, 2005, and adopted KOPT and until its purchase by Oregon Public Broadcasting in 2008, when it became KOPB-AM.

## KFLW-AM/KFLS-AM Klamath Falls

Oregon's first new post-war AM station was KFLW Klamath Falls (signifying K-Falls Land of Waters). The *Klamath Falls Herald and News* had flirted with radio as far back as 1922, when it sought a license for KDYU and on July 5, 1940, the paper's corporate parent Klamath Publishing Company filed an application for a 250-watt station operating at 1450 KHz (see chapter 2). World War II interrupted the FCC's processing of the application, but on November 21, 1944, the commission issued a construction permit and the *Herald and News* pushed to get the station on the air.

The paper had sought call sign KFHN for the station (intended to stand for the Klamath-Falls-Herald-News) but it was already in use elsewhere. The call letters KFLW were assigned. As 1944 came to a close, the newspaper printed the headline "1945 Expected to See New Radio Station Start Here" and forecast "it will be at least six months before the station is in operation."[52]

By granting the November 1944 construction permit, the FCC had effectively conveyed to the newspaper "go ahead and start building if you think you can get the equipment," which was in short supply due to wartime restrictions on strategic materials production. Because the *Herald and News* couldn't secure equipment, on July 3, 1945, the FCC extended the period allowed for construction—which finally began September 1. At 2 p.m. on March 31, 1946, KFLW signed-on from studios located in the newspaper's building at 1301-09 Esplanade Street. Its transmitter was located in the Balsiger Building at Main and Esplanade Streets. Following extensive promotion in the *Herald and News*—KFLW signed-on with an ABC affiliation.

Marshall Pengra of KRNR Roseburg (in which the *Herald and News* had an ownership interest) had written KFLW's original FCC application and generally oversaw the station's operations from Roseburg. Station manager Bud Chandler, who reported to Pengra, was assisted by chief engineer Gilbert Walters, Paul Alexander, and Bruce Hulse, who had previously been an announcer at KOAC Corvallis and KLBM La Grande before deciding to work in radio's more technical areas. Marjorie Eagle was the station's receptionist, and announcers Mel Baldwin (formerly with Portland stations KWJJ, KGW and KEX), Bob McCarl (who went on to work at KLIQ Portland and then became program director of KXL Portland) and Chuck Cecil (formerly of KFEC San Luis Obispo) filled out the station's roster. Cecil later went on to a career in Los Angeles that included announcing at NBC Radio mainstay KFI-AM.

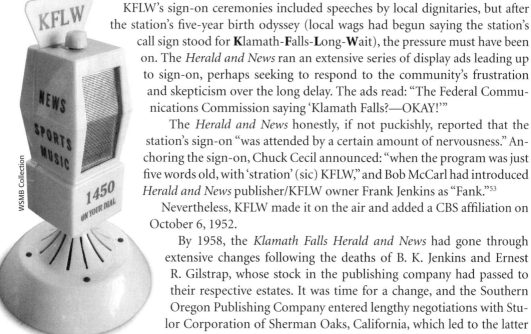

KFLW's sign-on ceremonies included speeches by local dignitaries, but after the station's five-year birth odyssey (local wags had begun saying the station's call sign stood for **K**lamath-**F**alls-**L**ong-**W**ait), the pressure must have been on. The *Herald and News* ran an extensive series of display ads leading up to sign-on, perhaps seeking to respond to the community's frustration and skepticism over the long delay. The ads read: "The Federal Communications Commission saying 'Klamath Falls?—OKAY!'"

The *Herald and News* honestly, if not puckishly, reported that the station's sign-on "was attended by a certain amount of nervousness." Anchoring the sign-on, Chuck Cecil announced: "when the program was just five words old, with 'stration' (sic) KFLW," and Bob McCarl had introduced *Herald and News* publisher/KFLW owner Frank Jenkins as "Fank."[53]

Nevertheless, KFLW made it on the air and added a CBS affiliation on October 6, 1952.

By 1958, the *Klamath Falls Herald and News* had gone through extensive changes following the deaths of B. K. Jenkins and Ernest R. Gilstrap, whose stock in the publishing company had passed to their respective estates. It was time for a change, and the Southern Oregon Publishing Company entered lengthy negotiations with Stulor Corporation of Sherman Oaks, California, which led to the latter company's purchase of KFLW for $80,000. In submitting the sale to the FCC for approval, the *Herald and News* reported that it "desires to withdraw from [the] radio broadcasting business."[54]

The buyers were Stuart Wilson, who had worked in radio in the Los Angeles area (including at KHJ, KFWB and KBIG) since 1934;

Given away as a sales promotion, this radio, shaped like a microphone, was fix-tuned to KFLW, c. 1965 his wife, Lorraine K. Wilson; and their son Robert S. Wilson, who was director of special events programming, public service and public relations at station KBIG Hollywood, California. The Stulor corporation took possession on October 15, 1958, but a year later sold the station for $80,000 to Caloretex Corporation so the Wilsons could return to Los Angeles. Caloretex Corporation, with Joe D. Carroll as its president, in turn sold KFLW to David F. Snow of Klamath Falls on October 16, 1960. A California broadcaster with previous radio experience at stations in Madera, Fresno, Santa Rosa, Merced and Marysville, Snow had spent six months looking for a station to buy before deciding on KFLW.

By coincidence, Floyd Wynne, who worked for KFLW when it signed-on, had the same initials as the station's original call sign. When he purchased it from Snow on January 1, 1971, some erroneously speculated that the call sign had been devised by Wynne, who owned and managed the station for many years. He changed the call sign to KFLS on October 16, 1972, which the station promoted as standing for: **K**lamath-**F**alls-**L**and-of-**S**unshine.

## KMCM-AM/KCYX-AM McMinnville

In 1946, another newspaper jumped into radio when the McMinnville *Telephone-Register* filed an FCC application for a new station in the paper's hometown. The *Telephone-Register* had first applied to build an FM station, but when growth in FM popularity seemed lagging, switched its application on September 9, 1948, to AM on 1260 KHz with 1 kilowatt daytime power. Jack B. Bladine, president of the McMinnville Broadcasting Company and publisher of the *Telephone-Register*, was joined in the effort by his brother Phillip N. Bladine, who was also involved in the newspaper. They requested the call sign KMCM, standing for **K**-**MCM**innville, and broke ground on January 28, 1949, having changed their corporate name to Yamhill Broadcasting, Inc., the previous month.

KMCM was built at an estimated cost of $27,500 with its 210-foot tower erected by C. H. Fisher and Son in February 1949. On March 31, construction began at 2163 Lafayette Avenue on the natural-cedar-clad 1,600-square-foot studio/transmitter building, which featured a green pylon next to the station's tower. The building's interior was trimmed in mahogany.

KMCM signed-on its Western Electric 443A-1 transmitter on June 18 at 11 a.m. with McMinnville mayor R. H. Windisher throwing the switch to initiate broadcasting. The inaugural program consisted of a special one-hour broadcast from the stage of the Mack Theatre at 510 NE Third Street, during where the broadcast's audience enjoyed musical performances by Steve Paietta and his Orchestra with vocals by Brad Reynolds. The program included the station's first newscast was live from that stage.

KMCM's inaugural staff included station manager Louis F. Gillette (formerly at KPQ, KHQ, KGA, KPOJ and KOIN), news director Gilbert Tilbury, sports director Bruce Brown, commercial manager and announcer Glasco P. Branson (formerly at KELA, Centralia, Washington), chief engineer George "Skip" Hathaway (later KUGN's chief engineer), receptionist/bookkeeper Phyllis Bladine, announcer Ivan Smith (who went on to a career in Portland) and announcer Eugene K. Kilgore (formerly at KRUL).[55, 56] Audio tape recording was a new technology that was just starting to replace wire recorders at local radio stations, and KMCM boasted an "Echo-tape" reel-to-reel tape recorder. The station broadcast local music programming such as *The Alarm Clock Club* (mornings), *Bargain Bulletins, Newberg On The Air, Sheridan On The Air, Amity On The Air, Noon News, Farmers Exchange, Yamhill County Today, Sports From The Sidelines, Northwest News* and *Kilgore Auction Time.*

While licensed for daytime-only operation, the station quickly secured approval for directional nighttime operation, which allowed it to be heard between North Bend, Oregon and Seattle. Its slogan was "Always Good Listening." The station joined the Keystone Broadcasting System on March 1, 1950, and the Liberty Broadcasting System on October 2, 1950.[57] KMCM retained its call sign for decades, through numerous ownership changes, until July 1, 1979, when it became KCYX.

## KYJC-AM/KRTA-AM Medford

While the *Medford Mail Tribune* had a longstanding interest in radio dating back to its early association with KFAY's founding in1922, it wasn't until 1947 that the newspaper moved to establish a station that it officially owned. The story of the paper's re-entry into radio is complex. Publisher Robert Ruhl, who had been involved with both KFAY and KMED in the 1920s, apparently initiated the new project but was drawn into extensive travel and other commitments that prevented him from supervising it. Other staff stepped in, among them Gerry Latham (then the *Mail-Tribune*'s circulation manager), who wound up supervising the station construction despite the fact that he had no previous radio experience.

Latham reviewed three potential locations for the station before selecting one on Barnett Road. Originally a slaughterhouse, its walls were more than a foot thick in places. Following a fire, the structure was being remodeled as a three-bedroom home—in an *art deco* style reminiscent of KMED's building—when Latham picked it as the station's studio/transmitter location. He purchased it before ever receiving FCC authorization. "I was asked what we would do with the building if the FCC turned us down," Latham recalled, "and I said we could always turn the building into a night club."[58]

FCC approval arrived on August 27, 1947, and on Friday, October 10, 1947 the Mail Tribune's new station KYJC signed-on with 250 watts on 1230 KHz. Initially, KYJC was a part-time ABC Network affiliate carrying some network programs such as the *Breakfast Club.*

KYJC's first general manager was Collin R. "Bob" Matheny, who was just completing an engineering degree at Oregon State University in 1946 when one of his professors got him the job at the station. Matheny presided over the opening ceremonies, which were followed by ABC's *Bing Crosby Program.* Following the Crosby program, KYJC broadcast the high school football game between Medford and Eureka, California, with sportscaster Ned Liebman on play-by-play, commercial manager Bill Woodford doing statistics and Jack Adkins engineering. KYJC didn't become a full ABC affiliate until March 1, 1949, when the change brought programs such as *Breakfast in Hollywood,* the *Breakfast Club, Milton Berle Star Theatre, Mr. President,* the *Lone Ranger* and the *Richfield Reporter* to the station. Matheny went on to found KRCO in Prineville in 1949 (see chapter 21).

Latham continued to supervise KYJC until the Medford Printing Company, owner of both the newspaper and the station, sold the *Medford Mail Tribune* to the Ottaway Corporation in April 1973. In October 1973, Medford Printing announced it was separately selling the station to Mattco, Inc., which installed Craig Findlay as station manager. Under the new ownership, Jerry Allen became an important figure. Allen had grown up in Grants Pass, Oregon, and had taken a part-time "gopher" job at KAGI during high school. While never contemplating a career in radio but having a life-long love of sports, Allen studied teaching at Southern Oregon University but he kept his hand in radio. Working part-time for KAGI and announcing at SOU's KSOR (he signed-on that station on May 21, 1969), Allen worked his way up the ladder at KAGI.

Courtesy of the Southern Oregon Historical Society photo 19889

After college, Allen remained at KYJC. There, he worked his way from music director to program director to general manager (succeeding Finley). But he also continued to do play-by-play sports, which was his real love. Following KYJC's sale in 1985, he moved to Eugene to become the "Voice of the Oregon Ducks" for the University of Oregon.

On May 24, 1983, KYJC vacated its original frequency of 1230 KHz, moving to 610 KHz, and increased its power to 5 kilowatts. In January 1985, Grants Pass resident and owner of that town's station KFMJ-FM, John Miner purchased KYJC under the name Lindavox Broadcasting (see chapter 27). While maintaining an FM studio in Grants Pass, Miner operated both KYJC and KFMJ largely from Medford. Eventually, KYJC's ratings slipped; the AM and FM encountered financial difficulty and went off the air for more than a year. In October 1990, KYJC was sold to a new owner, Encore Broad-

KYJC staff members, c. 1951. (left to right) Tom MacLeod, James Dunleavy, unidentified man. MacLeod arrived at KYJC as the station's sports director around the time this photo was taken. On Dunleavy's departure in 1957, MacLeod became KYJC's general manager.

casting Corporation. On January 3, 1995, KYJC switched to a Spanish-language programming format under the new call sign KRTA.[59]

## KNPT-AM Newport

Tom Becker got into electronics during a World War II Coast Guard stint. Afterward, he secured an FCC First Class operator license and took his first radio job at KOOS in 1947 as that station's chief engineer. At the time, Al Shade was the manager of KOOS and the two men formed a partnership to apply for a new station in Newport. KNPT (**K-NewPorT**) signed-on June 19, 1948, with 250 watts on 1230 KHz. KNPT's studios and transmitter were at 1940 North Oregon Coast Highway. On March 1, 1951, KNPT went to 1 kilowatt at 1310 KHz.

When KNPT started, Newport had a population of only 1,800. Attorney John C. Kendall, who handled the FCC application for Yaquina Radio, Inc. (the corporate name of the applicant), said to Becker: "Why go to Newport when you could go to McMinnville or some other [larger] location?" But Becker liked Newport, where he signed-on the station with a total staff of five.

One early KNPT staff member was Mo Niemi, whose father originally contacted Becker, asking, "Is there any chance of you hiring my daughter? She's got this restaurant down by the waterfront and it isn't making a dime." Becker not only hired Niemi, but after looking over the restaurant's operations, helped her put it solidly in the black while becoming her partner in that

John Haley (at console) and Tom Becker in KNPT control room, 1948

venture. Niemi did a talk show on KNPT and sold advertising. "She had a great radio voice," Becker recalled. "She knew everyone in town."[60]

Perhaps Becker's most long-lasting decision was his 1952 hiring of Robert Spangler, a newly minted broadcaster with a consuming passion for sports. Spangler had previously played for the Pacific Coast League's San Diego Padres, following his World War II military service, before deciding upon a career in broadcasting. He was KNPT's morning announcer—and the radio voice of the Newport High School Cubs—for more than 50 years. Likely holding the record of longevity of service at an Oregon station, he remained at the KNPT microphone (apart from two brief time-

Mohava Marie (Mo) Nieme, c. 1957

outs in Eugene and at KTDO) right up until his death in 2008. During his remarkable career at KNPT, he earned the love and respect of the entire community. Becker eulogized Robert Spangler, observing that he was "a person who gave his whole life to everyone else."[61] Known as "Mr. Newport," Spangler was honored in 1999 when Newport High School named its basketball court Spangler Court. On his passing, KNPT renamed a studio in his memory.

## KSRV-AM Ontario

Following World War II, in Oregon's far southeastern reaches, Gordon L. Capps was deep in preparation for the inaugural broadcast of Ontario's first radio station, 250-watt KSRV, which signed-on at 11 a.m. November 23, 1946. Plans for the station dated back to 1942, when land for a tower site was surveyed and studio plans were developed. However, it wasn't until March 1946 that Inland Radio, Inc., the station's owner, began construction.

Managed by Capps, the initial station staff included program director John W. Powell, head announcer Al Corwin, chief engineer Chuck Harland, news reporter Ted Loud and secretary Velma Morton. Ray L. Kozak, whom Capps brought to Ontario from KMMJ Grand Island,

Nebraska, was also among the station's inaugural staff. Kozak remained at KSRV until 1950, when he left to start a station in Kansas but returned to Oregon in 1957 when he purchased KPLK (see chapter 21). He was apparently sufficiently prominent at the station that his picture still hangs in the station's lobby.

Operating at 1450 KHz, the "Voice of the Snake River Valley" was warmly welcomed by the Ontario Commercial Club and local citizens with initial program including *The Sons of the Pioneers, Casa Loma Time, Presenting Harry Horlick, Singing Sam,* and Thursday evening's *The Haunting Hour* (sponsored by the Ontario Cleaners) as well as Oregon State football games.[62] The station's slogan was "Tune to the top of your dial for the summit in radio enjoyment."

Pat Wilkins, later of KATU-TV Portland, was the KSRV news director for three years. "When I was hired to be the newscaster at KSRV in Ontario, I had only two or three years' experience, but I thought I was pretty hot stuff, ripping and reading copy off the news wire machines," he remembers. "Boy, I was in for a surprise. I was told by the boss that I was to gather, write, and broadcast a fifteen-minute, completely local newscast each evening, six days a week," Wilkins says.[63] KSRV was successful, and it raised its power to 1 kilowatt and changed frequency to 1380 KHz in the early 1950s.

## KGON-AM/KYMN-AM/KSGO-AM/KFXX-AM/KKSN-AM/ KZNY-AM/KGDD-AM Oregon City

KGON was founded by Clackamas Broadcasters, whose president was Dr. John H. Fitzgibbon. He was joined in the venture by Roy Jarman, owner of Jarman's Buick and Chevrolet dealership, and Temple V. Ehmsen, who was KGON's chief engineer (see chapter 13).[64]

While the company originally requested 1490 KHz, the frequency was amended to 1230 KHz due to concerns expressed by KOCO Salem. Licensed for 250 watts, the station was built at a cost of $50,000 with studios on McLoughlin Boulevard (Pacific Highway) in Gladstone.[65] KGON signed-on at 7 a.m. on July 4, 1947, and was managed by Hale Byron. Other staff included Bob Roberts, program director and chief announcer (who later became KXL's news director); Douglas Bates, news editor; Ray Cummins, chief operator; Rod Cain and Gene O'Brien, announcers, and John Ford, opera announcer.

"The Voice of Clackamas County" was active in local programming—particularly in sports, beginning by carrying local high school games and then expanding into other Portland-area sports broadcasts. When KGON joined the Liberty Broadcasting System (LBS) on March 11, 1950, the station also began carrying major league baseball games but lost network service when LBS failed.

Local sports broadcasts were largely re-created. Wes Baaken was a teenager at the time and played steel guitar for his dad's country music band's Saturday afternoon broadcast, recalls Dick Novak announcing such events (see Chapter 45):

> Hanging from his microphone on a string was a small baseball bat about the size of a normal flashlight. To the left of (Novak) was a quarter-inch audio tape recorder with a loop of tape, containing crowd noises. Dick had a pencil in his hand and while reading the teletype, he would hit the bat with the pencil and say something like 'It's a hit into center field' and at the same time bring up the audio from the tape machine and the crowd would roar. I was about 15 at the time and was really taken with how he could make that game sound so real on the air.[66]

On July 30, 1956, KGON switched to 1520 KHz with 10 kilowatts power. Shortly thereafter, it became Portland's NBC Radio Network affiliate when KGW-AM abandoned NBC on

December 17, 1956 (see chapter 18). KGON's slogan was: "First in sports. Tops on your dial at 1520." The station took an additional Mutual affiliation on April 17, 1959, but lost NBC to KGW on January 7, 1960, when the latter took NBC back. The station made a huge jump when it raised its power to 50 kilowatts day and night from a new 12-acre transmitter site in Clackamas located at15201 SE Johnson Road.

KGON went to a top-40 format on September 3, 1962, dropping Mutual. On November 12, 1962, it received FCC permission to move the station's studios to the transmitter site.

On July 1, 1964, KGON was purchased by Republic Broadcasters, Inc., of Denver, Colorado. In Denver, Republic Broadcasters owned rock station KIMN, which was locked in a bitter struggle with another station partially owned by Don Burden, whose Star Broadcasting had purchased KISN in 1959 (see chapter 23). It was Republic's firm intention to challenge Portland's top-rated rock station KISN.

KGON ad, Oregon City High School *Hesperian* yearbook, 1956
Courtesy of Wes Baaken

On August 1, 1964, Republic changed KGON's call sign to KYMN (a play on the call sign of their Denver property) and adopted the slogan "Kim Radio 1520." Other slogans KYMN used included: "More music and more entertainment from fabulous Kim in Oregon;" "the 50,000 watt voice of the Great Northwest; the peak of your dial;" and "Move up to Kim." As counterpoint to KISN's highly promoted on-air use of its call letters, KYMN featured "Kimcasters," who reported "Kim Weather" in "Kimland" and "Kim Time." Douglas J. Taylor was installed as the station's general manager. Shortly after the call sign change, KYMN dropped its Mutual affiliation.

KYMN's attempt to unseat KISN failed, and the station adopted a beautiful music format on February 1, 1967. Republic re-organized on August 21, 1967, and Wally Nelskog became its vice president and James B. McGovern took over as general manager. On September 11, 1967, KYMN changed its call sign to KYXI and its slogan to "Beautiful music 24 hours a day."

On January 7, 1971, Republic sold KYMN (along with its Denver KIMN-AM and FM) to Pacific & Southern Company, Inc. (DeSales Harrison, president) for $6,493,550. On January 26, 1973, the station was again sold, this time to McCoy Broadcasting Company (Arthur H. McCoy, president) for $1.5 million. The station's licensee was renamed KYXI, Inc., on March 13, 1973. James B. McGovern remained general manager, and some months later the station switched to a popular music format.

On October 1, 1973, KYXI, Inc., announced its purchase of KLIQ-FM for $400,000. KLIQ-FM became KGON-FM on November 1, 1973, and in March 1974 Craig McCoy, the son of McCoy Broadcasting's president, became KYXI's general manager. In October 1974, KYXI affiliated with the NBC Radio Network (which KGW had again dropped). The station went to an all-news on July 12, 1976, with the NBC News & Information Service (NIS) using the slogan: "News 15" and claimed to have the largest news staff in the Northwest. When NIS folded, KYXI became KYTE and joined CBS on May 2, 1977, adopting an all-news format with Paul Hanson as news director.

On April 14, 1978, the station's licensee name was changed to McCoy Broadcasting of Oregon, Inc., and a year later on April 8, 1979, the station was sold to Western-Sun, Inc. (owned by the *Des Moines Register & Tribune* newspaper) for $27.7 million.[67] Craig McCoy became president of the licensee as well as general manager of KYXI, which also picked up CNN audio in 1982.

On February 20 1984, KYXI abandoned the expensive all-news format and switched to the Satellite Music Network's "Stardust" format. The station also changed its call sign to KSGO (**K**-**S**olid-**G**old-**O**ldies) on September 1, 1984. Dropping CBS Radio, the station began programming "Solid Gold Rock and Roll," under program director Michael Johnson. During this period KSGO's slogans were: "1520 KSGO solid gold" and "the music you grew up with." In December 1984, Jeff Davis took over as program director for "Solid Gold Oldies."

Apparently unsuccessful, on July 1, 1985, the Des Moines Register & Tribune Company announced that it had sold the stations to Ackerley Communications, Inc., of Seattle for $6.75 million. In April 1988, the KSGO/KGON studios moved to 4614 SW Kelly Avenue. The KSGO studios had been at the transmitter site at 15201 SE Johnson Road since November 1962.

The station went through a number of call sign changes in the 1990s and early 2000s, successively becoming KFXX (with the slogan "X marks the spot"), KKSN, KZNY and eventually KGDD—its current call sign.

## KBKO-AM/KLIQ-AM/KMJK-AM/KVIX-AM/KLVS-AM/ KPHP-AM/KKSL-AM Portland/Lake Oswego

Mercury Broadcasting Company planned KBKO for two years before the station officially signed-on at 7:30 a.m. on January 10, 1949. Mercury was founded by its president, general manager and chief announcer Gordon E. Bambrick, who began his career as an announcer on Portland's KXL in June 1937. Following seven years at KGW-AM as production manager, Bambrick was planning his own station for which he purchased the old KWJJ transmitting plant at Oaks Park.[68]

Besides Bambrick, initial staff included Helen Drill, previously at KWJJ; George Skiff, formerly at KPOJ; and announcer Lloyd A. Sutherland, who had come to Portland from KJBX San Francisco. Mercury's vice president and the station's chief engineer, Harold K. Krieger, had previously worked at both KGW and KOIN. Reportedly, the station's call sign, KBKO, reflected the first letters of Bambrick's and Krieger's last names with the "O" added for Oregon.

The 1290 KHz, 1 kilowatt, daytime-only station liked to boast that "combined, its radio staff represents a half century of radio broadcasting experience."[69] With studios in the Carmen Building at 3908 NE Sandy Boulevard, the independent daytime station specialized in "sweet-type" music.

On September 25, 1952, W. Gordon Allen and Thomas P. Kelly purchased 75 percent of Mercury's stock from Bambrick, who remained Mercury's president and general manager. The FCC would later maintain that the purchaser had transferred control back to Bambrick and Krieger in August 1953, without the commission's knowledge or consent.[70] Krieger's purchase of control in 1952 made change imminent at KBKO, which became KLIQ (with the station re-

**1290 ON YOUR DIAL**
BROADCAST SQUARE
OAKS PARK
PORTLAND
OREGON

KLIQ stationery letterhead, late 1950s
WSMB Collection

ferring to itself as CLICK Radio or Radio CLICK) on November 1, 1952. Kelly also apparently bought out Allen's interest in 1953.

The station has a rich history and was the first Portland station to drop block programming in favor of a popular music/DJ format in 1952, which essentially marked the beginning of rock 'n roll radio (later top-40) in Portland. KLIQ's on-air staff was a fine team consisting of: Bob Adkins (later known as "Addie Bobkins") from 4 p.m. to sunset (and noon to sunset on Sundays); Tom Kelly on the morning program from sunrise to 9 a.m.; Rick Thomas (who had become program director) from 9 a.m. to noon and Jeryll Burris taking over from noon to 1 p.m., when women announcers were a rarity. They were rounded out by Bob McCarl who was on the air from 1 p.m. to 4 p.m. KLIQ used a clicker sound on the air when giving its slogan: "This is KLIQ, Radio Click. (click!)" Adkins later recalled that he did his program seven days a week and sold air time for a gross income of $29.75 per week (against a 10 percent commission on sales). While Bambrick initially continued to manage KBKO/KLIQ under the Kelly ownership, Kelly took over as general manager in 1953. The station had both enjoyed—and suffered through—a rather remarkable opening of the decade, but things ultimately went wrong. On April 12, 1954, KLIQ signed-off when the IRS padlocked its doors over failure to pay 1953 tax withholdings. The station's assets were sold at auction on May 5, 1954. While it had received FCC authority to remain silent until July 12, 1954, the station failed to return to the air and ultimately its license renewal was set for hearing.

On March 12, 1956, the hearing examiner ruled against Mercury's renewal application and recommending awarding KLIQ's frequency to Robert E. Bollinger, a Portland resident who owned Oaks Park amusement park along with the land adjacent to KLIQ's studio/transmitter location. Bollinger promptly converted his licensee status from 100 percent personally owned to a corporation, KLIQ, Inc., in which he owned all of the stock. At noon on August 15, 1957, KLIQ returned to the air under Bollinger's ownership. The station promoted the occasion with a series of red cars driving around Portland with lettering that announced the station's impending return. On February 18, 1959, KLIQ, Inc., was sold to KLIQ Broadcasters, Inc., for $90,000. Stanley G. Breyer was its president and John F. Mallow its vice president. On March 18, 1959, the new owners changed KLIQ to an all-news format. It was Oregon's first all-news station and one of the first in the country. The revolutionary format, which was quickly profiled in *Newsweek* magazine, was short-lived.[71] On May 4, 1959, the station abruptly scrapped all-news to become a rock 'n roll station—again for a brief period—by hiring DJs who were fired at KVAN when that station became KISN four days earlier (see chapter 23). On June 13, 1959, the rock format was scrapped and KLIQ switched to good music (popular standards). It was not until 1966 that KLIQ returned to a talk format, when it hired the well-known *Oregon Journal* columnist Doug Baker to host a daily talk program.

David M. Jack became KLIQ's general manager in 1963 and purchased the station on April 1, 1967, along with silent partner Walter McNiff as Cascade Broadcasting Company (which

KLIQ's *Doug Baker Show* debuted on January 5, 1966. In this photo, Baker's guest is Bob Hazen (left), of Benjamin Franklin Federal Savings and Loan, who did programs on many Portland area stations including KEX, KOIN, KXL and KWJJ.

eventually became Tamarack Communications, Inc). KLIQ increased its power from 1 to 5 kilowatts daytime-only on April 16, 1961; changed its city of license from Portland to Lake Oswego on February 20, 1981, and received FCC approval to begin night operation with 5 kilowatts directional power on June 7, 1984.

On August 30, 1985, Vic Ives' 107 Ltd. purchased KLIQ from Tamarack Communications for $1,575,000. Ives was, and is, a larger-than-life radio figure. As Golden West's KEX program director from 1970 to 1975—during which time he achieved notoriety as host of KATU-TV's campy *Sinister Cinema*—he managed other Golden West properties from the company's headquarters but eventually returned to Portland to assume control of KMJK-FM. Jack reported that he sold the station because of changing conditions in radio. "In order to compete, you really need an AM-FM combination," he said.[72] Ives named the station KMJK-AM#1 as a companion to the FM station he had acquired in 1983. When Ives KMJK-FM was sold on December 31, 1986, Ives' AM station became KVIX (as in "Vic's station") on January 15, 1987. That short-lived call sign was succeeded by KLVS—all Elvis radio—on September 15, 1988. But it only lasted until December 31, 1988, when the station went silent. It returned to the air July 1, 1990, and then went dark again on September 12, 1991. The station was sold to the Christian broadcaster Crawford Broadcasting Company, who changed the call sign to KPHP on July 29, 1991, for $450,000. The buyer had not owned an Oregon station for almost 30 years since its ownership of KWAY Forest Grove, had ended in 1963 (see chapter 21). KPHP became KKSL on August 31, 1995, but was off the air in 2008.

## KPDQ-AM Portland

KPDQ was founded by John W. Davis, who received an FCC construction permit for a 250-watt station on 800 KHz on July 18, 1946. The original call sign issued was KJXD, but that was changed to KPDQ (along with a power increase to 1 kilowatt) on December 18, 1946. The station signed-on July 30, 1947, with an initial slogan of "Join the K-Pretty Darn-Quick Switch to KPDQ." The station's studio, Raytheon transmitter and 260-foot tower were located at the opposite end of Oaks Park from KWJJ's transmitter.

Don Dundell was KPDQ's program director for a schedule that consisted predominantly of news and transcribed programs. Rodney Johnson, who got his start in radio at KBPS while a Benson Polytechnic High School student, next worked briefly as a transmitter engineer at KXL. Johnson found that work tedious and switched to a position as studio announcer/engineer at KWJJ before Davis hired him to build and maintain KPDQ.

One of the station's local programs featured organist Leah Holt, who had played for Portland theatres for many years, and who regularly broadcast an organ concert from her home. Johnson, who had started the Rex Recording company to supplement his work at the station, was impressed by her performances and began marketing recordings of Holt.

In 1949, KPDQ opened a sales office in room 210 of Portland's Panama Building at 534 SW Third Avenue, and William E. Richardson took over as general manager that same year. In 1956, the station moved its studios to a brick building at 4903 NE Sandy Boulevard in Portland's Hollywood District. By 1959, KPDQ was being managed by David M. Jack, who remained until December 1962 when he assumed that same position at KLIQ. In the mid-1970s, KPDQ switched to a religious format and in 1977 changed its corporate name from KPDQ, Inc., to Inspirational Broadcasting Corporation to better reflect the station's focus.

On July 28, 1986, Portland-based Inspirational Broadcasting sold KPDQ-AM-FM for $6.5 million to Salem Media of Oregon, Inc., which was headquartered in Camarillo, California, and already owned KBMC-FM in Eugene (see chapter 26). According to the buyer, the word "Salem" in its name was not related to the Oregon capital. Rather, it referred to a word meaning "peace." Under Inspiration Broadcasting's ownership, the AM-FM stations were Portland's only full-time religious stations—programming that Salem pledged to continue.

Art work from a KPDQ promotional brochure, c. 1953
WSMB Collection

## KOCO-AM/KBZY-AM Salem

Around Christmas 1945, Salem resident B. Loring Schmidt filed an application for a new Salem radio station to operate on 1490 KHz. Because Clackamas Broadcasters' original application for KGON Oregon City specified the same frequency, the FCC was forced to designate the two mutually exclusive applications for hearing. To avoid costly litigation, Clackamas switched its application to 1230 KHz and on November 21, 1946, and the commission awarded 1230 KHz to Clackamas for KGON and 1490 KHz, at 250 watts, to Schmidt for KOCO (**K-O**regon's-**C**apitol-**O**utlet). The station referred to itself as "Cocoa."

Shortly thereafter, Schmidt and his wife, Jennie, purchased land for the station's tower, radial field and studio/transmitter building at 1426 Edgewater Street in West Salem, from R. L. Elfstrom. Schmidt separately negotiated the use of a strip of adjoining land, which was needed for the tower's radial field, from P. E. Bunnell for a $50 annual fee.[73]

KOCO signed-on at 6 p.m. on July 9, 1947. Early staff included Robert Suing, staff technician; Richard Nason, writer-announcer; and Al Schuss, sportscaster and commercial manager. One of the station's early features was Western International League baseball coverage.

KOCO was well-received by the community, and its success caused competitor KSLM to suddenly begin referring to itself as "Salem's pioneer station." Working to construct KOCO apparently proved too stressful for Schmidt, however, and he suffered a nervous breakdown nearly concurrent with the station's sign-on.

Schmidt's wife was appointed his guardian in September 1947, and an involuntary transfer of the station's license to her, as guardian of his estate, occurred on November 21. Jennie Schmidt operated the station successfully until her husband's recovery in July 1948, when the guardianship was discharged and the license returned to him.

Loring Schmidt's original lease of the Bunnell property, secured for the station's radial field, had been for a ten-year period and was not renewed. Apparently unable to deal with the responsibilities of relocating KOCO, the station signed-off in February 1957. It was then

KBZY top-40 survey, October 14, 1963

purchased by Salem Broadcasting Company, headed by Carl O. Fisher, who moved the station to newly leased property on Glen Creek Road NW in spring 1957.

Under its new ownership, KOCO became KBZY on May 1, 1957, when the station signed-on at 5 a.m. with an NBC Radio affiliation.[74] The station's logo was a cartoon bee, and the BZY call letters seem to have referred to "busy bee." To celebrate the new call sign and network affiliation, the station gave away ten NBC radios to help promote its blend of hourly network news and smooth, enjoyable music.[75]

On February 1, 1981, Friendship Communications Company, co-owned by Burns Q. Nugent and Donald D. Rosenburg, purchased KBZY from Salem Broadcasting Company. At the time, Rosenburg was a major radio DJ personality on KFRC San Francisco under the name Dr. Don Rose, and Nugent owned KACI-AM The Dalles. Following the purchase, KBZY renewed its affiliation with NBC but changed formats from top-40 to middle-of-the-road (popular) music. On June 15, 1982, the station was sold to Capitol Broadcasting Inc., James J. Opsitnik, 65-percent owner, and Michael D. Kern, 35-percent owner, for $365,000 plus a $23,750 non-compete agreement. Opsitnik was a former vice president and general manager of KWJJ-AM and KJIB-FM Portland and Kern had previously been a salesperson at KWJJ-AM. KBZY also affiliated with KWJJ's network of choice, the American Entertainment Radio Network, dropping NBC. KBZY's format was changed back to top-40 following the sale.

## KTIL-AM Tillamook

KTIL was conceived in 1946 when Fred H. Guyton filed an FCC application for the station in the name of Tillamook Broadcasting Company. The small coastal town didn't receive strong radio service from the inland stations, so Guyton, who owned a farm in the area, believed the community needed a local station. When KTIL signed-on at 1590 KHz on August 16, 1947, it was managed by Robert W. Harris (formerly with KOIN) and studios were located at 170 West Third Street.[76] Guyton was shortly succeeded by Mel Baldwin.

Perhaps Guyton's most enduring contribution to KTIL was a phone call he placed to neighbor Mildred Davy, who recalled:

> Fred Guyton had known me since I was a little girl because we lived around here on 3rd Street and he owned a big farm out here. So he called up one day and he said: 'Oh Mildred, if you just come out [to work at the station for a few days] to answer the phone, [we need] somebody out there who knows the difference between Neskowin and Nehalem.[77]

That was around 1960. When Guyton sold the station in 1962, the new owners wanted to know if there was anyone on staff doing a "woman's program" (then remaining a popular and frequently scheduled local radio programming staple) and Mildred—who had never been on the air—was "volunteered" into service. Her daily program, *It's a Woman's World*, took to the air January 7, 1963, and remained until August 19, 2005. It was one of the longest-lived radio programs in Oregon broadcast history.[78]

The common-sense Davy, who never went to college, intermittently managed KTIL over the years. She interviewed an incredible range of individuals—ranging from presidents to national and international politicians to sports figures and children. Her program, which she originated from six continents, included broadcasts from Brazil, Australia, England, Germany and Israel. She kept a map of the world near her desk at KTIL with pushpins marking all the places from which she had broadcast.

On December 20, 1993, KTIL-AM's call sign was officially changed to KMBD, adopting Davy's initials in her honor. One of the station's studios was also named after her.

Following Davy's 2005 passing, Barbara Trout, KTIL-FM/KMBD-AM news director, called her "a community icon." "She was our spiritual leader," proclaimed the

Mildred Davy, c. 1970

WSMB Collection

station's website. On her passing, Portland-based nationally-syndicated talk show host Lars Larsen said: "I have not found a community where one person is [so much] the center of the community. She knew everyone from children to people her own age, and she had an institutional memory of the community. She was an amazing lady."[79]

# Endnotes

1. Other terms that were used included radiovision and televisor. Hugo Gernsback, then editor of *Radio News*, claims to have coined the term television in an article in his magazine's August 1928 issue.
2. http://www.wsone.com/fecha/armstrong.htm.
3. Inventor Philo Farnsworth was a competitor of RCA's Vladimir Zworkin on whose patented experiments RCA based its own electronic television system. The Farnsworth system wasn't compatible with RCA's but the genius inventor devoted great attention to demonstrating and promoting his product. The RCA system was ultimately adopted as the nation's standard by the FCC.
4. "Application for Experimental Station license," filed with the Department of Commerce by Wilbur J. Jerman, Inc., approved on May 5, 1926 (Wilbur J. Jerman Collection, WSMB). This license application was presumably a renewal of an earlier 1925 facility, no copy of which can now be located in the National Archives at College Park, Maryland.
5. "Radio Pictures Contemplated: Television Set Will Be Put in Here," *Oregon Sunday Journal*, June 17, 1928, 8.
6. Ibid. The 7XAO license was converted to W7XAO in December 1928 when the FRC changed its call sign structure for experimental licenses.
7. "Gets Permit to Radio Pictures," *Oregon Journal*, December 28, 1928.
8. At that time, TV experimentation only produced the visual transmission; the marriage of sight and sound onto one station's signal was still in the future.
9. Department of Commerce, *Radio Service Bulletin #128*, November 29, 1930 (Washington, DC: Department of Commerce), 12.
10. Austin remained at KGPP until his retirement in 1955.
11. "Application Filed for FM Station," *Oregonian*, July 20, 1944 (KGW-FM file, NARA, College Park, MD). This was a low-band application for 36.1 MHz that was later amended to the high-band FM frequency of 95.3 MHz.
12. In 1960, an international convention adopted the modern terms Kilohertz (KHz) and Megahertz (MHz) to replace the earlier kilocycles and megacycles. The move honored pioneer electrical experimenter Heinrich Hertz
13. "FM Introduced to West: Oregonian Station on Air," *Oregonian*, May 9, 1946.
14. "Arrival of FM," *Oregonian*, May 21, 1946, editorial page.
15. Craig Adams, www.pdxradio.com.
16. Kendall, John C. 1950. Letter to T. J. Slowie, Secretary, FCC, dated February 20, and Pangborn, Arden X., 1950. Letter to T. J. Slowie dated March 27 (acknowledging Commission's letter advising that it had cancelled the KGW-FM license) (KGW-FM file, NARA, College Park, MD).
17. John W. Kendall (1911–96) was the son of Judge John C. Kendall (c. 1888–1951), who also practiced communications law. He took over representation of many of his father's clients late in his father's career and following his death in 1951. John W. Kendall's son, John S. Kendall, later acquired KRCO-AM, Prineville (see chapter 21).
18. While KGW-FM had signed-on with only 250 watts, the station was successively granted power increases, first to 5.1 kilowatts (with a change in frequency to 100.3 MHz) and later to 54 kilowatts on April 1, 1948 (Craig Adams, www.pdxradio.com). It is to that pending KGW-FM power increase that the Kendall letter refers.
19. Kendall, John W., 1947. Letter to T. J. Slowie, FCC, dated December 22 (KGWG file, NARA, College Park, MD).
20. "Oregon Faces Long Delay in Television," *Oregonian*, July 10, 1949.
21. The partners were John A. Masterson, Harold H. Holden, John W. Melson, John F. Reddy, Lester C. Bacon, W. E. Laughlin, Charles Wesley Turner, J. G. Moser, I. Ditmars, Charles B. Brown (the general manager of the company) and H. E. Moser.
22. The building was incomplete because an 18-foot-by-40-foot room on the transmitter side of the building wasn't finished.
23. This may have been the KPAM-KPFM building at 4700 SW Council Crest Drive.

24. FCC Inter-Office Memorandum to the Commission from The Commission's Acting General Counsel, Harry M. Plotkin, July 6, 1949 (KTVU file, NARA, College Park, MD).

25. Craig Adams, www.pdxradio.com.

26. Fisher, Carl O., 1964. Letter to Ben F. Waple, FCC Secretary, dated May 19 (KUGN-FM file, NARA, College Park, MD).

27. Ibid.

28. The university declined the donation of KUGN-FM on learning that operation on that station's commercial frequency involved obligations that significantly exceeded those attached to its existing non-commercial operation of KWAX-FM in areas such as required hours of operation.

29. Arnold maintains that KGPO signed-off in 1961, although the station is listed in the 1963 *Broadcasting Yearbook*. It is likely that the station's license wasn't promptly returned to the FCC at sign-off, which could account for its listing in the 1963 *Yearbook*.

30. KFLW changed call signs to KFLS and eventually KFLS-FM was constructed, licensed to Tulelake, California, in 1993.

31. Chipman, *KMED—The First Half Century*, 18, and Kramer, Ronald, "History of Radio in Southern Oregon," (unpublished manuscript, WSMB Collection). The Construction Permit was cancelled on February 15, 1949.

32. The location and history of the various Healy Heights transmitter sites is complex. KGW FM was built at 4545 SW Council Crest Drive and KEX-FM at 4504 SW Carl Place. When KGW-FM was sold and became KQFM-FM (see chapter 13), the property was still owned by King Broadcasting. King donated the property to the state's Oregon Educational Broadcasting (now Oregon Public Broadcasting) for a Portland satellite television station of OEB's KOAC-TV Corvallis. The new station, KOAP-TV, was constructed at 4545 SW Council Crest Drive. In November 1960, KQFM-FM's transmitter was moved across the street to the KGMG tower, at 4636 SW Council Crest Drive. When KEX-FM was donated to KOAP-TV and became KOAP-FM on April 30, 1962, KOAP-FM continued to operate at 4504 SW Carl Place, where it even had a studio. Then, in early 1972, KOAP-FM moved its studio and transmitter to 4545 SW Council Crest Drive and side-mounted its antenna on the KOAP-TV tower. OPB then sold the site at 4504 SW Carl Place to Al H. Herman for $53,000 on August 28, 1972 (Bob McClanathan via Craig Adams).

33. Most of this KPFM information comes from Craig Adams, www.pdxradio.com.

34. Jerman interview.

35. Dawson, Ben. Interview with author. Tape recording. October 15, 2004.

36. Both the 1941 and 1950 numbers include KVAN Vancouver, Washington.

37. Data from *Broadcasting Yearbooks*, 1941 and 1951.

38. Christopher Sterling. *Electronic Media: A Guide to Trends in Broadcasting and Newer Technologies, 1920–1983*, (New York: Praeger, 1984) 12–13.

39. Ibid., Table 370-C, 109.

40. MBS was still the largest network nationally although that wasn't true in Oregon where LBS's 11 affiliated stations beat MBS's 10. Oregon LBS affiliates were: KWIN Ashland, KBKR Baker, KRUL Corvallis, KASH Eugene, KLBM La Grande, KMCM McMinnville, KFIR North Bend, KSRV Ontario, KRCO Prineville and KOCO Salem.

41. Modeling KWIN's building after KMED was far more than casual. Apparently, Blanch Virgin made copies of her station's blueprints available to the new station.

42. Correy, Chet. Oral History interview by Ed Tomlin. Transcript. 1962 (WSMB Collection).

43. Some equipment had been previously ordered including a Western Electric console (presumably for a production control room). At the time of the fire it hadn't been delivered so the station's initial capitalization wasn't a total loss (Reinholdt, Robert. Oral history interview by Ed Tomlin. Transcript. May 29, 1962, 28–29).

44. Correy interview.

45. http://en.wikipedia.org/wiki/Disc_jockey.

46. Email post by John Callarman, DX Listening Digest 4-047, March 13, 2004, on http://www.worldofi-adio.com.

47. Read's career details from 1941-47 are taken from the KWRO FCC Application for a New Standard Broadcast Station Construction Permit, filed August 5, 1947 (KWRO file, NARA, College Park, MD).

48. It was established in January 1947.

49. Memorandum dated November 15, 1952 from Bill Smullin to "Pop" Fisher detailing negotiations for Smullin's potential purchase of one-third interest in KUGN. (KUGN folder, Smullin Collection/Briefcase A, Smullin Collection, WSMB).

50. Fisher, Carl O. Interview with author. Tape recording. August 30, 2004.

51. Memorandum of Agreement, May 2, 1954 (KASH file, NARA, College Park, MD).

52. "1945 Expected to See Radio Station Start Here," *Herald and News*, December 26, 1944, 1.

53. "Static," *Herald and News*, April 1, 1946, 5.
54. FCC Application for Consent to Assignment of Radio Broadcast Station Construction Permit or License, Southern Oregon Publishing Company to Stulor Corporation, August 8, 1958 (KFLW file, NARA, College Park, MD).
55. Gillette left KMCM in 1953 to work at ABC Radio in Hollywood. (Craig Adams).
56. Smith later went to KXL as a news reporter and then became prominent in Portland television (see Chapter 36).
57. Much of the material concerning KMCM comes from Craig Adams www.pdxradio.com.
58. Latham, Gerald. Interview with author. Tape recording. November 10, 1993.
59. KYJC was sold to Opus Broadcasting, Inc., on July 9, 1991, along with companion station KYJC-FM, Grants Pass.
60. Becker, Tom. Interview with author. Tape recording. April 20, 2005.
61. "Memories and Thoughts of Bob Spangler," Yaquina Bay Communications website, http://ybcradio.com, accessed on March 19, 2009.
62. *Ontario Argus*, November 28, 1946.
63. www.bearcreekpress.com/pat_wilkins.html
64. Ehmsen helped build KFIF (later KBPS) at Benson Polytechnic High School when that station signed-on in 1923, according to KBPS station manager Pat Swenson ("Student Radio Station Plans Birthday Party," *Oregonian*, March 21, 1968, 19).
65. The address was later assigned as 1065 McLoughlin Boulevard in the late 1950s. (Craig Adams)
66. Baaken, Wes. Email to author. May 16, 2008.
67. The sale price included KGON-FM Portland, KLAK & KPPL-FM Lakewood/Denver, KHON-TV Honolulu and its satellite KAII-TV Wailuku.
68. KWJJ reportedly left the Oaks Park transmitter site in August 1948. (Craig Adams www.pdxradio.com).
69. "Station KBKO Takes to Air," *Oregonian*, January 10, 1949, Sec. 3, 10.
70. The allegation that an unauthorized transfer of this type had occurred was one issue the FCC specified in its July 13, 1955, Hearing Designation Order to determine whether Mercury's license for KLIQ should be renewed.
71. "Now the Talk Jockey," *Newsweek*, April 6, 1959.
72. "Deal Reached to Sell KLIQ," *Oregonian*, June 26, 1985, C9.
73. Bunnell, P. E., 1946. Letter to Loring Schmidt dated December 12 (KOCO file, NARA, College Park, MD.
74. KBZY operated from the Glen Creek Road NW site until August 2006, when the station's lease expired and the station again relocated. (Craig Adams).
75. Jim Hunter went on to become Roger W. Morgan at KISN as well as at KOIL St. Louis, WIFE Indianapolis, and KYA San Francisco. Dick Middleton became similarly prominent as Dick Saint on KISN, KFRC San Francisco, KHJ Los Angeles and WLS Chicago.
76. Exact date comes from "About KTIL/KMBD," www.ktil-kmbd.com.
77. Davy, Mildred. Interview with author. Tape recording. July 12, 2004.
78. Davy worked the County Fair in August 2005, as she always did, but fell ill afterwards. She took some time off but her health was failing. She passed away October 4, 2005. "Voice of Tillamook County Falls Silent," *Oregonian*, October 7, 2005.
79. Ibid.

# 15

# Across the Dial:
# Radio Around the State

In post-war America, stations that had been founded in the previous decades were undergoing huge changes in both technology and programming. For most, these changes were producing evolutionary—rather than revolutionary—change and stations generally remained profitable. It was, in short, a good time for radio in Oregon.

## KAST-AM Astoria

Astoria Broadcasting Company's KAST remained closely affiliated with the *Astoria Budget*. But despite investment in new studios at 1006 Taylor Street in 1939; an affiliation with the Mutual/Don Lee Broadcasting System on October 1, 1941 and other improvements in frequency and power that year, the station was still not making money.[1] The stress of the war economy only aggravated the station's situation, and on January 7, 1943, the stockholders instructed station manager James C. Wallace to request FCC permission to sign-off for the war's duration. On March 13, 1943, the commission denied the request, essentially requiring that KAST remain on the air. Wallace promptly resigned and moved to Portland.

Hearing of these developments, Ed Parsons (who was working at KGW Portland as an engineer) contacted the *Astoria Budget* to inquire if they were interested in selling the station. Accounts vary but Parsons subsequently maintained that, while they were not initially interested, he was contacted a few weeks later with an offer to proceed with a sale. Parsons

KAST staff gathered at the station's new studio dedication, 1946. (left to right) Bob Holmes, Neil Norfitt of the American Legion, Stan Church, state representative Merle Chessman, Astoria mayor Orval Eaton, congressman Walter Norblad, Ed Parsons. Note the station's portable recorder in the foreground.

The Don Lee Net newsletter, January-February 1947, WSMB Collection

claimed he visited a couple of banks to borrow funds for the purchase and, in short order, owned KAST. FCC records do not reveal any transfer in ownership from Astoria Broadcasting. More likely, Parsons purchased a portion of the *Astoria Budget*'s stock. He succeeded Wallace as manager in April 1943.

By 1945, Parsons held nearly 55 percent of the Astoria Broadcasting Company's stock, with the remaining balance largely held by M. R. Chessman, president of the Astoria-Budget Publishing Company. Parsons later recalled that, as owner/manager, that "Within 30, days, I had the station in the black and had raised the prestige of the station tremendously by hiring more qualified personnel. Also, revenue shot up. Doing live newscasts was all it took to bring the station up to a profitable basis."[2]

In those years the station's identification announcement was: "Station KAST, the *Astoria Budget*, with studios in the Hotel Astoria."[3] Parsons hired Robert Holmes of Gearhart to manage KAST; it was Holmes' first job in radio. With the station running smoothly, Parsons, an experienced pilot, was able to pursue other interests, including running a flying school, managing the local airport and eventually launching the nation's cable television industry in Astoria (see chapter 17).

With KAST's new momentum, Parsons confidently moved the studios from Taylor Street to the former First National Bank building at Ninth and Commercial Streets in downtown Astoria. The new location featured a 150-seat auditorium and a 15-foot-by-21-foot stage. KAST announced plans to broadcast live shows three nights a week—the *League of Women Voters Forum*, an eighth grade spelling bee and a hillbilly musical program—in addition to making the auditorium available for a variety of other civic purposes.

With KAST-FM already under construction, the new plant also included an additional control room for the impending FM station. The dedication of KAST's new home on October 12, 1946 was a major Astoria news story.

Mary Ristola was a mainstay of KAST's operations for many years. Hired as a secretary in 1942, she was at times given the title of program director, but regardless of title, she was a central figure for decades. In the words of former KAST announcer Jean Hallaux, "It's really Mary's station but nobody knows it."[4] Recalling her various bosses, Ristola—whose husband George was KAST's chief engineer for many years—recalled Parsons as:

A Henry Ford of radio. He had little technical education but he could build almost anything he could imagine. Parsons was the first to conceive of and build a portable tape recorder [that consisted of] a toy wagon laden with heavy storage batteries and a tape recorder [that] Parsons pulled through the streets and did Astoria's first 'man-in-the-street' interviews. Parsons was the only sane man around who would touch the transmitter [even when] blue flames and sparks shot from it.[5]

A major technological and programming development occurred in August 1946 when KAST acquired its first portable (30 pound!) wire recorder, a new technology developed during World War II that allowed magnetic recording on wire as opposed to the previous practice of cutting discs on recording blanks. The wire recorder allowed delayed broadcast of events that previously would have required installation of expensive remote telephone circuits.

At the end of the 1940s, KAST sought a frequency change from 1230 KHz to its original 1370 KHz, a move that required additional tower construction. Parsons de-

KAST greeting card, c. 1953. (beginning top left): Bob Holmes, Hal Chase, Irving Steinbock, Vern Cimmyotti, Mary Ristola, George Ristola, Bruce Whitwell, Harvey Candeaux, Ester Rabell

signed the new antenna system in his capacity as the station's technical director but he resigned as KAST's manager in October 1949 to launch a new station, KVAS Astoria (see chapter 25).[6] On February 10, 1950, KAST received FCC approval for the station's permanent switch to 1370 KHz, with 1 kilowatt power, for full-time operation. With KVAS soon to come on the air as a competitor, KAST announced various studio improvements in February 1950, including a new record library and turntable equipment.

## KOAC-AM Corvallis

On June 2, 1942, KOAC raised its daytime power from 1 to 5 kilowatts and moved its transmitter to Granger. On October 16, 1942, former KWSC staff member Allen Miller became KOAC's program director, and on December 6, 1946, the FCC authorized KOAC to go to 5 kilowatts full-time.

In 1942, the station was honored with a prestigious Peabody Award for Outstanding Public Service by a Local Station for its program *Our Hidden Enemy, Venereal Disease.*

## KORE-AM Eugene

In October 1948, KORE was sold to Lee Bishop's Lane Broadcasting Company. Bishop was president and general manager, and by December 1949, Bob Eubanks was KORE's program director. Eubanks later went on to become host of ABC-TV's *Newlywed Game* show. Bishop's company owned the station until 1966, when KORE was

Billboard for George Hebert's *Man on the Street* program

purchased by the McKenzie Broadcasting Company which arranged a trade of frequencies between KORE and KEED. On August 14, 1966, KORE moved to KEED's 1050 KHz daytime-only frequency. Conversely, KEED moved to KORE's 1450 KHz frequency. On December 1, 1979, KORE was purchased by Intercontinental Ministries, Inc., which later sold the station to Support Christian Broadcasting, Inc., in August 1987.

## KMED-AM Medford

Just as World War II began, the new military training facility Camp White opened in White City just outside of Medford. Ex-KMED announcer James Dunlevy, who was posted at Camp White during the war, frequently emceed KMED broadcasts for the enlisted men. Some of these broadcasts were fed to the NBC Blue Network via KGW Portland.

Besides the technological changes that Blanch Virgin was making at KMED throughout the 1940s, she was clearly wrestling with the station's—and her own—future. Lionel E. "Eddie" Randle had been hired at KMED in 1936, following his service in the U.S. Army Signal Corps, but he left in 1942 to return to duty as an Army instructor. He returned to KMED in 1944 and Virgin, a widow for nearly 20 years, developed a romantic relationship with him and they married in 1947. While Virgin had adopted a son, William "Billy" J. Virgin Jr., shortly after her first husband's death, he was living in southern California, and no family succession considerations existed for KMED.[7] With FM and television looming on the horizon, Virgin wrestled with the decision over whether to sell the station. First, she filed an application for an FM frequency—but later withdrew it. Then, following her marriage to Randle, she decided it was time to leave broadcasting and enjoy retirement.

Industrialist/broadcaster Powel Crosley was president of Crosley Radio Corporation, which became the world's largest manufacturer of radios and associated businesses. One of the wealthy Cincinnati resident's properties was Cincinnati station WLW-AM, which was once the most powerful radio station in America. In 1945, Crosley sold his broadcasting interests to Aviation Corporation (AVCO) in a controversial decision that prompted the FCC to adopt "the AVCO Rule"—which was designed to solve commission concerns over multi-faceted corporations lacking broadcast experience acquiring stations. It was the commission's view that that radio station licenses are a public trust and should not be simply treated as investments by diversified holding companies. Although the commission narrowly approved Crosley's sale to AVCO, the resulting new rule required that an open public bid solicitation be conducted whenever an owner wished to sell a station and that the commission would select the station's purchaser from among all bidders.

On May 9, 1946, Virgin proposed selling KMED to Gibson Broadcasting Corporation, a California-based company headed by Luther E. Gibson. But the commission—under the AVCO Rule—determined that the station should instead be sold to a local, rather than a distant, buyer. On July 7, 1947, the commission ordered Virgin to sell KMED to the local group, the Medford Radio Corporation, which had matched Gibson's offer.[8] It was the FCC's first application of its new AVCO Rule.

On January 12, 1948, Virgin formally declined to complete the sale to Medford Radio Corporation and requested the commission's reconsideration. In the meantime, Gibson appealed the FCC's ruling all the way to the U.S. Supreme Court, which reversed the decision. Gibson, having invested considerably in fighting the case, then decided against completing the purchase, and on January 31, 1949, Virgin terminated all purchase discussions. In light of the Supreme Court's ruling, on June 13 the FCC repealed its AVCO Rule, stating that its purpose had not been successfully realized and had often inflicted "severe economic and other hardships" on buyers and sellers.

During the course of the abortive Gibson sale, Virgin had purchased a new 5-kilowatt Gates transmitter and the Gates factory sent engineer Ray Johnson out to install it in 1948. The new transmitter went into service on January 23, 1949. Virgin appreciated Johnson's skills and following completion of his work, hired him permanently for KMED's engineering staff. When the Gibson sale failed, Johnson assembled a local group of investors to form Radio Medford, Inc., which purchased the station. Joining Johnson as stockholders were company president Verne Robinson, a local insurance man; vice president Dwight Findley, a local physician; treasurer Bert Lageson, a local dentist; secretary William McCallister, an attorney; Les A. DeArmond, a mill and lumber operator; and Howell Murphy, who was associated with the local fruit industry. Blanch Virgin sold KMED to Radio Medford, Inc., in June 1950 and never returned to the station's studios.[9] An era had ended at KMED.[10]

KMED's Jimmy Dunlevy in the Camp White radio control room, c. 1944

Radio Medford quickly sought advice about recruiting a station manager from Jennings Pierce, NBC Radio's west coast manager of station relations at the time (see chapter 16). They were likely surprised when the much-respected Pierce—who had started at NBC as chief announcer in the network's early San Francisco Sutter Street studios and was just recovering from serious injuries sustained

Ray Johnson with Miss America 1958, and an unidentified engineer, at a 1958 KMED-AM remote broadcast from a Medford Kiwanis event.

during a Hollywood airplane crash—expressed personal interest. He arrived at KMED in July 1950 to manage the station and remained until around 1954, when he left to pursue a consulting business. He was succeeded by Johnson.

In the mid-1970s, Radio Medford sold KMED to Northstar Broadcasting, a company formed by Martin and Gary Hawke and Stanley M. Friden (a retired industrialist living in Siskiyou County). The Hawkes also owned and operated KSYC-AM in Yreka, California. The sale was announced on November 9, 1976, and consummated on August 2, 1977. Northstar, in turn, sold the stations to a limited partnership, KMED Radio, on October 6, 1981. That group encountered financial difficulties, and KMED was transferred to Sound Radio Enterprises, Inc., as receiver in the bankruptcy, on September 28, 1984. KMED was then purchased by Crater Broadcasting, Inc., (another entity associated with Duane Hill, who had started Gold Hill's KRWQ in 1980) on

December 14, 1984 (see chapter 27). With Crater headed by president Sherry Hill, her husband, Duane, took over as KMED's general manager. Crater held the station until July 17, 1998, when it was sold to Citicasters Licenses LLP of Tulsa, Oklahoma.

## KWJJ-AM Portland

From its 1920s inception until after World War II, with a few temporary exceptions, KWJJ had been an independent station in a radio world largely dominated by network affiliates. Rod Johnson describes KWJJ's independent status:

> Before the Second World War, radio was hardly more than a plaything. It wasn't taken seriously in the business community, which was completely dominated by the newspapers, unless a station had major network affiliation. As for a station like KWJJ that played mostly phonograph records, why, what kind of trash operation would play phonograph records? That was the attitude.[11]

Recognizing the disadvantage under which independent stations operated, several parties attempted to create new national radio networks after World War II. Among these was the Associated Broadcasting Corporation (ABC), which was launched by Storer Broadcasting Company-related interests in 1945 and anchored out of WWDC-AM Washington DC. KWJJ immediately joined ABC and carried the network's two-hour inaugural program on September 16, 1945. The Associated Broadcasting Company's initials were quickly of interest to the Blue Network, which paid ABC to change its name to Associated Broadcasting System (ABS) in December 1945. This paved the way for the Blue Network to become the American Broadcasting Company (ABC) that same year.

ABS offerings on KWJJ included a heavy schedule of such military bands as the United States Army Band, the Navy School Band and the United States Spar Band (a women's band), plus the *Old Fashioned Revival Hour*, Ray Schmidt's *The A to Z of Sports*, Lee Giroux's human commentaries on *S.F. Calling* and news commentators Ross McFarland and Mark Austad. Following much hoopla over the new network, ABS folded on April 28, 1946, and KWJJ was once again an independent station.

WSMB Collection

Sammy Taylor's early morning KWJJ program was the inspiration for this promotional photo, c. 1950.

Following his arrival at KWJJ in 1936, announcer/DJ Sammy Taylor had gradually become a Portland radio fixture. In the words of *TV-Radio Prevue*, he was a recognized "dean of DJs."[12] Art Morey, who had long been with KWJJ, was promoted to production manager in 1946. Assistant station manager Leon D. Henderson, who had been with KWJJ since 1927, had become a strong force on the station's sales staff. KWJJ was also featuring an African-American, Bass Harris, at the microphone nightly on the *Bronze Community Hour*. KWJJ's *Home Maker*, Polly Anne Knickerbocker, appeared the station's *Morning Musicale*,

*Hospitality House* and *The Adventures of the Little Tin Soldier. Greek Music on Parade* was hosted by Billy Polichananis, whom KWJJ claimed was the leading war bond salesman in the west. Organ music performed by maestro Pete Kraushaar was also piped in live from the Oaks Park Rink every Sunday. On September 5, 1941, KWJJ raised its power from 500 watts to 1 kilowatt full-time and in August 1948 to 10 kilowatts from a new transmitter site at 4350 Suttle Road.

Rod Johnson purchased KWJJ from Wilbur Jerman in 1952, and one of his first steps was firing John Egan—whom he found unreliable.[13] The sale stipulated that KWJJ remain in its SW Sixth Avenue studios, which Jerman owned, for five years. Johnson made one of the station's most memorable statements by moving KWJJ to the elegant Theodore B. Wilcox Victorian mansion, at 931 SW King Street, in October 1957.[14] On April 1, 1959, the station ended its independent status and joined the ABC Network when KGW went independent. Although the station remained a strong ABC affiliate for many years thereafter, KWJJ switched to country music on March 1, 1965. On December 10, 1965, KWJJ raised its daytime power to 50 kilowatts directional from a new transmitter site at 17200 NE Marine Drive. Johnson sold the station to Roy H. Park Broadcasting of Roanoke, Inc., on February 17, 1973.

## KGW-AM Portland

Just a few days after VE Day (or Victory in Europe Day, May 8, 1945), KGW announced that it had hired Wallace L. Kadderly as director of farm programs. Kadderly had originally been on the Oregon State University faculty and served as KFDJ/KOAC program director from 1925 to 1932 and station manager in 1933 before moving to the United States Department of Agriculture in Washington DC, where he was chief of the USDA's radio service. KGW had long paid significant attention to agricultural reporting which drew Kadderly back to Oregon. He remained at KGW into the 1950s.

Frank Hemingway at the Don Lee microphone, 1951. Heard morning and evenings, his slogan was "Twice a day with Hemingway."
Courtesy of Timothy Ellis

Frank Hemingway moved to KGW from KBND and became one of the station's prime announcers (among other assignments, his newscast was heard at 4 p.m. weekdays) before he moved to Hollywood for network assignments—first on the Don Lee Broadcasting Service and later for ABC Radio.

Another change at KGW was the promotion of Homer Welch, who had started out at KOIN in 1934 and moved to KGW as an announcer and producer in 1936. In January 1941, he was promoted to program director. Welch sparked numerous changes and one of the most ambitious was his creation of *Hospitality House* in the spring of 1949. *Hospitality House* started out as a half-hour program heard at 10 a.m. on Friday mornings and gradually grew to multiple weekday morning broadcasts. The *Oregonian* had long titled the newspaper's second section, which included radio program listings along with recipes and household tips, *Hostess House.* Welch borrowed that name for KGW's own effort, which was also targeted at women. The *Oregonian* also dedicated an area on the main floor of its building, likely set up as a product merchandising arena for some of its advertisers, as the *Hostess House*—which is where the radio program originated. Mounted on a large scale with a studio audience, it often drew on guest artists and stars such as Lillian Roth, who were

in town to perform in live theatre. Welch, an actor and vocalist who often performed in local theatrical productions, was highly effective as the program's genial emcee. Eventually, the program began to use the KGW orchestra, commanding more of the station's resources in the face of its clear success, and for a time *Hostess House* was carried on at least a portion of the NBC Radio Network.

In 1951, KGW was rocked by a series of resignations, including those from chief announcer Bob Thomlinson, who returned to Navy duty; announcer Wayne Roberts (known on the air as Robert Peart), who joined the Marine Corps; announcers Frank Billings and Ray Benningson, who simply left radio altogether; continuity chief Helen Alexieve, who had written *Hostess House*; and long-time education director Evelyn Sibley Lampman, who left to pursue her writing career (see chapters 9 and 16). The biggest surprise, however, was Homer Welch's resignation. Welch stayed long enough to celebrate the second anniversary of *Hostess House's* on April 13, 1951, and then left to join

Homer Welch on the KGW *Hostess House* set with an unidentified housewife, c. 1950

NBC Radio in Hollywood as a director. Ultimately, he became the assistant director of the network's Western Division, where he remained until NBC shuttered that division in 1957.

Welch left KGW just as the station was being sold as part of the *Oregonian*'s purchase by Newhouse Broadcasting Corporation (see chapter 13). Former KGW staff member Hank Norton, who had departed in 1944 to pursue a career as an author, returned to the station to take over Welch's *Hostess House* duties.

KGW Radio left NBC and switched to ABC when KGW-TV signed on in 1956, but dropped its ABC affiliation on April 1, 1959 (see chapter 18). The station operated as an independent for a year, re-joined NBC Radio on January 11, 1960, and then again went independent in October 1974. Craig Walker began doing middays on KGW in August 1972, the same year the station won a George Foster Peabody Award for its broadcast *Open Door*. On June 7, 1965, KGW-AM and KGW-TV moved to their new 50,000-square-foot studios at 1501 SW Jefferson Street and dedicated the KGW Broadcast Center on July 12, 1965. The station moved to a rock 'n roll format in 1970 and was sold, along with the rest of the King Broadcasting properties, in 1992. KGW-AM abandoned its historic call sign in 1993 and underwent a series of call letter changes ultimately becoming KPOJ-AM in 2003.

## KEX-AM Portland

KEX was rocked by a different type of change. In 1941, the Federal Communications Commission issued its *Report on Chain Broadcasting*, which reviewed network operations and crafted new regulations that addressed certain network-related problems the commission had identified. The report's major finding, to no one's surprise, was that ownership/operation of two national networks by one party—termed a *duopoly* by the commission—harmed the public interest. The FCC's subsequent order forbid stations from affiliating with networks that owned and operated more than one national network, and it prohibited any one party from owning more than one radio station in a given community (see also chapter 13).

In Portland, the duopoly ruling led to the sale of *Oregonian*-owned KEX, which Westinghouse purchased on December 28, 1944. Westinghouse, which had been involved in radio since the industry's earliest days, owned a powerful group of stations and was a major force in broadcasting. Leaving NBC's ownership for Westinghouse's certainly didn't diminish KEX, although it led to major changes, including its moving from joint KGW-KEX studio plant, which had been temporarily located at KWJJ in 1945 (see chapter 13). Westinghouse also raised KEX's power to 5 kilowatts in 1948.

When KLIQ went silent in 1954, Bob Adkins moved to KEX, doing his *Bob's Danceland* program from 7 p.m. until midnight. In addition to Adkins, the KEX DJ line-up, included Barney Keep, Bob Blackburn, Russ Conrad and Al Priddy on the all-night program.

In early radio it was common for radio stations to have their own theme songs. This undated sheet music for Call of the Northwest, "The Theme for KEX Radio," appears to be from the early 1960s. Its cover features iconic Portland-area images, including the Rose Gardens, Mt. Hood, the city's bridges, boats and fishing and the Portland Zoo's prize pachyderm, "Packy." The song was reportedly frequently broadcast by KEX in the late 1950s and early 1960s to acknowledge the station's 50,000 watt signal which blanketed the Northwest.

Also known as the "Big K of West Coast Radio," KEX moved its offices on May 28, 1960, to 2130 SW Fifth Avenue. The next day at 3:05 p.m., KEX switched to new studios in the same location. On May 14, 1962, KEX announced its acquisition by Golden West Broadcasting Company, a sale that became effective a few months later on September 1. Golden West had been created ten years earlier by cowboy actor/singer Gene Autry, who described the purchase as "completing Golden West's chain of radio stations in the major cities along the Pacific Coast."[15]

At the time, Golden West already owned KSFO-AM San Francisco and KVI-AM Seattle, plus stations in Arizona. A sale had been rumored ever since longtime KEX owner Westinghouse had purchased a New York radio station and was said to be exploring a Los Angeles station purchase. Under FCC regulations of the time, a single owner was limited to a small number of station ownerships, and it seemed possible that Westinghouse would sell KEX in order to purchase a station in a larger market. Westinghouse already seemed to be lightening its Portland presence with its donation of KEX-FM to the Oregon State System of Higher Education, which transformed the station into KOAP-FM, the preceding fall (see chapter 16). Now the longtime KEX owner's exodus from Portland would be complete. Noting the sale, Autry said, "I'm going to be spending a lot of time in Portland to get the station on a top keel."[16]

The Texas-born Autry had started out modestly, become an enormously successful entertainer and then parlayed his performance income into canny business ventures that eventually included ownership of the Gene Autry Hotel in Palm Springs, the Anaheim Angels American League baseball team, Los Angeles TV station KTLA-TV plus his radio holdings. He was the first country-and-western singer to receive a star on the Hollywood Walk of Fame and the only entertainer to ever receive five stars on—one each for radio, records, film, live appearance and television.

Autry's ownership took KEX from one golden age into another. KEX hadn't been profitable for Westinghouse and also wasn't for Golden West—at least initially. Richard Kale, who came to Portland as KEX's general sales manager, reported that he was surprised to discover at the end of the year that Autry had made less money from owning the station than Kale had as its general sales manager.[17] On becoming KEX's general manager, Kale dramatically improved the station's profitability.

Gene Autry, promotional still from the television program *The Gene Autry Show*

Autry, whose real passion was baseball, was good to his employees and well-liked. He normally came to Portland several times a year on visits that were often prompted by a baseball game. Each year, he threw a large Christmas party for KEX staff. Kale remembered:

> He had a kind of a standing policy during the years I worked for him that he wasn't a performer and he did not perform. Somebody would say, 'Gene, would you sing a song for us?' and his answer was 'No, I'm not a performer. I'm a businessman.' Well one Christmas I had rented the Grand Ballroom at the Westin Hotel for our staff Christmas party and [the wife of one of the staff] came over and said, 'Mr. Autry, I wonder if you'd be kind enough to sing a song for us,' and he kind of turned to me and said, 'Well, I might consider that.' So he went up and sang three or four songs. Of course everybody in the room thought it was wonderful and gosh what a great guy, and we know he doesn't perform, because he's not a performer, he's a businessman. You know, you could kind of see that sort of filtering around the room. And he came back, sat down and was very quiet for 30, 45 seconds. Then he turned to me and he said, 'Dick, did I do all right?' I thought, well here's a guy that could probably buy anything he wanted but he still had that [concern] 'Was my performance up to par? Was it acceptable?' I thought it showed great humility.[18]

One of KEX's major figures was Barney Keep, who ended a remarkable 35 years before the the station's microphone on Valentine's Day, February 14, 1979. On his retirement, he received a huge outpouring of public gratitude for his many years' as Portland's morning companion (see chapter 22 for a more complete history of Keep's career).

On November 29, 1978, KEX and KQFM moved into the new Golden West Broadcast Center at 4949 SW Macadam Avenue. Autry had owned KEX since 1962 and KQFM#1 "Q100," (that station became KKRZ "The Rose" on November 2, 1983) since 1977. The years of Autry ownership were great ones for KEX, but that era ended when Golden West Broadcasters sold both stations to Cincinnati-based Taft Broadcasting Company on March 14, 1984 for $8.18 million. Kenneth J. Bartell, who had served as general manager of both stations until his resignation shortly before the sale, was replaced by David Crowl as manager of KKRZ and David Milner as manager of KEX.

## KALE-AM/KPOJ-AM/KPOK-AM Portland

KALE-AM changed call signs to KPOJ-AM on June 6, 1948, the same day its sister station, KPOJ-FM, signed-on. It was a change made to reflect the stations' ownership by the *Portland Oregon Journal*. The licensee name was officially changed from KALE, Inc., to KPOJ, Inc., on July 7, 1948.

Under either call sign, the 1940s and 1950s were good to the station. On his return from World War II, Homer Welch's cousin Ted Hallock went to work at KALE/KPOJ on the station's announcing and production staff. In the late 1940s, Hallock began his *Spins 'n Needles* disc jockey program featuring "Tunes of the Times." Heard Monday through Friday from 12:45 p.m. to 4 p.m., the program was targeted at housewives who were encouraged to "Enjoy Home Duties with Smooth Melody."[19] The bright, articulate Hallock made the program a great success, and by the end of the 1940s he became KPOJ's program director. From that position, he led the station to many successes, including several major national awards such as the 1952 George Foster Peabody Award for Meritorious Local Public Service for its *Careers Unlimited* and *Civic Theatre on the Air* broadcasts. Hallock went on to become a leader in the Oregon senate, where he was influential in establishing the Land Conservation and Development Commission (LCDC) in 1973. Following his political career, he founded Portland's Hallock-Modey advertising agency. Part of him never left radio, however, and during his final years he did a weekly big band jazz program on Mt. Hood Community College's KMHD-FM.

KPOJ manager since 1949, Richard M. Brown guided the station through the many changes then overtaking radio. Sales manager, Bob LaBonte, was sales manager for 10 years before leaving to manage KERG-AM in Eugene in 1959. In 1956, KPOJ's longtime engineer Herbert Davidson came to KPOJ from KWIL Albany. According to Davidson, who remained at KPOJ for 19 years, KPOJ was number two in the Portland ratings on his arrival. Flirting with

KPOJ's *Million Dollar Music* promotion, c. 1955

emerging popular music trends, in 1955 the station made a home for Dick Novak's *Rhythm Room*, while also emphasizing traditional popular music hyped with gimmicks such as cash prizes for listeners on *Million Dollar Music* (see chapter 22). Eventually, the station also decided to "go independent"—perhaps following KEX's lead—and dropped its longstanding Mutual-Don Lee Network affiliation on April 15, 1959.[20]

On March 27, 1964, KPOJ-FM moved from 98.7 MHz to 98.5 MHz, and on April 15, 1968, KPOJ-FM became KPOK-FM, inaugurating stereo programming separate from KPOJ-AM. KPOJ-AM became KPOK-AM on June 9, 1970, and switched formats to "pop tunes blended with oldies" using the slogan "Now everything is OK."[21]

On May 16, 1973, KPOK-AM/KPOK-FM Portland were sold to Tracy Broadcasting Company for $1,050,000. The station—which had re-affiliated with Mutual Broadcasting on October 25, 1964—dropped MBS, and on July 11, 1976, the station's call sign was switched to KUPL-AM. KPOK-FM then became KUPL-FM in August 1976. The station moved to new quarters in the Sylvan Park Office campus at 6400 SW Canyon Court by December 1976.

## KXL-AM Portland and the XL Stations

Following Tom Symons' death, his company was carried on by his widow, Frances; daughter, Virginia; and son, Tom III. Plans for KXL to move from its longtime home in the *Portland Telegram* building had likely been initiated by the elder Tom prior to his death in 1941 but negotiations for the entire top floor of the Orpheum Theatre Building at 743 SW Broadway weren't completed until August 1942. On July 1 of that year, Hal Wilson became KXL manager and promptly arranged to complete the move, which occurred on November 1, 1942. The large plant included an auditorium studio, along with several smaller studios, all incorporating "the latest theories in acoustic engineering."[22]

KXL was the founding namesake for what became known as the XL stations, a regional group owned by Craney-Symons that included radio stations in Spokane and Ellensburg, Washington, and Butte, Helena, Great Falls and Bozeman, Montana. On January 4, 1947, all these stations (except for KXL) changed their call letters to ones that included XL—giving the group its name. They formally operated under the name Pacific Northwest Broadcasters, but the XL stations, as they were commonly known, were large enough to maintain offices in Hollywood, San Francisco, New York and Chicago, and their scope gave KXL added prominence.

KXL Broadcasters, Inc., had been watching the developments in television and tried desperately to get into the game. Anticipating that it would be expensive, the company had accumulated considerable cash, and when its TV plans went awry, couldn't directly reimburse its stockholders. As a result, the only way to really distribute the funds back to the owners was to sell KXL. Craney was, therefore, looking for a buyer.

In 1955, the Craney-Symons interest sold KXL to Mt. Rainer Radio and Television Corporation, which purchased their KXL Broadcasters, Inc., stock for $450,000. Mt. Rainier Radio and Television was owned by Lester Smith and Lincoln Deller. Smith had been a station broker, and through his extensive dealings with buyers and sellers of radio stations, was both experienced and well-known in the radio industry. Deller already owned a number of stations in California and knew Smith from his brokerage activity.[23]

Smith and Deller quickly assembled a purchase plan, and the FCC approved the sale on December 19, 1955. Several years later, Deller decided that he wanted out for personal reasons and Smith sought to buy out Deller's interest. Through his Washington attorneys, he learned that Julius Lefkowitz, who worked in the William Morris talent agency, might know

XL stations stationery letterhead, c. 1949

of parties interested in getting into broadcasting ownership. Lefkowitz did—and put Smith in touch with both Frank Sinatra and Danny Kaye. Sinatra's production company (Essex Productions) and Kaye's production company (Dena Pictures, Inc.) jointly acquired Deller's stock in Mt. Rainier Radio and Television and in the process also purchased the other stations which Smith and Deller jointly owned. The venture registered the assumed business name of Seattle, Portland and Spokane Radio for its operations. The FCC assignment application was approved on June 7, 1958, with a $2 million sale price (which included KJR Seattle). With capital newly available for expansion, KXL filed for a major power increase to 50 kilowatts, an upgrade that was implemented in August 1960.

Having now become a partner with Sinatra and Kaye, Lester Smith needed some documents signed and went to Las Vegas, where Sinatra was appearing at the Sands Hotel and was performing the Desert Inn. Smith recalls his conversation with Kaye:

I went over to see Danny and between the dinner show and the evening show, he says, 'What've you been doing?' Well, I just learned how to fly an airplane, and I just bought myself a single engine, Cessna 182. He says, 'That's funny. I just got my license, and I have a Piper-Aztec.' So, for the next two hours between the shows, we're talking aviation. Aviation is what brought us to become really very close friends. Later on, we'd buy an airplane together.[24]

According to Smith, the two became "like brothers, aviation was the key, not broadcast."[25] They bought Sinatra out on October 14, 1964.

Radio was changing, along with KXL's ownership, and the station was the second in Portland (after KLIQ) to switch to a popular music format and abandon the "block programming" that had been radio's staple since its founding. Rick Thomas and Bob McCarl moved from the then-silent KLIQ to KXL and helped convert the station to a rock 'n roll DJ format.

New to KXL in 1961 was John Salisbury, who began his broadcasting career at Minneapolis' WRHM in 1933. He'd moved to Salt Lake City in 1954 as a news editor and then came to Portland in 1955 as program coordinator and announcer/host for KLOR-TV channel 12. By the time KLOR-TV and KPTV-TV merged in 1957, Salisbury was one of the station's news anchors (see chapter 22).

Salisbury enjoyed a long and distinguished career as the news director of KXL, where he won a total of 14 George Washington Honor Medal awards from the Freedom Foundation at Valley Forge. Salisbury also rose within the broadcasting industry's national ranks, serving on the Radio Television News Directors Association (RTNDA) board and eventually rising to the RTNDA presidency. Salisbury was eventually named executive director of news and public affairs for KXL, the position from which he retired in 1982. He continued to deliver regular radio commentaries on the station until a year before his death in 1987.[26]

When KXL left the Orpheum Theatre Building studios, it no longer needed such large radio production spaces. KXL relocated to this converted house on SE 82nd Street, 1956.

In 1981, Lester Smith bought out the Kaye interest in KXL-AM-FM for $5.2 million and took sole possession of the stations through his Alexander Broadcasting Company. In 1998, he sold KXL to Rose City Radio Corporation for $55 million.

## KOIN-AM Portland

The 1940s brought major changes to KOIN. On May 20, 1942, C. Roy Hunt passed away. Hunt had been president and general manager of KOIN, since 1929 and part-owner of the jointly-owned KOIN and KALE. C. W. Myers, the presiding influence at KOIN since its first days on the air, died on November 3, 1947. "Myers believed in morality—he wouldn't even broadcast an aspirin advertisement if he thought it might be dishonest," recalled Bill Mears, a Hollywood radio actor and writer who came to KOIN in 1940 and eventually became the station's program director.[27] Mears further described Myers as "ruling with an iron hand. You were one big family until you didn't do your job and then out you went. We were a bunch of smart-mouths. I used to get fired more [often] than I got paid."[28]

1944 was a year of some glory for KOIN, when the station won an Honorable Mention in the prestigious Peabody Awards for the program *Song of the Columbia*.

Perhaps the biggest change of the 1940s was the sale of KOIN-AM-FM on March 30, 1946, to Field Enterprises, Inc., for $1,045,000. The Chicago-based owner of the Marshall Field department stores, which was diversifying into broadcasting, Field Enterprises assigned C. Howard Lane, vice president of its radio division, to oversee Portland operations. Harry H. Buckendahl managed the stations. Field Enterprises owned KOIN-AM-FM until 1952, when it sold the stations to a new company, Mt. Hood Radio and Television Broadcasting Corporation, formed principally around Portlanders Harry Buckendahl and Theodore R. Gamble. Field Enterprises explained the 1952 sale by saying, "the decision to sell the stations was dictated largely by the fact that the major business interests of Field Enterprises, Inc. are centered in Chicago and New York City."[29] Gamble, who had soft drink bottling interests, was the prime mover in the purchase.[30] Mt. Hood paid $1.5 million for KOIN-AM-FM and KJR Seattle (see chapter 18).

1955 also brought historic changes at KOIN, which hadn't broadcast a commercial phonograph recording since its 1926 sign-on. In the 1950s, the radio networks were retrenching and air time formerly occupied by network programs had to be filled. KOIN's nighttime schedule began to suffer from that shrinkage in 1953, and by 1955 it was no longer economically feasible to fill the evening openings with a live music schedule. That year, KOIN began its first disc jockey program with an announcer spinning commercial recordings. Given its long history as a station focused heavily upon music, however, KOIN was firm in its view that the central figure in DJ programming was the music—not the DJ.

Consistent with that philosophy, KOIN music director Johnnie Walker, who traditionally chose the sheet music for performances by the station's live musical groups, also assumed responsibility for selecting the recorded music DJs played. The station was particularly concerned about duplicating songs, and Walker screened the music lists of network programs to avoid repeating songs between the local live and commercially recorded KOIN programs.

Responding to the changing times, the station also moved out of the spacious Heathman Hotel studios it had occupied since 1927. With the exodus of KALE in 1944 and a reduction in live music programming, the Heathman location afforded far more space than was needed by the mid-1950s. KOIN-TV had signed-on two years earlier from its newly constructed television studios at 140 SW Columbia Street, and in 1955, KOIN radio joined it there. The move from the Heathman, which had been the site of KOIN-AM's days of national glory, must have been painful—and a clear indication that radio's era of grandeur was passing.

KOIN began experimenting with stereo broadcasting in 1958. Pre-recorded stereo tape recordings had been commercially available for several years when stereo LPs first hit the U.S. market in fall 1957. By that time, the public was increasingly curious about stereo sound. KOIN initially used the AM-FM simultaneous transmission method by transmitting left channel audio on KOIN-AM and right channel audio on KOIN-FM. Following several days' testing, the first KOIN-AM-FM stereocast occurred on May 2, 1958, and the station followed up with a regular schedule of AM-FM stereo transmissions at 11:05 p.m. on Fridays, Saturdays and Sundays (see chapter 22 for continuation of KOIN).

## KSLM-AM Salem

Glenn McCormick, president of Oregon Radio, Inc., died in 1959 and control of the company was assumed by his widow, Lou McCormick. She remarried and owned the station as Lou McCormick Paulus until October 30, 1977, when she sold KSLM to Holiday Radio, Inc., of Dallas, Texas.[31] Holiday Radio held the station until October 23, 1985, when KSLM and its sister FM station, KSKD ("**KaSKaD**e 105" for "Cascade") were purchased for $1.2 million by Ronette Broadcasting based in Daytona Beach, Florida. Greg Fabos was manager of the Salem stations at the time of the Ronette purchase.[32]

## Endnotes

1. In July 1938, KAST's power was increased to 250 watts, on 1200 KHz, from the station's early 100-watt, 1370 KHz, daytime-only FCC authorization (*Astoria Budget*, July 29, 1938).
2. Parsons, Leroy "Ed" E. Interview with Richard Barton. Transcript. Anchorage, AK. June 19, 1986, 2 [WSMB Collection].
3. *Astoria Budget*, September 28, 1938.
4. "Long-Time KAST Staffer Recalls Personalities, Events," *Daily Astorian*, June 25, 1969, 2.
5. Lavern Shadow had it built in 1933 and it was very fussy but couldn't be replaced because of war material shortages.
6. The date of his resignation as general manager is inferred based upon his use of the title technical director in FCC filings of October 29, 1949, through January 16, 1950. Whereas in September 1949, Parsons was still signing FCC documents on behalf of the corporation, by January 25, 1950, M. R. Pressman had again begun

signing for the corporation. On that basis it seems that Parsons' withdrawal from KAST was phased, first from the manager position in October, while he oversaw technical changes in progress as technical director through late January 1950. Robert Holmes, who served as station manager under Parsons' general manager position, began signing FCC materials as general manager as early as February 6, 1950 (KAST file, NARA, College Park, MD).

7. William J. Virgin Jr. died in Los Angeles in 1964 at age 37.
8. Medford Radio's principals consisted of John Tomlin, Alfred S. V. Carpenter, H. S. Deuel, John Moffat, Glenn Jackson, Ben Harder and Otto Frohnmayer (Source: *Medford News*, January 27, 1947, 1).
9. Johnson, Ray. Interview with author. Tape recording. Medford, OR. October 11, 1993.
10. Blanch Virgin Randle and Eddie Randle remained in Medford for a time. The couple later lived in Tracy, California, before moving to Marysville, Washington. Virgin died in Marysville on October 25, 1978.
11. Johnson and Artman, *A Tiger By The Tail*, 102.
12. "Show Biz" Salutes Sammy Taylor," *TV Radio Prevue*, February 19. 1956, 5.
13. Johnson and Artman, *A Tiger By The Tail*, 113.
14. KWJJ left the Wilcox Mansion on April 20, 1997, to move into new studios in the 2000 block of SW First Avenue.
15. "Gene Autry Buys Radio KEX for $900,000," *Oregonian*, May 15, 1962, 10.
16. Ibid.
17. Kale, Richard. Interview with author. Tape recording. Seattle, WA. October 15, 2004.
18. Kale interview, October 14, 2004.
19. *Oregon Journal*, January 12, 1949, Sec. 3, 6.
20. MBS moved to KGON; Don Lee to KWJJ.
21. Craig Adams, email dated October 17, 2008.
22. William Moyes, "Behind the Mike," *Oregonian*, August 27, 1942, 11.
23. He owned stations in Stockton, Chico and Sacramento.
24. Smith, Lester. Interview with author. Tape recording. Bellevue, WA. September 16, 2004.
25. Ibid.
26. Obituary, *Oregonian*, June 28, 1987, c6.
27. "Two KOIN Veterans Remember Heyday When 'Radio Was Place To Be,'" *Oregonian*, January 2, 1977, D5.
28. Ibid.
29. "KOIN Radio Sold by Field," *Oregonian*, July 5, 1952, 1.
30. Mt. Hood paid $1.5 million for KOIN-AM-FM plus Field's Seattle station KJR-AM.
31. Lou McCormick Paulus died in Riverside, California, on Christmas Day, 1982.
32. "Two Radio Stations Sold," *Oregonian*, October 24, 1985, C3.

# 16

# Noncommercial Educational and Public Broadcasting

## Evolution of Educational Broadcasting

Not only were all radio stations originally noncommercial, many had been started by schools or governments whose institutional goals were educational or social as opposed to financial. But by the mid-1920s, many privately-owned stations—such as KGW—had turned to commercial operation while others owned by non-profits had either folded or been sold. By the start of the Great Depression, few educational stations remained.

Oregon State University's KFDJ, which became KOAC on December 21, 1925, was a strong, continuing educational voice, as was Benson Polytechnic High School's KFIF (which became KBPS on March 17, 1930). The question of radio's educational role, however, remained central for the still-developing radio industry, as well as for the federal government. The Radio Act of 1927, which established the Federal Radio Commission, largely side-stepped the question of what educational or public service obligations should be expected of broadcasters, and that debate remained unresolved by passage of the Communications Act of 1934, which established the Federal Communications Commission (FCC).

During this time, educational and religious interests waged a vigorous, albeit largely unsuccessful, battle advocating for a federal licensing system that would assure greater commitment to educational programming by commercial stations.

Since the 1934 act gave the educators' interests little satisfaction, that pressure continued, leading to the initial reservation of some FM frequencies exclusively for noncommercial use in the late 1930s and ultimately the creation of public broadcasting with passage of the Public Broadcasting Act of 1967.

Yet, as radio developed under the 1927 and 1934 acts, virtually all commercial radio stations and networks devoted some air time to public service programming on a noncommercial, sustaining basis. The framers of the Communications Act of 1934 logically assumed those practices would voluntarily continue, which was one reason the 1934 act imposed no specific expectation of that type. These educational efforts by commercial broadcasters did persist well into the 1940s and produced some significant results in Oregon.

## Network Educational Broadcasts in the West

With educational programming now virtually absent from commercial radio, it's hard to imagine the programming to which Americans were listening in the early 1930s. In 1927, the Standard Oil Company began sponsoring the *Standard Hour,* an extremely popular 60-minute program devoted to classical music, that aired on the Pacific Coast NBC Orange network.[1] The series saved the San Francisco Symphony and remained on the air until 1955. In 1928, the *Standard School Broadcast* made its debut on the NBC Red Network, offering "in-class music appreciation and cultural studies for children in the primary grades."[2]

Standard Oil produced accompanying teachers' manuals that were distributed without charge to schools throughout the nation. In schoolrooms across America, students gathered around radios to hear the *Standard School Broadcast.* At its peak, the program was heard weekly by three million students in more than 9,000 schools across the nation.[3] The CBS Network followed suit with its own *American School of the Air* series.

Some Oregon stations devoted very significant efforts to their own sustaining and educational programming efforts.

Ray Johnson Collection, WSMB

The *Standard School Broadcast* originated from NBC's San Francisco studios. The program's original cast, pictured in this 1928 photo, included Jennings Pierce as announcer. Pierce was an NBC San Francisco staff announcer who was later promoted to manager of NBC's west coast affiliate relations. He relocated to Medford, as KMED-AM's general manager, when Blanch Virgin sold that station in 1950.

Children listening to an educational radio program at Rigler Elementary School, Portland, January 8, 1947

## Commercial Stations' Educational Efforts in Oregon

**KGW/KEX Portland:** KGW began Portland's first in-school listening programming—heard once weekly for 15 minutes—in 1931, at the request of the Portland School Board. Two years later, KGW added another program, *Talking Text Books*, heard twice weekly. In 1935, KGW began broadcasting *Current Events*, with content planned by local principals. That program expanded to five episodes a week later that year and continued until 1951. When KGW purchased KEX in 1933, educational programs were transferred from KGW to KEX, although they reverted to KGW upon KEX's 1944 sale. Far from delegating these programs to new staff recruits or interns, top-echelon programming personnel were assigned to them. KGW and KEX maintained a full-time education director to coordinate these efforts.

Even as television was dawning, KGW devoted new resources to education when program director Homer Welch and education director Evelyn Sibley Lampman created KGW's Summer Radio Workshop for Children. Predominantly an educational exercise, some of its output likely found its way onto the KGW air waves.

Following KEX's purchase by Westinghouse in 1944, the station created a number of educational programs, including *Adventures in Research*, *Making Friends with Science*, *Our Town* (rebroadcast over KBPS), *Intercollegiate Forum*, *Careers Unlimited*, *Music is our Business*, *Junior Town Meeting* and *Portland Hi Time* (see chapters 13 and 15). Tom Swafford directed and cast these educational programs which featured professional actors and borrowed KGW organist Glenn Shelley. Following carefully conducted auditions, children's roles were cast with pupils selected by the Portland schools. The entire effort was coordinated by KGW-KEX's then education director T. Robert Zimmerman, Lampman's predecessor in that assignment.

KGW and KEX were not alone in such efforts.

**KOIN Portland:** Luke Roberts (later the executive director of what is now called Oregon Public Broadcasting) was KOIN's director of education in 1939-41, when the station wrote and produced the *Dutch Uncles* program in cooperation with the vocational guidance office of the Portland school system. In 1941, that program won a prestigious Ohio State Institute for Education by Radio (IER) award. A year later, KOIN began the series *Kid Critics*, which featured

Evelyn Sibley Lampman and Homer Welch in the KGW studios for the station's Summer Radio Workshop for Children, 1950.

a panel of school children discussing their favorite library books, in cooperation with the Portland Library Association and the Portland school system. That program, which KOIN produced until 1948, also won an IER award in 1943. Other KOIN efforts included *Song of the Columbia*, a 26-program series in 1943-44, and *White Fires of Inspiration*, which offered stories of painters, poets, writers and musicians for teenagers listening in evening broadcast hours. KOIN launched a

The award-winning *Kid Critics* featured Portland school children critically reviewing young people's literature over KOIN.

new venture, Radio Institute for Teachers in 1944. The station offered this multi-week institute for a number of years as a service to Portland Public Schools. Portland's school superintendent, Willard B. Spalding, described as "A most outstanding contribution to the educational development of the Portland schools.[4]

**KPOJ Portland:** Another local effort was KPOJ's *Quiz 'em On The Air* program which appealed to the high school and collegiate audiences.

These efforts by commercial stations were notable exceptions in their predominantly commercial schedules. Oregon's educational stations, however, offered full-time educational programming.

# Oregon Educational AM Stations

KFDJ/KOAC Corvallis and KFIF/KBPS Portland, founded in 1922 and 1923 respectively, were among the few surviving educational AM stations at the start of the Great Depression. The economic collapse of the 1930s was especially hard on educational stations. In 1932, with public funding for higher education at one of its most challenging points, a serious effort arose to force KOAC's sale. The station was saved following a spirited defensive campaign spearheaded by the *Oregon Journal* and Governor Julius Meyer. Newspapers headlined the result as "Oregon Saves Her Station."[5] While still operated by Oregon State University, KOAC was transferred to the new Oregon State Board of Higher Education in 1932, and the station, which used the slogan "Oregon's Own Station," tenaciously clung to life against the Depression-enhanced odds.[6]

As the Depression was ebbing, the 1939 Legislature provided funding to increase KOAC's power to five kilowatts.[7]

Logo from cover of KOAC Broadcasting Schedule, spring 1945

Courtesy of the Oregon State University Archives

Similarly, KFIF/KBPS struggled through the Depression while benefiting from the educational efforts of commercial stations like KGW, as well as continuing support from the Portland School District. From the time of its birth in 1923, the station was somewhat casually managed by Benson Polytechnic High School faculty, chiefly led by W.D. Allingham and R.T. Stephens. In 1939, the school district decided to dedicate administrative staff time to KBPS and promoted Franklin High School teacher Helen Kenyon to be the station's manager. Kenyon brought new precision to its operation and was later hired as director of education by Seattle's CBS outlet, KIRO, in September 1941. She went on to a career with CBS Radio in Washington, DC, and was succeeded at KBPS by Mary Elizabeth Gilmore, who continued Kenyon's vision.[8] When Gilmore resigned in September 1947, she was succeeded by a new probationary teacher, Patricia Green, who became Patricia Green Swenson following her marriage to KOIN's Daryl Swenson.[9] Swenson managed KBPS until 1994 and was the driving force behind the station for those 47 years. KBPS was fortunate to enjoy leadership from this unusually talented trio of women, whose vision and drive propelled the station to national prominence.

Thus, Oregon emerged from the Depression era with two fine educational stations—at a time when only approximately 31 noncommercial, educational radio stations remained in the entire nation.

Pat Swenson with KBPS student Warren Weagant. Radio ran in Weagant's family. His father, Charles, and brother Ralph started KHFS/KKEY and both had worked for other Oregon stations (see chapter 21)]. Warren worked for KKEY while a student and, under the air name John Edwards, went on to become a DJ at KGON, and later program director at KPAM/KPFM, before moving to California. c. early 1960s.

KBPS Collection, WSMB

# Birth of Noncommercial Educational (NCE) FM

Notwithstanding the educational efforts of commercial networks and stations, educators continued to dream of an expanded role for education through radio fostered by nonprofit station ownership. Those plans began to mature in the later 1930s when the FCC reserved a few high frequency AM channels exclusively for noncommercial, educational use, a step that was feasible because the new frequencies were of dubious economic value. When the commission first authorized FM, it reserved the first five "low-band" channels for such use. When FM was "kicked upstairs" occupying the 88 to 108 MHz band in 1945, the band from 88–92 MHz was reserved for such use (see chapter 14).

Prior to 1938, when the FCC first reserved some frequencies exclusively for noncommercial education use, the Commission had a conception of educational radio through stations such as KOAC and KBPS but hadn't sought to formally describe and license a station specifically for such purposes. The creation of these reserved frequencies forced the commission to establish a noncommercial, educational (NCE) licensing category, and when the reserved FM band was established, schools and government agencies across Oregon and the nation, responded to this new opportunity.

# Oregon's First Noncommercial Educational (NCE) FM Stations

Several key individuals helped to establish and nurture Oregon's NCE stations including KOAC's James Morris, KBPS's Pat Swenson, KRVM's Roger Houglum and Luke Roberts at what is now called Oregon Public Broadcasting. Without their pioneering efforts to create a foundation for noncommercial public service broadcasting in Oregon, the state's other non-commercial and public radio and television stations could not have developed and flourished as they have.

**KRVM-FM Eugene:** The first Oregon station to be licensed for the new noncommercial, educational FM service was Eugene's KRVM—which was only the 13th NCE station on the high FM band to be licensed in the entire nation.[10] While KGW's Harold Singleton constructed the station's FM antenna, much of KRVM was built by Roger J. Houglum, who then headed up the Eugene Vocational School's Electronics Department and later became KRVM's first manager.

Community support for KRVM was strong. Houglum, who was also part-owner of KERG Eugene at the time, donated his time to construct KRVM. Local supporters also donated construction materials and sold the station a baby grand piano at a charitable price. Located at the school district's vocational high school, KRVM was envisioned as both a source of classroom educational programming and a vocational training laboratory for broadcasting students.

Licensed to Lane County School District Number 4 (now School District 4J), KRVM slipped onto the air without fanfare for test purposes at 10 a.m. on December 6, 1947. Oscar Johnson powered up the transmitter and chief announcer Leo Reetz read the announcement which KRVM signed-on with for the next 35 years: "You are in tune with K R V M in Eugene, Oregon. Operating with a power of 400 watts on channel 211. The station is licensed to School District Four, Lane County and carries on an educational and non-commercial broadcast service."[11]

Two days later on December 8, KRVM signed-on with 400 watts on 90.1 MHz to an over-flow crowd gathered at the station for the formal inauguration. At precisely 7:30 p.m., Oscar Johnson again energized the transmitter, and a student announcer signed-on the station and introduced the distinguished guests. A formal training program for announcers and broadcast engineers commenced the following morning.

Five full-time directors at various schools in the district assisted Houglum at KRVM. One was longtime KOAC staff member Elizabeth Patapoff, who was recommended to Houglum by KOAC's Jimmy Morris. Patapoff left KOAC to take that position, which she held for two years before returning to KOAC. While the Eugene Technical School was later consolidated with Lane Community College (LCC) upon that institution's founding, the school district elected to retain KRVM at the time.

Roger Houglum was a towering figure in Oregon's noncommercial/public radio activities during the mid-20th century. A man with a slight build, who stood 5 feet 10 inches and weighed only 150 pounds, Houglum devoted most of his adult life to teaching and educational radio. "Radio started off to be my hobby," he reminisced, "but it turned out to be my vocation."[12] Houglum remained at KRVM until 1965, when he became chairman of the electronics department at the newly formed Lane Community College. He also was the first manager of the radio station that LCC then developed, KLCC (see KPNW-FM/KLCC-FM in this chapter).

Many who started at KRVM went on to significant broadcasting careers. including Bob Litten, who worked at KERG and KEED; Glenn Nickell, who was at KORE and KUIN before becoming general manager of KVAL-TV; Bob Fulton, who served at KERG and later KFRE Fresno, California; Leo Reetz, who later was chief engineer of KEZI-TV; Don Anderson, who worked at KASH; Ralph Cook, who later was KASH's chief engineer; Dale Reed, a program director at KUGN and was known as "Uncle Fuzzy" on that station's *Morning Show*; Wendy Ray, who later worked at KASH, KOMB (now KNND), KERG and was KUGN's news director for many years; Dick Cross, who went on to KUGN and KPNW; Tom Worden, who later worked at and owned KRSB and KYES; and Russ Doran, a program director at KPNW.

**KTEC-FM Klamath Falls:** Another important educational broadcasting development was the Legislative request advanced from the Oregon State System of Higher Education for authority to install an noncommercial educational FM station at the Oregon Institute of Technology (OIT), which had been established in Klamath Falls in 1947. In 1949, the school successfully solicited legislation authorizing its application for a noncommercial FM station to which call letters KTEC were then assigned. The station signed-on December 19, 1950, as a 10-watt educational station on 88.1 MHz.[13] Originally licensed in the name of Oregon Technical Institute (the school's name was subsequently changed to Oregon Institute of Technology), the station was transferred to the institution's parent organization, the Oregon State Board of Higher Education, on September 7, 1961. Like KRVM, KTEC was viewed as a curricular adjunct/training facility for students.

**KWAX-FM Eugene:** Radio had been a part of the University of Oregon for decades prior to its first licensed radio station, KWAX, which sign-on April 4, 1951. At radio's inception in the early 1920s, the university had offered programs over Portland's KGG and KGW, as well as over Corvallis' KOAC. After World War II, interest in radio ran high at the university, and students created the unlicensed campus-only, closed-circuit (commonly known as carrier current because its signal was transmitted via the power lines in campus buildings) KDUK, which began operation on June 1, 1949, with a program called *Duck Soup's On*.[14] Professors such as Herman Cohen in the Department of Speech served as faculty advisors to KDUK, known as "the Voice of the Ducks."

By late 1949, KDUK had expanded from what the *Oregon Daily Emerald* had earlier described as a "one and two-room affair" to the entire third floor of the university's Villard Hall, where the Department of Speech was located. The third floor also housed two classrooms designed for radio instruction, which were also used by KDUK. It was abundantly clear, however, that a licensed, on-air radio station had long been a gleam in the eye of the radio division faculty of the department of speech, and like-minded students and faculty were using KDUK to test the waters toward that eventual goal. Like many student stations, KDUK operated only during the school year, and by late 1949, the station's failure to return to normal operation following the resumption of fall classes attracted attention from the *Oregon Daily Emerald*. While no explanation was offered, it eventually became clear that the faculty was deeply involved in exploring significant expansion of KDUK's transmission capability, whether by wiring the campus or securing an FCC license. This led the *Oregon Daily Emerald* to hope that "if we ever do get a station, it will aid all of us and will not be the plaything of one department."[15]

In early 1950, the radio division faculty decided to seek an FM station and then went public in April with a proposal to fund the station's construction using "breakage fees," which the university collected from dormitory residents. A student vote on the proposal was quickly authorized by Associated Students of the University of Oregon (ASUO).

Perhaps surprising to contemporary students, there seems to have been no expectation that KDUK (or a contemplated university FM station) would seek to particularly reflect student programming interests. Rather, KDUK seems to have operated with a general programming style consistent with the commercial radio stations serving Eugene, but with an occasional a university-focused orientation to topics, music and so forth—and that was also the implicit goal for an FM station.

Six hundred and eighteen students voted to pledge their breakage fees toward construction of an FM station, and an FCC license application for 88.1 MHz was apparently approved by the commission during the university's summer recess. While student funds would be used to build the FM station, it was to be operated entirely from Speech Department monies.

By fall 1950, Jack Vaughn had assumed the position of station manager in preparation for the launch and on November 18, the FCC issued a construction permit for the new 10-watt KWAX station. With an estimated February or March 1951 sign-on, Vaughn began assembling the needed staff but was set back by delays in receiving needed equipment, the result of a national railroad switchmen's strike.

KWAX signed-on at 7:30 p.m. on April 4 with the opening line, spoken by Bob Litten, "These are the first words to be spoken over radio station KWAX."[16, 17] "This is the one the campus has been waiting for" the *Oregon Daily Emerald* editorially observed. Besides Vaughn, the station's initial staffing consisted of Dave Strauss, business manager; Janet Harris, music director; George Drougas, continuity director; Jim Blue, announcer; Lionel Matthews, traffic director; and Dick Hardie, program director. Speech professor Glenn Starlin, who was heading the university's radio division, signed-on as KWAX's faculty advisor. Opening night programs included classical dinner music, a discussion of current popular novels conducted by freshman Alvin Jones and a news commentary on world affairs by political science junior Doug Ambers. *Radio Workshop*, "a transcribed drama produced by Oregon students," was also on the initial KWAX program schedule.

A series of power increases were partially assisted by the donation of KUGN, Inc.'s FM transmission equipment in 1964, growth in its academic connection, and the securing of charter status in the founding of National Public Radio (NPR). KWAX emerged as a leader, and in the decades following the station's launch, trained many of Oregon's most talented broadcasters (see chapter 14).

**KRRC-FM Portland:** In 1954, Reed College's KRRC had its genesis in the formation of the Reed Radio Club, which was established to rally support for a student radio station. Interested students assembled an unlicensed 40-watt AM carrier-current transmitter whose signal was distributed through the campus electrical system. Its coverage was limited to the campus (similar to KDUK's at the University of Oregon). Operating as KRCB-AM (**K-R**eed-**C**ollege-**B**roadcasters) at 660 KHz, the station signed-on in October 1955 from the basement of Doyle Dormitory. Classical music, which was largely unavailable on Portland radio, was a mainstay of the KRCB schedule.

However, student sights were set on an on-air FM station. Their goal was realized when the FCC approved a construction permit for the 10-watt KRRC, which signed-on 89.3 MHz on May 14, 1958, using a transmitter largely financed and constructed by student Roger Wiesenbach. At first, KRRC broadcast somewhat

Former KRRC student Dr. Demento in a 1976 promotional photo

sporadically but soon settled into a schedule with generous amounts of classical music, drawn largely from the library of the school's music department, interrupted by not-infrequent technical challenges. A 1958 *Oregonian* article noted that "austerity vies with ingenuity" at KRRC.[18]

On May 23, 1959, KRRC became the first Northwest station to broadcast a Spanish-language program, which featured news and interviews and ran weekly at 9:30 p.m. KRRC increasingly prided itself on providing unconventional programming that later came to be called "free-form."

Perhaps the station's most famous alum is Barret Hansen, who graduated from Reed in 1963 and came to be known as Dr. Demento. Obsessed with music and recordings from an early age, on his "Musical Museum" at KRRC Hansen interspersed country, blues, folk, rock 'n roll, rhythm and blues and other music in a highly eclectic mixture drawn from the thousands of recordings he had been collecting since the age of 11. Following graduation from Reed, Hansen worked at the legendary Pasadena, California "underground" station KPPC-FM, where he reportedly got his air name after playing Nervus Norvus' "Transfusion" in 1970.[19] When someone commented that he had to have been demented to play it, his air name was born. The *Dr. Demento* program went into national syndication in 1974 and is still on the air. Hansen was inducted into the Comedy Hall of Fame in 2005. Of his time at KRRC, Hansen says: "I wouldn't have had a career without it."[20] Other KRRC alumni include NPR correspondent Eric Westervelt, NPR producer Susan Davis and broadcast consulting engineer Gray Haertig.

In later years, KRRC faced numerous challenges because its tiny, 10-watt signal was constantly subject to preemption by more powerful stations. In 1984, KRRC moved to 107.5 MHz, in 1992 to 104.1 MHz and in 2003 to 97.9 MHz.

# Other Oregon FM NCE Stations

KRVM, KTEC, KWAX and KRRC, which all signed-on prior to 1960, were founded based upon the easy availability of NCE frequencies. It was the establishment of such stations across the nation that eventually provided the opportunity to create vastly more significant "public radio stations," as they came to be defined by the federal government following passage of the Public Broadcasting Act of 1967. Their existence also led to the establishment of noncommercial educational television, a service that began in Oregon in the late 1950s and matured into public television service in the late 1960s.

Beginning in 1960, other small NCE stations sprang up around the state including KSOR Southern Oregon University, Ashland; KCHC Central Point High School, Central Point; KBVR Oregon State University, Corvallis; KEPO Eagle Point High School, Eagle Point; KLCC Lane Community College, Eugene; KEOL Eastern Oregon University, La Grande; KSLC Linfield College, McMinnville; and KRBM Blue Mountain Community College, Pendleton (for additional details on some of these stations, see chapter 27).

**KBVR-FM Corvallis:** Corvallis got another FM station when Oregon State University's Speech Department spearheaded the effort to build the 10-watt (class D) noncommercial FM station KBVR, standing for **K**-Oregon State **B**ea**V**e**R**s, on 90.1 MHz. The station signed-on October 26, 1965, from studios in Shepard Hall and functioned as a student-staffed, faculty-supervised operation partially devoted to training would-be broadcasters and catering to student interests. In the 1970s, the class D station struggled to adapt to the FCC's evolving rules for 10-watt stations, which required either significantly expanding or giving way to larger operations. OSU opted to invest in KBVR and in 1981 filed an application to change KBVR's frequency and increase its power. It was not until 1988, however, that KBVR began transmitting on 88.7 MHz with 340 watts.

**KPNW-FM/KLCC-FM Eugene:** Roger Houglum was the driving force behind Eugene School District 4J's founding of KRVM-FM to train students for broadcasting careers (see elsewhere in this chapter). In 1965, Houglum was hired by Lane Community College for a similar assignment. Initially, Houglum made arrangements for his students to broadcast over KRVM to provide them on-air experience, but he had difficulty securing enough air time for his growing student enrollment. That pressure led to his recommendation to LCC president Dale Parnell that the college build its own station.

An FCC application for a 440-watt station on 90.3 MHz was approved on December 26, 1964. KPNW (LCC' first call letter choice—KLCC—had been unavailable) signed-on February 17, 1967, from studios it shared with KRVM. Initially, KPNW's antenna was located on KRVM's tower, and its control room was constructed in an unused KRVM studio area. The total cost of construction was $8,900.

The station signed-on without a great deal of fanfare. The *Eugene Register-Guard*, for example, didn't even acknowledge the station's arrival on the airwaves. Four-year-old KPIR-AM did notice, however, and apparently thought the KPNW call letters had value. In order for KPIR to inherit the KPNW call sign, the AM station offered to pay the costs of LCC securing the KLCC call sign—which had recently become available. While some students opposed the call sign change, it went into effect on August 1, 1967.

Initially, KLCC operated in a type of hybrid mode; it offered students the opportunity to hone their broadcast announcing skills while also offering "educational fare from various syndicated and network sources." To support the latter goal, the station joined National Educational Radio (NER), an early educational syndication network. Thus, in its early days, KLCC's program schedule included *Old Swedish Organs*, *Germany Today* and *London Echo*. In the summer of 1968, the station boosted its coverage by moving its transmitter to KFMY's site on Blanton Heights, and the station's studios and record library were simultaneously moved to the LCC campus.

At the time, LCC seems to have become more interested in using KLCC for community impact rather than as a student laboratory. In the first week of fall term 1970, all "educational" programs were dropped from KLCC, and a week later the station adopted a "hard rock" format designed to make the station more competitive. Broadcasts of campus events were also eliminated. The station was growing, and in February 1976, applied to move to 89.7 MHz and raise its power.

KLCC later joined National Public Radio (NPR) and ultimately became highly competitive in the Eugene radio market. Although its air time perhaps became less directly useful to students training for careers in commercial radio, it became a highly successful training ground for individuals seeking employment in public radio. In 1979, when NPR moved to the federally-funded satellite program distribution system that replaced telephone circuits, KLCC was selected as the first station in the U.S. for the installation thus becoming the first radio station, commercial or public, in the nation "to receive transmissions from other stations by way of satellite."[21]

**KBOO-FM Portland:** Listener-supported radio in America dates from the 1949 founding of KPFA-FM Berkeley, a station that was inspired by its visionary founding figure and first manager, Lewis Hill. In succeeding years, others were inspired by Hill's concept and other listener-supported stations developed, including Seattle's KRAB-FM, which was launched by Lorenzo Milam and several associates in 1962. Milam saw himself as a kind of Johnny Appleseed of listener-supported radio and sought to clone KRAB-type stations in other communities.

Some Portlanders desired more classical music than was available to them on the air waves of the 1960s and were perhaps also intrigued by the devilish, anti-establishment flair that KRAB exuded. In 1964, they formed Portland Listener Supported Radio. Recognizing an opportunity, Milam contacted them, and on April 21, 1965, KRAB announced that it wanted to bring "Free Form Radio" to Portland. With support from the Portlanders whose goodwill it had solicited, KRAB's licensee, the Jack Straw Memorial Foundation, filed an FCC application in November 1965 for a 10-watt Portland satellite station on 90.7 MHz.[22]

The application proposed locating a transmitter in long-time broadcast engineer Harold Singleton's garage, located at 4646 SW Council Crest Drive on Healy Heights, with a 50-foot tower erected in his backyard. Without funding for local studio facilities, the plan was to place a receiving antenna at the Healy Heights site to receive KRAB's off-air signal from Seattle, which the Portland transmitter would simply relay. However, KRAB's signal proved too noisy to broadcast in stereo and could therefore only be offered to Portland in monophonic sound. On June 14, 1967, a construction permit was issued under the call sign KBOO—which referred to a strain of marijuana known as "Berkeley Boo"—for the tiny station, which was predicted to only cover a portion of the Portland area. An inspiring figure from KRAB's Seattle coterie, David Calhoun, was dispatched to Portland to launch and manage the station. As KBOO relates the story, "Calhoun, an ex-monk and third-year medical student, packed his VW with a transmitter from Seattle, and moved south."[23]

KBOO signed-on at 1 p.m. on June 18, 1968, and simply repeated KRAB's signal. But the station slowly began to develop local programming from the ramshackle, cramped basement studios that it had hastily assembled in downtown Portland on Third Avenue and Salmon Street. Amid growing public support, KRAB raised its power to 1 kilowatt in 1970.

The KRAB/KBOO relationship, while entirely amiable during KBOO's founding years, gradually evolved with the Portland station developing an increasingly separatist stance. Having outgrown its studios at 234 SW Salmon Street, the station moved to a storefront at 3129 SE Belmont Street in 1971 and the Oregon nonprofit KBOO Foundation was formed in 1972. A three-year transition period ensued with the KBOO license being formally transferred from the Jack Straw Memorial Foundation to the KBOO Foundation on August 5, 1975.

In 1974, KBOO raised its power to 12.5 kilowatts and slightly moved its transmission plant by mounting its antenna on the KXL-FM tower. On June 26, 1977, KBOO moved it studios to 65 SW Yamhill Street. In 1981, KBOO again moved, this time to 20 SE Eighth Avenue, from which it continues to serve Portland with its unique, eclectic programming mix.

**KSOR-FM, Ashland:** On May 21, 1969, the Rogue Valley's first noncommercial educational radio station, KSOR, signed-on at Southern Oregon College (now Southern Oregon University). Operating at 90.1 MHz with a fledgling power of 10 watts, it could only be received in Ashland. The station's major purpose was to help train students for careers in broadcasting.

KSOR was spearheaded by former commercial broadcaster David Allen Borum (known professionally as Dave Allen), who was then teaching broadcasting at the university. The broadcast during the academic year and offered rock 'n roll, and beautiful music and classical music and also affiliated with the Metropolitan Opera network.[24] The station's tiny signal left most of the Rogue Valley with only a tantalizing sense of the possibilities more transmitter power and funding could provide.

In 1973, Allen suddenly became ill. His early death left a large void in the university's broadcast instruction program and at KSOR. During interim operations following Allen's death, SOU president James K. Sours—who wasn't necessarily persuaded that the station had achieved results sufficient to defend its continuation—contemplated KSOR's future. In 1974, he decided to acquire an independent analysis of the university's options and opportunities.

At this point, the author needs to make clear that the KSOR history that follows is informed by his personal experience and therefore necessarily suffers from a lack of objectivity.

The author, Ronald Kramer, who had recently resigned from the faculty at Portland's Lewis & Clark College, where he had launched a broadcasting curriculum, was recruited to Ashland as a temporary consultant to Sours. Prior to coming to Portland, Kramer had worked in commercial radio in Cleveland and for the ABC Radio Network in Los Angeles.

Arriving Ashland in September 1974, Kramer served as KSOR's faculty advisor, and in early 1975 presented Sours with a white paper detailing five potential options for developing the station. Among them, the most elaborate and risky contemplated raising KSOR's power to cover the entire Rogue Valley, along with a plan to grow the station into eligibility for membership in the fledgling National Public Radio (NPR). Sours selected that course, which he described as the "Cadillac" option, and Donald Larson, representing the Oregon State Board of Higher Education, expressed the state board's support for the growth plan and advocated for it in various public and private meetings that ensued.

In 1976, KSOR filed an FCC application to increase its power to 2.2 kilowatts with its transmitter located on 3,500-foot Mt. Baldy east of Phoenix. A concurrent application for federal financial assistance was submitted to the Educational Broadcasting Facilities Program (EBFP) of the Department of Health, Education and Welfare. Proceeds from that EBFP grant, along with local fundraising initiatives, enabled the station to commence construction. When KSOR signed-on its new transmitter on February 25, 1977, the *Medford Mail Tribune* proclaimed "Now the entire Valley may hear KSOR."[25] The expanded station began offering a great deal of locally produced programming with a schedule that included rock 'n roll. The station gradually developed, and in 1980 qualified for support from the Corporation for Public Broadcasting (CPB) and joined NPR at the same time. In response to a landlord dispute, KSOR's transmitter was relocated in 1986 to the 5,300-foot King Mountain near Wolf Creek. Its power increased to 35.5 kilowatts.

KSOR began exploring the use of FM translator technology to respond to a request from Grants Pass' Rogue Community College for KSOR service. The station installed its first translator, K217AB on 91.3 MHz in

Khayam the cheetah participates in a 1981 interview at the KSOR/JPR Ashland studios accompanied by Winston, Oregon's, Wildlife Images staff.

Grants Pass, but it didn't work properly because then-current translator technology didn't properly handle the relatively narrow input/output frequency spread on the 4 MHz-wide reserved FM band. Soon, KSOR was being asked to install translator service to other adjacent communities as invitations arrived from the Yreka city council and the Weed California chamber of commerce in California and Roseburg's Umpqua Community College in Roseburg. The station worked with a major translator manufacturer, Television Technology Corporation (TTC) of Arvada, Colorado, which designed a new-style translator unit to KSOR's specifications. The station purchased the first 18 units off the assembly line to service its existing translator locations, as well as the many new installations that had been funded under a new Public Telecommunications Facilities Program (PTFP) grant.[26] The construction project included the first federally funded, solar-powered translators in the U.S.

KSOR's translator construction had transformed the station from a local to a regional service. In a 1983 study of Oregon's public radio stations, University of Oregon researcher Alan Yorty, wrote:

> Southern Oregon has a significant public radio service, not due to a regional planning mechanism, but as a result of one local station—KSOR—defining itself as a regional service. Through a system of translators, most cities in southern Oregon with a population of over 3,000 have access to a public radio service.[27]

KSOR had made a huge investment in translator technology and ultimately constructed 36 translator installations—the largest public radio translator plant in the nation.

Over time, however, the translators' ability to serve the region was adversely impacted by changes in FCC rules, which both minimized translators' maximum power and authorized remotely feeding translators and repeater stations by satellite. The combination of these events created greater competition for translator frequencies as distant entities sought to install new radio satellite-fed stations in the region, forcing translators, which were subordinate to such stations, off the air.

Shortly after moving KSOR's transmitter to King Mountain, the station expanded by installing a small 227-watt station, KSMF, on 89.1 MHz. Although it was on Mt. Baldy, it as in a different location than KSOR had originally been. While the KSMF installation was largely made to fill in shadow areas not well-served by KSOR from King Mountain, it also afforded KSMF the opportunity to occasionally counter-program KSOR, providing a taste of running multiple program services. That led to SOU's filing applications for other radio stations in Klamath Falls, Coos Bay, Roseburg, Burney/Redding, Mt. Shasta and Yreka where KSKF, KSBA, KSRS, KNCA, KNSQ and KNYR were respectively built between 1988 and 1991. In 1992, SOU filed an application to increase KSMF's power to 2.2 kilowatts and used the original KSMF transmitter to launch another new Rogue Valley FM station, KSRG, which signed-on in 1995 at 88.3 MHz with 227 watts.[28] The small transmitter had originally been purchased for KSMF from KTEC Klamath Falls—who had in turn originally secured it from KBOY Medford, which had used it when it first signed-on in 1959.

The number of stations SOU was at the time operating increasingly caused call-letter confusion among listeners and led to the March 1989 adoption of a common name, Jefferson Public Radio (JPR), for the university's network of stations. The name referred to the mythical state of Jefferson, which had been the object of various serious and humorous succession movements in northern California and southern Oregon dating back more than 100 years.

In 1989, Perry Atkinson donated his 1230 KHz AM station to SOU, which led JPR's launching an entirely new program, the *News and Information* service, over the re-christened KSJK-AM. Its programming consisted almost entirely of network and syndicated programming, which the station purchased from NPR and other sources. While KSJK's initial operations didn't cause an explosion of public interest, the station steadily gained an audience, and its operation taught JPR how to run a network with multiple, simultaneous program streams. On July 11, 1991, Bill Smullin donated KAGI-AM Grants Pass, his original Oregon radio station and the last radio station his company owned, to JPR (see chapter 10). The 5-kilowatt KAGI-AM simulcast KSJK and began JPR's expansion of its *News and Information* service to a larger region.

By 1991, JPR had enough FM stations to separate them into distinct groups. One was assigned to carry a newly established *Classics and News* service; the remaining FM stations carried the other new offering, JPR's *Rhythm and News* service. Thus, in October 1991, JPR began operating three fully separate program services, *Classics and News*, *Rhythm and News* and *News and Information*, on its network of stations.[29] JPR was one of the first public radio broadcasters in the nation to begin operating three fully separate streams simultaneously from one central network headquarters, a model that public radio operators in other parts of the country later came to emulate.[30]

To make all three program services as widely available to the region as possible, JPR continued to launch new FM stations, as well as purchase a series of AM and FM stations through the allied JPR Foundation, which had been incorporated in 1998. Whereas in 1998 it owned/programmed ten radio stations and 33 translators, by 2008 it owned and/or programmed 22 radio stations plus its translator network and had FCC applications pending for additional facilities.

## Oregon Public Broadcasting/KOAC-TV Corvallis

As broadcasting changed in the post-World War II environment, the question of how KOAC should keep pace with radio's evolving technical and social evolution was a constant question. While both FM and TV prospects were under discussion, simply maintaining funding for KOAC-AM alone had proven no small feat. How could Oregon finance new services like FM or TV?

When both governors McKay and Patterson encouraged adding television to KOAC's mission, KOAC staff initiated some experimental programming over KVAL-TV in Eugene to explore the medium.[31] With funding from the state government, KOAC's own 29-kilowatt TV station, KOAC-TV, subsequently signed-on channel 7 on October 7, 1957, from studios in OSU's Gill Coliseum and a transmitter at Vineyard Hill. KOAC-TV operated largely as a daytime teaching tool but other hours were used for general public offerings.

## KOAP-TV Portland

Portlanders who wanted educational television couldn't receive KOAC-TV from Corvallis. As a result, they formed Community TV, Inc., to apply for a channel 10 license and seek funds to build a station. Important assistance was provided by the Bullitt Foundation, King Broadcasting Company's charitable division. On June 14, 1960, the foundation gave them the former KGW-FM Healy Heights transmitter site, worth an estimated $65,000.

While Community TV received a channel 10 construction permit, it ultimately concluded that the fundraising required to build a station presented too great a challenge. Community TV then turned over the channel 10 construction permit, the transmitter site and the funds and equipment that had been donated for the project to the Oregon Department of Higher Education, which assumed the task. A legislative appropriation provided the final impetus, and KOAP-TV (which some have suggested stood for **K-O**regon-**A**ir-**P**ortland) signed-on February 6, 1961, as a companion to KOAC-TV—giving Oregon a two-station educational TV network.

From *The Remembered Years*/Courtesy of Oregon Public Broadcasting

KOAC-TV Capitol Reporter Don Dill, filming interview with David Cameron, Oregon Employment Commissioner, c. 1959

# KEX-FM/KOAP-FM/KOPB-FM Portland

Westinghouse had given KEX-FM two tries in Portland and neither had been successful (see chapter 14). Across the country, other FM station owners were also tiring of sustaining FM operating losses and had accordingly donated some of these stations to nonprofit groups. By 1961, the state of Oregon's educational broadcasting activities had been grouped into a new division of the Department of Higher Education called Oregon Educational Broadcasting Network (OEBN), which included KOAC-AM, KOAC-TV and KOAP-TV. Noting the state's expanding broadcasting horizons, KEX-FM's general manger, Herbert L. Bachman, approached OEBN about Westinghouse's possible donation of KEX-FM.

A formal announcement of the gift was made on October 25, 1961, and the station was formally accepted by the Oregon State Board of Higher Education on March 15, 1962. Westinghouse's donation included the KEX-FM equipment, FCC license and the station's classical music library, which had been assembled to support the classical music programming that Westinghouse had launched in 1957.

KEX-FM signed-off April 8, 1962, and the 92.3 MHz frequency returned to the air under the new KOAP-FM call sign on April 30, 1962, as part of OEBN. Thus, the radio operation became a two-station network—KOAC-AM in Corvallis and KOAP-FM in Portland—although all programming originated in Corvallis. KOAP-FM picked up an off-air signal from KOAC-AM for FM rebroadcast. By May 1963, a microwave interconnection was established between the two stations, and the radio operation had changed its name to Oregon Educational Radio Network (OERN). On September 26, 1963, KOAP-FM moved from its Westinghouse-inherited frequency to 91.5 MHz and raised the station's antenna to improve coverage.

# Oregon Educational Broadcasting (OEB) Becomes OEPBS

By February 1965, the Oregon Educational Broadcasting Network shortened its name to Oregon Educational Broadcasting (OEB) and the radio side began identifying itself as OEB Radio. In January 1966, the OEB radio stations became members of the National Education Radio (NER) network, which used tape syndication to distribute educational programming across the country. TV facilities were dramatically enhanced with the May 1966 move of OEB's administration and television studios to the Northwestern Building at 2828 SW Front Street in Portland, a facility that was replaced by an entirely new plant constructed on SW Macadam Avenue in 1988.

The 1960s and 70s were periods of considerable growth for OEB. Passage of the federal Public Broadcasting Act of 1967 created the Corporation for Public Broadcasting, which in turn led to the founding of the Public Broadcasting Service (PBS) for television and National Public Radio (NPR) for radio. Equally important, it led to the replacement in both name and goals of "educational broadcasting" with "public broadcasting."

On October 5, 1970, PBS replaced the earlier National Educational Television (NET) tape network, and OEB joined PBS on that date. On May 3, 1971, OEB joined NPR, which had absorbed NER. The following year, KOAC won a George Foster Peabody Award for the series *Conversations with Will Shakespeare and Certain of His Friends*, which drew upon Oregon Shakespeare Festival resources.

Recognizing the evolution in public broadcasting as well as its own heritage, OEB became Oregon Educational and Public Broadcasting Service (OEPBS) on March 13, 1972. That same day, it moved its transmitter and FM studios a few hundred yards to 4505 SW Carl Place.

This was also a time when OEPBS worked hard to extend its signal beyond the Willamette Valley. Initially using television translators such as those first installed in the 1950s by Bill Smullin and others, OEPBS extended its reach to the Oregon Coast and eastern Oregon. Radio, while much slower to experience translator development, also began extending its signal using FM translators.

## Changes in OEB/OEPBS Personnel

Following Wallace Kadderly's 1933 resignation, Luke Lamb (who had previously been manager of KOAC) became director of OEB/OEPBS. In 1963, Lamb asked James Morris, who had been at KOAC-AM since the mid-1920s and program director since 1945, to become assistant to the director. Bill McGrath and Lester Mock moved into the general manager positions at KOAC and KOAP respectively and OEB/OEPBS initiated a growing emphasis on cultural programming, along with adopting a more elaborate administrative structure.

In 1967, Lamb left to join the extensive public broadcasting operation of the University of Wisconsin. Robert Mundt succeeded him and served until 1971, when Donald R. Larson assumed that position. During Larson's tenure, Robert Hinz served as general manager of stations, Tom Doggett as broadcast manager, Les Mock as director of statewide services, Bob Mundt as station operations manager for the Corvallis stations and Bill McGrath as station operations manager for the Portland stations. In 1972, Larson authored the OEPBS Campaign for Excellence, which was designed to greatly expand the newly renamed OEPBS's scope and public service value for Oregonians.

While OEPBS was growing, what has more recently come to be viewed as a predominantly listener/viewer-supported service was then still in its infancy. As OEPBS's Campaign for Excellence was concluding, the statewide service boasted a total of only 535 members.[32]

In 1971, Donald S. Bryant joined OEPBS as director of instructional services, and, when Larson left in August 1973 to become executive assistant to the Oregon State System of Higher Education's (now Oregon University System) chancellor Roy E. Lieuallen, Bryant succeeded him as OEPBS director. Bryant had initially been hired by OIT in Klamath Falls in 1958, but left his position as OIT's dean of educational services there to join OEPBS.

While Bryant's background apparently suited him in his first OEPBS assignment, his experience in broadcasting remained modest by the time he assumed the OEPBS director assignment. He was always alert to opportunities to expand OEPBS's reach, however, and under his administration the service significantly expanded its transmission system.

## OEPBS Purchases KVDO-TV Salem

Salem's struggle to have its own television station had been a long one, dating all the way back to the UHF/VHF fights of the 1950s. "A television station will be a reality in Salem at least by this fall," Salem channel 22 construction permit holder Laurence Harvey promised on March 19, 1953. But it wasn't until 17 years later that Harry Godsil, a veteran of KPTV Portland, successfully put a Salem TV station on the air under the auspices of Channel 3, Inc.

In October 1967, Channel 3, Inc., had filed an FCC application to build that station under its then-president Urlin S. Page, a Salem attorney. Approximately $500,000 had been subscribed by a local group of stockholders toward the effort and the group's FCC application had been endorsed by U.S. senators Mark Hatfield and Bob Packwood, as well as Oregon governor Tom McCall. On March 5, 1969, Channel 3, Inc., received a construction permit with call sign KVDO—standing for **K-ViDeO**. The station signed-on at 7 p.m. on February 24, 1970, from studios located in a remodeled warehouse at 3000 Portland Road NE, with a transmitter on Prospect Hill.

By then, Godsil had succeeded Page as president, and station staff included news director Jim Hollon, chief engineer Robert Ridgeway and weatherman James F. Ransom. The inaugural ceremonies featured a filmed summary of the station's construction. Immediately following sign-on, KVDO broadcast the movie *Trapeze* followed by its first news program. The *Capitol Journal* was apparently pleased that Salem finally had its own station and described the inaugural evening's programming as "rough and jittery but promising." Initially, KVDO operated between 3 p.m. and midnight.

As an independent, KVDO was struggling. On October 31, 1972, the FCC approved a merger of Channel 3, Inc., with Liberty Television, which gave the latter control over KVDO and changed the station's function to that of a partial satellite station of Eugene's KEZI-TV. A condition of the FCC's approval of the merger, however, was that Liberty sell KVDO within three years.[33]

KVDO's signal was picked up by a large portion of the television market in south Portland and it effectively added significant audience to Liberty's from Eugene. The merger was, therefore, strongly opposed by Portland's KATU, which like KEZI, was an ABC-TV affiliate. The result was an agreement that KVDO would "black out" any ABC Network programming that was being broadcast over KATU, a restriction that significantly minimized KVDO's value to Liberty.

Bryant astutely read the situation as opportune for OEPBS and set about negotiating the purchase of KVDO. OEPBS took possession of the station on February 19, 1976. Just more than a week later, a Corvallis viewer who was unhappy about KVDO's sale brought the station's tower crashing to the ground by severing its guy lines. The vandal was ultimately jailed, and a rebuilt KVDO signed back on September 20, 1976.

## Oregon Commission on Public Broadcasting

While OEPBS had vastly extended its transmission reach under Bryant's leadership, criticism of him steadily grew during the 1970s. Some believed his major focus was on equipment to the detriment of programming, while many at OEPBS believed that he was uncomfortably detached from core institutional challenges. In the late 1970s, the Portland *Willamette Week* newspaper published a scathing series of articles critical of what it perceived to be OEPBS's lack of direction under Bryant's leadership.

The author, however, needs to acknowledge a personal attachment to that *Willamette Week* series, which resulted from a 1975 summer-long assignment during which he produced nine hours of local weekly programming for OEPBS Radio. One program the author created was a live, 90-minute Friday night interview/live entertainment program, *Friday Night in Studio A*, which might best be described as a kind of poor man's *Tonight Show*. The program was co-hosted by Penny Avila, a Lake Oswego poet, and Ron Buell, then editor of *Willamette Week*, and originated from OEPBS's radio studios on Healy Heights. Buell's summer inside the organization apparently taught him more about OEPBS than he'd bargained. *Willamette Week's* harsh, but fair, indictment of OEPBS was published about 18 months after the Friday night program ended. Following *Willamette Week's* critical series, the *Oregonian* picked up where *Willamette Week* left off and published its own series of articles critical of Bryant's leadership.

These public lashings spurred senator Jack Ripper to sponsor legislation in 1979 that transferred OEPBS from the state board's jurisdiction to the newly created Oregon Commission on Public Broadcasting (OCPB). Ripper's interest in OEPBS had initially been sparked by his son,

John, who first served as an OEPBS producer and then went to work for the highly regarded Maryland Public Broadcasting Authority. His experience there apparently helped him better understand OEPBS's shortcomings, which he detailed to his father.

The OCPB was constituted in early 1980 to hold the OEPBS stations' licenses and direct operating policy. Travis Cross, a widely respected figure who had previously served on governor Mark Hatfield's staff, was appointed as the OCPB's initial chair. Commissioners included KUMA radio's Ted Smith and KGW-TV's Patricia Joy.

While the department of higher education served as a vehicle for administering station operations during OCPB's first two years, it formally separated from higher education in 1981 and began operating as a separate state agency. OEPBS was also renamed Oregon Public broadcasting (OPB) at that time. The OCPB clearly believed a new administrative direction was needed and, reportedly at its first meeting, discussed replacing Bryant. The embattled director took a sabbatical commencing in October 1980, and OCPB initiated a national search for his replacement. During the interim, E. Dean Anderson served as acting director until the announcement of Gerald "Jerry" Appy's appointment as OPB's new executive director on December 12, 1980. Appy, who started in broadcasting as a Hollywood radio actor in 1946, had served as associate director of the Georgia Center for Continuing Education and vice president and director of communication for WNET-TV New York before coming to Oregon.

Appy inherited a system challenged by paltry financing and racked with serious morale problems. "Some staff members feel the Commission does not know enough about public television to run the system," the *Oregonian* observed.[34]

A year after Appy's appointment, Cross resigned the OCPB chair position and was succeeded by Katherine Boe, wife of former Oregon Senate president Jason Boe.

Pat Joy had been appointed to the OCPB by governor Vic Atiyeh and served as vice chair under Cross. An industrious, highly regarded KGW-TV news producer, she had grown up in broadcasting as the daughter of legendary network radio announcer Dick Joy. A KGW-TV staffer since the late-1960s, she was only the second woman journalist in Portland television and quickly became an esteemed member of the commission. In 1982, Appy invited her to join the staff of OPB, where she was eventually placed in charge of radio operations. While it was not the focus of her professional background, she quickly grew into the assignment and brought new energy and direction OPB radio. Tragically, while traveling in Europe in the mid-1980s, she contracted a then-mysterious and highly aggressive disease that began degrading her neurological and muscular functions.[35] Her capacity ebbed during 1986 and 1987. By then under a guardianship, she was placed on leave in October 1987. Her resignation from OPB was tendered by her guardian in January 1988, and she passed away in August of that year—widely mourned.

Appy significantly altered OPB's course and fortunes by emphasizing programming and public service and redressing the lingering critical attitudes toward OPB both inside and outside the organization. In 1985, in one of his last acts at OPB, Appy created a furor by quietly proposing to the governor that licenses for certain of the campus-based FM stations held by the department of higher education be forcibly transferred to OPB. A nasty battle ensued between OPB and most of the other public FM stations in the state, and even stations that were not directly affected took up the fight. Listener meetings were held across the state and in the state capital. Ultimately, construction of OPB's new Portland headquarters was halted pending a resolution of the dispute, and HB 2490—designed to blunt the OPB initiative—was introduced by representative Peter Tarzian. In 1986, in response to an undefined element of legislation which charged the commission with coordinating public broadcasting in Oregon, the commission convened a statewide conversation to assess public radio service throughout Oregon. In

1987, the resulting study led to an informal "truce" under whose terms all stations—including OPB—agreed to observe a defined consultation process before initiating construction of any new services in areas already served by another Oregon public station.

In 1985, ill health forced Appy to resign, and following another national search, he was succeeded by Maynard Orme in August 1986. Orme, who had been the general manager of public TV station KTEH in San Jose, California, remained in charge of OPB for the next 19 years.[36] OPB flourished during Orme's tenure, growing stronger and achieving both regional and national recognition. When Orme retired on December 31, 2005, he was succeeded by Steven Bass.

In June 1988, KOAP-FM and KOAP-TV moved into the new OPB Broadcast Center at 7140 SW Macadam Avenue and on February 19, 1989, changed their call signs to KOPB-FM and KOPB-TV respectively—to better reflect OPB's identity.

The OCPB was abolished in 1993 and in September of that year, the station licenses and property were transferred to a new non-profit corporation—Oregon Public Broadcasting, Inc., which continues to operate the system.

# KSYS-TV Medford

When planning for public television in southern Oregon began in the mid-1960s, the state's only public TV facilities were Willamette Valley stations KOAC-TV and KOAP-TV and their associated translators.

Seeking to expand into southern Oregon, OPB noted that the FCC had allocated channel 8 to Brookings, which could scarcely support a full VHF television station. Accordingly, OPB asked the FCC to move that channel to Medford and indicated it would apply for the Medford facility. While the channel 8 Brookings assignment was for a commercial TV station, OPB failed to ask that the relocated channel be reserved for noncommercial use in Medford.

As a result, three commercial parties joined OPB in submitting applications for channel 8 once it was reassigned to Medford. The commercial applicants consisted of Don Tykeson's Liberty Television of Eugene, a group of Rogue Valley investors assembled under the name Siskiyou Broadcasters and the *Medford Mail Tribune* (which also owned KYJC-AM), whose interest in broadcasting dated back to 1922. Legal skirmishing between OPB and the three commercial applicants ensued, and eventually, when the state officials concluded it was inappropriate to compete with commercial interests, OPB withdrew.

The three remaining commercial applicants fought intensely for several years, but when the channel was finally awarded to Liberty, the company demurred. Perhaps Medford seemed, on reflection, too small a community to support service from a third commercial television station.

Bill Smullin had clearly anticipated these events because, in 1969, he caused a new Oregon nonprofit corporation, Southern Oregon Education Company (SOEC), to be founded for the purpose of establishing a public television station in southern Oregon.

In 1973, Smullin and Ray Johnson, president of Radio Medford, Inc., which owned Medford's KMED-AM, KTMT-FM and KMED-TV, donated funds to SOEC, enabling it to purchase the channel 8 construction permit from Liberty for $16,000. Smullin and Johnson's funding the purchase of the Liberty construction permit to launch of SOEC's station was deemed controversial in some quarters. OPB and its executive director Don Bryant were particularly bitter over being outmaneuvered in establishing public television in Medford. Nevertheless, the 131.8-kilowatt KSYS signed-on January 17, 1977, and southern Oregon had a public television station. KSYS's studios were located at 34 South Fir Street and the station's transmitter was located at King Mountain. Bill Smullin owned or controlled both sites, which he made available to SOEC on charitable terms. SOEC hired commercial radio and television executive Ed Barnett—who had previously worked for Johnson's KMED and Smullin's KOBI—to manage the new station.

While SOEC clearly struggled with the high cost of a television operation in a relatively small community, Smullin and Johnson had already demonstrated that cost-effective television operation in the market required development of an extensive network of TV translators and repeater television stations to extend audience reach. Over time, SOEC added translators, as well as satellite television station KFTS Klamath Falls in 1989, to its system.

Around 1981, Art Knoles, executive imported from commercial television executive, was brought in as KSYS's assistant manager. On Barnett's 1985 retirement, Knoles took over as station manager.

KSYS's relationship with OPB was complex. For years, OPB remained tender over the loss of channel 8 in Medford to SOEC. Even following Bryant's retirement, OPB periodically explored absorbing KSYS throughout the 1980s. While the SOEC board periodically engaged in cordial discussions on the topic, it consistently decided against transferring KSYS's license to OPB.

During the 1990s, SOEC changed its corporate name to Southern Oregon Public Television (SOPTv). It increasingly began to operate like an affiliate of OPB, who encouraged such a relationship by extending programming and technical courtesies to the Medford-based operation. This support strengthened SOPTv's programming choices, elevated its technical plant and provided cost-saving labor in certain operational areas. Under that arrangement, OPB began handling SOPTv's program scheduling functions and continues to do so today.

## KVDO-TV Salem Becomes KOAB-TV Bend

Because Salem's KVDO-TV significantly duplicated the signals of KOAP-TV and KOAC-TV, an FCC application was filed in 1981 to move KVDO-TV to Bend. KMTR-TV wanted to purchase the station from OPB and opposed the move, but OPB persevered and secured federal funding for the relocation. OCPB commissioner Ted Smith particularly championed the Bend relocation, and the FCC approved the move in August 1982.

KVDO signed-off on August 6, 1983, and moved to Bend, where the station returned to the air from Awbrey Butte on December 22, 1983, under the call sign KOAB-TV. As an extension of the project, a new OPB radio station, KOAB-FM Bend, commenced operation on January 23, 1986.

## KTVR-TV La Grande

KTVR channel 13, "Television for Eastern Oregon," signed-on at 6 p.m. on December 6, 1964, with a broadcast ribbon-cutting ceremony that featured state and local dignitaries, an introduction of station personnel and interviews. The station (whose call sign stood for **K**-**TV**-Grande-**R**onde) was located at 1605 Adams Avenue, and former Portland broadcaster Cy Smith was the station's general manager.

KTVR began as a satellite station of Boise, Idaho, station KTVB-TV, which was owned by KTVB, Inc., and the company's president, Georgia Davidson, presided during the station's inaugural program. KTVR had rushed to get on the air to meet a published sign-on date, and the opening program, held together "by nerves of steel," did not go entirely as planned. Then next day, the *La Grande Observer* reported the sign-on under the headline "Mish Mash—TV Station Opening Posed Some Problems."[37] One of the station's early features was a weekday live program from 3:00 p.m. to 3:30 p.m. called *Periscope*, which covered "people and events in eastern Oregon."[38]

However, KTVR wasn't profitable, and the station was sold to OEPBS on August 31, 1976. While some accounts suggest that this is the date when the station signed-off, newspaper reports at the time indicate that KTVR had its last broadcast about 18 months earlier.[39] OEPBS took possession on September 29, 1976, when Roy Lieuallen, chancellor of the Oregon University System, handed a $50,000 check to Robert Kreuger, then-president of seller KTVB, Inc.

When the station resumed operation on February 1, 1977, OEPBS did not have a method of relaying its own signal to the station's transmitter on Mt. Fanny and made arrangements to rebroadcast the signals of public stations KWSU-TV Pullman and KSPS-TV Spokane. Plagued by technical problems, OEPBS shut KTVR down on September 1, 1977, implemented its own microwave system to relay OEPBS programming to KTVR, and returned the station to the air on January 1, 1978.

## KEPB-TV Eugene

Channel 28 had long been designated by the FCC for educational use in Eugene, and in 1967 Lane Community College filed an application to construct a 9-kilowatt station on that channel—but it was never built.[40] Eugene didn't get its own public TV station until OPB's KEPB-TV signed-on February 27, 1990, from a transmitter located just off Blanton Road. While Eugene had previously received OPB service from KOAC-TV Corvallis, that signal was not satisfactory throughout Eugene, and KEPB—which relays KOAC-TV—was designed to resolve OPB-TV's reception shortcomings in Eugene.

## KRBM-FM Pendleton

With the exception of the donation of Portland's KEX-FM, which created KOAP-FM, OEPBS had focused on television expansion during the 1960s and 70s. In the late 1970s, however, FM radio newly attracted its attention. KRBM (standing for **K-R**adio-**B**lue-**M**ountain) broadcasting at 90.9 MHz from Pendleton's Blue Mountain Community College (BMCC) was struggling with growth questions, which encouraged discussions about a cooperative relationship with OEPBS.

In 1968, KRBM's genesis was in the hiring of veteran broadcaster Blaine Hanks, who was charged with establishing a broadcasting education program at BMCC. Initially, Hanks' students vocational had the use of air time provided by Harmon Springer over his KOHU but BMCC soon sought its own 10-watt station, KRBM, which signed-on 90.9 MHz in spring 1970. While the station was doing a fine job of training students, it was modestly financed and 1970s revisions in FCC procedures for 10-watt stations forced BMCC to face up to the challenges inherent in raising the station's power and costs.

In September 1979, OEPBS announced an agreement with BMCC under which OEPBS assisted KRBM with technical expansion, such as making OEPBS programming available for broadcast over the Pendleton station. On the strength of that assistance, KRBM, which was under FCC pressure to increase power, filed an application to do so.

Following FCC approval, KRBM-FM began broadcasting on March 17, 1981, with 440 watts from an 80-foot tower constructed by the newly renamed OPB on Black Mountain, to which OPB's Portland signal was relayed. KRBM began offering some OPB evening programming on that same date.

Like KRBM, many of Oregon's 10-watt noncommercial educational FM stations were established to serve as laboratories for collegiate training programs in broadcasting. This excerpt, from a circa 1969 BMCC brochure, pictures Blaine Hanks with some of his early students.

In September 1985, KRBM began stereo transmission using equipment provided by OPB, and on March 28, 1986, Blue Mountain Community College transferred the KRBM license to OPB. After hiring BMCC students to staff the station during the summer, while it broadcast solely OPB programming, OPB again allowed BMCC students to program some evening hours in fall 1986. OPB also announced plans to upgrade KRBM to 25 kilowatts, a power increase that went into effect in October 1987 from a new transmitter site on Warren Hill.

Through its joint radio/TV operation, OPB had some advantages in seeking to extend its radio coverage. The television operation used video microwave units to send programming to distant television transmitters, and those microwave links hopped sequentially from mountain to mountain to arrive at their intended destination. This made it possible for OPB to carry the radio program signal along the way, install FM transmitters on various mountain tops and add radio stations to the network in a more cost-effective manner than a radio-only network could have done.

## KOAB-FM Bend

With KOAB-TV already in operation in Bend, OPB established the 25 kilowatt KOAB-FM, which signed-on January 23, 1986, relaying KOPB-FM's programming at 91.3 MHz transmitting from Awbrey Butte.

## KOAP-FM Lakeview

Lakeview had been receiving public radio programming since 1981, when Jefferson Public Radio began serving the community by translator on 89.5 MHz. OPB began offering its radio

service by translator on 91.9 MHz in November 1987. Lakeview acquired its first full-power
full-power public radio station in 2000 (in the same fashion as had Bend) when OPB constructed a video microwave link to feed a television translator there and carried its radio signal
along. Reconstituting OPB's original FM call sign, KOAP-FM Lakeview signed-on in September
2000 with 170 watts at 88.7 MHz. The video microwave plant installed at Lakeview also enabled
OPB to install several FM translators along its route, included including installations serving
Silverlake, Valley Falls and Wagontire.

## KTVR-FM La Grande

Like Lakeview, La Grande gained OPB radio service because of the ease of installing an FM
station there along with an OPB television outlet. Previously, La Grande had been served by
OPB's 89.9 MHz translator, which signed-on in November 1987. That translator was replaced
by OPB's 90.3 MHz, 400-watt KTVR-FM, which signed-on August 27, 2003.

## KTMK-FM Tillamook

OPB been interested in serving the northern Oregon coast with radio for a long time but
had demurred, pursuant to the statewide consultation process adopted in 1987.[41] The Tillicum
Foundation, which owned KMUN, had sought and received an FCC construction permit for a
small, 140-watt Tillamook station operating on 91.1 MHz. Eventually, OPB sufficiently resolved
KMUN's concerns about competition, and the Tillicum Foundation sold its Tillamook construction permit to OPB on October 1, 2002. Construction wasn't completed until February 14,
2006, and KTMK-FM Tillamook signed-on shortly thereafter.

## KASH-AM/KEED-AM/KOPT-AM/KOPB-AM Eugene

In 2008, OPB purchased KOPT-AM Eugene and changed its call sign to KOPB-AM. While
OPB remains the largest public broadcasting entity in Oregon, neither its TV nor its radio
operations cover the entirety of the state and some portions of the state are covered exclusively
by public radio or public television services that have no connection to OPB. OPB's combined
radio and TV operations, however, cover more of Oregon than any other single public broadcasting enterprise and represent the largest such activity in the state.

The combination of OPB and the state's other independent public radio and television stations has provided Oregon with an exceedingly rich complement of public broadcast services.
Oregon is nationally recognized for possessing innovative public radio services that are among
the nation's most highly effective, highly rated, and strongly publicly supported.

## Endnotes

1. The program's slogan was "With an accent on music—and an ear to the future." (www.chevron.com).
2. Ibid.
3. Ibid. http://www.coutant.org/standard/index.html includes the sheet music and educational materials as well
   as an audio excerpt from the program's stirring opening.
4. "KOIN Institute for the Study of Radio: Triumph in Public Service," *KOIN Radio Advertiser*, August 1945, 1.
5. Ibid., 16.
6. James M. Morris, *The Remembered Years!*, (Corvallis, OR: Continuing Education Division, Oregon State
   University, 1972), 17.

7. KFDJ/KOAC, like all stations in the early 1920s, initially broadcast on a common frequency of 833 KHz. In successive changes, the station moved to 1180 KHz, 1060 KHz, 1070 KHz, 1110 KHz, 560 KHz, 570 KHz and—on October 1, 1929—to 550 KHz. Using the 1939 appropriations, KOAC moved its transmitter to Granger OR, on the Albany-Corvallis Highway (US 20) on June 2, 1942, and raised its daytime power from one to five kilowatts directional on October 16 of that year. On December 6, 1946, the FCC authorized an increase of KOAC-AM's nighttime power from one to five kilowatts directional. (Craig Adams)

8. Kenyon married and took the name Helen Kenyon Markel during her World War II military and subsequent CBS career.

9. Swenson, *Radio in the Public Schools of Portland, Oregon,* 42, 53, 101.

10. Houglum, Roger J., undated. *Educational Broadcasting Comes To Lane County: A Short History of Radio Station KRVM,* Lane Community College, 1. (WSMB Collection)

11. Ibid., 0.

12. "Houglum Radio Pioneer," *Lane Community College Torch,* January 26, 1967, 3.

13. KTEC-FM changed frequencies to 89.5 MHz in April 1983.

14. "The First 30," *KWAX Program Guide,* April 1981, 6. This name was possibly influenced by the Marx Brothers' famous 1933 Paramount movie, *Duck Soup.*

15. Ibid.

16. "After a Slight Pause…KWAX," editorial, *Oregon Daily Emerald,* April 4, 1951, 2.

17. "The First 30," *KWAX Program Guide,* April 1981, 6.

18. MacRae, Patti. "KRRC—The (barely audible) radio voice of Reed College," *Reed Magazine,* August 2002.

19. This station should not be confused with the subsequent Pasadena Community College public radio station, KPCC-FM.

20. Hansen, Barret (Dr. Demento). Email to author dated March 26, 2009.

21. "Eugene to Tie Radio Station to Satellite Communication," *Oregonian,* May 11, 1979, C8.

22. The playful name was taken from a character in Chaucer's *Canterbury Tales.*

23. *KBOO Volunteer Handbook,* excerpted from website http://wgdr.net/doc/kboo_history.doc, accessed on August 14, 2008.

24. Allen had worked for various local stations, including KAGI-AM, and did news and sports for KOBI-TV. He also worked in media relations for Southern Oregon University and shot 16 mm news film of university events for both Medford TV stations.

25. *Medford Mail Tribune,* February 25, 1977, Tempo, 1.

26. PTFP was the successor agency to the Educational Broadcasting Facilities Program (EBFP).

27. Alan R. Yorty, Public *Radio Under Fire: One Approach to Surviving the 80s.* Graduate paper (University of Oregon, 1983), 32 (WSMB Collection).

28. KSRS-FM signed-on with 2.2 kilowatts at 91.5 MHz in 1995; KSBA-FM with 2.2 kilowatts at 88.5 MHz in 1988; KSKF-FM with 2.2 kilowatts at 90.9 MHz in 1988; KNSQ-FM with 5 kilowatts at 88.1 MHz in 1994; KNCA-FM signed-on in 1992 with 2.2 kilowatts on 89.7 MHz; KNYR-FM signed-on with 400 watts on 91.3 MHz in 1995. In 1995, KSKF-FM raised its power to 6.5 kilowatts horizontal and 2 kilowatts vertical.

29. In 1991, KSOR-FM, KSRS-FM and KSRG-FM—and all of JPR's 33 KSOR translators in Oregon and California, carried *Classics and News* service; KSMF-FM, KSBA-FM, KSKF-FM, KNCA-FM and KNSQ-FM carried *Rhythm and News*; KSJK-AM and KAGI-AM carried *News and Information.*

30. The record for being "first" isn't totally clear.

31. Morris, The *Remembered Years,* 111.

32. Don Larson, "The Hungry Eye Speaks," *The Hungry Eye, Program Guide for the Oregon Educational and Public Broadcasting Service,* August 1972, 1.

33. "TV Station Merger Approved by FCC," *Oregonian,* October 31, 1972.

34. "New Public Broadcasting Chief Hopes to Find Untapped Funds," *Oregonian,* December 14, 1980, D7.

35. Joy's condition wasn't really definitively diagnosed until an autopsy after her death.

36. After receiving a master's degree in Theatre Arts and a PhD in Education from UCLA, Orme was a TV producer/director from 1966 to 1968 at KVCR-TV, San Bernardino, CA and Director of Educational Services at KCET-TV, Los Angeles from 1968 to 1973. (Orme, Maynard. Email to author. April 18, 2007).

37. "TV Station Opening Posed Some Problems," *La Grande Observer,* December 8, 1964, 3.

38. Ibid.

39. "E. Oregon Gets Educational TV," *Oregonian,* September 3, 1976, B4.

40. "For the Record," *Broadcasting,* September 4, 1967, 81.

41. Concerns were expressed by KMUN-FM Astoria, which feared that competition for the northern Oregon coast's relatively small population might financially threaten KMUN's existence.

# The 1950s

# Inventing TV Land and Radio's Rebirth

# 17

# Television Arrives
# in Oregon

Television had been slow to arrive in Oregon (see chapter 14). Even when it became realistically available following World War II, it was in the form of small sets with screens so tiny that many viewers used external magnifying lenses to provide reasonable group viewing. Television arrived in the Pacific Northwest on Thanksgiving Day 1948, when Palmer K. Lieberman signed-on KRSC-TV Seattle. A shoestring, struggling operation, the station probably both benefited and suffered from the fact that it was Seattle's only TV station. Because television sets were expensive, few people were able to watch Seattle's only television station sign-on and cover the state championship high school football game that Thanksgiving Day.

## Dorothy Stimson Bullitt

One key Seattle resident, however, was intently watching: Dorothy Stimson Bullitt. Born into one of Seattle's most prominent and wealthy families, Dorothy Stimson had married Alexander Scott Bullitt of Louisville, Kentucky, on May 18, 1918. An attorney and politician, Bullitt was descended from one of Kentucky's most distinguished families. Handsome and charismatic, he had instantly captured Dorothy's heart, and—following their wedding and a brief life together in Kentucky—the couple moved to Seattle.

King Mike as
originally drawn
by Walt Disney
Courtesy of Belo Corporation/
King Broadcasting Company

Bullitt fathered three children, and ran three times for public office (albeit unsuccessfully), before succumbing to liver cancer on April 10, 1932. While Dorothy had inherited considerable business holdings centered in real estate, times were tough and tenants were having a hard time paying their rent during the Depression. On paper she was wealthy, but on a cash basis, she was in a pinch along with the rest of the country.

Facing her problems with steely resolve, she began learning the ins and outs of business, for which she demonstrated an aptitude that others, and perhaps Dorothy herself, found surprising. As the 1940s dawned, Dorothy Bullitt and her children were again financially secure.

From the time her father first brought a set home, radio had always fascinated her. Large, elegant radios had always been a prominent element of her own family furnishings, and as an adult, she thrilled at live broadcasts of opera and classical music. Radio itself gave her a charge.

Following World War II, Bullitt was in a position to explore investing in radio, and in 1946, she founded the Western Waves company to apply for new Seattle AM and FM stations. FM wasn't much of a problem but finding an available AM frequency proved difficult until fate stepped in. Learning that "the worst [AM] station in town" was for sale, she jumped at the chance to buy it.

KEVR had a 10-kilowatt AM signal with surprisingly slight coverage—but it also had an attractive FM companion station. Taking the leap, Bullitt bought the AM-FM pair on May Day 1947. With a nod to Seattle's home of King County, and with an obvious expression of her aspirations, she changed Western Waves' name to King Broadcasting company in late 1947—and then wrestled the KING call letters out of the FCC.[1] Previously acquainted with the famous cartoonist Walt Disney, she casually asked if he "might be willing to create a logo for the KING stations" Shortly thereafter, a drawing of an impish figure that became known as King Mike arrived in the mail. Disney billed Bullitt $75 for his work.[2]

## Dorothy Bullitt Gets Into Television

Television had interested Bullitt since she first saw it demonstrated in 1939, and she was thrilled as she watched KRSC sign-on. She quickly sent congratulatory flowers to the station—the only acknowledgement it apparently received for the accomplishment. While Dorothy Bullitt was exhilarated by KRSC's sign-on, Palmer Lieberman was likely terrified. The station was significantly undercapitalized and quickly was losing $10,000 per month. When KRSC was just three months old, he remembered the flowers and called Bullitt to inquire if she was interested in buying the station. She was—and scraping together the funds, she signed the purchase contract on May 9, 1949. It was the first television station in the nation to be sold. Her friends and her broadcasting competitors all thought she had taken an expensive and foolhardy step. The former was true; the latter was not—because fate stepped in.

## FCC Freeze on Television Applications

During the later part of 1946 and throughout 1947, applications for new Very High Frequency (VHF) TV stations had flooded the FCC's offices, and the commission was concerned that the nation's limited capacity for stations would soon be exhausted. When the FCC imposed a freeze on receiving new TV applications in late 1948 in order to study the matter, KRSC became the sole television station authorized in the entire Pacific Northwest. Dorothy Bullitt and her King Broadcasting company had received a *de facto* exclusive TV franchise of unknown duration.

## Ed Parsons and the Birth of Cable Television

Two other special viewers had also been watching when KRSC signed-on that Thanksgiving Day in 1948. They were Ed and Grace Parsons—in Astoria, Oregon.

Leroy E. "Ed" Parsons had been part of the radio industry for years. Born in Latourell Falls along the Columbia Gorge, he'd attended school in Corbett, Oregon, before enrolling in engineering trade schools. Always interested in radio, Parsons built a wireless system to communicate with a friend, as well as radio receivers for pay, during his high school years. His 1925 high school yearbook entry reads: "Talent and manliness are his/At Math he's a wonder, at Radio a whiz."[3]

Ed Parsons, c. 1946, (from *KAST—The Voice of the Lower Columbia*, promotional brochure)

Parsons' route to Astoria had been circuitous. Following engineering school, he worked as the chief engineer for Bridal Veil Timber Company and in other radio jobs before coming to KGW and then to Astoria's KAST in 1943 (see chapter 15).[4]

In 1946 and 1947, Parsons attended the National Association of Broadcasters (NAB) conventions. Accompanying him in 1947, his wife, Grace, was immediately fascinated by a TV demonstration and told her husband that she just "had to have it." With the closest TV station to Oregon then in Chicago, Parsons told her that wasn't possible. Given his technical background, if anyone could figure out how to get a television signal to Astoria, it would be him she told him. "I want television with my radio," she insisted—so Parsons purchased a nine-inch Howard TV set, which he had flown home.[5] "It wasn't under a $1,000 and we weren't that flush. [Grace] had to do without other things to have the set," Parsons later recalled.[6]

Coordinating with Bob Priebe, a friend who was managing KRSC, Parsons first learned the timing of the station's scheduled transmitter tests. Working closely with KAST's chief engineer, Jimmy Titus, Parsons checked KRSC's signal throughout Clatsop County by listening to its audio signal. Sometimes he used his own airplane to cover more ground. Eventually, he concluded that an adequate signal was available on the roof of the elegant Hotel Astoria, located on Commercial Street across from the Parsons' penthouse apartment.

With his primitive efforts bearing success, when KRSC signed-on November 25, 1948, Ed and Grace Parsons were watching in their Astoria apartment—along with Dorothy Bullitt in Seattle. For the next month, people converged on the Parsons' home to watch the marvel, something the Parsons hadn't anticipated. Ed Parsons recalled "We literally lost our home. People would drive for hundreds of miles to see television. And when people drove down from Portland or came from The Dalles or from Klamath Falls to see television, you couldn't tell them no."[7]

With his home life in chaos, Parsons ultimately ejected all of his visitors—reportedly on Christmas Eve 1948—and confronted the realization that he had to figure out how to provide TV to others in order to preserve his own domestic tranquility. Puzzling about how to secure, amplify and deliver a TV signal, he suggested to the Hotel Astoria's manager that placing a

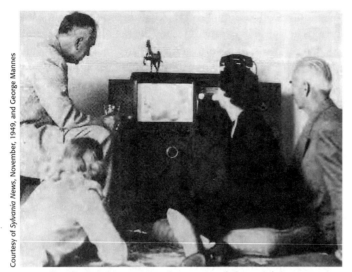

From the Parsons' apartment in Astoria, (left to right) a reporter, a friend, Grace Parsons and Ed Parsons, watching KRSC-TV Seattle in 1948.

TV in the lobby might prove good for business. Securing consent, he ran a line from his equipment located on the hotel's roof to the lobby, where he set up a receiver. The Hotel Astoria's lobby became "a theater every night with two rows of chairs and divans drawn up before the 12-inch television screen," he recalled.[8]

Soon, the TV traffic became too much even for the hotel, so Parsons next ran a wire across the street to Cliff Poole's music store. There, even more Astorians could watch television on a receiver placed in the store's display window. Poole's Music Store had become the first official cable television customer in the nation. The attraction quickly drew crowds, causing the police to complain over the impediment to street traffic.

Clearly, Parsons needed to establish more TV viewing locations, so beginning in February 1949, he started running coaxial cables through downtown Astoria.[9] Over the next three months, wires were plumbed through elevator shafts and underground tunnels, across buildings and along utility poles—all terminating in residences, taverns and businesses where TV could then be seen. One of Parsons' customers was the Elks Club, which set up a television set and published a schedule of programs. Group viewing was possible at the Elks Club, although reserved solely for members, and that location helped relieve some of the pressure on other viewing locations in town.

Responding to requests from friends that he "hook them up," Parsons had about 25 subscribing neighbors by the summer of 1949.[10] Parsons treated the cables as common property of the "system," in which all the customers were essentially participants in a cooperative. Although the financial arrangements were neither permanent nor precise, everyone connected to the system had become Parsons' cable customers. While not entirely certain that it was necessary to secure KRSC's permission to distribute its signal in this way, Parsons nevertheless requested such authority as a precautionary step—because cable subscriptions were growing. In a letter dated May 18, 1949, KRSC general manager Robert E. Priebe, Parsons authorized Parsons to relay KRSC's signal to his subscribers.[11, 12]

## Developing the Astoria Cable Television System

Parsons' system was primitive and suffered from bugs that required time and money to resolve. At one point, he brought a friend, KNPT's Tom Becker, into the venture. Becker recalled:

> I raised $50,000 and spent three months trying to get the cable reception to work. At the end of 3 months, I gave back all of the $50,000 to the friends of mine that had invested. The problem was herringbone in the TV and we could not get the picture clear. We later found

out that the cable was not uniform and the line amplifiers were not uniform. I got out of cable TV but got several others in the business that stuck with it and made millions.[13]

By May 1950, Parsons had sufficiently resolved the technical problems to begin operating on a commercial basis as the Pacific Television Company. He had 150 subscribers. News reports about the Astoria system began producing inquiries from across America, and Parsons established a consulting business with Byron E. Roman to offer consulting services on community antenna television installations, as well as sell associated equipment. The company helped design and construct numerous cable television systems, including installations in Aberdeen/Hoquiem and Centralia, Washington, and Lewiston, Idaho.

## Parsons Invents the Translator

Parsons' initial cable TV approach had been to carefully locate a master antenna, boost the signal it received and then redistribute it by wire. Since wires were hard to run in some locations, he eventually constructed a device to receive KRSC's channel 5 signal on-air and retransmit it on channel 2 to receivers throughout Astoria. Parsons installed the device without notifying the FCC, and for the time being both he and the commission more or less mutually ducked the issue of whether his unit required a license. Parsons had designed and built the first television translator, a device that eventually became critically important in extending television—and later FM—signals to distant communities.[14]

## Parsons Leaves the Astoria Cable System Behind

In the beginning, no one really questioned whether Parsons had the authority to run wires around Astoria just as no one questioned whether his translator required a license. But later, the City of Astoria was anything but clear about the propriety of the cable installation. After considerable legal wrangling, Pacific Television was ultimately granted a city franchise to make "pole attachments" to Astoria's utility poles.

All of these matters—the debugging of the Astoria installation, the municipal franchise negotiations and the explosive growth of the cable installation consulting business—took their toll. In March 1953, Parsons collapsed and was hospitalized with exhaustion. His doctors ordered him to rest completely for a full 30 days, but stories differ about what happened next.

Parsons' recalled that, once he was well enough to leave the hospital, he hopped onto his plane. While the publicly released story was that he was flying to visit his wife's aunt in Vancouver, BC, his real destination was Fairbanks, Alaska. There, he found so much challenge and opportunity that he never returned to Astoria. Pacific Television went into receivership and was acquired by a newly founded Clatsop Television Company composed of 13 Astoria businessmen. As part of the settlement of Parsons' business affairs, KVAS was sold to Lower Columbia Broadcasting Company in January 1954.[15]

However, there are other accounts of Parsons' exit from Astoria. William Bright was a Portlander who had founded Western Products, Inc., which produced and marketed equipment for the electric utility industry. Learning of Parsons' work in Astoria, Bright helped Parsons in his fight to use the city's utility poles and set up other cable TV installations, including the Pasco-Kennewick-Richland system. Bright was a fan of Parsons and later described him as "some kind of electronic genius."[16]

Notwithstanding that admiration, Bright reports that the signal instability issues in the equipment Parsons had developed caused customers to drop their subscriptions. The business, he later reported, had been undercapitalized and was thus ill-equipped to resolve these challenges. Bright claims he put together a recapitalization plan with a group of investors—including Portland attorney John C. Kendall—under which Parsons would have retained 50 percent of the company's stock. But at the last minute Parsons proved intransigent. "This is my company. I don't want anyone to own me," Bright reports Parsons as saying.[17]

Tom Becker, later owner of KNPT Newport, essentially corroborates this account and must have been one of Parsons' "radio station owner friends" that Bright reports having solicited to join the effort. According to Bright, after the investor opportunity failed, Parsons couldn't keep the system properly functioning and worked himself into exhaustion. Bright remembers that the morning after Parsons fled the hospital in the middle of the night, Grace Parsons called to tell him that Ed had left for Alaska and had no intention of returning. She was panicked. He had left her in the lurch, and she had no money for payroll or accounts payable.

While Bright's company was owed $7,000, there were other significant creditors as well. With Grace's consent, Bright convened the creditors and pushed through a plan under which Bright became receiver for the company. While Grace couldn't get Parsons to return for the meeting with the creditors, she did secure his power of attorney to authorize the arrangement.

Under Bright's management, staffing was normalized and the signal instability resolved. With the business stabilized, it was sold to a new group of local investors named Clatsop Television Company. That group later sold the system to Cox Cablevision.

In later years, Parsons did not believe his founding of the cable television industry was his most important professional achievement. He was prouder of his work on polar communications in Alaska.[18]

While Mahanoy City, Pennsylvania vies with Astoria for recognition as the founding location of the cable TV industry, Astoria's claim was recognized by the National Cable Television Association (NCTA) in 1968 when it installed a monument at the base of the famed Astor Column on Coxcomb Hill (where Parsons had located one of his system's receiving antennas).[19] Its inscription reads:

> Site of the first community antenna television installation in the United States completed February 1949 Astoria, Oregon. Cable television was invented and developed by L. E. (Ed) Parsons on Thanksgiving Day, 1948. The system carried the first TV transmission by KRSC-TV Channel 5, Seattle. This marked the beginning of Cable TV.

## Portland Awaits Television

Oregonians were eagerly awaiting television—but had to suffer a considerable delay. Television was suddenly all the buzz across the nation. Active promoters such as educator Angelo Patri wrote: "Youngsters today need television for their morale as much as they need fresh air and sunshine for their health. Not to have it [television], well, that is unthinkable."[20] Housewives saw television offering potential excitement and valuable new vistas for their families. Women's magazines offered floor plans and advice about how to properly incorporate a television set in a home. *Family Circle* offered helpful diagrams of suggested placement in budget-sized rooms, L-shaped rooms and rooms decorated with 18th-century furnishings.

But for virtually all Oregonians, these were tantalizing—yet distant—glimpses of the new marvel. The FCC's freeze on new station TV applications meant that Oregonians had no access to this new medium for the duration of the freeze (see elsewhere in this chapter). Indeed, Portland had the unwelcomed distinction of being the largest city in the nation without a television station. Portlanders' frustrations were exacerbated by the fact that both the *Oregonian* and Video Broadcasting Company had received FCC authorization to construct TV stations and both had either declined or squandered their authority (see chapter 14). But for those missteps, Portlanders might have been easily enjoying television.

FCC chairman Wayne Coy visited Portland in May 1950 and tried to quell the complaints, which had grown to include Oregon's governor and congressional delegation. In 1951, the Oregon senate entered the fray and passed a bill calling upon the FCC to grant Portland an exemption to the freeze, stating that it was unfair to deprive Oregonians of "the delights of Hopalong Cassidy and Faye Emerson's plunging neckline any longer."[21]

## KPTV-TV Signs-On Portland

Finally in April 1952, the FCC lifted its freeze and issued its *Sixth Report and Order*, which created the UHF band of channels to add to the national bank of available frequencies. In the document, the commission indicated it would begin receiving television applications that spring.

Empire Coil, Inc., located in upstate New York, manufactured television coils and transformers used in television broadcasting. It had already branched out to include TV station operation when it started Cleveland, Ohio's, second television station, WXEL-TV, which was affiliated with the DuMont Television Network.[22]

The article "Does Your TV Set Feel t Home," which appeared in *TV Show* magazine in May 1952, illustrated examples of pleasing arrangements and décor for incorporating a television into the home. Showing a DuMont TV, this photo's caption reads: "Here is an excellent example of how a television can be placed to provide the focal point in a room. The handsome painting above and the wicker fruit lead the eye in a continuous, graceful curve to the screen."

Empire Coil's president, Herbert Mayer, was pleased by WXEL's success, and with the freeze newly lifted, was watching TV developments with interest. Mayer, who had never been west of Chicago, saw a unique opportunity to put a station on the air in the nation's largest metropolitan area without one. Given that the FCC had recently created the new UHF band of channels, it could also be first UHF station in the U.S. and the world. The opportunity seemed to offer a potential public relations bonanza, in addition to a good investment opportunity.

Things happened quickly. On June 19, 1952, Empire Coil filed an FCC application for Portland's UHF channel 27, which was granted on July 11. On July 25, the company requested the call letters KPTV and they were assigned the same day. Other forces were also at work to accelerate KPTV's birth.

The Radio Corporation of America (RCA) had been a major proponent of television ever since its president, David

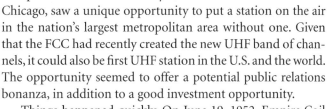

Herbert Mayer, c. 1952

The station identification slide used by KPTV in its earliest days prominently featured its slogan "the world on view."

Sarnoff, committed the company to developing TV in the 1930s. Through its wholly-owned National Broadcasting Company (NBC), RCA owned television stations in key cities as well as patent rights on various components used in transmitters, receivers and studio equipment. RCA was also a major manufacturer of broadcasting equipment. Since the freeze had halted most of the company's television manufacturing for four years, no one was more eager to see it lifted than Sarnoff, who knew that establishing UHF would dramatically increase the potential number of stations that could use RCA broadcast equipment. And there was one more piece of the puzzle: RCA's UHF experiments had been largely responsible for the FCC's decision to create the UHF band. In fact, RCA had constructed a UHF prototype transmitter—the only one in the world.

To help quickly establish UHF, Sarnoff approached Mayer and offered two plums. First, he would sell Mayer RCA's prototype UHF transmitter—which had cost $3 million to build—"at a fair price." Second, and most important, he would guarantee Mayer an affiliation with the NBC Television Network for Empire Coil's Portland station, a valuable inducement. Sarnoff stipulated just one condition—that KPTV be on the air in time for the opening of the NBC Television 1952 fall season. That left only three months in which to construct the world's first UHF television station from the ground up. Before accepting Sarnoff's offer, Mayer needed someone trustworthy to meet the challenge.

Among the eager, young TV engineers in Ohio was Russell Olsen, who worked at Mayer's Cleveland competitor, WEWS-TV. Olsen began working in television at the DuMont Laboratories under the supervision of Allan DuMont and his chief technical wizard, Thomas Goldsmith. Olsen had also worked at the DuMont network's flagship station—WABD-TV New York City—and the network's Washington DC facilities. He was, therefore, well-known to both DuMont and Goldsmith.

Through the DuMont affiliation held by Empire Coil's Cleveland station, Herbert Mayer and Russell Olsen became acquainted, and Mayer soon approached Olsen about going to Portland to build KPTV. Sarnoff also encouraged Olsen to take the KPTV assignment, and Olsen recalls first hearing about the project in a conversation with Sarnoff.[23] DuMont also apparently vouched to Mayer that Olsen would be an ideal choice to supervise building the world's first UHF television station. Olsen agreed to go to Portland—and launched a television frenzy.

Portland was agog. Newspapers followed KPTV's construction nearly on a daily basis with headlines like:

Russell Olsen (left) and David Sarnoff, c. 1952

"Heave-Ho for TV," "Fast Job Raises Portland TV Building," "Tip-Top of TV Tower is Up," "Everybody's Got The TV-Jeebies!" and "Portland TV Station Tests Get Under Way."

Retailers were busy selling TV sets all summer despite the fact that there was nothing yet to watch. Meeting Sarnoff's stipulated sign-on schedule was a huge challenge that required an incredibly accelerated construction schedule, which unfolded as follows:

---

**KPTV Construction Timeline (1952)**[24]

**July 7:** FCC construction permit is granted.

**July 25:** Call letters KPTV are assigned.

**Mid-August:** RCA's UHF transmitter is dismantled in Bridgeport, Connecticut, and trucked across the country. Custom-made RCA UHF antenna is sent by railroad.

**August 20:** Russ Olsen arrives in Portland to supervise construction and installation. Phone company begins construction of microwave to bring NBC network programming from the roof of phone company's downtown Portland building to KPTV's Council Crest transmitter. Ground is broken at 3405 SW Council Crest Drive for the transmitter building, and work on KPTV's 250-foot-tall tower commences.

**August 28:** Floors one and two of transmitter building are finished and work begins on the third floor.

**September 11:** Transmitter arrives in Portland; rapid installation begins.

**September 9:** Antenna work begins on the tower at Council Crest and concludes in two days.

**September 17:** FCC grants permission for KPTV to initiate broadcasting.

**September 18:** KPTV goes on the air at 12:01 a.m. with test broadcasts.

**September 20:** KPTV formally signs-on at 4:30 p.m. from its transmitter with NBC network programming.

**October 1:** KPTV begins regular broadcasting with programming from all four TV networks: ABC, NBC, CBS and DuMont.

---

Given the tight schedule, KPTV was reluctant to publicly commit itself to a sign-on date. Much depended upon the arrival of the transmitter and antenna which, although expensive, had been shipped by truck rather than rail because it was thought to be faster. While the front of the truck contained the RCA equipment, the rear held Olsen's household furnishings.

RCA and the awaiting KPTV staff had some anxious moments when they lost contact with the truck for an extended period of time. According to Olsen "The driver of the van had a girl-friend in Texas and no one could find him any place [for days]. RCA and the state police helped us quite a bit."[25]

On September 16, the *Oregon Journal* launched a contest offering a $350 television set to the person who most accurately predicted the exact day, hour and second of KPTV's inaugural broadcast. Much of the public believed the station would sign-on in time to cover the upcoming

# TV's Here; Turn Knob At 4:30 P.M

Look What Flew In

TV BUG

PORTLAND HOME LIFE

Courtesy of the Oregonian

(Top) *Oregonian* headline, (above) *Oregonian* cartoon, both September 18, 1952

November elections but were skeptical that it would debut significantly earlier. So when the actual sign-on happened on September 20, it was all the more a surprise. The station began transmitting just 26 days after breaking ground for its transmitter building.

Throughout the nation, NBC-TV's Milton Berle was known as "Mr. Television" and was famous for his *Texaco Star Theatre* program. He is credited with having done more to sell sets in television's early years than any other person, program or event. But to Portland and the *Oregonian*, the title "Mr. Television" belonged to Herbert Mayer.

Mayer arrived in Portland on September 17, 1952, with nearly his entire family in tow. His wife, Frances, and their children (Sandra, 14, Tommy, 12; Margot, 9 and Carlie, 6) all came to Portland for the inauguration of UHF television in America. Five hundred people crowded into the Benson Hotel's Crystal Room to watch the station sign-on. Meier & Frank invited people to watch at their sixth-floor headquarters ("the West's largest television department"). Since it was a pleasant September day, crowds lined up in front of appliance stores across the city to watch the TV sets placed in display windows.

Finally, at 4:30 p.m. on Sunday, September 20, Portland's "teleblindness" (as the *Oregonian* dubbed it) ended. In preparation, dignitaries had gathered in the Multnomah Hotel for an inaugural luncheon "in a gala burst of party atmosphere, speeches and mutual pats on the back."[26] Mayer assured the assembled Portlanders that "public service would always be KPTV's principal objective."[27] Then he left for the Council Crest transmitter to sign-on KPTV with these words:

> Ladies and gentlemen, good afternoon. This is Television Station KPTV Portland, the World on View, Channel 27. We are signing on the air this 20th day of September 1952 in accordance with authority granted to us by the Federal Communications Commission. And so, let us now witness the inauguration of television in Portland and the first commercial UHF broadcast in history.[28]

KPTV then broadcast *Success Hill*, a special which consisted of a filmed tour sponsored by RCA showing the Bridgeport, Connecticut, UHF station, which had been shipped to Portland to form the core of KPTV's transmission plant. It was followed by the film *Beautiful Oregon*, sponsored by King Building Materials. The *Oregonian* was quick to note it was Oregon's first paid television commercial. At 5 p.m., KPTV joined the NBC Network for the *All-Star Revue* program, starring Jimmy Durante and Margaret Truman. *Your Show of Shows* and *Your Hit Parade*, both from NBC, followed until KPTV's scheduled sign-off at 7:30 p.m.

Mayer had clearly made a personal, as well as a professional, investment in KPTV. He had also written a children's book, *The Story of Little Ajax*, to welcome young viewers of his Cleveland station, WXEL. Illustrated by his wife, the book was re-issued for Portland-area youngsters shortly after KPTV's sign-on.

An interesting sidelight of KPTV's birth is that it coincided with the visit of vice presidential candidate Richard M. Nixon. While the visit of any vice-presidential candidate would have been newsworthy, this particular one had riveted the nation. During an appearance in Medford the previous day, Nixon had first encountered questions about his possible use of campaign funds for personal expenses. By the time he arrived in Portland, a full-scale national debate was in progress, and many believed that presidential candidate Dwight D. Eisenhower was going to drop him from the Republican ticket. Just as KPTV was signing-on, Nixon was in his Portland hotel room furiously writing what became the famous "Checkers" speech, which he delivered in a national broadcast (including over KPTV) the following Tuesday. It saved his political career.

Portland mayor Dorothy McCullough-Lee speaking at the KPTV Inaugural Luncheon on September 20, 1952, at the Multnomah Hotel.

KPTV signed-on with a staff of 28. Charles White, who became the station's commercial manager, was the first employee; another early employee was Gene Phelps. Later, in 1953, Russell Olsen was promoted to KPTV's station manager.

Following sign-on, the national attention paid to Portland and the world's first UHF station hardly lulled. Since neither KPTV nor Sarnoff knew precisely when the station would begin broadcasting, he and NBC had made elaborate plans to salute the new station during the World Series broadcast slated for October 1. Concurrent with KPTV's daylong inauguration of programming (noon through 11 p.m.) on that date, NBC nationally broadcast a *Salute to KPTV, Portland Oregon* as a prelude to the World Series.[29] The program featured NBC commentator Morgan Beatty, FCC chairman Paul Walker and a special appearance by Mayer's 14-year-old daughter, Sandra, who presented Sarnoff with a scroll "honoring all NBC has done for television."

In response to the station's "exceptional send-off," *Television Digest* reported that the "pioneer UHF station is becoming a sort of petted darling of the industry." [30] Portland and the rest of [the] network saw and heard FCC chairman Paul Walker welcome KPTV as "a harbinger of

(Left) KPTV's *Story of Little Ajax* promotional book, (right) inside cover

Barbara Angell on the set in 1953

Betty Davis on *Freezer Fancies,*
who moved her kitchen to
KOIN-TV in 1954.

the more abundant TV to come."[31] Sarnoff referred to Mayer's effort as being "in the traditional pioneer spirit of the great Northwest," and likened the opening of 'new UHF frontiers' to the Lewis and Clark expedition."[32]

KPTV's sign-on originated from the station's Council Crest transmitter because the studio hadn't yet been built. Mayer had purchased the former Sawyers Viewmaster plant at 735 SW 20th Place, which he enlarged to create a full television studio. It wasn't completed until early 1953, so much of KPTV's large output of locally produced programs awaited the studio building's completion. The station's first local newscast, featuring newsman Norman Wallace and weatherman Bill Clayton, was broadcast from the new studio on April 24, 1953. At that point, KPTV sailed into a broad range of locally developed programs, which were clearly designed to reflect the culture of Portland and Oregon.

KPTV's women's programs began with the arrival of Barbara Angell. According to Russ Olsen, Angell wound up at the station when a caller from a Portland radio station mentioned a woman who was interested in getting into television. "Can she cook?" Olsen asked. When assured that she could, Olsen said: "Send her over."[33] On April 27, 1953, Angell began hosting KPTV's first locally produced daily program, *What's Cooking,* which began at 9:30 a.m.[34] Always smartly dressed, Angell was extremely popular. Later in the series, she began incorporating visiting celebrities into the program. She failed, however, with a leopard named Chui. A reluctant participant throughout the live program, Chui camped out on a sofa in the reception area despite Angell's entreaties. Another inhabitant of the KPTV kitchen set was home economist Betty Davis, who appeared on *Freezer Fancies.* KPTV's locally produced programming ran the gamut of news/public affairs, children's programs, women's programs, sports and entertainment. Children's programming was extensive and created deep, abiding loyalties that continue to resonate with baby boomers who watched those programs as youngsters.

One of KPTV's first children's programs was *The Toymaker* which debuted on May 4, 1953, and was produced by Albany native John R. Ralston. Russ Olsen recalls: "Alpenrose Dairy had one of the first programs for children, which was a toymaker program. They dressed up like Swiss toymakers and they would make toys for children. It was a pretty good children's show."[35]

KPTV studio floor during production of the Alpenrose *Toymaker* program, 1952.

The 15-minute weekday program, which was also seen for an hour on Saturdays, received 1,500 letters a month according to *TV Life Magazine.* On the program, the toymaker crafted toys that then became the show's characters. Often the program had guests, such as firemen or circus performers, and content was keyed to real-life events such as the circus visiting. Besides Alpenrose Dairy, other sponsors included The Toy House, Sperry Wheathearts, Polt-O-Products and Grandma's Cookies.

Frederick Giermann played the German toymaker, and on the Saturday program, was assisted by his wife, Gail. Five children rounded out each show's cast. Both Giermanns had previously spent many years in motion pictures, Gail appearing under the stage name Gail Gardner. According to early KPTV-staffer, Gene Brendler, Frederick Giermann had an uncanny knack for memorization and would sit down and read through the script an hour before air time. That brief review was all he needed to commit the entire script to memory.[36]

Graham Archer on *Mr. Smiles Reads the Funnies*

At 9:15 a.m. on Saturday, September 27, 1953, Graham Archer, a longtime KGW staff member, made his debut on KPTV as the title character in *Mr. Smiles Reads the Funnies.*[37] Sponsored by Sunshine Dairy, Archer weekly dramatized the *Oregonian*'s comic pages with dramatic flourish. He later started and managed an audio service for the visually handicapped, Golden Hours, for Oregon Public Broadcasting.

Heck Harper's *Bar 27 Corral*, which signed-on November 9, 1953, was by far the most long-lived

The *Toymaker* with one of his characters

Tarantula Ghoul's *House of Horror* on KPTV-TV featured Susanne Waldron hosting horror movies on Wednesdays at 10:30 p.m., c. 1957–58. As "Tarantula Ghoul and her Gravediggers" she also released a recording *Graveyard Rock*.

KPTV's Heck Harper

of KPTV's early children's programs. Harper, whose real name was Hector V. Flateau, had been an entertainer since the age of age 11 and got his TV start at KING in Seattle. He was working at Portland's KXL-AM when KPTV signed-on in September 1952 and soon found favor with the station's younger viewers as Foreman Heck on the *Bar 27 Corral* show. Typically, the program opened with Heck telling his "ranch hands" a story and singing a few songs. He also acknowledged birthdays of children in the audience with his own special birthday song. The program featured 15 minutes of a western film, presented in serialized form over a week's time.

While Gene Brendler did not arrive at KPTV until nine months after the station signed-on, he quickly became an important staff member with one of the longest KPTV careers. Brendler got his first taste of radio in the Armed Forces Radio Network in Berlin, but hadn't really sought a broadcasting career. After the war, he was working in sales in Portland when he substituted as host on Bill Sawyer's *Make Believe Ballroom* on KWJJ. That led to a job at KXL-AM in 1950. He auditioned for KPTV in June 1953, and left KXL to start there on July 1, 1953.

Brendler was involved in many early KPTV programs, but perhaps one of the most stylized was his *Wedding Belles* show, which offered advice to brides-to-be. Beginning on August 9, 1953, *Wedding Belles* was concocted by Showalter Lynch, a Portland advertising agency that represented several wedding-related businesses. Completely live and unrehearsed, the program consisted of three series of questions put to prospective brides. Those with the best answers won prizes worth $500 provided by the sponsors.[38]

From 1957 to 1961, Brendler also hosted *High Time*, a local popular music program similar to *American Bandstand*. He was a news announcer/anchor and a frequent master of ceremonies on many KPTV programs. Brendler remained with KPTV for more than 30 years, later serving as the station's public affairs director.

KPTV's *Wedding Belles* with Gene Brendler

While early live remote program origination was complex and expensive, KPTV was active in the community with this remote van, c. 1954.

KPTV *Treasure Hunt* ad, 1953

*Hoffman Hayride*, a country-and-western program sponsored by TV set manufacturer Hoffman Television, made its debut on May 8, 1953, and featured Taylor Morris and The Country Gentlemen.

The show *See Hear* came a bit later, debuting on September 27, 1954. The 25-minute program, described as Portland's first daily variety television show, featured vocalist Patty Baldwin, formerly with Ray Anthony's Band; pianist Al Davis; organist Charles Fendall; and KPTV announcer Gene Brendler, who served as emcee.

KPTV even launched a game show, *Treasure Hunt*, which featured host Cretoria Thompson, model Pat Carmen and Portland radio personalities Thomas Lawson McCall from KGW-AM, Bob McAnulty from KWJJ-AM and Bob McCarl from KXL-AM.

KPTV's *See Hear*, 1954

Another early hit program among KPTV's entertainment offerings was *What's On Your Mind?* The program originated when someone on Mayer's staff saw "mentalist," Myrus, who had attracted considerable attention, including from NBC's David Sarnoff, when he'd seen the performer's Manhattan night club act. Myrus debuted over KPTV on October 19, 1953.

Russell Olsen recalls: "He pretty much had us and the *Oregon Journal* convinced that he was legitimate." In an article entitled "These Portland TV Viewers Have Myrus in their Mind," the *Oregon Journal* reported that Myrus was "the best thing that ever happened" to the station.

According to Olsen, KPTV's promotion director Sally Savane was in the sponsor's booth and noticed that "he was palming stuff and from that direction you could see that. That's why he got a lot of information correct. We arranged for him to leave town fast."[39] The program lasted about five weeks.

Myrus at work

KPTV also launched a news department that began modestly but quickly achieved stature. Its first effort was *Northwest News Digest*, which began on May 18, 1953. Hosted by Norman Wallace, the program featured national and international news supplemented with United Press International wire photos.

*Newspaper of the Air,* c. 1953

Famous baseball figure Leo Durocher (center) with KPTV's sportscaster Hal Childs (left) and newsman Ivan Smith.

*Newspaper of the Air* came next on July 20, 1953. Hosted by Bill Clayton, this five-minute news summary covered the local scene.

Portland Federal Savings sponsored *News Scene,* which aired twice weekly at 11 p.m. The show was an early attempt to take television news into the community. Hosted by Chuck Foster, who had previously been KGW-AM's news director and was KXL-AM's news director when he took on the KPTV assignment, *News Scene* used movie film that was often shot the day of broadcast by Foster or his wife, Betty.[40]

KPTV's *News Scene* with Chuck Foster

The ten-minute *World on View* program took its title from KPTV's sign-on slogan and was structured like what would eventually became traditional television news programs. Gene Brendler read the news, Bill Stout covered sports and George Sage presented the weather. Over time, KPTV assembled a highly regarded news team, including anchor Ivan Smith (who had first been KMCM-AM McMinnville's news director and later its program director) and commentator Tom McCall. A youthful, fresh and innovative feeling—still evident more than 50 years later—pervaded KPTV's first efforts and Portland's first TV. UHF television seemed to be off to a promising start.

KPTV's *World on View* (left to right), Bill Stout, Gene Brendler, George Sage

## KPTV's UHF Challenges

While KPTV had captivated Portland, and was initially successful, the station suffered from the handicap of being on a UHF channel. Despite the favorable attention it received as America's first commercial UHF station, it was battling the odds.

Sarnoff and the FCC had intended KPTV to be the vanguard of a whole new UHF television era, and in the year following its sign-on, 82 other UHF were born started.[41] With the arrival of KPTV and these other stations, manufacturers began offering UHF tuners as *optional* receiver

KPTV studio at night

equipment. But the vast majority of existing and new VHF sets didn't have UHF tuning built-in, and the aftermarket addition of external UHF tuners never achieved popularity. UHF stations found themselves at a disadvantage, with fewer potential viewers than VHF stations.

UHF stations such as KPTV also faced challenges in transmission equivalency. VHF reception was easier and better than UHF reception at that time. Recognizing this, KPTV migrated to the VHF band as channel 12 in 1957 (For a more complete discussion of the competitive factors KPTV faced as a UHF station and its channel change, see chapter 20).

## KBES/KTVM/KOBI Medford

KBES-TV logo from stationery letterhead, c. 1953
Smullin Collection, WSMB

Other AM radio station owners may have been wondering whether to move into FM or television, but Bill Smullin wasn't one of them—he was going into both. Having launched KGPO-FM in Grants Pass before the FCC announced its 1948 freeze, he closely monitored the phone company's plans for providing west coast circuits for network television connection.[42] He also spent a great deal of time consulting with Russ Olsen and others while planning TV stations for the Medford, Oregon, and Eureka, California, markets as well as working with the National Association of Broadcasters (NAB) on issues facing small-market TV.

Smullin recommended to Amos Voorhies, his *Grants Pass Daily Courier* partner in KUIN-AM radio, that their company—Southern Oregon Broadcasting Company (SOBC)—file an FCC application for Medford's channel 5. Following the FCC's lifting of its TV freeze on July 1, 1952, SOBC promptly filed the application on August 18.[43]

Half of the Southern Oregon Broadcasting stock was owned by Voorhies, with the balance held by Redwood Empire Broadcasting Corporation (licensee of Eureka station KIEM), which was wholly owned by Smullin.

TV Rogue logo used on KBES letterhead, c. 1953

Smullin Collection, WSMB

Still a Eureka resident, Smullin was already involved in launching KIEM-TV in Eureka and was thus deeply involved in the technical and business issues associated with launching a new TV station.

Following the FCC's awarding him a Medford TV construction permit on March 4, 1953, Smullin promptly requested the call sign KBES. While some didn't pay a great deal of attention to call-sign selection, Smullin did. Sometimes he'd try out a call sign, and if it didn't turn out as successfully as he had hoped, he'd change it and try something else. So it was with KBES.[44] Smullin liked the way the KBES-TV call sign included the word " best," affording a clever advertising opportunity. However, in his view the call sign never really caught on, and in the 1960s he changed it twice.

Racing to get on the air before the fall television season, KBES was constructed on an aggressive summer timetable. While Smullin initially planned a studio in Medford, he ultimately decided to program from the station's transmitter, which was constructed on Blackwell Hill 2.3 miles east of Gold Hill.

Standing in front of the KUIN transmitter, Amos Voorhies (left) and Bill Smullin re-affirm their "handshake" partnership on its tenth anniversary. They had co-founded KUIN-AM Grants Pass in 1939 and would launch KBES-TV Medford three years later.

Public anticipation over the arrival of southern Oregon's first television station, and a VHF station at that, was high. Beginning in July, KBES broadcast a test pattern "so that many of you who already have your television sets can have them properly adjusted by [the] dealer who sold them to you. If your set is adjusted to the test pattern, then you will be able to get perfect reception of the KBES-TV programs"—and people throughout southern Oregon watched the test pattern.[45]

While KBES publicly targeted a July 1 sign-on in its May 23 *Ashland Daily Tidings* ad, construction on the Blackwell Hill building didn't begin until that date. Smullin was simultaneously making arrangements with the power company to import electric service to the hilltop and Pacific Telephone and Telegraph for installation of the necessary circuits to bring in network programming. Given these factors, an August 1 formal sign-on was announced.

The decision to build KBES must not have been an easy one. When the station signed-on, Medford was reportedly the smallest community in America to have a VHF TV station. Because there were no stations to watch, there were virtually no television receivers in public hands. Predicting reasonable expenses for a new station based entirely on anticipated revenues must have required considerable acumen and soul-searching.

As KBES's sign-on approached, an open house for local dignitaries was held on July 29.

# KBES Signs-On

KBES signed-on at 6 p.m. on Saturday, August 1, 1953, with a studio orchestra playing for much of the first hour. Local attorney Frank Van Dyke presided over the inaugural ceremonies, which included on-camera appearances by Oregon's acting governor Eugene Marsh, secretary of state Earl Newbry, state treasurer Sig Unander, state representative Bob Root and other local officials. Senators Guy Cordon and Wayne Morse—along with congressmen Harris Ellsworth, Walter Norblad, Homer D. Angell and Sam Coon—all participated from Washington via filmed statements.

While a primary CBS-TV affiliate, KBES carried programming from all four networks, including Ed Sullivan's *Toast of the Town, Lux Theatre, Flash Gordon, Buck Rogers, Foreign Intrigue,*

Bill Smullin hosting KBES-TV's *The Answer Man,* c. 1955

*Cisco Kid, Red Buttons* and, once the star returned from his summer hiatus, the *Jack Benny Program.* Locally produced programs included *Val Rogue, High Noon Hi-Jinks* and *Feminine Fancies,* plus two programs aimed at youngest audience members: the *Uncle Bill Show* and the *Aunt Polly Show.* The former was conducted by hosted by various "Bills," including Bill Smullin at times. Bill's red-headed wife Patricia, known to all as "Rusty," played Aunt Polly.

Besides hosting her program, Rusty was deeply involved in Bill Smullin's growing broadcasting business and joined him on visits to manufacturers' factories when it came time to purchase transmitters for the Eureka and Medford TV stations. Bill and Rusty managed to dovetail their business and family matters, such as when they took a vacation to Europe around 1954 and letters from Aunt Polly were read on the air during her broadcast absence.

One of KBES's early and most enduring programs, *Adventures in Medicine,* is still airing as of this writing in 2007. The show began in 1954 in cooperation with the Jackson County Medical Society and the Jackson County Health Department. Over the years, numerous physicians and health professionals have appeared on the program, which the station bills as "the longest-running program in television history" along with the program's current host, Dr. Robin Miller, as the program's longest-enduring host.[46]

In early 1954, Smullin purchased approximately nine acres of land alongside Medford's Bear Creek, at 2000 Crater Lake Avenue, and the next year installed a 40-foot-by-100-foot prefabricated-style building to hold the station's studios and offices.

Smullin's business style was highly original, particularly his written and spoken communication, which apparently was heavily influenced by Colonel B. J. Palmer, a chiropractor who helped develop modern chiropractic. A highly effective salesman, Palmer was also an early broadcasting legend through his radio station, WOC-AM Davenport, Iowa. Smullin once brought Palmer, who apparently helped Smullin appreciate the value of economy in communication, to Eureka as a trainer for KIEM's sales staff. Palmer's influence helped Smullin develop

*Bobby Champion and the Melody Wranglers,* in the KBES-TV studio, c. 1955

what his friends and business associates came to call "Smullinese."[47] Gradually but progressively, his memos and notes shrank in length and their terseness became legendary. His memos weren't impudent, arrogant or ill-conceived. They were simply crafted with laser precision. Words that earlier in his career might have been more fully written out, later distilled down to: "re ur's 7th"(meaning "regarding your letter of the seventh"). Recipients often devoted considerable effort to be certain they understood his communications in order to craft a reply. Speaking at an honorary roast, Smullin's long-time San Francisco attorney, Vic Reed, once genially chided the honoree by saying that his firm was going to promote itself with the phrase "Smullinese Spoken Here." Smullin's conversation was similarly concise.

By 1964, Smullin had concluded that the "K-Best" identity hadn't caught on as he'd hoped and the station was renamed KTVM on September 21, 1964. That call sign, which stood for **K-TV-M**edford, also didn't seem to gel. The station was again renamed, in conjunction with its major transmitter move to King Mountain, on August 19, 1968, when it became KOBI standing for **K-O**regon-**B**roadcasting-**I**ncorporated (see chapter 26).[48]

## Endnotes

1. Bullitt apparently considered this date to be the signal one for the acquisition since it is cited in her authorized biography: Delpine Haley, Dorothy *Stimson Bullitt: An Uncommon Life* (Seattle, WA: Sasquatch Books, 1995). Technically, KEVR-AM-FM owner A. W. Talbot sold the stations for $190,000 to Western Waves, Inc. on May 5, 1947, and the FCC approved the purchase late in June of that year.

2. O. Casey Corr, *KING: The Bullitts of Seattle and Their Communication Empire* (Seattle, WA: University of Washington Press, 1996), 35.

3. George Mannes, "The Birth of Cable TV," *American Heritage Invention and Technology Magazine*, Fall 1996, Vol. 12, Issue 2, 44.

4. In 1930, while in Bridal Veil Falls, he was married to Lossie L. Parsons and they had a daughter, born in 1927, named Mildred (1930 Census).

5. "Astorian Brings Seattle's Video to Home City," *Oregonian*, July 28, 1949.

6. Parsons, Leroy "Ed" E. Interview with Richard Barton. Transcript. Anchorage, AK. June 19, 1986 (WSMB Collection).

7. Ibid.

8. "Television Effects Change In Habits of Young, Old," *Oregonian*, March 26, 1950, 1.

9. The Cable Center (previously the National Cable Television Association), Denver CO., website: http://www.cablecenter.org/education/library/collectionDetail.cfm?id=91&type=manuscriptn, http://ieee.cincinnati.fuse.net/reiman/02_1996.html. The Cable Center's data is not necessarily to be taken as 100 percent accurate. Its website cites Parsons as having died in 1990 when his actual death was May 23, 1989 (Obituary. *Daily Astorian*, May 25, 1989, 4). The Cable Center, however, has acknowledged Parsons' claim to having first invented CATV.

10. R. J. Reiman, historian. Cable Television (CATV) http://ieee.cincinnati.fuse.net/reiman/02_1996.html

11. "Television Schedule," *Astorian Evening-Bulletin*, April 4, 1950, 7.

12. Phillips, *CATV: A History of Community Antenna Television*, 14.

13. One investor Becker solicited was attorney John Kendall; another was broadcaster Gary Capps, who ultimately remained involved in the cable television industry (Becker, Tom. Interview with author. Tape recording. Silverton, OR. April 20, 2005).

14. Parsons interview.

15. KVAS-AM became KKEE-AM on January 11, 2001.

16. Bill Bright. Two Bills From Boston. (Wilsonville, OR: Bookpartners, 2000), 86.

17. Bright, *Two Bills From Boston*, 89.

18. Mannes, "The Birth of Cable TV."

19. John Walson claims that he designed and installed a system as early as June 1948 but the documentation to support his claim was reportedly destroyed in a 1952 fire. His claim, therefore, is difficult to verify.

20. Steve Kosareff, Window *To The Future* (San Francisco, CA: Chronicle Books, 2005), 35.

21. "State Senate Asks Thaw On Television Freeze Here," *Oregonian*, April 25, 1951, 12. The amply-endowed Emerson appeared on numerous early television programs, including one of her own, and was often called the "First Woman of Television" in the industry's early years.

22. The DuMont Network was launched in 1945 and only survived until 1956 notwithstanding that it was the home of some of television's most innovative early programming.

23. Olsen, Russell. Interview with author. Tape recording. Eugene, OR. July 15, 2004.

24. The construction timeline information is largely taken from *Television Digest*, Vol. 8, No. 35, September 20, 1952.

25. Olsen interview.

26. "UHF Television Enters Portland," *Oregonian*, September 21, 1952, 1.

27. "World Series Slated on Air," *Sunday Oregonian*, September 28, 1952, TV section.

28. KPTV-TV used the "World on View" slogan in its earliest broadcasting days.

29. KPTV used programs from all four national television networks to operate for a full day.

30. *Television Digest*, October 4, 1952.

31. Ibid.

32. Ibid.

33. Ibid.

34. Material on KPTV's early programs largely taken from *Yesterday's KPTV* website, http://home.comcast.net/~kptv/kptv.htm.

35. Olsen interview.

36. Brendler, Gene. Oral History, February 26, 1982 (Oregon Historical Society, transcript of OHS cassette 384.55 B837w), 17.

37. Archer's legal name was Louis Graham Archer but he was professionally known as Graham Archer.

38. Brendler oral history, 9.

39. Olsen interview.

40. The significance of film being shown the day it was taken might be missed by a contemporary reader. The 16 mm film had to be processed, and early television stations had extensive equipment and staffing to develop movie film in their studios.

41. "KPTV, On Birthday, Salutes New Station," *Oregon Journal*, October 1, 1953, 22.

42. Smullin had saved among his papers a 1948 copy of Pacific Telephone and Telegraph's *Management Bulletin*, August 18, 1948, detailing AT&T's West Coast television circuit plans.

43. Subsequently, the FCC reassigned channel 4 from Medford to Roseburg, where it became KPIC-TV (see chapter 21).

44. The KBES call sign never caught on the way Smullin had hoped and he changed it to KTVM in 1964. The change also failed to meet his expectations and in 1968 the station became KOBI—standing for Oregon Broadcasting Incorporated—which it remains.

45. "When TV?" display advertisement. *Medford Mail Tribune*, July, 1953.

46. KOBI-TV website, www.localnewscomesfirst.com.

47. Material on Smullinese largely taken from *WmB* by J. Edwin Arnold, chapter 11 (Smullin Collection, WSMB).

48. "TV Station Changes Its Call Letters, *Ashland Daily Tidings*, August 20, 1968, 1.

# 18

# Portland Television:
## KOIN-TV, KLOR-TV, KGW-TV and Dorothy Bullitt

## Founding of KOIN-TV

K PTV's time as Portland's sole telecaster was relatively short. Just 13 months after its sign-on, Mt. Hood Radio and Television Broadcasting Company's KOIN-TV inaugurated channel 6.

The impetus to form Mt. Hood originally came from the company's major stockholder, Theodore R. Gamble, whose prior broadcast holdings included KLZ Denver, Colorado; KCMJ Palm Springs, California; and a sizeable ownership interest in Mount Rainier Radio and Television Broadcasting Corporation, which was then engaged in buying KJR-AM Seattle. Additionally, Gamble had business interests in movie theatres across the country and was a 25 percent shareholder in a major Portland soft drink bottler.

Another Mt. Hood Radio and Television Broadcasting stockholder was C. Howard Lane, who had been a director of KOIN, Inc., for more than five years. Harry H. Buckendahl, who was also a founding stockholder as well as general manager of KOIN-AM-FM, and an applicant for a Seattle commercial TV station.

On July 14, 1952, the newly formed Mt. Hood Radio and Television filed an FCC application to purchase KOIN-AM-FM from Field Enterprises, Inc. It filed the channel 6 application at nearly the same time. That channel 6 application set in motion a chain of events.

KOIN-TV

Channel 6 – Portland, Oregon

CBS

THE **BIG**
MR. SIX
IN THE WEST

KOIN-TV Logo from *Television Age* ad, June 1956
WSMB Collection

In 1950, KGW had moved from the *Oregonian*'s direct ownership to a wholly controlled subsidiary, Pioneer Broadcasting Company, when Newhouse family's Newhouse Broadcasting Corporation purchased the newspaper and KGW (see chapter 13). Subsequently, Pioneer Broadcasting filed an application for TV channel 6. In May 1953, *Oregonian* publisher Matthew J. Frey announced that Mt. Hood Radio and Television had agreed to sell 50 percent of its stock to Pioneer Broadcasters, thereby merging the competing channel 6 applications. Eliminating the costly contest made sense, and both parties heralded the merger. Portlanders also liked the deal because, by avoiding a lengthy competitive application process, the merger hastened the time when Portland would get a second TV station (see section on North Pacific/KING later in this chapter).

The merger forced Pioneer Broadcasters to sell KGW-AM-FM to avoid violating the FCC's duopoly rule (since Mt. Hood also owned KOIN-AM-FM). Mt. Hood's decision to ally itself with Pioneer, therefore, provided Dorothy Bullitt the opportunity to purchase KGW-AM-FM (see section on North Pacific Television, Inc./KING-TV elsewhere in this chapter).

Portland was clearly excited about securing a second TV station—and its first VHF outlet. On July 17, 1953, the FCC authorized construction, which began almost immediately at the KOIN-AM-FM transmitter site at 5516 SW Barnes Road and the TV studio plant at 140 SW Columbia Street. C. Howard Lane, who had relocated to Portland, was designated managing director for the new station, which planned to sign-on October 15, 1953. While KOIN radio was abandoning its longtime home in the Heathman Hotel to move to its Columbia Street headquarters, the station retained its lease for the prominent "KOIN" neon sign on the Heathman's roof, which radiated the station's name nightly over the Portland skyline until at least 1985.

Art Kirkham had joined KOIN radio on November 4, 1928, and, in recogni-

Frank Kinkaid as Mr. Duffy on KOIN-TV's *Cartoon Circus*, 1966

WSMB Collection

tion of his long service, he was given the honor of signing-on KOIN-TV at 3:53 p.m. on October 15, 1953. The time had been selected to allow the station to carry *Strike It Rich* from CBS following the sign-on ceremony. Studio construction had been rushed, and once Kirkham had officially launched the station and *Strike It Rich* had begun at 4 p.m., painters picked up their brushes to resume work on the studios.

Like KOIN radio, KOIN-TV was a primary CBS affiliate, and immediately following the sign-on program went to CBS Network powerhouse programs such as the *Garry Moore Program* (which followed *Strike It Rich*).[1]

Initially, KOIN-TV operated from 3:30 p.m. until midnight daily. While remaining a primary CBS affiliate, KPTV and KOIN-TV shared programs from ABC, which was without a full-time Portland affiliate. Thus, it was over KOIN-TV that Portlanders first saw ABC-TV's *Davy Crockett* as part of the highly popular *Disneyland* series' 1954–55 season.

Many of KOIN radio's long-established local personalities migrated to the KOIN-TV screen, including Art Kirkham, Frank Kinkaid, Johnny Carpenter and Red Dunning. Newsman Chuck Foster came over from KPTV to anchor KOIN-TV's local news, and the station grew and prospered throughout the 1950s and 60s.

KOIN-TV attracted national attention in a most unwelcomed manner when two of the station's Sylvan transmission towers crashed to the ground after heavy icing on February 28, 1971. The station operated at decreased power for several months until new facilities could be installed.

Chuck Foster, c. 1952

Courtesy of the Oregon Historical Society, photo 011189

Sections of KOIN-TV towers in mangled heap following their collapse on February 28, 1971

Courtesy of Joel "JR" Miller

Longstanding Portland broadcast owner Newhouse Broadcasting Corporation (a subsidiary of S. I. Newhouse's enterprises) sold its 50 percent interest in Mt. Hood Radio and Television, Inc., to Lee Enterprises, Inc., of Davenport, Iowa, for $13.5 million in April 1977. A large scale media owner, Lee's holdings at the time included four other television stations and 15 newspapers (including the *Corvallis Gazette-Times*). A week after Newhouse's sale of its interest, Lee Enterprises purchased the remaining 50 percent of the Mt. Hood Radio and Television stock for another $13.5 million. Its ownership of the station was consummated on October 21, 1977.

## The Applicants for Channel 12

On July 1, 1952, Oregon Television, Inc.—a company that had been formed entirely by local Portland business interests—filed an FCC application for channel 12 in Portland. Board members included company president Henry A. White, a retired financier; Steven Eberly Thompson, vice-president of M&M Wood Working Company; William A. Healy, former president of Portland Furniture Manufacturing Company and vice president in charge of sales for Dorenbecher Furniture Company; Jack Meier, of the Meier & Frank department store; and Kathleen Elizabeth Malarkey and Robert L. Sabin, co-executors of the estate of Huntington Malarkey (who had died in May 1953 but had purchased stock in 1952 when Oregon Television was).[2]

Another party who'd filed channel a 12 application was Columbia Empire Telecasters, Inc. Its principal stockholders were the Journal Publishing Company (publisher of the *Oregon Journal*) and its wholly owned subsidiary KPOJ, Inc., and Wesley I. Dumm, whose broadcast interests included San Francisco's KPIX-TV and KSFO-AM.

The third applicant, Northwestern Television and Broadcasting Company, dated back to a joint effort in 1951 between Ed Parsons, John Keating and J. Elroy McCaw to bring the KRSC-TV Seattle, signal to Portland with a translator-relay. Following Parsons' departure from Astoria, McCaw and Keating explored an alliance with Ted Gamble for a channel 12 application, but Gamble instead decided to purchase KOIN radio and subsequently applied successfully for channel 6. The channel 12 venture was, thus, McCaw and Keating's second attempt to enter the Portland television market.

By 1952, when Northwestern actually filed an application for channel 12, McCaw and Parsons had been replaced as stockholders by Lester L. Hunter and Winston W. Casey. Keating, the only Northwestern stockholder with a broadcasting background, began his radio career in parts sales in Portland and had earlier been a part-time announcer for various Portland radio stations following his work at KFJI-AM Klamath Falls (see chapter 10). Eventually, he started the John D. Keating Company, a successful business specializing in sound and film recording, as well as a sales representative for regional radio stations.

According to its FCC application, Northwestern had secured a contractual commitment from Heck Harper to work for the station. Because they were unsuccessful in securing channel 12, however, Harper remained at KPTV. His willingness to jump ship from KPTV to an uncertain Northwestern operation may have indicated some unease on his part over KPTV's future as a UHF operation.

FCC hearings over the three competing applications lasted many months but were finally resolved on July 22, 1954, when Oregon Television received a construction permit. Thirty-two months elapsed between Oregon Television's initial application and the station's sign-on March 9, 1955.

## Planning for Color Television

At the time of Oregon Television's initial application, the future of color TV remained unclear. The Columbia Broadcasting System (CBS), Radio Corporation of America (RCA/NBC) and Color Television, Inc., of San Francisco were all competing for FCC approval of their respective color TV systems, which were fundamentally different. Color-compatible meant color transmissions could still be received in black-and-white on those existing sets. Some created compatibility issues for the existing black-and-white sets that had already been sold. While the FCC had authorized the CBS system in 1950, that technology never became commercially successful. In 1954, the FCC reversed its earlier designation and declared the color-compatible system controlled by RCA/NBC as the national standard. Expecting that color television would catch on quickly, channel 12 selected the call letters KLOR and the station was constructed at 4700 SW Council Crest Drive in the basement of the KPAM/KPFM studio building.

# KLOR Signs-On

KLOR assembled an impressive staff, which was managed by S. John Schile, formerly executive vice president of Salt Lake City's Rocky Mountain Television, Inc. KLOR's program director was Sam

KLOR logo
WSMB Collection

Herrick, who had originally worked at various Portland radio stations in the 1930s and was returning from Los Angeles, where he had been working as a director at KTTV-TV.

KLOR's chief engineer was Michael McMullen. The station's promotion manager was Bill Nutt, whose background was in non-broadcast public relations and promotion. Production manager Bill Plummer had previously worked in radio in Los Angeles, San Diego, Salt Lake City and San Francisco. Harry Godsil was the station's lighting director, and Fred Oppenheimer was the studio manager.

Perhaps because it was the only station entirely owned by local interests, KLOR heavily emphasized local programming. Promising the "latest on sports," KLOR hired sportscaster Charlie LaFranchise, a Portland area radio veteran who had started out at KVAN-AM Vancouver before moving to KPOJ-AM in 1945. KLOR's sales staff included sales manager Jack Watson, who had held the same position at KGW radio for ten years before coming to KLOR, and salesmen John Hunt and C. E. McMorine. Patti Throop, Miss Oregon of 1953, was the station's receptionist.

The station's studios clearly sought to make a statement. Their dark walnut paneled offices and modern lamps reminded one visitor of the elegance of the Benson Hotel's London Bar.

On Tuesday, March 8, 1955, the station threw a pre-sign-on party for the trade in its studios, which were located in a newly-remodeled factory building at 915 NE Davis St. The managers of all competing TV (and most radio) stations showed up to meet the newcomer, and they all took out display ads in the following day's *Oregonian* to welcome KLOR.

KLOR signed-on March 9, 1955, with a 3 p.m. broadcast of a public service program "on the wilds and wonders of the Pacific Northwest." The station then offered its first local studio program, the daily 30-minute *Ron Myron Show*—one of KLOR's signature offerings—for "the housewife who wants entertainment as a garnish for her afternoon coffee break." With a theatrical background, Myron had earlier been associated with both KOIN radio and KGW radio (see chapter 9). He was assisted on his KLOR program by co-hostess Doni Hurd, who doubled as the program's weather girl. She had to learn how to write backward on the station's glass weather map—in addition to her duties as KLOR's assistant program manager. Hillsboro organist John Emmel, who had earlier been on the KOIN-AM staff, provided live music for the program. Primarily an interview program, the *Ron Myron Show* included a "Tiny Tot" slot, which invited children ages three to six to speak their mind. The show offered a similar teenage segment.

Long-time Portland broadcast personality Vree Kneeland hosted the weekday *Lady of the House*

Courtesy of the Oregonian

KLOR's general manager, John S. Schile, with receptionist Patti Throop

KLOR building entry, 1955

women's program, which aired at 4:30 p.m. Kneeland began her Portland radio career in 1929 doing a similar program—*It's a Woman's World*—on a number of Portland radio stations and was known by various air names. She had been Betty Buyer on KOIN radio and Kay West on KEX's award-winning *At Home with Kay West*.

KLOR's local news effort was headed up by Sherman Washburn, who appeared daily on *The World, The West and the Weather* weekdays at 6:15 p.m. The station also relied upon its ABC Network connection, which offered *John Daly and the News* at 4:15 p.m. Monday through Friday.

Long-time Portland broadcast personality "Uncle Nate" Cohn was already familiar to Portland radio listeners for his *Stars of Tomorrow* program, which had been broadcast over KGW and KEX since 1935. He moved the program to KLOR from KPTV, where it was also being telecast (see chapter 13).

Another veteran Portland radio personality, KEX morning announcer Barney Keep, contributed a weekly half-hour effort called *The Show,* which was broadcast on Tuesday at 8 p.m. It was Portland's only live song and dance program on television, and Keep emceed it in his customary "slow-tempo style."

A KLOR voice that would become familiar to generations of Oregonians belonged to the station's chief announcer, John Salisbury, who came to KLOR from Salt Lake City's KUTV-TV (see chapter 22).[3] Salisbury went on to enjoy a long career in Portland with both KPTV and KXL radio.

Thus by 1956, Portland had three television stations, one UHF and two VHF. All three major networks (DuMont had collapsed in 1956) had local outlets. Television in Oregon's largest metropolitan area was thriving.

## Channel 8 Portland

While Portland's KPTV and KOIN-TV and Medford's KBES-TV had all secured their channels without competition, they were exceedingly fortunate. The television industry was growing—along with interest in TV station ownership. It soon became the norm for any television station aspirant to wrestle with competitors for the increasingly valuable channels—whether VHF or UHF. In Portland, for example, four parties filed applications for TV channel 8. They were Portland Television, Inc.; Cascade Television Company; North Pacific Television, Inc.; and Westinghouse Radio Stations, Inc., owner of KEX, which it had acquired in 1944 (see chapter 9).

## Portland Television Inc.

Portland Television, Inc. was a broadcast newcomer. Caroline Burke, an NBC-TV producer in New York with a longstanding interest in developing a Portland station, was the company's first vice president and the only stockholder with any broadcasting experience.[4] Joining her in the venture was her brother, Forrest Berg.[5]

Caroline and Forrest were the children of Charles F. Berg, a founding KGW Hoot Owl and owner of the Charles F. Berg apparel store (see chapter 3). Forrest's broadcasting experience was essentially limited to his association with the Hoot Owls, which had ended in 1933. In Portland Television's FCC application, he stated that he had no previous broadcasting experience but "was interested in television" as a result of his sister's work. The other stockholders were all Portland residents without prior broadcasting experience, including company president Ralph E. Williams, who was a 25-percent shareholder.

Caroline Burke prepared virtually all of the programming exhibits for Portland Television's FCC application and among those people she consulted was American Federation of Musicians' Herman Kenin, who had been closely involved with KGW and the Hoot Owls (see chapter 3). Assuming Portland Television would successfully secure channel 8, Burke committed to remaining in Portland during the station's first six months of operation but intended to return to NBC in New York.

## Cascade Television Company

Cascade Television Company was another locally based applicant. In 1953, Cascade sought the commission's consent to enter additional information into the FCC record—from which a choice would be made among the four applicants. When the commission denied that request, Cascade continued to file repeated Requests for Reconsideration—which so irritated the FCC that it concluded that Cascade was putting more energy into that effort than to supporting its pending application. Ultimately, the commission charged Cascade with failing to diligently pursue its application, which was effectively dismissed on July 20, 1953.

That left three remaining contenders for channel 8.

## North Pacific Television, Inc./KING-TV

North Pacific began in 1952 when Dorothy Bullitt, who owned and operated KING-TV, the oldest television station in the Pacific Northwest, decided to pursue a new television channel in Portland. Even though the FCC's freeze was still in effect, Bullitt decided to become "more local" in the minds of Portlanders in preparation for filing a future TV application.

First, to avoid being seen as an outsider, she researched the names of prominent Portland businessmen and invited several to purchase stock in her new company, North Pacific Television, Inc. While King Broadcasting maintained majority control of North Pacific, other stockholders included Prescott Cookingham, a Portland attorney; Henry Kuckenberg, owner of a Portland construction company; W. Calder McCall, president of McCall Oil Company; Paul

Murphy, president of Oregon Iron and Steel; and Gordon Orput, state general agent for New England Mutual Life Insurance Company. Collectively, the non-King interests held 40 percent of the new company's stock.

Next, the tenacious Bullitt began spending a great deal of time in Portland, meeting people and learning about the community. Bullitt's close friend Gloria Chandler had joined the KING-TV staff in 1952 and was particularly interested in children's programming. In Seattle, Chandler conceived shows such as *Televenture Tales* and *Wunda Wunda,* a program for very young children in which she cast Ruth Prins—dressed in a pointed hat and tights—as that program's "Story Lady." Besides her programming duties, Chandler was a close business confidante of Bullitt's and also had strong Portland connections. Chandler and Bullitt frequently traveled together to Portland. Chandler introduced Bullitt to people like Helen Platt—whom Dorothy promptly enlisted to her cause of promoting North Pacific's application for channel 8.

Dorothy Bullitt at KGW Radio's 50th anniversary celebration in 1972

When it came time to go to Washington, DC, for the hearings, Bullitt prepared like a college student gearing up for finals. Coached by her close friend and business advisor, attorney Andrew Haley, she studied voluminous FCC applications from morning to night.

Once the FCC lifted its freeze, North Pacific promptly filed an application for channel 8. As the FCC deliberations among the four contenders ground on, another opportunity arose for Bullitt. Pioneer Broadcasters, Inc., had decided to sell KGW-AM-FM to allow the Newhouse interests to ally themselves with Mt. Hood Radio and Television Broadcasting in the channel 6 contest (see elsewhere in this chapter). Sensing that ownership of a local radio station might help her television application, Bullitt persuaded her North Pacific business partners to purchase Pioneer Broadcasters and thus acquire KGW-AM-FM. In that ownership, King would be the minority stockholder at 40 percent while the Portland interests would collectively control 60 percent of the company's stock. Announced in October 1953, the KGW-AM-FM purchase was consummated in January 1954, reportedly for $500,000. Ten months later, on October 20, 1954, KGW-FM was sold to KGW radio general manager Quentin H. Cox for $3,750. Cox, known as "Q" Cox, left KGW to operate his new property, whose call sign was changed to KQFM-FM on December 1, 1954 (see chapter 13).

## Westinghouse Radio Stations Inc.

Westinghouse was a well-financed major broadcast owner with decades of radio experience, including its prior ownership of KEX-AM-FM in Portland. Its record before the FCC was strong—although legally complex.[6] Indeed, Westinghouse's position appeared so strong that the company considered itself essentially invincible when matched against North Pacific and Portland Television.

Westinghouse Radio Stations was a wholly owned subsidiary of Westinghouse Electric, a vast company whose board of directors consisted of prominent individuals from across the country. Yet, none of the officers or directors of either Westinghouse Radio Stations or Westinghouse Electric lived in Oregon or were even very familiar with the state. The most that could be claimed was that one or two may have briefly visited.

The FCC likely had some concern that the newest TV station, in what would become a four-station TV, might have a difficult economic future. Westinghouse unquestionably possessed the funds to both construct and operate a TV station, regardless of whether it was profitable. So, where the other applicants had no record of broadcast ownership to review, the FCC paid considerable attention to examining Westinghouse's KEX operation to assess whether it was likely to adhere to the programming proposals it had submitted in its channel 8 application. Following that review, the commission seemed unimpressed with KEX's commitment to educational and public service/public affairs programming. Indeed, Westinghouse relied extensively upon John B. Conley, KEX's general manager and proposed TV station manager, and Melvin M. Bailey, KEX's program manager and proposed TV station program manager, to ensure there was a suitable amount of "local flavor" in the company's application.

## Dorothy Bullitt Secures Channel 8/KGW-TV Signs-On

The stage was fully set as the FCC convened its final hearings in Washington, DC, and assessed the applicants' virtues. Westinghouse, whose corporate slogan was "You can be sure if it's Westinghouse," exuded confidence. Bullitt's energy and drive sparked North Pacific.

When Bullitt entered the FCC hearing room, competitors' counsel were taken aback. A grandmotherly looking figure who didn't make major fashion statements, she seemed anything but serious or dangerous. Yet, Bullitt was clever and determined. Early in the hearing, she realized that Westinghouse intended to use to its advantage the fact that Hearst Newspaper syndicate's ownership of three percent of King Broadcasting's stock. At the time the commission looked unfavorably upon "cross-media" ownerships between press and broadcasting entities. Bullitt took the risky step of buying Hearst out during the hearing. Normally, an FCC applicant couldn't improve its competitive standing or change its ownership during a comparative hearing, but Bullitt gambled and bought out Hearst's interest anyway. Somewhat surprisingly, the FCC hearing examiner admitted the ownership change to North Pacific's record.

Children's programming had always been especially dear to Bullitt, and indeed, KING-TV had long-devoted special attention to it with efforts well-beyond Chandler's *Wunda Wunda*. The hearing examiner was impressed.

Westinghouse spent huge sums advancing its case and was represented by a highly experienced counsel. When one of Bullitt's partners, Paul Murphy, was put on the stand, he was quizzed by a Westinghouse attorney about a provision of North Pacific's bylaws that governed stock sales. Because of the division of the Seattle/Portland interests, Dorothy Bullitt had stipulated various conditions in North Pacific's bylaws governing stock sales, and the attorney artfully posed a hypothetical question to Murphy. On the witness stand, Murphy was made to realize that, if Bullitt chose to exercise her majority control prerogatives in a way that neither she nor the Portland stockholders had contemplated, Murphy would have his interest in the business taken from him for nothing. He was embarrassed by this revelation, all the more so in a public setting. Bullitt had never intended that she have such an option, but Murphy retired from the stand with a bruised ego, angry that he had been made to look foolish. While not a turning point in the case, it later proved a turning point in KGW's history when Paul Murphy's

Courtesy of the Oregonian

W. Calder McCall "throws the switch" to sign-on KGW-TV on December 15, 1956, as Dorothy Bullitt and KGW-TV station manager Walter Wagstaff observe.

embarrassment opened a rift between Bullitt and her Portland investors.

Ultimately, it seemed that the hearing examiner just wasn't very impressed by Portland Television or Westinghouse. Having reviewed the applicants, the commission ultimately found "Very Favorably—with respect to North Pacific's proposed programming."[7] When the hearing examiner awarded channel 8 to North Pacific on June 22, 1954, a stunned Westinghouse apparently hadn't seen it coming. Playing against Westinghouse's slogan, *Variety*'s headline the next day read "Westinghouse Cannot Be Sure."

Because the FCC's commissioners were not obliged to accept the hearing examiner's recommendation, a paper war ensued for over a year while Westinghouse unsuccessfully sought to reverse the decision—but on June 23, 1955, the FCC affirmed the award to North Pacific. Now it was Westinghouse's turn to be embarrassed. It had been totally defeated by a relative broadcasting newcomer, a woman no less—and someone it had read as a western "hick."

In addition to the rift that had been created between Bullitt and the Portland investors, stockholders had not initially appreciated just how expensive launching a television station would be and were uneasy about purchasing the additional shares necessary to capitalize the project. Eventually, Bullitt bought out the Portland investors' stock (except for W. Calder McCall's) in North Pacific Television for $320,000, as well as their 60 percent interest in KGW radio's owner, Pioneer Broadcasters. McCall was invited to join the board of King Broadcasting, which by then owned virtually all of the stock in North Pacific and Pioneer Broadcasting. Merging those interests, North Pacific eventually adopted the Pioneer Broadcasters name as its own. With the ownership interests of Pioneer Broadcasters Company and King Broadcasting now virtually identical, King moved to abandon the Pioneer Broadcasters name, and on May 10, 1957, formally sought FCC permission to transfer ownership of KGW-AM-TV to King Broadcasting.[8]

With the channel 8 construction permit in hand, Bullitt assigned one of her trusted Seattle employees, Ancil Payne, to Portland to serve as general manager of KGW-TV. Payne was a talented, longstanding broadcasting executive who skillfully guided KGW-TV's development and operation. Where Westinghouse had underestimated Bullitt, Payne later reported that people in Portland had entirely the opposite view. "They [the Portland business community] thought she was one of the meanest, toughest [in business] old ladies they'd ever come across. You didn't cross Mrs. Bullitt an awful lot."[9]

With the stock transfers and changes in station ownership unfolding, KGW-TV signed-on December 15, 1956. Newsman Richard Ross, imported from KING-TV Seattle, was channel 8's news director and presided over the 8 p.m. inaugural ceremonies. "'Stand by. Quiet in the studio. This is it!' crackled over the loudspeaker in the studio" wrote the *Oregonian*. An audience of 120 gathered in Studio A of "Broadcast House," KGW-AM-FM-TV's home at 1139 SW 13th Avenue, while a Marine color guard snapped to attention as the station signed-on. Other participants were the station's program director, Tom Dargan (also imported from KING-TV); James Middlebrooks, KGW-TV's director of engineering; and John Eichorn, manager of KGW radio. Eichorn gave a speech, as did Gordon Orput, president of Pioneer Broadcasters.

The celebration included one more speaker, Joseph Merkle from the American Broadcasting Company (ABC), because KGW-TV was an ABC affiliate. That choice was a portent of change that soon cascaded across the Portland broadcasting community.

One of KGW's earliest acquisitions was Heck Harper, who left KPTV for the new channel 8 affiliate when it signed-on. Harper remained on the air with a daily KGW-TV program until 1967. At that time, the station wanted to place an adult program in the slot Harper had occupied, immediately preceding the early evening local news, so Harper moved to Saturday mornings, where he remained until 1971. By the time he left the air, Heck Harper's program had enrolled more than 42,000 Portland-area youngsters as members.

## KGW-AM Leaves NBC

KGW-AM had been an NBC affiliate since the network's west coast inception in 1927. But David Sarnoff had played a key role in getting UHF KPTV-TV on the air and had guaranteed that station an NBC affiliation (see chapter 17). With NBC committed to channel 27 and CBS to KOIN-TV, KGW-TV had little choice but to affiliate with ABC. While KGW-AM could have remained an NBC affiliate as a business separate from KGW-TV, that wasn't customary in the broadcasting world of 1956. On December 17 of that year, KGW-AM ended its nearly 30-year association with NBC radio and affiliated with ABC radio. In Portland, it was called "the big network switch" day when KGW-AM, KGON-AM, KGW-TV and KLOR-TV all switched networks and KEX-AM went independent—all within 24 hours. To promote the change, KGW-AM began billing itself as "Radio-Active 6-2-0, KGW, pioneering new sounds and concepts for 1957." At KGW-AM, the switchboard reported that the most frequently asked question was "Where's *One Man's Family*?" referring to the nearly 25-year-old NBC radio drama that had been on KGW's schedule since the program's inception. KGON-AM was enthusiastic about inheriting the west's most prominent news program, the *Richfield Reporter*, and for weeks ran newspaper ads promoting the program's addition to its schedule.

## KEX-AM Goes Independent

KEX had been an NBC Blue/ABC affiliate since 1931 but now had been "trumped" by its former sister station, KGW-AM.[10] In 1956, network affiliation didn't mean as much for a radio station as it previously had. While KEX could likely have taken over the NBC radio affiliation abandoned by KGW, it chose instead to go independent.

Independence Day ad, *Oregon Journal*, December 16, 1956

Touting its new, "More Music, More News, More Community Service" programming goals as an independent, the station—with photos of its staff dressed in Revolutionary War garb—ran an extensive advertising campaign declaring Monday, December 17, KEX's "Independence Day." NBC radio, now needing a Portland affiliate, hooked up with KGON-AM that same day.

## KGW-TV Signs-On

KGW-TV took to the air on December 15, 1956, from the KGW studios at Jefferson Street and 13th Avenue—as an ABC-TV Network affiliate. With Dorothy Bullitt's Seattle stations KING Radio and KING-TV as ABC affiliates, she had substantial influence to push ABC to move its Portland TV affiliation from KLOR to King's Portland properties.[11] The result was that ABC abandoned KLOR for KGW-TV. It was a huge blow to KLOR, which had signed-on with ABC affiliation and pushed the station into churning waters as Oregon's first independent TV station (see chapter 26).[12]

Dorothy Bullitt took an intensely personal interest in KGW-TV's sign-on. She frequently visited Portland to help in planning and to cheer on her team, and she was widely admired both by her employees and the community at large. Longtime KGW meteorologist Jack Capell summed her up, saying:

> She ran that station in the most conscientious way a person could. She had commitment to the public and a commitment to quality and useful broadcasting. She didn't care about ratings that much. She wanted quality. In those days when Dorothy was heading it up, you can bet if it was worthwhile information, wise and good entertainment, that's what interested Dorothy.[13]

## Oregon's First Local Color TV Transmission

For its sign-on, KGW-TV produced the special program *Salute to Portland,* which was a 30-minute color film narrated by Tom McCall (who was going by the air name Lawson McCall at that point in his career). The color telecast was the city's first color transmission and took the in-studio audience and viewing public by surprise—since there had been no announcement that the station would transmit in color. KGW-TV had equipped its studio with color cameras and began Portland's first regularly scheduled, locally produced color programs the following Monday, December 24, when *Telerama* and *Pioneer Club* both made their debuts.

McCall's path to KGW-TV was an interesting one. He began his broadcasting career at KGW and KEX radio, as Lawson McCall, and later did commentaries for KPTV as that station expanded its news operation (see chapter 13 and elsewhere in this chapter). McCall's articulate and strong-willed mother was a major influence in his life, and their close relationship was legendary. At KGW-AM, he typically came into the station shortly before his scheduled five-minute commentary. She would often call and try to influence what he was going to say. Sometimes, he would set the telephone down on the desk while she was lecturing him. Times when they would argue right up to air time, he would say "Mother, I can't talk with you now" and hang up. Once, he hung up on her under such circumstances, and about 15 minutes later Western Union delivered a telegram that read: "Call me, Mother."[14]

In 1956, both McCall and Ivan Smith abruptly left KPTV for KGW-TV and some intrigue was reportedly involved. Both had been heavily recruited by KGW-TV. The 1956 election was at hand, and KPTV and ABC-TV had put a great deal of effort into the coverage. With Ivan Smith anchoring the *Alka Seltzer Newspaper of the Air* program on KPTV, the network had made a deal

KGW-TV's promotion manager Chris Christensen (center), Patricia Reynolds (left) and Silvia Taylor from the station's programming department, planning a broadcast in Studio B, c. 1957.

with Peak Antifreeze for additional sponsorship of the program with the condition that Smith deliver a Peak Antifreeze commercial. By then, Storer Broadcasting had acquired the station, and Russ Olsen had left as general manager—creating a temporary vacuum in the top KPTV management. Sales manager Don Tykeson, then only 29, was the senior executive and had to ask Smith to do the commercial. Smith, who was already obligated to do a Prestone Antifreeze commercial, refused. The network was insistent. Peak Antifreeze was an important client with lots of money, and a valued relationship was at stake. Tykeson recalled "it was sweaty palm time." With greater insistence, he again asked Smith—who quit on the spot. When Tykeson requested McCall as a substitute, he refused and also quit on the spot. Eventually, Gene Brendler did the commercial. Smith and McCall promptly went over to KGW-TV and became important elements of that station's news team. Tykeson always felt that it was an orchestrated exit.[15]

So it was that when KGW-TV signed-on December 15, 1956, the narrator for *Salute to Portland* was none other

KGW Newsbeat ad for the station's new news team, *TV Guide,* September 14, 1963

KGW's cooking program hosts Konnie Worth and chef Gino Airaldi, preparing for their inaugural broadcast.

# CHANNEL 8 IS ON THE AIR!

**WITH A FULL SCHEDULE OF ABC AND LOCAL TELEVISION SHOWS**

Headline from KGW sign-on ad, *Oregonian*,
December 17, 1956
Courtesy of the *Oregonian*

than Lawson McCall, better known as Tom McCall, future governor of Oregon.

Some KGW staff such as **Konnie G. Worth** (whose real name was Florence Pickett) migrated over from radio. With an assumed name—owned by the station—that borrowed KGW's initials, the Worth character had been part of KGW Radio for many years in a hostess/homemaker program capacity. Konnie transferred to KGW-TV for the station's local cooking program.

The KGW-TV news team came together quickly. Joining Smith and McCall were newsman Richard Ross and sportscaster Doug LaMear. Within the team's first year on the air, Jack Capell joined as weatherman. The KGW-TV news team was distinguished, popular and durable. Ross didn't depart until 1975, when he moved to KATU to anchor that station's evening news. After many years at KGW-TV, Smith left for King's Spokane station, KREM-TV, where he served as news director before returning to KGW. He retired from KGW on June 5, 1980; LaMear remained until 1991.

Among KGW-TV's early accomplishments was the creation of *The Children's Doctor* by the station's program director Tom Dargan. Portland pediatrician Lendon Smith starred on the program. With KGW-TV an ABC-TV affiliate at the time, the program was picked up by that network for national release for two years.

In 1984, KGW-TV won a coveted George Foster Peabody Award for its *Rajneesh Update* special coverage dealing with the controversial cult that had taken over the town of Antelope in Wasco County.

Following Dorothy Bullitt's death in 1989, King Broadcasting continued its record as a distinguished broadcasting owner, but eventually Bullitt's children decided it was time to sell the stations. After an intense search for the type of owner their mother would have thought suitable, King sold its broadcast properties to the Providence Journal Corporation in 1992. In 1998, Belo Corporation, a media company based in Dallas, Texas, purchased the Providence Journal Corporation's broadcast properties, including KGW.

## Endnotes

1. The station also carried some ABC-TV Network programs as did KPTV-TV.
2. Sabin had been a Portland attorney since 1920 in addition to also being a stockholder in his own right. Decision, FCC 54-926, July 27, 1954, 8 (KLOR file, NARA, College Park, MD).
3. Information in this chapter about KLOR-TV's initial programming, staff and sign-on activities is taken from extensive coverage in the *Oregonian*, March 8–11, 1955.
4. Burke had first joined NBC in 1939 and had been continuously employed by the network in a variety of radio and television production capacities by the time of Portland Television's application. Decision in Re: Applications for Construction Permits for New Commercial Television Stations (Channel 8) Portland OR, FCC 55-715, Released June 29, 1955, para. 98 (KGW-TV file, NARA, College Park, MD).
5. At the time of the FCC application's submission, Caroline Burke held 16.67 percent and Forrest Berg held 8.33 percent of the company's stock. Decision in Re: Applications for Construction Permits for New Commercial Television Stations (Channel 8) Portland OR, FCC 55-715, Released June 29, 1955, para. 93 (KGW-TV file, NARA, College Park, MD).
6. While Westinghouse Radio Stations had a "clean" record, its parent company, Westinghouse Electric, had been involved in various proceedings involving possible violation of federal antitrust statutes. FCC regulations essentially barred licensing a station to a party that had been found guilty of antitrust violations. Westinghouse Electric had never been found guilty on such charges but the commission seemed to take note of the presence of some "smoke," if not fire, in this area.
7. Summarized from Decision, FCC 55-715 (19948), dated June 29, 1955. Federal Communications Commission, Washington, D.C. (KGW-TV file, NARA, College Park, MD)
8. FCC approval was granted on December 10, 1957 FCC Consent to Assignment of License. (KGW-TV file, NARA, College Park, MD).
9. Haley, *Dorothy Stimson Bullitt: An Uncommon Life*, 256.
10. KEX had originally been an affiliate of the NBC Gold and Blue Networks (the latter having become ABC in 1945).
11. KGW-TV's transmitter was located at 299 NW Skyline Blvd.
12. Material regarding the multiple radio and television network affiliation changes taken from "Radio, TV Switch Due Saturday," *Oregon Journal*, December 14, 1956, 2.
13. Material quoted from Jack Capell interview contained at: http://www.eou.edu/~mmustoe/easpaperc.html
14. LaMear, Doug. Interview with author. Tape recording. Portland, OR. October 13, 2004.
15. Tykeson, Donald. Interview with author. Tape recording. Eugene, OR. August 30, 2004.

# Television Across the State in the 1950s

Across the state, people were inspired by the arrival of television in Portland and began exploring creating local stations for their own communities. In Eugene, numerous parties were fervently planning for TV just as the FCC's freeze on new television station applications was expiring.

## Failed Eugene UHF Applications

W. Gordon Allen filed an application for Eugene UHF channel 20 on January 9, 1953, and received a construction permit with the call sign KVTF-TV. Later reflecting concern over the viability of a UHF station, he abandoned the effort. Another newly formed company, Television Airways, Inc., filed an FCC application in 1953 for Eugene channel 26. It was dismissed by the commission in March 1954 for "failure to follow through."

## KVAL-TV Channel 13 Eugene

While C. H. "Pop" Fisher already owned 50 percent of Eugene's KUGN-AM, he aspired to enter the television game and became the major instigator, incorporating president and one-third shareholder of Eugene Television, Inc. Joining him were S. W. McCready as vice president and 1 percent shareholder; his son Carl O. Fisher, treasurer and 21 percent shareholder; Thomas Winn, secretary and 24 percent shareholder, and Robert P. Booth, 24 percent shareholder. Their FCC application for a 56-kilowatt station on channel 13 was filed on July 2, 1952. Ownership

KVAL-TV news department, c. 1975. (left to right) Standing: Bryce Zabel, Pat Hellberg, Rachel Gille, Paul Reiss, Liz McCale, Bill Bradbury, Diane McCarthy, Tom Hickey, Tom Cooke, Julie Brown, Ken Crocket. Seated: Mike Mekela, Deanna Dvorak, John Doyle, Jim Bradley.

changes prior to sign-on included Carl O. Fisher's exit from the company and the addition of Glenn E. McCormick, who owned KORE-AM Eugene and KSLM-AM Salem.[1] When the FCC balked at the prospect of channel 13 being controlled by the owners of Eugene radio stations KUGN and KORE, Pop Fisher sold his KUGN radio interest to his son, Carl, and board assignments were modified. Stockholder Robert P. Booth (a partner in Tillman-Booth Company, a wholesale plumbing and electrical jobber outfit) assumed the presidency; Pop Fisher became the vice president; Thomas Winn, a partner in certified public accountants Winn, Shinn, Synder and Company became the secretary; and Lee P. Bishop became the treasurer.[2]

W. Gordon Allen, who had abortively applied for channel 20 in Eugene, protested the reorganization as a sham transaction, but the FCC nevertheless granted Eugene Television's construction permit in May 1953 and assigned the call letters KVAL-TV standing for **K-VAL**-ley. Pop Fisher wasn't happy with the call sign and tried to secure KPIC-TV, which was then held by an unbuilt channel 24 in Salem, but ultimately concluded that station development had gone too far to make a change. A joint KVAL studio/transmitter facility was constructed on Blanton Heights, and the station signed a primary NBC affiliation, although it carried some programming from CBS, ABC and DuMont.[3]

KVAL-TV signed-on at 6 p.m. on April 15, 1954, with an hour-long inaugural program featuring majors V. Edwin Johnson of Eugene and Edward C. Harms Jr. of Springfield. Oregon governor Paul L. Patterson also appeared on film. The station's board of directors participated by reading congratulatory telegrams from Oregon congressmen. Most of the program consisted of "a preview of personalities who will appear locally on TV," following which KVAL broadcast *The Range Rider* at 7 p.m., *Liberace*, and then network features beginning at 8 p.m. Much of the evening was devoted to the sport of wrestling—including *Famous Fights* from Madison Square Garden at 10 p.m. and *Wrestling from Hollywood* at 10:30 p.m. The station began releasing color network programs in early January 1957 after spending about $30,000 on the necessary equipment.

Eugene Television owned KVAL-TV until 1996 when it was sold to Retlaw (Walter spelled backward) Broadcasting, a subsidiary of the Walt Disney corporate interests. On April 20, 1999,

Retlaw sold the station to Seattle-based group broadcast owner Fisher Broadcasting (unrelated to the Fishers who founded KVAL-TV).

## KEZI-TV Channel 9 Eugene

KVAL had enjoyed a television monopoly in Eugene since its 1954 sign-on. Its position was buttressed by the fact that the FCC's Table of Allocations provided Eugene with only UHF channels as potential commercial competitors to KVAL. Some local individuals decided that additional commercial television in Eugene was both desirable and a good investment—but they weren't willing to launch a UHF channel, which they believed could not compete with KVAL's entrenched position. They formed Liberty Television, Inc., hoping the company could persuade the FCC to allocate a new commercial VHF channel for Eugene. On April 16, 1957, Liberty filed an FCC Petition for Rule Making, seeking a suitable amendment to the Table of Assignments, in which it argued that:

a) Eugene deserved and could support another commercial television station,

b) A UHF commercial TV station in Eugene could not effectively compete with KVAL's VHF advantage,

c) The assignment of channel 9 to Eugene—which the Table had reserved entirely for noncommercial educational purposes—was unnecessary because the Oregon State Board of Higher Education was activating channel 7 in Corvallis. (Channel 7 Corvallis became KOAC-TV, a noncommercial educational station for the region. See Chapter 16),

d) The FCC should remove the noncommercial reservation on Eugene's channel 9 and permit its commercial operation.

The FCC granted that petition and Liberty promptly filed an application for channel 9. So did Thomas B. Friedman and Dawkins Espy (as Northwest Video) from Pacific Palisades, California and Springfield radio station KEED-AM, headed by Glen M. Stadler.

Liberty was headed by Eugene resident Donald A. McDonald. Its other officers were vice president C. E. Carlson of Portland, secretary Richard Miller, and treasurer Julio William Silva, both of Eugene. Silva owned a local automotive dealership, and both he and his family would prove unusually important to the effort. Other stockholders included Earl McNutt, Elisabeth M. Silva (wife of Julio Silva), Gordon Ramstad, Durward L. Boyles and Carolyn Silva McDonald (wife of Donald McDonald and daughter of Julio and Elisabeth Silva). [Carolyn Silva McDonald is now Carolyn Chambers, which is how she will be identified hereafter.] The company's board members and stockholders were all Eugene residents who were significantly drawn from Silva's business acquaintances from the Rotary.[4] Donald McDonald's goal and vision was to make the station the anchor of a "regional broadcast operation."[5]

The FCC had reservations about Northwest Video's financial capabilities and the company soon exited the contest, leaving behind a tough fight between KEED, Inc., and Liberty.[6] During the FCC comparative hearings, Carolyn Chambers was a key witness for Liberty and Glen Stadler principally represented his company. Because KEED was an established broadcaster, it had a record of accomplishments to review. Various parties took issue with KEED's compliance with its stated objectives and its past performance as an FCC licensee. Former KEED announcer Ron Ogle testified that he had been repeatedly instructed by Stadler to play popular music on KEED's evening devotional program but log the time as religious programming.[7] Ogle was the son-in-law of Liberty stockholder C. E. Carlson and was slated to be channel

9's program director if Liberty was successful in securing the channel, according to Carolyn Chambers. Ogle's testimony directly contradicted Stadler, who maintained that he was traveling on at least one of the occasions mentioned in Ogle's allegation. The testimony further called into question the integrity of the station's program logs.

Carolyn Chambers had worked for KASH in Eugene, where she had done all of the bookkeeping during the period when the station was located on Day Island. She had other unofficial duties at KASH as well. KASH's owner used to joke with her that she "did everything except engineering" at the station, where she sometimes handled traffic (scheduling of programs and commercials) and substituted for many staff members during their vacations.[8] While Julio Silva was the treasurer at Liberty's founding, Carolyn Chambers actually handled the company's financial records and did most of the preparatory work for the FCC comparative hearing.

Liberty's president, Donald McDonald—Chambers' husband at the time—didn't testify. Rather, Carolyn Chambers and Glen Stadler represented their respective interests in the hearings, which dragged on for six weeks. Much of Chambers' testimony involved allegations that KEED, Inc., had misrepresented its KEED-AM operating record to support its channel 9 application. Her claim was supported by tape recordings of KEED-AM, which indicated that the station had engaged in excessive commercialism—in contradiction of KEED, Inc.'s, FCC filings and Stadler's testimony—and had falsified station logs in the manner to which Ogle had testified.[9] The FCC frowned upon, but did not prohibit, commercials longer than one minute but Chambers' tape recordings also contradicted the station's previous claims in the 1956 KEED-AM-FM FCC license renewal applications. Chambers' testimony also contradicted KEED, Inc.'s, testimony in the hearing.

While the hearing officer discounted the significance of KEED-AM's lengthy commercials, the contradiction between KEED, Inc.'s, assertions and the evidence Liberty presented must have carried weight. Stadler, trying to remain optimistic, publicly promised to have the TV station on the air within six months of FCC authorization if KEED, Inc., was awarded the channel.[10] Following the bitterly contested proceeding, hearing examiner Thomas Donohue reported that it would take him several months to review all testimony and render a decision.

Liberty won—and was awarded channel 9 under a construction permit dated July 27, 1960. The call letters KEZI were assigned to the station, whose transmitter was to be constructed on Coburg Ridge, north of Eugene. That was originally also to be the site of the station's studios but a newly recruited stockholder, physician Alan Baugh, owned land at 2225 Coburg Road, "just over the Ferry Street Bridge," where the station built a new 10,000-square-foot studio and corporate offices.

On Monday, December 19, 1960, KEZI channel 9 signed-on at 6:30 p.m. with an hour-long inaugural program featuring "dignitaries, entertainers and television station personnel." Participants included Donald A. McDonald, South Eugene High School's Purpose Pipers, the Eugene Gleemen and the Fay Knox Dancers of Eugene. Following the station's inaugural program, the ABC affiliate went to network programs. Marvin Krank was station manager. According to Chambers, from the station's inception Liberty believed that "you compete [based on] on your news." The station devoted great emphasis in that area.

In 1960, Don Tykeson, who had remained sales manager at KPTV Portland, was increasingly "disappointed by the way they [KPTV] handled some of the executives." He wanted to find an opportunity for professional growth in broadcasting and possible ownership.[11] Just as KEZI was preparing to go on the air, Tykeson initiated a meeting with McDonald to explore possibilities at the new station. Nothing came of that meeting, and Tykeson continued his career exploration while remaining at KPTV.

McDonald took his own life in 1962. Later that year, KEZI's lack of financial progress caused a new Liberty representative, attorney Dick Miller, to contact Tykeson. He stated his terms for leaving KPTV to manage KEZI—and they included some ownership in the company. While Liberty initially declined Tykeson's proposal, two months later Miller offered Tykeson the job.[12]

While his wife wasn't particularly enthusiastic about the move, Tykeson assumed the KEZI managership on January 2, 1963. According to Tykeson, KEZI had not been profitable during its first two years. But he was confident that he could turn the station around financially in fairly short order. Tykeson anticipated selling his interest after 18 months and leaving to pursue other opportunities, which reassured his wife.

Tykeson's prediction about profitability was accurate. "I started in January and [in] March [the station] was profitable. [We] never had an unprofitable month after that." But instead of a quick turnaround and exit, Tykeson grew Liberty into a major regional and national player with television and cable TV properties. Chambers was a part-time bookkeeper at KEZI on Tykeson's arrival, and he quickly spotted her talents. She "did a remarkable job for KEZI and for Liberty Communications, and over the years I kept advancing her [first] to vice president [and then to] executive vice president."[13]

Liberty was a dynamic company and by 1967 had acquired cable systems in Albany and Lebanon. Sensing a significant growth opportunity, Tykeson broadened Liberty's management capabilities and then spearheaded the company's serious entry into the cable television world. First, he bought the North Bend-Coos Bay system, which had about 8,000 subscribers. He next acquired another cable group owner with systems in Bend, Sweet Home, Corvallis, Newport and Toledo. The move brought principals Ray Siegenthaler and Bill Elkins into Liberty's stockholder fold. While the purchases were highly leveraged, they greatly broadened Liberty's scope. Recognizing the expansion, the company's name was changed around 1968 from Liberty Television, Inc., to Liberty Communications, Inc., and eventually to Liberty Media, Inc.

While Tykeson's interest was in purchasing new broadcast stations, few meaningful opportunities emerged. However, he did note that other cable system owners were purchasing systems located at great distances from the purchasers' headquarters—so he set about purchasing additional cable systems around the country. He started with Birmingham, Alabama, and M. M. Victory, "a talented individual, very good on public relations" came along with the deal.[14] Victory's expertise was particularly helpful when Liberty profitably restructured some of that cable system's existing lease-back arrangements with the South Central Bell Telephone Company. The arrangement worked so well that in 1972, when General Telephone wanted to sell its cable systems—which served mostly rural areas in seven eastern states—Liberty used its expertise and growing prominence to purchase the systems at far lower than the original sale price.

In 1975, Liberty purchased a regional television network in Wisconsin; built a TV station in Eau Clair, Wisconsin; and then acquired UHF station channel 27 in the Dallas-Fort Worth market. As a pay-TV station, the UHF station was leased to Time, Inc.

By 1977, Tykeson was interested in taking Liberty to the next step. He explored making the company public but was unhappy with the type of return he thought it might bring the stockholders. By 1983, the company had grown from an initial staff of 30 to a payroll of about 1,200 employees—and the stockholders were looking for a return on the company's huge success.

On August 4, 1983, TCI, Inc., of Denver merged with Liberty by purchasing the company's stock for $186 million in a highly leveraged transaction. Some of Liberty's holdings were, in turn, purchased by a few existing Liberty stockholders as part of that transition. Tykeson acquired the Bend cable system. He later purchased KVAL-TV and other properties.

The most visible result in Oregon of TCI's sale, however, was Carolyn Chambers' driving desire to acquire KEZI. It was, after all, a station born out of her family's founding efforts and one to which she had devoted many years. According to Tykeson, Liberty didn't believe that it had the latitude at the time to split KEZI off for sale to an individual stockholder. Everyone involved was pleased when she arranged to purchase KEZI directly from TCI. At the same time, Chambers acquired cable TV systems in Marysville, California, and King County, Washington, and went on to build a regional television empire founded upon her purchase KEZI.

## KPIC-TV Channel 4 Roseburg

Having constructed KBES-TV in Medford and KIEM-TV in Eureka, Bill Smullin had hoped to interest national advertisers in his two stations as a combination advertising buy. To his disappointment, they apparently didn't see the regional picture like he did, and little such interest developed. As a result, Smullin began seeking ways to expand his regional television footprint. His Southern Oregon Broadcasting Company filed an application in late 1954 for channel 4 in Roseburg, for which he proposed building a transmitter on the 4,250-foot Mt. Scott near Glide.

At approximately the same time, Eugene Television, Inc., owner of the relatively new KVAL-TV, helped organize the South West Oregon Television Broadcasting Corporation, which also filed a Roseburg channel 4 application. Signed by South West Oregon Television's president Noble Goettel, the application proposed transmitting from Rose Mountain.[15]

Neither Southern Oregon Broadcasting Company nor South West Oregon Television Broadcasting proposed building a local studio in Roseburg. Rather, each applicant contemplated operating channel 4 as a satellite of their respective parent stations, although both held the prospect of constructing a local Roseburg studio at a future date.

As the FCC was gearing up for the traditionally lengthy and expensive comparative hearing process to select among the two, the applicants decided to join forces. In a letter dated March 4, 1955, South West Oregon Television Broadcasting Corporation advised the commission that the two parties had decided to merge, with the Smullin interests withdrawing and acquiring 50 percent of the amended South West application. They also agreed that KVAL would be the "managing partner," with the programming carried on KPIC (duplicating KVAL's rather than KBES's). The merged board of directors consisted of president Pop Fisher, vice president/treasurer William Smullin, secretary Harvey S. Benson and board members Robert P. Booth (of Eugene Television's original ownership) and Everett A. Faber (of Southern Oregon Broadcasting Corporation's original ownership). No individuals directly owned stock in the new company, half of which was held by Southern Oregon Broadcasting Company (owner of KBES), with the remaining half held by Eugene Television, Inc. KVAL general manager S.W. McCready requested the call letters KPIC for the Roseburg station—the call sign Pop Fisher had originally sought for KVAL—and the FCC approved channel 4's construction permit on June 8.

A video microwave system was constructed to link KVAL's Eugene studios and KPIC's transmitter. Oregon's sixth television station, KPIC, went on the air on Sunday, April 1, 1956 at 6 p.m. Gene Pierce was appointed KPIC manager. "Initially, the station will carry a duplicate of the Eugene schedule [but] at some time in the future, KPIC will carry local programming" the owners promised.[16] Some KVAL shows, such as Beverly Brunton's *Guest Book* interview program (which aired at 4 p.m., Monday and Wednesday), were already well-known in the community from Abel cable distribution, but they were newly available to the entire community when transmitted over KPIC.

## KOTI-TV Channel 2 Klamath Falls

Nearly simultaneously with the KPIC project in Roseburg, Smullin was exploring other TV expansion opportunities. W. D. Miller's KFJI Broadcasters, which owned KFJI-AM in Klamath Falls, had received a Klamath Falls channel 2 TV construction permit in December 1954. Early in 1955, Smullin filed to move KBES's transmitter from its original 2,000-foot Blackwell Hill site to a 6,200-foot Soda Mountain site above Siskiyou Pass and raise the station's power to 79 kilowatts. Clearly, Smullin was looking to better serve northern California and the Klamath Basin from the more southerly transmitter site. But Smullin's proposal further aggravated Miller's agonizing over whether a community as small as Klamath Falls could support the TV station he had proposed. Smullin had the opportunity to use KBES as a hub for a smaller Klamath Falls station, whereas Miller had only his radio operation on which to rely. In December 1955, when the FCC approved KBES's relocation despite Miller's objection, Smullin purchased Miller's Klamath Falls TV construction permit, and abandoned the move.

In a symbolic partnership, Smullin constructed his Klamath Falls TV studios at the Oregon Institute of Technology in 1973 at OIT's then-current loca-

The *Uncle Bill Show* originated at KBES/KOBI Medford in that station's earliest days. A locally-produced Klamath Falls version was created at KOTI, which was hosted by several different "Uncle Bills" including Bill Clark, pictured here c. 1957.

tion. Smullin and the school administration envisioned that electronics students could gain helpful experience at KOTI while the station would enjoy a ready supply of student employees/interns. OIT also stood to gain public attention through KOTI's presence on its campus.

In recognition of the partnership, the call letters KOTI—standing for **K-O**regon-**T**echnical-**I**nstitute—were assigned and the station signed-on August 12, 1956. KOTI operated as a satellite of KBES but with a local studio and some local staff who prepared material that was inserted to the program feed from KBES.

Bill Clark (later KOTI news director) was the station's first production director and worked in the original KOTI studios, which were constructed in a converted Marine Corps building that had earlier been used as an OIT dormitory. Clark recalled those studios:

> We tore out the second [floor and other walls] and had a huge studio complex. Unfortunately, we didn't have a zoom lens [on the camera and] because the flooring was two-inch tongue-and-groove, we were forced to dolly the camera [over its grooves] and every time we dollied the camera, the audience got seasick. We didn't even have 16-millimeter cameras yet—the state of the art was the Polaroid [instant] camera. So, they designed a turntable that was just large enough to put Polaroid pictures on [and] you could rotate this turntable slowly in front of a close-up lens on a camera and it was at least current as far as [breaking news].[17]

## KCBY-TV Channel 11 Coos Bay

Having successfully expanded into Roseburg with KPIC, Eugene Television next set about replicating that success in Coos Bay. A new corporation, Pacific Television, Inc. (which was controlled by the same individuals who owned Eugene Television), was formed and an application was filed for Coos Bay channel 11—which drew both competition and considerable scrutiny.

# KOOS-TV Channel 16 Coos Bay

On June 27, 1952, Sheldon Sackett, president of KOOS, Inc., filed an FCC application for channel 16 in Coos Bay. The FCC granted it on August 29, 1956, under the call sign KOOS-TV. Sackett repeatedly postponed construction and was likely re-evaluating his business plan for the station. Fearing competition from a VHF station, he sought to move KOOS-TV's construction permit to channel 11—in direct competition with Pacific Television. On February 20, 1959, KOOS-TV asked that the FCC dismiss its application after negotiating an agreement with Pacific Television for reimbursement of KOOS-TV's application expenses to date, which amounted to $8,700.

Yet, concerns about possible KVAL ownership of a Coos Bay station remained because of KVAL's ownership of stations in both Eugene and Roseburg. The FCC expressed concern that— given Coos Bay's close proximity to both—a station there would create too great a concentration of control over television facilities in so small a regional area.[18] Pacific Television argued that the communities involved were simply too small to support any ownership that wasn't connected to a larger regional hub and thus *required* joint ownership. Hearing examiner J. D. Bond agreed, and on September 23, 1959, the commission awarded channel 11 to Pacific Television. Dissenting from the majority, FCC commissioner Bartley said: "In my judgment, a grant here resulting in common ownership of three VHF television stations, particularly in areas as closely contiguous as here, would result in concentration of control of television broadcasting."[19]

KCBY (**K-C**oos-**Ba**Y) signed-on October 1, 1960, at 9 a.m. from its Noah Butte transmitter. The station's sign-on came just in time to offer Coos Bay viewers coverage of the World Series, which began October 5.

# Endnotes

1. He was also an applicant for Channel 3 in Salem.
2. Other stockholders included: Willis B. Shepard, a Eugene physician; William N. Russell, owner of Russell's Department Store in Eugene; and C. Philip Tillman, also a partner in Tillman-Booth Company.
3. In 1960, the station dropped all networks other than its primary NBC affiliation.
4. Tykeson interview.
5. Ibid.
6. Morris, Mary Jane, Secretary, FCC, 1958. Letter to Northwest Video dated April 3 (KEZI-TV file, NARA, College Park, MD).
7. At that time, broadcasting was more heavily regulated by the FCC than has recently been the case and stations were required to keep detailed logs of all programs broadcast. Mandated log entries included the "type" of programming broadcast according to FCC-defined categories. Stations were expected to provide programming that was broadly responsive to the community—which included some offerings in many, or most, of those categories. A station's performance in that regard was theoretically a factor in periodic license renewal proceedings before the commission.
8. Chambers, Carolyn. Interview with author. Tape recording. Eugene, OR. August 30, 2004.
9. Ibid.
10. "Stadler Plans to be On Air in Six Months," by A. Robert Smith, *Eugene Register-Guard*, January 22, 1959, B1.
11. Tykeson interview.
12. Ibid.
13. Ibid.
14. Ibid.
15. He was later succeeded by Pop Fisher.
16. "Station KPIC Goes On Air Sunday Evening," *News-Review*, March 31, 1956, 1.
17. Clark, Bill. Interview with author. Tape recording. Klamath Falls, OR. April 18, 2005.
18. Coos Bay is only 42 miles from Roseburg and 66 miles from Eugene.
19. "Dissenting Statement of Commissioner Bartley," FCC Order 59-980, 77910, Docket 12200, September 25, 1959 (KCBY-TV file, NARA, College Park, MD).

# UHF's Early Triumph and Failures

As television was dawning in Oregon, Salem would not have appeared to be a particularly attractive opportunity for a new station. Notwithstanding its designation as the state's capital, Salem was and still is of modest size. Yet, the city became the object of a long series of intricate maneuvers for rights to construct new television stations, efforts that were more motivated by proximity to Portland than by Salem's own economic potential.

When the FCC lifted its freeze on applications for new TV stations in 1952, its channel allocation system contemplated full-power television stations with the ability to cover significant geographic areas. As a result, Salem's location between Portland and Eugene meant that TV stations built to serve Salem would command significant viewing in both the Portland and Eugene television markets (neither one of which was close enough to the other for their own television stations to serve their mutual audiences). As a result, the battle over rights to build television stations in Salem lasted for decades and became intertwined with other contests over rights to build new stations in Portland and Eugene.

## Channel 24 Salem

As Portland's channel 27 (KPTV) received enormous regional and national attention following its 1952 sign-on, UHF television must have looked inviting. And the FCC allocated channel 24 to Salem, several parties applied. Westways Broadcasting Company of Torrance, California, filed an application in mid-1952. On December 8 of that year Laurence A. Harvey, a prominent Los Angeles industrialist with important political connections, filed an application for the same channel. By that time, Westways had apparently withdrawn its own application. Harvey received a construction permit on January 29, 1953, and secured the call sign KPIC for the station, but he apparently became pessimistic about the station's financial prospects.[1,2] On March 22, 1954, Harvey reported to the FCC through his legal counsel that he "determined that the many problems attendant on the establishment of a UHF television service in this area both preclude the completion of construction at this time and do not justify the commitments to the commission necessary to secure an extension of time within which to construct [the station]." Harvey surrendered KPIC's construction permit on that date.

## Channel 3 Salem and UHF Issues

Oregon Radio, Inc., had purchased Salem's KSLM-AM in 1943. Nine years later, its president, Glenn McCormick, watched television's arrival in Oregon and decided to get into the act. On June 26, 1952, he filed an application for Salem channel 3, which proposed studios in Salem's Senator Hotel and indicated that the station wasn't interested in a network affiliation. It's debatable whether the station's proposed independent status was a concession to localism, which was what the applicant asserted, or simply an acknowledgement that the existing Portland network affiliates would certainly have blocked a network affiliation because of their signals' overlap with the proposed station.

On July 1, 1952, Salem's KGAE radio owner W. Gordon Allen also filed an application for Salem channel 3 under the name Willamette-Land Television, Inc. Allen quickly ran into opposition when the FCC inquired into Willamette-Land Television's financial qualifications and explored whether Allen improperly engaged in "editorial broadcasts [that] may not have been presented in a responsible, fair and impartial manner," as well as investigating a character issue. When the commission indicated that it intended to schedule a hearing to further explore these points in question, Willamette-Land Television withdrew its application in August 1953. That left Oregon Radio unopposed for channel 3, and the commission granted the application on September 30, 1953, with the call letters KSLM-TV assigned. A jubilant McCormick announced plans to have the station in operation by January 1, 1954.[3]

Then the plot surrounding Salem's securing its own television station thickened. Clearly, McCormick was rethinking the project as he engaged in a multi-year effort to expand the station's potential coverage through several FCC application amendments that sought both to raise power and to move the transmitter site 31 miles closer to Portland thereby including large portions of the Portland-metropolitan area. Portland stations naturally opposed the move and charged that these changes were being sought "in order to obtain a Portland rather than a Salem transmitter location for network purposes."[4] While the FCC approved numerous requests for additional time to construct channel 3 at the original Salem location, it never authorized the northerly move.

Storer Broadcasting, which became involved in Oregon television through its acquisition of the original KPTV channel 27 in Portland, grew interested in acquiring Salem's channel 3 and proposed that it be reassigned to Portland as a substitute for Storer's failed channel 27. Storer also appears to have considered operating KSLM-TV in Salem as a KPTV "satellite" and simulcasting programming on both stations. Such an approach would have given Storer simultaneous UHF and VHF coverage of portions of the Portland market while stretching its television coverage well south of the area that channel 27 covered. On May 2, 1956, Oregon Radio filed an application to sell its KSLM-TV permit to Storer Broadcasting and cited as motive McCormick's illness and the death of one of his partners in an unrelated California broadcast venture. It was a daring move because FCC rules prohibited one party from owning two television stations whose signals significantly overlapped one another.[5] In support of the sale, Storer argued that KPTV's UHF status had created challenging financial conditions and that the FCC should grant it a waiver of that rule. The move drew immediate opposition, including the filing of a competing application for channel 3 Salem from Pop Fisher (as Salem Television Company).

Suddenly, John Kendall—vice president of Oregon Radio and the company's attorney—had a real fight on his hands. In an editorial titled "Channel 3 is Salem's," the *Oregon Statesman*, edited by former Oregon governor Charles A. Sprague, blasted the various McCormick proposals for moving channel 3 to the Portland site. Senator Richard L. Neuberger (R-OR) wrote FCC chairman George McConnaughey to complain, as did Salem mayor Robert White.[6, 7]

As if the situation wasn't already sufficiently volatile, in 1952 KVAN of Vancouver, Washington, filed an application for UHF channel 21 in Portland, which was granted on September 23, 1953. Press coverage suggested construction progress was being made. On December 7, 1953, the *Oregonian* reported that the proposed station had leased transmitter space in the KPAM-KPFM building at 4700 SW Council Crest Drive (the location from which KLOR-TV would sign-on two years later). The station also announced purchase of the old Coca-Cola bottling building in Vancouver for its studios. The problem was that the transmitter hadn't yet been built.

In 1956, KVAN, Inc., amended its FCC application (asking to use substitute channel 2 in Vancouver for channel 21 in Vancouver by deleting channel 3 from Salem whose presence in Salem would preclude the proposed change). The KVAN proposal fundamentally challenged the McCormick/Storer proposal to significantly move its proposed Salem channel 3 closer to Portland and predictably drew a caustic response from Storer. Ultimately recognizing that the transmitter relocation wouldn't succeed, McCormick withdrew Oregon Radio's longstanding request to move the Salem transmitter to the Portland area, while continuing to perfect the sale of KSLM-TV's construction permit to Storer. But on November 15, 1956, the FCC refused to grant the necessary waiver the parties had requested and returned Oregon Radio's application as "unacceptable for filing." Its decision was based on the overlap between Storer's existing Portland station and the proposed Salem station.

At this point, one might have anticipated that Oregon Radio would have built KSLM-TV—but it didn't. First, Oregon Radio entered into negotiations with Shasta Telecasting Company—owners of KVIP-TV in Redding, California, to sell them the KSLM-TV permit.[8] Then on May 14, 1957, Oregon Radio filed an attendant FCC application to relocate the KSLM-TV transmitter to Bald Mountain, 30 miles *south* of Salem, a move that would have given KSLM-TV significant penetration of the Eugene market. On June 17, 1957, Eugene station KVAL-TV jumped into the fray with an FCC "Petition to Designate [KSLM-TV] Application for Hearing."[9]

Pop Fisher of KVAL filed a supplementary letter alleging that Oregon Radio was also exploring selling KSLM-TV's permit to the *Tacoma News Tribune*, which owned and operated KTNT-TV Tacoma, Washington. Fisher complained that Oregon Radio clearly had no interest in building KSLM-TV and was just seeking someone—anyone—to buy the permit.

On October 21, 1957, an increasingly impatient and sour FCC responded to Oregon Radio's request for yet another extension of its construction permit by ordering a hearing to determine whether it "had been diligent in proceeding with the construction of television station KSLM-TV as authorized in its construction permit." The result was a tentative finding on March 26,

1958, that Oregon Radio would receive no additional time in which to construct the station. While Oregon Radio claimed it had been unable to construct the station due to circumstances beyond its control, the FCC disagreed: "Those factors were of Oregon's own creation and volition." The commission further stated that "Oregon has not been diligent in proceeding with construction of television Station KSLM as authorized [and that] Oregon has not been prevented from completing the aforesaid construction by causes not under its control."[10] On March 4, 1959, the FCC decisively rejected Oregon Radio's renewed request for additional time to construct KSLM-TV and extinguished the station's call letters on March 13. Salem would have to wait years for its own television station.

## KPTV-TV Channel 27 and KLOR Channel 12 Portland

While KPTV had entered uncharted waters when it launched as America's first commercial UHF television station, it became profitable shortly after initial start-up operating losses.[11] The arrival of competing VHF KOIN-TV channel 6, however, created a significant challenge.

Under the best of circumstances, the contest between UHF and VHF television stations could hardly be described as a fair match. UHF stations operate at higher frequencies than VHF stations, and therefore, transmit with lower efficiency. Even 50 years later, the general rule of thumb is that it takes a high multiple, perhaps as much as ten-fold, for a UHF station to equal the coverage of a VHF station. When Portland's KOIN-TV signed-on in 1953, it boasted 100 kilowatts power. Portland's KLOR-TV signed-on channel 12 in 1955 authorized for 316 kilowatts. At that time, no one could even manufacture a UHF transmitter that that would produce such powers. Even if one could have been built, such a monster UHF transmitter would have saddled the station with an uncomfortably high operating cost compared to a VHF station. Moreover, in the pre-transistor era of vacuum tubes, UHF equipment was considerably more fussy, and UHF transmitters required greater maintenance.

Russ Olsen reflected afterward that the only way UHF stations could have succeeded at the time was if the FCC had allocated whole markets to either UHF or VHF stations so that UHF stations competed only with one another. The mixture of UHF and VHF stations in the same market was a sufficiently unfair match that it was, Olsen later laughed, "something that never should have happened."[12]

Still, KPTV was clearly making progress at its outset. Just four months after the station signed-on, there were 64,846 TV sets in its viewing area. Eighteen months later, with KPTV just two years old, set ownership had nearly tripled to 181,034.[13] So KPTV's challenge wasn't in the public's ability to receive the station so much as it was in the quality of the station's signal versus its VHF competitors.

As the television marketplace flourished, KPTV's struggle increasingly grew more difficult. The station tried valiantly—adding a stellar news team, including newsman Ivan Smith and commentator Tom McCall. Seeking to stay the competitive course, it secured the capital to buy more powerful transmission equipment and in September 1954 increased its power from 17.6 to 204 kilowatts. Unlike KLOR (whose call sign hinted at color television), it was KPTV that first transmitted a network color program in Oregon on August 11, 1954. On April 23, 1955, KPTV became the first Oregon station to originate local color programming when it offered *Colorama*.[14] Yet beginning in 1953 when KOIN-TV signed-on, KPTV's profitability began slipping, and the station's struggle to survive against VHF competition deepened.

The professional goals of KPTV owner Herbert Mayer also seemed to be changing. Competing with Portland's VHF stations was clearly going to require considerable capital both for more powerful equipment with color capability and expanded investment in local programming. Empire Coil (Mayer's company) seemed disinclined to make such commitments, and on November 17, 1954, sold its television stations in Cleveland and Portland to Storer Broadcasting.

## Storer Broadcasting

In 1927, Storer Broadcasting began when George B. Storer, who started in business as the operator of auto service stations along with his brother-in-law J. Harold Ryan, purchased radio advertising time on a Toledo, Ohio, radio station to promote his stations. Both impressed and intrigued by radio, Storer decided to concentrate his future business activity in broadcasting—eventually becoming a significant group station owner. He even tried to establish a full-scale national network, the American Broadcasting System (ABS), to compete with ABC, NBC, CBS and Mutual (see chapter 15). In the early 1950s, Storer decided to enter television by purchasing several stations. When he added Empire Coil's KPTV Portland and WXEL Cleveland to the Storer TV station group, he helped make it the sixth largest broadcasting enterprise in the nation by 1961.

KGW-TV's channel 8 sign-on threw the entire Portland television market into disarray and particularly affected KLOR, which lost its ABC Network affiliation to the newcomer. KLOR was thus left to make its way as Portland's only independent, non-network TV station. While KLOR reported to the FCC that it was operating in the black in July 1956, the loss of its ABC affiliation shortly thereafter hit hard, and station losses were steadily mounting by early 1957.

Although a network affiliate, UHF KPTV was struggling to compete with VHF stations KOIN-TV and KGW-TV. On February 27, 1957, George Haggarty—a Detroit, Michigan, attorney and businessman—purchased all of the stock of in KLOR's licensee, Oregon Television, Inc., for slightly more than $1.1 million. At approximately the same time, Haggarty purchased an option from Storer Broadcasting that allowed him to purchase the physical assets of KPTV channel 27. On April 17, 1957, Haggarty's acquisition of controlling interest in Oregon Television, Inc., was approved by the FCC. Just five days later, Haggarty advised the commission that:

    ◖ under the terms of his [Haggarty's] option, Storer would surrender the KPTV channel 27 license to the FCC "within two or three days,"

and notified the FCC that he was:

    ◖ exercising his option to purchase KPTV
    ◖ exercising his option to purchase KPTV's physical assets
    ◖ requesting that the KPTV call letters be reassigned to channel 12
    ◖ requesting that the KLOR call letters be deleted.

He asked that the FCC officially delete channel 27's use of the KPTV call sign at midnight on April 30, 1957, and that the call sign be associated with channel 12 immediately thereafter.

Thus, channel 27 disappeared from Portland TV sets—and channel 12 became KPTV. "Remember to tune channel 12 for NBC programs as the world's first commercial UHF station goes off the air Wednesday," the *Oregonian* reminded readers.[15]

While KPTV channel 27 had successfully launched a variety of programs, the UHF signal wasn't fully competitive and VHF KLOR's independent status portended ruinous losses. Haggarty's solution was to combine the two stations and move the KPTV programming—including the station's NBC schedule—to channel 12. Some of KPTV's most popular features, such as *Rusty Nails'* cartoon programs, continued on KPTV channel 12 for many years.

By 1959, KPTV channel 12 was producing "a substantial profit."[16] Indeed, the station became sufficiently successful that Haggarty sold all of his stock in Oregon Television on June 4, 1959, for approximately $4 million, to the NAFI Corporation, whose board chairman was Bing Crosby. The company later merged with Chris Craft Boats to form Chris Craft Industries. Long-time KPTV general manager John Hansen took over management of KPTV on September 1, which was the date of formal ownership transfer to NAFI. Thus began the KPTV career of one of the station's most important and enduring staff members.

*Oregonian* ad, May 1, 1957

Hansen originally had no particular interest in radio but was taken on as a page at the NBC Network's Rockefeller Center headquarters in New York. Following military service, he held a series of odd jobs in California and was eventually hired in the Los Angeles research department of the young ABC-TV network on the strength of his experience at NBC. Eventually, he became promotion manager of the network's western division but, realizing that sales was a more lucrative field than promotion, he transitioned to the sales staff of the network's Los Angeles station KABC-AM.

Following work at ABC's San Francisco station KGO-AM, Hansen moved to television and went to work for Chris Craft's Los Angeles station KCOP-TV. There, his broad training proved useful, and when NAFI purchased KPTV in 1959, he was sent to Portland to manage the acquisition. It was a fortuitous choice. KPTV was enduring a rocky bout of growing pains for which Hansen seemed to possess unique managerial talent.

Notwithstanding the failure of KPTV channel 27, the nation's first commercial UHF station, it seemed that UHF wasn't quite dead in Portland—at least not yet.

## KHTV-TV Channel 27 Portland

A little more than five months after channel 27 faded to black, the Trans-Video Company of Oregon filed an FCC application to put it back on the air in Portland. The effort was spearheaded by Wally Matson, who was the owner of Portland's Regal Engineering Company, which specialized in cable TV systems and electrical engineering. Trans-Video stockholders included Paul S. Forsythe, owner of the Blue Mouse and Bagdad Theatres; Willis E. Early, a partner in Don Burcham Company, a manufacturers' agent; attorney C. E. Wheelock; and Matson's wife, Clara, who was an *Oregonian* newspaper employee. Others—such as Pop Fisher, William A. Elsasser, J. Benton Heald and Carl W. Boehme—had originally been stockholders but left the company within weeks of its founding. Those defections must have significantly

KHTV stationery letterhead, 1957

A KHTV-TV studio public affairs program broadcast during the station's brief three and one-half months. (left to right) Buzz Buzzell, James Goodsell, Phil Frost, Ed Whelen and unidentified moderator.

helped destabilize the company, which struggled from the outset. Another change occurred on February 11, 1959, when the company changed its name to KHTV, Inc. With an FCC construction permit issued on May 8, 1959, KHTV, Inc., was under FCC pressure to complete construction and sign-on the station. Seeking to put a positive spin on these developments, KHTV boasted in press coverage that it was installing the latest development, transistor cameras, in its studio.

With it transmitter and studios located at 4636 SW Council Crest Drive, KHTV channel 27 signed-on at 8 p.m. on Monday, July 6, 1959.[17] Participants in the opening ceremony included Howell Appling, Oregon's Secretary of State, representing Governor Mark Hatfield; Portland mayor Terry Shrunk; and a variety of religious leaders. Senators Wayne Morse and Richard Neuberger provided filmed congratulations. The station's published program schedule is its own indication of the serious challenges it faced. KHTV signed-on at 2:30 p.m. daily with the *Liberace* show and relied heavily on movies that were shown on *Family Theatre* at 7 p.m. and *Curtain Call Theatre* at 11 p.m. The *Liberace* program was neither new nor competitive and had earlier been presented on other Portland stations. The pianist was quoted as saying: "We love those returns [re-runs]. We start making money on the residuals the third time around."[18] Liberace may have been making money, but KHTV was not.

Since its final FCC license hadn't yet been issued, KHTV was still operating under Program Test Authority when it notified the commission on October 30, 1959, that it was filing for bankruptcy and terminating broadcasting at 9:30 p.m. on Sunday, November 1. The FCC could hardly have been surprised. On October 6, Matson had reported to the commission on the station's precarious financial situation. Even before sign-on, KHTV had peddled stock to 32 new investors. In August, the station began conversations with various new potential stockholders in Seattle, but those talks failed. Still hopeful of new stock sales, Matson, in his October 30 letter, also held out the prospect that KHTV might reorganize and continue—but that was not to be. After a lengthy bankruptcy proceeding, the FCC extinguished KHTV's construction permit and deleted its call sign November 4, 1964.

For the second time, UHF had failed in Portland—home of commercial UHF television in America.

# Endnotes

1. FCC Decision (in re: KSLM-TV), FCC 59-175 (69384), March 9, 1959, 5, footnote 2 (KSLM-TV file, NARA, College Park, MD).
2. Fisher, Henry G. 1953. Letter to George L. Kramer, Bureau of Customs, Treasury Department, Washington, D.C. dated February 20 (KPIC-TV file, NARA, College Park MD).
3. "FCC Grants Salem Plea," *Oregonian*, October 1, 1953, 1.
4. "Petition to Vacate or revoke Construction Permit or Declare Permit Forfeited," regarding channel 3, Salem, OR filed June 28, 1956, by Pop Fisher (KSLM-TV file, NARA, College Park, MD).
5. This was a television extension of the duopoly rule under which NBC had been forced to divest itself of one of its two radio networks (the Red and the Blue) because their affiliated stations' signals overlapped one another.
6. Neuberger, Sen. Richard L. 1957, Letter to McConnaughey dated January 8 (Willamette-Land Television, Inc., file, NARA, College Park, MD).
7. White, Roger, 1956. Letter to FCC dated August 10 (Willamette-Land Television, Inc., file, NARA, College Park, MD).
8. Russell Olsen, who had been KPTV's manager, left the station following its purchase by Storer and went on to KVIP-TV Redding, where he was vice president at the time McCormick sought to sell KSLM-TV to the Redding interests.
9. "Petition to Designate Application for Hearing," filed by Eugene Television, Inc., on June 11, 1957, File No BMPCT-4687 (KSLM-TV file, NARA, College Park, MD).
10. FCC Decision re: For Extension of time to Complete Construction of Television Station KSLM-TV, Docket 59-175, File BMPCT-4564, released March 9, 1959. (KSLM-TV file, NARA, College Park, MD).
11. Olsen interview.
12. Ibid.
13. Data taken from Yesterday's KPTV website, http://kptv.home.comcast.net/Timeline/timeline.htm
14. Ibid.
15. "Behind the Mike," by B. Mike, *Oregonian*, May 1, 1957, B2.
16. KPTV FCC. License Renewal application, Exhibit No 3, April 25, 1959 (KPTV file, NARA, College Park, MD).
17. Previously the site of KPRA-FM, the first KWJJ-FM and Ed Parsons' attempt at building Oregon's first television station (as a relay of KING-TV Seattle, WA).
18. "Behind the Mike," *Oregonian*, July 6, 1959, Sec. 2, 2.

# 21

# New Radio Stations of the 1950s

The post-war boom of new radio stations continued in the 1950s. Despite the arrival of television, many saw lucrative business opportunities in radio, particularly in smaller markets where good frequencies remained available. Network radio was fading, and by 1950 evenings were no longer radio's prime time as audiences were shifting toward daytime hours.

The radio networks' decline was reasonably swift. For example, in 1947 only 18 percent of the programming on Medford's KMED was locally generated with 82 percent coming from network and syndicated sources. By 1955, insufficient radio listenership made it difficult for networks to cover the cost of expensive programs and they ceased offering continuous day-long programming. Local stations filled the time with disk jockey programming—which rapidly became radio's staple. In KMED's case ten years later, in 1957, 52 percent all air time was local. Two years later in 1959, the figure had jumped to 69 percent. To distinguish themselves from one another, stations began individually concentrating on different types of music and moved to what came to be called "specialized format" radio.

But just as radio was struggling to accommodate television's advent, new AM stations began sprouting up with increasing speed. In Oregon, 38 new radio stations signed-on in the 1950s, and their arrival added to the competition from television.

## KABY-AM/KRKT-AM Albany

Albany Broadcasting Corporation's 250-watt daytime KABY, the "Voice of Albany," signed-on January 16, 1959, at 990 KHz. An important feature on the station's first program schedule was *Sandy's Beat*, which was heard from 4:30 p.m. to 5 p.m., Monday through Saturday. Chet Wheeler, who had gotten his start at KBND Bend, was the licensee's president and Fred Henshaw the station manager. Other key staff included Sandy Rhodes, program and promotion director; Ken Burford, chief engineer; Melvin Miller, news director; Delores Berg, farm director; and Carley Copenhaver, women's director. KABY's studios were located at 233 West 3rd Avenue.

By October 1962, KABY had been purchased by station KNND, and its call sign changed to KRKT.

## KVAS-AM Astoria

KVAS's birth was complex. Ed Parsons had been involved with Astoria's KAST since 1944, and as he increasingly became intrigued by television he also developed plans for a new Astoria radio station to compete with KAST.

Following several unsuccessful attempts to establish partnerships to found the new station, Clatsop Video Broadcasters (the corporate entity under which he was conducting his cable television business) filed an application in 1949 for a new Astoria 250-watt daytime station on 1050 KHz. At the point that he was planning the operation of a competing station, Parsons had to sever his connections with KAST although his departure from that station doesn't seem to have occurred at a precise moment. While he reportedly resigned as KAST's general manager in October 1949, Parsons continued to transact FCC business on KAST's behalf into early 1950, signing correspondence as the station's technical director.

Following the FCC's granting of a construction permit for the new station, Parsons secured the call letters KVAS. The station was heavily connected to the cable TV system, with its transmitter site co-located with the cable system's head end on Astoria's Coxcomb Hill.

KVAS signed-on May 10, 1950, from studios in Suite 302 of the Astoria Building at 612 Commercial Street and operated from 6:30 a.m. until 9 p.m. Without a network affiliation, the station depended on "local events, local programs, local news and music," according to Parsons, who managed the station.[1] Richard F. Denbo served as sales manager, Elmer Littlehales as production manager, James Titus as chief engineer, Harvey Lipsit as news director, and Dale Cooper as operator. Parsons' wife, Grace, was program director.

KVAS was not entirely successful as a competitor with KAST and appears to have gone dark later in 1950. Following litigation to resolve the dissolution of a partnership between Parsons and Denbo, it returned to the air in November 1950. By 1952, the station had switched to 1230 KHz with 250 watts full-time. When Parsons left for Alaska in 1953, KVAS faced serious financial challenges (see chapter 12). On November 12, 1953, KVAS was sold by order of Judge H. K. Zimmerman to T. R. Williams of Astoria and A. I. Capstaff of Portland.[2]

In 1955, Tracy Moore Sr. purchased KVAS, which by then was located on the second floor of the Astoria Motors Building on Commercial Street. In 1963, the station moved to a waterfront location next to Englund Marine. Charles Farmer moved to Astoria in 1959 and purchased an interest in the station from Moore. In 1972, Farmer bought out Moore's remaining interest and assumed total ownership.

## KRNS-AM/KZZR-AM Burns

Co-owners and co-managers Jim Ward and Howard McDonald secured a license for KRNS and signed-on the station September 28, 1957. The 250-watt station, operating at 1230 KHz with its studios and transmitter on Fairground Road, received reception reports from as far away as Winnemucca, Nevada. A Keystone transcription network affiliate, KRNS immediately began broadcasting local high school football games. The station also added Joan Lee to its staff. Lee was both the station's secretary and host of a household show that aired weekdays at 10:15 a.m. Around 1964, the station raised its power to one kilowatt daytime and 250 watts nighttime. By 1968, Rich Watkins was program director and Marie Barrett news director. On April 10, 1984, the station changed call signs to KZZR.

## KURY-AM Brookings

In February 1957, Joseph F. Sheridan of Crescent City, California, filed an FCC application for a new one-kilowatt Brookings station on 690 KHz. Following some technical opposition, the application was amended to specify 910 KHz at 500 watts daytime-only on September 25, 1957. Approved by the FCC on January 30, 1958, and with the call letters KURY later assigned, the station's tower, studios and transmitter were constructed on Oceanview Drive in the town of Harbor.

KURY stationery letterhead, c. 1960
WSMB Collection

KURY signed-on May 2, 1958, and observed its first birthday with a large celebration on the station's front lawn. A large cake, decorated with an antenna, was served to the crowd along with live music, public tours of the studios and interviews with local citizens.[3]

Jack Heald, who came from the Rogue Valley, was KURY's first manager but didn't remain there for long. Sheridan replaced him with Norman Oberst from Coos Bay, who stayed at KURY for many years.[4] Robert Vitto was his program director.

KURY was originally intended to also serve Crescent City and Gold Beach, but the station soon discovered that terrain blocked most of its signal from reaching that far. In 1959, KURY remedied that by seeking permission to increase its power to one kilowatt on 910 KHz and to raise its tower by 100 hundred feet—although still as a daytime-only station. That power increase apparently occurred in 1962.

KURY tower being helicoptered to the station's new transmitter site in 1972

In 1964, KURY station manager Norman Oberst purchased KURY from the Sheridans in partnership with Brookings resident Vernon Garvin. In 1972, KURY moved from Oceanview Drive to Dawson Road, just north of the Brookings city limit. To accomplish the move, the station hired a Sikorsky Sky Crane helicopter that picked up the 284-foot tower and moved it four air miles to its new location in 45 minutes. It proved to be a historic event and was reportedly the first time a standing commercial radio station tower was moved by helicopter.[5]

## KCBY-AM/KYNG-AM/KMHS-AM Coos Bay

On December 7, 1956, Coos Bay got its second radio station when KYNG took to the air. The 1420 KHz station had a rocky birth when KGW's Harold Singleton filed an FCC application for the one-kilowatt, daytime-only operation in 1955.[6] When that application was granted on January 4, 1956, with the call letters KCBY, existing Coos County stations KOOS, KFIR and KWRO jointly asked the FCC to rescind KCBY's construction permit, arguing that its addition would cause them irreparable "economic injury." In April 1956, the three stations withdrew their complaint, after which Singleton established a partnership with Walter N. Nelscott under the name Coos County Broadcasters. Until then, Nelscott had been associated with a variety radio stations in Washington state.

Coos County Broadcasters requested its KCBY call sign be changed to KYNG, which is how the station began broadcasting at 5:30 a.m. on December 21, 1956, from studios in the Tioga Hotel at 275 North Broadway Street. When the call sign was changed, the partnership also changed its name from Coos County Broadcasters to KYNG Radio.

Phillip F. Waters, who had been managing Albany station KWIL, was hired to manage the station, which was sold to KYNG Radio, Inc., in 1957. The buyer consisted of Phillip Waters; George F. Brice Jr., president of Oregon Mutual Savings Bank and owner of other realty-related companies; and Milton A. Foland, vice president and manager of Pacific National Advertising Agency. KYNG Radio, Inc., also acquired KQEN Roseburg shortly thereafter, following which the corporation's name was changed to Pacific Western Broadcasters.

In 1976, KYNG made unwelcomed news when Waters was convicted by a federal grand jury of both income tax evasion and falsifying the company's tax returns. The result of that shakeup was the station's sale to Sequoia Broadcasting, Inc., on April 3, 1978. Bud Hutchinson managed the station for Sequoia, which later sold KYNG to Calegon in Buena Vista, California, on August 26, 1987.

KYNG was clearly struggling by the 1990s, and Calegon's own well-being was also in decline. The company arranged a sale to Ray Sparks of Bandon in 1990, but that failed. KYNG then became KYYG on February 18, 1992, and KRSR on March 19, 1992. By October of that year, the station was bankrupt. At that point, KRSR was turned over to Ronald Sticka as trustee and was successfully sold to Joel W. Lemon, Harry Abel Jr. and Dan Seleshanko in May 1993 under the name Lighthouse Radio Group.

In 1995, owner Lighthouse Radio Group approached Marshfield School District Number 9 to determine whether it had an interest in receiving a gift of the station's license and equipment—valued at $8,506. The School District readily accepted, and the station became KMHS—referring to K-Marshfield-High-School – on July 22, 1997. Its studios are located at Marshfield High School at 10th and Ingersoll Streets. Unlike other government-owned stations in Oregon, however, KMHS remained licensed as a commercial station.[7]

Marshfield High School, whose name dates back to the time before Marshfield became Coos Bay, has long used "Pirates" its mascot. Where it is true in the radio world that "pirate" refs to an outlaw who makes unlicensed use of the radio spectrum, KMHS is the "Pirates' station" and proudly flies that flag.

KMHS is operated entirely by students who work under the guidance of a faculty advisor. The students announce, do sports broadcasting and sell commercial air time, revenue from which supports the station's operating costs.

## KCTG-AM/KSGA-AM/KOMB-AM/KNND-AM Cottage Grove

Philip S. Holt, owner of Creswell Radio and Electric and Drain Radio and Electric stores, was 35 years old when he applied to build a new radio station in Cottage Grove. The May 1951 FCC application requested 1400 KHz at 250 watts day and nighttime power was submitted under the assumed business name Coast Fork Broadcasting Company. Granted in early 1952 with the call sign KCTG, Holt apparently needed construction capital and converted Coast Fork Broadcasting into a corporation whose stock sales provided the necessary funds. The majority stockholder thus became W. Gordon Allen with 60 percent, which was purchased for $9,000. Robert R. Bruce, a one-third owner of Prineville's KRCO, and Harold J. Davis, general manager of the Salem station KGAE, each purchased ten additional shares for $1,500.

The FCC approved the transfer of control on February 11, 1953. Because he was a 50-percent owner of Redmond's KSGA, Allen knew that station was switching call signs to KJUN and asked that KCTG become KSGA—a change made on March 13, 1953.[8] Prior to KSGA signing-on in Cottage Grove, Bruce withdrew from the venture and Allen purchased his ten shares as well.

KSGA signed-on in August 1953 with W. Gordon Allen officially serving as general manager, Anthony Maucione as station manager, Jack Vaughn as program director and Robert Kenedy [sic] as chief engineer. Within eight months, however, ownership of the station changed, with John Truhan holding 21 percent of the stock, Laurence Morley 1percent and Walter H. Dodd 19 percent. Allen, until then a 59-percent owner, exited as a shareholder along with Holt and Davis.

On March 31, 1954, Coast Fork Broadcasting Company's shareholders sold their stock, along with virtually all of the company's assets, to Orlo M. Bagley for $27,000. Bagley was a 48-year-old Cottage Grove businessman who also owned half of that city's Daughtery Piling Company. In January 1955, he changed KSGA's call sign to KOMB (Bagley's initials) and transferred the station to a new partnership, which he established with his wife, Thelma D. Bagley. While KOMB changed its call sign to KNND around 1959, the station remained under the Bagleys' active control for the next two years. With a longstanding sports interest, Orlo Bagley was KNND's principal sportscaster for many years.

While the Bagleys retained ownership, daily operations seem to have been turned over to others around 1961. The station was purchased by Interstate Radio Corporation around 1968, by which time Orlo Bagley was Cottage Grove's mayor. The 1968 sale began a long string of ownership changes. In 1972, KNND was purchased by Keith L. and Eleanor B. Stiles, who then sold the station to KTOB, Inc., in 1974. KNND was again sold, this time to Thornton Pfleger, Inc., on December 1, 1976, with Mary T. Pfleger as president of the licensee and David R. Pfleger serving as general manager and program director. On December 3, 1989, Robert L. and Diane C. O'Renick purchased the station.

## KCOV-AM/KFLY-AM/KEJO-AM Corvallis

On June 17, 1953, the FCC granted an application of Mid-Land Broadcasting Company for a new station in Corvallis operating with one kilowatt daytime-only on 1050 KHz.

Portland attorney Donald B. McCormick was president of Mid-Land. Prior to construction, the company asked to switch from 1050 KHz to a full-time, 250-watt operation on 1240 KHz. At approximately the same time, W. Gordon Allen filed an application for a new Salem station that proposed using the same power and frequency. KRXL Roseburg, which also operated on that frequency, protested both applications and the FCC ordered a hearing to resolve the conflict.

Ultimately, Mid-Land's application was granted, and W. Gordon Allen appears to have been quite upset by that decision. Tower construction was completed on November 2, 1954, and Corvallis' KCOV signed-on two months later with its final license issued on the January 13th. Allen continued to hector KCOV with complaints and asked various members of congress to echo his concerns. Whereas prior to KCOV's construction all of Allen's complaints were technical, afterward his objections alleged that McCormick was simply a front man and that the real party behind KCOV was Lee Bishop of KORE.

On June 17, 1955, Donald McCormick sold his interest in KCOV to Lane Broadcasting Company, which was controlled by Bishop, and to Oregon Radio, Inc., controlled by KSLM's Glenn McCormick.[9] The FCC approved that sale on July 20, 1955, and Bishop took over the presidency of Mid-Land Broadcasting. On May 16, 1957, he wrote the FCC requesting that KCOV's call sign be changed to KFLY, which occurred on May 24. Shortly thereafter, KFLY affiliated with the Mutual Broadcasting System.

On January 14, 1958, Mid-Land's stockholders sold all of the company's stock to David E. Hoss and Leander Quiring. The former was KSLM's program manager from 1948 to 1953 and manager from 1953 to 1957. The latter was a Hermiston, Oregon, resident who owned a variety of local retail businesses.

On October 27, 1958, Quiring sold his stock in equal amounts to Leon C. Boner and Douglas Whipple while additionally selling a small amount of stock to David Hoss in order to give him majority control of the company. Boner, who had worked at KUIN from 1951 to 1958, was KFLY's program director, engineer-announcer and traffic and office manager. Whipple was KFLY's chief engineer, having come to the station after serving in that role at KWRL Pendleton, and KPQ Wenatchee.

KCOV/KFLY's original studios had been located at the Corvallis Hotel, but by the time Hoss acquired majority control, it was operating out of the Hotel Benson. Within a year, the station had relocated to Oregon State University's M. U. Building and was billing itself as "Radio Corvallis." In January 1963, the station was purchased by Radio Broadcasters, Inc., headed by James L. Hutchens and owned jointly by him and his father, C. C. Hutchens.

In 1972, KFLY-AM and KFLY-FM suffered the extreme and rare penalty of license revocation in a proceeding dating back to the mid-1960s. The case involved James L. Hutchens' ownership of both Corvallis stations, as well as construction permits for KPTN Central Point and a construction permit for a new AM station in Gold Beach. It revolved around the allegation that Hutchens had provided false information to the FCC. In May 1970, the Commission revoked the KFLY-AM and FM licenses, in addition to dismissing the Central Point and Gold Beach applications. Its decision stated: "a licensee should not be provided with a profitable escape route from the consequences of his own wrongdoing."[10]

KFLY-AM and FM were allowed to remain on the air temporarily, and on September 2, 1970, the FCC announced that it would accept applications for new operators of the two frequencies. Three parties filed such:

    ℭ Ted Jackson, son of Philip D. Jackson, both men were associated with Grants Pass Broadcasting Company's KAJO and formed Beaver Broadcasting System, Inc.

- Mario D. Pastega, with Pepsi-Cola bottling interests in both Corvallis and Klamath Falls, and Vernon L. Bowlby, a certified public accountant in Corvallis. The two men formed Corvallis Broadcasting Corporation.

- Western Radio, Inc., whose president was John S. Brandies Jr., and who was joined by 10 other local stockholders in the enterprise.

Realizing that the FCC processes to choose between them would be time-consuming, the three applicants jointly formed KFLY Interim Broadcasters and then received FCC permission to operate the stations effective March 1971, pending the commission's permanent decision between them. By then, while Radio Broadcasters, Inc., was in bankruptcy, Hutchens leased his personally owned equipment to the KFLY Interim Broadcasters to permit them to operate the stations.

As the FCC hearings began, each party had reasons for concern. But on July 17, 1972, Beaver Broadcasting and Corvallis Broadcasting met and agreed to merge into a new entity, Corvallis Radio, Inc., and jointly agreed to purchase Western Radio's application for $3,000. The FCC accepted these arrangements and awarded the KFLY-AM and FM licenses to Corvallis Radio. Ted Jackson held 50 percent of the company's stock, while Bowlby and Pastega held 25 percent each. Philip D. Jackson held no stock but served as a director.

So life went on for KFLY-AM and FM. KFLY-AM changed its call signs to KEJO-AM on January 31, 1994.

## KPLK-AM/KROW-AM/KWIP-AM Dallas

Polk County Broadcasters was a partnership between Portland resident Edward C. McElroy Jr. and Leland M. Tucker of Lebanon. Tucker was the majority partner with 51-percent interest and also the "money man," agreeing to fund up to $15,000 in construction costs. McElroy made no such financial commitment. In September 1954, the pair requested 1540 KHz at 250 watts daytime-only power for a new station in Dallas. Following an apparent amendment, the commission approved a 1460 KHz construction permit on December 15, 1954. The call sign KPLK, which stood for **K-PoLK** County, was assigned on January 20, 1955. During the course of the application process the station's authorized power was also changed to 500 watts and KPLK then proudly proclaimed "500 Watts in All Directions" on its letterhead. The station's studios and transmitter were located on the Willamina-Salem Highway (Oregon 22), a little more than 20 miles east of the Dallas city limits.

In March 1955, the partnership was converted to a corporate ownership under the same name. Tucker served as president and McElroy as vice president and general manager—and KPLK signed-on April 17, 1955.

On August 1, 1957, Tucker left KPLK and McElroy brought in a new partner, Ray L. Kozak, who became president of Polk County Broadcasters, Inc. Kozak, who took over as general manager, had earlier helped start KSRV-AM Ontario (see chapter 14). His teenage son, Craig, often helped around the station, including doing air shifts, and later became one of Oregon's major radio personalities under the air name Craig Walker (see chapter 22).

In 1960, KPLK raised its power to one kilowatt daytime. On April 1, 1962, it switched call signs to KROW, raised its power to five kilowatts daytime-only and opened a Salem news bureau headed by Leigh Hess.

KROW then went through a series of administrative changes. Dick Robinson was general manager in October 1965 but was succeeded by Arthur "Bo" Westergard by 1967 and Clifford Murray by 1969. Dave Meholovitch took over in 1971, and by 1974 the station had switched to a top-40 format and was an affiliate of the American Contemporary Radio Network.

In September 1975, KROW was purchased by KROW Broadcasters with D.H. Maves as president and David Meholovitch as general manager. The station's program director was Don Richards, and Cal Applegate was chief engineer. Shortly after the sale, KROW converted to an all-news format and affiliated with the NBC News and Information Service (NIS). When NIS folded on August 1, 1977, KROW continued as an NBC Radio affiliate.

On October 23, 1980, KROW was sold for $170,000 to Firebird Communications, Inc., which was headed by Mark Blinoff. The buyer's principals included Blinoff, who was vice president of Merv Griffin Productions and former program director of KMPC-AM Los Angeles, and Roger Carroll, chairman of Firebird and former an ABC-TV announcer who had also worked at KMPC. Eric G. Norberg was appointed general manager and program director. Norberg had also previously worked as KMPC's assistant program director, as well as KEX's program director. Firebird changed the station's call sign to KWIP on October 23, 1980, switched to an oldies-based adult contemporary format and adopted the slogan "The Parade of Hits."

On November 13, 1981, the area was racked by a hurricane-force storm that swept in without warning. Damage was extensive, with winds gusting above 100 miles per hour on the Oregon coast and exceeding 71 miles per hour in the Salem and Portland areas. A half-million people in Oregon and Washington lost power, and 11 died. As the only radio station in Polk County, KROW activated the Emergency Broadcast System (EBS) and carried special coverage well into the night (even though the station was officially a daytime-only broadcaster at that point). Its coverage was unique in the Pacific Northwest and drew praise from the *Oregonian* and other regional newspapers.

In 1983, KWIP switched frequencies from 1460 to 880 KHz with five kilowatts daytime power and, for the first time, began night operation with one kilowatt. The station also moved its studio and transmitter to 1405 E. Ellendale Avenue (Oregon Highway 223/Dallas-Rickreall Hwy). Largely because Norberg was a champion of AM radio stereo broadcasting, KWIP inaugurated it in 1983.

On June 10, 1991, KWIP was sold to Jupiter Communications Corporation for $21,000. Jupiter's president, John Burns, also served as the station's general manager. In summer 1992, KWIP switched to a Spanish-language format and in 1993, Diana Burns became president and general manager.

## KFMY-FM/KUGN-FM Eugene

Lyle "Duke" Young was president of Music, Inc., the licensee of KFMY Eugene, and the driving force behind the FM-only station. An FCC application to build KFMY was filed in 1958. It was granted on January 17, 1959, and KFMY signed-on that same day operating on 97.9 MHz with 3.6 kilowatts power. Originally, the station's studios were located in the Eugene Medical Center at 132 East Broadway, with the transmitter located at 66 Prall Lane, but they were both relocated to 4555 Blanton Road on Blanton Heights in mid-1962. Another Music, Inc., stockholder was KFMY's chief engineer, Laurence "Curt" Raynes, who pioneered the station's stereo broadcasting activities. By 1963, he had been succeeded by James L. Brock.

Young first entered radio in 1938, while working at KORE while a student at the University of Oregon. Following his World War II service, he went to work for Eugene's KUGN and eventually moved to KVAL-TV. But Young had always wanted to run his own radio station and KFMY gave him that chance. He needed help for a successful launch, and "pulled friends and family together." Thus, from the beginning KFMY was a family affair. Initially, the station struggled as an FM-only operation, but Young nevertheless energetically developed significant local programming, including a Sunday evening series that featured University of Oregon faculty and visitors; *KFMY Forum*, also produced in cooperation with the university; and *Open Mike, Ladies Only,* scheduled at 9:30 a.m. When male listeners objected to the latter program, it was re-titled *Coffee Time* and opened the phone lines to both genders. KFMY intentionally operated with limited commercial announcements.

A major KFMY claim to fame was its inauguration of FM stereo multiplex broadcasting. On June 1, 1961, the FCC authorized stations to begin stereo multiplex operation.[11] While radio stations had been experimenting with AM/FM stereo—originally called "binaural"—operation since 1953, FM multiplex was the first convenient and true stereo broadcast system.

KFMY notified the FCC on November 6, 1961, that it would inaugurate stereo multiplex transmission at 8 p.m. on November 17 using a Standard Electronics 935 transmitter exciter. It was the first station in Oregon to launch multiplex stereo FM, and only the fourth on the West Coast, and the fifteenth in the nation.

Young died at age 86 on December 17, 2003, and is fondly remembered as a legend by several generations of broadcasters. One former employee described her feelings about him as follows:

> His office at KFMY [had] stuff that used to hang on the walls, including a pair of boxing gloves and a handwritten sign that said 'Yard by yard, life is hard. Inch by inch, life's a cinch….' We all learned so much from Duke. I really was fond of him, and I adored Hazel, his wife who was the traffic director. It was Duke's world of radio, and he did things his own way. On any level, you have to admire that. It was Duke's world; we were just broadcasting in it.[12]

Young's son Jeff carried on the family radio tradition, serving as a radio instructor at Mt. Hood Community College. Raynes went on to become chief engineer of Eugene's KEZI-TV by 1965 and later turned to teaching as an assistant professor in Lane Community College's electronics division, a position from which he retired in 1982.[13]

In 1968, KMFY became an affiliate of the newly launched American FM Radio Network, which began on January 1, 1968, when ABC Radio split itself into four separate program services: the American Information Radio Network, the American Entertainment Radio Network, the American Contemporary Radio Network and the American FM Radio Network. KFMY was Oregon's first affiliate of the new network.

In 1978, KUGN owner Obie Communications purchased KFMY, and the station's call sign was changed to KUGN-FM effective October 5, 1978. The new owners received permission to raise the station's power to 100 kilowatts.

## KFGR-AM/KRWC-AM/KGGG-AM/KWAY-AM Forest Grove

KFGR—standing for **K**-**F**orest **G**rove **R**adio—signed-on November 16, 1950, with 250 watts on 1570 KHz. The station was owned by Irving Vincent Schmidtke, who was also the station's general manager and chief engineer. Other staff included Schmidtke's wife, Eleanor, who served as the women's director, and Robert Roberts, who was program director. KFGR's studios and transmitter were located on Sunset Drive between 26th and Willamina Avenues.

Lois Olson replaced Roberts as program director in 1952, but by then the station must have been struggling and in 1953 Schmidtke added the program director assignment to his own. On December 28 of that year, the station changed call signs to KRWC, standing for Radio Washington County, and raising its power to one kilowatt on September 1, 1955. On September 10, 1958, KRWC was sold to the Christian Broadcasting Company for $50,000, although Schmidtke retained ownership of the studio/transmitter building and the land on which it was located.[14]

The station's call letters were re-conceived by the new owners as Keep Right With Christ and KRWC, now known as the "Station of Inspiration," KRWC embarked upon programming that it described as cultural and religious.

Schmidtke apparently wished to recover his land and building for another of his businesses, Smitty's Radio and Television Clinic, and KRWC moved to a mobile home located at 2740 Pacific Avenue on October 1, 1958. Christian Broadcasting apparently decided KRWC was not sufficiently successful and sold it to Triple G Broadcasting Company for $47,500 on November 8, 1959.

The new ownership included Lester L. Gould, Dorothy R. Gould, Leroy A. Garr and Esther L. Plotkin. Lester Gould was president. With a nod to the owners' initials, Triple G promptly changed the station's call sign to KGGG on December 1 and assumed a new slogan, "The Voice of the Valley." At times, KGGG also called itself "The Station with a Smile at the Top of the Dial." Patrick W. Larkin and his wife, Jean, became KGGG's co-managers under the new ownership.[15]

Triple G's ownership was short and it sold KGGG to group owner Crawford Broadcasting Company for $65,000 in fall 1960. Headed by Dr. Percy B. Crawford, the company changed the station's call sign to KWAY (standing for **K-WA**shington-**Y**amill counties) on January 1, 1961. The station used the slogan "K-Way." Rick Blakely was its station manager and chief engineer, and with his wife, Pixie Blakely, served as program director.

On June 1, 1963, KWAY was sold to fuel dealer Harold O. Savercool for $37,500. His son, Paul W. Savercool, became the station's president and general manager, but in early 1965, Harold Savercool assumed the presidency and Robert T. Fletcher became general manager.

Clearly, things were not going well for KWAY, which was reflected in a sharp drop in the station's value between 1960 and 1965. On October 31, 1965, KWAY permanently left the air. The last song it played before its final sign-off was "Eve of Destruction" by Barry McGuire, which was a hit that summer. Some sources indicate that the station was "removed from the air." Its license was returned to the FCC for cancellation in late 1966.

## KAJO-AM Grants Pass

On August 15, 1957, Grants Pass's second AM station and third radio station, KAJO, signed-on at 1270 KHz with one kilowatt. At the time, the station was owned by a 50-50 partnership between James O. Wilson Jr. (brother of Clarence E. Wilson, who was then engaged in constructing KBOY-FM in Medford) and James T. Jackson (brother of Philip D. Jackson, who was an applicant for a new station in Weed, California). The Wilson/Jackson partnership used the assumed business name of Grants Pass Broadcasting Company, and the FCC approved its application for KAJO—which billed itself as the "tallest tower, lowest frequency, greatest coverage" in Grants Pass—on May 1, 1957. Wilson served as KAJO's general manager and Jim Jackson as chief engineer. Because of its proximity to the Oregon Caves, Grants Pass has long identified itself with the cavemen, and KAJO's early letterhead featured a caricature caveman speaking into a microphone.

One of the first things Wilson did for the station was to call upon his lifelong friend, Texan Elzie Parker, "to drop everything and join [KAJO]."[16] The men had been friends since their boyhood in Oklahoma. Parker became a KAJO staple, hosting a noon program that was described in a station publication as "The Early Bird, usually found out when everyone else is in bed. Frequently found swapping lies with Big Jim [Wilson]. Former Oklahoman. Has two mattresses. Raises chicken fat for a hobby."[17] Wilson did KAJO's sign-on programs preceding Parker's broadcast.

KAJO stationery letterhead, c. 1960
WSMB Collection

Several months after the station signed-on, the original partners concluded that they needed additional capital, and each sold half of his interest in the company to Philip D. Jackson "to bring into ownership the experience of Philip D. Jackson and also to obtain additional funds to insure adequate working capital."[18] Eventually Wilson acquired the Jackson interests, and the Wilson family continues to own KAJO today.

## KGRO-AM/KRDR-AM Gresham

KGRO, with a power of 100 watts at 1230 KHz, signed-on at 12:30 p.m. (a time that recognized its frequency) on September 28, 1956. The station's birth was enabled by Oregon City station KGON's move from 1230 KHz, a frequency it had occupied since 1947, to 1520 KHz on July 30, 1956.

KGRO was partially owned by the *Gresham Outlook* newspaper's president and publisher, Thomas B. Purcell, who held 45 percent of that company's stock. The station took its call sign from the newspaper's name (as in **K-GR**esham **O**utlook). Other stockholders included Dr. Herbert H. Hughes, who was Gresham's mayor, and local investors Sylvester B. Hall and Guy E. Mathews. They held 20, 20 and 15 percent of the station's stock respectively. KGRO's studios and 154-foot tower were located on four-and-one-half acres at 1230 Melody Lane. At sign-on, Alex de Schweinitz was general manager, Herb Smith was program director, and Jack Par (sic) and Cal Lehman were announcers. Broadcasting "sparkling music," KGRO operated from 6 a.m. to 10 p.m. daily.

In early1958, KGRO raised its daytime power to 250 watts and by March 1958, the station was referring to itself as K-grow. Perhaps the power increase was designed to boost the station's value because the *Outlook* sold KGRO to Daniel M. Peak on April 11, 1959, for $44,000. Peak took over as station manager and chief engineer and quickly raised its nighttime power to 250 watts. By the end of the decade, KGRO was referring to itself as "Radiant Radio. Hi-Fi and Happy Sounds."[19]

On May 1, 1963 KGRO was again sold—this time for $72,000—to John E. Grant's Action Broadcasting Company. Grant was president, general manager and 40-percent owner, and George O. DeWitz Jr. was vice president. DeWitz also owned 40 percent of the company with the remaining 20 percent owned by Marion G. McKeown, secretary-treasurer.

On June 6, 1963, the new owners quickly changed the station's call sign to KRDR (or "KaRD- Radio) and switched formats from big band to country-and-western music under the slogan "You're in Card Country." The station's DJs were known as "The Card Country Gentlemen."[20] KRDR was the Northwest's first 24-hour country-and-western music station. Ed Keebler was program director, Buddy Simmons was music director, and Dan MacDonald news director.

## KOHU-AM Hermiston

Daytime KOHU bowed in on February 7, 1956, at 1570 KHz with 250 watts. The "Radio Voice for Western Umatilla and Morrow Counties" was owned and managed by Carl F. Knierim, and his wife, Sarah, of Hermiston. KOHU's staff featured E. A. Phaneuf as commercial manager, Don McGowan and John M. Welsh as announcers, Sam Whitsett as chief engineer, and Eleanor Davis as program director and receptionist. KOHU's studios were located at 420 West Ridgeway Avenue. The station was purchased on June 9, 1966, by Robert Chopping, his wife, Margaret, and their son Gerry. The Choppings also owned KAST-AM-FM Astoria at the time.

## KRTV-AM/KUIK-AM Hillsboro

Under the business name Hillsboro Broadcasters, Harold Singleton filed an application for a new station to serve Hillsboro, in March 1954. Because he planned a daytime-only operation, he requested 1360 KHz at one kilowatt, and the application was routinely granted on June 9, 1954. Singleton promptly requested the call sign KRTV, standing for **K-R**adio-**T**ualatin-**V**alley, and the station was rapidly constructed with its transmitter situated at Oregon Highway 219 at a location that would now be 2400 SW Hillsboro Highway in what is known as the Jackson Bottom Wetlands Preserve (three-quarters of a mile south of the city limits). The station's studio was located at 155A South Second Avenue in Hillsboro.

"Your Good Neighbor Station" KRTV signed-on October 29, 1954, and broadcast from 6 a.m. to 5:30 p.m. daily. In 1954, the licensee was changed to Harold C. Singleton (doing business as Tualatin Valley Broadcasters). The station, whose first general manager was Herbert Everitt [sic], claimed over a half million listeners and proclaimed that it was "Oregon's No. 1 Suburban Market Radio Station." It changed call signs to KUIK on February 21, 1957.

## KIHR-AM Hood River

On November 25, 1949, father and son team Pop and Carl O. Fisher, doing business as Oregon-Washington Broadcasters, filed an application for 1340 KHz with 250 watts unlimited time in Hood River. At the time, the 51-year-old father and his 24-year-old son were equal partners in a variety of enterprises, including Tower Sales and Erecting Company and C. H. Fisher and Sons (a sales agent for Tower Sales and Erecting and Valley Construction Company in Portland). The elder Fisher also held a substantial interest in Cyl-Ray Antenna Corporation, which manufactured FM antennas, and Eugene's KUGN-AM-FM. He had also filed an application for a new AM station in Seaside.

The FCC granted the application for the Hood River station, and KIHR signed-on October 16, 1950. S.W. McCready was the new station's general manager. Hood River finally had its first radio station since KQP/KOIN moved to Portland 25 years earlier (see chapter 5).

Others employees of KIHR during its early years include station manager Don McCutcheon and DJ Robert Lowell Houglum (see

KIHR's Don Norris during the station's inaugural open house, 1950

Radio stations frequently provided stand-up cards like this Christmas display item to retail advertisers to jointly promote the station and help support the client's on-air advertising campaign. c. 1955.

chapter 14). To comply with an FCC divestiture requirement in connection with an FCC grant to Eugene Television, Inc., for KVAL-TV in 1953, Carl O. Fisher transferred his 50 percent interest in Oregon-Washington Broadcasters to his father, as part of the son's acquisition of KUGN, Inc. (see chapter 19). That made Carl O. Fisher the sole owner of KIHR, a position he retained for two years—although in 1955 the Oregon-Washington Broadcasters partnership was converted to a corporate structure under the name Oregon-Washington Broadcasters, Inc. In 1967, Paul Walden purchased the station and began building a new family-owned broadcasting station chain. The following year, Walden secured FCC approval to increase KIHR's power to one kilowatt.

## KLAD-AM Klamath Falls

Following World War II, Clarence E. Wilson and Philip D. Jackson were actively founding radio stations. After 1945, their partnership—and others involving their brothers—constructed/operated stations in Redding, Eureka and Weed, California; Hobbs, New Mexico; and Bend, Medford and Klamath Falls. The scale of their activity even prompted FCC concern over whether C. O. Wilson and Philip Jackson were engaged in "trafficking in licenses" and were in violation of the commission's rules limiting the number of stations any individual party could own. KLAD Klamath Falls was one of their ventures.

The station signed-on at 900 KHz with one kilowatt daytime power in September 1955 and was an equal partnership between C. O. Wilson and Philip Jackson. The station was originally owned by the Wilson/Jackson equal partnership, doing business as K-LAD Broadcasters, but became Wilson's sole property under a partnership dissolution on April 6, 1957, which also conveyed a Bend FCC construction permit to C. O. Wilson. As part of the deal, Jackson received KBOY-AM and a Weed construction permit application—but that wasn't the end of the complexities. At that same time, Jackson was managing KLAD and Wilson's brother, Jim, was an announcer at the station. Jackson's brother, also named Jim, was KLAD's commercial manager. Both of the brothers named Jim were also partners in Grants Pass Broadcasting Company, owner of KAJO-AM.

Following the partnership's dissolution, Philip Jackson in fairly short order arranged a sale of KLAD-AM for $165,000 to a partnership (headed by Burton Levine) that called itself KLAD Broadcasters. Following the July 1958 FCC approval, KLAD switched to 960 KHz at with one kilowatt power daytime-only.

The new KLAD Broadcasters consisted of: Myer Feldman of Roanoke, Virginia, an attorney and special counsel to the Securities and Exchange Commission; Bessie Von Zampft of Miami Beach, Florida, who was married to Martin Von Zampft, board chairman of the Miami National Bank; Rose L. Lerner of Upper Darby, Pennsylvania; and Melanie D. Thurman of Miami Beach, Florida. Rose Lerner was the mother of Arnold Lerner, a partner in Radio Oklahoma and owner of KOMA Oklahoma City, Oklahoma. Melanie Thurman was married to Harold Thurman, president of Miami National Bank and a partner in KOMA.

While Gene Riesen managed the station, Feldman apparently represented the partnership in most matters. When he "undertook a responsible position in government service" in 1961, the partners decided to sell the station because Feldman could not "devote the time and effort to KLAD that the operation deserves and needs" and because "the remaining partners have been dependent upon the advice and leadership of Mr. Feldman."[21] One could also assume that the station had been only modestly successful because it was sold on December 1, 1960, for only $10,000 more than the partnership had paid Jackson for it. The new KLAD buyer, Ogden Knapp, had been a station relations manager for the National Broadcasting Company in New York until July 1960 but relocated to Klamath Falls to assume the general manager position at KLAD. The FCC approved the sale on April 3, 1961.

Knapp retained the KLAD staff, which included Lucille Hutchinson, program manager and bookkeeper; Lee Craig, Fritz Egger and Larry Chaplin, announcer-operators; Douglas Walker, chief engineer and announcer-operator; Bill Grimes, technical director; and Patricia Johnson, continuity director. Riesen was apparently also retained in an executive capacity.

KLAD increased its power to five kilowatts daytime-only by October 1962. Knapp owned KLAD-AM until August 1, 1969, when he sold the station to Radio 960, Inc. (see chapter 27). KLAD-AM did not go full-time on its frequency until the early 1980s.

## KQIK-AM Lakeview

Lakeview's first radio station began as a partnership between Lynn C. Thomas and A. E. Freeman jointly doing business as Pacific Northwest Radio. Thomas had been general manager of KWRO Coquille since 1952, while Freeman was a Brookings logging and timber business-man who also owned a Coquille livestock ranch.[22] Freeman was clearly the "money" man, with assets in excess of $130,000, while Thomas apparently intended to continue managing KWRO while simultaneously serving as manager of the proposed Lakeview station. Their FCC application, requesting a 250-watt day and night operation on 1230 KHz in Lakeview, was filed on February 2, 1956, and granted on July 11, 1956.

Shortly before sign-on, the partnership was converted to a corporation under the name Pacific Northwest Radio, with Thomas and Freeman each holding 25 percent of the stock and each of their spouses a like amount.

KQIK has at times claimed a sign-on date of August 1956, but the station likely began oper-ating in early December because a letter to the FCC dated January 2, 1957, reported that KQIK was operating under Program Test Authority, notice of which had been filed with the commis-sion prior to December 19, 1956.

KQIK's transmitter was constructed at 17968 Highway 395, where it remains today. But the station's studios were initially located at Hunter's Lodge, which is most noted for the adjacent "Old Perpetual," the Pacific Northwest's only geyser. The studios were located in a small, single-story building on the south side of the lodge, several hundred feet away from the transmitter, and were connected to the transmitter with a privately run wire across the inter-vening pasture land.

From the start, KQIK must have had a very difficult time. An early FCC filing suggests that Thomas may have been living in Lakeview at least part-time but by April 1957 "desired to leave Lakeview, Oregon, immediately."[23] Wishing to preserve KQIK, Freeman purchased Thomas' stock for $500 "to enable [Thomas and his wife] to take care of personal obligations."[24] "Only by a valiant effort on the part of the Freemans in April 1957 was the station able to keep its doors open and to remain in operation," Freeman's attorney reported to the FCC.[25]

KQIK was housed at Hunter's Lodge in a small, single-story building not shown in this picture, behind the lodge's left side.

The struggle continued. Lacking experience in broadcasting, Freeman hired Don Anderson to manage the station, but in September 1957, it was operating under FCC Special Temporary Authority to permit signing-off at 7 p.m. in order to keep expenses down. In an apparent effort to expand the station's resources, small additional amounts of stock were sold in May 1957 to Harold Pate (and his wife, Irma) of Brookings and to J. K. Ragland (whose initials stood for Jewell King) and his wife, Etta, of North Bend. This was done largely for the purpose of enabling the purchasers to serve on the company's board of directors.

Normally, radio stations wish to use all of the air time available to them. It was, therefore, unusual for a station whose license specified unlimited hours of operation to seek a reduction in the time it was allowed to broadcast. However, KQIK's financial situation must have remained precarious because in September 1958, it moved to further reduce its operating time to 6:30 a.m.-7 p.m., Monday through Saturday, and 9 a.m.-5 p.m. on Sundays. The FCC's Special Temporary Authority to broadcast less than the hours authorized in KQIK's license was not intended to be a long-term waiver of the station's responsibilities, but it must have reluctantly concluded that formally reducing its licensed authority for broadcasting hours was the only sure means of holding down its operating expenses.

At the same time, the station moved its studios from Hunter's Lodge to 413 North First Street in Lakeview. By 1960, KQIK began a period of serial staff changes. Anderson had departed the station and Harry Kirk was managing KQIK. Following Kirk's departure, the position was held by Wayne Whitehead (1962), Clifford L. Sheel (1963) and Pauline Walsh (1965). By then, Walsh owned the station along with the Raglands and the Pates. In 1966, KQIK moved its studios from downtown to the station's transmitter site on Highway 395, probably to further reduce operating expenses, and at the same time it raised its power to one kilowatt.

In 1968, a buyout of the company's stock occurred with Ernest L. McKinney, who was a Lake County employee, the company's major stockholder and station manager. The company's other stockholder was Frederick Phillips Jr. who worked for Kennewick, Washington's KSNK-AM. Pacific Northwest Radio sold the station on April 1, 1974, to Lake County Communications, Inc., whose president, Ernest Riedelbach, managed the station. Staff included news director Richard Carter, and chief engineer Robert Leland. Sometime during the 1970s, the station, which had a country-and-western and middle-of-the-road format, began a regular morning feature presented by Lloyd Tatro, a community icon who has broadcast *Lloyd's Outlook* at 7:35 each morning for decades. A folksy five minutes, the *Outlook* consists of Tatro acknowledging birthdays, as well as his own version of a weather forecast—which he creates without benefit of weather instruments. Walt Lawton, who worked at KQIK for ten years, remembered: "His forecasts weren't always extremely scientific. He based a lot of his stuff on looking at the clouds [and] how he felt. How accurate is he? About average for a weather forecaster."[26]

In October 1994, KQIK was sold to New Start Enterprises, Inc., headed by Art Collins, who was both general manager and news director. By then an ABC Direction Network affiliate, the station changed call signs to KRIT on October 21, 1994, but very quickly returned to its original KQIK call sign on November 7 of that year.

On April 9, 1999, KQIK was sold for $190,527 to Clause Charitable Remainder Trust, which was headed by trustee Beverly J. Clause. The price included KQIK-FM, which had been launched in 1987.

## KGAL-AM Lebanon

Throughout the time Gordon Allen was working as an account executive at KSLM-AM Salem, from 1946 to 1948, he wanted to move up.[27] In 1948, he went to KYAK-AM Yakima, Washington, as that station's executive director and business manager and then moved on to WGEZ-AM in Beloit, Wisconsin, as general manager from January to July 1950. But Allen wanted to own his own station, and while in Beloit, he filed an application for a new one kilowatt station on 930 KHz in Lebanon. The FCC granted a construction permit on October 4, 1950, with the call sign KGAL. The station signed-on November 1, 1951, from its six-room studios in the Marion Hotel.

But Allen had much bigger ambitions than just starting KGAL. On August 24, 1951, he changed his KGAL ownership from a sole proprietorship to a corporation named Linn County Broadcasters, Inc., in which he held 59.1 percent of the stock. Other stockholders included Harold Singleton at 9.9 percent; Donald F. Whitman, former KOIN production director, at 20 percent; and Kathryn B. Hayden, whose husband owned the *Lebanon Express* newspaper, at 10 percent.[28] Holding 1 percent of the company, Allen's wife, Madeline, rounded out the stockholders, and served on the corporation's board of directors. Allen was contemplating broadcast expansion and recognized that he needed to bring in new stockholders in order to capitalize that growth.

Shortly after establishing the corporation, Allen filed an application to move KGAL's frequency to 920 KHz and switch from daytime-only to full-time using a directional antenna array. Allen's move drew protest from KVAN's Sheldon F. Sackett, but too late to affect the FCC's approval of the upgrade, which occurred on January 2, 1953.

KGAL became the cornerstone of what quickly grew into a small broadcasting empire and Allen took to recognizing his burgeoning broadcasting family by adding "Affiliated through Gordon Allen Radio Interests" on each station's stationery.[29] Allen's group rapidly expanded to include KBKO-AM Portland; KGAE-AM Salem; KSGA-AM Redmond; KRGA-AM Springfield; and various television applications, including KVTF-TV Eugene.

On July 1, 1961, Linn County Broadcasters Inc., sold KGAL to Radio Wonderland Willametteland, Inc., headed by president Alex Dreier and general manager Glen Stadler. Dreier was an NBC radio network reporter during the 1940s and subsequently worked for various broadcast organizations in Chicago and southern California. The sale to Radio Wonderland

Willametteland began a chain of ownership changes for KGAL. Radio Wonderland Willametteland, Inc., owned the station until 1970 and then sold it to Lebanon Broadcasting Corporation, whose president was Robert W. Chandler. Robert Esty, who had a long career in Oregon radio, was KGAL's general manager.

Lebanon Broadcasting operated the station for four years and then sold it to Juniper Broadcasting—which owned four other Oregon stations in addition to one in Idaho—in November 1974 for $340,000. By the time Juniper acquired the station, KGAL was a top-40 station and was managed by Ronald L. Hughes. Juniper eventually changed its name to Capps Broadcasting Corporation, reflecting the name of its primary stockholder, Gary Capps. On October 1, 1981, Eads Broadcasting Corporation purchased KGAL from Capps. Eads' vice president, Richard C. Eads, took over as general manager for the station, which by then was airing adult contemporary music.

## KDOV-AM#1 Medford

On August 17, 1958, Medford's KDOV signed-on at 1300 KHz with five kilowatts daytime-only power as a "music, news and weather station."[30] It was launched by Kenneth C. Laurence of Gold Hill, who also managed the station. Vernon C. Ludwig was the sales manager and chief engineer, and Paul M. Ward was program director and announcer. By 1960, the ownership had converted to a corporation under the name Medford Broadcasters, Inc., and the station was managed by J. Silkwood, who was succeeded by William Stamps. By 1963, Bill Hansen, who had initially worked for KBOY but had become involved in KDOV's technical operations early in the station's life, acquired control of Medford Broadcasters, Inc., and was managing the station.

Late in the evening of December 15, 1963, a fire destroyed the station's studios and transmitter, located at 2741 South Pacific Highway. A one kilowatt spare transmitter in an adjacent building wasn't damaged and apparently was used to get the station back on the air pending arrival of a full-power unit. However, the daytime-only station, by then on a top-40 "contemporary music" format, was having a hard time competing with fulltime stations. Hansen believed KDOV needed to operate both daytime and nighttime to succeed and he explored that possibility.

In 1966, Robert W. Brier was managing KDOV when it was abruptly announced on September 19 that the station was going off the air "temporarily." Medford Broadcasters attributed the action to "a problem with the Federal Communications Commission and a desire to operate on a full time basis. When KDOV receives authority to operate on a full time basis it will resume broadcasting."[31] While the station publicly indicated an intention to return to the air, it never did. In 1968, Hansen unsuccessfully competed with Radio Medford, Inc., for the frequency, which became KMED-FM/KTMT-FM. He then unsuccessfully sought to renew KDOV's license in 1969.[32, 33]

## KBOY-AM Medford

Medford's third radio station, KBOY-AM, was the result of an FCC application filed in July 1952 by Puyallup, Washington, resident Clarence Wilson and Philip D. Jackson of Chickasha, Oklahoma.[34] The station signed-on May 27, 1954, at 730 KHz, with one kilowatt daytime-only. It was managed by Wilson and programmed beautiful music. Bill Hansen was KBOY's commercial manager; Chuck Field and Paul Ward were the station's announcers; and Delores Berg was receptionist, copywriter and women's program director. Originally, the station's transmitter was located on Medford's Barnett Road which had been subdivided for an early settler's large rural tract, which led the station, whose studios were located downtown at 43 North Peach Street, to promote itself as the KBOY Radio Ranch.

By 1960, the station's original beautiful music programming had at least partially given way to country-and-western with Phil Holman hosting the *Wake Up to Western* program at 5:30 a.m., Monday through Saturday.

## KBOY-FM Medford

On January 20, 1959, Medford's first FM station, KBOY-FM (companion to KBOY-AM) signed-on at 95.3 MHz with 800 watts broadcasting "good music" in "Hi Fi" (short for high fidelity). In the station's early years, it offered Christian programming, general and western music DJ'd by local radio personality Phil Holman among others. In the early 1980s, it moved to 95.7 MHz.

Rock 'n roll was the first specialized format widely offered on radio, and such was the case in Medford when KBOY-FM eventually became Medford's first rock 'n roll station.

## KFIR-AM/KBBR-AM North Bend

Two parties filed applications to build a North Bend station on 1340 KHz. Bay Broadcasting Company—owned entirely by Josephine E. Edwards, who also owned North Bend's Edwards Hardware Store—applied for a 250-watt station on January 10, 1950. Two Portland residents, Donald B. Carmichael and attorney John W. Kendall, served on Bay Broadcasting's board of directors as secretary/treasurer and vice president respectively.

On April 6, 1950, Bartley T. Sims filed an application for the same frequency. Various parties, including the North Bend Chamber of Commerce, quickly endorsed Edwards' application, complaining that Sims wasn't even a local resident.

Bay Broadcasting requested an FCC hearing to decide between the two applicants. Sims quickly asked that his application be dismissed, and the commission granted Bay Broadcasting's application on July 7. Liberty network affiliate KFIR signed-on in February 1951 from its studios and transmitter located on The Glascow Road (East Bay Drive), one-half mile east of U.S. Highway 101.

At sign-on, Roger L. Spaugh, who managed the station, was the corporation's secretary/treasurer, replacing Carmichael. Following the Liberty network's demise on May 26, 1952, KFIR affiliated with CBS radio near the end of that year, and the station seems to have opened downtown studios at 1937 Union Avenue by 1954 (see chapter 14). Around 1960, KFIR changed its call sign to KBBR.

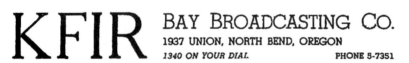

KFIR stationery letterhead, c. 1951. The station had recently joined the Liberty Broadcasting System and typed its new affiliation over an earlier "Progressive" broadcasting reference.
WSMB Collection

## KBCH-AM Oceanlake

Robert G. Beattie established Electronics, Inc., which applied for a 250-watt station on 1400 KHz in Oceanlake on September 30, 1954. The station signed-on as KBCH on May 27, 1955, from its studios at the corner of Columbus Street and Knobb View Avenue.

Portland resident Willard L. Guthrie, who had previously worked at KWRO Coquille, was vice president and Pat Seldon Mason of Camas, Washington, was secretary. Beattie, Guthrie and Mason were equal shareholders in the new company. Beattie and Guthrie hailed from Portland's KPDQ, where Beattie had been chief engineer since 1952 and Guthrie program director for the same period. Mason, the only corporate officer who wasn't a broadcaster, owned a skating rink and ballroom, Wagon Wheel Park, in Camas and later became KBCH's station manager.

Robert Chopping, who was working in logging in Lincoln City while KBCH was being planned, found himself suddenly out of work when weather shut down logging operations. Chopping's wife was working as a bookkeeper for the KBCH partners, and because the station had no building of its own, she worked in a bedroom of the Choppings' home. When one of the partners was there on business, he learned that Bob was heading to Portland to look for work and invited him to work for KBCH—despite the fact that he had no previous radio experience. Thus began Chopping's 36-year-long radio career. Eventually, Chopping managed KBCH but left to work for Sheldon Sackett's KOOS in Coos Bay because "there was constant fighting between the three [KCBS owners] which became unpleasant" for both Choppings.[35]

Guthrie sought to sell his shares to William B. Comer, a step that was opposed by Pat Mason, who protested to the FCC. Ultimately, Comer did become KBCH's manager in 1956. By then, several of Comer's relatives were staffing the station, including Clayton S. Comer as general manager and Connie Comer as women's director. Don Lyle was news director, Hazel Smith was promotions manager and Ralph Heyser was chief engineer and farm director.

KBCH struggled and ultimately failed. Yaquina Radio, Inc.—which owned KNPT-AM Newport—took control of KBCH on November 16, 1959. According to KNPT's Tom Becker, "the Lincoln Bank said if [I] took it over they'd finance it. So I never had a dime in it. I got it into the black and [then] I sold it."[36] The sale took place on March 1, 1974.

## KUMA-AM Pendleton

KRWC-AM was Pendleton's only local radio station until Pop Fisher decided to build one in the "World's Roundup City." Like other stations that Fisher started, he formed a partnership, Pendleton Broadcasters, with his wife, Edna, to apply for the license. Its application for a one-kilowatt daytime-only station on 1370 KHz was filed on February 7, 1955, and granted on May 11 of that year.[37] Fisher learned that the maritime ship Seapearl was due to abandon its radio call sign KUMA and hastily requested it shortly before the station signed-on.

KUMA studios December 1954, shortly before sign-on

Ted Smith (center) reporting as governor Tom McCall (right) presents an award at the Pendleton Roundup.

WSMB Collection

Ted Smith had been managing KRWC, but as he later recalled, "it became evident that Pendleton was going to get a second radio station and I didn't want someone else to do it." So in 1955, Smith joined Fisher's effort as the new station's general manager. In August of that year, Smith notified the FCC that construction had been completed and that program tests were scheduled to begin August 17. But his attempt to file that notification was unsuccessful and some mystery, therefore, surrounds KUMA's actual sign-on date. The station subsequently published its official sign-on date as noon on August 26, although the FCC authorized an October 8 sign-on following resubmission of the missing application.

In any event, Smith recalled that the station signed-on from its studios at 1815 Southwest Emigrant Street with A.C. "Art" Holmes, president of the Pendleton Chamber of Commerce, throwing the switch at high noon. KUMA's transmitter was located on Riverside Avenue on property purchased from the John Nooy family. Smith also recalled that the daytime-only operation had serious drawbacks "especially in the short months of winter," and KUMA soon sought to switch to full-time operation on 1290 KHz with five kilowatts and a directional tower array—a change that occurred on October 14, 1956. Because it had become Pendleton's most powerful station, KUMA attracted the ABC Network affiliation away from KRWC in 1960. Along with Smith, the station's early staff included Willie Slater, Jack Web, Howard Schwartz and Bob Eaton, who served as the station's engineer.

## KUBE-AM Pendleton

KUBE (standing for **K-U**matilla-**B**roadcasting-**E**nterprises) was founded by John M. Carroll, who had owned a Pendleton farm implement business since 1940. Carroll, also a long-time amateur radio operator, believed that Pendleton was large enough to support another local station in addition to KRWC and submitted his FCC application under the business name Umatilla Broadcasting Enterprises. KUBE signed-on June 26, 1956, with one kilowatt operating at 1050 KHz daytime-only.

KUMA signed-on following Carroll's submission of his KUBE application, so KUBE actually turned out to be Pendleton's third local radio station instead of its second, although it was the only station that was locally owned. Unfortunately, KUBE quickly ran into serious financial difficulty that was evident from the station's letter to the FCC dated June 25, 1957. It requesting authority to sign-off at 6 p.m. in the summer months when the daytime-only station would nor-

# UMATILLA **KUBE** BROADCASTING ENTERPRISES

## 1050 KCS ✦ 1000 WATTS

236 S. E. 1ST.

TELEPHONE CR 6-1961

PENDLETON, OREGON

KUBE stationery letterhead, c. 1960
WSMB Collection

mally have been on the air later. Whether to hold onto key staff or to secure needed capitalization, Umatilla Broadcasting Enterprises filed an FCC transfer of control request on February 19, 1958, "to allow members of the present KUBE Staff to buy into the Broadcast Station." Robert E. Thomlinson had departed from his long-time KGW assignment to become KUBE's manager at sign-on, and the FCC request proposed transferring station ownership to a newly formed corporation, Umatilla Broadcasting Enterprises, Inc., and dividing its shares equally between Carroll and Thomlinson (who contributed $5,000 for his stock). However, the handwriting must have been on the wall, at least in Thomlinson's eyes, because just nine months later he sold his shares back to Carroll and left KUBE shortly thereafter.[38] He was succeeded as manager by Paul A. Schumacher.

By 1960, KUBE appeared to be gaining strength. It had a net worth of approximately $8,500 and began fully using its available air time—but things quickly started to go awry. A year later, the station had a negative net worth. By 1963, the station (which was then being managed by James L. Hyndrick) was having a hard time paying its bills.[39] KUBE went silent, but in a burst of hope, bravado or desperation filed for renewal of its license. A suspicious FCC sent an inspector from its Portland office who found that the tower had been dismantled, the transmitter removed and the studios were up for rent. When Carroll failed to reply to an FCC request for explanation, the commission terminated KUBE's license on December 4, 1964.[40]

## KPAM-AM Portland

Stanley Goard and his partners had been operating Portland's KPFM since 1946 but FM had proven to be financially risky, which led Goard to conclude that an AM-FM station combination would provide additional strength. Goard's group, doing business under the name

KPAM-KPFM stationery letterhead c. 1955

Broadcasters Oregon Ltd., filed an FCC application for a daytime-only one kilowatt station on 580 KHz, a step that drew a complaint from Eugene's KUGN, which operated on 590 KHz. Broadcasters Oregon Limited, choosing not to fight KUGN, switched its application to 1410 KHz, and the FCC granted it on June 6, 1951, under the call sign KPAM. Operating from their FM station's Healy Heights transmitter site located at 4700 SW Council Crest Drive, KPAM signed-on September 20, 1951, and simulcast considerable portions of KPFM's classical, opera and organ music programming. KPAM-KPFM also experimented with stereo broadcasting using the AM and FM stations to individually carry the left and right channel stereo signals.

While KPAM predominantly simulcast KPFM on December 1, 1973, it ceased broadcasting what had by then become KPFM's top-40 format and launched its own "oldies" format. Simultaneously, the station changed call signs to KLSC standing for **K**-c**L**as**S**i**C**. The KLSC oldies format endured until April 30, 1976, at which time the AM station reverted to simulcasting KPFM's top-40 format and returned to its original call sign of KPAM (see also chapter 14).

## KBEV-AM Portland

KBEV is the station that never was. While an application for the 1010 KHz one-kilowatt daytime-only Portland station was granted to James R. Roberts of Farmington, Missouri, on September 6, 1956, Roberts was never able to capitalize the station's construction. On July 31, 1958, he sold the construction permit for $5,000 to Coast Broadcasting Corporation, headed by engineer Dawkins Espy of Beverly Hills, California. Espy was no more successful at raising the necessary funds to build KBEV. Following an abortive 1959 sale of the construction permit, the KBEV project went into a bankruptcy from which it never recovered. The FCC cancelled KBEV's construction permit in 1966, although the 1010 KHz frequency was eventually activated in Milwaukie as KZRC in 1988 (see chapter 27).

## KRCO-AM Prineville

Prineville's KRCO was Oregon's first station of the 1950s.

Its owner, Radio Central Oregon, was incorporated by Collin R. "Bob" Matheny along with a number of his then-present or former co-workers. Matheny had been general manager of KYJC from July 1947 through February 1949 and was joined in forming Radio Central Oregon by other former KYJC staffers. Robert M. Bruce had been KYJC's sales manager for several months ending in February 1949. Chester J. Stuart had been chief engineer. Matheny was also joined by Norbert A. "Mike" Misksche, who came to KRCO as program director but was also president of Radio Central Oregon, Inc., by 1951. Matheny's wife, Rita, was the station's first traffic director.

KRCO tower being erected, January 1950 sign-on ad

Other stockholders included CPA and Portland resident Howard N. Dietrich; Dietrich's partner in the CPA firm, J. W. Oswald; Paul B. Kelly, owner of a Prineville lumber company; Oregon Legislator (and later U.S. Senator) Wayne B. Morse; rancher Robert T. Lister; and farm owners Claude F. Williams and Roscoe Hopper, both from Prineville. Williams offered a portion of his ranch, on which he granted a perpetual easement for $500, for the station's tower and radial field.

An FCC application requesting daytime-only use of 690 KHz with one kilowatt power was filed on April 25, 1949, and granted by the FCC November 16, 1949. KRCO signed-on January 31, 1950, from its studios located on Madras Road.[41]

KRCO was co-founded, owned and managed by Bob Matheny, from 1950 to 1979.

With stock subscriptions totaling $28,800, the company was tightly capitalized and devoted considerable attention to the careful purchase of necessary equipment and items.

On February 1, 1979, Bob Matheny sold KRCO to High Lakes Broadcasting Company, which was owned by John S. Kendall, a broadcast executive who moved to Prineville from Dallas, Texas, upon the station's purchase. Kendall, who also launched KRCO-FM (see chapter 27), was also the grandson of John C. Kendall and the son of prominent Portland broadcast attorney John W. Kendall (see chapter 7). By 1981, he had led KRCO into affiliation with Mutual Broadcasting. Kendall owned the station until December 1, 1995, when he sold it to Jonathan Mann, a veteran member of the New York City music industry who had moved to Eugene.

*Courtesy of John S. Kendall*

John S. Kendall owned KRCO from 1979 until 1995.

## KPRB-AM/KSGA-AM/KJUN-AM/KPRB-AM Redmond

On March 9, 1951, partners Harold C. Singleton and W. Gordon Allen—under the assumed business name Redmond Broadcasting Company—filed an FCC application for a 250-watt radio station on 1240 KHz for Redmond. Singleton, who had been KGW's chief engineer since 1933 and planned to remain there, was the secretary/treasurer. He had also been part-owner of Walla Walla Broadcasting Company/KWWB since 1946. He had an extensive technical background working both as a consultant and an applicant/owner of various other broadcasting properties. Allen had worked in an executive capacity at KSLM, KYAK and WGEZ between 1945 and 1950 before launching KGAL in Lebanon in 1950.[42] At the time of the Redmond filing, he was also an applicant for a new station in Salem.

The commission granted Redmond Broadcasting's application in March 1952 and assigned KPRB as the call sign. Allen promptly filed a request to change the call sign to KSGA (which may have stood for the partners' initials as **K-S**ingleton-**G**ordon-**A**llen) and the station signed-on in October 1952 as an ABC network affiliate.[43]

It seems likely that Singleton and Allen filed the KPRB/KSGA application with the intent of founding the station and then selling ownership interests to others, both to help capitalize the construction as well as to take some profit from successfully securing the frequency. A new corporation—Juniper Broadcasters, Inc.—was formed for that purpose. F. Gilbert Lieser, an experienced broadcaster, purchased 39 percent of the new company's stock. Lieser was also brought in as KSGA's manager.[44] Singleton purchased 59 percent and both his wife and Lieser's each purchased 1 percent. The FCC approved the sale from Redmond to Juniper on February 18, 1953, and KSGA became KJUN (for **K-JUN**-iper Broadcasters) on March 15. Seeking to tie itself to the community, KJUN almost immediately began offering Sunday programs featuring members of the Redmond Toastmasters Club, who read a 15-minute Associated Press summary of the preceding week's news.

Orlo M. Bagley and his wife, Thelma, doing business as Radio Station KPRB, purchased KJUN on June 1, 1958, and reversed the call sign back to KPRB. The Bagleys sold KPRB to Donald S. and Rita M. Anderson on September 3, 1959 (see also KCTG/KSGA/KOMB/KNND Cottage Grove elsewhere in this chapter).

Richard E. Combs purchased KPRB on January 13, 1970, but on March 1, 1975 sold it to Big Sky Broadcasters, Inc., originally headed by president/station manager Ronald E. Post. By the time of the sale to Big Sky, the station had affiliated with the American Information Radio Network. Shortly thereafter, Bill Moller became president of Big Sky, but the station was transferred to BBS Communications (also headed by Moller) on March 23, 1978.

KJUN stationery letterhead, c. 1955

California-Oregon Broadcasting, Inc., (COBI) acquired BBS on July 30, 1980, but the station was subsequently transferred to Don Smullin, son of Bill Smullin. He acquired a number of radio properties in the name of KRC Broadcasting as part of a division of COBI's radio properties, which occurred when Don Smullin left COBI to start his own business. On March 3, 1989, Don Smullin sold KPRB to Don McCoun, owner of KUIK-AM Hillsboro. Subsequently, KPRB-AM failed and the license was remitted to the FCC on August 1, 1994.[45] In June 2004, a new station, KRDM, signed-on the 1240 KHz frequency in Redmond. KRDM, however, is an entirely new station unrelated to KSGA/KJUN/KPRB-AM.

## KRXL-AM/KQEN-AM Roseburg

On September 19, 1950, under the corporate name of Umpqua Broadcasters, Inc., KRXL signed-on in Roseburg with 250 watts on 1240 KHz. The company's president was Donn W. Radebaugh and the station was represented by John W. Kendall. KRXL's studios and transmitter were originally located at 1640 Medford Street in Roseburg, and the station's initial staff consisted of Iris Rise Helliwell, general manager; Del McKay, program director; Jerry Oliver, sports director; Lon D. Hunt, commercial manager; and Ralph E. Smith, chief engineer. Some Mutual Broadcasting System programs had previously been carried by Roseburg's KRNR, which became a CBS Network affiliate on October 10, 1952. This cleared the way for the Mutual-Don Lee Network affiliation to move to KRXL (which occurred by December 1963). The station's call sign was changed to KQEN around 1959 or 1960.

## KYES-AM/KRSB-AM/KTBR-AM Roseburg

Douglas Broadcasters, Inc., was founded in 1955 by E. Leroy Hiatt, who had worked at Roseburg's KRNR since 1943 and managed that station beginning October 1, 1949. His FCC application for a one-kilowatt daytime-only station at 950 KHz was filed on March 15, 1955. Originally, the application was competitive with Harold Singleton's application for KYNG Coos Bay, but Singleton switched his proposed Coos Bay station to 1420 KHz, which paved the way for a smooth sign-on for KYES in November 1955 (see KYNG, this chapter).

KYES's transmitter was located two miles south of the Roseburg Post Office in a pasture near McLain Avenue (where it remains today), and the studios were at 762 SE Pine Street. Leroy Hiatt was president, general manager and chief engineer of the station, and Warren Ward was commercial manager. While Hiatt remained president, Kenneth Bushey took over as general manager in 1959. He was succeeded by Elliott Motschenbacher, who also became president of Douglas Broadcasters, Inc., around 1967. Motschenbacher remained in those positions until 1981, when

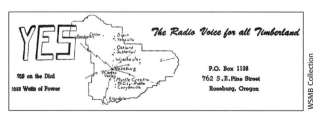

KYES stationery letterhead, c. 1955

KYES was purchased by Bcst House, Inc. Karen Worden was president and her husband Tom was general manager under Bcst House. The Wordens, who also owned KRSB-FM Roseburg at the time, changed KYES-AM's call sign to KRSB-AM at the time of the purchase (see chapter 27).

The station changed its call letters to KTBR on October 1, 1987, concurrent with its station's purchase by K/S Riggs Broadcasting. It became a public radio station, when it was purchased by the JPR Foundation, Inc., on April 19, 2002, and is still associated with the Jefferson Public Radio network of stations.

## KGAE-AM/KGAY-AM, Salem

With a strong engineering background, W. Gordon Allen did his own engineering research before filing an application for a new daytime-only station on 1120 KHz with 250 watts for Salem, Oregon. Allen partnered with John B. Truhan to file the application on January 10, 1951. Subsequently, the Allen/Truhan partnership brought in a third, Justin H. Clark, with each partner having apparently invested $6,000 in the undertaking. It was jointly in their names that the FCC issued the station's construction permit on September 19, 1951, and the call letters KGAE were promptly assigned. True ownership of the Salem station would, however, remain the subject of considerable litigation for five years.

Shortly after receiving a construction permit, KGAE applied to switch to 1430 KHz with one kilowatt daytime power and that change was approved on May 1, 1952. The station apparently began broadcasting around May 10, 1952, which was the date upon which the station sought FCC Program Test Authority. Studios were located in the Marion Hotel at sign-on but were subsequently relocated on August 1, 1954, to KGAE's transmitter site at Carrol Avenue and Lancaster Drive in Salem.

Allen kept the FCC busy with documents and frequently filed complaints, inquiries or cross-applications in connection with any number of radio and television applications/station modifications in various parts of Oregon. The ownership struggle that ensued over KGAE, however, was unusually protracted and intense.

On September 2, 1954, the licensee of KGAE filed an FCC assignment application to switch the license from partners Allen, Truhan and Clark to a new corporation, KGAE, Inc. That step produced a wave of litigation that ultimately extended to the Oregon Supreme Court. Clark alleged that Allen and Truhan had jointly sought to convey the partnership's principal asset, the KGAE license, to the corporation without having bought out his interest, thus depriving him of the value of his partnership investment. He claimed that "since the day I first invested $6,000.00 cash in this station I have never received one cent of return for my one-third share of the station although both Allen and Truhan have each taken substantial sums of money from it."[46]

In his suit, Clark sought an accounting of the partnership because "it was apparent to me that I was being 'frozen out.'"[47] Allen and Truhan undertook various legal actions to forcibly extinguish the partnership with Clark—which he understandably opposed. The trial record reports various alleged improprieties, including the allegation that Allen forged Truhan's signature on the initial partnership agreement to bring Clark in as an equal partner.

Correspondence filed with the FCC on March 14, 1956, reports that the matter had been appealed to the Oregon Supreme Court. The FCC subsequently received copies of the numerous court pleadings, filings and depositions that ensued. Clark asked the commission not to authorize the transfer of control prior to conclusion of the litigation, while the Allen/Truhan group argued that the transfer of control to KGAE, Inc., should be approved because Clark had no legitimate interest to preserve.

The FCC apparently didn't relish being in the middle of the civil dispute. On April 11, 1956, the commission approved the transfer to KGAE, Inc., with the stipulation that Allen and Truhan be permitted to purchase Clark's interest in KGAE once the value of his holdings had been definitively established by the courts. Perhaps to help distance itself from the swirl of litigation, KGAE changed its calls letters to KGAY on June 11, 1956, and promoted itself as "Radio K-Gay," according to then-manager Earl Headrich. The corporation duly followed suit, renaming itself KGAY, Inc. Around 1956, KGAY secured a power increase to five kilowatts and billed itself as "5,000 watts of Hi-Fidelity."

Establishing the value of Clark's interest dragged on for nearly five more years before an agreement was reached for Clark to sell his one-third interest in KGAY to Allen/Truhan for $7,045.49. That sale occurred on January 4, 1961. The agreement was no doubt spurred by KGAY, Inc.'s, having already tentatively negotiated the sale of the station to Eugene-based Radio Wonderland, Inc.[48] KGAY, Inc. explained to the FCC that its reason for selling the station was "to withdraw from radio broadcasting in this area and concentrate on pursuing application for TV station in Salem, Ore."[49]

## KEGA-FM/KEED-FM/KORE-FM/KSND-FM Springfield

For Glen Stadler's KEED-AM, 1959 was a busy time. The station had filed an application for TV channel 9 and was engaged in a bitter fight over it (see chapter 19). Testy FCC hearings over the outcome of that battle were nearing conclusion just as KEED-AM's FM counterpart, licensed to Springfield, took to the air with the call sign KEGA on January 25, 1959 (at 93.1 MHz with 1.35 kilowatts power). The AM-FM combination began presenting a "Sunday afternoon stereo broadcast" with the AM and FM stations each transmitting one of the two channels necessary for stereo sound (see KFMY/KUGN-FM elsewhere in this chapter). Eugene was well-served by classical music FM stations, with KUGN-FM offering regular classical programming and KEGA additional classical hours. KEGA, however, also offered Broadway and Hollywood music in its schedule.

The separate identity from KEED-AM must not have been helpful, and KEGA became KEED-FM by March 28, 1959. Around 1968, the station's call sign changed to KORE-FM. In 1976, the station became KSND and later changed to KKNU on February 3, 1993.

## KRGA-AM/KEED-AM/KRXX-AM/KKXO-AM/ KOPT-AM/KLZS-AM Springfield

"Springfield's Own KRGA," owned by W. Gordon Allen, signed-on September 7, 1954, at 1050 KHz daytime—but its arrival did not go unchallenged. KUGN, KASH and KORE all complained to the FCC in January 1954 that the approval of W. Gordon Allen's construction permit could potentially injure their stations, but the FCC rejected their arguments.

"Nifty Ten-Fifty" signed-on from studios located at 2100 Laura Street and was managed by the Pulitzer Prize-winning Glen M. Stadler, who had been a United Press chief in Spain.[50] Other initial staff included Robert Litten, program director; Robert Crites, engineer; Carrieanne Ayres, salesperson and receptionist; Rad Lowden, DJ-announcer; and Ralph Guempelein, salesperson. In May 1955, KRGA was sold to KEED, Inc., the president of which was Glen Stadler. Stadler's wife, Helen, was vice president. The new owners promptly changed KRGA's call sign to KEED. In 1966, a very unusual move occurred when KEED 1050 KHz and another Eugene station, KORE 1450 KHz, swapped dial positions. In 1985, KEED abandoned its call sign and has used a number of call signs, including KRXX, KKXO, KOPT and KLZS since then.

## KRMW-AM/KACI-AM The Dalles

"Lucky 13 on Your Dial" signed-on June 2, 1955, at 1300 KHz as a daytime, one-kilowatt, non-directional station. As was the case with KHFS Vancouver, Washington (later KKEY), KRMW billed itself as a "hi fidelity station," meaning that its transmitter and studio plant had been installed to transmit a fuller frequency signal than was customary for most AM stations. In practice, the difference would have likely been indistinguishable for many listeners.

With studios in the Bank Hotel building "in the heart of The Dalles," KRMW was owned by Radio Mid-Columbia, Inc., which was controlled by five mostly local residents: Jerry Webb, Collin "Bob" Matheny, Hal Newhouse, Chester Stuart and Larry Phillips. Initially managed by Chester Stuart (formerly with KYAK Yakima, Washington, and KRCO Prineville, Oregon), the station featured "music for every mood." It also offered news prepared by news director Chuck Staufacker, who had just completed his studies at the University of Oregon. Hal Newhouse was the station's commercial manager. Jerry Webb, program director, came from KYAK. Farm director Larry Phillips had been a news dealer in North Bend and had earlier been associated with KCNO-AM in Alturas, California. Matheny served as technical director from his Prineville station KRCO. In 1959, the station was purchased by Idaho interests who changed its call sign to KACI. In 1963, it was purchased by Juniper Broadcasting.

## KHFS-AM/KKEY-AM Vancouver WA

KHFS was owned by father-and-son partners Charles A. and Ralph C. Weagant, operating under the name Western Broadcasting Company. Licensed to Vancouver, Washington, the station was issued its construction permit on November 5, 1953, and signed-on July 3, 1954, as a daytime-only station with one kilowatt on 1150 KHz.

With its studios and transmitter located at 5500 Fourth Plain Road in Vancouver, the station described itself as a "high-fidelity AM station" and was committed to a music programming format.[51] Charles had been in radio since 1923, including a 12-year stint as chief engineer of KBPS Portland, and Ralph had been a member of both the KVAN and KXL staffs. It was, indeed, a radio family. Ralph's younger brother, Warren, also announced part-time while he was in high school during KKEY's eventual top-40 format (see photo in chapter 16).

Charles designed and built KHFS while seriously ill, and management responsibility fell entirely on Ralph from the station's inception. A bedridden Charles died 15 months after KHFS signed-on.[52]

The Weagants apparently selected the station's call letters—Kilowatt-High-Fidelity-Station—to promote the station's intended technically superiority. At sign-on, Ernest Crater was the commercial manager, Jack Nino the promotions and marketing manager, and Bryce Howard was chief engineer.

In August 1956, KHFS apparently concluded that the call sign was too obscure a marketing device and requested KKEY, which was assigned effective May 29, 1957. The station adopted the slogan "The KEY Radio Station of the Northwest."

KKEY changed its city of license from Vancouver to Portland on November 29, 1967 and in November 1968 raised its power from one to five kilowatts daytime-only. By December 1969, the station had opened an additional studio in Portland at 1226 West Burnside Street.

Ralph Weagant at the KXL mike, c. 1945

WSMB Collection

KKEY began its long-standing talk format on October 4, 1971 when Jack Hurd, formerly of KLIQ/KLIQ-FM and KGAR, came to the station. In 1975, KKEY began an affiliation with the Mutual network and also added NBC in 1991. Ralph's sons, Craig and Todd, grew up in radio and were both working for KKEY at the time of Ralph's death in 1987.

On September 24, 1997, Ralph's widow, Florinda J. Weagant, sold KKEY, which had been continuously owned by her family since its 1954 inception. The station was sold for $345,000 to Portland radio personality J. J. Mckay, whose real name was Jeanine J. Wells. Mckay revised the station's long-standing talk format by bringing in new network/syndicated programs, as well as locally hosted shows with Bill Sizemore and herself at the mike. The station's Mutual and NBC Network affiliations were dropped at that time.

The station changed call letters to KKGT-AM (for **KK-G**reat-**T**alk) on February 28, 1998, to reflect the changes made by Mckay. On September 2, 1999, KKGT was sold to Bill and Cynthia B. Sizemore for $165,000, and the studios were moved to 15240 SE 82nd Drive in Portland.

# KRIV-AM/KPVA-AM/KVAN-AM#2/KARO-AM/KAAR-AM/ KBMS-AM Camas/Vancouver, WA

In April 1955, Camas-Washougal Radio, Inc., received an FCC construction permit for KRIV Camas, Washington, and the station signed-on February 2, 1956, at 1480 KHz with one kilowatt daytime-only power. The company's president, Gene R. Johnsick, was also the chief engineer of KRIV, as well as KJUN Redmond. Johnsick selected a call sign standing for **K-RIV**er, that referred to the transmitter's location beside the Washougal River.[53] KRIV's other staffers included Donald R. Nelson serving as general manager, program director, news director and sports director and Rod Walters as assistant general manager.

Just six months after KRIV signed-on, the worst Columbia River flood since the 1948 Vanport Flood caused the Washougal to back up and threaten the station's transmitter. It was saved, and at the request of local officials, KRIV broadcast emergency information 24 hours a day. Following the flood, the station requested reimbursement of $1,200 for the overtime help and the sandbagging that had saved the transmitter, but the Camas City Council refused the request. Since the young station's finances were already precarious, the emergency costs put KRIV out of business and forced Johnsick to put it up for sale.

Two KRIV staff members, William B. Murphy and his wife, Cathryn C. Murphy, purchased the station on February 8, 1957. The Murphys changed the call sign to KPVA (which stood for **K-P**ortland-**VA**ncouver on June 6, 1958, and shortly thereafter moved the studios to the Crown-Zellerbach Hotel at 714 NE Fourth Avenue.

Unfortunately, the Murphys were soon involved in a bitter divorce that deeply affected KPVA. In early 1960, Cathryn became station manager, and on May 13, 1960, the station's call sign was again changed to KVAN, standing for **K-VAN**couver. Apparently, the Murphys had actively been trying to secure the KVAN call sign and pounced on it when it became available following the FCC's dismissal of the KVAN-TV construction permit a week earlier (see chapter 9).

On November 2, 1960, Cathryn Murphy assumed sole ownership of the station. Under her leadership, KVAN#2, had a colorful life. It was a relatively minor player in the Portland/Vancouver radio market and struggled through a series of format changes and studio/transmitter locations. Ad sales were difficult, staffing was erratic and paychecks often bounced. On October 23, 1964, United Press International sued the station for non-payment of newswire fees totaling $1,132. Eventually, KVAN#2 couldn't afford the rent for its Vancouver studio/transmitter site, and in December 1961, the station settled on Hayden Island, adjacent to the Jantzen Beach Amusement Park.

Murphy's young daughter, Adah Louise Murphy, increasingly played a role in helping her mother run the station. Using the name "Adah Louise" on the air, she was one of KVAN's Mono Maniac star DJs. She took over as program director in 1966, and on August 1, 1968, crafted a progressive format that drew attention as Portland's first exclusive album rock format. KVAN#2's business side remained erratic, however.

When its leased transmitter site on Hayden Island was sold, the station again needed a new home—a change it could ill-afford. Out of desperation, Cathryn moved the station into a mobile home, which she parked in various locations—all without notifying the FCC. With the station using a long-wire transmitting antenna (instead of a tower) stretched from the trailer to a convenient tree and no running water or toilet facilities, it was primitive. DJs were told that, when it necessary to use the restroom, to put on long songs and walk to the gun club down the road. In early 1970, the trailer was replaced by a house that also had no running water. At the same time, a simple tower was erected.

In the face of such problems, FCC district engineer-in-charge Francis McCann tried to be both lenient and understanding—but the station's deterioration couldn't be ignored. Moving a station without FCC permission simply wasn't acceptable, and KVAN#2's hazardous operation compounded the situation. When its license renewal was set for review on March 3, 1972, the hearing examiner recommended against it, saying: "Rarely has there been a license of this commission who has been so seriously deficient in the conduct of the affairs of a station as Mrs. Cathryn C. Murphy, nor so lacking in candor."[54]

Since revocation of the station's license would have left Cathryn Murphy essentially destitute, the commission, spurred by McCann, authorized a transfer of KVAN#2's license from Murphy to her mother, Ada C. Brown, in November 1972—with the proviso that Brown would sell the station within six months. That outcome enabled the family to convert the station's value into cash.

On February 22, 1974, the station was sold to New Broadcasting Corporation for $150,000. The buyer was 90-percent owned by Howard R. Slobodin, its president, with the balance of the stock held by his brother Alan. Continuing a progressive format, the station used the slogan "You're driving home in your K-Van." The staff included program director Bob Ancheta ("the Big BA"), Gloria Johnson, Mike Waggoner and Jeff Clarke (whose air name was Freddy Flack).[55]

Former Capitol Records representative Stan "the man" Forman recalled his visits to KVAN#2 beginning in 1976:

> The studios had a real gang-plank walkway to get to the front door. There was no indoor plumbing. The toilet was in another building about 50 yards from the studio. When I walked

in, a couple of doggies got up from the front office and moved on. The GM, we later called him "Dr. Slo" [Howard R. Slobodin] was sitting behind a desk cleaning a pistol, a Smith & Wesson 38. He was wearing a vest, cowboy hat and boots, which were propped up on the desk as he cleaned the gun. They played a lot of music and reported to the trades and Portland music retailers loved them because they played mostly new music and, of course, the record companies loved them, too, for the same reason. I have to say, it was the funkiest radio station I have ever seen but the place had soul and they broke a lot of acts.[56]

Following the 1972 revocation hearing, which it barely survived, the station retained its historic call letters KVAN until January 18, 1980, when it became KARO. The station's time under that call sign, when it used the slogan "Car Radio," was relatively brief, and the station became KAAR on March 25, 1981. The studios were moved to 6301 NE Highway 99 in Hazel Dell, Washington, at the same time. KAAR joined the ABC Direction Network in 1983 and on February 14 of that year switched to an oldies format. As KAAR, it used the slogan "K-double A-R, Classic Gold" which originally stood for **K**-**A**ll-**A**merican-**R**adio. KAAR left ABC for CBS's young adult "RadioRadio" Network in 1984. In 1985, the station moved to The Tower Mall at 5411 East Mill Plain Boulevard in Vancouver, Washington.

# Endnotes

1. "New Astoria Radio Station, KVAS Is On Air at 1050 Kc's," *Astorian Evening Budget*, May 10, 1950, 1.
2. *Oregonian*, November 12, 1953.
3. Edward G. Olsen and Leo H. Appel, *Then Till Now in Brookings-Harbor: A Social History of the Chetco Community Area* (Rotary Club of Brookings, Oregon: Brookings, OR), 161.
4. Before coming to Coos Bay, Oberst had worked for stations in Mt. Shasta, CA, Medford and Klamath Falls.
5. Olsen and Appel, *Then Till Now in Brookings-Harbor: A Social History of the Chetco Community Area*, 161.
6. Singleton had originally requested 950 KHz, which conflicted with the Douglas Broadcasters Roseburg application. Singleton then voluntarily amended his Coos Bay application and changed frequencies to 1420 KHz.
7. All educational or public FM stations in Oregon are licensed as noncommercial stations. Educational or public AM stations do not have unique dial positions such as the 88–92 MHz FM band, to set them apart from commercial stations. While educational or public AM stations are owned by nonprofit or government entities, they are licensed and/or can choose to operate non-commercially (as opposed to being required to by their dial position). KMHS's commercial AM operation is an exception.
8. FCC notations on Allen, Gordon W., 1953. Letter to FCC requesting call sign change dated February 10 (KCTG/KWGA file, NARA, College Park, MD).
9. It is unclear whether Donald McCormick and Glenn McCormick were related.
10. Decision in the Matter of: Revocation of License of Radio Broadcasters, Inc., Dockets 18079–18084, FCC 70-527, Federal Communications Commission, released May 26, 1970. (KFLY file, NARA, College Park, MD)
11. History of American Broadcasting website maintained by Jeff Miller, http://members.aol.com/jeff560/jeff.html.
12. Posting on Portland Radio Message Board by Radiowoman, on December 18, 2003.
13. Raynes died at age 87 on November 29, 2005. Obituary, *Oregonian*, November 29, 2005.
14. Rev. F. Demcy Mylar, president, became general manager on January 1, 1958 (Craig Adams, www.pdxradio.com).
15. Information about KFGR/*KGGG* is drawn extensively from material assembled by Craig Adams.
16. Josephine County Historical Society, History *of Josephine County, Oregon* (Grants Pass, OR: Josephine County Historical Society, 1988).
17. Undated KAJO publication (KAJO file, NARA, College Park, MD).
18. KAJO FCC Application for Consent to Assignment of Radio Broadcast Station Construction Permit or License, BAP-366 (KAJO file, NARA, College Park, MD).
19. Information on KGRO from Craig Adams, www.pdxradio.com.
20. "Radio Station KRDR Changes Ownership," *Oregonian*, July 8, 1986, B5.
21. KLAD Application for Assignment of Radio Station License FCC Form 314, BAL-4082 (KLAD file, NARA, College Park, MD).

22. Thomas had previously worked for KROP Brawley, CA, as assistant manager.
23. Rowell, Russell, attorney for Pacific Northwest Radio, Inc., 1959. Letter to Mary Jane Morris, Secretary, FCC, dated June 3 (KQIK file, NARA, College Park, MD).
24. Ibid.
25. Ibid.
26. *Klamath Falls Herald and News*, August 25, 2007, C1.
27. Allen had an engineering background. He graduated with a BS degree from Louisiana Polytechnic Institute and did other undergraduate engineering work at Oregon State University, the, at Princeton and Massachusetts Institute of Technology. Prior to the World War II, Allen was an announcer-engineer at WMIN St. Paul, MN, and KDLR Devils Lake, ND.
28. KGAL was apparently an investment transaction for Singleton who was still KGW-AM's chief engineer.
29. During the 1950s, Allen had ownership interests in KGAL Lebanon, KBKO/KLIQ Portland, KSGA/KPRB Redmond, KGAE/KGAY Salem, KRGA/KEED/KORE Springfield, the KSPF/KVTF Eugene construction permit and a TV channel 3 application in Salem.
30. "New Radio Station Goes On Air Here," *Medford Mail Tribune*, August 17, 1958, 3.
31. "Radio Station KDOV Goes Off The Air," *Medford Mail Tribune*, September 19, 1966, 1.
32. "For the Record," *Broadcasting*, July 28, 1969, 60.
33. "For the Record," *Broadcasting*, December 8, 1969, 75.
34. Wilson and Jackson also co-owned KWCO Chickasha, OK, and KPUY Puyallup, WA. ("Broadcast Permit Sought for Medford," *Medford Mail Tribune*, July 31, 1952, 1).
35. Chopping, Robert. Interview with author. Tape recording. Astoria, OR. July 12, 2004.
36. Becker, Thomas. Interview with author. Tape Recording. Aumsville, OR. April 20, 2005.
37. Allen was also an applicant for a new station in Pendleton, for which he was competing with John M. Carroll. Allen alleged collusion between Fisher and Carroll to "impede" his Pendleton application. The commission dismissed Allen's complaint saying it was without merit. (Morris, Mary Jane. 1955. Letter to W. Gordon Allen dated May 11. KGAL file, NARA, College Park, MD).
38. Contract between John M. Carroll and Robert E. Thomlinson submitted to FCC in connection with KUBE Application for Consent to Transfer of Control, dated November 22, 1958 (KUBE file, NARA, College Park, MD).
39. Round-Up Electronics, 1963. Letter to FCC dated January 11 (KUBE file, NARA, College Park, MD).
40. Waple, Ben F., 1964. Letter to Umatilla Broadcasting Enterprises, Inc., dated December 4 (KUBE file, NARA, College Park, MD).
41. The sign-on date is not clear from traditional sources, such as FCC records or *Broadcasting Yearbook*, but is reported in the station's own online history at http://www.krcoam.com/history.shtml, which was accessed on August 16, 2008.
42. Allen had an engineering background according to the FCC application for KPRB.
43. The call sign was changed when the partnership ended.
44. Lieser had previously worked for KYAK Yakima, WA; KANA Anaconda, MT; KGVO Missoula, MT; and KBMY Billings, MT before coming to KSGA on September 17, 1952 as general manager.
45. www.recnet.com.
46. Sworn Declaration by Justin H. Clark presented to Mary Jane Morris, Secretary, FCC, in re: Pending Application for Assignment of License (KGAE, Salem Oregon) BAL-1864, January 6, 1956, 1 (KGAE, NARA, College Park, MD).
47. Ibid.
48. The FCC application for approval of the sale was filed on January 11, 1961.
49. KGAY FCC Application for Consent to Assignment of Radio Broadcast Station License, dated January 11, 1961 (KGAY file, NARA, College Park, MD).
50. The address changed slightly to 2080 Laura Street by 1955.
51. This address changed in 1959 to 5500 NE Fourth Plain Road and, in 1965, to 5500 NE Fourth Plain Boulevard.
52. Weagant died on September 15, 1955 (Warren Weagant).
53. The transmitter's street address was 1916 NE 2nd Avenue.
54. *Oregonian*, September 16, 1972, sec 2, 11.
55. Craig Adams, www.pdxradio.com. Prior to moving to KVAN-AM#2, Clarke had been Jeff Thomas on KBZY and KSLM, Jeff Clarke on KGAY, Charlie Stevens on KISN, and Jeff Clarke again on KQIV-FM and KGON-FM.
56. Post on www.pdxradio.com on May 11, 2008.

# 22

# Play Lists:
# Radio's Changing Face
# in the 1950s

The nation's entertainment options were changing. In the 1950s, television was causing network radio programming to become more sparse in local stations' program schedules. Fewer listeners were tuning in for particular programs—"appointment listening" as it later came to be called. As opposed to tuning in to *programs*, listeners began seeking *stations* whose overall sound consistently appealed to their particular tastes. More stations were competing for audiences that were shifting toward television, and radio stations began developing individual identities, or formats, to capture audiences.

Moreover, 1949 brought the "battle of the speeds," with RCA Victor's introduction of the 45-rpm record, its answer to the 33 1/3 Long Playing (LP) which Columbia Records had introduced in 1947. What no one really envisioned was that the advent of 45 rpm "singles" would spawn virtually an entirely a new radio industry—rock 'n roll radio—in just a few years.

These changes had a profound effect on announcers. Radio of the past had featured vocally precise, highly erudite announcers who presided over live performances and announced station breaks and commercials with great decorum. But as the 1950s dawned, that type of radio was dying, and announcers who anguished over correct diction and dressed in formal attire for work were increasingly becoming anachronisms.

Courtesy of the Oregonian

The KGW String Orchestra at the station's "temporary" KWJJ home, 1947 (see chapter 13)]. (from left) Glenn Shelley (piano), unidentified, unidentified, unidentified, unidentified, Gerry Peterson, Abe Bercovitz, Stephen Paietta

# KGW-AM Portland— Orchestra Disbanded

During the era of network-dominated radio, only independent stations broadcast phonograph records hosted by local announcers, but, in the 1950s, radio's course was increasingly charted by the conversion of announcers to DJs. Music was also changing. Big band tunes of the previous decades had given way to Percy Faith, Perry Como, the Four Aces, the Mills Brothers, Rosemary Clooney and Teresa Brewer. An early 1950s DJ who wanted to play something "edgy" might program one of Johnny Ray's records. Increasingly, DJs were learning how to assemble and present those recordings in ways that would engage listeners, and they were increasingly inventing radio personalities to do so.

Oregon's oldest radio stations and their most cherished traditions grappled with these changes. When KGW-AM, the second-to-last station in Portland with a studio orchestra, disbanded that group in 1954, it was simply acknowledging the inevitable. Radio no longer commanded a large enough audience to support that type of program, and those that musicians originally accompanied no longer existed.

## KOIN: The Last Chord

That left KOIN-AM as the last station in Oregon with a studio orchestra. When KGW canceled its group, organist/pianist Glenn Shelley moved over to KOIN, and the other KGW musicians faded out of radio.

By 1955, even KOIN could no longer afford to program solely live music and for the first time since its 1926 sign-on, the station began playing phonograph records between CBS Network features and the station's own live music.[1]

Radio was clearly changing, but more than any other Portland station, KOIN-AM was the one station that had seemingly changed the least.

Some personnel changes had, of course, occurred. Ted Gamble's death on May 18, 1960, saw C. Howard Lane became president of Mt. Hood Radio and Television Broadcasting. By then, KOIN-AM's middle-of-the-road music was principally coming off phonograph records rather than live performances in the KOIN studios. A longtime CBS mainstay affiliate, KOIN saw its network progressively reduce its programming output. The last network radio soap operas—*Ma Perkins, Right to Happiness, Young Dr. Malone* and *The Second Mrs. Burton*—bowed out on Thanksgiving Day 1960. *Art Linkletter's House Party* signed-off in October 1967. That left only *Arthur Godfrey Time* on the CBS Radio Network's non-news schedule, but Godfrey bid his daily listeners *adieu* on April 30, 1972.

As the 1960s were ending, the KOIN musicians continued to broadcast each day. They were one of only two radio station studio orchestras remaining in the nation—but change was in the air even at KOIN. "Red" Dunning, a KOIN mainstay since Labor Day 1929, retired in 1968, and Fred McKinney took over as director of the KOIN Orchestra.

Bill Mears had been KOIN radio's program director since 1953. In the late spring of 1972, shortly after Godfrey's last broadcast, the noon-time *Come and Get It* program had scheduled one of its periodic audience participation programs. Listeners had been invited to come watch the program, while it originated outdoors in the station's large parking lot. Watching from his second-floor office window while smoking his perennial pipe, Mears was visiting with the author of this book while watching the audience arrive—largely on canes and walkers. He'd seen the audience ratings, and while KOIN was still highly rated, he knew the station's audience was seriously aging. Watching them struggle into the parking lot presented a harsh truth. Taking a draw on his pipe, Mears quietly observed that, within a few years, *Come and Get It* and *KOIN Klock* wouldn't have an audience—and neither would KOIN.

It must have been difficult for Mears, who had been *Come and Get It*'s master of ceremonies when the program launched as *Red's Gang* in 1942. With little choice, Mears pulled the plug on live music shortly after the 1972 parking lot broadcast.

*Courtesy of Blaine Hanks*

KOIN Klock crew late in the show's run, c. 1967 (from left) Dean Norton, Don Bottari, Blaine Hanks, Bob Douglas, Jack Lenard, Fred McKinney

*Courtesy of the Oregonian*

The KOIN Orchestra, which performed for both KOIN radio and television, is pictured here preparing for a TV broadcast, likely the mid-morning "Hi Neighbor" program, c. mid-1960s (left to right) Dean Norton, Jack Lenard, unidentified, unidentified announcer, Don Bottari at the organ.

*KOIN Klock* had been on the air 41 years; *Come and Get It* for 30 years. The KOIN Orchestra—which in 1972 featured Jack Lenard, Kash Duncan, Bob Douglas, Harry Gillgam and Fred McKinney—dated all the way back to 1926. But the group played its final notes during the week of August 21, 1972 with former *KOIN Klock's* staff gathered for the final programs. KOIN promptly switched formats to popular contemporary and adopted the slogan "KOIN's Flipped."

KOIN radio was struggling to compete in the evolving industry, and on May 1, 1977, KOIN-AM-FM was sold for $1.5 million to Gaylord Broadcasting Company (Edward L. Gaylord president, and Lee Allen Smith, vice president). On May 12, KOIN radio terminated its 48-year-long CBS radio affiliation and became independent. [The CBS affiliation moved to KYXI-AM.] That day marked another change when KOIN abandoned its historic call letters and became KYTE-AM and KYTE-FM.

It was truly the end of an era.

## Radio Rocks

Change was everywhere in the 1950s. The baby boom that followed the return of America's GIs from World War II meant that throughout the 1950s a bumper crop of teenagers was asserting its presence. And, just as teenagers have done since the advent of recorded sound, they were rejecting their parents' music in favor of something uniquely their own.

While parents watched *Leave It To Beaver, Lawrence Welk* or *The Rifleman* on TV, their teenage children were increasingly seeking *their* music on *their* radio stations. Thus, rock 'n roll radio was born at a conjunction of technology, economics and sociology.

Rock 'n roll transformed radio—many would say it saved it.

The history of rock 'n roll has long been debated. Variants occur in rhythm and blues (R&B) and jazz recordings of the 1940s, such as Wynonie Harris' 1947 *Good Rockin' Tonight* on the King label. Though likely not the first entry in the genre, the song most prominently identified with the founding of rock 'n roll is *Rock Around the Clock*, which was recorded in April 1954 by Bill Haley and the Comets. It was the first rock song to hit the number one spot on the record charts.

The origin of the term rock 'n roll radio is equally ambiguous. Most authorities cite Alan Freed as the DJ who first applied it to a radio program format, during his time at WHK-AM Cleveland around 1953. Introducing teenagers to this emerging music, Freed created a kind of *sub rosa* "us" culture to which teens felt they belonged. Freed's program featured music that was intrinsically opposite of the music of his listeners' parents, so his program implicitly conveyed an "us versus them" message. This cultural divide was extended by the use of "hip" words that Freed's listeners understood but whose meaning was supposedly unknown to their parents. At least, that was the idea that Freed's program suggested.

Yet, while Freed is generally credited with first applying "rock n roll" to radio, nationally recognized broadcast historian Barry Mishkind credits KPOJ's Dick Novak with first using "rock 'n roll" on the air when playing Bill Haley's *Rock Around the Clock*.[2]

As radio and the music it offered began to change, two Oregon DJs led the way.

## Richard "Dick" Novak

Portland native Dick Novak was raised during the Depression by a foster family. Following his service in World War II, he won a contest that allowed him a trial DJ shift on KGON-AM—and the station quickly hired him. It's likely that he began *Dick Novak's Rhythm Room* on KGON but quickly moved to KPOJ (reportedly on April 11, 1955) by assuring that station's manager that within 30 days he would make KPOJ number one in his time slot, and he did![3] Novak opened every program with a recording of "Open the Door Richard." Eventually, Scotty's Hamburgers, a Portland teenage hang-out located at 1221 NE Sandy Boulevard, began sponsoring the program. *Scotty's Party Line* became part of the Novak's evening—which he broadcast live from the restaurant from 7 p.m. to 2 a.m. Monday through Saturday.

Novak made Scotty's busy and famous. It reportedly served up to 2,000 hamburgers nightly to teens who came to see Novak's broadcast and each other. Eventually, the Portland Police decided that the crowds drawn by the "teen pied piper" were a public hazard and threatened to revoke Scotty's business license revoked if the broadcasts continued to originate there.[4] Novak's response was to don a coat and tie and take his remote broadcast to Amato's Supper Club at 706 SW Main Street, where he continued to hold forth.

Musically, rock 'n roll sprang from both jazz and R&B, which was called "race" music at the time because it was created by and for African-Americans. Before rock 'n roll radio was ten years old, it had fully embraced its R&B origins. Many of rock 'n roll's greatest vocalists, and the rhythm and blues "Motown sound" they grafted into rock, were predominantly black. But in the early and mid-1950s, race music was banned on the all-white radio stations that served most of America.

Novak is credited with being the first Oregon DJ to play R&B. It is speculated that he initially snuck the music past program directors who either didn't know what it was or weren't listening that late at night.[5]

*Courtesy of Wes Bakken*

Dick Novak DJs an Oregon City High School dance, 1955 (OCHS Hesperian Yearbook)

In 1975, when Novak left KPOJ (which by then had become KPOK) he moved to KYXI-AM, where he was heard from 7 p.m. to midnight. Beginning in 1977, he moved to KXL's evenings. In 1978, he went to work for KATU as the station's booth announcer and remained with that station for 14 years before retiring in 1992. He died in Portland in 2002.

## Fitzgerald "Eager" Beaver

Another early Oregon R&B DJ was Fitzgerald R. Beaver. Initially heard in Portland on KPDQ and later over KLIQ, he was known on the air as "Eager Beaver." Off-air, he went by the nickname "Fitz."

Following his work in the Portland shipyards during World War II, Beaver began his radio career at North Bend's KFIR. He moved on to radio work in Los Angeles before returning in 1955 to Portland, where he co-owned the Bop City Music Shop on Union Avenue. At the time, the shop was Portland's only outlet for R&B records, and Beaver began a weekly program on KPDQ devoted entirely to R&B, perhaps to promote his shop. Sometimes broadcasting live from Bop City, the program was highly successful and eventually moved to KLIQ. While Novak's program played predominantly mainstream music and simply included some R&B, Beaver's show played R&B exclusively. Beaver likely

*Courtesy of Vic Condiotty/Seattle Times*

Fitzgerald Beaver standing near the Seattle newspaper he founded, c. 1985

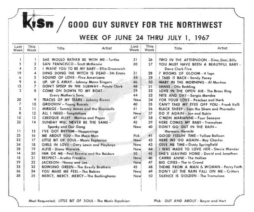

KISN Portland music survey, June 24, 1967

suffered from being on a less-prominent station than Novak's KPOJ-AM, but he clearly influenced Novak and a host of upcoming DJs.

In 1961, Beaver left for Seattle to manage the Pacific Northwest's first black-owned radio station, KZAM-AM. The following year, he left that station to found *The Facts*, Seattle's first African-American community newspaper—which is still publishing.

James Brown reportedly described Beaver as someone who did a lot in the Northwest to provide opportunities for performers like Brown, as well as help build a bridge between the races through his radio programs and the dances he sponsored in Portland and Seattle. At the time of Beaver's death in 1992, Portland city commissioner Dick Bogle said of the program, "It was just a relief to hear the music."[6]

## Promoting the Music

Evolving music increasingly offered radio new life, and stations responded led by Novak, Beaver and others. In January 1958, KVAN changed formats to rock. As station manager Larry Lau described KVAN's new direction: "There will be an entirely new KVAN in 1958. We will introduce new sounds we call 'Instant Radio.'"[7]

KEX was an early station to abandon the old network-centered program schedule. On December 17, 1956, it held an Independence Day kick-off celebrating the station's network-independent status (see chapter 18).

Stations promoted their unique identities in different ways. A new technology called cartridge tape (a professional application of the eight-track tape cartridge) allowed stations to replace electrical transcriptions and reel-to-reel recordings with self-cueing tape cartridges. Used to punctuate programming with jingles, station breaks and other musical identifiers, cartridge tape helped establish a station's personality. Portland's KISN was reportedly the first in Oregon to install such equipment.

Stations of all sizes that switched to rock music heavily promoted it by publishing play lists or supposed surveys of local record sales, which were conducted with widely varying levels of statistical precision. While such playlists helped promote record sales by cueing buyers to what was "hot," they also cemented stations' relationships with record companies and helped strengthen stations' identities.

While rock 'n roll was the biggest change in American music in the 1950s, the biggest change in radio as a whole was the rise of DJ-centered programming for music of all styles. The ability to project a strong, engaging personality through the radio became an announcer's key strength. Many of the Oregon announcer/DJs who began their careers in the 1950s have become radio legends in the state and the nation. In many respects, they became institutions unto themselves, much as stations had been in the previous era. While it was generally DJs alone that became a station's signature, on some stations it was a duo composed of a DJ and a news or weather reporter sidekick.

## Some of Oregon's Top DJs/Announcers

The list of Oregon's most notable DJs/announcers is lengthy and subject to enormous personal interpretation. No list could ever meet the test of any single reader, radio listener or radio professional. Given that challenge, in 2007 the author posed the question "Who are the top Oregon DJs and news personalities of all time" to an online community of Oregon radio professionals—both past and present—who maintain a lively listserv dialogue. While these individuals didn't entirely agree who should be on that list or how they should be ranked, some clear winners emerged.

More than 60 names were submitted. Since Portland is and has been Oregon's largest media market, more Portland-area individuals were nominated than those who worked in other markets. The nominations also reveal an age bias. Few individuals can now recall hearing Oregon announcers/DJs of the 1940s and 1950s. Ted Hallock, for example, was a widely acknowledged DJ at the time but had retired from the air waves by the time most of the listserv participants first listened to radio (see chapter 15). Accordingly, Hallock was never mentioned. Some people advanced sportscaster Rollie Truitt but did so based upon reputation rather than having heard him. For reasons such as these, the list is neither definitive nor balanced over time or geography. Nevertheless, such a list helps capture the flavor of the changes that engulfed Oregon radio in the 1950s and 60s.

Among those nominated as top in their field were (listed alphabetically):

- Dave Allen (Borum) (KUIN/KAGI and in Medford/Ashland)
- Paul Oscar Anderson, "POA" (KISN and KGAR)
- Bob Anthony (KGW)
- Bill Barrett (KKNU)
- Alan Budwell/Kent Phillips (KMJK)
- Jeff Clarke (KBZY, KSLM, KGAY, KISN, KQIV, KGON, KVAN and KINK)
- Russ Conrad (KEX)
- Jerry Dimmit (KLIQ, KYXI, KXL and KKEY)
- Jeff Douglas (KINK)
- T. L. Fuller (KSLM)
- Rick John Garrigus (KICE)
- Iris Harrison (KFMY, KVAN and KGON since 1977)
- Gloria Johnson (KQIV, KVAN and KGON)
- Ron Leonard (KROW, KODL, KUIK, KFLY,KBZY, KYTE, KPAM-FM, KB101, KBOY, KKRZ, KXYQ-FM, KSLM, KKSN-FM, KXPC, KWJJ-FM and KPPT)

- ℂ Tom Michaels (for his work in Eugene and on KISN, KPAM-FM and KEX)
- ℂ Chris "Ichibod" Murray (KEED)
- ℂ John Napier, "Ted Rogers"(KZEL)
- ℂ Dave Paull (KGW)
- ℂ Jim Pierson, "Fenwick" (arguably Oregon's first talk show host) (KUIK, KPOJ, KGW, KPOK and KKEY)
- ℂ Bill Prescott (KASH, KRCK, KBDF, KPNW, KZEL and KGON)
- ℂ Dale "Uncle Fuzzy" Reed (KUGN and KATR)
- ℂ Ron "Ugly" Thompson (KISN)
- ℂ Mike Turner (KGON, KLIQ-FM, KPAM/KPFM, KQFM and KINK)

The group of radio professionals consulted also didn't entirely agree on who warranted placement on a "best of the best" list. However, there was consensus, hands down, that Barney Keep was the number one DJ/announcer. In addition to Keep, there was a general agreement that the other individuals profiled below were among the best of the best.

## Byron "Barney" Keep

Born Byron William Keep in 1917, the Portland native graduated from Washington High School and enrolled at Oregon State University (OSU), where he pursued a degree in forestry. While at OSU, he worked part-time at KOAC, and by the time of his 1942 graduation, he had firmly decided on a career in radio. James Morris, who managed KOAC for many years, remembered Keep as "the funniest student" he encountered during his teaching/radio career.[8]

Barney Keep began his commercial radio career at KXL in 1942 immediately following his college graduation.[9] In late 1943, he moved to KGW-KEX, where co-worker Tom McCall told him he'd "never make it in radio" (see chapter 13). When KGW and KEX split ownership, Keep remained at KEX, where he began his morning program in 1944. His acerbic wit took aim at all manner of men and women, from station owners to politicians to sponsors. Few were safe from his frequently satiric—but never mean—barbs and Keep slowly became a Portland tradition. "Sweet Lovable Old Barn" (Keep loved the initials of this nickname) had married his college sweetheart, the former Eleanor (née) Cleveland, while at OSU, and she was a frequent guest on his KEX program.

Keep's humor and his sense of connection with his audience, as well as the numerous program gimmicks he created (such as reading "Today's Chuckle" from the front page of the *Oregonian* and ringing the "Goody Gong" when he read the Portland Public Schools lunch menu) estab-lished traditions that helped make *Keep Time* an Oregon tradition. His impact was broader than he sometimes appreciated, such as when his affectionate dubbing of the Fred Meyer superstore chain as "Freddy's" became so pervasive that the company adopted the nickname in its advertising.

Hi! I'm Barney Keep the morning man at KEX Radio with a message! . .We'd like to UP YOUR PLEASURE!

Display ad, c. 1975
Courtesy of the www.PdxHistory.com website

Keep's colleague Bob Miller said of him, "Barney spoke to his listeners. He didn't try to be cute. He just tried to be Barney."[10] Keep himself once said, "If you're serving the listeners, if you're giving them what they want, if you're speaking directly to them, then the rest kind of takes care of itself, doesn't it?"

In short, Keep became a Portland radio institution. When he retired on Valentine's Day 1979, KEX staged his final broadcast from Portland's Civic Auditorium to hold the crowd of mayors, governors, sponsors, county commissioners and listeners who had assembled to honor "Ol' Barn." Described by the *Oregonian* as a "four-hour extravaganza," Keep's swan song included his wife—"the

Keep receiving a retirement acknowledgement from the *Oregonian*'s Francis Murphy, 1979.

biscuit burner"—and a host of other figures who gathered to salute the morning radio veteran. Congressman Bob Duncan phoned in, saying, "I've found out that everyone doesn't love me but they do you." Senator Bob Packwood reported: "I would be happy to spend as many years in the Senate as you have on the radio." Governor Vic Atiyeh rang in from Salem to recall some of Keep's special moments on the air and to proclaim that date "Barney Keep Day in Oregon." Tom McCall showed up on stage and commented on Keep's reaction when McCall arrived at the Civic Auditorium for the broadcast: "I saw how you warmed up when I arrived because it was someone who was older than you." Keep rejoined: "You said I'd never make it."[11] McCall spoke eloquently, "There's never been anyone like you, as far as I'm concerned, anywhere in the world on radio or television." Portland Mayor Neil Goldschmidt joined in the broadcast, saying: "I've been practicing this speech for two weeks" to which Keep punted back, "You mean you've been practicing for two terms."

Well-wishers included Portland city commissioner Mildred Schwab, Multnomah county commissioner Dennis Buchanan; and fellow broadcasters Doug LaMear from KGW-TV, Jim Bosley from KATU-TV and Bob Hazen, president of Ben Franklin Savings and Loan, who dated his own broadcast career back to 1948 when he worked with Keep. All joined in saluting "Ol' Barn."

For his final broadcast, Keep did most of his regular program. Reading the Chuckle from the *Oregonian*'s front-page, he dead-panned: "Old disc jockeys never retire, they just go off the record." It turned out that the *Oregonian* had salted the front page with the joke, anticipating that Keep would select it for the broadcast. Keep rang the Goodie Gong and read the Portland Public Schools lunch menu for the day. He selected the music for his final program, which included Monte Ballou's *Green River*, and danced on-stage with his wife to *For the Good Times*. As the broadcast neared conclusion, KEX presented the Keeps with a trip to Hawaii and announced establishment of the Barney Keep Scholarship in Speech Communication at OSU.[12]

Barney Keep retired from radio to "waves of applause."[13] Upon his death in 2000, KEX's "morning-drive gab king" was eulogized by many, including *Oregonian* reporter Norm Maves Jr., who wrote:

> He made his listeners wince, squirm and hide with his understated needle. No social or political balloon stayed inflated for too long when Keep was at his mike, particularly if the balloon was filled with hot air. He made everybody laugh at one time or another as KEX's morning-drive gab king. Keep didn't just live and work in Portland; he was Portland.[14]

# Robert "Bob" Adkins (Addie Bobkins)

Robert Adkins was born in Los Angeles on February 22, 1932. A professional drummer since high school, Adkins originally envisioned a career in the ministry and attended the Lewis & Clark College with that goal—but wound up in radio. At age 20, he got his first broadcasting job at KBKO/KLIQ as part of the Radio Click DJ lineup that launched at the time of the station's call letter change in 1952 (see chapter 14).

At KLIQ, Adkins (working under his own name) handled air shift from 4 p.m. to sunset (when daytime stations had to sign-off). When the station was closed by the Internal Revenue Service in April 1954, Adkins moved on to a station in Aberdeen, Washington, but returned to Portland around 1955 to work weekends at KXL and filling for the station's weekday announcers. Moving over to KEX in 1956, he hosted *Bob's Danceland* from 7 p.m. to midnight weekdays—but in 1957 television beckoned.

In fall 1957, Adkins moved to KVAL-TV for his first show as "Addie Bobkins" weekdays from 4:30 to 6:00 p.m. Seen on both KVAL Eugene and its satellite stations, KPIC Roseburg and KCBY Coos Bay, the program was an immediate hit. Adkins also took a DJ job at KEED on a program that preceded his daily TV appearance.

Ad for the *Addie Bobkins Show* on KVAL/Triangle Television, June 1961

Adkins remained in Eugene until fall 1961, when he moved his TV program—which he continued to host as Addie Bobkins—to KPTV Portland. He also did a weekday slot from 10 a.m. to noon on KISN radio.

In 1964, a major market opportunity beckoned and Adkins left for KPTV's sister station, KCOP-TV Los Angeles, where he created his own special world on television for southern California. Following his retirement from broadcasting, Adkins worked in real estate, was active in his church and led choruses that performed at senior organizations and in retirement homes. He passed away on February 2, 2005, in Portland.

# Robert Ancheta (The Big B.A.)

Bob Ancheta got his first radio job at KVAN-AM#2 on March 1, 1970, while still a senior at Portland's Madison High School. Ancheta's fascination with radio dated back to childhood and included his building and operating an AM station from his parents' attic throughout his high school days. Using equipment he purchased at Goodwill, Ancheta rigged up a one-watt pirate station whose signal reached about five blocks. "I'd be up there all night broadcasting," he recalled.[15] His neighbors became his fans, and according to Ancheta, "The neighborhood kids came up with the nickname 'The Big BA,'" which he carried into his professional career.[16]

At KVAN#2, Ancheta did a blues program and eventually became program director. In 1973, he moved to KQIV-FM, and when that station failed, returned to KVAN#2. In January 1978, Ancheta moved to KGON-FM, where he did the 10 a.m. to 2 p.m. slot (see chapter 14).[17] In August 1980, he announced that he was taking over the afternoon drive 3 p.m. to

7 p.m. shift at KQFM-FM, an AOR (album oriented rock) station that proved unsuccessful at competing with KGON-FM. He returned to his afternoon KGON assignment in 1983.

In September 1985, the Big BA moved to KAAR (formerly KVAN#2) as program director and afternoon DJ. He became KAAR's general manager on November 7, 1986, but switched to KMJK in the summer of 1987, where he did evenings. He returned to KGON as assistant program director, music

Bob Ancheta at KVAN#2, 1976

director and evening DJ in May 1988. Along the way, Ancheta also began his *Sunday Night Blues* show on KGON.

By September 1991, Ancheta was again doing the afternoon drive on KGON. In 1993, he teamed up with KC Caldwell for the afternoon traffic. Caldwell and Ancheta had great on-air chemistry, so with Ancheta's blessing, she began co-hosting with him in 1994 on the renamed "The Big BA & KC" show.

At that time radio really started to change according to Ancheta: "When [media ownership] consolidation happened, it took me out of the business."[18] After leaving KGON-AM in 1996, both the Big BA and his listeners felt the loss. Two months later, KKRH-FM Earth 105 put him back on the afternoon drive shift with K C Caldwell—in direct competition with KGON—and also invited him to bring his *Sunday Night Blues* program back. After KKRH-FM went through a sale-induced format change, Ancheta left on March 10, 1998, but moved seamlessly to KINK-FM for the *Sunday Night Blues* program from 7 p.m. to 10 p.m. That same year, he also started an independent voice-over business, *Internet Jock*.

## William Calm (John Erickson)

William Calm describes his younger self as a "relentlessly determined teenager" interested in radio. "I was lucky to begin my career at a time when some hardboiled guardians of the old school were willing to mentor a willing learner," he says.[19]

He got his start in news at KBTR-AM Denver in 1968 working under his own name. The next year found him at KLSI-AM Salina, Kansas. By 1971, he was back in Denver, still as Bill Calm, at KIMN-AM. He moved over to Denver's KLAK-AM in 1973 and briefly left for WOW Omaha, Nebraska, in 1974, but he returned to Denver on KTLK-AM that same year.

In 1975, King Broadcasting brought him to Seattle for its flagship station, KING-AM, and suggested that he take an air name. Thus, "John Erickson" was born. The following year, Erickson transferred to King's KGW-AM Portland where he was both news

John Erickson KGW promotional photo, c. 1978

director and news sidekick for the morning drive period. When Craig Walker took over the morning drive shift in 1977, Erickson teamed up with him.

Erickson reflects that:

> KGW Radio was unique among contemporary music stations in the 1970s for the emphasis it placed on news and information. At a time when many stations in our format ran long newscasts on the overnight shift to fulfill an FCC commitment, we placed ours front-and-center, in the drive times and at midday. King Broadcasting Company's corporate philosophy, which President Ancil Payne articulated and we all understood and respected, consisted of three equal goals: to earn a profit, to serve our communities, and to excel. King Broadcasting Company's citizenship ethic pervaded the radio stations, as it did TV, and set a very high bar. My orders were to create a news product that matched the standards of the rest of the station. [In the News Department] we were all very young, mostly under 30, and when we met each morning to collaboratively plan the day's assignments, the questioning of authority was one of our principles.[20]

Soon, KGW's Walker/Erickson duo dominated the Portland radio market. Erickson left KGW-AM in 1984 for KTRH Houston, working again as Bill Calm, and was there less than a year before returning to Portland to rejoin Walker—this time on KKCW-FM/K103. They continued as a very successful morning radio team. Erickson has been called the "dean of news readers" for his contributions to the Portland morning radio scene. While Walker retired in 2005, Erickson remained at KKCW-FM.

## James Howe

From the age of ten, Jim Howe knew he wanted to be behind a microphone. Radio fascinated him, and he knew he wanted to be on the air. Howe often listened to Barney Keep, who was among his radio heroes. After graduating from high school in his home town of Tigard, he hung around at KUIK Hillsboro, which convinced him to pursue a career in radio. Following his graduation from the University of Portland, Howe spent a year at Portland's Northwest School of Broadcasting before landing his first professional radio job at KCRE-AM Crescent City, California—mostly as a disc jockey. He was there only six weeks when he was transferred to a co-owned station in Montana, where he mixed DJing with news announcing. Eager to get out of Montana, he secured a list of open positions at Oregon radio stations and was quickly hired as news director of the one-person KUMA Pendleton news department. Howe recalled his work under KUMA owner Ted Smith:

Jim Howe, c. 2001
Courtesy of Jim Howe

> … I was very green [and] Ted was very patient. I thought Ted was probably the best broadcaster I ever worked for. He really understood the relationship between the radio station and the community better than anybody I ever knew. I really enjoyed it.[21]

But Howe knew that he wanted to be in a big city, particularly Portland:

> I had listened to KEX for years, Barney Keep and all those people. So I decided that I would become their stringer in Pendleton so I used to send them stories and I did that for probably a year or more. One day they said they had an opening if I'd be interested in trying for the job—I did and I got it.[22]

In January 1962, Howe was hired by KEX as a street reporter on a three-person news staff working under news director Pat Wilkins. "It was like getting out of the pickup [and going] into the limousine," Howe recalls. Promoted to KEX's news director in 1965, he gradually became the station's morning newsman and worked with Barney Keep during his last decade on the air. Keep had beckoned Howe into radio and their relationship each morning on the air was easy and close.

Howe also got into sportscasting as far back as the days of Bob Blackburn's play-by-play coverage, when the young Howe provided stats for the veteran sportscaster. Howe continued with Darrell Aune, who took over for Blackburn when he moved to Seattle to become the radio voice of the Seattle Sonics. Then in 1972, Howe inherited the sports commentating job, an add-on to his KEX news director assignment. He retained the sports assignment until 1986, when he relinquished it to concentrate on news.

Retiring in June 2001 after nearly 40 years at KEX, Howe's record was pretty much unequaled as a KEX fixture and as part of many Oregonians' mornings.

## William Howlett

One broadcaster who heard Howlett as a youth and then became a DJ himself describes Howlett as "The gold standard [to] whom I compare other news anchor people."[23] Originally a newspaper reporter, Bill Howlett started out in radio at KUIK Hillsboro in 1957 before moving to KVAN#1 the following year. There, he hosted the enormously popular *Uncle Bill's Bandstand*. When Don Burden purchased KVAN#1 and converted it to KISN in 1959, he fired virtually the entire KVAN staff, including Howlett. KLIQ immediately hired a number of the former KVAN#1 staffers, including Howlett, and four days after KISN's launch, KLIQ jumped into a rock format that was in direct competition.

In the summer of 1960, Howlett returned to Burden's station to join the KISN "Swingin' 91 DJs" as news director. There he did *KISN Action Central News Live at 55* (which became *KISN Total Information* in 1964).[24] In 1968, he began doing *KISN 20/20* news from 7 p.m. to midnight. Before Tom Murphy left KISN in 1965, one of Howlett's regular bits during Murphy's program was an 8:30 p.m. feature called *Meet Your Neighbor*, in which Murphy interviewed a fictitious, wacky guest played by Howlett, who wrote and performed the very popular and funny bits. Murphy recalls: "Bill was truly a 'renaissance man' and a very gifted writer. Some of my happiest memories are of time spent working with Bill. He was truly 'One Of The Good Ones.'"[25]

While Howlett relinquished the news director position to George Sanders in 1963, he remained a commanding presence under the title night news editor until KISN's very end. When the station left the air in 1976, Howlett briefly moved over to KWJJ but later left the microphone to work as a radio engineer. He was engineering for KKEY Vancouver, Washington, at the time of his death in 1984. "When Bill Howlett spoke, God stopped what he was doing to listen! A great broadcaster and the nicest guy I ever met," says colleague and fan Mark Andrews.[26]

Bill Howlett at KISN, *KISN Bugle*, June 10, 1966

# Richard Johnson (Bwana Johnny)

Portland native Rick Johnson was interested in radio from an early age. As a 12- or 13-year-old, he often hung out at KISN late at night. According to Tom Murphy, Johnson was on most of the record companies' mailing lists and loved finding hits he could pitch to his KISN buddies. Relishing his contacts with the KISN jocks, Johnson even engineered an invitation to have Murphy visit his high school. Murphy believed he would be speaking to a group of students, but it turned out to be an opportunity for Johnson to have a private lunch with Murphy. During high school, he was called "Dick," but after he took the air name "Bwana Johnny," he became known to his friends as "Rick."

"Bwana Johnny" at KYA, 1971

In 1964, Johnson got his start in professional radio at middle-of-the-road KLOO-AM Corvallis, where he worked afternoons and early evenings under the name "Dick Johnson." His colleague Bob Kuhn recalls Johnson sitting in the control room after sign-off one night, playing hits and rocking out. When station owner Bob Houglum walked in, Johnson said, "This is what we should be doing in the nighttime," and Houglum decided to let him switch his nighttime program to rock—which was successful. [27]

After competitor KFLY-AM lured Johnson away from KLOO-AM, he progressively worked his way up to larger markets through stations in Kelso, Washington, and Cincinnati, Ohio—where he first took the name "Beautiful Bwana Johnny." He carried the name with him to the morning DJ slot at KJR-AM Seattle. KYA-AM brought him to San Francisco in 1969, and a year later, he moved on to KGB-AM San Diego, where he remained until 1971.

Next, Johnson was off to the legendary WWDJ-AM New York as both music director and afternoon drive DJ. The station was already struggling when a strike by the American Federation of Television and Radio Artists (AFTRA) brought an abrupt format switch to religious programming. Listeners thought it was an April Fool's Joke—but it wasn't—and Bwana Johnny moved on to WFUN-AM Miami.

In 1975, Johnson returned to Portland to work at KISN, where he used the name "Crazy Dick Simms" on the afternoon drive shift. He also served as KISN's music director. But when KISN's license was revoked, Johnson first moved to KGW, working under the name Dick Kilpatrick, and then to KIOA-AM Des Moines (see chapter 23).

He returned to Portland in 1980 to take over as KARO-AM's program director while also holding down the morning drive shift at the Vancouver station. In 1982, he became music director of KLLB-FM Portland/KB101 where Bwana Johnny became "BJ" for the afternoon drive shift. According to Robin Mitchell, who was then the station's operations manager, the switch to "BJ" was motivated by KB101's manager, Ron Saito, who felt that racial sensitivities had changed since Johnson first launched the name "Bwana Johnny" nearly 15 years earlier. Saito was uncomfortable with Johnson using the name at KB101, although Johnson still occasionally interspersed it within his program.

In late 1982 or early 1983, Johnson moved to KKCW-FM/K103, where he did the overnight shift using his real name. In 1983, he moved on to Cheyenne, Wyoming, where he became "Bronco Johnny" DJing country-and-western records. He also simultaneously worked at KLAK-FM Denver using the name "Buffalo Claude Keeley" as a lark.[28] In 1986, he moved to KSND-FM Eugene and from 1991to 1991 was on KZEL-FM Eugene. In 1993, he moved to KODZ-AM Eugene and then, in 1998, went to KKBR Billings, Montana, where he remained until 2000.

Struggling with health issues, he began work in September 2000 as music director for the Jones Radio Networks out of Seattle. He also did music programming and consulting before failing health caused him to retire. He passed away from congestive heart failure on October 28, 2005, at age 59, at an extended care facility in Mercer Island, Washington.

## Thomas Murphy

Courtesy of Tom Murphy

Tom Murphy at KISN, 1961

Tom Murphy grew up in Portland and began his broadcast career as a Grant High School junior in 1957 when he debuted on carrier-current (a non-licensed limited range station) KFOJ, which was owned by Murphy's schoolmate Phil Boyer and was operated from Boyer's family home. In fall 1958, Boyer was working weekends at KPDQ-AM, which was playing popular music of the day, and he got Murphy a weekend shift there. In mid-June 1959, about six weeks after KISN's debut, Murphy was hired as a weekender at the station. Three weeks later, KISN hired him full-time. As one website devoted to KISN put it: "'Tiger' Tom Murphy was KISN 1959–1962!!!"[29]

Because Murphy's original time slot was in the evenings, he started using the phrase "TM in the PM." After about a year on the air, he became "Tiger Tom" not because of a conscious decision but because it was something that drew positive comments after he tossed off the phrase casually during a program. Not much older than the audience he was dazzling, Murphy often drew attention for his involvement in drag racing. In 1964, KISN's then-program director the Real Don Steele moved Murphy to the morning drive time slot but the evening ratings suffered so severely that Murphy was quickly moved back to nights. By the time he left KISN in 1965, Murphy was the only on-air person left from KISN's early days in 1959.

In 1965, Murphy moved briefly to KNEW-AM Spokane before being transferred to KJR-AM Seattle. In Seattle, he dropped the name "Tiger Tom" because:

I thought maybe Tiger had worked in Portland because it just sort of 'happened' and perhaps it was peculiar to Portland and that period of time. [So] as a bit, I called myself the Famous Tom Murphy. Then I thought, what the heck, that wasn't big enough so I called myself 'World Famous.'[30]

In February 1971, The World Famous Tom Murphy headed to Los Angeles to take over mornings for the powerhouse KRLA-AM. He returned to Seattle about a year later, and in 1972, went to WCFL-AM Chicago before moving on to Cleveland's WIXY-AM in 1975. In 1977, he returned to Los Angeles and has remained there.

Murphy was on KIIS-AM from 1977 to 1981, on KPRZ-AM from 1981 to 1985, and on KFI-AM from 1987 to 1988. In 1993, he started working for the Salem Radio Network from Los Angeles, but when Salem Radio moved its operations to Dallas in the summer of 1994, he joined KGRB-AM until a format change took that station to Spanish-language programming. He has remained active and does daily programs from Los Angeles for Portland's KPOJ-AM (which was formerly KGW-AM) and Chicago's WRLL-AM.

## Pat Pattee

Like a lot of other teenagers in the 1950s, Pat Pattee was glued to a transistor radio that connected him to the nearly mythic DJs with whom he identified. In 1958, he built his own carrier-current station, which he called KDAG, in his parents' Portland home in St. Johns. Somehow he even managed to get the station listed in the 1959 *Oregon Blue Book*'s list of radio stations. While he originally intended to be an engineer, Pattee switched to DJing and got his first professional post at KCAP Helena, Montana. He moved on to KWIK-AM Pocatello, which was owned by Don Burden, who promoted Pattee to his flagship station, KOIL Omaha.

Reportedly following an episode in which he was snowed in at the KOIL-AM transmitter, Pattee appealed to Burden to let him return to his hometown. By April 1962, Pattee was back in Portland, joined the KISN Good Guys and took on the KISN overnight shift (generally either midnight to 6 a.m. or 1 a.m. to 6 a.m.), which the station called *The Nightwatch*.

Pat Pattee at KISN, *KISN Bugle*, June 10, 1966

KISN used a jingle package produced by PAMS, a company that specialized in creating station breaks and short identifiers. In the early 1960s, KISN's PAMS package included a special *Nightwatch* theme in which Pattee came in over the PAMS jingle, following its sung portion, and launched his nightly music jam with his unique brand of patter. His announcing style eventually caused him to be dubbed "The Preacher." A phrase frequently used by Pattee was "The Groove Juice Special"—a reference to the older R&B music he liked to feature on his program.

Pattee handled the KISN overnight shift for more than ten years but left the station (before it was shut down by the FCC) because KISN believed the music he was playing—which focused heavily on music of the 50s and 60s—was too dated. In 1973, he went to KLSC-AM, which had adopted an oldies format, and remained there until the station reverted to simulcasting its FM sister station's top-40 format in April 1976 (see chapter 21). Following a period when he appeared in Portland-area clubs spinning oldies music, Pattee moved to the afternoon slot on KAAR-AM Vancouver in September 1983. After leaving KAAR-AM in 1985, Pattee continued to DJ the music he loves in Portland clubs.

# Robert "Red" Robinson

Red Robinson's Portland tour was relatively brief—but memorable. It began in 1959 when he came to KGW quite early in his career but already showing extreme talent. The only entry in the author's Top Oregon DJ's list to be inducted into the U.S. Rock and Roll Hall of Fame, the native Canadian got his start in radio in at age 16 while still in high school in Vancouver, B.C.[31] Named "Red" for his full shock of red hair, Robinson was fascinated by radio from an early age and loved staging pretend shows for his family and friends. When he heard local radio DJ Jack Cullen on the air, he knew what he wanted to do with his life.

From his start in radio, Robinson played rock 'n roll and featured Elvis Presley, Buddy Holly and similar performers at a time when their music was seldom on the air. He had to personally buy black performers' race recordings because his stations didn't stock such music. Robinson recalls having to carry music by black artists "out of the store in brown paper bags 'like pornography.'"[32] His prominence with listeners gave him wide access to performers, and at an early age he was hanging out with Elvis Presley, Buddy Holly, Bill Haley, Roy Orbison and others.

Red Robinson hosting KGW-TV's *Portland Band Stand*.

Courtesy Robin Mitchell Associates

Robinson arrived at KGW in 1959. In addition to his show that aired Monday through Friday from 2 p.m. to 6 p.m., he also hosted KGW-TV's *Portland Band Stand/Teen Canteen* program on Saturdays.

Robinson was lured away from KGW-AM by KJR-AM Seattle but never got to the station because the draft board came calling. He wound up doing a stint in the U.S. Army and afterward returned to radio in Vancouver, B.C.—first as a DJ and later as a program director. He has subsequently hosted many television programs and emceed concerts and was inducted into the Canadian Broadcast Hall of Fame in 1997 and the Rockabilly Hall of Fame in 2000. Robinson officially retired in 2001 but continues to broadcast on a weekly basis in Canada.

# John Salisbury

Originally from Minneapolis, Minnesota, John Salisbury got his start in radio in 1933 at his home town's WRHM-AM, and he continued to work in radio until World War II intervened. Following his military service, he taught broadcasting in Washington, DC, and Minneapolis and then returned to active broadcasting as news director at Salt Lake City's KUTA-AM/KUTV-TV. An avid writer, Salisbury liked to combine his work in broadcasting with writing, and he penned plays, articles and essays for much of his life.

In 1955, Salisbury came to Portland from Salt Lake City to be chief announcer at then-new KLOR (see chapter 18). In short order, he became KLOR's program coordinator and picked up other duties such as hosting the station's Saturday night *Academy Theatre* movie presentations. Following the merger of KLOR and KPTV, Salisbury became KPTV's news director and anchored the station's 6 p.m. *News Central* program.

John Salisbury as host of KLOR's *Academy Theatre, TV Prevue,* July 22, 1956

Salisbury left KPTV in mid-1961, but given his news background, he made a natural transition to KXL-AM-FM on September 1, 1961, as director of news and special projects. For decades, he remained at KXL, where his morning newscasts included a daily commentary, several collections of which were published. The commentaries also brought him the Freedom Foundation's George Washington Medal of Honor in 1962 and that organization's Certificate of Merit the following year. In 1970, Salisbury's *This Is Law Day* editorial, which had been broadcast the previous year, was also awarded the George Washington Medal of Honor. During the course of his career at KXL, Salisbury received a total of 15 Freedom Foundation medals—the first broadcaster ever so honored.

Salisbury joined the Radio Television News Directors Association (RTNDA) in 1969 and rapidly achieved prominence. In 1972, he was elected RTNDA's western regional director and became the organization's vice president in 1974. In 1975, he was elected to the presidency of RTNDA—a prestigious post that had previously been held by former CBS News presidents Sig Mickelson and William Small. In 1980, Salisbury was awarded the association's John F. Hogan Award, which honors individuals for distinguished contributions to journalism and freedom of the press. At the time, he was only the tenth individual ever to be honored with the award. Previous recipients include former NBC president and chairman David Sarnoff, former CBS president Frank Stanton, and former NBC and ABC president Robert Kintner.

In 1977, Salisbury ended his daily KXL newscasts while retaining his daily commentary assignment. In March 1978, he relinquished the news director title to Brian Jennings and became KXL's executive director of news and public affairs. On January 26, 1982, Salisbury retired from active KXL duty while continuing as a senior advisor for news and commentary. He retired from that post on January 1, 1986, although he continued to handle special assignments. KXL broadcast his last recorded commentary on January 3, 1986.

Salisbury died on June 27, 1987, at age 71 and posthumously was given the Oregon Association of Broadcasters' Tom McCall Award later that year.

## Donald S. Revert (The Real Don Steele)

Donald S. Revert was born in Hollywood, California, in 1936. His mother, who had a background in show business, gave her son the middle name Steele because she thought it sounded like a better name for an entertainer than Revert. He grew up accompanying her on the performance circuit and in United Service Organizations (USO), canteens and rehearsal halls filled with singers, clowns, strippers and animal acts voluntarily entertaining military personnel. While young, he played music and started his working career as a newspaper boy. When he was given a star on the Hollywood Walk of Fame in 1995, he asked that it be placed at the corner of Hollywood Boulevard and La Brea Avenue, the same corner from which he had hawked newspapers as a kid.

Listening to radio as a youth, Steele was fascinated by the baritone voices of announcers, particularly big band remote announcers, and he spent a great deal of time cultivating his own voice. Steele credits nightclub singer Francis Faye and actor Elisha Cook Jr. for the act he created, which was based on a movie in which Cook plays a maniacal DJ and Francis offers a lot of double entendre word play. Steele blended the two together to form his own radio personality.

Following training at the Don Martin School of Broadcasting in Los Angeles, Steele got his first radio job in Corona, California, in 1960. He moved on to Kennewick and Yakima, Washington, and then spent 18 months in Omaha at Don Burden's KOIL-AM before returning to Washington on Spokane's KXLY-AM in 1963.

Emperor Don the First (Don Steele) broadcasting from KISN's "Window to the World" studio, c. 1963

*Courtesy of www.therealdonsteele.com and REELRADIO, Inc.*

In Portland, he did an afternoon drive shift for Burden's KISN, in addition to serving as the station's program director, from July 1963 until August 1964. Following his stint at KISN, he returned to California. After six months in San Francisco, Steele moved to Los Angeles to work at KHJ-AM—where he helped to create the station's powerful "Boss Radio" format—and did *The Real Don Steele Show* on KHJ-TV from 1965 to 1975. He later worked at KIQQ-AM, KTNQ-AM, KRLA-AM, KODJ-AM, KCBS-FM and, finally, at KHJ-AM's KRTH-FM. He remained at KRTH until shortly before his death in 1997. Along the way, he took the air name "The Real Don Steele" to distinguish himself from another announcer with the same name. By the time he got to Los Angeles, his style made one author, referring to his pacing, dub him as "the fastest in the west."[33]

A rock jock who hated to over-analyze what he did, Steele said: "You take the Motown sound and the British Invasion and throw in Elvis Presley and Roy Orbison, and you have a music mix that's hard to beat at any time or any place."

## Craig Walker

Craig Walker was born into a broadcasting family. Originally Craig Kozak, the youngster hung out at KPLK/KROW Dallas, which was owned by his father, Ray. He remembers:

> I grew up in and on that station. I did my first air shift on a Sunday morning in 1959. I was 13 and I made sure that all the usual Sunday morning tapes were threaded through the heads of the two Magnecorders and ready to go. I also made sure the teletype had paper. It was big time radio![34]

Courtesy of Craig Adams

Craig Walker, at KPAM, 1971

Following a stint at KFLY Corvallis and a 1969 arrival at KPAM/KPFM Portland (where he became program director when the stations were KPAM-AM/KPAM-FM), Walker started as KGW-AM's mid-day DJ in August 1972. He took over that station's morning slot in January 1977, and his time period was consistently first or second in the Portland audience ratings. In 1986, he left KGW for KKCW-FM, where he was equally successful. During a portion of his 14 years at KGW, he also co-hosted KGW-TV's *Good Evening* program.

Three generations of Portland-area listeners awakened to Walker before his retirement in 2005. Described by the *Oregonian* as: "The well-read guy who shares his opinions without making them mad," he had habitually accompanied his listeners' breakfasts and morning commutes. At the time of his retirement from KKCW-FM, he was hailed as Portland's most beloved broadcaster. The *Oregonian* once affectionately described him as "nauseatingly normal," but his casual manner was genuine. Unlike some other DJs, he answered his own phones to the surprise of most callers. Colleague John Erickson, who at various points over a nearly 20-yer period spent mornings on the air with Walker, said: "[He's an] extraordinary guy with an extraordinary amount of talent. He's just always been himself" (see chapters 5, 14 and 21).[35, 36]

## Don Wright

The son of Lithuanian parents, Donald Nomako was born on Chicago's South Side and had become Don Wright by the time he chose a career in radio. He came to KGW-AM by 1968 to do the morning drive slot. By 1970, "Uncle Don" was the station's very successful morning man heard from 6 a.m. to 10 a.m. He remained at KGW until April 1975, when he joined KISN.

Listeners loved his easy manner and his "groaners." Wright was the last addition to the KISN "Good Guys" and the station's last morning man before it lost its FCC license in 1976 (see chapter 23). After Wright's brief tenure at KISN, it seemed as if his short-term status there dogged him. His career moved through a series of short- or medium-term stints at different Portland-area stations.

Courtesy Don Wright

"Uncle Don" Wright at KGW

After working at KOIN-AM (which became KYTE-AM in May 1977), he wound up doing the afternoon drive on KYTE-AM's FM side, KLLB/KB101, in 1982. In the summer of 1984, he took on a talk radio role at KEX-AM as host of *Northwest at Night*, heard from 8 p.m. until midnight. On Friday nights, he was also *Dr. Love* on the station's *Loveline* program. In January 1984, Wright moved to KEX-AM's FM side, KKRZ

"The Rose," and did mornings until the station became "Z100" in a format switch in March 1984.

In late 1988, in an economy move Wright was replaced with the satellite feed of Sally Jessy Raphael's talk program. While he continued to handle some KEX-AM weekend programs for a time, Wright returned to his original DJ role when he went to oldies station KSGO-AM in September 1988 for the morning drive slot. General manager Dan Hern wanted "someone who had a name that people 35-to 44-years-old—that's our target audience—would have a remembrance of."[37] But Hern wasn't happy with the ratings, and four months later Wright was out. "There's no business like show business," Wright observed.

At the age of 54, following a 30-year broadcasting career, Wright was unemployed and seemingly at a dead end. And then he decided to use his vocal assets, which had sustained him throughout his adult life, to pursue a different career path.

First, he created Don Wright Productions, a communications consulting firm specializing in teaching corporate executives how to become effective public speakers. Then someone told Wright that he could do a great imitation of Jack Benny, and he tackled that with characteristic energy. He decided to "become" Jack Benny, channeling the legendary comedian into a successful series of stage performances.

While continuing his consulting work, Wright still performs his Jack Benny recreations at retirement centers and nursing homes.

## Endnotes

1. Singletary, *Radio Station KOIN: A Case Study of Music Programming*, 83.
2. Barry Mishkind on http://www.oldradio.com/current/bc_hoaxe.htm.
3. The date comes from Mark Moore's www.pdxhistory.com accessed on July 12, 2008.
4. Robin Mitchell on www.pdxradio.com.
5. Following KPOJ-AM, Novak worked at KYXI-AM and KXL-AM before settling into work in 1978 at KATU-TV, where he was the booth announcer for many years.
6. Ibid.
7. *Oregon Journal*, January 5, 1958, TV Tab.
8. Morris, *The Remembered Years*, 145.
9. KXL staff listing dated 11/16/1943 (KXL file, WSMB).
10. Bob Miller on www.pdxradio.com.
11. Francis Murphy, "Barney Keep's Finale Sentimental Air Affair," *Oregonian*, February 15, 1979, C11.
12. Quoted material from Keep's final broadcast, and much of the detail, taken from: "Behind the Mike," *Oregonian*, February 15, 1979, C11.
13. Ibid.
14. http://alumni.oregonstate.edu/eclips/carry/oct11_2002.html.
15. Marge Boule, "An Ex-Pirate Fondly Recalls Making (Radio) Waves," *Oregonian*, October 31, 2004, L1.
16. Ibid.
17. While also appearing on KQFM-FM in 1980.
18. Ancheta reminiscence posted on KQIV-FM history website, www.rockinquad.com.
19. Erickson, John. Email to author dated May 8, 2008.
20. Erickson, John. Email to author dated May 10, 2008.
21. James Howe. Interview with author. Tape recording. Portland, OR. October 12, 2004.
22. Ibid.
23. Unidentified writer on www.pdxradio.com.
24. Which became "KISN Total Information" in 1964.
25. Tom Murphy. Email to Craig Adams.
26. www.pdxradio.com
27. Ibid.

28. Robin Mitchell post on www.pdxradio.com, May 11, 2008.
29. Robin Mitchell Associates' website www.rma1.com.
30. Murphy, Tom. Email to author dated May 10, 2008, and *LA Radio People, Vol. 2 (1957–1997)* (Los Angeles, CA: dbMarketing, 1997).
31. In 1995.
32. Rockabilly Hall of Fame website, http://www.rockabillyhall.com/RedRobinson1.html.
33. Arnold Passman. *The Deejays,* (New York: Macmillan Company, 1971), 288.
34. www.pdxradio.com.
35. *Oregonian,* October 3, 1993, Northwest Living, 1.
36. *Oregonian,* January 3, 2005, 1.
37. Peter Farrell, "An All-Elvis Radio Station? I'm All Shook Up," *Oregonian,* September 15, 1988, B11.

# Don Burden and KISN

Don Burden, c. early 1960s

In 1939, Sheldon Sackett founded KVAN#1 Vancouver, Washington, in partnership with Walter L. Read (see chapter 9). Twenty years later, in March 1959, an aging Sackett opened discussions with Don Burden, president of Star Broadcasting, Inc., about selling the station.[1]

The young Burden, who had been valedictorian at Iona High School in Idaho, majored in advertising at Idaho State University but was bitten by the radio bug following a two-year stint in the Navy. He started out at KWIK-AM Pocatello, Idaho, where he became sales manager in 1950. Moving to KOIL-AM Omaha, Nebraska, in August 1953 as sales manager, he purchased the station four months later and launched his broadcasting empire. Sackett was involved in an extraordinarily bitter divorce in spring 1959 and wanted to trim his radio holdings. In a fairly rapidly negotiated deal Burden purchased KVAN, Inc. (KVAN#1), at a reported price of $580,000. The FCC approved the sale on April 15, 1959, and he requested a call sign change to KISN, on May 1.[2]

Burden was 30 years old at the time and already had significant broadcasting interests, including stations in Omaha, Indianapolis, Denver and Pocatello—but his purchase of KISN began one of the most colorful sagas in Oregon radio history.

Where Sackett had been widely acknowledged as an eccentric character, the brilliant, driven Burden soon achieved his own legendary status for being colorful, as did KISN#1.

Burden, who had been described as cherub-faced and youthful, had lusted after the call letters KISN.

K-I-S-N—I always wanted those letters. I wanted them so badly we went ahead and cut our tapes and we were right down to the day before [the station's] opening before we negotiated and brought them here.[3]

Ever the showman, Burden ordered that on KVAN#1's last day on the air—Thursday, April 30—the station would continually broadcast the song *Teen Age Bill of Rights: The Revolution* by Robby John and the Seven Teens.[4] Following the switch from a more conservative music format to rock 'n roll, KISN soon became a radio powerhouse riding on its clever programming, massive promotional and public relations support and highly talented on-air crew dubbed the "The Swingin' 91 DJs" (who became "The KISN Good Guys" in 1962).

KISN took the Portland radio market by storm. KISN's inaugural staff included Charles J. Vais, general manager; Chris Lane, program director; and Jon Doe, news director. The station typically had a lot of turnover in its senior staff, as Burden continually tinkered with his invention. In July 1964, Steve Shepard became KISN's general manager, as well as vice president of Star Broadcasting. Shepard was also heard on-air presenting commentaries on topical items to which KISN invited listener response.

On October 1, 1966, the station moved its transmitter site from Smith Lake in north Portland to 4617 NE 158th Avenue and raised its power from one kilowatt to five kilowatts directional. Building steadily, the station reportedly had 30 percent of the Portland radio audience by 1967.[5]

Burden was a tough radio competitor, and the station was known for taking chances. On November 28, 1959, the station moved its studios to NW 10th Avenue and Burnside Street in downtown Portland. The building became known as "The KISN Corner," where it had a prominent studio with picture windows called "the Window on the World Studio," which attracted considerable attention. KISN also heavily promoted itself through audience contests, some of which prompted complaints to the Portland Better Business Bureau over allegations of rigging and failure to award prizes.

In 1962, a Multnomah County sheriff's deputy attempted to serve papers to KISN DJ Bill Western for "an overly spirited broadcast" and a fight broke out in the studio.[6] Western was subsequently fired and replaced by Frank Benny. When KISN wanted to hold a rock 'n roll dance for its listeners at the 1964 Portland Exposition, the station's aggressiveness—and its audience's fervor—apparently spooked the Portland Exposition Recreation Commission, which refused the dance proposal out of concern that "kids by the thousands [could] possibly get 'out of hand.'"[7] Each time *Oregonian* columnist Francis Murphy "criticized the KISN sound, Burden would write a vituperative letter, then, when he'd cooled down, request that it not be published."[8]

KISN got into a scrape with the FCC over what the commission called repeated violations of its rule requiring accuracy in stations' required broadcast of identification (ID) announcements. The FCC believed the station sought to appear as a Portland-licensed station (as opposed actually to a Vancouver-licensed one), and following a formal admonishment on June 12, 1961, the commission fined KISN $2,000 for the station's "apparent willful and repeated improper identification" of itself. KISN's response attributed the fine to disagreement over the length of the pause taken between words in the IDs and puckishly compared it to Coca-Cola's prominent use of the "pause that refreshes" slogan. Burden probably thought the value of all the advertising involved was well worth $2,000.

In 1966, the station became involved in a nasty lawsuit when DJ Paul Oscar Anderson, known on-air as POA (real name Paul E. Brown) moved over to KGAR after being fired from KISN. The station filed suit to force him off the rival KGAR based upon a non-compete clause in his KISN employment contract. Brown was silenced on KGAR for 60 days. As part of the litigation, he claimed that he had been fired "after refusing to participate on one-sided coverage of the [1966] Oregon senatorial campaign." According to Brown, Burden had said that "he intended 'to put Mark Hatfield in the Senate' and that, to that end, Hatfield would receive special campaign coverage while comment about his opponent would be derogative."[9]

While some KISN employees disputed Brown's charge, others substantiated it and his allegations of news slanting simmered. In mid-1969, Washington syndicated columnist Jack Anderson reported on missing documents detailing gifts Burden had given to a senator and aide, both of whom had responsibilities for the Senate committee that had oversight of the FCC. Shortly thereafter, investigators from the House Foreign and Interstate Commerce Committee, which had jurisdiction over the FCC in the U.S. House of Representatives, began probing KISN by interviewing individuals in Portland and inspecting station records.

Former KISN employee Don Kennedy told investigators that "in 1966 he was assigned to cover the Hatfield campaign for six weeks but had been pulled off after [Paul Oscar] Anderson alleged preferential treatment for Hatfield."[10] He also testified about a contest in which a camper was to be awarded to the individual who found a "lucky key" in a fishbowl hidden at an automobile dealership lot. But, Kennedy alleged, the contest was rigged because the key wasn't hidden until well after the contest began.[11]

Courtesy of Gino Rossi

KISN participated in Capitol Records' "The Beatles Are Coming" promotion, which helped create the Beatlemania craze in preparation for the band's arrival in the U.S. in February 1964. To support the campaign, Capitol provided Beatles-style wigs to radio stations, which the KISN staff donned for this promotional photo staged outside the station's downtown studios, January, 1964. From top: Paul Oscar Anderson, Frank Benny, The Real Don Steele, Tiger Tom Murphy. An unidentified Capitol representative stands watching.

While senator Hatfield denied that KISN had ever given him anything, in May 1970 the FCC held a hearing in Portland. In December of that year, the FCC denied Star Broadcasting's application for renewal of KISN's license—as well as the company's renewal requests for WIFE-AM Indianapolis and KOIL-AM Omaha—on grounds that Star Broadcasting had given "illegal campaign support to senators Vance Hartke (D-IN) and Mark O. Hatfield (R-OR)."[12] The FCC further held that the chairman of Star Broadcasting's board, Don Burden, "was intimately involved in and had knowledge of the misconduct," although Burden vigorously denied the charges.[13] The commission didn't comment on other allegations, such as contest rigging.

The matter slogged through federal processes for five years. During that period, KISN threw itself into a laudable series of public service campaigns and other good works, under the guidance of station manager Sol Rosinsky. Such initiatives were doubtless, at least in part, a precautionary measure. Star Broadcasting appealed the commission's action to the U.S. Court of Appeals, which generally only reverses an FCC ruling when it perceives that due process has not been observed. On December 11, 1975, the court upheld the FCC's decision, and on May 23, 1976, the Supreme Court refused to hear Star Broadcasting's appeal of the court's decision.

Many believed that KISN would have only 30 days in which to continue operating before the FCC named an "interim operator" for the frequency. The commission actually gave Star Broadcasting 90 days in which to wind up business. The company, believing its $20 million in assets would be totally extinguished by the FCC's action, proclaimed that the denial of its stations' license renewals was "the severest sanction which the FCC has ever levied upon a broadcast licensee."[14] KISN was near the end of its rope. On June 5, the FCC ordered Star the company to cease broadcasting on September 2.

Rosinsky—working in concert with Don Dudley, president of KYAC-AM Seattle (which claimed to be the only African-American-owned station in that city)—filed an FCC proposal for the two stations to jointly operate on 910 KHz with the commitment that any profits would go to charity. Part of Rosinsky's goal was to keep KISN's more than 30 staff members employed. One of those staff members was William Failing, KISN's sales manager. The situation was somewhat unclear because both Rosinsky and Dudley also indicated their intent to compete for permanent use of the frequency. Additionally, Rosinsky and "about eight other Portland and Vancouver radio broadcasters" formed a new corporation—Rose Broadcasting, Inc.—which also filed an application for permanent use of the frequency. Despite these efforts and a last-ditch request from Star Broadcasting to the FCC for another 30 days in which to operate KISN, the commission took no step to appoint an interim operator. When September 2 arrived, KISN's morning DJ, a flustered Don Wright, intended to play George Harrison's "My Sweet Lord" as his final song but punched the wrong button. He ended his show by saying: "I'm a talented man and I'm unemployed."[15]

Despite a desperate—and unsuccessful—last-minute effort by Star Broadcasting to secure injunctive relief from the Court of Appeals, the ax fell at midnight on September 2. It was evening DJ Dave Stone who officially signed-off the station when he ended his program with the last full song played on KISN, "She's Gone" by Daryl Hall and John Oates. Then Stone said: "At this time KISN leaves the air for an indefinite period of time. Good night from the KISN Good Guys." While he spoke, Stone began playing "Someday We'll Be Together," by Diana Ross and the Supremes. He punctuated KISN's exit with an ID cartridge containing station breaks in rotation by all the KISN Good Guys.

At 12:01 a.m., chief engineer Byron Swanson shut off the transmitter, which had run continuously for 17 years.[16] "Well that's it," Rosinsky said as he shook Stone's hand. They all walked out of the control booth to meet the assembled reporters and well-wishers.

Rosinsky believed the station would be back on the air within 30 days under an interim authority with the same call letters—but that optimism proved misplaced.[17]

The FCC set as the deadline of November 3 for new applications for the frequency, and five materialized:

   ❧ Rose Broadcasting, headed by Rosinsky
   ❧ Don Dudley of Seattle

- Viking Broadcasting of Vancouver, Inc., comprised of lawyers and business interests in Maryland, Virginia and Washington
- Longwood Broadcasting of Vancouver, Washington, headed by a Vermont advertising executive with the majority stock held by an operator of nursing homes in Indiana and Ohio
- Ft. Vancouver Broadcasting Company, whose president was Bill Failing Jr., KISN's former sales manager

The FCC indicated that cooperation among the applicants would speed its ability to again allow the frequency on the air, but they fell to arguing among themselves. "It's a classic case of people who are ready to battle each other to the death being unable to sit down and work out an agreement," said one man who was involved in the negotiations.[18] Given the fractious nature of the proceedings, the FCC began predicting that it would be years before anything would again be broadcast on 910 KHz in Portland.

A paper war ensued in Washington, DC, and matters were not helped when Rosinsky died unexpectedly on November 9, 1977. Phil Jacks of Tigard bought Rosinsky's interest in Rose Broadcasting, but Rosinsky's death created mountains of new paperwork at the commission's offices. By July 1979, the five competing applicants had been reduced to three through merger and withdrawal. Longwood Broadcasting, Ft. Vancouver Broadcasting and Rose Broadcasting remained.

To expedite matters, Failing's Ft. Vancouver Broadcasting proposed a deal under which Longwood Broadcasting and Rose Broadcasting would take minority interest stock positions in Ft. Vancouver, leaving it as the only remaining applicant for the frequency. The other parties accepted the proposal, and Ft. Vancouver was awarded the frequency on October 25, 1979. The 910 KHz AM dial spot once again came to life on April 1, 1980, as KKSN.

Don Burden eventually returned to radio, owning KPEN Altos, California, until shortly before his death in 1985.


# Endnotes

1. Sackett died in 1968.
2. KVAN, Inc., was owned 75 percent by Sackett, 20 percent by D. Elwood Caples and 5 percent by its vice president, Jack Irvine. (*Broadcasting Yearbook*, 1958).
3. Gerry Pratt, "Teen Market Builds Radio Fortunes," *Oregonian*, May 28, 1967.
4. "Behind the Mike," *Oregonian*, May 1, 1959, Sec. 2, 9. The recording was released as Del-Fi 4115.
5. Ibid.
6. "KISN Plagued by Problems from Beginning," *Oregonian*, September 2, 1976.
7. "E-R Board Denies Permit for Rock 'n Roll Dance," *Oregonian*, June 19, 1964.
8. Francis Murphy, "As KISN Folds," *Oregonian*, September 4, 1976.
9. Ibid.
10. Doug Baker, "House Committee Probers Shift Emphasis to KISN," *Oregon Journal*, December 16, 1969.
11. Ibid.
12. "FCC Refuses License Renewal For KISN, Four Other Stations," *Oregonian*, December 4, 1970.
13. Sue Hobart, "Supreme Court Rejects Review of KISN Ruling," *Oregonian*, May 25, 1976.
14. "KISN Radio Halt Ordered For Fall," *Oregonian*, June 8, 1976.
15. Fred Leeson, "KISN Kisses Fans Goodby," *Oregon Journal*, September 1, 1976.
16. Swanson was known to *Nightwatch* listeners as Johnny Dark.
17. Presumably to cover the interval he anticipated, Rosinsky had taken a position as general manager of KMJK-FM Lake Oswego several months before Rose Broadcasting's founding.
18. Joe Berger, "KISN Given Slim Chance to Return Soon," *Oregon Journal*, February 3, 1977.

# The 1960s
# In Full Color

# 24

# Mother Nature's Wrath:
## Columbus Day 1962 and
## Other Calamities

On Friday, October 12, 1962, Bob Chopping, owner/manager of KAST Astoria, picked up the phone in the afternoon and called a friend—the manager of KPOD-AM Crescent City, California. Chopping had seen some weather reports about a storm forming over the Pacific Ocean and wanted to know what the weather was like further south down the coastline. "Oh, it's kicking up like you couldn't believe," he was told. Thinking there might be reason for concern, Chopping called KOOS in Coos Bay. "Eh, it isn't so bad, Bob," was the report. But in short order, KOOS called back with an update. "The wind's gusting so hard, it's blowing boats out of the water and up onto the beach and streets and breaking windows…." Then the phone went dead.

Chopping dialed Tom Becker, owner/manager of KNPT Newport, who reported that it was a normal day." Chopping was just digesting these divergent accounts when Becker called back. "Boy, this looks like it's going to be a wild one."

KAST went on the air and put out an alert to Astoria: "Button down the hatches; take in all your lawn chairs, everything!" it warned.[1] Oregon was set to encounter the worst natural disaster in its history—the 1962 Columbus Day Storm. No one who lived through it will ever forget it. By then, radio had grown in its ability to provide important civil defense information during emergencies—an ability developed from earlier challenges.

## Tillamook Burn

Broadcasting had always been squarely in the forefront of emergency communications—particularly at times of natural or man-made disaster. But early radio was hampered by the bulkiness of the equipment used for live field reporting. Thus, radio's coverage of events like the Tillamook Burn of 1933, which destroyed nearly a quarter-million acres of coastland timber, suffered from radio's youth and primitive technology. Accordingly, radio coverage of the fire drew more from wire-service accounts than local stations' own coverage.

## Bandon Fire

By 1936, that had started to change. KGW-AM made a serious attempt to cover the Bandon Fire on September 26, 1936, which destroyed virtually the entire town of and killed 11 people. KGW's news director, Virgil Smith, sent a two-person team, which included Bob Thomlinson, to Bandon and scheduled a live report for broadcast on both KGW and the NBC Network. According to Smith:

> We didn't have very many telephone communications in those days. As a matter of fact, there was only one line into Bandon and [authorities] were keeping this line open for emergencies. But we had it set up [that] at a certain time, those fellows would go on the line and their feed would go on over the network. Well, Bob Thomlinson came back the next day quite proud of the program that they had put together [but] we had to tell him we didn't get a word of it because the government had taken over the lines—so he had spoken to dead air.[2]

## Vanport Flood

By the time of the 1948 Vanport Flood, radio's capabilities had vastly increased. Portable recording equipment was smaller, and it was easier to go live on the air using remote transmitters without resorting to phone lines.

Early in World War II, Vanport city had been rapidly constructed on the Columbia River floodplain north of Portland. Thousands of workers who had been imported from across the nation to fulfill industrialist Henry Kaiser's maritime ship-building contracts lived there.[3] By 1948, Vanport (built as temporary housing) was Oregon's second-largest city and home to 19,000 people living in 5,300 homes. It was the largest public housing project in the nation.

Courtesy of the *Oregonian*

Live remote news coverage was still a cumbersome two-person affair when this photo was taken in 1938 of Bob Thomlinson (left) and Bill Mock (right) interviewing Jim Hefty.

WSMB Collection

KOIN's Johnny Carpenter, broadcasting with smaller more portable equipment, is piloted over Oregon coastal timberland to report on forest fires. *KOIN Radio Advertiser*, August 1945

Postcard showing Vanport following the flood, May 1948

In May of that year, unusually heavy winter snows and unseasonably warm spring temperatures caused so much snow melt-off that adjacent river levels rose perilously. By late in the month, the Columbia River was 15 feet above the delta on which Vanport sat, and the community's only protection was a system of dikes.

Shortly after 4 p.m. on Memorial Day, May 30, 1948, a 200-foot section of dike broke—and a ten-foot wall of water cascaded through Vanport, obliterating the city. Fifteen people died in what was reportedly the second-largest flood in the Columbia River's history.

On June 11, President Harry S. Truman traveled to Portland and delivered a radio address to the community from Portland Civic Auditorium. It was broadcast over KGW and KXL. Truman reported that an emergency Joint Resolution of Congress had been passed earlier that day, which would appropriate $10 million for immediate relief of the flood victims.

KALE's Lou Gillette (left) interviewing a survivor of the Vanport Flood. KALE used shortwave radio, airplanes and a blimp to cover the flood.

Portland radio stations heavily covered the Vanport disaster and attempted to provide emergency communication assistance. KXL requested and received Special Temporary Authority from the FCC to broadcast 24 hours a day. "…thousands of lives are imperiled plus millions in property damage," KXL reported in a telegram to the FCC.

Wilbur J. Jerman rafting through the flooded interior of the KWJJ Smith Lake transmitter building, 1948

Radio itself wasn't immune to the flood. KGW-AM's transmitter, which had been located at Delta Park since 1931, was thrown off the air when a 635-foot tower toppled over after a floating apartment building crashed into it. A 300-foot wooden transmission pole, which KEX had erected in 1934, also toppled over. Mud and water made their way halfway up the third floor of the KGW-AM transmitter building, which was essentially destroyed. Using KALE's auxiliary transmitter at Mt. Scott, KGW-AM resumed operations after 14 hours of silence.[4]

KPDQ, while not located in the Vanport Delta, was also flooded out at Oaks Park but resumed operation at reduced power from 3115 NE 35th Avenue under the supervision of the station's chief engineer Rod Johnson.

In early April, KWJJ had moved to its new 24-acre transmitter site at Smith Lake, located at 4350 North Suttle Road, about a half-mile west of Vanport. The move had allowed the station to boost its daytime power from 1 kilowatt to 10 kilowatts directional. But KWJJ was still broadcasting at night from its old site at Oaks Park, pending FCC approval to go to 10 kilowatts directional at night. The flood inundated the KWJJ transmitter building at Smith Lake, forcing the station to abandon the site and return operation to the Oaks Park facility. KWJJ didn't complete repairs at Smith Lake until August 1948.

Eight months before the flood, KVAN#1 had also relocated to Smith Lake and remarkably was the only station with a transmitter in the flood plain that remained in operation. According to a KVAN#1 ad placed in the *Oregonian*:

[The station needed to place] thousands of pounds of sand in the transmitter house to keep it from floating away. The roof was torn away and the transmitter and other essential control equipment was hoisted through the roof and suspended on scaffolding. As the water rose, it was necessary to repeat the moving operations over and over again. KVAN stayed on the air except for brief periods when it was necessary to turn off the power to move the equipment. KVAN operated with eight feet of water in the transmitter building.[5]

With all circuits between the Vancouver studios and the transmitter out of service, KVAN#1 had to operate from its transmitter building.

## Columbus Day Storm

Thus, Oregon broadcasters had considerable experience dealing with disasters by the time of the 1962 Columbus Day Storm.

In Astoria, the storm was intense. Chopping reports:

> We did get some gusts out at the radio station [of] 110 miles an hour. You could actually feel the building going up and down on that concrete foundation. But it missed Astoria and went through the woods out here 10-15 miles away, just like a giant had gone through there with a scythe and just cut the forest down in an absolutely clear path.[6]

What neither Chopping, Becker nor anyone else could have known at the time was that when the storm hit Newport, it veered inland. The Oregon coast had missed the worst of the storm's intensity, which was reserved for the inland communities.

The Columbus Day Storm was an extratropical wave cyclone and was the most powerful storm of that type recorded in the U.S. in the 20th century. Wind gusts exceeded 170 miles per hour in parts of Oregon, and afterward the state's entire electricity distribution system had to be rebuilt from the ground up.

Virtually all radio and TV stations were thrown off the air. Tom Murphy reports that Mike Phillips was on the air at KISN when the tower fell over on the transmitter building, knocking the station off the air.[7] Bob McClanathan was at KPAM-AM when the storm hit. According to McClanathan:

> By 5:30, the electricity was off and the neighbor's roof blew across. We were up there [on Healy Heights] looking out the window overlooking the whole city and all of the lights in the City of Portland were off—except for downtown Portland. We didn't have electricity up there then for about three or four days. And, of course, some towers blew down. The KGW-TV tower collapsed and then the three KPOJ-AM-FM towers over on Mount Scott, folded up like jack knives.[8]

KPOJ-FM was off the air for four months and didn't fully return until February 9, 1963.

The damage also extended to other stations. KOIN-AM lost one of its two towers at Sylvan Hills. KWJJ-FM lost one tower and a portion of its transmitter building. KEX's Jim Howe, a street reporter who had just begun doing helicopter traffic reports, recalled:

> The pilot and I were over Ross Island and he said to me, "Something is wrong. It's not good news".... He had looked at the air speed indicator and were doing about 75 miles per hour in the helicopter [but if you] looked at the ground, we were going backwards. He said, "We have got really strong winds up here." And I said, "We'd better get this back on the ground." He turned it around and it seemed like it wasn't five seconds that we were back at Swan Island, and the wind was blowing so hard he couldn't land. He couldn't get the rotors to slow down and so he kept going down and coming back and going down and coming back. So, finally, he said. "I am going to go down this time and get close to the ground, and you just jump out and lay on the ground." So, I just jumped out and lay on the ground and he hit the power and took off.[9]

Courtesy of Wes Luchau and Western Oregon University

Campbell Hall on the campus of Oregon College of Education (now Western Oregon University), Monmouth, after the storm

Jack Capell, KGW-TV's weatherman for decades, was in the habit of going out to the Portland airport weather station at 5 p.m. to gather data for his 6 p.m. TV newscast. Capell recollects:

> I [had] taped that [5 p.m. radio] broadcast so I could [go to the airport and] be back to the studio [for television] air. We didn't have any idea if it was actually going to hit us or whether it might stay off-shore. But, it seemed to me that it was getting up to an 80 or 90 percent chance we would get some effect from it—a major effect—so I decided this was one time I was going to go all-out. And I didn't actually intend to forecast the intensity of it, but I did say, "It's the worst I've ever seen and it's going to have serious consequences for Portland." And so I put my car radio on, [and] was listening to what I had said [on the taped 5 p.m. radio newscast] as I drove along the Columbia River. There was a light easterly breeze; the sky was brightening, and the barometer had started to rise again. And I said, "Oh, my gosh!" I don't know what happened. It's going to miss us.
>
> [I got] down to Vancouver Avenue and that's where I saw this great, black mass right across the street ahead of me. It was just blowing debris and garbage cans, and everything was flying around. And everybody else was worried when they saw that thing.... I said, "There it is. We're going to get it!"[10]

When Capell had gotten to the airport, the weather bureau personnel were still skeptical that a major storm was going to hit. But, Capell was certain of it and rushed out of the airport heading back to KGW-TV. He remembers the trip:

> I was stuck trying to get across the Broadway Bridge because there was scaffolding between one side and the other, right across the lanes of traffic, so they stopped all traffic from going across the bridge. I knew I had to get to the studio, so I broke through the blockade and drove by and the scaffolding was swinging and "bang!" it came, just missing my car.

After the Columbus Day storm in Polk County, October 13, 1962
Courtesy of the Salem Public Library Historic Photograph Collections

A grain elevator in Newberg, following the storm
Courtesy of the National Oceanic and Atmospheric Administration

I got to Burnside and that was closed off. They weren't letting traffic through there so the cars were lined up on 11th. I had to get off, and actually go up on a curb and drive along the sidewalk until I got to the end of the line of cars—and then I busted across Burnside and was thinking, "Well, if the police start following me, that's fine. I'll get them to escort me up to the station." On 14th, a tree came down and crashed right across a car behind me. Those trees in the old park blocks were blowing over. When I got to the station, I pulled in the back parking lot—fast. They were at the back door waving at me, saying, "Take it easy. Calm down. We're not going on the air. Our tower's down." So, I'd risked my neck to get there, went through all that, and we were off the air.

So, I get inside the station and there's no power. The lights are out; windows are blown out. And I was so frustrated. Here's the biggest story and I can't do anything. And then, the radio manager came running over and says "Jack, come here quick. Radio's on the air." They had emergency power over there and they had not lost their tower—so they were broadcasting. He said "Get on the air and tell them the story." So I got on the air but the window was blown out in the radio booth. They had a candle set up inside some glasses, so we had a little bit of light, but [the] wind was blowing in that window like everything—and I broadcast like that. Jim Miller and Hal Starr were the guys there [with me] and Miller says to me that Hal Starr is getting tired and he's starting to not make sense. So, he says you better start wrapping things up—and that was about 4:00 in the morning. I broadcast like that until 4 a.m.

With towers down at KGW-TV and other stations, and most of the city, without electricity, KGW-AM was the only Portland radio or TV station on the air. KGW-TV news director/anchor Richard Ross recalled:

The guys at the transmitter [which was running from a generator] said: "We can't last without more fuel. We've got to have more gas. Can you see if you can round up some fuel for us?" That announcement went out on KGW radio and a guy called in and said: "Listen, I have a 55-gallon drum but you're going to have to come get it." And I said, "Hell, I'll deliver it.' I got in the news car and drove north on 13th and got on Burnside heading east. I had the radio on, and they said: "Richard Ross, if you're listening, we don't need you to get that. We've got another source and the fellow will deliver it." I made a U-turn right then and there. I mean glass, metal, aluminum [was flying around]. It was hazardous to be out.[11]

Capell spent the whole night writing up an account of the storm and the station published 300 mimeographed copies for distribution. Inquiries poured in and the station produced another 10,000 copies. When those ran out, KGW ran a third printing of another 20,000, and that was followed by a fourth. Ultimately, KGW sent out 40 to 50,000 copies of the report Capell wrote by candlelight that night.

Stations recovered gradually. According to McClanathan, KPTV brought a generator up to its transmitter the day after the storm to get channel 12 back on the air. Other stations similarly improvised until commercial power was restored.

The catastrophe had hit statewide.

In Newport, KNPT's Tom Becker had been right. It was indeed a "big one." Becker recalls:

We had a station at Bandon and the manager there called me up and says: 'Man, we got a storm coming down here.' There was a school bus [headed out]. I guess it was to a football game in town. And he says, 'Stop that bus.' I called the high school and stopped the bus, thank God. It took all the power out for a week.[12]

In Eugene, Gordon Bussey was at KVAL:

Columbus Day, we were blown off the air. We didn't have a generator for back-up power and there were candles everywhere. I went riding around with the news crew and we went out to Junction City and filmed a grange being burned down. We filmed a guy on the street in Eugene picking up walnuts out in front of his house as limbs were coming down.[13]

In Oregon, 25 people lost their lives during the storm, 98 percent of Portland General Electric's (PGE) customers were without power and the PGE grid sustained $3.5 million in damage. The storm was a terrifying experience—made all the worse for lack of broadcast communication.

Roger Avrit, who was trying to listen to the radio that night, recalls:

The night was long and dark with no power and no communications. The power had long since gone out, but we had battery powered radios. I remember turning mine on and the only stations I could get were in California and they were broadcasting totally unaware of what had hit the Northwest. There were no Oregon radio or TV stations on the air—none. No signals from Washington state.[14]

Off the air for almost four days, KGW-TV returned to the air on October 16 using a temporary tower with a temporary antenna borrowed from KTNT-TV Tacoma. KGW limped back on the air at reduced power, and it was unclear whether its signal would be strong enough to power the station's coastal translators. KGW didn't permanently replace the damaged antenna and tower until January 28, 1963.

Several weeks after the storm, like other stations, KGW-TV broadcast a documentary—called *Twelfth Day Tempest*—chronicling the storm." Pat Krafton, KGW's general manager at the time, spoke for the station:

What was done by radio that Friday night of October 12 and the following days of recovery is what you have every right to expect of us. But there are lessons to be learned for the future. No transmitter can be of value to you unless you have a receiver to remain in touch with your fellow human beings. To know what is going on and where your help is needed, to aid those less fortunate than yourselves, or merely to follow instructions and thereby minimize confusion and tragedy, the role of the portable transistor radio receiver certainly became an extremely important one. It became the link to reassurance and vital information. In time of need, radio will be there again to give immediate help when you need it. I would like to express our heartfelt appreciation to all of you who helped us at KGW. The many public officials, the police and fire departments throughout our listening area: the ham radio operators and many others too numerous to name. But particularly, we want to thank you, our listeners, who tuned to KGW the night of the terrible 12th. Thank you for helping us and thank you for your many heart-warming letters and calls which have poured into the station these past few days. It has been our privilege to serve you.[15]

# Endnotes

1. Chopping's telephone conversations concerning the Columbus Day Storm recounted in an interview with the author. Tape recording. Astoria, Oregon. July 14, 2004.
2. Smith, Virgil. Interview "KGW Reminiscences" as part of KGW Radio 50th anniversary, 1972 (Oregon Historical Society collection).
3. The area is now the site of Delta Park and the Portland International Raceway.
4. The site remained a continuing potential flooding problem for KGW, which in June 1961 requested emergency FCC authority to operate from another location as rising Columbia River waters again "threatened [a] flood of the Columbia River [which] precludes operation of the station's regular facilities." Also Andrew G. Haley, attorney, 1961. Letter to Ben F. Waple, FCC Secretary dated June 9 (KGW file, NARA, College Park, MD).
5. KVAN ad, *Oregonian*, June 21, 1948.
6. Quoted material taken from Chopping interview.
7. Quoted from "Mike Phillips Tribute" website, http://www.cfmm.com/sites/MikeP/Content.asp?ID=456.
8. Robert A. McClanathan. Interview with author. Tape recording. Portland, OR. October 13, 2004.
9. Howe interview.
10. Jack Capell. Interview with author. Tape recording. Seattle, WA. September 15, 2004.
11. Richard Ross. Interview with author. Tape recording. Lake Oswego, OR. October 13, 2004.
12. Becker interview.
13. Gordon Bussey. Interview with Brian Mount. Tape recording. Portland, OR. August 2004.
14. Recollection of Roger W. Avrit, as posted online December 4, 2007, at http://bztv.typepad.com/newsviews/2005/10/storm_memories_.html.
15. Mustoe Jr., Dr. Myles. Pat Krafton quotation in *"Part II: The Emergence of the Emergency Alert System,"* Eastern Oregon University, online at http://www.eou.edu/~mmustoe/easpaperc.html.

25

# New Radio Stations
# of the 1960s

S urprising to some, radio survived television's arrival and continued to grow during the 1960s. While new AM stations developed, the major growth occurred on the FM band as new stations, often companions to existing AMs, developed.

## KWIL-FM/KHPE-FM Albany

KWIL-AM built an FM sister station, KWIL-FM, which it abandoned around 1955 (see chapter 14). Revisiting that decision more than a decade later, KWIL again ventured into the FM band and signed-on a second KWIL-FM on January 12, 1969, this time at 107.9 MHz with 100 kilowatts. Initially, the station was a Mutual Broadcasting System (MBS) affiliate and duplicated KWIL-AM's programming, but in the early 1970s, it began programming separately. The FM station changed its call sign to KHPE-FM in 1972, at which point it dropped the MBS affiliation.

## KRVC-AM/KDOV-AM#2/KSJK-AM Ashland

On September 3, 1958, Faith Tabernacle in Ashland filed an FCC application for a new radio station that was spearheaded by its president and pastor, Leo C. Wine. He cobbled together the construction funds by securing nearly 20 "sponsors," who executed promissory notes offering to loan amounts ranging from $100 to $1,500 (the high figure being pledged by Wine himself) for the project.

KRVC-AM signed-on November 19, 1960, from its studios in the Faith Tabernacle building at 840 Faith Avenue in Ashland. A formal 90-minute dedication program began at 2:30 p.m. and featured Mike Martin, president and founder of King's Garden in Seattle, an operator of religious radio stations in Washington and Montana. Ashland mayor Richard Neill also participated, along with a wide variety of regional religious leaders.

Broadcasting at 1350 KHz with 1 kilowatt daytime-only power, KRVC offered its own religious and Mutual Network programs. Mutual's switch to KRVC left Ashland's KWIN an independent. In a confusing series of events in 1977, KRVC took the call sign KDOV#2, which had been abandoned by the old KDOV#1 in Medford in 1966. A new 1300 KHz station in Phoenix then adopted the call sign KRVB (see chapter 27).

Perry Atkinson, who had been involved in broadcasting in Sacramento, first heard KDOV#2 while vacationing in the Rogue Valley and stopped by Faith Tabernacle to ask pastor Wine if he wanted to sell the station.[1] Wine thought briefly and then replied: "Yes, I think I do."[2] Two years later, on September 9, 1983, Perry Atkinson purchased KDOV#2 from Faith Tabernacle, re-licensed it to Talent and moved the transmitter to Ashland's north Interstate 5 freeway exit. With 1230 KHz newly available as a result of a frequency change by KYJC, Atkinson moved KDOV#2 from 1350 to 1230 KHz on January 23, 1984 (see chapter 16).

In 1988, Atkinson was exploring the possibility of acquiring the 5-kilowatt KHUG-AM Phoenix, and initiated discussion with Southern Oregon University about donating his KDOV#2 to SOU for use by its regional public radio network, Jefferson Public Radio (JPR) (see evolution of the JPR network elsewhere in this chapter). On July 28, 1989, the FCC approved that donation. It was the largest gift JPR had ever received.

Concurrent with that donation, Atkinson changed KHUG's call letters to KDOV#2 (see chapter 27). JPR secured the call sign KSJK for its newly acquired, 1230 KHz AM station.

## KGRL-AM/KXUX-AM/KMGX-AM/KICE-AM Bend

Bend's KGRL signed-on February 4, 1960, on 940 KHz with 1 kilowatt daytime-only power. By late spring 1960, the "Good Music Station" was aggressively promoting its "K-GIRL Smiley Contest," which offered a "luxurious weekend for four at Luxurious King-Surf Resort" as a prize. The station, which claimed to be number one in central Oregon, used a photo of a young girl holding the sign "I'm Miss KGRL" as its logo. John H. McAlpine purchased KGRL on June 8, 1961, through his McAlpine Broadcasting Company, and Gary Capps purchased the station from him on October 1, 1964. Capps also started KXIQ-FM Bend in December 1974.

Following the stations' longest period of continuing ownership, Capps sold KGRL and KXIQ to Engel Communications on October 3, 1985. Owned by Bruce and Teri Engel, the company promptly affiliated KGRL with NBC. Capps, however, remained with the stations, serving as chief operating officer of Engel Communications. Concurrent with the purchase of the two Bend stations, Engel Communications also acquired KVAN-AM#3 Vancouver and KMJK-FM Lake Oswego (see KGAR-AM elsewhere this chapter).

In early 1991, Engel Communications announced the sale of KGRL and KXIQ to Michael and Sarah Burnette for $1,625,000. In anticipation of the purchase, the couple had moved to Bend from Phoenix, Arizona, where Michael had been general manager of KMEO-AM-FM. Previously, he had been national programming director for Westinghouse's FM stations from 1982 to 1985.

The sale was called off when the Burnettes' financing fell through in August 1991, but Burnette arranged for the sale of the stations to Oak Broadcasting—who made him manager of both stations. Subsequently, KGRL became KXUX on July 5, 1994, when it and KXIQ were sold to Stewart Broadcasting Corporation for $975,000. KXUX briefly became KMGX on April 25, 2000, following the station's purchase by GCC Bend, LLC (commonly known as the Bend Radio Group) on December 7, 1999. Ultimately, the station settled in as KICE-AM on May 4, 2000.

Additionally, KXIQ became KXIX on June 9, 1995, when it was part of the Oak Broadcasting group.

## KPTN-AM Central Point

The FCC authorized a 1400 KHz station in Central Point on December 1, 1967, for Radio Broadcasters, Inc. Its president was James L. Hutchens, who also owned KFLY-AM and KFLY-FM in Corvallis along with members of his family. On May 27, 1970, the commission rescinded the Central Point construction permit for "conscious fabrications" and "deliberate misrepresentations" by Hutchens (see chapter 21).[3]

## KFLY-FM Corvallis

Shortly after purchasing Corvallis' KFLY-AM Corvallis in 1963, Radio Broadcasters, filed an application for an FM station in Corvallis to operate on 101.5 MHz with 27.72 kilowatts power.

A construction permit was issued on January 24, 1964, and in 1966 James Hutchens personally leased to the corporation most of the equipment necessary to construct KFLY-FM. The station was built at 351 1/2 Madison Street, where it shared studios with its AM sister station. An ABC affiliate, KFLY-FM went on the air October 1, 1966. Following FCC hearings scheduled to explore alleged violations of commission rules by Hutchens, KFLY-FM's license was revoked in May 1970. The station's facilities were eventually acquired by Corvallis Radio, Inc. (see chapter 21).

## KWVR-AM Enterprise

Two Lewiston, Idaho, residents—Robert Edwards and Gene W. Wilson—wanted to own their own radio station and chose Enterprise as a location. On July 24, 1958, they formed a partnership under the name of Wallowa Valley Radio, to which they each contributed $500 and pledged an additional $3,000 upon FCC approval for a construction permit. At the time, Edwards was program director of Lewiston's KLEW-TV channel 3, and Wilson was an engineer at that station.

On February 10, 1960, the FCC authorized the Enterprise station's construction and assigned the call sign KWVR, which the owners said stood for **K**-**W**allowa **V**alley **R**adio.[4] Following preliminary testing, KWVR signed-on May 25, 1960, with 250 watts at 1340 KHz from its studios at 307 West Main Street.[5] It was Wallowa County's first radio station.

Gene Wilson served as both manager and chief engineer and envisioned KWVR as having a strong commitment to local news programming. He had relocated to Enterprise to manage KWVR, and on January 17, 1961, he bought out Edwards' interest in the partnership. Station staff at the time included Virginia M. Wilson, program director; Ray G. Wilson, news director; and H. G. Rhoads, commercial manager. In 1962, the station moved its studios to 203 East Main Street.

In contrast to stations that fought for additional nighttime hours, small market stations—such as KQIK Lakeview and KUBE Pendleton—had the opposite problem as they struggled with operating costs under FCC rules requiring that they maintain minimum hours of operation. Beginning in 1963, Wilson sought to have KWVR's station license modified to stipulate limited broadcasting hours. He advanced his case by explaining that KWVR's advertising revenues had shrunk from $30,918 in 1961 to only $16,834 in 1963. He related that he had reduced staffing in 1962 to cut costs and that his net income from operating the station that year had only been $6,909. On March 4, 1964, the FCC placed KWVR on a specified hours license of 6 a.m. to 6 p.m., Monday through Saturday, and 8 a.m. to noon on Sunday. Even with that reduction, KWVR was still struggling, and a further reduction in hours that eliminated Sunday broadcasts was sought and granted in 1972. That same year, KWVR moved its studios to 102 SW First Street.

In June 1974, Wilson sold KWVR to David D. Dirks and his wife, Pamela. Dirks was a young Walla Walla, Washington, resident with a background in radio sales, news, announcing and management. By 1981, KWVR had affiliated with the ABC Information Network, and by 1983 its daytime power had been raised to one kilowatt.

Lee and Carol-Lee Perkins purchased KWVR (known locally as "quiver") from the Dirks on September 1, 1984. The Perkins had moved to Enterprise from Tacoma, where Lee had managed the public radio station at L. H. Bates Technical College and Carol had been a staff member at the college. The new owners quickly made plans to add an FM station, which signed-on in 1985 (see chapter 27).

## KPIR-AM/KPNW-AM Eugene

On February 1, 1960, brothers Richard B. and Thomas F. Thompson, owners of a record and audio equipment store in Eugene, filed an application—along with Hobart Wilson—for a new Eugene radio station. The three parties organized Emerald Broadcasting Corporation in which Wilson, who owned Eugene's Wilson Insurance Agency, held 50 percent of the stock and the Thompson brothers equally held the balance. Richard Thompson and Thomas Thompson were respectively president and vice president of the company and Wilson was its secretary-treasurer. They proposed a daytime-only operation on 1500 KHz with 10 kilowatts power. Following approval, the station signed-on February 12, 1962, with Laurence C. "Curt" Raynes as the station's chief engineer.

KPIR changed call signs to KPNW on August 1, 1967 (see KPNW-FM/KLCC-FM in chapter 16).

## KWFS-FM/KZEL-FM Eugene

Willamette Family Stations, Inc. filed an application for a new Eugene FM station on July 23, 1960. Company president Marvin R. Steffins Jr. was a Detroit, Michigan, resident who had previously been general manager of WGEI-AM Detroit until shortly before the Eugene application was submitted.

Steffins was joined in the Eugene venture by his father, Marvin R. Steffins Sr., who was chairman of Willamette Family's board. The elder Steffins was an engineer with prior broadcasting experience through his 59 percent ownership of WGEI-AM. The Steffins were joined

KWFS-AM-FM stationery letterhead, c. 1965
WSMB Collection

by several Oregon residents, including K. Ray Barnes, with Security Light and Accident Company of Salem, and Jack W. Gossard, an employee of Willamette Valley Lumber Operators Association. Steffins Sr. held 24 percent of the company's stock, and Steffins Jr. held 26 percent. Barnes held 12 percent; Gossard held 8 percent; and Clarence E. Brenneman, owner of various sign companies in Eugene, Roseburg and Medford, held an additional 12 percent. The balance of the shares was issued to Eugene C. Venn, Lane County district attorney; John O. Chatt, majority owner of Lane County Escrow Services, Inc., and other individuals.

Willamette Family's FCC application, which requested 96.1 MHz with 70 kilowatts power, was approved on March 16, 1961, and station construction was completed on March 31, 1962. KWFS-FM signed-on April 22, 1962. Both broadcast religious programming.

Early in 1967, Steffins sold the religious station to George L. Zellner, who changed the corporation's name to K-ZEL, Inc., in June. Zellner assumed the presidency of the company, and his name presumably served as the basis for a call sign change to KZEL-FM at the same time. Under Zellner's ownership, the station became a CBS radio affiliate and was managed by Cottonseed Clark. Simulcasting its sister AM station, both stations offered a country-and-western format. The AM station had also changed call signs from KWFS-AM to KZEL-AM. KZEL-FM station wasn't successful, and Zellner took it off the air in mid-1969 to stem its operating losses.

Later that year, an enterprising group of University of Oregon students approached Zellner and proposed that he entrust them with programming and operating the then-silent FM station. Tom Ballantyne, Marc L. Marsh and Matt McCormick were all journalism majors; Gary Palmatier was a political science major and Stan Garrett was an English major. Most had previously worked at the university's KWAX-FM, and all shared an interest in playing rock music, which wasn't being broadcast by the AM top-40 dominated stations. "The FM industry in 1969 was agricultural reports from South America, classical music and Muzak," recalled Palmatier, and they wanted to make KZEL "a seminal force in the underground FM movement."[6]

Marsh made the pitch to Zellner, who approved, and in mid-December 1969 they returned KZEL-FM to the air with a staff that largely worked without pay and presented free-form underground rock. The station was precedent-setting and highly popular, and it gradually became a community institution.

In 1970, Ballantyne left KZEL-FM, and in 1972, Jack "Jay" Arthur West and his wife, Barbara, purchased the station under the corporate name FM/96, Ltd. Jay West was president of the company, and his wife was its secretary-treasurer. Other stockholders included John S. West and Stan Garrett, who had remained at the station since 1969.

Jay West had a background in the music industry and was an astute music programmer who continued the station's success. On November 22, 1978, KZEL-FM was sold to Jayar Communications Corporation, which also owned KBDF-AM 1280 Eugene.

KZEL bumper sticker, c. 1970

## KWFS-AM/KZEL-AM Eugene

After having submitted an FM station application for Eugene, Willamette Family Stations filed another one—this time for an AM station on 1540 KHz with 1 kilowatt power. KWFS-AM signed-on May 6, 1962, just slightly after its FM sister station and the AM-FM pair simulcast programming.

As part of the stations' 1962 license renewals, KWFS received an FCC inquiry.[7] The AM-FM pair must have encountered some financial difficulties because one of the commission's questions involved the stations' $45,000 debt. Steffins Jr. reported that members of the board had agreed to provide funds to liquidate the debt. The commission apparently also questioned some programming as departing from the type originally proposed in the stations' FCC application. Steffins acknowledged such variations and explained that, since the time that the original KWFS-AM and FM applications had been submitted, five new stations had signed-on in Eugene and intense competition for talent and news/public affairs resources had required changes in the their plans.

In early 1967, Steffins sold KWFS-AM and KWFS-FM to George L. Zellner (see KWFS-FM/KZEL-FM for details of the sale). Following or concurrent with the sale of KZEL-FM to FM/96, Ltd., the station seems to have been turned back to Willamette Family Stations, although George Zellner remained in operational control. The AM station appears to have then not operated for long, and the 1540 KHz daytime facility was abandoned around 1970.

## KAPT-AM/KATR-AM/KZAM-AM/KHNN-AM/
## KZZK-AM/KNRQ-AM/KSCR-AM Eugene

Diana Crocker Redington, William H. Crocker II, Thomas J. Davis Jr. and Robert Sherman were equal partners in forming Eugene Broadcasters, Inc., which filed an application on March 24, 1959, for an AM station on 1320 KHz with 1 kilowatt power in Eugene. With the call letters KAPT assigned, station construction was completed on May 12, 1962. KAPT, which was located at 130 East 13th Avenue, considers its official sign-on date to be June 12, 1962.

The station, which was managed by David Miles, underwent ownership structure change in November 1962 when Davis sold his interest to Redington.[8] Following a call sign change to KATR, the station was sold to Westone Broadcasting Company on August 1, 1971, and then to KATR Communications, Inc., on April 1, 1977. The station was purchased on June 1, 1983, by

Visionary Radio Euphonics of Oregon, Inc., which changed the call sign to KZAM-AM on August 20, 1985. The station went through more call sign changes and became KHNN on May 1, 1990; KZZK on October 1, 1992; KNRQ on September 29, 1995; and KSCR on April 26, 2001.

# KBMC-FM/KMGE-FM Eugene

On May 5, 1961, Milan Corporation filed an FCC application to build a new station on 94.5 MHz in Eugene. A moving force in the enterprise was its vice president Sidney G. Smith, who owned 44 percent of the company's stock. John R. Riedinger was president and the majority stockholder with 55 percent, and secretary David N. Andrews, also of Eugene, owned the remaining 1percent.

Riedinger was employed by an engineering firm, Smith had previously been an announcer and commercial manager at Eugene's KFMY and Andrews was a Eugene lawyer.

Accompanying the FCC application, Milan submitted a modest petition signed by Eugene-area residents who supported the application because they believed the station would offer "high-quality programming similar to that now offered by Portland, Oregon stations KGMG and KPFM."[9] The petition went on to complain about the programming offered by radio stations that existed in Eugene at the time.

On January 3, 1962, Milan was granted an FCC construction permit for a 3.4-kilowatt station on 94.5 MHz with the call letters KBMC. The studios and transmitter were to be located at 858 East Park Street, and Milan spent $12,552 in constructing the station. It was ready for operation on June 30, 1962.

KBMC signed-on September 3, 1962, with a staff of four and very thin financing. Newspaper listings for the station were sporadic and perhaps reflected similarly inconsistent operation. In March 1963, Milan secured FCC permission to move KBMC's studio to 2041 East 26th Avenue and took the station off the air pending the relocation. KBMC was in over its head—and on July 2, 1963, Milan agreed to sell the station to Alan C. Graves (operating as F-Empire Broadcasters) while receiving FCC authority on July 22 to remain off the air. F-Empire Broadcasters, which consisted of Graves and his wife, Ruth, purchased the station for $22,571, including the discharge of approximately $8,000 in debt that Milan owed to various equipment suppliers. The sale was consummated on January 22, 1964. The station, which now re-conceived its call letters to mean **K**-**B**est-**M**usic-**C**ountry-style-FM, resumed operation under the new ownership on January 28, 1964.

KBMC also promoted itself as "The New Nashville Sound." Later that same year F-Empire moved KBMC's studio and transmitter to 600 Ridgewood Drive. However, the Graves' seemed to enjoy no greater success in operating KBMC than had Milan. On March 30, 1964, they requested FCC permission to go silent—which prompted public inquires to the FCC about the station's status.

The Graves then negotiated a sale of KBMC for $28,200 to Good Shepherd Broadcasting, Inc., of Eugene. The cited "lack of operating capital and continued operating expenses exceed[ing] financial capabilities" as their reason for selling.[10] The FCC approved the sale on September 16, 1965.

Good Shepherd reported that it intended to "enter the field of religious music in which no other local station specializes" and moved the KBMC studios to 2895 Hilyard Street. Key staff included Leonal Fiksdal, station manager, and Larry Jonas, sales manager. Good Shepherd also utilized volunteer students and community members who volunteered to work as announcers, disc jockeys, bookkeepers and sales people. However, KBMC continued to operate at a loss. In spring 1966, Larry Jonas assumed the company's presidency, and Bernice Poling of Eugene became vice president. The station also added farm and ladies' news programs; a weekly, 15-minute report from the Oregon Department of Continuing Education; and the five-day-a-week, 15-minute program *Psychology for Living*, hosted by Clyde Narramore. By May 1965, Fiksdal was president of Good Shepherd, as well as station manager, and KBMC was apparently operating in the black. The station changed call signs to KMGE on January 6, 1987.

## KPNW-FM Eugene

In 1967, KUGN, Inc., and Pacific Northwest Broadcasting, Inc., competed for the 99.1 MHz FM frequency in Eugene. The latter company, which owned KPIR-AM, successfully secured the new frequency but waited until Lane Community College changed its station's call sign from KPNW to KLCC before adopting KPNW as its own. KPNW-FM signed-on in November 1968 on 99.1 MHz with 86 kilowatts power from its studios at 1345 Olive Street, where it shared studios with its AM sister station (although the AM and FM programmed separately).

## KJDY-AM John Day

According to long-time KJDY staff member J. Leroy "Buss" Jolley, some minor interest had been shown in the 1940s and early 1950s in establishing a radio station in Grant County. However, it was KUMA's Ted Smith that brought KJDY onto the air on Decem-

KJDY Scrapbook, WSMB Collection

KJDY's inaugural program, December 13, 1963. In the studio were Herman Oliver (left), "Buss" Jolley (right) and Jim Bradley (foreground), who was engineering.

ber 13, 1963, when he and his long-time partner Pop Fisher established John Day Valley Broadcasters, which filed an FCC application for the 250-watt 1400 KHz facility.[11]

Smith's interest was originally sparked by a conversation with Herman Oliver, a well-known Grant County rancher and banker. While planning for the station was in progress, Smith decided to stimulate local interest by launching a non-broadcast version of KJDY prior to the station's actual sign-on. In 1960, he hired John Day's Ernie and Sally Sharp to gather Grant County news, which was mailed to Pendleton and broadcast over KUMA. That station's signal was carried by the Blue Mountain Cable TV Company, which meant that KUMA and its Grant County news coverage could be heard in John Day, Canyon City and Mt. Vernon over TV cable channel 6.

While still awaiting FCC approval to sign-on KJDY, Smith installed a full radio studio in December 1962 that allowed programmed the cable channel full-time just as though the channel was a radio station. When KJDY's FCC construction permit was issued on October 31, 1963, plans were made to inaugurate the station on December 1 and the cable version of KJDY was abandoned on November 30.

"Five Foot and Rising," captions this photo in the KJDY Scrapbook, December 1964.

"Went thata way" captions this photo of KJDY's tower after the flood, in the KJDY Scrapbook, December 1964.

Constructed by KUMA chief engineer Jim Bradley, KJDY was located in a 20-foot-by-40-foot portion of Keerins Hall at the Grant County Fairgrounds. Jolley, who had previously managed KNPT Newport, moved to Canyon City/John Day in September 1963 to prepare KJDY for sign-on, which took place at noon on Friday, December 13, 1963. Participating in the inaugural broadcast were Herman Oliver, president of Grant County Bank, who "threw the switch," and Jolley, who served as master of ceremonies. The program also featured John Day mayor Cliff Benson; Chamber of Commerce president Joe Cahill; Chamber president-elect John Gardner, and reverend Phil Ryan, who gave an invocation. Senator Mark Hatfield sent a tape-recorded message of welcome. Joining Jolley as initial staff members were Gary Hill, Robert Wiley (who was a John Day mail carrier) and grade school teacher Tom Switzer. Jolley's wife, Dorothy, was the station's receptionist.

Smith's three-year promotional effort paid off in strong community support for the new station. In a town of less than 2,000 people, 508 attended the station's weekend inaugural open house. On November 24, 1964, the FCC granted KJDY permission to increase its power to 1 kilowatt—but nature got in the way.

On December 22, 1964, a disastrous flood hit Grant County and resulted in more than $4 million in damage. Ranchers suffered extensive losses; county roads sustained in excess of $500,000 in damage; and KJDY was wiped out, with flood waters rising to five feet inside the station's studios. An essential community emergency communication link, KJDY was forced off the air. The studio and transmission plant were a total loss, and all that remained of the station's tower was a crumpled mass of metal.

Owners Ted Smith and Pop Fisher immediately committed to rebuilding KJDY. Smith sent emergency equipment from KUMA Pendleton and requested FCC authority to establish a temporary studio and transmitter at Jolley's home. On Christmas Day 1964, KJDY resumed operation from a spare bedroom in the Jolley residence.

Referred to jokingly as "the BBC," (for the Bedroom Broadcasting Company), KJDY operated from the temporary quarters until April 9, 1965, when the station entered "a new era." It moved into new studios in the Grant County Bank building located at 160 East Main Street and activated its new 1-kilowatt daytime transmitter.[12] It had been an epic struggle.

# KSHA-AM/KISD-AM/KMFR-AM/KTMT-AM/KCMX-AM Medford

KSHA was another Oregon station developed by individuals who had participated in establishing stations in Eugene and Salem. For the Medford operation, the group consisted of Genevieve de Dampierre Casey, Alexander M. Casey, William H. Crocker II and Diana Crocker Redington. Their partnership agreement for a Medford station was struck on February 27, 1959, and an FCC application was filed on April 9 of that year.

Because the parties were involved in a number of other radio station applications, their partnership agreement referred to the undertaking as "The Medford Project." The application was approved by the FCC on October 12, 1960, but construction did not proceed quickly. The group hired Russell K. Olsen (founding chief engineer and general manager of KPTV channel 27 in Portland) as the station's technical director.

KSHA signed-on April 4, 1962, at 860 KHz with 1 kilowatt power from studios located at 27 West Main Street. The station was managed by Robert J. Wells, with Barton Cronin as program director. Alexander M. Casey withdrew from the venture on July 14, 1964, and assigned his interest to Genevieve de Dampierre Casey—perhaps as part of a property settlement. Around 1972, Westone Broadcast Company purchased the station, which was then managed by Virgil Watkins. Bob Thomlinson, a long-time figure in Oregon radio, was briefly on staff. Robin Lawson served as program director, and Mel Tynan was chief engineer.

By 1980, the station was being managed by Fergus Prestbye, with Dave Michaels as program director, Bob Merrill as music director, Dick Huston as news director and Don Bennett as chief engineer. In June 1980, the station was sold to CBF Broadcasting, Inc. Craig Finley was president of the buyer and general manager of the station—which changed call signs to KISD. On April 27, 1984, the station was sold again, this time to Rogue Valley Broadcasting, Inc., whose president was Ray Johnson (who had

British-born Robin Lawson was seen and heard over numerous Rogue Valley stations, including KCMX-AM, KISD-AM and KOBI-TV, for decades. In 1987, he inaugurated Saturday Morning Jazz (pictured here during his first program) over Jefferson Public Radio's KSMF-FM.

sold KMED-AM in 1977 and KTVL-TV in 1981). Johnson's son, Robert Johnson, served as vice president and general sales manager, Jack Earl was program director, Robin Lawson was news director and Sam Croskell was sales manager. The station also shifted frequencies to 880 KHz and became KMFR.

Rogue Valley Broadcasting sold the station to DRB-Medford License, LLP, on May 14, 1996. Co-owned with KTMT in 1999, the station became KTMT-AM and then, in a switch of several Medford stations' call signs, became KCMX. The station was later acquired by Mapleton Communications, LLC.

## KGMG-FM/KXL-FM/KXJM-FM/KXTG-FM Portland

KGMG was conceived by International Good Music, Inc. (IGM), a manufacturer of broadcast automation systems which played recorded music from large tape reels. Founded in 1958, IGM was located in Bellingham, Washington, and was headed by Lafayette "Rogan" Jones, president, and David Mintz, executive vice president. In addition to manufacturing broadcast automation systems, IGM owned and operated KVOS-AM-TV in Bellingham.

On August 5, 1959, IGM filed an FCC application to expand into Portland with an FM station, and the commission granted that application for 95.5 MHz, at 68.35 kilowatts, on September 23, 1959. The call letters KGMG were issued on October 28, 1959. On December 22, 1959, the station purchased KHTV channel 27's former Healy Heights land, building and tower (which had originally been constructed by Wilbur Jerman for his company's first FM station, KPRA-FM) for $45,000 through its parent company, Tower Sites, Inc. The call sign KGMG (standing for Good Music) referred to the focus of the station's classical music programming.

The station was managed by Marc Bowman, who had extensive radio, newspaper and theatre experience in Portland. KGMG signed-on September 25, 1960, and was referred to by the *Oregonian* as "the marriage of automation and the classics." KGMG was conceived by Jones as part of an intended chain of stations to be operated under the name Heritage FM Stations. They were to be run, with time sold to advertisers, as a network of 25 stations across the country using common taped programming designed to offer "balanced excellence in performance and reproduction." By 1962, Heritage was programming stations in Seattle, Los Angeles and San Bernardino, in addition to Portland and Bellingham. On March 17, 1962, KGMG became Portland's second FM station to convert to FM stereo multiplex broadcasting.[13]

In 1963, William J. Trader became station manager. On April 20, 1964, Trader guided the station from its previous classical/broadway/jazz/folk music format to middle-of-the-road music, which was supplied to the station on tape from

Courtesy of the Oregonian

Models demonstrating one of the new IGM broadcast automation systems that allowed for KGMG's automated music format, 1959.

IGM's Bellingham headquarters. Six months later, Trader was succeeded by John S. Mackwood as station manager and chief engineer. Virginia C. Kupfer was program director.

On June 18, 1965, KGMG was sold to Portland and Spokane Radio, owner of KXL-AM, for $125,000. It relocated to KXL's studios on SE 82nd Street and Sunnyside Road. On July 5, the station changed call signs to KXL-FM and began duplicating KXL-AM's beautiful music format. KXL-AM staff Melvin Bailey program director; John Salisbury news director and Bryce Howard chief engineer served both KXL-AM and FM. Bailey became KXL-AM-FM's station manager on June 15, 1966. The station later changed call signs to KXJM-FM on April 30, 1999 and became KXTG on May 27, 2008.

## KPDQ-FM Portland

On November 9, 1960, John W. Davis filed KPDQ, Inc.'s, application for an FM companion to its Portland AM station. The application requested 93.7 MHz with 49.7 kilowatts power with the station's antenna on the KGMG tower. That application was granted on March 22, 1961, along with a power increase request for 56.7 kilowatts. The station's chief engineer, Donald C. Wilkinson, oversaw construction.

KPDQ-FM quietly signed-on October 11, 1961, simulcasting its AM counterpart from studios at 4903 NE Sandy Boulevard. Managed by Robert W. Ball, the young station soon confronted the FCC order that, after October 15, 1965, jointly owned AM-FM stations could no longer simulcast programming. KPDQ protested and secured a delay in complying through the duration of the station's existing license term.

Station owner KPDQ, Inc., changed its corporate name to Inspirational Broadcasting Corporation in 1976. Ten years later, it sold the station, along with its sister station KPDQ-AM, to Salem Media of Oregon, Inc. (see chapter 14).

## KLIQ-FM Portland

On March 17, 1967, Cascade Broadcasting Corporation applied for a new Portland FM station on 92.3 MHz with 59 kilowatts power. Cascade's president and 50-percent stockholder was David M. Jack, who was joined in the effort by Willis M. Coil of Portland, who served as secretary-treasurer, and Walter McNiff of Woodside, California, who served as vice president.[14] (Cascade Broadcasting also concurrently filed an application for approval of its purchase of KLIQ-AM, which Jack had been managing since January 1963.)

The call letters KLIQ-FM were assigned, and construction of the new FM station was completed on November 9. The station's studios were located at "Broadcast Square" at Oaks Park,

**1290 KC**
PORTLAND, OREGON 97202
234-8448

While this 1967 letterhead promotes KLIQ-AM's talk lineup, KLIQ-FM simulcast the daytime AM station and then continued at night with its own talk host complement. While KLIQ-FM's talk format was short-lived, this letterhead illustrates much of its flavor.
WSMB Collection

while its transmitter was installed at the KXL-FM site. KLIQ-FM signed-on December 6, 1967, and five days later on December 11, began 24-hour talk programming. It was said to be the first all-talk FM format in the nation.[15]

On April 1, 1968, KLIQ-AM-FM abandoned talk and began carrying what it described as "Town & Country Sound" under the slogan "Country Click."

## KINK-FM Portland

KGW gave up its license for KGW-FM in March 1950—which was the second such instance of KGW-AM giving up on FM (see chapter 14). KGW-FM entered its third incarnation when the station returned to the air in February 1952, but it was sold to "Q" Cox in October 1954 (see chapters 13 and 15).

A promotional piece for KINK's impending arrival, 1968
WSMB Collection

By the mid-1960s, FM radio was gaining strength as an industry, and while FM stations were not necessarily profitable, it was clear that they would eventually become valuable properties. King Broadcasting filed for another FM sister operation to KGW-AM in the mid-1960s and received a construction permit for KGW-FM in mid-June 1967. King constructed new studios for the FM station on the second floor of the KGW Broadcast Center at 1501 SW Jefferson Street, and the FM station's transmitter was installed at 299 NW Skyline Boulevard with its antenna mounted on the KGW-TV tower.

KGW-FM manager John David did most of the planning for the new station and outlined his thoughts in a 1968 memo to King Broadcasting president Ancil Payne:

> Two important trends are occurring in music today. First, Middle-of-the-Road music is beginning to reflect population demographics; the Big Beat sound is becoming today's Standard Pops as the original rock & roll generation of the 1950s grows older.
>
> Trend number two is the emergence of a new style of popular music. New Rock or Progressive Rock evolved from rock & roll but bears little similarity to popular music of more than two or three years ago. Progressive Rock is the sound of today's young people, just as Big Beat Rock belonged to an earlier generation of teenagers.
>
> Top-40 stations, which originally catered to teenagers and achieved dominance as that segment of the population grew older and larger, and as our society grew more youth oriented, are now faced with a dilemma; whether or not to program New Rock. If they do play it in large amounts it will alienate the older portion of their audience which took them 10 years to build, but does not identify with or understand the new music. If they don't play it, they will lose today's young listeners and tomorrow's mass audience.
>
> This new direction in popular music will make it necessary for radio broadcasters to begin another cycle of establishing a young audience and growing with it.[16]

That's precisely what King Broadcasting authorized David to do. He wanted slightly quirky call letters and settled on KINK, using the slogan "the Underground Link." The KGW-FM call sign was changed to KINK-FM on December 12, 1968, and the station signed-on Christmas Day.

David hit his target. KINK was an immediate success with programming that was a clear alternative to other Portland rock formats.

Among the staff changes at KINK in the mid-1980s were the arrival of Les Sarnoff as host of the *KINK Morning Show* on February 13, 1986; Carl A. Widing's appointment as program director; and Stan Mak's appointment as vice president and general manager.[17]

# KJIB-FM/KWJJ-FM Portland

KJIB signed-on at 6 a.m. on September 21, 1968, at 99.5 MHz with 35 kilowatts power. Owned by the newly-formed Contemporary FM, Inc., the station was the inspiration of 26-year-old Bernard Seitz, who had previously worked for Sears Roebuck in Illinois and California. KJIB was a family operation, with Seitz's wife, Christine, serving as Contemporary FM's secretary-treasurer and Seitz's father, who invested $45,000 to launch the venture. At that time, no one had successfully sold FM radio time to Portland advertisers, and Seitz openly acknowledged that KJIB was a gamble.

KJIB letterhead logo, c. 1969
WSMB Collection

While Seitz originally planned to locate KJIB's transmitter at KXL-FM's site on Healy Heights and to lease the upper floor of KXL's transmitter building for a studio location, KJIB actually built its studios at 309 SW Fourth Avenue. The genial Seitz owned the station for nearly six years but could never quite get the stand-alone FM station to financial stability, and Contemporary FM's stock was purchased by the owner of KWJJ-AM on June 6, 1974. Initially, the station kept its call sign and middle-of-the-road music format but eventually took the KWJJ-FM call sign.

# KRAF-AM/KLLU-AM/KDUN-AM Reedsport

On October 23, 1958, Walter J. Kraus—who had various business interests in the Reedsport/North Bend area—filed an application for a daytime-only station at Reedsport to operate on 1470 KHz with 5 kilowatts power under the name Oregon Coast Broadcasters. John W. Kendall was Kraus' attorney, and Grant Feikert engineered the station's design.

Under call sign KRAF (which stood for **K**-**R**eedsport-**A**nd-**F**lorence), station construction was completed on May 14, 1961, and the self-proclaimed "Mighty K-RAF Radio" signed-on June 2. It was managed by Gless Connoy and used the slogan "Listening is Heavenly on 1470." A Keystone Broadcasting System affiliate, the station also referred to itself as "The Big Wave of the Oregon Coast." Connoy's wife, Katie, was the program director.

KRAF was struggling and on May 23, 1963, Kraus and Connoy signed an agreement under which Connoy was to purchase the station for $48,000—but the deal was called off six months later. The sale was reactivated and consummated on November 20, 1964.

KRAF's call sign later changed to KLLU, changed frequencies to 1030 KHz, and on September 25, 2002, became KDUN.

THE BIG WAVE OF THE OREGON COAST — 5000 WATTS

REEDSPORT, OREGON
Number **1** Melody Lane

FLORENCE, OREGON
790 Highway Avenue

Radio **KRAF**

MIGHTY **K-RAF**
REEDSPORT AND FLORENCE

"LISTENING IS HEAVENLY ON 1470"

LAND OF THE DUNES — REEDSPORT AND FLORENCE

KRAF stationery letterhead
WSMB Collection

## KAPT-AM Salem

On January 15, 1960, Reid W. Dennis, Diana Crocker Redington and Genevieve de Dampierre Casey filed an FCC application, as joint venturers, for a new 1 kilowatt radio station on 1220 KHz in Salem under the name Salem Broadcasters. Dennis was half-owner, and the other two venturers each held 25 percent. Dennis was involved in radio stations in El Centro, California, and Reno; Redington in Eugene and Medford; and Casey in Medford and Honolulu. The daytime-only station's application was granted on March 29, 1960, and the station signed-on December 12, 1961, from studios at 212 High Street NE. In its early years, KAPT was managed by Colonel Carl W. Nelson and was affiliated with the Mutual and Keystone Networks.

## KOHI-AM St. Helens

On March 2, 1960, St. Helens got its own radio station when KOHI signed-on at 2 p.m. with 1 kilowatt power at 1600 KHz. L. Berenice Brownlow was the owner of KOHI, Inc., which created the station. Her husband, Charles T. Brownlow, was the company's vice president and the station's general manager. Mrs. Brownlow was also a 19-percent owner of KSEM, Inc., of Moses Lake, Washington, and a 7 percent owner of Washington Telecasters, Inc., of Seattle, with which Charles was also associated. KOHI, Inc.'s, secretary-treasurer was Kathleen Ward. Charles Brownlow was later succeeded by Bill Anderson, who served as vice president, general manager, program director and commercial manager. Anderson was later the Portland Buckaroos hockey play-by-play announcer on KPOK, KOIN and KYXI in the 1970s.

KOHI's slogan was "Dial high, Dial KO-HI" but the station also used "The sweet 16" (referring to its 1600 KHz frequency). KOHI's studios and transmitter were located on the Columbia River Highway. The station was an affiliate of the Keystone Broadcasting System transcription network. By 1975, KOHI was an ABC Entertainment affiliate.

## KSWB-AM Seaside

Seaside Broadcasting Corporation, with Gerald "Jerry" B. Dennon as its president, filed an FCC application for a Seaside radio station to operate on 750 KHz, and KSWB signed-on the air July 11, 1968. The *Seaside Signal* headline trumpeted the town's very own station as "KSWB, the New Giant on the Coast."

Dennon had earlier worked for KOIN-AM-FM-TV and KUIK before founding the Jerden record label in Seattle in 1960. Interestingly, the 45-rpm single *Louie, Louie* by Portland's Kingsmen, was originally released on the Jerden label. Joining Dennon at Seaside Broadcasting were the members of the Seattle-based folk music group "The Brothers Four."[18]

Jon C. Ogle was KSWB's general manager, and Steve McNally was program director—both of whom were formerly with KACI. KSWB, which used the slogan "Radio 93," operated from studios at 120 North Holladay Drive, while its transmitter was located on Avenue South. The station's jingles were recorded by The Brothers Four and listener Eric Swedberg remembers them as: "93, by the Sea, KSWB" (with a sustained B). Dennon adds: "We signed off each broadcast day with The Brothers Four Columbia recording of *What Now My Love*."[19]

On June 30, 1972, Seaside Broadcasting Corporation's stock was purchased by Robert E. Gilbert, who became the company's president and KSWB's chief engineer. Kenneth E. Karge took over as general manager and Sam D. Kirkaldie as program director. The station then affiliated with the ABC Contemporary Network. Around 1984, KSWB switched to 840 KHz with 1 kilowatt daytime and 500 watts of nighttime power.

## KFIR-AM Sweet Home

Sweet Home got its own radio station when the daytime-only KFIR signed-on August 7, 1968, with 1 kilowatt power at 1370 KHz. Promoting the station's impending arrival, Sweet Home's *New Era* weekly newspaper printed an ad saying "We're Not Fir Off!" The August 8 edition of the *New Era* reported that the inauguration ceremonies held at noon the day before included a statement of purpose: "Our emphasis will be on local news of Sweet Home and the Northwest," read by KFIR general manager Dennis Celorie, who was also president of licensee Santiam Broadcasters, Inc. Celorie, who had previously been the program director at Eugene's KWFS-AM-FM, owned Santiam Broadcasters in partnership with Sweet Home's pharmacist, Ken Groves, and Dick Groves of Seattle. The ABC Entertainment Network-affiliated station held a subsequent public inauguration party on August 17 at the station's Pleasant Valley Road studios featuring free hot dogs and cold drinks.

The station's early staff included sales manager Herbert A. Schacher, program director/chief engineer Kenton E. Sturdevant, announcer and salesman Dave Hudson, and office manager Linda Brown. Sturdevant recalls that he was the "morning man, [who] did a little part-time sales, mowed the lawn and chased news in my spare time. KFIR was really a ball."[20]

## KCIV-FM The Dalles

The Dalles' first FM station and the first commercial FM station in Central Oregon, KCIV signed-on Thanksgiving Day, 1968, at 104.5 MHz with 25 kilowatts power. Initially, the station operated from 9 a.m. to 10 p.m., Monday through Saturday, and its slogan was "Beautiful Music in Stereo Radio."

Identified on-air as Q-104, the KCIV call sign was chosen for its somewhat obscure reference to the Roman numeral for 104: CIV. KCIV was conceived and founded by Leslie L. Cunningham, a 13-year resident of The Dalles, who had initially gained radio experience both in Portland and at The Dalles' KODL. Cunningham built KCIV on Stacker Butte in the Columbia Hills, eight miles north of town. Cunningham's stated goal in starting the station was to provide "a class and quality of music not available to the area," although he clearly acknowledged that his own financial rewards would be modest. Cunningham served as his own program director and employed only one other full-time person, and the station operated with "a gross income of slightly under $25,000 per year.[21]

In 1982, the station was sold to Mid-Columbia Broadcasting, Inc., which was owned by Greg Walden (son of Paul Walden and future U.S. Representative), and Greg's wife Mylene. The new owner changed the station's call sign to KMCQ on June 20, 1984. KMCQ disappeared on March 30, 2007, as part of Mid-Columbia's sale of its five-station group, which included the transfer of KMCQ's frequency for use in the Seattle area.

## KLUU-AM/KTDO-AM Toledo

KTDO signed-on in 1960 after a troubled start. The station originated with a 1957 application filed by Robert G. Beattie and his wife, Reve, who were both Corvallis residents. Doing business as Toledo Broadcasters, the former Portland Television College instructor and his wife filed the application—perhaps on a speculative basis—for a full-time station with

250 watts at 1230 KHz. Beattie had built radio stations in Walla Walla and Anacortes, Washington, and had been chief engineer for KPDQ Portland and KPIC-TV Roseburg. His first broadcast ownership venture, KBCH Oceanlake, had been unsuccessful (see chapter 21).

The FCC granted Toledo Broadcasters' application with a required construction completion date of May 5, 1958. The call sign KLUU was assigned, but construction was delayed—which Beattie attributed to litigation with KBCH's Clayton S. Comer. The construction permit was ultimately extended, but the station wasn't built. In early 1960, Beattie sought to sell the KLUU construction permit to Edward C. McElroy Jr., a Dallas, Oregon, resident. McElroy had previously been a co-founder of KPLK-AM, Dallas, and later established KBBM-AM, Waldport. Although an objection was promptly filed by KNPT Newport, the FCC approved that sale. On July 28, 1960, McElroy requested that the KLUU call sign be changed to KTDO, under which the station signed-on September 26 with its studios and transmitter located on Highway 20 at Dundon Road, one-quarter mile from Toledo's center.

Staff at sign-on included McElroy's wife, Josephine as program director, and Kent Freeman Jr., news director. By 1965, KTDO's power had increased to 1 kilowatt daytime, and the station had affiliated with the ABC Radio Network.

## KGAR-AM/KVAN-AM#3/KMJK-AM/KVAN-AM#3/ KKAD-AM Vancouver WA

Gordon Arthur Rogers was president and program director of KBLA-AM Burbank, California, when he applied on May 1, 1959, for a new 1 kilowatt daytime station on 1550 KHz for Vancouver, Washington. Rogers sold KBLA to finance his Vancouver venture, which the FCC authorized on January 10, 1962. Rogers requested the call sign KGAR (for his own initials), and the station signed-on at 5 a.m. on August 10, 1963. Its studios and transmitter were located at 2808 Walnut Street in Vancouver.

The modestly financed station was constructed at a cost of $13,675, including the 100 feet of sewer pipe used for KGAR's tower. Most of the station's equipment consisted of KBLA's castoffs.

Initial staff included Rogers as general manager, Bob Van Roy as news director, Tom Cauthers and Gordon Short (whose air name was Al Gordon) as news announcers.[22] The station's slogan was "All news, All day."

The all-news KGAR broadcast the *KGAR News Wheel*, which Cauthers recalls as:

> The reporters, us three guys, would rotate doing shifts. All the news was rip 'n read off the UPI teletype machine. The first newscast was assembled off the wire and had to last at least 30 minutes. It was recorded as it was delivered live on the air. Then, about 3 minutes of PSAs ran while the reporter re-wound the tape to air it. That newscast would run again, while the reporter assembled the next half hour newscast. When the first tape was over, the reporter would read another half hour while the tape recorded.
>
> When it was over, the first tape ran. Then the second tape while the reporter got ready to read the third segment while it was being recorded. After that, every other half hour was fresh, and recorded for later playback.[23]

KGAR ran on all-news format for six years but switched to top-40 in January 1966. By this time, KYMN had abandoned top-40, leaving the field to KISN, and KGAR positioned itself to compete directly with Don Burden's top-rated KISN.

Robert T. Fletcher, whose air name was Bob Duke, assembled a strong team at KGAR, including chief engineer A. J. Harold (who was later known as Bobby Noonan on KISN) to launch KGAR's "Boss Radio" format on May 1, 1966. The station's slogans for the new format were: "Boss Radio at 1550," "The in Sound in Town," "The Boss 1550," "More Rockin' Rhythm," "KGAR Plays More Music" and "Much More Music Machine."

In a direct challenge to KISN, Rogers leased the Flatiron Building at the corner of SW 10th Avenue and Burnside Streets—directly across the street from KISN's "window on the world" studio at NW 10th and Burnside. Rogers also challenged KISN by running satiric, low-cost

KGAR radio brochure, 1966

promotions, such as the Bat Guanomobile campaign—during which the station gave away a wheelbarrow of guano manure and a trip to Scappoose—which spoofed KISN's expensive Batmobile promotion.

The gutsy Rogers was in for the long haul. He had signed a ten-year lease on the space opposite KISN and eagerly hired such talent as Paul Oscar Anderson, formerly of KISN and known on-air as POA, and Bob Duke (see chapter 23).

In December 1966, KGAR dropped its "Boss Radio" slogan and became "KGAR, The Hard Rock of the Northwest." Anderson left several months later, and Fletcher again took the program director reins. When the ABC Radio Network split itself into four specialized formatted news services on January 1, 1968, KGAR took the American Contemporary Radio Network affiliation for the Portland-Vancouver market.[24] Some months later, KGAR started to enter the rhythm and blues genre. Its program schedule noted that it was playing "Negro music 6 hours weekly."[25] Not long afterward, KGAR was describing itself as a "Top-30 and Rhythm and Blues" music" station.

Having abandoned the Flatiron Building studio, in late 1969 KGAR also closed its Oak Street studio in Portland and began operating exclusively from its original Vancouver location at 2808 NW Walnut Street. On December 15, Fletcher took over as general manager for Rogers, while retaining his program director position, and took KGAR from a Top-30 to a "Golden Hits" format, with afternoon talk programming featuring Jack Hurd (who had come over from KLIQ). When Michael W. Johnson took over as program director, he dropped the American Contemporary Radio Network affiliation and moved the station to a country-and-western format—which debuted on January 18, 1971.

In the early 1970s, KGAR was clearly having a hard time finding its niche. On September 13, 1972, it switched back to rock and two years later added soul music on weekends. In 1975, the station opened an additional Washington studio at the Inn at the Quay on the Columbia River, and Dave Beck came over from KOIN as the station's news director. When KISN signed-off the air on September 2, 1976, following its license revocation, KGAR could finally declare victory in its long battle with Burden's station.

That same year, Rogers transferred KGAR's license to the corporation KGAR, Inc., which he controlled. KGAR, Inc., aggressively pursued expansion and in 1976 secured FCC permission for a new four-tower directional antenna array on ten acres in Evergreen, Washington, and an increase in power from one to five kilowatts along with nighttime authority. KGAR eventually secured permission to operate at ten kilowatts directional and began 24-hour operation from its studio/transmitter site at Orchards, Washington, on December 24, 1976.

KGAR again switched from rock to country music on August 1, 1977, and dropped its ABC Contemporary Network affiliation in the process. In December 1978, the station moved its studios to 5620 NE Gher Road, Suite H, in Vancouver.

Brothers David and Gary Capps already owned KSRV-AM Ontario; KGAL-AM/KXIQ-FM Bend; KTIX-AM Pendleton; KGAL-AM Lebanon; and KEEP-AM and KEZJ-FM Twin Falls, Idaho. On December 1, 1978, their company, Inland Radio, Inc., added KGAR to that list when it purchased KGAR, Inc. On May 4, 1981, KGAR became KVAN#3 after the call letters were once again available after having been relinquished by the 1480 KHz Vancouver station—which became KARO (see chapter 21).

With the call sign change, the station's slogan became "K-Van is Clark County Proud." In July 1985, KVAN#3 moved its transmitter site to Sifton, Washington at 15307 NE 34th Street. Gentry Development Corporation purchased KVAN#3 from Inland Radio for $1,289,964 on October 3, 1985.

Gentry's majority stockholder was David Capps, who held nearly 40 percent of the company's stock. Bruce L. Engel (president of Tigard-based forestry company WTD Industries, Inc.) and William G. Williamson held the balance of the stock. Gentry switched the station's format to adult contemporary and then purchased KMJK-FM at 106.7 MHz for $3.9 million under the corporate name Magic Radio, Inc., which was owned by Engel, Gary L. Capps and Gary's son, Mark.

Following a Mutual network affiliation in February 1988, the KVAN#3 and KMJK licensees merged on December 23, 1988, such that both stations were owned by Engel Communications Group, whose president was Bruce L. Engel. On February 4, 1989, KVAN#3 was purchased by Rogue Broadcasting Corporation, a subsidiary of Fairmont Communications Corporation, for $7.4 million. Eight months later, most of the station's staff was suddenly laid off "for economic reasons," leaving the affected employees in a state of shock. At the time the stunned staff was discharged, KVAN#3 abandoned independent programming and began simulcasting KMJK-FM. The station also switched its call letters to KMJK-AM#2 ten days later on October 12, 1989.

On February 15, 1991, KMJK-AM#2 returned to the call sign KVAN#3, ceased simulcasting its FM sister station, and adopted a light contemporary format. However, the station had nearly hit bottom, and Rogue Broadcasting filed for bankruptcy the following August.

Emerging from that bankruptcy, the station entered into a local management agreement with KWBY-AM Woodburn and began simulcasting the Woodburn station's country-and-western format, along with some KVAN#3 talk programming. The station slowly began adding Spanish programming.

On July 12, 1993, KVAN#3 was sold for $177,750 to Vancouverradio, Inc., whose president was former Clark County commissioner Richard A. Granger Sr. On November 20, 1998, the station was sold to Pamplin Broadcasting Corporation for $1.65 million, and on March 25, 2003, KVAN#3 became KKAD-AM.

# KWRC-AM Woodburn

On March 5, 1962, Oliver Lee Withers, who was generally known as O. L. Withers, filed an application for a 250-watt Woodburn radio station on 940 KHz. A local businessman who owned the Withers Lumber Company and the Mt. Angel Lumber Company, Withers was eager to get on the air and found the FCC's customary application process frustrating. When the commission authorized construction on December 12, 1963, and assigned the call sign KWRC, Withers sailed into constructing the station, which signed-on July 10, 1964, from its studio and transmitter site at 698 Pacific Highway (Oregon 99E). Bryon M. Stephenson was the station's original general manager and news director. Others on staff included Pat Stephenson, commercial manager; Dean Norton, program director; and Archie Brush, chief engineer.

## Endnotes

1. Atkinson had been the weather helicopter reporter for KCRA Radio and TV, and then the weather/traffic reporter for Sacramento station KFBK-TV which he later managed.
2. Perry Atkinson. Interview with author. March 27, 2007.
3. "KFLY Radio License Lost," *Oregonian*, May 27, 1970.
4. The owners had originally sought the call signs KRST, KMFY, KTOP or KOBY, none of which were available. (Shoemaker, George W., attorney, Wallowa Broadcasters. 1958. Letter to Mary Jane Morris, Secretary, FCC, dated July 30. KWVR file BP-12406, NARA, College Park, MD).
5. Sign-on date based on news story "Radio KWVR Takes to Air," *Oregonian*, June 2, 1960.
6. Eric Mortenson, "DJs Take Look Back at Good Ol' Radio Days," *Eugene Register-Guard*, January, 2005.
7. The stations had come on-line just at the close of the previous license term and thus faced the need to file for renewal after only being on the air for a comparatively brief period.
8. The FCC filing reports that "Mr. Thomas J. Davis, Jr., finds it necessary for personal reasons to terminate his interest in Eugene Broadcasters" (KATR file, NARA, College Park, MD).
9. KBMC-FM FCC Form 301 Application for Authority to Construct a New Broadcast Station in Eugene, BPH-3379, filed May 5, 1961 (KBMC file, NARA, College Park, MD).
10. KBMC-FM Form 314 Application for Consent to Assignment of Radio Station License, dated June 21, 1965 (KBMC file, NARA, College Park, MD).
11. Power was subsequently raised to 1 kilowatt.
12. The station remained at 250 watts nighttime power.
13. "KGMG Set For Stereo," *Oregon Journal*, March 15, 1962, 11.
14. The balance of the stock was held by Pacific Insurance Investment Company, which sold its interest to Trans-Pacific Leasing Inc. in May 1970. Consent to Transfer of Control, BTC-6236, FCC (KLIQ-FM file, NARA, College Park MD).
15. Craig Adams, www.pdxradio.com.
16. David, John. Memorandum to Ancil Payne dated September 16, 1968. (http://www.kink.fm/Early-Brainstorming-Memo/131265)
17. Sarnoff, who began his Portland career on KGON-FM in 1974, died on April 29, 2009.
18. The Brothers Four consisted of vice president of Seaside Broadcasting Robert L. Flick, Richard Foley, Michael Kirkand and John Paine.
19. Jerry Dennon, email message dated May 21, 2008, posted on www.pdxradio.com.
20. From www.pdxradio.com post by Sturdevant.
21. KCIV-FM License Renewal Application Amendment, dated April 9, 1975 (KCIV-FM file, NARA, College Park, MD).
22. Cauthers had previously worked at KGON, KYJC, KRVC, KNND, KKEY and KGRO.
23. Craig Adams, www.pdxradio.com.
24. On January 1, 1968, the traditional ABC affiliate KWJJ-AM took the American Information Radio Network affiliation; KKEY (which had carried the *Don McNeill Breakfast Club* program since 1965, when KWJJ took a country-and-western format, became the American Entertainment Radio Network affiliate. The American FM Radio Network went to KLIQ-FM on April 1, 1968. When the Don McNeill program ended on the American Entertainment Radio Network in December 1968, KWJJ took the American Entertainment Radio Network affiliation away from KLIQ-FM in January 1969, and the American Information Radio Network affiliation moved to KXL on January 13, 1969.
25. *Broadcasting Yearbook*, 1969.

# 26

# New Television Stations
# of the 1960s

## KCBY-TV Coos Bay

While KVAL had served Coos Bay via cable for some time, the construction of a full Coos Bay TV station on channel 11 finally gave KVAL the third side of what it called the "Triangle TV Network," consisting of KVAL Eugene, KPIC Roseburg and KCBY Coos Bay. KCBY signed-on at 9 a.m. on Saturday, October 1, 1960—just in time to carry the World Series between the New York Yankees and the Pittsburgh Pirates on October 5. "Southwestern Oregon's Own TV Station" was managed by Milt Lindley, who had been assistant manager at KPIC. The station's Coalbank Slough studios stood at the foot of Bunker Hill, and its transmitter was on Noah Butte (see chapter 19 for KCBY's pre-history).

The KVAL signal, including NBC Network programming, was fed to KCBY with a newly installed microwave system, construction of which had been supervised by S. W. McCready in his role as general manager for all three stations in the TV Triangle group. Glynn McCready was KCBY's first chief engineer, assisted by Max Dick (former chief engineer at KXL Portland) and Dick Lee. Cliff Engle, whose career dated back to KGW's earliest days, was the new station's sales manager, and Wink Guthrie was hired from KOOS as staff announcer. Ed Davis was KCBY's photographer and film editor, and Mrs. Evelyn Larson was traffic manager.

# KTVR-TV La Grande

(See chapter 16)

# KMED-TV/KTVL-TV Medford

Medford's second television station began in an interesting fashion. When the FCC allocated channel 10 to Medford, Bill Smullin knew that his monopoly on TV in the Rogue Valley would eventually come to an end. The only questions were when that would occur and who would be his competitor. Learning that Radio Medford—owner of KMED radio—was interested in entering television, Smullin decided to help things along.

He contacted Radio Medford's president, Dwight Findley, and invited the Radio Medford board of directors to tour KBES in the dark of night to avoid "tipping any hands." There, he offered them the use of his transmitting site on Blackwell Hill (at what Smullin later described as a give-away price of $100 per month) and advice on how to get started. It was a very attractive offer, and Radio Medford promptly filed an FCC application for channel 10.

Radio Medford faced two challengers for channel 10. One bid came from a group of KMED radio's own employees and the other from Bill Hansen, who had earlier launched KDOV#1. Radio Medford prevailed before the FCC, and on October 3, 1961, at 9:55 a.m., KMED-TV signed-on from Bill Smullin's Blackwell Hill transmitter site. KMED's radio building on Ross Lane was enlarged to accommodate television studios.

Where portions of the NBC Network schedule had previously been seen over KBES, with KMED on the scene, the full NBC schedule shifted to the new station. KBES remained a primary CBS affiliate, and both stations picked what they wanted from the ABC schedule. Somewhat surprisingly, the enormous newspaper attention that attended KBES's 1953 sign-on was absent when KMED-TV arrived. Only a few short newspaper announcements noted the arrival of Medford's second TV station.

Bill Smullin and Ray Johnson, KMED's general manager and part-owner, were good friends. Both had grown up in the radio industry, so they had a great deal in common.[1] Johnson had been a vaudeville performer in Montana as a youth and had first broadcast over KFDB in Grand Falls in 1937. He wound up in radio engineering, working on the KMED technical staff, from which he became the radio station's general manager (see chapter 15). While Smullin eased the way for

Ray Johnson Collection, WSMB

Hank Henry, on assignment for KMED-TV, gathering news on 16 mm film, which was used before the advent of portable video equipment, c. 1965.

KMED-TV's birth, the two men and the two stations were intense business rivals when seeking advertisers or negotiating for programs—but they remained personally friendly. Their children relate that Smullin would spontaneously call Johnson to ask what his plans were for lunch, pick him up, and the two would drive to a mountain top, where they would eat sandwiches Smullin had prepared—and discuss their professional and personal lives.

Television was a young, invent-on-the-fly industry. Johnson later recalled that he imported top-notch people from throughout the nation to launch KMED-TV "but they all had different ideas" and couldn't get along. After a sleepless night's deliberation, Johnson came into the station, fired the imported crew and put his long-time radio employee Russ Jamison in charge of television programming. "We may ruin this thing but at least we're going to do it ourselves," he told him. They went on to make the station highly successful.[2]

KMED-TV news team, c. 1978 (left to right) weatherman Leon Hunsaker, co-anchor Ann Curry, co-anchor Marvin Rhodes

KMED built its news operation around Hank Henry, its radio news director, who came to Medford in 1963 from KGW radio in Portland. Radio Medford, Inc., reorganized under the name Sierra Cascade Communications, Inc., around 1979 and went on to purchase Redding's KQMS-AM and launch KTVZ-TV Bend (see chapter 27).

Notwithstanding such expansion, as Johnson approached retirement age he explored selling properties. In 1977, KMED-AM was sold. On September 4, 1981, KMED-TV channel 10 was sold for $12.1 million to Freedom Newspapers, Inc., of Santa Ana, California. The station's call sign was changed to KTVL-TV as a result of the sale. The three original partners—John R. Dellenback, J. L. "Les" DeArmond and Johnson—had been in business together for more than 30 years. Johnson noted to the press that he had "mixed feelings" about the TV sale, which arose because DeArmond, who was more than 80 years old, wished to liquidate his Sierra Cascade interests. The partners were so close that Johnson "did not wish to go on without DeArmond."[3] The buyer—which then owned 31 daily and 5 weekly newspapers in 11 states—was taking its first step into television. It was Medford's first instance of a TV station that wasn't locally owned.

One of the station's major finds was a recent University of Oregon graduate who was hired as KMED-TV's first female reporter. An Ashland High School graduate, Ann Curry had studied for a career in the magazine industry but, in 1978, jumped at a job opening at KMED-TV, where she rapidly won acclaim. King Broadcasting Company president Ancil Payne spotted a Curry broadcast while attending the Oregon Shakespeare Festival, which led to her move to his company's KGW in Portland in 1981. From there, she moved on to CBS-TV's Los Angeles KNXT-TV in 1984, NBC-TV in Chicago in 1991 and was quickly tapped by the network to anchor its *NBC News at Sunrise*. In May 1997, she was promoted to the news anchor spot on NBC-TV's *Today* show.

## KBES-TV and KMED-TV Move Their Transmitters

Shortly after KBES became KTVM in 1964, both KTVM and KMED-TV began think-ing about relocating their transmitters to enlarge their coverage. Reportedly, the two stations considered which station would go north (relocating to King Mountain) and which would go south (to Mt. Ashland), and the decision was worked out over one of Smullin and Johnson's mountaintop lunches. Smullin developed the transmission facilities at King Mountain, above Wolf Creek, believing that from that location he would be able to serve Douglas and southern Lane counties while also reaching the Oregon coast.

Eyeing northern California coverage, Johnson opted to move KMED-TV to Mt. Ashland, where a major road had recently been installed for the Mt. Ashland Ski Park. The station's move was overseen by KMED-TV's chief engineer, Ellis Feinstein, who had served at KWIN-AM be-fore joining Radio Medford's stations.[4] The power imported for the ski park and the associated road significantly reduced the costs for developing the Mount Ashland TV transmitter site.

In September 1966, KMED-TV signed-on the new transmitter site from Mt. Ashland, and in September 1968, KTVM signed-on from King Mountain with the new call sign KOBI. The moves dramatically increased both stations' coverage.

## KATU-TV Portland

In March 1961, Fisher Broadcasting was award-ed a construction permit for Portland channel 2—but KATU's start would not be an easy one. By the late 1950s, the Portland television market seemed to have settled. KPTV had moved from channel 27 to channel 12 by absorbing KLOR and had become an ABC affiliate. KOIN-TV was a solid CBS affiliate on channel 6 and KGW-TV channel 8 was NBC's Port-land outlet. Because KHTV had failed on channel 27, Portland had no independent television station. All three networks were represented, and the market appeared stable (see chapter 18).

KATU-TV's sign-on test pattern, 1962

When channel 27's owner George Haggarty announced he was returning that station's li-cense to the FCC, the Tribune Publishing Company of Tacoma, Washington, petitioned the commission to add a Portland VHF channel 2 to the Table of Allocations (see chapter 20).

There was already a considerable history of maneuvering for allocating VHF channels in Vancouver, and Salem—surrounding Portland—which would potentially have impacted the use of channel 2 in Portland. Those proceedings eventually settled, however, leaving channel 2 available in Portland.

Three parties filed applications for channel 2:

❰ KPOJ, Inc., which had previously competed for channel 12 in Portland and later for channel 2 in Salem (see chapter 18)

❰ Tribune Publishing Company—publisher of the *Tacoma News* and licensee of Tacoma stations KTNT-AM, KTNT-FM and KTNT-TV

❰ Fisher Broadcasting, which had previously explored filing an application for a Salem channel 2 station but now filed for that channel's use in Portland

Jim Allen began his *Rusty the Clown* program, which soon became *Rusty Nails*, on KPTV. The popular program moved to KATU in 1962 when that station signed-on. (promotional postcard produced by the program's sponsor, Alpenrose Dairy)

These three mutually exclusive channel 2 applications were designated for an FCC hearing. In Fisher's application, the company stated that it contemplated operating the station as an independent, since while it desired either an ABC or NBC Network affiliation, but had "no commitment" from either network.

The hearing examiner found in Fisher's favor, positively citing the company's record as a licensee, the fact that its principals had ties to the community and the diversity of their backgrounds. KATU (which was often rendered as K-2) signed-on at 7 p.m. on March 15, 1962, as an independent station. Its studios were located on 2153 NE Sandy Boulevard in the former Crystal Laundry building, which was substantially expanded for the station's use.

KATU's inaugural program, *Standby for K-2,* introduced "KATU personalities and guests" and was narrated by Leslie Nichols with entertainment featuring the Emery Clay Dancers and the Johnny Reitz orchestra. Among the station's special guests was former Portlander Jane Powell, who introduced a telecast of her 1951 MGM movie, *Royal Wedding* (see chapter 13).

Once on the air, KATU took various steps to strengthen its position, including moving its transmitter from Camas, Washington, to Portland's Skyline Boulevard at Stone Road. KATU's signal improvement apparently paid off, and the Portland television market was rocked by the announcement on November 30, 1963, that ABC would be leaving KPTV for KATU on March 1, 1964.[5] That left KPTV to become Portland's independent TV station. KATU owner Fisher Broadcasting had a strong association with ABC at the company's Seattle KOMO-TV station, which was seen by many as the driving factor in the switch.

KPTV eventually thrived as an independent, but at the time, most staff and observers wondered if the station could survive without a network. Station manager John Hansen guided KPTV to financial health as, eventually making it the most successful independent television station in the U.S.

KGW-TV's program director, Tom Dargan, who later took over management of KATU, c. 1956

Tom Dargan was a vice president at Fisher and station manager of KATU. Dargan, whose background was in theatre and journalism, had been on staff at KING-TV Seattle before transferring to Portland as KGW-TV's program director when that station launched in 1956. Moving back to Seattle, he managed KING-TV from 1959 until Fisher offered him the chance to manage KATU in 1963. Dargan is credited with introducing the magazine format to Portland television on *Sunday Morning, Faces and Places,* and *A.M. Northwest,* as well as launching the Iris Award-winning *Town Hall.* The latter show is credited with establishing a national model for issue forum-programs. Dargan died of cancer in 1988 after managing KATU for 25 years and guiding the station to a position of both prominence and success.

One of Dargan's widely respected achievements was convincing his old KGW-TV news crew members, Richard Ross and Tom McCall, to move to KATU. McCall became KATU's news analyst in 1975, following his service as Oregon's governor. When he came to KATU, he was already writing news analyses for the *Oregonian,* as well as airing radio commentaries over KEX and a "McCall radio network" of stations assembled by Vic Ives (see chapter 14).

Ross, referred to by the *Oregonian* as the "dean of Portland newscasters," had originally been imported from Seattle's KING-TV. He was part of the ten-person contingent King dispatched to Portland to launch KGW-TV in 1956. Ross was a towering media figure in Portland and the announcement that he was leaving KGW for KATU came as a major surprise. On September 1, 1975, Ross became KATU's news director and anchor of the early evening news, along with Dick Bogle, Jim Bosley and David Carr. Ross continued at KATU until his retirement from broadcasting in 1986 at age 75. Retiring to his home in Lake Oswego, Ross passed at in July, 2007 at age 86.

Jim Bosley ("the Boz") was a KATU icon, having come to the station in 1962 after starting out at KOTI Klamath Falls in 1958. KATU's weatherman since shortly after his arrival there, he became an institution at the station. Additionally, Bosley hosted *AM Northwest* for KATU from 1975 until he retired in 2000. He passed away in April, 2008 at age 73.

In 1981, KATU twice won the prestigious George Foster Peabody Award, sometimes called the Pulitzer Prize of broadcasting, for producing two docu-

Jim Bosley, c. 1968
Courtesy of KATU/Fisher Broadcasting Company

mentary programs—*To Begin Again* and *Out of the Ashes*—both of which focused on the effects of Mount St. Helens' volcanic eruption.

One of KATU's most famous alumni is Bill O'Reilly, who came to the station from KMGH-TV Denver in 1984 to anchor KATU's 6:30 p.m. news. O'Reilly moved on to ABC News in 1986 and later to the Fox cable television network. Another well-known former KATU staffer is Lisa Stark, who began as a researcher/reporter for National Public Radio in Washington, DC, then moved to radio reporting in San Francisco, Salem and Portland before getting into television. She anchored the 5:30 p.m. newscast on KEZI-TV Eugene before moving to KATU, where she anchored the 6:30 p.m. and 11 p.m. newscasts. Following her tenure at KATU, Stark moved on to the ABC-owned KGO-TV San Francisco before being named an ABC Network correspondent in 1994.

## KVDO-TV, Salem

(See chapter 16)

## Endnotes

1. Johnson had first broadcast over KFDB in Grand Falls as a youthful vaudeville performer in Montana in 1937. He wound up as part of the KMED technical staff and eventually purchased the station.
2. Johnson interview.
3. "Television Station KTVL Sold," *Medford Mail Tribune*, January 19, 1981, 3.
4. Radio Medford, Inc. eventually purchased Scala Electronics, Inc., a major U.S. antenna manufacturer, and relocated the manufacturing to Medford from San Francisco. Scala was spun off as a separate company as part of the sale of Radio Medford, Inc.'s properties in 1981 with Feinstein as Scala's president. Scala Electronics was subsequently purchased by Kathrein, Inc. a worldwide manufacturer of professional antenna systems based in Germany.
5. KATU-TV moved its transmitter 21 miles southwest to 225 NW Skyline Boulevard in Portland's west hills on January 14, 1964.

# The 1970s & '80s
# TV Roars, FM Soars

# New Oregon Radio and Television in the 1970s and Beyond

## The FM Decade: New Radio Stations of the 1970s

The 1970s were definitely FM's time. Many long-established AM stations, such as KCMX-AM Ashland, KLOO-AM Corvallis, KIHR-AM Hood River, KOOS-AM Coos Bay and KSLM-AM Salem, started new FM companion stations. Whereas the FM stations of AM-FM operations had largely relied on a simulcast basis in previous decades, the combination of evolving FCC regulations and market forces pushed AM-FM operators to find separate programming formats for their FM outlets.

Experimentation was the order of the day, and FM stations' frequent call-sign revisions marked the changes those explorations produced. FM standalone stations, which had largely been unsuccessful in the 1950s and 60s, became financially viable in the 1970s. By the end of the decade, FM radio as a whole had surpassed AM radio in listenership.

Another area of growth occurred in the 88 to 92 MHz noncommercial portion of the FM band. In the wake of the passage of the Public Broadcasting Act of 1967, a push to establish rechristened public radio stations emerged and brought with it accelerated interest in noncommercial FM as a whole. Some earlier educational FM stations, such as KWAX-FM, KOAP-FM and KLCC-FM, made the transition to public radio stations. (These stations met certain standards, making them eligible for support from the Corporation for Public Broadcasting, which had been founded as a result of the 1967 Act's passage.) Other stations, such as KCHC-FM Central Point High School, KEPO-FM Eagle Point High

School, KSLC-FM Linfield College/McMinnville and KRBM-FM Blue Mountain Community College/Pendleton signed-on as new ten-watt noncommercial educational stations.

The following AM and FM Oregon stations signed on in the 1970s.

| Call sign | City | Sign-On date | Frequency | Power | Originally owned by | Early staff | Slogan | Affiliated station |
|---|---|---|---|---|---|---|---|---|
| KRKT-FM | Albany | 8/1/1977 | 99.9 MHz | 100 kw | Linn-Benton Broadcasters, Inc. | Robert A. Esty (p); Gary Grossman (vp, gm) | 99 FM Stereo Oregon Country | KRKT-AM |
| KKIC-FM/ KCMX-FM | Ashland | 7/20/1978 | 101.9 MHz | 3 kw | Rogue Radio Corp. | | | KCMX-AM |
| KQHV-FM/ KICE-FM/ KMGX-FM | Bend | 7/1973 | 100.7 MHz | 50 kw | Paulina Broad-casting Company | Richard E. Gervais (p) | | |
| KXIQ-FM/ KXIX-FM | Bend | 12/1974 | 94.1 MHz | 50 kw | Juniper Broad-casting, Inc. | Gary L. Capps (p) | "What Gives Johnny Cash" | |
| KURY-FM | Brookings | c. 1976 | 95.3 MHz | 3 kw | KURY Radio, Inc. | | | |
| KCHC-FM | Central Point | 9/1974[1] | 91.7 MHz | 10 watts | School District #6 | | | |
| KICR-FM | Coos Bay | 11/19/1978 | 98.3 MHz/ 98.7 MHz | 700 watts/ 30 kw | Intercontinental Ministries | Gary A. Randall (p); Don Morningstar (m) | | |
| KYNG-FM | Coos Bay | 12/21/1979 | 105.5 MHz | | SGB Broadcast-ing, Inc. | Richard J. Behrendt (p) | K105 FM Stereo Rock | |
| KWRO-FM/ KSHR-FM | Coquille | 2/1981 | 102.3 MHz/ 97.3 MHz | 300 watts/ 25 kw | KWRO Broad-casting Corp. | | | KWRO-AM |
| KLOO-FM/ KFAT-FM/ KLOO-FM | Corvallis | 1/1973 | 106.1 MHz | 27.5 kw | KLOO, Inc. | Marvin "Kent" Frandsen (p) | | KLOO-AM |
| KEPO-FM | Eagle Point | 2/3/1976 | 89.1 MHz | 10 watts | School District #9 | | | |
| KOHU-FM/ KQFM-FM#2 | Hermiston | 9/18/1978 | 99.3 MHz | 3 kw | Hermiston Broadcasting Company | | FM 99 | KOHU-AM |
| KIHR-FM/ KCGB-FM | Hood River | 12/4/1978 | 105.5 MHz | 3 kw | Columbia Gorge Broadcasters, Inc. | | K105 | KIHR-AM |
| KLAD-FM/ KJSN-FM | Klamath Falls | 7/19/1974 | 92.3 MHz | 27.5 kw | Radio 960, Inc. | Cyrus Smith (p, gm) | | KLAD-AM |
| KAGM-FM/ KAGO-FM/ KJFF-FM | Klamath Falls | 10/15/1973 | 98.5 MHz | 26.5 kw | Klamath Broad-casting Company | John L. Ferm (p,gm) | | KAGO-AM |
| KLBM-FM KKUC-FM KUBQ-FM | La Grande | 8/15/1977 | 98.3 MHz | 1.3 kw | KLBM, Inc. | Kenneth Lillard (p,gm) | Your Sound Alterna-tive | |
| KEOL-FM | La Grande | 2/1974 | 89.1 MHz | 10 watts | Eastern Oregon University | | | |
| KQIV-FM/ KMJK-FM | Lake Oswego | 9/15/1972 | 106.7 MHz | 100 kw | Willamette Broadcasting, Inc. | Walter J. M. Kraus (p) | Rockin' In Quad | |
| KOMS-FM/ KIQY-FM/ KXPC-FM | Lebanon | 4/8/1974 | 103.7 MHz | 30 kw | Cary T. Isley | Cary T. Isley (gm) | | |

| Call sign | City | Sign-On date | Frequency | Power | Originally owned by | Early staff | Slogan | Affiliated station |
|---|---|---|---|---|---|---|---|---|
| KSLC-FM | McMinnville | 1/17/1972 | 90.3 MHz | 10 watts | Linfield College | Craig Singletary (gm) | | |
| KNPT-FM | Newport | 10/25/1976 | 102.5 MHz | 100 kw | Yaquina Radio, Inc. | Tom Becker (p,gm) | | KNPT-AM |
| KOOS-FM | North Bend | 12/10/1979 | 100.9 MHz | 800 watts | Larson-Wynn, Inc./Gold Coast Communications Corp. | Brent T. Larson (p) | | |
| KXBQ-FM/ KSRV-FM | Ontario | 7/4/1977 | 96.1 MHz | 27 kw | Duane Kressly; Duane Kerrula | George Bain (gm); John and Shirley Jennings (sls); Bill Gentry | | |
| KMED-FM/ KTMT-FM | Medford | 11/15/1970 | 93.7 MHz | 18.5 kw | Radio Medford, Inc. | Ray Johnson (p); Richard Huston (gm) | | KMED-AM |
| KUMA-FM | Pendleton | 10/1/1978 | 107.7 MHz | 18.5 kw | Pendleton Broadcasting Company | Ted Smith (p)(gm) | | KUMA-AM |
| KRBM-FM | Pendleton | 4/18/1970 | 90.9 MHz | 10 watts | Blue Mountain Community College | Blaine Hanks (gm) | | |
| KFMT-FM/ KWHT-FM | Pendleton | 1984 | 103.5 MHz | | KSRV, Inc. | | | KSRV-AM |
| KRVB-AM/ KHUG-AM/ KDOV-AM#2/ KAPL-AM | Phoenix | 1/2/1977 | 1300 KHz | 5 kw | Rogue Valley Broadcasting Company | Jay Jones (p); Mack Lochrie (om); Rick St. Clair (pd); Rich Brown (cm); Barry Mayd (ce) | | |
| KRSB-FM | Roseburg | 10/1/1970 | 103.1 MHz | 2.75 kw | W.R.R., Inc. | John Worden (p); Thomas Worden; Karen Worden | All Stereo KRSB | |
| KSLM-FM/ KORI-FM/ KSKD-FM/ KXYQ-FM/ KKRH-FM/ KRSK-FM | Salem | 7/3/1970 | 105.1 MHz | 100 kw | Oregon Radio, Inc. | Bruce Kerr (vp,gm); | | KSLM-AM |

gm = general manager · p = president · vp = vice president · m = manager · pd = program director · md = music director
om = operations manager · ce = chief engineer · cm = commercial manager · sm = sales manager · sls = sales

# Bill Schonely and the Portland Trailblazers

Sports and radio in Oregon had a long relationship. Rollie Truitt's broadcasts of the Pacific Coast League's Portland Beavers had been a staple since the early 1930s and made him a well-known figure in the state. Oregon would see its first major league sports team when entrepreneur Harry Glickman entered the scene with a consuming determination to bring a major league franchise to Portland. Glickman's passion led to one of the most exciting developments in the history of Oregon radio.

In 1970, Glickman snagged an expansion basketball team that became the Portland Trailblazers. Occupied with the many details associated with launching a major league sports team, Glickman was, if anything, too casual in putting together the play-by-play radio package necessary for any sports team's success. When he requested suggestions for a sportscaster, he was steered in the direction of Seattle's William Schonely.

Schonely, universally known as "The Schonz," had been in radio since his World War II military service when he did play-by-play sports coverage for the Armed Forces Radio Service (AFRS). After his discharge, he took his first commercial radio job in Louisiana but soon moved to Seattle, where he was hired by KOMO-AM and shared announcing duties with Keith Jackson (who eventually moved on to the ABC Radio Network in Los Angeles). Sports announcing was Schonely's passion. Switching to Seattle's KAYO-AM in 1959 to do play-by-play for the Pacific Coast League's Seattle Totems, he remained there until 1965, when he again moved—this time to Golden West's KVI-AM Seattle as sports director.

At KVI-AM, he got his first taste of major league play-by-play when broadcasting for the Seattle Pilots with radio star, Jimmy Dudley, who for many years had been the voice of the Cleveland Indians. When the Pilots moved to Milwaukee, where they became the Brewers, Schonely had no play-by-play assignment and deeply missed it. That's when Glickman arrived and invited Schonely to Portland. Schonely recalls: "Harry and his big, big deep voice says 'Schonz, how would you like to do NBA basketball?' So I came down from Seattle, and we met over a famous Harry Glickman handshake. That's all it was then, and I've been here ever since."[2]

The Trailblazers' launch was magical. Against most betting, the team won its first game and then went on to win 29 games in its first season—an unequaled new team record. Public interest soared, especially with such talented and genial men on the court as Geoff Petrie.

Schonely recalls: "One of the first things Harry said was "I don't know what we're going to do, Schonz, but I need a network, and you're going to put it together." [3]

Schonely traveled throughout Oregon to line up stations for the fledgling Trailblazer's network, sometimes personally calling on prospective sponsors with representatives of local stations. By the Blazers' second season, the network had picked up stations in Klamath Falls, Grants Pass, Coos Bay and Bend. Schonely says:

> I got in my little car and we went to Astoria; we went to Bend; we went to Pendleton; we went to all of life's little cities of our state. I talked to the radio people in those days and had to get down on one knee and beg them to carry the Portland Trailblazers.[4]

Portland and the entire state quickly became infected with Blazermania. Fans were in love with the team—and with its voice, Bill Schonely.

Part of Schonely's appeal was his straight forward approach to the games. He never tried to apologize for lapses in performance and just called the plays as he saw them. His specialty was putting radio listeners "in the game" with a uniquely colorful and eloquent vocabulary which included: "moving left to right on your radio dial," "through the cyclops at mid court," and "ocean to ocean." Reportedly, a three-point play by Blazer Jim Barnett caused the net on the basket to rip, prompting Schonely's spontaneous exclamation "Rip City."[5] The phrase went on to become an Oregon catch-phrase as well as an alter ego for Portland. When a ball gracefully went through the center of the basket, it "tickled the twine." A ball that went off-target was "laying in the weeds." Then there was "bingo, bango, bongo,"—another of the Schonz's unique colloquialisms.

Schonely wasn't confined to play-by-play, either. His *Calling All Sports*, heard over KOIN, was Portland's first all-talk sports program. Schonely's passion for his work was all consuming. Said his wife, Dottie, "It's not his job. It's his life."[6]

When Schonely finally put down his Blazers' mike on April 30, 1998, after 2,252 broadcasts, both he and his audience were overcome. Protests rained across Portland and Oregon. Schonely signed-off with typical humanity and modesty, saying, "I thank you from the bottom of my heart, wherever you may be."[7]

# FM Continues Its March: New Radio Stations of the 1980s

With the dawn of the 1980s, FM continued its march toward radio prominence. Twenty-three new Oregon stations signed-on in the 1980s, only two of which were AM. A listing of the new radio stations of the 1980s (and a few of the 90s) follows:

| Call sign | City | Sign-On date | Frequency | Power | Originally owned by | Early staff | Slogan | Affiliated station |
|---|---|---|---|---|---|---|---|---|
| KAST-FM/ KBKN-FM/ KAST-FM | Astoria | 5/10/1981 | 92.9 MHz | 99 kw | KAST Broadcasting Company | | | KAST-AM |
| KMUN-FM | Astoria | 4/17/1983 | 91.9 MHz | 3 kw | KBOO Foundation, Inc./Tillicum Foundation, Inc | Doug Sweet (gm) | | |
| KBKR-FM/ KKBC-FM | Baker City | 2/1981 | 95.3 MHz | 3 kw | Oregon Trail Broadcasting Company | Kenneth Lockwood (p); C. Ray Jones (gm) | | KBKR-AM |
| KKCW-FM | Beaverton | 2/24/1981 | 103.3 MHz | 100 kw | Columbia-Willamette Broadcasting Company | John Q. Tilson (p) | | |
| KJII-FM/ KWBX-FM/ KQAK-FM | Bend | 9/5/1986 | 105.7 MHz | 40 kw | University of Oregon[8] | Paul Bjornstad (gm) | | |
| KBEY-FM/ KSHR-FM | Coquille | 11/1/1981 | 97.3 MHz | 25 kw | KWRO Broadcasting, Inc | | | |
| KZAM-FM/ KAVE-FM/ KNRQ-FM/ KKTT-FM/ KUZJ-FM | Cottage Grove | 9/1/1983 | 95.3 MHz | 3 kw | Visionary Radio Euphonics of Eugene, Inc. | John Detz (p); Steve Feder (gm); Joe Losi (sm); Jeff Hanley (pd); "Sparky" Schneider (ce) | | KZAM-AM (Eugene) |
| KWVR-FM | Enterprise | 9/1/1984 | 92.1 MHz | 3 kw | Wallowa Valley Radio Corporation | Lee Perkins; Carol-Lee Perkins | | KWVR-AM |
| KBGR-FM | Gold Beach | 6/1987 | 92.7 MHz | 2.6 kw | Chambers Broadcasting | George L. Chambers; Bonnie L. Chambers | | |
| KRWQ-FM | Gold Hill | 8/11/1980 | 100.3 MHz | 30 kw | Hill Radio, Inc. | Duane Hill (p) | | |
| KFMJ-FM/ KYJC-FM/ KROG-FM | Grants Pass | 10/2/1981 | 96.9 MHz | 25 kw | Lindavox | John Miner (p,gm) | | KYJC-AM (Medford) |
| KMHD-FM | Gresham | 1/1984 | 89.1 MHz | 7 kw | Mt. Hood Community College | | | |
| KDOV-FM | Medford | 8/1/1995 | 91.7 MHz | 1.25 kw | Family Life Broadcasting, Inc. | Perry Atkinson (gm) | | |
| KRKX-AM/ KZRC-AM/ KGUY-AM/ KZNY-AM/ KSZN-AM | Milwaukie | 2/28/1988 | 1010 KHz | 4.5 kw | 1010 Broadcasting, Inc. | John Grant (p) | Z-Rock | |
| KHUG-FM/ KROG-FM/ KAKT-FM | Phoenix | 8/1991 | 105.1 MHz | 52 kw | | | | |
| KIJK-FM/ KRCO-FM/ KMJZ-FM/ KLTW-FM | Prineville | 4/8/1981 | 95.1 MHz | 50 kw | High Lakes Broadcasting Company, Inc. | | | KRCO-AM |
| KLLR-FM | Redmond | 6/17/1985 | 101.7 MHz | 23 kw | KBND, Inc. | | | KBND-AM |

| Call sign | City | Sign-On date | Frequency | Power | Originally owned by | Early staff | Slogan | Affiliated station |
|---|---|---|---|---|---|---|---|---|
| KSBC-FM/ KZKD-FM/ KPRB-FM/ KSJJ-FM | Redmond | 11/1/1980 | 92.7 MHz | 2.5 kw | Sunshine Broadcasting Corporation | Robert Nash (p); Dan Kennedy (gm); Ray Westbrook (cm); Robert King (pd,md); Barbara Mason (nd) | | KPRB-AM |
| KTIL-FM/ KJUN-FM/ KFIS-FM | Tillamook | 1987 | 104.1 MHz | 950 watts | Beaver Broadcasting System, Inc. | | | KTIL-AM |
| KLWJ-AM | Umatilla | 6/1980 | 1090 KHz | 2.5 kw | Umatilla Broadcasting, Inc. | Darrell Marlow (p); John Marlow (gsm) | | |
| KWSO-FM | Warm Springs | 9/22/1986 | 91.9 MHz | 3.3 kw | Confederated Tribes of Warm Springs Oregon | Billiejo McConville (gm); Aaron Grey Horse Garcia (md) | | |
| KHQE-FM/ KWSI-FM/ KTWI-FM/ KWEG-FM/ KWPK-FM/ KRCO-FM/ KWLZ-FM | Warm Springs | 1/17/1985 | 96.5 MHz | 100 kw | Confederated Tribes of Warm Springs Oregon | | | KWSO-FM |
| KKSN-AM/ KFFX-AM/ KOTK-AM/ KKSN-AM/ KTRO-AM | Vancouver, WA | 4/1/1980 | 910 KHz[9] | 5 kw | Fort Vancouver Broadcasting, Inc. | William Failing Jr. (p) | | |

gm = general manager · p = president · vp = vice president · m = manager · pd = program director · prod = production manager
md = music director · om = operations manager · ce = chief engineer · cm = commercial manager · gsm = general sales manager
sm = sales manager · sls = sales

# The UHF Era: New Television Stations of the 1970s and Beyond

By 1970, television had entered a more mature phase and only two new TV stations—KTVZ-TV Bend and KSYS-TV Medford—signed-on in the decade. Spurred by the growing financial viability of UHF, which helped spark the launch of the Fox Network and smaller "netlets," a host of new UHF stations signed-on in the 1980s, while only two new VHF arrived during that decade—KDRV-TV Medford and KFFX-TV Pendleton. Most of these new stations, located outside of the Portland metropolitan area, developed as satellite operations associated with a parent station in a larger community.

This next listing groups together new TV stations of the 1970s and 80s because the real growth spurt of TV stations in Oregon occurred in the latter decade.

| Call sign | City | Sign-On date | Channel | Power | Originally owned by | Early staff | Network | Affiliated station |
|---|---|---|---|---|---|---|---|---|
| KTVZ-TV | Bend | 11/6/1977 | Ch 21 | 77.6 kw | Sierra Cascade Communications, Inc. | Ray Johnson (p); John Larkin (gm) | NBC CBS (sec) | |
| KVPP-TV/ KMTZ-TV/ KUCW-TV/ KMCB-TV | Coos Bay | 7/8/1991 | Ch 23 | 12.3 kw | KMTR, Inc. | | NBC | |

| Call sign | City | Sign-On date | Channel | Power | Originally owned by | Early staff | Network | Affiliated station |
|-----------|------|--------------|---------|-------|---------------------|-------------|---------|--------------------|
| KMTR-TV | Eugene | 10/4/1982 | Ch 16 | 1919 kw | KMTR, Inc. | Robert Davis (p); Cam Wilson (gsm); Donn Doak (nd) | NBC | |
| K25AS/ KEVU-LP#2 | Eugene | 5/1/1987 | Ch 25/ Ch 23 | 46 kw | John Field | John Field (p); John Mielke (gm) | —/Fox | |
| KEVU-TV/ KLSR-TV#2 | Eugene | 10/31/1990 | Ch 34 | 4470 kw | Telecasters of Eugene, Inc. | John Mielke (gm) | —/UPN | |
| KEPB-TV | Eugene | 2/27/1990 | Ch 22 | 389 kw | Oregon Public Broadcasting | | PBS | |
| K65EJ/ KBLN-TV | Grants Pass | 1992 | Ch 65/ Ch 30 | 12 kw | Better Life Television | | Better Life Television | |
| KFTS-TV | Klamath Falls | 12/13/1988 | Ch 22 | 9.33 kw | Southern Oregon Education Company, Inc. | Art Knoles (gm) | PBS | KSYS-TV (Medford) |
| KSYS-TV | Medford | 1/17/1977 | Ch 8 | 131.8 kw | Southern Oregon Education Company, Inc. | Boyce Stanard (p); Ed Barnett (gm) | PBS | |
| KDRV-TV | Medford | 2/26/1984 | Ch 12 | 190 kw | Sunshine Television, Inc. | Dunbar Carpenter (p); Ronald Kramer (vp); Keith Lollis (gm); Tom Craven (prod) | ABC | |
| KMVU-TV | Medford | 8/8/1994 | Ch 26 | 28.5 kw | 914 Broadcasting, Inc. (managed by Salmon River Broadcasting, Inc.) | Robert Hamacher; Peter Rogers (gm) | Fox | |
| KFFX-TV | Pendleton | 4/5/1999 | Ch 11 | 314 kw | Communication Properties, Inc. | | Fox | |
| KTDZ-TV/ KNMT-TV | Portland | 11/16/1989 | Ch 22 | 2,690 kw | National Minority TV, Inc. | | Trinity Broadcasting Network | |
| KLSR-TV#1/ KROZ-TV/ KTVC-TV | Roseburg | 3/13/1992 | Ch 36 | 42.7 kw | Metrocom of Oregon, Inc. | Glenn R. Edwards (p) | | |
| KLSR-TV#1/ KROZ-TV/ KTVC-TV | Roseburg | 4/8/1992 | Ch 36/ Ch 46 | 9.77 kw | KMTR, Inc. | Robert Davis (p) | NBC | |
| KECH-TV/ KWVT-TV/ KHSP-TV/ KBSP-TV/ KPXG-TV | Salem | 11/21/1981 | Ch 22 | 1702 kw | Greater Willamette Vision, Ltd. | Chris Desmond (ptnr); Arnold Brustin ( ptnr) | Subscription | |
| KUTF-TV/ KEBN-TV/ KWBP-TV/ KRCW-TV | Salem | 5/8/1989 | Ch 32 | 97.7 kw | Channel 32, Inc. | | Dove Broadcasting Network | |
| KLRK-TV/ KPDX-TV | Vancouver, WA | 10/9/1983 | Ch 49 | 2950 kw | Columbia River Television, Inc. | Richard Schwary (p) | Independent | |

gm = general manager · p = president · vp = vice president · m = manager · pd = program director · prod = production manager
md = music director · om = operations manager · ce = chief engineer · cm = commercial manager · gsm = general sales manager
sm = sales manager · sls = sales · sec = secondary affiliation · — = independent

# Endnotes

1. KCHC-FM returned its license to the FCC in 1981.
2. Schonely, William. Interview with Brian Mount, Tape recording. Portland, OR. June 7, 2005.
3. Ibid.
4. Ibid.
5. www.wikipedia.com.
6. Kerry Eggers. *The Bill Schonely Story: Wherever You May Be* (Portland, OR: Bookpartners, Inc., 1999), 218.
7. Ibid., 1.
8. KWBX-FM was sold to Norm Louvau on September 21, 1990, for commercial operation.
9. KKSN-AM was the successor to the frequency originally held by KVAN-AM/KISN-AM after the FCC revoked KISN-AM's license in 1976 (see chapter 23).

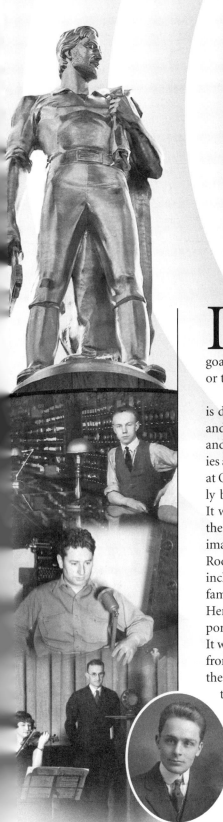

# 28

# The Kicker

I n the radio and television industries, the short, frequently funny or poignant moment that often occurs after a radio or TV program's last commercial interruption is called a "kicker." Its goal is to either send the audience away with a particular thought or to provide a sense of completion to the program.

Writing a kicker for the story of radio and television in Oregon is difficult. It would need to express the dreams of such tinkerers and inventors as Jerman, Austin, Hallock, Watson, Weed, Parsons and Read. It would need to convey the aspirations of such visionaries as Haller, Piper, Morris, Sackett, Bullitt and Smullin, who looked at Oregon's spectacular mountains and high deserts and saw equally broad vistas of public service opportunities for their stations. It would need to encompass the humanity of the Hoot Owls and their central figure, Charles F. Berg, along with the youngsters' imaginations fired by Addie Bobkins, Heck Harper, Rod Anders and Frank Kinkaid. It would need to include the professional achievements of the many famous figures, like Blanc, Huntley, Hansen, Steele, Hemmingway and Powell, who passed through the portals of Oregon's radio and television studios. It would have to capture broadcasting's role in confronting the danger and death of the Bandon Fire, the Vanport Flood and Mt. St. Helens' eruption and the spirit of dedicated news professionals like Jack Capell, Jim Miller and Hal Starr— broadcasting by candlelight during the Columbus Day Storm, when their work mattered the most. And it would need to recount the significance of the millions of hours of programming—the laughter, drama, pleasure and challenge it provided—and what that has meant to Oregonians.

It's a tall task.

Radio and television stations, in the strict legal sense, belong to their owners. But they tend to have established such deep public bonds that listeners and viewers often come to think of them as their own. If we read the histories of broadcasting in many states, we find they are filled with a sense of pride, awe, and "ownership" at what radio and television have brought to them—and so it is here in Oregon. Having read those histories of broadcasting, I still find that Oregon—while a relatively small state in population—has a big tale to tell. It is the story of a local program, the Hoot Owls, which swept the nation; the very beginnings of television experimentation in Portland by Wilbur Jerman; the founding of the cable television industry; KPTV's role as the nation's first UHF station; and the local and national recognition, too broad to recount on this page, that so many of Oregon's broadcasters have achieved.

One of the state's most prominent symbols is the gold-leafed figure that was installed atop Oregon's capitol in 1938, a time when radio was still in its formative years. Commonly referred to as the "pioneer," this figure was more particularly known as "Pioneer Mike," a little-known fact. Looking out over Oregon's vistas, guarding the people's rights and symbolizing their common aspirations, "Pioneer Mike" is a central symbol of Oregon. He might well have been cast holding a microphone out in front of him instead of a lowered axe, because he also symbolizes the pioneering Oregon spirit that the thousands of radio and television broadcasters—the famous and those now largely forgotten—brought to their professions and to the state. Their tools were their microphones and cameras, and they truly were pioneers.

Their work has stood the test of time as they have helped build an important industry. And they have helped make Oregon the unique and majestic place over which they have transmitted their work.

*Previous page, clockwise from top:* Oregon's Pioneer Mike; Dorothy Bullitt; Clif Watson; Art Kirkham; Harry Read; Wallace Kadderly; David Rees; Wilbur Jerman. *This page, top to bottom:* Russell Olsen; William B. Smullin; Doug LaMear; Cliff Engle; Mel Blanc; Blanch Virgin.

All photos from WSMB collection except LaMear, *Oregon Journal*/Courtesy of *The Oregonian*

# Selected Bibliography

Adams, Craig. www.pdxradio.com website

Andresen, Paul and Kip Carlson. "The Portland Beavers." Mt. Pleasant SC: Arcadia Publishing, 2004.

*Antique Radio Classified*

Armstrong, Herbert W. "Autobiography of Herbert W. Armstrong, Vol 1." Pasadena CA: Worldwide Church of God, 1987.

Arnold, J. Edwin. Wm. B. An unpublished biography in the Smullin Collection of the Western States Museum of Broadcasting.

Banning, William Peck. "Commercial Broadcasting Pioneer: The WEAF Experiment." Cambridge MA: Harvard University Press, 1946.

Barnouw, Erik. "A Tower in Babel." New York: Oxford University Press, 1966.

Bensman, Marvin. "Beginning of Broadcast Regulation in the Twentieth Century." Jefferson NC: McFarland and Company, 2000.

Bjorkman, Bruce W. "History of Salem's First Salem Electric Co." An unpublished paper compiled in 1998 in the possession of Salem Electric Company, Salem, Oregon.

Blanc, Mel and Philip Blashe. "That's Not All Folks!" New York: Warner Books, 1988.

Bright, Bill. "Two Bills from Boston." Wilsonville OR: Bookpartners, 2000.

*Broadcasting Magazine*

*Broadcasting Yearbook*

Carrillo, Leo. "The California that I Love." Englewood Cliffs NJ: Prentice Hall, 1961.

_____U.S. Census Bureau. Census of the United States.

Chasen, Daniel Jack. "On the Air: The King Broadcasting Story." Anacortes WA: Island Publishers, 1996.

Chipman, Art. "KMED The First Half Century." Medford OR: Pine Cone Publishers, 1972.

Chlupac, Robin Ann. "Airwaves over Alaska: The Story of Augie Hiebert." Issaquah WA: Sammamish Press, 1992.

Collins, Dean. "Hoot Owl Classics – Vol. 1." Portland OR: Sunshine Division, 1928.

Corr, O. Casey. "KING: The Bullitts of Seattle and their Communication Empire." Seattle WA: University of Washington Press, 1996.

Eggers, Kerry. "The Bill Schonely Story: Wherever You May Be." Portland OR: Bookpartners, Inc. 1999.

Edmiston, Fred W., "The Band that Made Radio Famous." Boone NC: McFarland and Company, 2003.

Faber, Daniel M. "Television and FM Translators: A History of their Use and Regulation." Online paper. http://www.danielfaber.com/translators.pdf

*Family Circle*

_____Federal Radio Commission. Files and papers held in Record Group 173, Accession 52A51, in the Textual Records section of the National Archives and Records Administration, College Park MD.

_____Federal Communications Commission. Files and papers held in Record Group 173, Accessions 54A390, 52C51, 55A639, 58A4, 60A132, 62A55, 69A1333, 72A451 and 75A24 of the Textual Records section of the National Archives and Records Administration, College Park MD.

Felsenthal, Carl. "Citizen Newhouse: Portrait of a Media Merchant." New York: Seven Stories Press, 1998.

*FMedia!* newsletter

Grannatt, Harry S. "Hoot Owl Classics, Vol. 2." Portland OR: Sunshine Division, 1929

Haley, Delpine. "Dorothy Stimson Bullitt: An Uncommon Life." Seattle, WA: Sasquatch Books, 1995.

Houglum, Roger. "Early Day Broadcasting in Lane County." Lane County Historian. Eugene OR: Lane County Historical Society: Spring 1974.

Houglum, Roger J. "Educational Broadcasting Comes to Lane County: A Short history of Radio Station KRVM." Eugene OR: Lane Community College, undated.

Hoover, Herbert. "The Memoirs of Herbert Hoover: the Cabinet and the Presidency, 1920–1933." New York: Macmillan and Company, 1952.

"Hungry Eye," monthly magazine. Corvallis OR: Oregon Educational and Public Broadcasting Service.

Jaker, Bill, Frank Sulek and Peter Kanze. "Airwaves of New York." Jefferson NC: McFarland and Company, 1998.

Johnston, Lyle. "Good Night, Chet." Jefferson NC: McFarland and Company, 2003.

Johnson, Rodney Forney and Robert Artman. "A Tiger By the Tail." Portland OR: privately published, 1985.

_____"History of Josephine County, Oregon." Grants Pass OR: Josephine County Historical Society, 1988.

_____"KGW and the Pacific Northwest: What They Offer the Radio Advertiser." Portland OR: KGW Radio, c. 1930.

_____"KGW Reminiscences." Audio tape recording of a KGW Radio program, broadcast in 1972 in connection with that station's 50th anniversary, held in Archives of KBPS collection of the National Public Broadcasting Archives, located in the Hornbake Library, University of Maryland.

_____"In Tune with the West." Portland OR: KOIN Radio, c. 1931.

Kosareff, Steve. "Window to the Future." San Francisco CA: Chronicle Books, 2005.

Kramer, Ronald. "History of Radio Broadcasting in Southern Oregon." Online article. www.wsmb.org.

Kuechler, Lori. "The Portland Police Sunshine Division: An Early History." Portland OR: Sunshine Division, 2003.

_____KWAX Program Guide. Monthly magazine. Eugene OR: KWAX/University of Oregon.

_____"Radio in Victory." (KWJJ) Peoria IL: National Radio Personalities, 1946.

_____"LA Radio People, Vol 2 (1957–1997)." Los Angeles CA: dbMarketing, 1997.

Lampman, Evelyn Sibley. Papers. Knight Library Special Collections, University of Oregon.

Levine, Lawrence W. and Cornelia R. Levine. "The People and the President." Boston MA: Beacon Press, 2002.

Lindley, Walter R. "Hard Times, Good Times in Oregon." Manhattan KS: Sunflower University Press, 1995.

Mannes, George. "The Birth of Cable TV," American Heritage Invention and Technology Magazine. Fall 1996

McCall, Tom and Steve Neal. "Tom McCall: Maverick." Portland OR: Binford and Morts, 1977.

McNeal, William H. "History of Wasco County Oregon." The Dalles, OR: William H. McNeal, 1953.

Morris, James M. "The Remembered Years!" Corvallis OR: Continuing Education, Oregon State University, 1972.

Mullins, William H. "The Depression and the Urban West Coast 1929–1933, Los Angeles, San Francisco, Seattle and Portland." Bloomington IN: Indiana University Press, 1991.

_____U.S. Department of Commerce. Files and papers of the Department of Navigation, Radio Division, held in Record Group 173 Accession 52A51 (filed by city of license or by call sign) the of the Textual Records section of the National Archives and Records Administration, College Park MD.

Nelson, Harold L. and Dwight I. Teeter, Jr. "Law of Mass Communication: Freedom and Control of Print and Broadcast Media." Mineola NY: The Foundation Press, Inc., 1969.

Nelson, Willie and Bud Shrake. "Willie, An Autobiography." New York: Cooper Square Press, 2000.

Olsen, Edward G. and Leo H. Appel. "Then Till Now in Brookings-Harbor: A Social History of the Chetco Community Area." Brookings OR: Rotary Club of Brookings, 1979.

_____Oregon Blue Book. Published annually by the Secretary of State of the state of Oregon.

Oregon Historical Society. Oral history collection.

_____Papers, files, photographs, sound recordings and manuscripts in the collection of the Oregon Historical Society, Portland OR.

Parker, Elliott. "The News Box: Re-evaluating Radio News in the 1920s." (paper, Association for Education in Journalism and Mass Communications Conference, 1996, Anaheim CA)

Passman, Arnold. "The Deejays." New York: Macmillan and Company, 1971.

Peterson, Emil R. and Alfred Powers. "A Century of Coos and Curry." Coquille OR: Coos-Curry Pioneer & Historical Association, 1952.

Phillips, Mary Alice Mayer. "CATV: A History of Community Antenna Television." Evanston IL: Northwestern University Press, 1972.

Platt, Helen. "KGW- Portland's Pioneer Radio Station." Oregon Historical Society MSS1134, unpublished manuscript, c. 1955.

Polks Directories for various Oregon cities.

Powell, Jane. "The Girl Next Door." New York: William Morrow and Company, 1988.

Radio Digest Illustrated

Radio News

_____U.S. Department of Commerce. Radio Service Bulletins. Washington, D.C.

Radio Waves. Monthly publication. Portland OR: Radio Waves Publishing Company.

Richards, Ron P. "A History of Radio Broadcasting in Montana." (Masters thesis, Montana State University, 1963)

Richardson, David Blair. "Puget Sounds: A Nostalgic Review of Radio and Television in the Great Northwest." Seattle WA: Superior Publishers, 1981.

Ross, John R. "Against the Odds!" Portland OR: Salem Electric and Carolina Pacific Publishing Company, 1991.

Rundell, Hugh (editor). "They Took To the Air." Unpublished collection of oral history interviews, produced for the Washington State Association of Broadcasters, conducted in the 1960s and 70s by Hugh Rundell and others. Manuscript in the collection of the Western States Museum of Broadcasting.

Saalfield, Rev. Lawrence J. "Forces of Prejudice in Oregon 1920–1925." Portland, OR: Archdiocesan Historical Commission, 1984.

Sand, Joseph Russell. "Sheldon F. Sackett: Flamboyant Oregon Journalist." (Masters thesis, University of Oregon, 1971)

Schiling, Jr., Lester Lorenzo. "The History of the Theatre in Portland, Oregon 1846–1959." (master's thesis, University of Wisconsin, 1961)

Schneider, John. "History of KFRC and the Don Lee Network." Online article. www.adams/net/jfs.

Schneider, John. "NBC Pacific Coast Network." Online article. http://members.aa.net/~jfs/nbc.htm

Singletary, Craig. "Radio Station KOIN: A Case Study of Music Programming." (Masters thesis, University of Oregon, August 1963)

Sisemore, Linsy, editor." History of Klamath County Oregon: Its Resources and Its People. 1941." Klamath Falls OR: no publisher cited, 1941.

Smith, Ted. "History of Radio in Umatilla County." *Pioneer Trails.* Pendleton OR: Umatilla County Historical Society, Spring 2003.

_____Social Security Administration. Death Index. Washington, D.C.

Stadler, Matthew. "At Liberty: A Town's Story & A Theatre's History." Portland OR: Oregon Council for the Humanities, 2006.

Staff of the *Oregonian.* "The Oregon Story 1850–2000," Portland, OR: Graphic Arts

Sterling, Christopher. "Electronic Media: A Guide to Trends in Broadcasting and Newer Technologies, 1920–1983." New York: Praeger, 1984.

Stingley, Douglas. "Salem's First," *Popular Communications.* October 1993.

*Sunset Magazine*

Swenson, Patricia Green. "Radio in the Public Schools of Portland, Oregon." (PhD diss. School of Education, New York University, 1958)

*Television Digest*

*The Hungry Eye*

*Time*

*TV-Radio Prevue*

*What's On the Air*

*Wireless Age*

Woodfin, Jane. (Evelyn Sibley Lampman). "Of Mikes and Men." New York: McGraw-Hill, 1951.

_____(The Radio staff of the Detroit News) "WWJ – The Detroit News." Detroit: Evening News Association, 1922.

Yorty, Alan R. "Public Radio under Fire: One Approach to Surviving the 80s." (graduate paper, University of Oregon, 1983)

# Index

St. Clair, Richard 437
St. Dell, Kippy 212
Stadler, Glen M. 319–20, 348, 358
Stamps, William 349
Stanard, Boyce 441
Standard Hour 252
Star Broadcasting 225, 387–90
Star Furniture Company 191–2
Stark, Lisa 431
Starlin, Glenn 258
Starr, Hal 401, 443
Staufacker, Charles 359
Steele, Donald (Donald Revert) (The Real Don Steele) 365, 379, 382–3, 389
Steffins Jr., Marvin R. 409–10
Steffins Sr., Marvin R. 408–9
Stephens, Roy T. 82, 255
Stephenson, Bryon M. 424
Stephenson, Pat 424
Stevens, Charles 363
Stevens, Fred W. 185
Stewart, Walter 132
Stewart Broadcasting Corporation 407
St. Helens, city of 419
Stiles, Eleanor B. 337
Stimson, Lloyd H. 23–4
Stockenburg, Stuart 142
Stockman, Jay 87, 94–5
Stone, Ben E. 144, 158, 161
Stone, David 390
Storer, George 329
Storer Broadcasting 240, 313, 326–7, 329, 332
Stout, William 294
Strandborg, Willliam 43–4, 52
Strauss, David 258
Strickland, James 212
Stuart, Chester J. 354, 359
Stubbs Electric Company 10–12, 18–19, 66, 71, 96
Stubbs, Osmon 10–11
Sturdevant, Kenton E. 420, 424
Suing, Robert 229
Sumner, Walter Taylor 42, 44, 51, 53, 56, 60
Sunday Oregonian 21, 38, 82–3, 106, 121, 299
Sunset Magazine 42–3, 59, 61

Sunshine Broadcasting Corporation 440
Sunshine Division 53–6, 59–61, 126
Sunshine Television 441
Sutherland, Lloyd A. 226
Swafford, Tom 253
Swanson, Byron (Johnny Dark) 390
Swartwood, Milton 170
Sweet, Douglas 439
Sweet Home, city of 321, 405, 420
Swenson, Patricia Green 82, 234, 255–6, 275
Switzer, Thomas 413
Symons Broadcasting Company 141
Symons Jr., Thomas W. 141–2

## T

Tacoma News Tribune 327
Talent, city of 167, 281, 406
Tatro, Lloyd 348
Taylor, Douglas J. 225
Taylor, Sammy 240, 250
Taylor, Silvia 313
Teague, Cecil 130
Teeter, Dwight L. 121
Television Airways 218, 317
The Dalles, city of 65, 183–5, 231, 281, 333, 359, 405, 420
Thomas, Dolph 88
Thomas, Lou L. 33–4
Thomas, Lynn C. 215, 346
Thomas, Rick 227, 247
Thomas Music Company 34, 68
Thomlinson, Robert E. 53, 171, 242, 353, 363, 396, 414
Thompson, Lewis Irvine 78–9, 84, 110, 120
Thompson, Richard 408
Thompson, Ronald (Ugly) 372
Thompson, Thomas F. 408
Thompson, Tommy 110
Thornton, Louis P. 158
Throop, Patti 305
Thurman, Melanie D. 345
Tigard, city of 376, 391
Tilbury, Gilbert 220

Tillamook, city of 49, 201, 274, 440
Tillamook Broadcasting Company 231
Tillicum Foundation 274, 439
Tillman, Philip 324
Tillman-Booth Company 318, 324
Tilson, John Q. 439
Titus, Ben 189
Titus, James 334
Toledo, city of 321, 329, 421
Toledo Broadcasters 420–1
Toleman, Toley 46, 60
Tomlin, Ed 212–13, 233
Tomlin, John 250
Tonkin, Marvin R. 210
Tower Sales and Erecting Company 216
Tracy Broadcasting Company 246
Trader, William J. 415–16
Trailblazers 435, 437–8
Trammell, Niles 51, 204, 382
Trans-Video Company of Oregon 330
Travers, Richard C. 8
Trevor, Frank 130–2
Triangle Network 75
Triangle TV Network 374, 425
Trinity Broadcasting Network 441
Trommilitz, Lionel 156
Trout, Barbara 231
Trout, Robert 185
Troy, Helen 102
Truhan, John B. 337, 357–8
Truitt, Arthur Roland (Rollie) 60, 133–4, 146, 172–3, 194, 204, 217, 371, 437
Truman, Harry S. 397
TTC (Television Technology Corporation) 263
Tualatin Valley Broadcasters 344
Tucker, Leland M. 339
Turner, Barry 161
Turner, Michael 372
Tykeson, Donald 270, 313, 315, 320–1, 324
Tynan, Mel 214, 414

Photo by Steve Sutfin

## About the Author

Ron Kramer has worked in, and been fascinated by, broadcasting since his teenage years. He worked at radio stations in Cleveland and Chicago, and as a director for the ABC Radio Network in Los Angeles, before settling into a career teaching radio and television at Lewis and Clark College in Portland and Southern Oregon University (SOU) in Ashland. Since 1974, he has served as Executive Director of SOU's 22-station public radio network, Jefferson Public Radio, and consulted for the Metropolitan Opera International Radio Network, the Corporation for Public Broadcasting and a variety of other broadcasting organizations. With an undergraduate degree in history and a deep appreciation of the foundations on which radio and television have been built, Kramer enthusiastically answered the Oregon Association of Broadcasters' request to write a history of broadcasting in Oregon. He holds bachelor's degrees in both speech and history from Baldwin-Wallace College, Berea, Ohio; a master's degree in radio-television-film from Northwestern University and advanced certificates in executive management from Harvard and Stanford universities. Kramer is currently working on a project to create the Western States Museum of Broadcasting in Ashland. The ability of sound and pictures to invisibly travel to listeners and viewers, and their potential for elevating our society, still fascinates him.